mexico

FODOR'S TRAVEL PUBLICATIONS
NEW YORK • TORONTO • LONDON • SYDNEY • AUCKLAND

WWW.FODORS.COM

Contents

Understanding Mexico 4–10

Living Mexico 11–24
- People and Society 12–13
- The Arts and Architecture 14–15
- Beauty and the Beasts 16–17
- Popular Culture 18–19
- Urban and Rural 20–21
- Festivals and Traditions 22–24

The Story of Mexico 25–38
- Prehistory–1500BC: Prehistory to the Maya 26–27
- 1500BC–AD900: The Maya 28–29
- 1325–1519: The Aztecs 30–31
- 1519–1821: Spain and the Conquest 32–33
- 1821–1876: Mexican Independence 34–35
- 1876–1920: Dictatorship and Revolution 36–37
- 1920–Today: Mexico Today 38

On the Move 39–58
- Arriving 40–44
- Getting Around 45–57
- Visitors with a Disability 58

The Sights 59–168
- The Yucatán 60–80
- Southern Mexico 81–98
- Mexico City 99–120
- Central Mexico East 121–136
- Central Mexico West 137–155
- Northern Mexico and Baja California 156–168

What to Do 169–206
- General Information 170–179
  - Shopping 170–171
  - Entertainment 172
  - Nightlife 173
  - Sports and Activities 174–177
  - Health and Beauty 178
  - For Children 178
  - Festivals and Events 179
- Listings 180–206
  - The Yucatán 180–185
  - Southern Mexico 186–189
  - Mexico City 190–195
  - Central Mexico East 196–199
  - Central Mexico West 200–203
  - Northern Mexico and Baja California 204–206

Out and About 207–238
- Walks and Tours 208–238
  1. Drive: Isla Mujeres 209
  2. Drive: The Riviera Maya 210–211
  3. Drive: The Convent & Puuc Routes Highlights 212–213
  4. Drive: Indigenous Villages Near San Cristóbal 214–215
  5. Walk: Oaxaca City 216–217
  6. Drive: Craft Villages Around Oaxaca 218–219
  7. Walk: Exploring Mexico City's Centro Histórico 220–221
  8. Walk: San Angel and Coyoacán 222–223
  9. Drive: The Churches of Puebla 224–225
  10. Drive: The Missions of the Sierra Gorda 226–227
  11. Drive: Silver Towns of the Bajío 228–229
  12. Drive: Around Lago de Pátzcuaro 230–231
  13. Walk: On the Edge of the Copper Canyon 232–233
  14. Drive: Cave Paintings and a Mountain Mission 234–235
  15. Drive: The Sea of Cortés: Lorteo to Mulegé 236–237
- Organized Tours 238

KEY TO SYMBOLS

- Map reference
- Address
- Telephone number
- Opening times
- Admission prices
- Bus number
- Train station
- Ferry/boat
- Driving directions
- Tourist office
- Tours
- Guidebook
- Restaurant
- Café
- Bar
- Shop
- Toilets
- Number of rooms
- No smoking
- Air-conditioning
- Swimming pool
- Gym
- Other useful information
- Shopping
- Entertainment
- Nightlife
- Sports
- Activities
- Health and Beauty
- For Children
- Cross reference
- Walk/drive start point

Eating and Staying 239–280

Eating	240–263
Eating Out in Mexico and Menu Reader	240–243
Eating Listings	244–263
The Yucatán	244–247
Southern Mexico	248–251
Mexico City	252–255
Central Mexico East	256–258
Central Mexico West	259–261
Northern Mexico and Baja California	262–263
Staying	264–280
Staying in Mexico	264–265
Staying Listings	266–280
The Yucatán	266–268
Southern Mexico	269–271
Mexico City	272–274
Central Mexico East	275–276
Central Mexico West	277–278
Northern Mexico and Baja California	279–280

Planning 281–304

Before You Go	282–284
Practicalities	284–285
Money	286–287
Health	288–289
Communication	290–291
Finding Help	292
Opening Times and Tickets	293
Books, Maps and Films	294
Tourist Offices	295–296
Media	296
Useful Websites	297
Spanish Words and Phrases	298–302
Mexican Glossary	303
Key Figures in Mexican History	304
Aztec and Maya Deities	304

Maps 305–322

Atlas	306–317
Atlas Index	318–322

Index 323–331

Acknowledgments and Credits 332–334

HOW TO USE THIS BOOK

Understanding Mexico is an introduction to the country, its geography, economy and people. **Living Mexico** gives an insight into Mexico today, while **Story of Mexico** takes you through the country's past.

For detailed advice on getting to Mexico—and getting around once you are there—turn to **On the Move**. For useful practical information, from weather forecasts to emergency services, turn to **Planning.**

Out and About gives you the chance to explore Mexico through walks, drives and organized tours.

The **Sights, What to Do, Eating** and **Staying** sections are divided geographically into six regions, which are shown on the map on the inside front cover. These regions always appear in the same order. Towns and places of interest are listed alphabetically within each region.

Map references for the **Sights** refer to the atlas section at the end of this book or to the individual town plans. For example, Acapulco has the reference ✚ 314 K10, indicating the page on which the map is found (314) and the grid square in which Acapulco sits (K10).

UNDERSTANDING MEXICO

Mexico is difficult to encapsulate. The regional differences are huge. Manic Mexico City is a world away from the serenity of the country's quieter spots, and underlying everything is the heavy weight of history. The growth of regional powers such as the Olmecs was the precursor for the Maya in the southeast and the Aztecs in the Central Highlands. The Spanish Conquest exploited regional differences to impose its own beliefs and traditions on the population, while the more recent cultural invasion from north of the border, helped by the free trade agreement, has added another dimension to this already complicated country.

Conchero dancer in pre-Hispanic costume, Mexico City

GEOGRAPHY

Mexico is the second largest country in Latin America (after Brazil), covering an area of just under 2 million sq km (772,000sq miles), making it four times the size of France and roughly a quarter the size of continental USA, with which it has a frontier of 2,400km (1,490 miles).

Put simply, the land mass consists of a plateau flanked by ranges of mountains roughly paralleling the coasts. The northern part of the plateau is low, arid and thinly populated; it takes up 40 percent of the total area of Mexico, but holds only 19 percent of its people. Farther south, the level rises considerably; this southern section of the central plateau is crossed by the volcanic cones of Orizaba (5,760m/18,897ft), Popocatépetl (5,452m/17,888ft), Iztaccíhuatl (5,286m/17,343ft), Nevado de Toluca (4,583m/15,036ft), Matlalcueyetl or La Malinche (4,461m/14,636ft), and Cofre de Perote (4,282m/14,049ft). This mountainous southern end of the plateau, the heart of Mexico, covers only 14 percent of the area of the country, but holds nearly half of its people, including the roughly 20 million inhabitants of Mexico City.

Geographically, North America may be said to come to an end in the Isthmus of Tehuantepec. South of the Isthmus the land rises again into the thinly populated highlands of Chiapas.

CLIMATE

Climate and vegetation depend upon altitude. The *tierra caliente* (hot land) takes in the coastlands and plateau lands below 750m (2,460ft). The *tierra templada*, or temperate land, lies at 750m to 2,000m (2,460ft–6,560ft). The *tierra fría*, or cold land, is from 2,000m (6,560ft) upwards. Above the tree line at 4,000m (13,125ft) are *páramos* (high moorlands).

The climate of the inland highlands is mostly mild, but with sharp changes of temperature between day and night, sunshine and shade. Generally, winter is the dry season and summer the wet season. There are only two areas where rain falls year round: south of Tampico along the lower slopes of the Sierra Madre Oriental and across the Isthmus of Tehuantepec into Tabasco state; and along the Pacific coast of the state of Chiapas. These wetter parts get most of their rain between June and September. Apart from these regions, the rest of the country suffers when the rainy season doesn't lives up to its name and when the dry season does. Extremes of weather do happen, however. In 2001 both the Caribbean and Pacific coastlines were battered by severe storms and hurricanes.

PEOPLE

Out of a total population of around 103.4 million, about 9 percent are white, 30 percent *indígena* (indigenous) and 60 percent *mestizos*, a mixture in varying proportions of Spanish and *indígena*. A small percentage (mostly in the coastal zones of Veracruz, Guerrero and Chiapas) are a mixture of black and white or black and *indígena* or *mestizo*. Mexico also has infusions of other European peoples, Arabs and Chinese. There is a national cultural prejudice in favor of the indigenous rather than the Spanish element, though this does not prevent *indígena* from being looked down on by the more Hispanic elements.

LANGUAGE AND DEMOGRAPHY

The official language is Spanish, and though English is widely spoken, especially in the most tourist-oriented parts, your stay will be all the more rewarding if you try to communicate with people in their native tongue. As well as Spanish, the estimated 24 million *indígenas* are divided into 54 groups or subdivisions, each with its own language. The most common native language after Spanish is Nahuatl, the ancient language of the Aztecs.

Generally, indigenous people are far from evenly distributed; 36 percent live on the Central Plateau (mostly Hidalgo, and México); 35 percent are along the southern Pacific Coast (Oaxaca, Chiapas, Guerrero), and 23 percent along the Gulf Coast (mostly Yucatán and Veracruz). In effect 94 percent of them live in these three regions. There are also sizeable concentrations in the states of Nayarit and Durango, Michoacán, and Chihuahua, Sinoloa and Sonora.

The main groups are: Pápago (Sonora); Yaqui (Sonora); Mayo (Sonora and Sinaloa); Tarahumara (Chihuahua); Huastec and Otomí (San Luis Potosí); Cora and Huichol (Nayarit); Purépecha/Tarasco (Michoacán); scattered groups of Nahua (Michoacán, Guerrero, Jalisco, Veracruz and other central states); Totonac (Veracruz); Tiapaneco (Guerrero); Mixtec, Mixe and Zapotec (Oaxaca state); Lacandón, Tzoltzil, Tzeltal, Chol and others (Chiapas); and Maya (Campeche, Yucatán and Quintano Roo).

The massive natural rock arch (El Arco) at Cabo San Lucas

The belfry of the Church of Santa Maria de Tonantzintla

Mist-covered mountains in the Chiapas Highlands

POLITICS

Under the 1917 Constitution, Mexico is a federal republic of 31 states and a Federal District containing the capital, Mexico City. The president, who appoints the ministers, is elected for six years and can never be re-elected. The next elections are scheduled for 2006.

Congress consists of the 128-seat Senate, half elected every three years on a rotational basis, and the 500-seat Chamber of Deputies, elected every three years. The states enjoy local autonomy and levy their own taxes, and each has its own governor, legislature and court. The president has traditionally appointed the chief of the Federal District, but direct elections were held in 1997 for the first time.

ECONOMY

As an emerging global market, Mexico's economy ebbs and flows with the tide of world trade, yet in rural communities market stallholders barter produce as they have for millennia. City wealth contrasts with rural poverty, and globalization creeps in through fast-food outlets and shopping malls as centuries-old cultures cling to ancient traditions.

Mexico has been an oil producer since the 1880s and led the world in 1921. By 1971 the country had become a net importer, a position reversed in 1972 with the discovery of major new reserves. Today Mexico benefits greatly from the reserves and is the world's sixth largest producer, with 65 percent of production coming from offshore wells in the Gulf of Campeche. Agriculture has been losing importance since the beginning of the 1970s and now contributes only 5.8 percent of GDP.

While the capital used to be a focal point for manufacturing, the government now offers incentives to companies relocating away from major industrial hubs. The boom came with the creation of 3,600 *maquiladoras* (assembly plants) along the US border, which employ some 1.3 million people, earning $1.5 billion annually for the economy. The country also benefits from over $10 billion sent home from families living north of the border. Tourism is a large source of foreign exchange and the largest employer (about a third of the total workforce). Around 6.7 million visitors come to Mexico every year, 85 percent from the US. Since 1994, Mexico has been a member of the North American Free Trade Agreement (NAFTA; ▷ 13).

RELIGION

Though 90 percent of the population is ostensibly Roman Catholic (with another 7 percent Protestant and 3 percent atheist), the principal religion is a hybrid of Catholicism and pre-Conquest beliefs and traditions. Despite the apparent piety of many Mexicans, the country is determinedly secular. Because of its identification firstly with Spain, then with the Emperor Maximilian and finally with Porfirio Díaz, the Church has been severely persecuted in the past by reform-minded administrations, and priests are still not supposed to wear ecclesiastical dress.

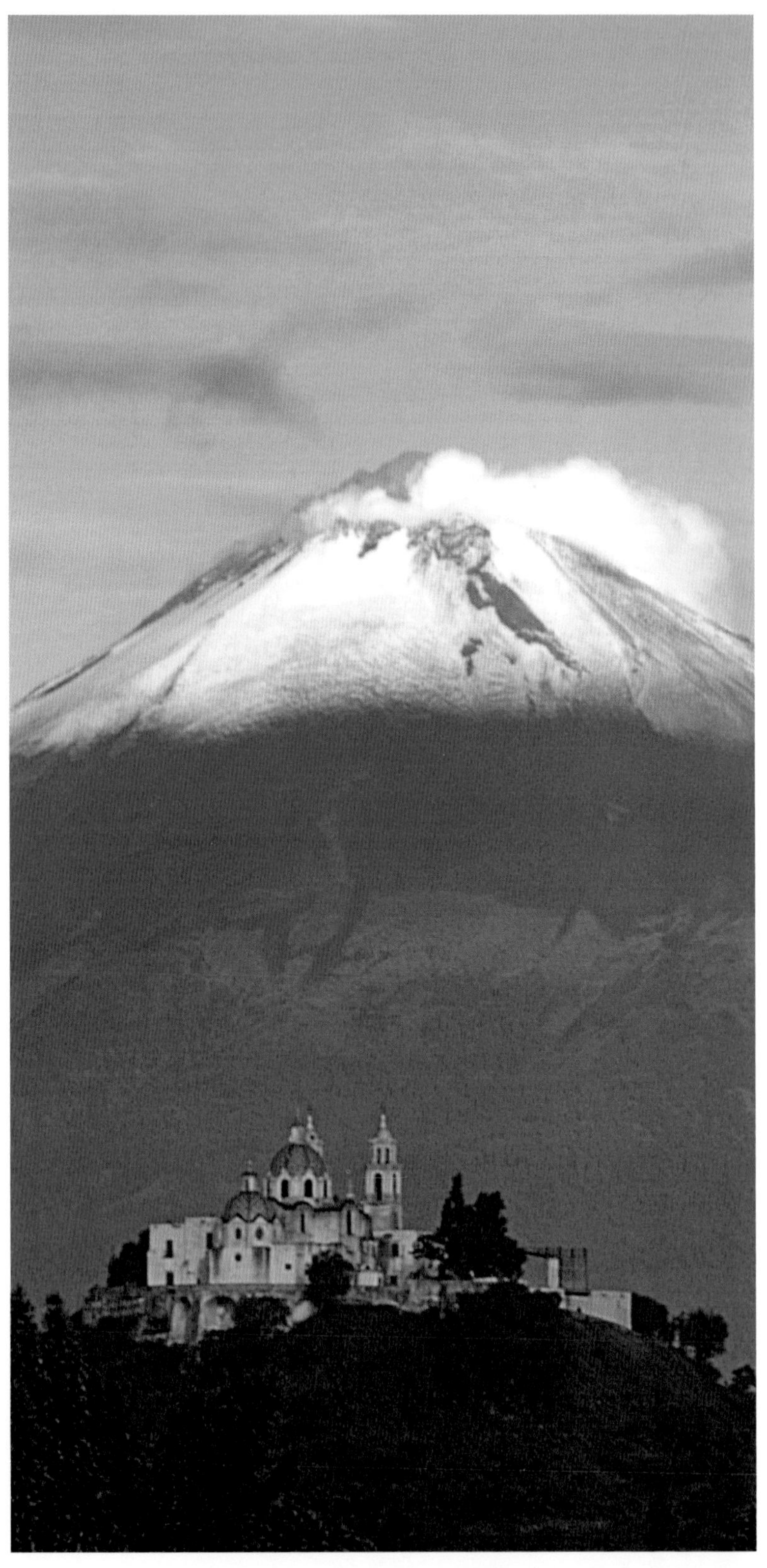

Church in Cholula, with Popocatépetl in the background

THE REGIONS OF MEXICO

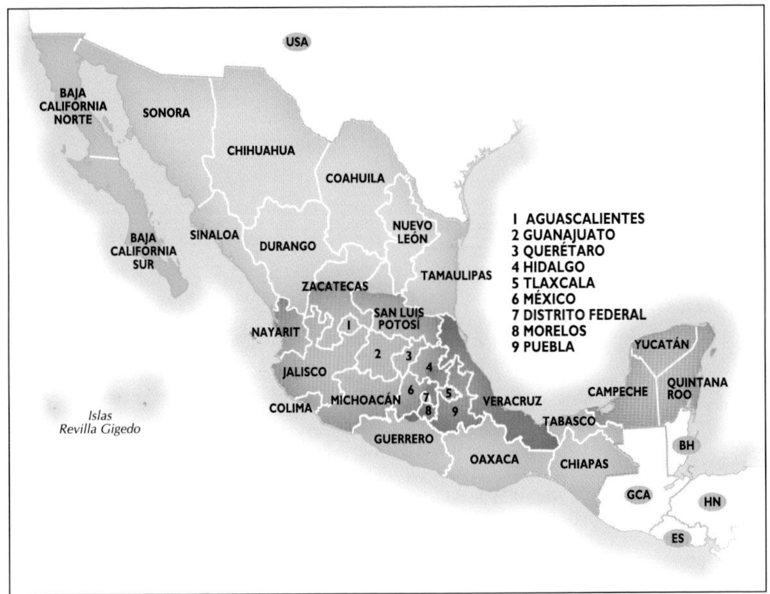

The Yucatán Comprising the states of Campeche, Yucatán and Quintana Roo, the Yucatán Peninsula includes Mexico's Mayan Riviera, a tourist hotspot full of great Maya archaeological sites and Caribbean beach resorts.

Southern Mexico This vast area of the country spreads out from its narrow waist of isthmus. On the southernmost edge, bordering Guatemala, is the fiercely traditional state of Chiapas, land of the Classic Maya, whose descendants still inhabit the highland villages today. To the north, Tabasco gave rise to the first great civilization of Mesoamerica, the Olmecs, while lively, cosmopolitan Oaxaca is one of the country's cultural highlights and the state of Guerrero is home to Acapulco, Mexico's most famous resort.

Mexico City Mexico City is one of the world's great capitals—its architectural magnificence and vast public plaza survive side by side with the noise and pollution of traffic and 24 million people. At once bawdy, vibrant, gaudy, cultured, noisy, sometimes dangerous and always fascinating, the ancient Aztec capital is a celebration of chaotic humanity, good and bad.

Central Mexico East Not far from the capital lie the colonial jewels of Puebla—the City of Angels—to the southeast, and the silver-mining town of Taxco to the south, while northeast the magnificent ruins of El Tajín host the spectacular *voladores* (flying men) ritual, an example of surviving pre-Hispanic traditions. The green, fertile coastal plain backs the Gulf Coast, largely given over to the oil industry. The port of Veracruz, Spain's gateway to the New World, has a distinct culture and is home to the liveliest pre-Lenten carnival in all Mexico.

Central Mexico West Spanish-style architecture, built with the fortunes amassed from silver and gold, is at its most opulent and impressive in the magnificent towns and cities of the Colonial Highlands, while the Mexican stereotype is alive and well in the state of Jalisco, where you'll find tequila, the lasso-swinging *charros* and the romantic *mariachis*. The state capital, Guadalajara, is Mexico's second city—a huge, modern metropolis with an elegant Spanish core. West of Mexico City the state of Michoacán is home to the ancient Tarascan people, and is the best place to witness the spectacle of the *Día de los Muertos* (Day of the Dead), one of the most important dates in the Mexican calendar.

Northern Mexico and Baja California The miles of endless deserts and vast, barren landscapes of the north hold some of Mexico's most spectacular surprises. Baja California, the long, narrow peninsula that dangles southwards from the US border between the Pacific Ocean and the Gulf of California for 1,300km (800 miles), is a stark and beautiful wilderness and one of the world's prime whale-watching sites, while in Chihuahua, Mexico's biggest state, is the Chihuahua-al-Pacífico, billed as "the world's most scenic railroad."

THE BEST OF MEXICO

THE YUCATÁN

A boat at rest on the beach at Isla Mujeres

Beaches Relax in the warm turquoise sea fringed with fine white-sand beaches and palm groves of the Riviera Maya (▷ 210–211).

Maya ruins Visit the sensational ruins at Uxmal (▷ 78–79), Tulúm (▷ 75) and Chichén Itzá (▷ 64–67).

Wildlife The Sian Ka'an Biosphere Reserve covers tropical forest, savanna and coastline and protects many bird species (▷ 74).

Diving Cozumel (▷ 68–69), the Island of the Swallows, is one of the most popular diving bases in the world, due to its rich variety of coral and underwater creatures.

Nightlife If you like to party, you'll love Cancún (▷ 63). It's also a good alternative entry point to Mexico City.

The archaeological site of Uxmal

Snorkeling in the clear waters of the Yucatán

SOUTHERN MEXICO

Architecture Visit Oaxaca City for its colonial architecture (▷ 88–91) and nearby ruins of Monte Albán (▷ 86–87).

Scenery Follow Route 190, from Oaxaca to Tehuantepec (▷ 97), as it serpentines unendingly over the beautiful Sierras.

Indigenous culture Soak up the atmosphere of the indigenous town of San Cristóbal de las Casas (▷ 96), from where you can explore the jungle waterfalls and multihued lakes.

Maya ruins The jungle setting of Palenque makes it the most atmospheric and beautiful of all the Maya sites (▷ 92–95).

Temple of the Foliated Cross, at Palenque

MEXICO CITY

History Wander the colonial Centro Histórico, Mexico City's heart; fascinating, chaotic and exotic in equal measure (▷ 220–221).

Museums The Museo Nacional de Antropología (▷ 108–111) is crammed with pre-Hispanic art and culture—a must before exploring the rest of the country.

Eating and shopping The district of Condesa (▷ 191–194) has become *the* place to eat, drink and be seen, while the more refined Polanco (▷ 116 and 191–192) is home to the city's finest shops and restaurants.

Café society Visit the beautiful, bohemian suburbs of San Angel (▷ 117) and Coyoacán (▷ 106), with their leafy, cobbled streets and chic pavement cafés.

Art The Palacio de Bellas Artes houses many works by the great artist Diego Rivera, but don't miss the Museo Mural Diego Rivera on the opposite side of Alameda Central (▷ 104).

Music Visit Plaza Garibaldi (▷ 115) on a Friday or Saturday night and you'll be besieged by persistent *mariachi* bands.

The Aztec Calendar, Mexico City

Diego Rivera mural in the Palacio Nacional, in Mexico City

Monarch butterfly

THE BEST OF MEXICO

Green Talavera tiles adorning a house in Puebla (above)

CENTRAL MEXICO EAST

Shopping Take a trip to Puebla, the City of Angels, to buy beautiful Talavera tiles—after admiring them first on the colonial buildings (▷ 197).

Sightseeing The spectacular *volador* ritual, an example of surviving Totonac traditions, is performed regularly in Papantla and outside the magnificent ruins of El Tajín (▷ 129).

Ancient ruins Don't miss the awesome ruins of Teotihuacán, one of Mexico's most important pre-Hispanic sites and a short, easy trip from the capital (▷ 132–134).

Museums Xalapa (Jalapa) is home to the excellent Anthropology Museum, one of the best of its type in the country (▷ 136).

Carnival Enjoy the legendary hospitality of the Veracruzanos and the eternally festive, tropical-port atmosphere that reaches its climax in spring during the liveliest carnival in Mexico (▷ 199).

Totonac *voladores* (flying dancers) at El Tajín (above)

CENTRAL MEXICO WEST

Culture To experience the Mexican stereotype go to Jalisco. Here you'll find the town of Tequila, the lasso-swinging Jaliscan *charros* (cowboys) and the country's most famous *mariachis*, those roving musicians dressed in their fine, tight-trousered suits.

Architecture A relatively short circuit north of Mexico City brings you to the Colonial Heartland, taking in the towns of Querétaro (▷ 148), Guanajuato (▷ 142–144), San Miguel de Allende (▷ 149) and Dolores Hidalgo (▷ 139–140), architectural gems built on the wealth from silver production.

Festivals The *Día de los Muertos* (▷ 24), a key date in the Mexican calendar, is especially celebrated in Michoacán, particularly around Pátzcuaro (▷ 147), where on November 1 every village around the lake commemorates its dead.

Nature People flock to El Campanario Ecological Reserve each year in spring to see millions of monarch butterflies take to the wing as they migrate north, one of the most impressive sights in all of Mexico (▷ 16 and 148).

Decorated papier-mâché skull, Museo Anahuacalli

A *charro* demonstrates his skills at a *charrería* (rodeo)

Cactus (below) and gray whale (right) in Baja California

NORTHERN MEXICO AND BAJA CALIFORNIA

Wildlife Head down the Baja California Peninsula through spectacular desert scenery to bask on idyllic beaches and, if you time it right, to watch the migrating whales at Laguna Ojo de Liebre (Scammon's Lagoon; ▷ 164).

Train journey Board the Chihuahua-al-Pacífico (▷ 159 and 232–233), billed as "the world's most scenic railroad," which wends its way across bridges, through tunnels and over the Sierra Madre to Los Mochis.

Hiking Stop off at Creel or El Divisadero to absorb the views, discover the awe-inspiring landscapes, rock formations and wildlife, visit Mexico's tallest waterfall and penetrate the vertiginous depths of the Barranca del Cobre (▷ 159).

TOP EXPERIENCES

Girl wearing traditional Oaxacan costume (above)

Gaze in awe at the 17th-century Franciscan Church of Santo Domingo, in Oaxaca, one of the best examples of baroque style in Mexico (▷ 90).

Soak up the sights, sounds and aromas of Oaxaca's Mercado de Abastos, the second-largest craft market in Mexico after Toluca. Beware of vendors trying to persuade you to taste *chapulines*—grasshoppers fried in huge vats (▷ 90–91).

Be pampered at the Reserva Ecológica Nanciyaga on Lake Catemaco (▷ 123), where you can lie in a steaming patchouli-scented bath, followed by a vigorous massage and a vegetarian meal, all in a lush, tropical setting.

Witness the spectacle of Oaxaca's Guelaguetza, an impressive carnival celebration in July, when many different cultural groups gather in one place (▷ 189).

Get off your horse and drink in the authentic Wild West atmosphere of Durango (▷ 161), backdrop for many Hollywood Westerns and more recent classics such as *The Mask of Zorro*.

Wallow in the sumptuous surroundings of Bar La Opera, one of the capital's most sophisticated dining experiences (▷ 252).

Dive into the deep blue waters of one of Yucatán's many *cenotes* (sink holes). At Tres Rios "eco" park, near Cancún (▷ 181 and 210), you can follow it up with horseback-riding on the beach and snorkeling on the reef.

Drive through spectacular scenery to the 1,000m-deep (3,280ft) Cañon del Sumidero, where trails wind through lush vegetation with orchids, cascading waterfalls, crystalline rivers, frolicking monkeys and amazing birdlife (▷ 83).

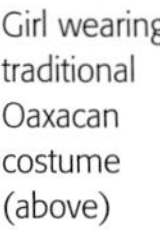

The quetzal (right), the sacred bird of the Maya

The Sumidero Canyon (left) home to the acrobatic spider monkey

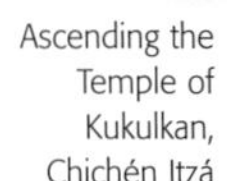

Ascending the Temple of Kukulkan, Chichén Itzá

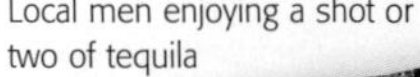

Local men enjoying a shot or two of tequila

Peer into the crater of Volcán Paricutín, near the town of Uruapan, following a 16km (10-mile) trek on horseback and a final 400m (440-yard) scramble on foot across the cold lava (▷ 153).

Climb the giant stepped pyramid of El Castillo at Chichén Itzá, one of the most visited and spectacular Maya sites (▷ 64–67). It's a steep haul to the top, best attempted before it gets too hot.

Attend a *charrería*, an authentic Mexican rodeo, where you can see wild-mare riding and team bull riding—accompanied by trumpets and local delicacies (▷ 176).

Down a shot of tequila, Mexico's national drink, in Cantina la Guadalupana (▷ 253), Mexico City, one of the best-known *cantinas* in the country.

Living Mexico

People and Society 12–13
The Arts and Architecture 14–15
Beauty and the Beasts 16–17
Popular Culture 18–19
Urban and Rural 20–21
Festivals and Traditions 22–24

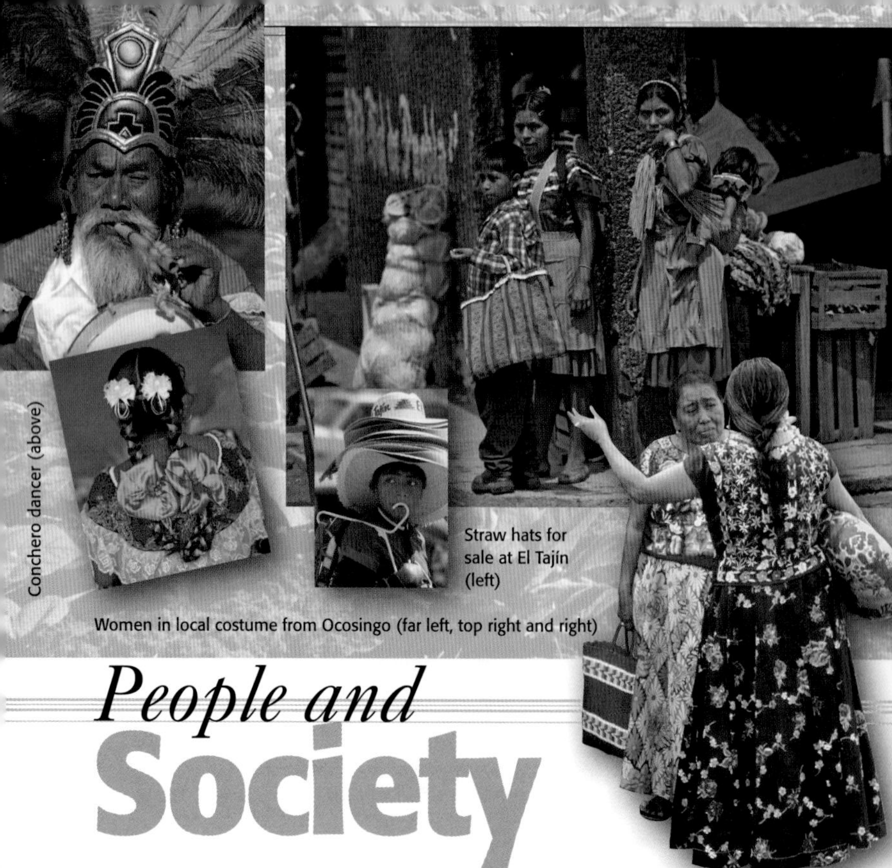

Conchero dancer (above)

Straw hats for sale at El Tajín (left)

Women in local costume from Ocosingo (far left, top right and right)

People and Society

Few countries in Latin America have such a large percentage of *mestizos* (mixed indigenous and European blood) and indigenous groups. Out of a total population of 103.4 million, almost 30 percent are indigenous while 60 percent are *mestizos*. Though the Spanish invaders set about converting the natives to Catholicism with a near hysterical zeal, pockets of resistance held out and today many indigenous groups have maintained their own cultural and religious identities. In Oaxaca, for example, some 20 percent of the population converse primarily in the Zapotec language, while the Lacandon and Huichol cultural groups, though small, have managed to avoid significant contact with the outside world thanks to their remoteness.

That said, however, Mexico's indigenous people remain the most marginalized sector of society. The uprising by the Zapatista National Liberation Army (EZLN) in Chiapas in 1994, which deliberately coincided with the inauguration of the North American Free Trade Agreement (NAFTA), was a warning to the government that they cannot ignore the rights of indigenous people. The rest of the country, too, is showing signs of unrest as NAFTA fails to deliver prosperity to the masses and increased globalization leads to a creeping Americanization that is threatening the Mexican way of life.

Girl Power

In this most macho of countries, one particular race stands out as a striking exception. The Zapotec women of the Isthmus of Tehuantepec are renowned for their strength, beauty and commercial acumen. Distinctive in their elaborately embroidered *huipils* (blouses) and long, flowing *enaguas* (skirts), they can be seen running the daily markets in the towns of Juchitán and Tehuantepec. One local custom that illustrates who wears the pants in this matriarchal society is the *tirada de fruta* (fruit throwing), which takes place at various fiestas throughout the year. Sweets, toys and mangoes are distributed among the crowd, before women climb onto the rooftops and hurl fruit at the males below.

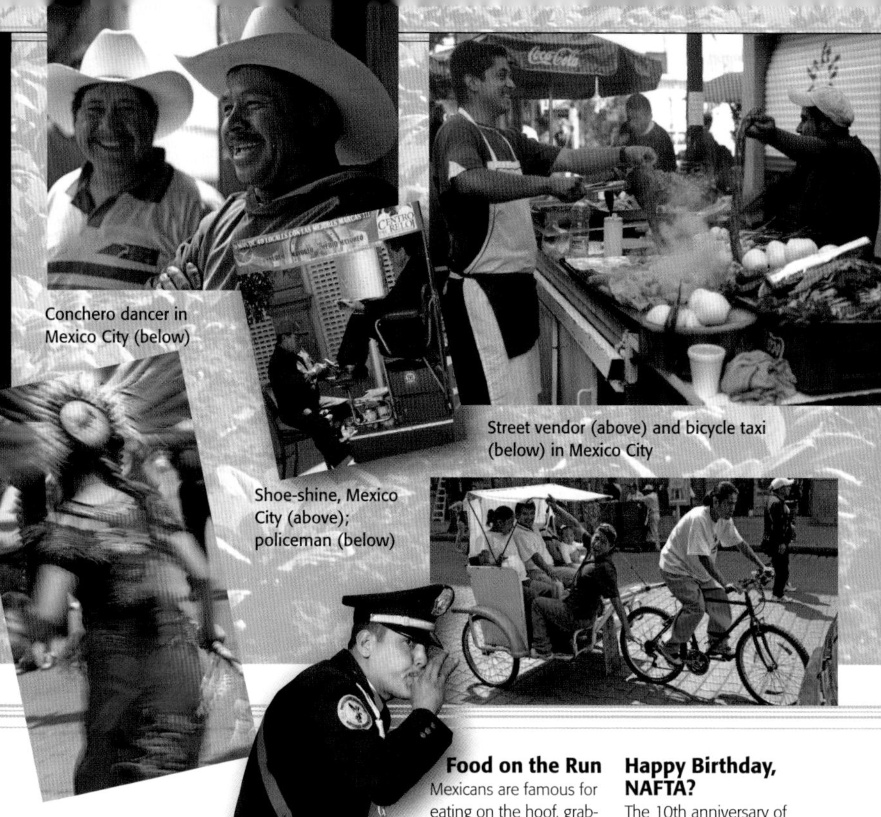

Conchero dancer in Mexico City (below)

Shoe-shine, Mexico City (above); policeman (below)

Street vendor (above) and bicycle taxi (below) in Mexico City

Super Barrio

Is it a bird? Is it a plane? No, it's Super Barrio. Unlike his comic book contemporaries, however, Super Barrio is a real-life character who concentrates his efforts on campaigning for Mexico City's poor. He first emerged after the devastating earthquake of 1985, which killed many thousands of people, as one of three superheroes who took it in turns to don red and yellow tights, cape and wrestling mask, and assist the victims of the disaster. Since then he has been a constant source of energy and inspiration. Other people who have tried to follow in his footsteps include Super-Eco, an environmental crusader who wears bright green spandex, and El Chupacabras Crusader, defender of middle-class people experiencing financial difficulties.

Drug Trade

Mexico's "informal" sector accounts for up to a third of the country's economic output and employs a quarter of the working population. At the bottom of the heap are the armies of street kids selling *chicles* (chewing gum), while at the top are Mexico's shadowy drug lords who earn vast sums from the narcotics trade. Despite a series of joint US–Mexican anti-drug initiatives, the drug traffickers have continued to prosper. In 1999, General Jesus Gutiérrez Rebollo, ex-head of the country's anti-drug agency, was found guilty of being in the pay of the drug barons and sentenced to 40 years. His story has since been dramatized in Steven Soderbergh's Oscar-winning movie *Traffic* (2000).

Food on the Run

Mexicans are famous for eating on the hoof, grabbing *tacos* or *quesadillas* at stands along roadsides. But sales of *tacos*, *tortas* and *tortillas* have been in decline because of competition from their fast-food equivalents north of the border, namely burgers, pizzas and hot dogs. Between 1998 and 2004, tortilla consumption fell by 25 percent, according to the National Corn Processors Chamber, who cite the sheer convenience of foreign imports and the social connotations attached to *tortillas*, which are viewed as the food of the poor, as reasons for the decline. Another reason is the mega marketing power of the big chains. It would be hard to imagine roadside *torta* stands offering a free toy with every sandwich!

Happy Birthday, NAFTA?

The 10th anniversary of NAFTA (North American Free Trade Agreement) between the US, Canada and Mexico fell in 2004, but although it was hailed as the panacea for the country's economic ills at its inception, few Mexicans now rejoice in its birth. True, Mexico's exports to the US grew threefold and its per capita income rose 24 percent, but most of the benefits of the agreement have been felt along the US border, where many US companies have taken advantage of a cheap workforce and relocated, creating thousands of new jobs. Being tied so closely to the US economy has meant that Mexico has suffered directly from the economic slump in the US since 2000. Now most Mexicans see NAFTA as having a negative impact on their lives, leading to a growing dissatisfaction with President Vicente Fox Quesada.

The Templo de San Francisco, in Acatapec (left); mural of Father Hidalgo by Orozco in the Palacio de Gobierno, in Guadalajara (right)

Teatro de Los Insurgentes, Mexico City (above)

Frida Kahlo and Diego Rivera (below)

The Arts and Architecture

Throughout Mexican history, art and architecture have been a fundamental part of the country's culture, from the massive Olmec heads of the mid-12th century BC to the eighth-century AD Mayan murals in the Temple of the Paintings at Bonampak, in southeast Chiapas. With the arrival of the Spanish in the 16th century came changes in style and content, but Mexico's indigenous painters and sculptors never completely abandoned their roots. This fusion of European and indigenous styles became a defining feature of the country's artists, architects and writers.

Twentieth-century Mexican art was dominated by the great muralists Diego Rivera (1886–1957), José Clemente Orozco (1883–1949) and David Alfaro Siqueiros (1896–1974), who brought art to the people through a series of huge murals on public buildings depicting themes from Mexican history. Rivera and his fellow artists were devoted to the idea of *mexicanidad*, glorification of their native heritage, environment and culture.

In literature, too, this notion of "Mexicanness" dominated intellectual thought, most notably that of Octavio Paz in his 1952 novel *The Labyrinth of Solitude*, an acute analysis of Mexican society and the way in which pre-Columbian cultures continue to influence the modern state.

This synthesis of the ancient and modern has also been used to dazzling effect by the country's leading architects, Ricardo Legorreta (born 1931) and Luis Barragán (1902–88).

The Cult of Kahlo

The turbulent life of Frida Kahlo (1907–54) was brought to the world's attention by the big-budget 2002 movie *Frida*, starring Salma Hayek in the title role. But long before the film hit the screens, the cult of this great feminist icon had spread far beyond Mexico. Kahlo's often shocking art was driven by the physical pain she endured from horrific injuries sustained in a bus crash at the age of 18 and the mental anguish she suffered during her passionate and tortured relationship with revolutionary muralist Diego Rivera. The mystique surrounding her will only be fuelled by a new book, written by her niece, Isolda Pinedo Kahlo, claiming that Rivera helped her to die.

Modern sculpture in Guadalajara (left)

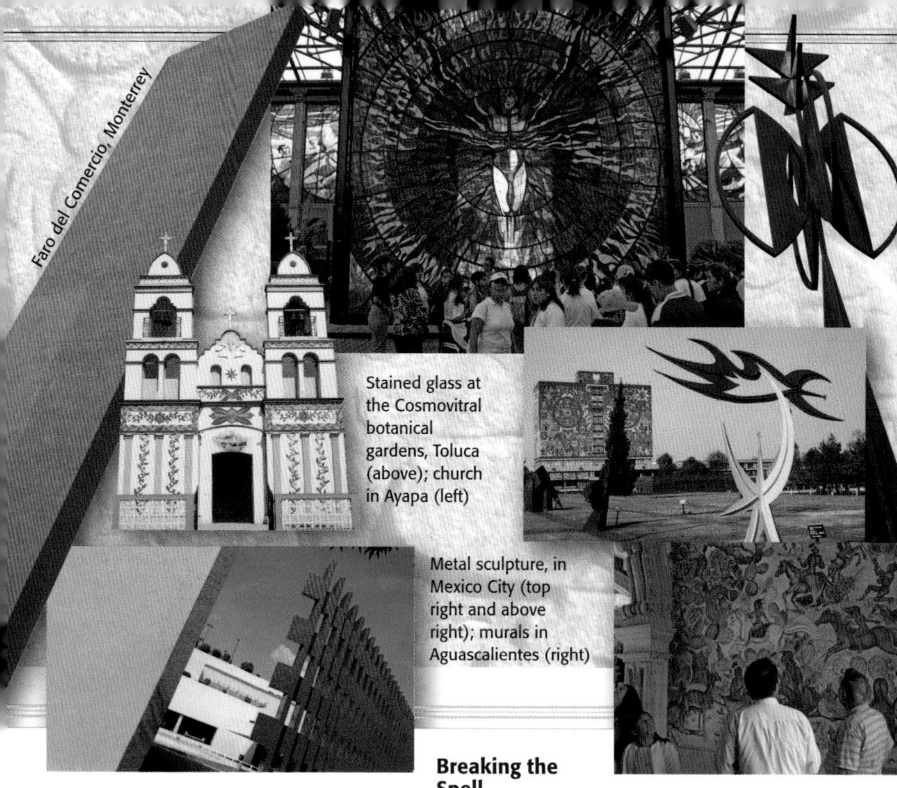

Faro del Comercio, Monterrey

Stained glass at the Cosmovitral botanical gardens, Toluca (above); church in Ayapa (left)

Metal sculpture, in Mexico City (top right and above right); murals in Aguascalientes (right)

New Identity

Carlos Fuentes is Mexico's most celebrated novelist. Among his best-known works are *The Death of Artemio Cruz* (1962), which won international acclaim, and *The Old Gringo* (1985), which was made into a film starring Gregory Peck and Jane Fonda. Fuentes' work has mostly explored the history and cultural identity of Latin America, especially Mexico, but this search for national identity no longer permeates his writing, as witnessed in his latest novel, *Inez* (2002), a love story based around Berlioz's opera *The Damnation of Faust*. Fuentes says: "You have an absolute freedom in Mexican writing today in which you don't necessarily have to deal with the Mexican identity…because we have an identity… we know who we are. We know what it means to be a Mexican."

Inspiration from the Past

One of the great landmarks of Polanco is the Camino Real Hotel (above), with its unmistakable hot-pink and canary-yellow walls. Opened in 1968, it was the result of collaboration between two of Mexico's leading architects, Luis Barragán and Ricardo Legorreta. Barragán was, without doubt, the most influential Mexican architect of the 20th century, having been awarded architecture's Nobel Prize, the Pritzker Laureate, in 1980. His most famous disciple, Legorreta, has gone on to enjoy a career of unbridled success and international acclaim. The work of both men may be at the cutting edge of contemporary architecture, but their use of clean, simple lines and vivid color to reflect the natural elements is based on pre-Hispanic, indigenous building principles.

Breaking the Spell

In 1967 Colombian writer Gabriel García Márquez wrote *One Hundred Years of Solitude* and lit the fuse of the so-called Latin American literature boom. Now a new boom is under way, led by thirtysomething Mexican writer Jorge Volpi, whose 1999 novel *Looking For Klingsor*, a spy thriller set in World War II Germany, has been translated into 16 languages. Together with Ignacio Padilla, Pedro Angel Palou, Eloy Urroz and Vicente Herrasti, Volpi forms the self-dubbed "crack generation," who have broken with literary conventions, particularly "magic realism," which has dominated the Mexican literary scene in recent decades. Controversially, the "crack generation" have criticized "boom" followers such as fellow Mexican Laura Esquivel and the Chilean writer Isabel Allende, who, they claim, reduce their literature to a mere formula.

Last of the Muralists

Alfredo Zalce (1908–2003) was the last of Mexico's great revolutionary muralists, but unlike the "Big Three" (Rivera, Siqueiros and Orozco), he remains virtually unknown outside his native country. Zalce spent his entire life avoiding fame and fortune and shunning all forms of publicity. When the name of Michoacán's museum of contemporary art was changed to the Museo de Arte Contemporaneo Alfredo Zalce, the artist had to be tricked into attending the inauguration ceremony. Many of Zalce's huge murals and statues are in Morelia, in parks and government buildings such as the Palacio de Gobierno (State Capital building) and the Camara de Diputados (House of Representatives), but they can also be seen in Mexico City's Museum of Anthropology (▷ 108–111).

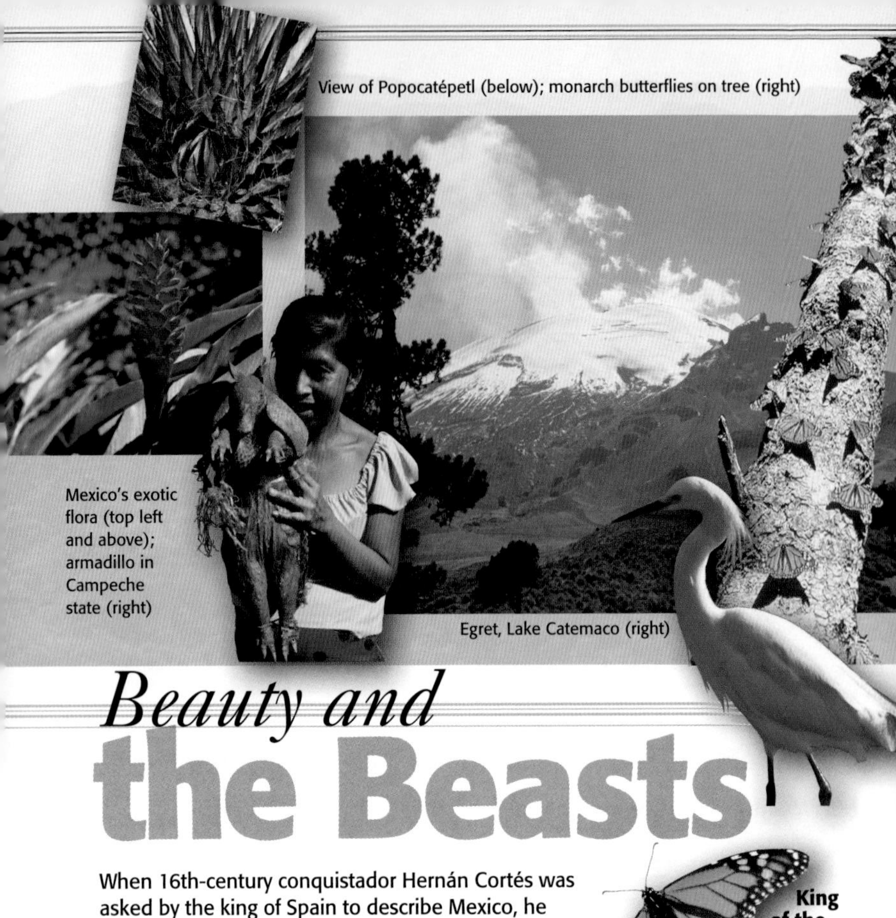

View of Popocatépetl (below); monarch butterflies on tree (right)

Mexico's exotic flora (top left and above); armadillo in Campeche state (right)

Egret, Lake Catemaco (right)

Beauty and the Beasts

When 16th-century conquistador Hernán Cortés was asked by the king of Spain to describe Mexico, he scrunched up a sheet of paper, dropped it on the table and said, "That is Mexico." From the scorched deserts of the north down to the steaming, tropical jungles of the south, this most geographically diverse of countries is dominated by mountains. Running down its flanks from the US border are the Sierra Madre Oriental (East) and Occidental (West), with a series of smaller ranges rising from the plateau in the middle of the country and in the northern deserts. These mountains were shaped by millions of years of geological activity and the process continues to this day: spectacular volcanic eruptions are a dramatic, and often tragic, feature of life for many Mexicans.

The diverse landscapes are home to a rich mix of wildlife. Mexico is the world's third most biologically diverse country, after Brazil and Colombia. It has 700 species of reptile (more than any other country in the world) and 450 species of mammal. Unfortunately, the protection of Mexico's precious natural assets comes low on the list of priorities when compared with economic necessity, and many rare species, including the leatherback turtle, are under threat of extinction.

An iguana suns itself

King of the Butterflies

In the insect kingdom, one creature reigns supreme, the monarch butterfly *(Danaus plexippus)*. In autumn tens of millions of these orange-winged marvels make the 3,000km (1,865-mile) migration south from the northern US and southern Canada to mountainous sites in central Mexico, most notably at the El Campanario Ecological Reserve in Michoacán (▷ 148). The following spring the butterflies begin the return trip north, breeding along the way, but they do not survive the journey; it is their offspring that arrive at their northern home in the summer, and the cycle starts again. The mystery is how each generation of monarchs finds the winter sites each year.

Toucan (above); sea-fishing (below); spider, Chiapas state (bottom)

Eagle, symbol of Mexico (top left); whale-watching (above); cardon cactus (left)

Seismic Matters

Less than 80km (50 miles) southeast of Mexico City and only 45km (28 miles) west of Puebla is the active volcano Popocatépetl (5,452m/17,888ft) and its dormant neighbor, Iztaccíhuatl (5,286m/17,343ft). Popocatépetl, or "smoking mountain" in the Aztec language, had lain dormant for 65 years until it began to spew out ash and red-hot rocks in a series of spectacular eruptions from 1994 to 2001. The authorities fear that this activity may have been a by-product of the massive earthquakes of 1985, which measured 8.1 and 7.5 on the Richter scale and left an estimated 6,000 people dead. Today, the volcano's snow-covered slopes remain out of bounds and "Popo" serves as a constant reminder of just how vulnerable this country is to seismic activity.

Plight of the Turtles

Though the sale of turtle meat and eggs has been banned in Mexico since 1990, the threat of up to nine years in prison has not been enough to deter poachers. The massacre of hundreds of olive ridley turtles at San Valentin in Guerrero state in January 2004 by armed poachers was only one in a long line of sickening incidents. Prized for their supposed aphrodisiac qualities, turtle eggs are sold on the black market for up to $1.35 each. Though poverty is a major factor in this illegal trade, lack of resources to enforce laws is another. Mexico's environmental watchdog, Profepa, has only 300 agents to protect the country's wildlife and relies heavily on support from the army, navy and police.

A Zone of Contention

Scientists studying the fragile desert environment of the Mapimi Biosphere Reserve, near Durango in northern Mexico, face an unusual problem. The so-called Zona del Silencio (Zone of Silence) has developed from a half-baked local rumor into a full-blown conspiracy industry. It all started when a US missile flew off course and landed in the reserve. The US military hastily removed the wayward craft, leaving the way open for a cult of so-called *zoneros* to develop. Among the many outrageous claims made for the area's mystical powers is a magnetic vortex attracting objects from outer space and acting as a conduit for extraterrestrial communication. The result is that the reserve has been overwhelmed by hordes of curious visitors and itinerant oddballs who are putting genuine scientific research at risk.

Alive and Pecking

The success of the campaign to save the thick-billed parrot *(Rhynchopsitta pachyrhyncha)* in the face of powerful logging interests made Mexico's hard-pressed environmentalists cheer. The endangered bird, which is endemic to the Sierra Madre Occidental, only nests above 2,300m (7,600ft), which is where the most valuable timber is found. Some 98.5 percent of the forests of the Sierra Madre have already been logged, and the Cebadillas de Yaguirachic, the parrot's most important nesting area, was targeted for logging in 2002. A cross border agreement between Pronatura (Mexico's largest conservation organization) and the Wildlands Project based in Tucson, Arizona, has ensured a 15-year moratorium on any logging in the area, during which time local communities will hopefully replace lost revenues with income gained from eco-tourism.

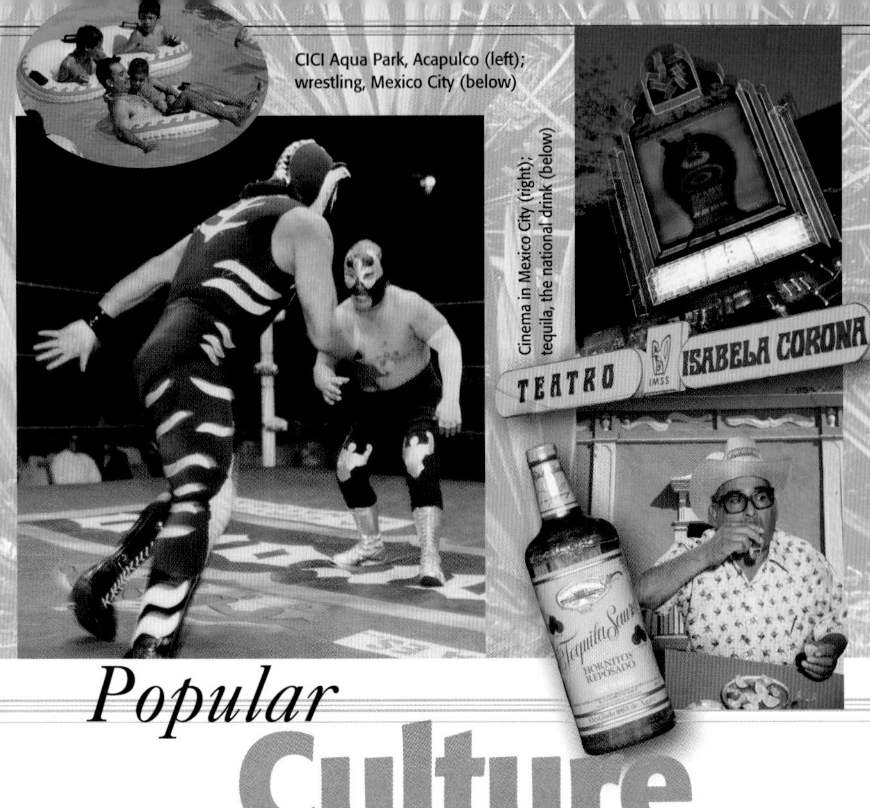

CICI Aqua Park, Acapulco (left); wrestling, Mexico City (below)

Cinema in Mexico City (right); tequila, the national drink (below)

Popular Culture

Mexican New Wave

Mexican cinema exploded onto the international stage in 2000 with the Oscar-nominated *Amores Perros (Love's a Bitch)*, directed by Alejandro González Iñárritu. He went on to make the critically acclaimed *21 Grams*, starring Benicio del Toro, but it was Gael García Bernal who grabbed the attention of the world's media with his role in the 2001 road movie *Y Tu Mamá Tambien (And Your Mother Too)*, which established him as the pin-up of Latin American cinema. Since then Bernal has shown his remarkable breadth of ability in two contrasting roles, first as a transsexual in Pedro Almodóvar's *Bad Education* (2004) and then as a young Che Guevara in *The Motorcycle Diaries* (2004). Could the next James Dean be Mexican?

When it comes to mass entertainment, US influence is ever present, yet Mexicans still prefer their own versions. Take TV, for instance—by far the most powerful medium. It is dominated by the huge number of *telenovelas* (soap operas), and every day millions of Mexicans tune in to watch their particular choice.

The music scene, meanwhile, is a richly diverse one. Traditional genres such as cumbia, which originated in Colombia, salsa and merengue are as popular as ever in dance clubs, while Mexican rock, rap and hip-hop are getting more exposure through satellite channels such as MTV.

In cinema, Mexico's image abroad has not always been a positive one, from the awful B-movies of the 1940s and 1950s to the evil villains of the Spaghetti Westerns. That screen image has been given an extreme makeover with the popularity of internationally acclaimed films such as *Amores Perros* and *Y Tu Mamá Tambien* that have proved homegrown talent can compete against the might of Hollywood.

Carlos Santana was born in Autlán de Navarro, Jalisco

Barbarroja nightclub in Acapulco (left and bottom left)

Painted pots for sale in Chilpancingo (right)

Gael García Bernal (front) in *The Motorcycle Diaries* (above)

Astrid Hadad (right)

Hard Rock Café, Cancún (above); wrestling (below)

Telenovelas

In Mexico, *telenovelas* (soap operas) are not so much an entertaining diversion as an addiction. Prime-time TV (between about 4 and 10pm) features an endless stream of *telenovelas*, each one aimed at a specific target audience, from teenagers to housewives. So gushy and melodramatic are they that they make the 1980s *Dynasty* saga look like a gritty and hard-hitting slice of social realism, but every day millions of mostly working-class Mexicans tune in to follow the twists and turns of each plot, no doubt treating the escapist fantasy as an antidote to the daily grind of their own lives. With viewing figures of up to 25 million, *telenovelas* are big business for the two main TV channels, Televisa and Azteca, and the actors are huge stars, heavily featured in celebrity magazines.

Mexican Rock

One of the most fertile musical genres to emerge from Latin America in recent years is Latin rock. The Mexican band Café Tacuba is a leading exponents of *rock en Español* and their 2003 album "Cuatro Caminos" won a Grammy for best Latin/alternative album. They formed in Mexico City 15 years ago, and their mix of rock, hip-hop, techno, merengue and ranchera, and famously electric live performances, have earned them a huge following far beyond their homeland. It wasn't always so, however. Seen by the left as US cultural imperialism and by the right as a threat to traditional values, Mexican rock music was driven underground in the 1970s. Even the country's most famous rock export, Carlos Santana, was once barred from playing in the capital.

Deadly Diva

In such a macho culture as Mexico, it is ironic that one of the country's most effective political satirists is a woman. Astrid Hadad is the outrageous diva whose notorious stage show has earned her not only national headlines, but also a devoted international audience and the label "Mexico's Madonna." Hadad's distinctive style—dubbed "Heavy Nopal," after the cactus used in the making of tequila—mixes ranchera, bolero, rumba, rock and jazz with performing art, political barbs and a range of surreal and extravagant costumes (she can appear as the Virgin of Guadalupe, an Aztec pyramid covered in writhing snakes or even the bleeding heart of Jesus). Her razor-sharp wit is aimed at everyone and everything, from the Mexican government to macho culture.

Behind the Mask

Since making its first appearance in the 1930s, professional wrestling, or *lucha libre*, has become one of the country's best-loved forms of entertainment. Many of the top *luchadores* wear distinctive masks to hide their real identity. This serves as a metaphor for a country that has concealed its true face from the outside world since the time of the Conquest. Fights are sometimes billed as "mask vs. mask" and the most bitterly contested will result in the loser having to give up his mask to the victor. The most famous of all Mexican wrestlers, *El Santo* (The Saint), went on to become a star of 1950s horror B-movies with titles such as *Santo versus The Mummy*.

Border patrol (above); Mexico City's cathedral at night (below)

Panoramic view of Mexico City (above); scenes from Oaxaca's Benito Juárez market (right)

Urban and Rural

That Sinking Feeling

Though not quite on the scale of the Leaning Tower of Pisa, Mexico City's cathedral suffers from serious subsidence. Inside, the two opposing side walls differ in height by about 1.5m (5ft) and there's a 6m (20ft) difference between the entrance and the high altar. In common with the rest of the city's central buildings, the cathedral's foundations are sinking. Pre-Hispanic Mexico City was a maze of canals, similar to those of Venice, and the Spanish built their new version directly on top, adding billions of tons of weight to a fragile foundation. The population explosion of the last century has added to the problem. At the beginning of the 1900s Mexico City stood more than 1m (3ft) above Lake Texoco; it now lies 3m (10ft) below.

As you fly into Mexico City you get the impression that the capital is lit with 20-watt light bulbs. In fact, the lights are as bright as those of any other big city, but they have to penetrate a haze of pollutants. With more than 24 million inhabitants, Mexico's capital is one of the largest conurbations in the world, with pollution levels and traffic congestion to match. And the problem gets worse as each year the capital, along with the country's other major cities, has to accommodate thousands of poor *campesinos* (peasant farmers), mostly from the south. From Mexico City to Ciudad Juárez in the north, city boundaries are shifting as shanty towns *(colonias)* appear, seemingly overnight, to house the new arrivals.

Life for Mexico's rural population is tough. With only 13 percent of the land suitable for agriculture, farmers need all the help they can get, but the North American Free Trade Agreement (NAFTA) has not benefited them as they had hoped. The flow of migration from the countryside to the cities is likely to increase, and many more thousands will join the army of economic migrants heading for the US border and the hope of a better life in the First World.

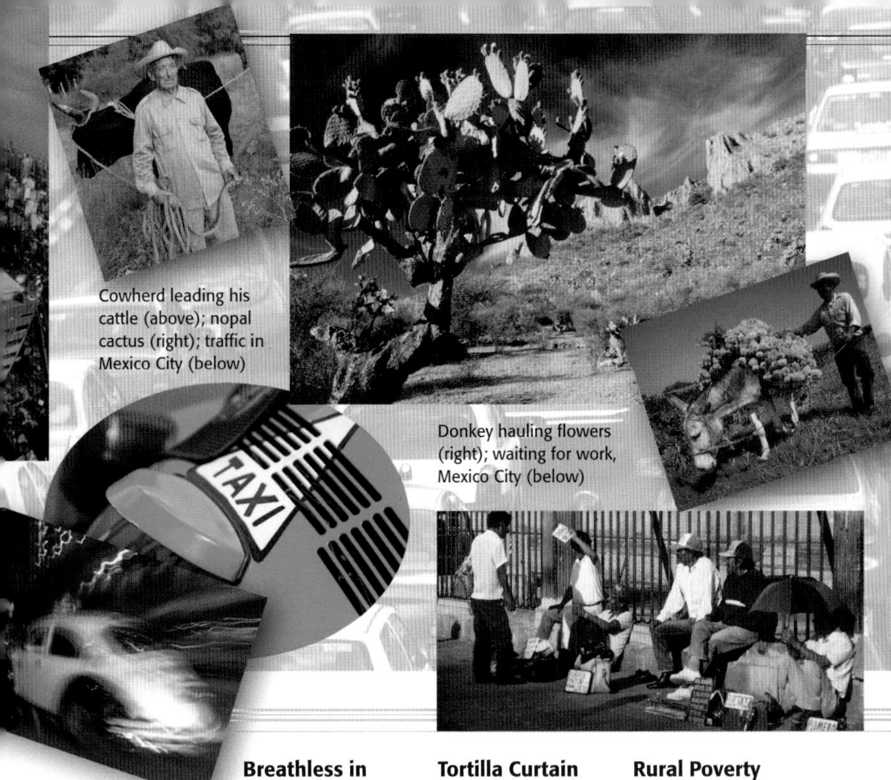

Cowherd leading his cattle (above); nopal cactus (right); traffic in Mexico City (below)

Donkey hauling flowers (right); waiting for work, Mexico City (below)

Beetlemania

On July 30 2003, the world's last original Volkswagen Beetle (number 21,529,464) rolled off the assembly line in Puebla. Though the "Vocho," as it is known, was superseded elsewhere by a new model, in Mexico demand was such that production in the country continued unabated for almost 40 years. Nearly 2 million Beetles have been built at VW's Mexico plant in Puebla, many ending up as taxicabs, and one of the most distinctive features of the capital's traffic-choked streets is the sheer number of these cars, painted in their conspicuous yellow or green. The last 3,000 to be made in Puebla, called the Ultima Edición (Last Edition), came with special features such as a CD player, and the very last one of those now stands in the VW museum in Wolfsburg, Germany, the car's spiritual home.

Breathless in the Capital

In 1958, Mexican novelist and elder statesman Carlos Fuentes wrote his remarkably prescient novel of life in the nation's congested capital, *Where the Air is Clear*. Within 40 years of publication, Mexico City was the air pollution capital of the world. By 1995, emissions of carbon monoxide, nitrogen dioxide, lead and sulfur dioxide all exceeded acceptable levels nine days out of ten, causing migrating birds to fall dead from the sky. In November 1996, 300 people died from respiratory illnesses. Since then, various government measures have helped to improve the city's air quality: the introduction of lead-free gasoline, fitting catalytic converters to all new vehicles and the relocation of industry. But there's a long way to go before *chilangos*, as the capital's residents are known, can breathe more easily.

Tortilla Curtain

One of the most contentious issues in US–Mexican relations is the policing of the 3,168km (1,968-mile) border. Every night, under cover of darkness, tens of thousands of Mexicans desperate for a better life slip into the waters of the Río Grande and strike out for *el otro lado* (the other side). More than a million are apprehended each year by the US border patrol, but hundreds of thousands succeed, adding to the 3 million Mexican-born unauthorized residents in the US (Los Angeles has the largest population of Mexicans after Mexico City). In 1994 the US government erected the "Tortilla Curtain," a huge steel fence with infrared cameras, lights and ground sensors, but the flow continued. In contrast, President Fox's government proposed to provide each of the economic migrants with a survival kit in order to reduce the risk of death from exposure or thirst.

Rural Poverty

Mexicans eulogize the countryside in countless *ranchero* ballads, but with only one in four of the population living outside towns and cities, such nostalgia may seem misplaced. Though one in five Mexican workers are directly involved in agriculture, it accounts for only 5 percent of GDP. The majority are subsistence farmers working plots as small as 1ha (2.4 acres). NATFA (▷ 12–13) has only made things worse for Mexico's millions of *campesinos*, who have had to compete with cheap agricultural imports from north of the border, as well as cope with a sharp fall in government subsidies. With the ending of all tariffs on food imported from the US and Canada in 2003, many rural Mexicans will be forced to abandon their tiny plots and head for the cities—or across the border.

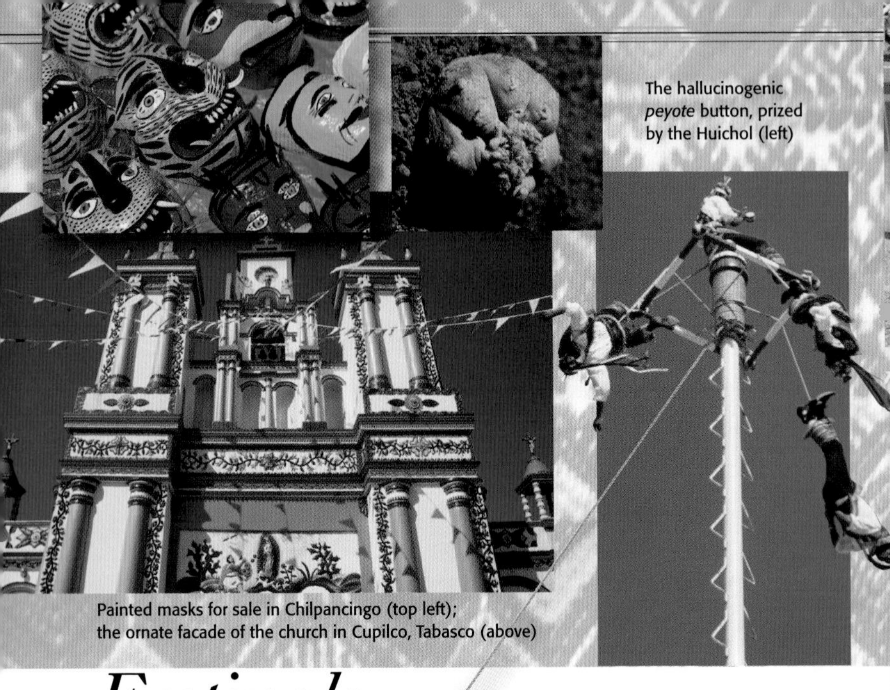

The hallucinogenic *peyote* button, prized by the Huichol (left)

Painted masks for sale in Chilpancingo (top left); the ornate facade of the church in Cupilco, Tabasco (above)

Festivals and Traditions

The Flying Men of Papantla (right and top right); mask in San Luis Potosí's Museo Nacional de la Mascara (bottom right)

Mexicans love a party, whether it's a child's birthday celebration where blindfolded guests try to smash open a *piñata* (papier-mâché donkey filled with sweets), or a tequila-fueled Carnaval with lavish parades and all-night dancing. In this predominately Catholic country, the festival calendar is full of religious events, *Semana Santa* (Holy Week) being the largest and most solemn affair, particularly in Taxco, San Luis Potosí and throughout Oaxaca. *Pascua* (Easter) is also celebrated throughout the country, but most spectacularly in the suburb of Iztapalapa, in the south of Mexico City, where more than a million visitors arrive annually to see its inhabitants stage a Passion play.

Many festivals have their roots in pagan customs, such as Oaxaca's *Guelaguetza*, an exhausting two-week dance extravaganza, while others are a fusion of indigenous and Christian traditions, most notably the *Día de los Muertos* (Day of the Dead). Music, too, stirs the blood of the Mexican people. Most famous are the *rancheras*—passionate and soulful ballads that reach to the core of the national psyche.

Serenading diners in Veracruz (below)

Aside from music and fiestas, Mexicans also express themselves through a huge diversity of folk art, crafting beautiful objects from anything they can get their hands on: wood, clay, silver—even root vegetables.

Charros at a Mexican charrería (rodeo; above)

Church of San José, Tlaxcala (below)

Religious celebrations (above and below)

Musicians in Garibaldi Plaza, Mexico City (left)

Flying Tonight

One dance craze unlikely to sweep Europe and North America is that performed by the daring Voladores de Papantla (the flying men on Papantla). This ancient Totonac ritual takes place every Sunday beside the cathedral in Papantla, and most days outside the ruins of nearby El Tajín (▷ 129). Five men dressed in elaborate costumes climb a 30m (100ft) pole crowned by a tiny platform. The leader then begins to play his flute and beat his drum while his four colleagues, each tied at the ankles to a rope that's fastened to a frame at the top of the pole, launch themselves backwards into midair. With arms outstretched to greet the sun, each *volador* (flyer) spins precisely 13 times before reaching terra firma. The total number of revolutions, 52, equals the number of years in the pre-Colombian religious cycle.

Mariachis

The only thing more Mexican than tequila is *mariachi*, the musical ensemble born in the state of Jalisco in the 19th century. Today, the most prestigious bands still hail from the town of Cocula. With their silver-studded *charro* (Mexican cowboy) suits and wide-brimmed hats, these Latin wandering minstrels sing songs of love, death, honor, betrayal, machismo, politics and revolutionary heroes, all to the accompaniment of violin, guitars and trumpet, with often a Mexican harp doubling the bass line. Seen all over the country, the bands are part of a deep-seated and much-loved tradition, expressing an essential part of the Mexican soul.

Radishing Beauties

Every year, on December 23, one of Mexico's most unusual festivals takes place in Oaxaca. *La Noche de Rábanos* (The Night of the Radishes) is a bizarre mix of folk art and horticulture, when local artist-gardeners create ornate radish sculptures ranging from animals and famous people to nativity scenes. The radishes are harvested on December 18, giving the contestants five days in which to fashion these humble root crops into a sophisticated tableau. The winner receives 12,000 pesos. The strange event has its origins in colonial times, when a Spanish friar suggested that farmers carve their radishes into imaginative shapes in order to entice people to their market.

Cactus Visions

Every year many Huichols, a native people who number only 15,000, make the pilgrimage from their homelands in Jalisco and Nayarit some 485km (300 miles) across the Sierra Madre to the *Wirikuta* (Field of Flowers) in the searing desert of San Luis Potosí, all for the sake of an innocuous-looking, potato-sized cactus. This cactus, the *peyote*, is at the heart of their sacred rituals and considered the fount of life. Through the chewing of the hallucinogenic *peyote* "button" in mystical ceremonies, the Huichol shamans believe they can communicate with the gods to predict the future and ensure the success of the maize crop. For the rest of the group, the visions resulting from eating *peyote* are interpreted through their art, in particular the creation of their vivid *nierika* (yarn paintings) and *chaquira* (beadwork).

Day of the Dead papier-mâché figure (left) and celebrations in a cemetery in Mixquic (below); Chinelo mask (right)

Traditional costume from Ocosingo, in Chiapas state (below)

The Tree of Life (above and below) has become a quintessential symbol of Mexican culture

Tree of Life

The village of Metepec, south of Toluca, is known as the heart of production of the *Árbol de la Vida* or Tree of Life. These brightly painted and elaborate clay sculptures portraying Adam and Eve in the Garden of Eden and their imminent fall from grace are decorated with flowers and foliage, angels and saints, devils, a snake and the ubiquitous Mexican skeleton. Originating in the Middle East and arriving in Mexico via Spain, the trees have become the best-known expressions of Mexican folk art and are collected all over the world. Among the most avid collectors were Frida Kahlo and her husband Diego Rivera (▷ 14), who did much to promote interest in the trees in the country's capital.

A Dying Art

Of all Mexico's religious festivals, one that stands out as the closest in spirit to indigenous traditions is the *Diá de los Muertos* (Day of the Dead), celebrated on November 1 and 2. During these two days and nights, families communicate with their departed relatives by placing offerings of food and drink on elaborately prepared altars, and candlelit family picnics are held in cemeteries across the country. Markets sell all manner of decorative candles and wreaths of flowers, while bakers and confectioners create tiny candy coffins, bread rolls shaped like human bones and little sugar-coated *calaveras* (skulls). The most famous symbols of Day of the Dead, and one of the most potent expressions of Mexican folk art, are the grotesque papier-mâché skeletons, which were inspired by the macabre, late 19th-century political cartoons of José Guadalupe Posada (▷ 37).

Costume Drama

One of the most famous of all Mexican folk legends is that of the erroneously named China Poblana (Chinese-Pueblan). In the early 17th century, a Chinese princess (or Indian, depending on which version you read) was captured by Portuguese slave traders and taken to Manila, in the Philippines, where she was then sold to Captain Miguel de Sosa and his wife and shipped back to her new home in Puebla. Raised more as an adopted daughter than a slave, she went on to devote the rest of her life to helping the poor. Eschewing the elegant Spanish fashions of the day, she wore simple, full skirts and a loose, delicately embroidered *huipil* (blouse) covered with a shawl—a combination of the local indigenous dress and her own native costume—thus creating the distinctive peasant style which has become Mexico's national costume.

The Story of Mexico

Prehistory–1500BC:
Prehistory to the Maya **26–27**
1500BC–AD900:
The Maya **28–29**
1325–1519:
The Aztecs **30–31**
1519–1821:
Spain and the Conquest **32–33**
1821–1876:
Mexican Independence **34–35**
1876–1920:
Dictatorship and Revolution **36–37**
1920–Today:
Mexico Today **38**

Prehistory to the Maya

Though the earliest evidence of human life in Mexico dates from around 20,000BC, it wasn't until around 7000 to 6000BC that the numerous tribes of nomadic hunter-gatherers, collectively called the Chichimecas, began to settle in Mesoamerica, the geographical and cultural area extending south from the deserts and great plains of the present-day United States to northern Honduras and El Salvador.

By 1500BC basic agricultural societies were forming and during the early Pre-Classic Period (1500BC–AD250) some were constructing large public buildings. One of the earliest of these, dating from around 1350BC, at San Lorenzo, near Veracruz, was built by the Olmecs, the oldest known civilization of Mesoamerica. Their origins remains a mystery, but their artistic, social, numerical and astronomical achievements had a major influence on all of Mexico's subsequent cultures.

The ascendancy of the Olmecs was relatively short-lived and by around 650BC they had been eclipsed by the Zapotecs, whose seat of power at Monte Albán, in Oaxaca, prospered from 500BC until AD700, when they lost out to the nearby Mixtecs. By this time, the metropolis of Teotihuacán, in the Valley of Mexico, had fallen into decline, while on the Gulf coast the Classic El Tajín civilization was still at its peak, and would remain so until around 1100.

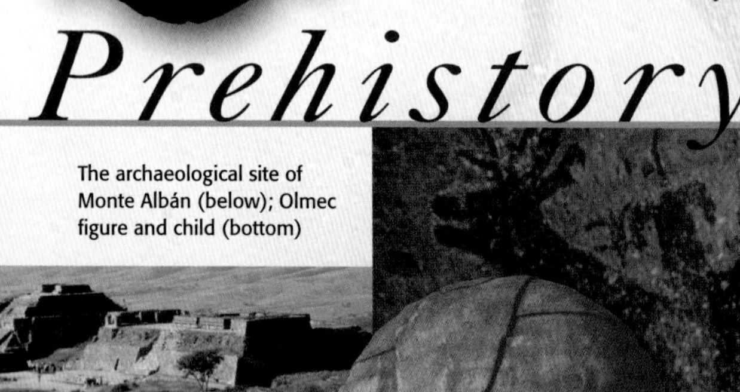

Exhibit from Monte Albán (left)

Finding their Berings

It is traditionally accepted that man first came to America from Asia across a land bridge formed over the Bering Straits at the end of the Ice Age. However, recent discoveries, including that of a skull found in Baja California, suggest that the first Americans may not have come from Siberia or Mongolia. Scientists now suggest that initial settlement of the continent was driven by people from the South Pacific and Southeast Asia, and that they may have arrived by boat via a coastal route. They lived in small nomadic groups as hunter-gatherers but, from around 7000BC, they planted and harvested crops like beans, avocados, fruit and, most significantly, maize, which was to become their staple diet and spiritual source of life.

Prehistory

The archaeological site of Monte Albán (below); Olmec figure and child (bottom)

Heads you Win

The Olmecs' greatest achievement was their massive carved basalt heads, measuring up to 3.4m (11ft) tall and weighing more than 20 tons. They all feature thick-set, flattened faces and typically wear "helmets," which may have been used for protection in war or in the traditional Mesoamerican ball game (▷ 29). The heads are thought to have been made as tributes to Olmec rulers, possibly recarved from the rulers' thrones, leading to the explanation that the stones which supported the rulers during their reign were thus refashioned to become "portrait-memorials" to them after their death. It was the discovery of one of these heads in 1939, with the date marked, which led archaeologists to conclude that the Olmecs, and not the Maya, were the "mother culture" of Mexico.

5,000 Years...and Counting

Though the Maya were famed for their mathematical and astronomical genius, their calendars were based on earlier Olmec versions. The Olmecs had several, including a 260-day ritual calendar and a 365-day solar calendar. These worked using cogs, which were meshed to produce a 52-year cycle in which every day had a religious and prophetic significance. Another calendar was the "long count" that measured time in a linear fashion from the first day of creation. The beginning of the "long count," according to most scholars, was on or around August 13, 3114BC, leading to one unorthodox theory that this date equates to the beginning of the Olmec civilization. Evidence gleaned from Olmec—and later Maya—glyphs (ancient symbols representing numbers and letters) suggests that the present epoch will be completed in AD2012.

Where Men Become Gods

Regarded as one of the most important archaeological sites in Mexico, Teotihuacán—"the place where men become gods"—was the largest city in the pre-Columbian New World. It covered more than 21sq km (8sq miles) and had a population of up to 200,000, which, by AD600, made it the sixth largest city in the world. How Teotihuacán grew to be such a powerful city remains largely a mystery. Examples of Teotihuacán-style objects have been found as far afield as Tikal and Kaminaljuyú in Guatemala, suggesting that the city-state must have benefited from long-distance trade links. Nevertheless, after thriving for almost 1,000 years, the culture collapsed dramatically after the heart of the city was destroyed around AD700, possibly by Totonac invaders from Veracruz, or the Totomí from the north of Mexico.

Animal Magic

The transmutation of man into wolf, or werewolf (half man, half wolf), has become a staple of the horror genre in film and literature, but the Olmecs were worshipping such notions many centuries ago, as shown by the recurring motif of the were-jaguar (half man, half jaguar) in their sculptures and pottery. The principal deity of the Olmecs was the jaguar, the most powerful creature in the jungle, and it was believed that the were-jaguar possessed the intellect and spirit of man and the strength and ferocity of the jungle feline. Only shamans could transform themselves into jaguars, which they achieved through the consumption of mind-altering plants. By taking on animal form the shaman could communicate with the spirit world and use his visions to guide his prophecies.

Olmec heads from Veracruz (left and below left inset)

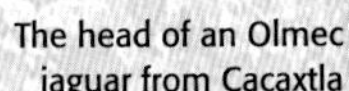

The head of an Olmec jaguar from Cacaxtla

1500BC

Prehistoric cave paintings at Las Flechas, Baja California (left); the Pyramid of the Sun (below left), carving of Quetzalcóatl (below middle) and the Pyramid of the Moon (below right) at Teotihuacán

The Maya

One of the great civilizations of human history was the Maya, who occupied the Yucatán Peninsula, Chiapas and Central America for more than 1,500 years, building great urban complexes at Calakmul (with some 60,000 inhabitants), Uxmal, Kabah, Mayapán, Cobá and Chichén Itzá. The Maya culture, which began to flourish just before the Christian era, made extraordinary developments and discoveries in mathematics, astrology and hieroglyphics. But disaster struck around AD900, bringing about the abandonment of all their ceremonial bases. The cause of this sudden collapse remains a mystery, though theories include famine brought on by drought, internal uprising and massacre by invading foreign tribes.

Whatever the truth, the downfall of the Maya marked the end of the Classic period, and with it the end of the era of great imperial urban cultures in Mexico. Understanding the Maya has been a slow process because much was thought to have been destroyed by the Spanish in the years following the Conquest–including burning hundreds of Maya books (codices). What is known comes from deciphering hieroglyphics carved on monuments and ceramics that were buried in the forest for centuries. Their descendants, Mexico's largest group of indigenous people, still practice the culture's traditional customs and beliefs.

The Flat Earth Society

The Maya belief held that the earth was flat, formed on the back of a basking crocodile that was bathing in a lake covered with water lilies. The earth had four corners, each with a cardinal point and an associated color. East was red and symbolized the sunrise, birth and fertility; west was black (the setting sun and death); north was white (upward and the heavens); south was yellow (downward and the underworld). The middle was represented by blue-green *(yax)*–the combined shades of water, jade and young maize. These four corners were also represented by deities *(bacabs)* who ruled over the days at the end of the year. The sky, which was the overworld, was also held up at four corners by gods.

Pre-Hispanic exhibit, Museo Rufino Tamayo in Oaxaca (above)

Maya stone carvings (right)

1500 BC

Maya codex or ancient manuscript (above); classic view of Chichén Itzá with Chac Mool in the foreground (right)

Giving Blood

As the gods had given life to the Maya, along with life-sustaining maize, the Maya sought to praise their largesse by offering their own blood. Self-mutilation was carried out on the nose, tongue, ears and penis—often by using stingray spines or needles to pierce the skin. The blood would be spilt on tree bark, which was then burnt as an offering to the gods. Another way of praising the gods was through human sacrifice. Ball-game losers (or possibly winners) and enemy captives would have their hearts ripped out or be decapitated and their blood offered to the gods. Such was the value of the enemy's blood that they would be kept imprisoned for years and their blood sapped on a regular basis, before finally being disposed of in suitably gruesome fashion.

In the Eye of the Beholder

In Maya society great weight was placed on physical beauty, and body mutilation for aesthetic purposes was a common practice. A broad, elongated forehead was held in high regard and this led to the custom of children having their heads compressed between concave wooden boards to generate the desired effect. Being cross-eyed was also deemed to be attractive, so beads were dangled in front of children's eyes to achieve this. The Maya filed their teeth and encrusted them with obsidian and the much-prized jade. Quite what a bunch of cross-eyed, flat-faced kids with razor-sharp teeth must have looked like is anybody's guess, though many of the sculptures at Palenque (▷ 92–95) portray the results of such beautification treatments.

Bitter Experience

Cocoa beans were revered by the Maya and used as cash currency. So valuable were they that fakes were made. Tricks of the trade included putting avocado seeds inside the cocoa pod to dye poor-quality beans and improve their appearance. This kind of dishonest behavior, however, landed many a Maya in hot water. The bean also had another use—one that prevails today. It was drunk by the Maya (and also the Aztecs) as a cold, bitter drink with spices such as vanilla, chili and honey added to the foaming broth. The beans would be roasted, ground down and mixed with water, then the extra ingredients added according to taste. It's said that the word chocolate derives from the Maya word *xocolatl*, which means "bitter water."

Sudden-death Play-off

The ball game, invented 3,500 years ago by the Olmecs, was the first team sport in history and became a highly significant ritual for the Maya. The path of the heavy rubber ball represented the movement of the sun across the sky, and by playing the game the Maya were ensuring that this daily celestial journey continued. Each team had to move the ball around a stone court using only their hips, knees, elbows and heads, and the ball was not allowed to touch the ground. Points were scored for propelling the ball through a hoop attached to the walls of the rectangular court. For the participants, winning and losing was a matter of life or death. The losers (or winners—this remains uncertain) were decapitated in human sacrifice after the game.

Cocoa—one of Mexico's gifts to the world (left); wall of skulls (Tzompantli) at Chichén Itzá (far left)

AD900

Well-preserved Maya murals at Cacaxtla (left inset); the ball court at the Zapotec capital of Monte Albán (below); carved jaguar heads at Chichén Itzá (right)

The Aztecs

From humble beginnings on their island home of Aztlán, in northwest Mexico, the belligerent Aztecs—also known as the Mexica—migrated south to the Valley of Mexico in the late 13th century. Within 50 years, they prevailed over the rival city states who had been competing for power in the vacuum left by the demise of the great Toltec civilization, wiped out by drought in the mid-13th century.

The Aztecs were first and foremost a supremely efficient military force. From their base at Tenochtitlán, on an island in the middle of Lake Texcoco, they set about expanding their territory, extracting tribute and victims for human sacrifice as they went, and by the late 1400s they were the most powerful state in the whole country. Their royal advisor, Tlacaecel, declared that the Aztecs were the chosen race who would keep the sun moving through the sky. Following this declaration of divine destiny, the Aztecs began a wave of military conquests across most of central Mexico and south as far as Guatemala, creating an empire to surpass that of the Toltecs, from whom they claimed to be descended. In 1502, Moctezuma II became the ninth Aztec emperor, his reign coinciding with the arrival of the Spanish conquistadors on Mexican soil.

Unlucky for Some

The Aztec calendar comprised the *tonalpohualli*, used for religious purposes, and the *xiuhpohualli*, the agricultural and ceremonial calendar. The former counted days in a 260-day cycle, which was divided into 20 periods of 13 days. The latter was for counting years and worked on a 365-day solar cycle, divided into 18 periods of 20 days, with each "month" dedicated to a particular god and ritual. For example, the 11th month, *Ochpanitztli*, was for the mundane practice of road sweeping, while the 13th month, *Tepeihuitl* (feast of the hills), was marked by human sacrifices and cannibalism. There were also five "empty" or "nothing" days *(nemontemi)*—a bit like our public holidays—which signified the transition from the old to the new year.

Statue of Cuauhtémoc, the last Aztec emperor (left)

Stone mosaic of the Aztec calendar (right)

1325

Brightly dressed Conchero dancer in Mexico City (above)

Diego Rivera mural in the Palacio Nacional, Mexico City (right)

Food of the Gods

The Aztecs worshipped many hundreds of gods but the one they revered most was Huitzilpochtli, god of the sun and god of war, who controlled their every decision and who inspired their notorious ferocity and blood lust. It was Huitzilpochtli who ordered the Aztec people to head south and settle in the place where they would find an eagle with a serpent in its mouth, perched on a cactus sprouting from a rock—Tenochtitlán. To sustain the god in his daily battle with the forces of darkness, and ensure that the sun would rise every day, the Aztecs had to feed him the blood and hearts of human victims. They did this by constantly waging war and taking prisoners for sacrifice.

Heart of the Empire

The heart of the Aztec empire was its capital, Tenochitlán, founded on an island in the middle of Lake Texcoco in the mid-14th century. By the late 15th century Tenochitlán had grown to become a vast city of magnificent temples and plazas, palaces, marketplaces and schools. These were all linked to the mainland by a series of causeways and surrounded by *chinampas*, floating gardens that produced enough crops to feed a population estimated at 200,000. At the heart of the city was the Great Temple, built in tribute to the god Huitzilppochtli, complete with skull rack on which to display the heads of sacrificial victims. At the dedication ceremony, in 1487, 20,000 prisoners of war were sacrificed in a non-stop, four-day bloodbath.

Crime and Punishment

The judicial system of the Aztecs was, in many ways, similar to that of modern western democracy, with accused criminals brought before a jury and a judge pronouncing guilt or innocence and meting out the appropriate punishment. That is where the similarity ends, however. Any breach of the laws in Aztec society was punished harshly. Adultery and major theft carried the death penalty, as did the heinous crimes of commoners wearing cotton clothing or moving a field boundary, while kidnappers appeared to get off lightly by being sold into slavery. Drunkenness was not tolerated. The first occurrence resulted in offenders having their heads shaved and their property destroyed, and if they then proceeded to drown their sorrows, they'd face the death penalty.

Return of the King

The Spanish invaders overthrew the mighty Aztec empire with ease, partly because of an ancient legend, which claimed that Quetzalcóatl would return from the east to restore the Toltec empire. Quetzalcóatl, the plumed serpent, is said to have originated as a priest-king during the rule of the Toltecs in the 10th century. Banished for his pacifist views, he ended up on the Gulf coast, where he then set sail for the Yucatán Peninsula, promising to return. When the Spanish arrived, the Aztec ruler, Moctezuma II, mistook Hernán Cortés for Quetzalcóatl and welcomed him, granting him special protection and offering him treasure. The Spanish were quick to propagate this mythical interpretation of their presence to help them win over their new subjects.

Aztec rain goddess, Chalchiutlicue, (above)

Tzompantli (skull wall) at Templo Mayor (left)

Portrait of Hernán Cortés (right)

1519

Relief carving depicting the Spanish invasion on the base of Cuauhtémoc's statue, Mexico City (left)

Line illustration showing Indian sacrifice (above); carving on Aztec throne (left)

Spain and the Conquest

When Hernán Cortés set sail from Cuba, landing on the island of Cozumel in 1519, before founding present-day Veracruz, he had one thing on his mind. So strong was his lust for gold and silver that he ignored orders to return to Cuba and even scuttled his ships to prevent his soldiers having any thoughts of retreat. So began 300 years of colonial rule, characterized by unprecedented greed, cruelty and an obsession with wiping out all traces of indigenous religious beliefs and practices. For their efforts, Cortés' men were rewarded with massive land grants *(encomiendas)*, giving them complete ownership of everything and everyone and reducing the indigenous population to the role of virtual slaves. African slaves were even imported to boost a workforce decimated by European diseases such as smallpox, and by exhaustion resulting from forced hardship and drudgery.

The Spanish also imposed a rigid social hierarchy, with the pure Spanish-born occupying the top government and church positions, educated *criollos* (Creoles or Mexican-born Spanish) becoming wealthy landowners, and the *mestizos* (mixed Spanish and indigenous blood) and *indigenas* (indigenous Mexicans) at the bottom of heap, with no place in the emerging colony.

La Malinche

One of the most controversial and important figures in Mexican history is La Malinche, known to the Spanish as Doña Marina. Born an Aztec princess but captured in war, she was made a slave before being passed to Cortés as a gift by the *cacique* (military chief) of Tabasco. With her understanding of the Mayan dialects and Aztec tongue, Nahautl, La Malinche was employed by Cortés, first as interpreter, then, when she had learned Spanish, as his military adviser and finally his mistress, bearing him several offspring in the process. Having proved such an invaluable asset in the conquest of Mexico, she was branded a traitor by the indigenous people. To this day, to be called *un malinchista* in Mexico is to be called a person of questionable patriotism or even a traitor.

1519

Cortés on horseback, surrounded by his armed troops and Indian allies, arriving in Mexico City (right)

Rivera mural, Mexico City (above); Cuauhtémoc is brought before Cortés (right)

Eighth Wonder of the World

Perhaps the greatest legacies of the colonial period were the exuberant baroque churches of the mineral-rich cities of central Mexico. Imported from Spain in the mid-17th century, the baroque style came to dominate Mexican architecture, its outlandish decoration and expansive, curvaceous forms reflecting the growing social and economic confidence of the time. By the early 18th century it had evolved into the even more extravagant Churrigueresque, which was named after the Spanish architect José Benito Churriguera (1665–1725). One of the most astonishing precursors to the Churrigueresque style was the dazzling Capilla del Rosario in Puebla (▷ 126). Completed in 1690, the richly decorated interior was described by contemporaries as the eighth wonder of the world and now stands as testament to the ecclesiastical excess of the period.

What the Lord Giveth…

Every bit as ruthless as the Spaniards' search for gold and silver was their campaign of religious conversion. One of the most zealous practitioners was Father Diego de Landa (1524–79), first head of the Franciscans in the Yucatán. In 1562, on hearing that many Maya were still practicing their own faith in secret, he had the perpetrators tortured, then burned every Maya idol, object and manuscript he could find. Four years later, he wrote a painstakingly detailed account of Maya life before the Conquest, entitled *Relaciones de las Cosas de Yucatán (Relation of the Affairs of Yucatán)*. Rediscovered in the 19th century, this book tells us much of what we know of the Maya today. How ironic that its author also did so much to destroy all evidence of this great civilization.

A Very Mexican Miracle

Every Mexican knows the legend of the humble peasant, Juan Diego, who was stopped by a vision of the Virgin of Guadalupe at Tepeyac Hill in the northern outskirts of Mexico City on December 9, 1531. When the local bishop demanded proof of the miracle, the Virgin showered Diego in roses. Returning to show the doubting bishop the roses wrapped in his cloak, he found that they had disappeared, to be replaced by an image of the dark-skinned Virgin imprinted on the cloth. Now the Virgin is the country's patron saint and her feast day, December 12, is the largest nationwide religious holiday—proof that the Catholic Church was willing to turn a blind eye to the occasional Mexican adaptation of their precious tradition in order to ensure the success of their quest for wholesale conversion.

Image of the Virgin of Guadalupe (left)

Vasco de Quiroga and the Utopian dream

One of the most remarkable of the first Spanish settlers was Vasco de Quiroga (*c.*1470–1565), sent by the Crown to arrest Nuno Beltrán de Guzmán, head of the first *audencia* (judicial body) in Mexico City and virtual dictator. Guzmán's reign of terror and corruption had almost wiped out the Purepechan (later known as Tarascan) kingdom, and Quiroga's duty was to repair some of the damage that had been done to the Crown's reputation. Influenced by Sir Thomas More's ideas of Utopia, Quiroga's appointment as Bishop of Michoacán gave him the opportunity to put his dreams of an ideal community into practice. He built schools and hospitals, converted the Tarascans to Christianity, and gave them instruction in arts and crafts. These skills have been passed down and today the Tarascan people are among the finest craftspeople in Mexico.

1821

Statue of the last Tarascan king in Colima (left); outside Puebla's Iglesia de Santo Domingo (below) and inside the gold-decorated Rosary Chapel (right)

Mexican Independence

Cry Freedom
On the morning of September 16 1810, in the village of Dolores (now Dolores Hidalgo; ▷ 139), the 60-year-old Creole priest, Father Miguel Hidalgo y Costilla, rang the church bells as usual to call the local people to Mass. What he had to say to them, however, would change the course of Mexican history. He urged his congregation to rise up against their Spanish oppressors and seize back the lands that had been stolen from their forefathers. With the now legendary cry *(grito)* of *Mexicanos, Viva Mexico!* (Mexicans, long live Mexico), he signalled the start of the long and bloody struggle for independence from Spain. Though he was tracked down and executed by Royalist forces, Hidalgo is revered as the father of Mexican independence.

Mexico finally threw off the shackles of Spanish rule in 1821, under the Treaty of Córdoba, but it was a long and bloody struggle. An estimated 600,000 lives were lost over the 11 years from Father Hidaglo's *grito* (see left) to liberation. Several decades of reconstruction and political and economic chaos followed, characterized by weak government and foreign intervention. In the 30 years between 1821 and 1851, Mexico went through 40 governments, invasion by France and war with the United States , which resulted in the US gaining Texas, New Mexico, Arizona and Alta California—more than half of Mexican sovereign territory—for $25 million.

The second half of the 19th century was wracked by war between the Liberals, who preferred secular federalism, and the Conservatives, who longed for the old days of a centralized and oligarchic system. Two men bestrode this period like political giants. The first, President Benito Juárez (1808–72), nationalized church property, with disastrous results for *campesinos* (peasants) who lost out to wealthy hacienda owners. While Juárez is seen as a hero of Mexican history, his successor, Porfirio Díaz, who came to power in 1876, is reviled as a dictator, whose methods of repression would lead ultimately to revolution.

1821

Statue of Father Hidalgo, in Guadalajara (right)

Monument to Benito Juárez in Mexico City's Alameda (right); carved eagle, symbol of Mexican independence (right inset); mural in the elegant Palacio de Gobierno, Saltillo (below)

A Losing Streak

Many tales surround Antonio López de Santa Anna, who occupied the presidency no fewer than 11 times between 1833 and 1855, and who insisted on being referred to as "His Most Serene Highness" instead of the usual "His Excellency." The most bizarre incident, however, dates from 1842 when his left leg, amputated in 1838 after being hit by cannon fire in a battle with a French army at Veracruz, was disinterred, paraded through the capital and placed in an urn on a huge stone pillar at a ceremony attended by high government officials. Santa Anna not only lost his leg, but also more than half of Mexican territory to the United States following the Mexican-American War (1846–48).

Maximilian and Carlota

One of the strangest events of Mexico's strife-ridden 19th century was the meeting, in October 1863, of Yucatán lawyer José Maria Gutiérrez with Maximilian, the Habsburg archduke of Austria, and his Belgian wife, Carlota. Gutiérrez was there on behalf of a group of hardline Conservative émigrés to persuade the Emperor and Empress to come to Mexico and govern as puppets of Napoleon III of France in order to enforce their own political agenda. The gullible couple agreed, but their reign was a short one. Maximilian turned out to be more Liberal than Conservative and Napoleon, fearing trouble, pulled out his occupying army. Carlota set off for Europe to drum up support for her isolated husband, leaving him to face capture and the firing squad alone. Maximilian was finally executed in 1867 in Querétaro, while Carlota ended her days, insane, in Belgium.

Hero or Villain?

One of the most famous participants in the Mexican-US War of 1846 to 1848 was John Riley, from County Galway in Ireland. Before the war began, the Legión Extranjera (Foreign Legion) was formed from European residents in Mexico, and expanded by the addition of deserters, mainly Irish, from the US army. Riley renamed them the St. Patrick's Brigade and gave them their distinctive green flag, with the shamrock on one side and St. Patrick on the other. The San Patricios, as they came to be known, were eventually captured by the US army and convicted of desertion. Most were hanged, but those who had deserted before the outbreak of hostilities were flogged, branded and set free, Riley among them. His story was dramatized in the 1999 film *One Man's Hero*, starring Tom Berenger.

Flour Power

It sounds like something out of a Marx Brothers movie, but the Pastry War, fought between Mexico and France in 1838, was a serious affair. It all began in Puebla, when a French baker's shop was ransacked by an angry mob of Mexican soldiers. The baker demanded compensation of 60,000 pesos, which the Mexican government refused to pay. News of the incident reached the French King, Louis-Philippe, who was already infuriated with Mexico for defaulting on its huge debt. The King demanded a 600,000-peso payment as compensation and when Mexico again refused to pay, he ordered the blockade of all Caribbean ports. The Mexican government remained defiant, leading in turn to the French invasion of Veracruz, during which Santa Anna lost his leg (see left). The conflict ended when Mexico agreed to pay the compensation of 600,000 pesos in return for a French withdrawal.

Antonio López de Santa Anna

***The Execution of Emperor Maximilian* by Edouard Manet**

1876

The Freedom Bell, rung by Father Hidalgo (above)

Detail of a mural by Orozco in Guadalajara (left)

Dictatorship and Revolution

The 19th century ended with Porfirio Díaz still reigning supreme over a relatively peaceful and stable country, and a widening chasm between a wealthy elite and a poor, repressed majority. It was this stark contrast that led to growing demands for change, culminating in his imprisoned challenger, Francisco Madero, escaping to Texas and issuing a call for revolution to begin at 6pm on November 20 1910. Madero was supported initially by the five main regional leaders—Pascual Orozco, Pancho Villa, Venustiano Carranza and Álvaro Obregón in the north, and Emiliano Zapata in Morelos—forcing Díaz to flee to safety in France. Madero championed a schedule of political and social reform, including the restoration of stolen lands, but during his presidency (1911–13), he managed to alienate both his revolutionary supporters and his reactionary enemies. After a coup in February 1913, led by General Victoriano Huerta, Madero was brutally murdered, but the great new cry *Tierra y Libertad* (Land and Liberty) was not to be quieted until the the election of Álvaro Obregón to the presidency in 1920. By that time, well over a million Mexicans had died or fled the country, and it wasn't until the regime of President Lázaro Cárdenas (1934–40) that some of the more important economic objectives of the revolution were fulfilled.

The Porfiriato

One of Mexico's most notorious leaders was Porfirio Díaz. After promising not to seek re-election, once he took the reins of power he simply refused to let go. He won the presidency no fewer than eight times over a period of 34 years, which became known as the Porfiriato. Under the slogan "order and progress" he suppressed all opposition using the dreaded *rurales*, a rural police force made up of the country's most notorious bandits. With peace restored, he sold off the country's oil fields, mines and railways to foreign interests, while rural workers had their lands seized by the hacienda owners. The Porfiriato may have been a prosperous time for the few wealthy investors, but for the vast majority it couldn't end soon enough.

A poster offering a reward for the capture of Pancho Villa (right). Painting of Emiliano Zapata by Diego Rivera (below)

Pancho Villa (middle) with generals Obregón and Pershing (below)

1876

Mounted statue of Villa in Cuernavaca (above)

Gunning for Pancho

Mexico's other great mustachioed hero of the revolution was Doroteo Arango (1877–1923), or Francisco "Pancho" Villa, as he is better known. The cattle rustler turned bandit ruled over much of northern Mexico, and his resistance against the 1913–14 Huerta dictatorship made him a hero, not only in Mexico but also north of the border as Hollywood filmmakers and newspaper reporters came to witness and record his exploits. This acclaim soon turned to hatred, when Villa's men looted and burned US border towns in retaliation for the US government's support for the new president, Venustiano Carranza. Villa evaded capture by the US government's "punitive expedition" of 5,000 troops, but his luck ran out when he was gunned down by assassins in the city of Parral, on July 20 1923.

Revolutionary Hero

The charismatic guerrilla leader Emiliano Zapata (1879–1919) has become the most famous symbol of the Mexican Revolution. Impatient for the implementation of land reforms promised by newly elected President Francisco Madero, Zapata's guerrillas took control of Morelos state in the south and began the process themselves under Zapata's "Plan of Ayala," which called for the expropriation and redistribution of hacienda lands to the rural poor. Zapata was ambushed and murdered by rival revolutionary leader Venustiano Carranza, two years after his land reform plan was enshrined in the revolutionary constitution of 1917. Successive Mexican governments failed to realize Zapata's dream, but his name has lived on as a symbol of social justice.

Cristero War

In 2000, Pope John Paul II canonized 25 of the clergy killed in the Cristero War (1926–29), the bloody civil conflict between government forces and Catholic rebels, which was provoked by violent Catholic resistance to the increasingly anti-clerical policies of the government of President Plutarco Elías Calles (1924–28). It remains one of the most tragic episodes in Mexico's history and cost some 30,000 lives. In one particularly odious incident, on April 19 1927, Father José Reyes Vega led a raid on a train allegedly carrying money. In the resulting shoot-out with the army escort, Father Vega's brother was killed and, in a vengeful rage, he ordered the wooden carriages to be set alight, killing 51 innocent civilian passengers. He was later killed in battle on 19 April 1929. Needless to say, Father Vega wasn't one of the Vatican's 25 new saints.

Art and the Revolution

The Mexican Revolution inspired the country's great muralists José Clemente Orozco (1883–1949), David Alfaro Siqueiros (1896–1974) and Diego Rivera (1886–1957)—Los Tres Grandes—whose powerful, stylized depictions of indigenous history and class struggle cover huge areas of government buildings across the country. Their fame has overshadowed another of the country's artistic geniuses—José Guadalupe Posada (1851–1913), the greatest political and social satirist of his day. Using Mexico's Day of the Dead skeletons as a metaphor for the corrupt society of the Porfiriato, Posada's lampooning of tyrannical politicians earned him several spells in jail. He died penniless, his talent unrecognized. Now his art, and his place in Mexican history as an important revolutionary catalyst, can be appreciated at the Bellas Artes National Institute and Biblioteca de Mexico (Library of Mexico) in Mexico City.

A relief of Francisco "Pancho" Villa (far left); portrait of General Emiliano Zapata (left)

Statue of Carranza in Ensenada (right); the Pancho Villa Museum in Hidalgo del Parral (below)

Mexico Today

Twentieth-century Mexican politics was dominated by the Institutional Revolutionary Party (PRI), which had governed continuously since its creation in 1929 as the PNR, later PRM. Often compared to the former Soviet Communist Party, the PRI controlled political, social and economic life. Things began to change towards the end of the 20th century, however. The party's old-style corruption and cronyism cut little ice with Mexico's burgeoning urban middle class and its support waned. Growing internecine strife reached a violent crescendo in 1994 with the assassinations of the party's presidential candidate and secretary general. This proved the final nail in the electoral coffin. The victory of the Centre Action Party (PAN) candidate, Vicente Fox, in July 2000 marked the beginning of a new era in the country's history.

Political Earthquake

One of the main developments in Mexican political life in recent years has been the rise of "civil society" (non-partisan, single-issue, campaigning groups). From farmers and students to the gay and lesbian community, many thousands of Mexicans are finding their voice. One of the largest groups is the feminist movement, which has been growing in strength ever since their key role in helping victims *(damnificados)* of the 1985 Mexico City earthquake. In the south of the country, women have been playing an active role in events for the past decade, not only comprising a third of the Zapatista rebel troops but also as leaders of the General Command, and inspiring local women to stand up against entrenched misogynist attitudes. But feminism has come late to Mexico, and women have only had the vote since 1954.

Style over Substance?

Mexico's first 21st-century president, Vicente Fox, is the most US-style president the country has seen. An admirer of Bill Clinton, he has often been compared to the former US president. Fox promotes himself as a down-to-earth man of the people—he spent much of his election campaign touring the country on horseback—and prefers to appeal directly to Mexican voters, over the heads of Congress. Critics have dismissed him as being all style and no substance, and with the Mexican economy slipping into recession, a knock-on effect of the economic downturn in the US, the knives are being sharpened. Mid-term elections saw the PRI scoring gains over the government. For Fox, the honeymoon may be over.

Cuauhtémoc Cardenas, leader of the PRD (below left); Vicente Fox (below right)

1920–Today

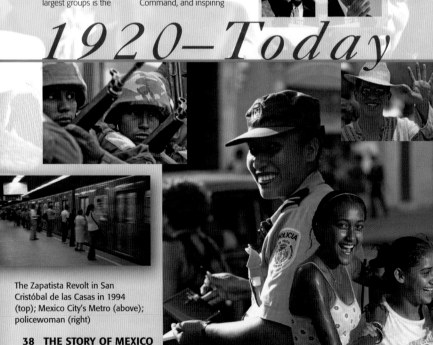

The Zapatista Revolt in San Cristóbal de las Casas in 1994 (top); Mexico City's Metro (above); policewoman (right)

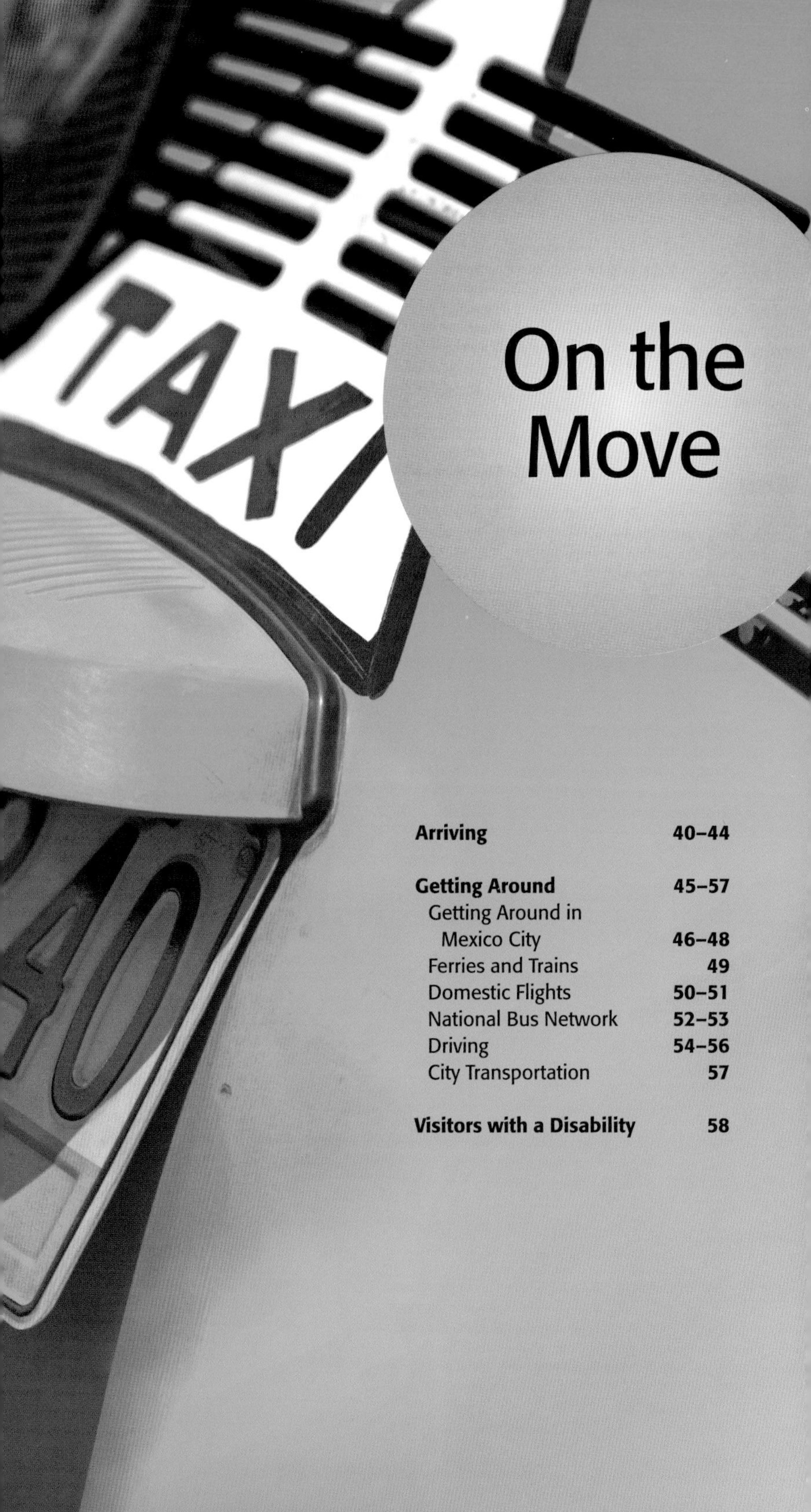

On the Move

Arriving	**40–44**
Getting Around	**45–57**
Getting Around in Mexico City	46–48
Ferries and Trains	49
Domestic Flights	50–51
National Bus Network	52–53
Driving	54–56
City Transportation	57
Visitors with a Disability	**58**

ARRIVING

By Air

Mexico is easily reached by air from the US, Canada, Europe, Australia, New Zealand and the rest of Latin America, with many international airlines flying direct to the country's two main airports—Mexico City (Ciudad de México) and Cancún in the Yucatán. In addition, airlines from the US and Canada fly to as many as 30 other Mexican destinations.

AIRLINES

Mexico's main national and international carriers are AeroMéxico and Mexicana. Most internationally recognized companies such as British Airways, American Airlines, Iberia, KLM and Lufthansa offer flights to at least Mexico's two major airports.

AIRPORTS

Aeropuerto Internacional Benito Juárez (MEX) is 13km (8 miles) east of central Mexico City (tel (55) 55 71 36 00, ext. 2208 for international arrivals and departures, ext. 2259 for domestic flights). The main terminal is divided into six sections, each designated by a letter, containing shops and services. **Sala A** receives all national arrivals, while international arrivals are received at **Sala E**. All national and international departures leave from **Sala D**; however, international check-in is carried out at **Sala F**.

There is a tourist office (tel (55) 57 86 90 02) in Sala A, generally open for most of the national and international arrivals, but the representatives speak only Spanish. In addition to this there are airport information kiosks at Salas A, D, E and F.

Hotel reservations can be made at the hotel desk, prior to going through customs, and at the airport information kiosks throughout the building. The tourist office in Sala A has phones for making free calls to hotels. There is a travel agency at the east exit of the airport, which will book hotels and reconfirm flights for you ($0.50).

There are *casas de cambios* and banks throughout the airport, where foreign currencies, travelers' checks and credit cards are accepted. The rate offered varies so it is best to compare first. Those in salas E and F are usually less crowded than the others. The opening hours of the banks and *casas de cambios* ensure that a 24-hour service of some kind is always on offer.

Car rental offices are near the international arrivals in Sala E, along with 24-hour luggage lockers ($5 per day).

GETTING TO THE CITY FROM THE AIRPORT

AIRPORT	MEXICO CITY	CANCÚN	PUERTO VALLARTA
DISTANCE TO CITY	13km (8 miles)	16km (10 miles)	6km (4 miles)
TAXI	Fixed-price taxis by zone. Tickets available from booths by exits of salas A, E and F. Price: approximately $14–$16 or more depending on distance. Journey time: 1 hour minimum.	*Colectivos* to the Hotel Zone or central Cancún from Main terminal. Pay at kiosks outside airport. Price: $9. Journey time: 30-45 minutes to central Cancún, 15-30 minutes to Hotel Zone.	Taxi: Available directly outside terminal. All prepaid at kiosk. Price: $10. Journey time: 30 minutes
BUS	Services from Boulevard Puerto Aéreo, 200m (220 yards) from Sala A. Frequency: at least every 45 minutes. Price: very cheap. Journey time: 1 hour minimum.	Services from airport to center via Avenida Tulúm. Price: $5. Frequency: half-hourly. Journey time: 30–45 minutes	Buses from opposite airport in main road (take walkway across). Price: $0.40. Frequency: 15–20 minutes. Journey time: 30 minutes
METRO/TRAINS	Metro: From Terminal Aérea, outside Sala A. Line 5, change at Pantitlán for Line 1 to city center. Advisable only if limited luggage, as often very crowded. Operates from 6am–1.30am on weekdays, 6am–1.30pm Sat and 7am–-3am Sun. Price: $0.20. Journey time: 45 minutes.	N/A	N/A

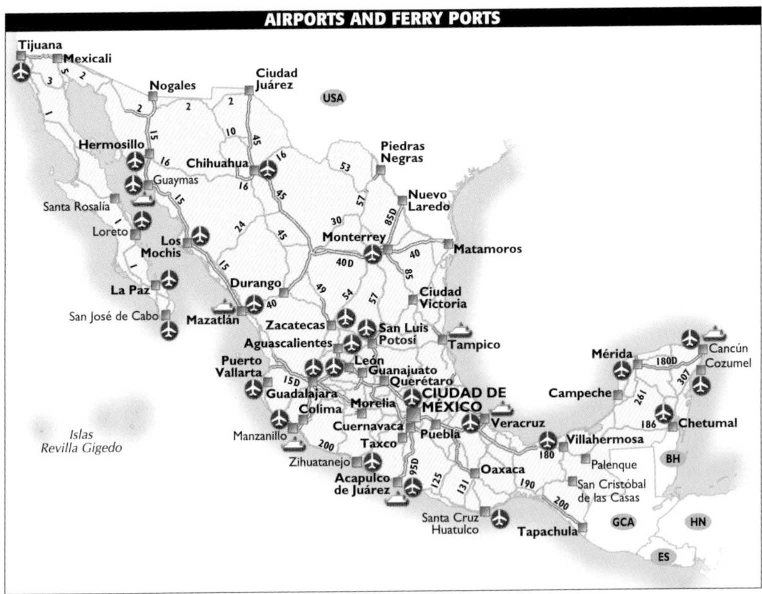

The domestic arrivals hall at Mexico City's Benito Juárez airport (left) with taxis waiting outside (right)

Cancún Aeropuerto Internacional (CUN) is 16km (10 miles) south of the city. It has two terminals, Main and South (or "FBO" building). The **Main** terminal handles mostly domestic and international flights and has many of the major airline operators such as American Airlines, Iberia and AeroMexico. The **South** terminal is generally used for chartered and private flights.

The **Main** terminal contains the essential services you are likely to need on arrival or departure. There are numerous shops and restaurants, but these are very expensive. Also here are tourist information booths, hotel reservation agencies, exchange facilities (which offer poor rates) and car rental agencies. In contrast, the **South** terminal offers only limited facilities. A free bus transfer service runs between the two terminals.

Puerto Vallarta's Aeropuerto Internacional Ordaz (PVR) is 6km (4 miles) north of central Puerto Vallarta and has very good domestic and international connections. The terminal is split into two levels, with check-in and arrivals on the main level and departure gates on the second level. The terminal holds all the necessary services such as money exchange, tourist information, telephone booths, restaurants, a post office and a number of small shops.

Acapulco's Aeropuerto Internacional General Juan N. Alvarez (ACA) is 23km (14 miles) east of the city. It has direct connections with the US, including Atlanta, Miami, Chicago, Dallas, Houston, Los Angeles and

USEFUL TELEPHONE NUMBERS AND WEBSITES	TELEPHONE	WEBSITES
AIRPORTS		
Mexico City	(55) 571 36 00	
Cancún	(998) 848 72 00	
Puerto Vallarta	(322) 221 13 25	
Acapulco	(744) 466 94 34	
Guadalajara	(33) 36 88 52 48	
Monterrey	(81) 83 69 07 53	
AIRLINES (MEXICO CITY)		
AeroMéxico	(55) 56 25 26 22	www.aeromexico.com
Air Canada	(55) 91 38 02 80	www.aircanada.ca
American Airlines	01-800-9046 000	www.aa.com
British Airways	(55) 53 81 03 00,	www.ba.com
Delta	01-800-123-4710	www.delta.com
Iberia	(55) 51 30 30 30	www.iberia.com
Lufthansa	(55) 52 30 00 00	www.lufthansa.com
Mexicana	(55) 54 48 09 90	www.mexicana.com
CRUISES/SHIPPING		
Strand Voyages (UK)	020 7766 8220	www.strandtravel.co.uk
The Cruise People (UK)	020 7723 2450	www.cruisepeople.co.uk
SGV Reisezentrum Weggis (Switzerland)	41 390 11300	www.frachtschiffreisen.ch
Freighter World Cruises (US)	800 531 7774	www.freighterworld.com
BUSES		
ADO GL (Yucatán, Southeast, Gulf, Northeast)	01 800 702 8000	www.adogl.com.mx
ETN	01 800 360 4200	www.etn.com.mx
Grupo Estrella	01 800 507 5500	www.estrellalanca.com.mx
CAR RENTAL OFFICES		
Alamo		www.alamo.com
Avis		www.avis.com
Budget		www.budget.com
Hertz		www.hertz.com
TAXIS		
Mexico City Airport	(55) 55 71 36 00, ext. 2299 (for losses or complaints) or (55) 55 71 93 44 (for reservations).	

Tucson. These destinations are served mainly by Mexican and US airlines, but there are also a number of European airlines in operation.

The airport is well represented by car rental agencies, including Alamo, Budget, National, Hertz and Avis. Facilities here are good—banks, *casas de cambios*, tourist information, restaurants and bars are all available.

Guadalajara's Aeropuerto Internacional Miguel Hidalgo y Costillo (GDL) is 20km (12.5 miles) south of the city. It has good domestic and international connections, which makes it an excellent alternative to Mexico City. There are decent facilities for arrivals and departures, such as money exchange and car rental agencies, but no tourist information kiosk.

Monterrey's Aeropuerto Internacional General Mariano Escobedo (MTY) is 24km (15 miles) northeast of the city. With two terminals (connected by a subway), it has flights to and from many Mexican cities, as well as connections with the US (Dallas, Houston, Los Angeles and San Antonio), Canada and Cuba.

Monterrey has standard facilities—a bank, *casa de cambio*, car rental agencies, tourist information, duty free shops, bars and restaurants.

By Land

Arriving in Mexico overland from the US is a popular option. The large number of border crossings ensures that entry into Mexico is relatively easy for foot passengers and those with their own vehicle. You must purchase Mexican automobile insurance before crossing the border as most US policies are invalid in Mexico. Almost every crossing now has a long-distance bus terminal, making travel from the border easy and relatively efficient. Below are the most widely used crossings between Mexico and the US, Guatemala and Belize.

US

Tijuana

- There is a 120km (74-mile) "buffer zone" south of the Mexican border that allows people from the US to travel in this area without a tourist card. If planning to go any farther afield, be sure to get the correct documents and stamps in Tijuana. The border crossing is open 24 hours.
- The nearest American town is San Diego and it is recommended that you take time here to familiarize yourself with Tijuana (bus times, hotel prices, etc).
- If coming from San Diego airport, take the No. 992 bus from the terminal to the Greyhound station in the city. From here, the city trolleybus service will go right up to the San Ysidro border with Tijuana.
- The number of people and vehicles crossing the border each day makes it very easy to forget or miss the essential border formalities.
- There are no passport checks at the border, so it is possible to get through without completing US exit formalities. However, it is recommended that you seek out the correct place to do this as it will make the return trip much easier.
- If arriving on foot, it is important to get a Mexican tourist card from the office just over the pedestrian bridge. Having done this, it is another short walk to Tijuana itself.
- If arriving by vehicle, progress may not be so fast, as the massive freeway on the US side is cut to just three lanes on the Mexican side.
- Once again, it is important to carry out the correct exit and entry formalities—find the Migración office by heading through the right-hand lane called "Customs." Here, be sure to get a US exit stamp as well as a tourist card with a Mexico entry stamp on the card and your passport.
- It is also possible to get a vehicle permit here, but you will have to head 100m (110 yards) south to get the correct stamp at the vehicle registry office.
- Be sure to have all documentation regarding the vehicle available when crossing as the officials will require a copy of the documents (for example, vehicle permit, insurance, driving license).

Otay Mesa

- This border crossing, 8km (5 miles) east of Tijuana, is far quieter. If arriving from the US you can find this on the SR-117 highway.
- It is open 6am to 10pm daily, but insurance and vehicle permit facilities do not exist.

Mexicali

- Mexicali borders the Californian city of Calexico (although it is heavily Mexicanized). The crossing is open 24 hours and progress is faster when leaving the US than when entering it.
- Be wary of the potential lack of interest from immigration officials on the Mexican side of the border—it is very important to go to them and get the correct entry formalities completed, as it will make later travel far easier.

Nogales

- If entering Mexico on foot, there is no checkpoint to go through. However, there is a customs area that may or may not be manned—you will be under official discretion as to whether you get searched or not when crossing. Open 24 hours.
- About 50m (55 yards) after the checkpoint is the immigration office where a tourist card and relevant stamps can be acquired. As with Tijuana and Mexicali, it is relatively easy to leave the border area without getting the official documentation. While doing this will not be an issue at the time, you run the risk of being returned to the border after a routine check later on in your journey.
- If entering Mexico with a vehicle, it is best to use the truck crossing 4km (2.5 miles) north of Nogales on the US side. The crossing is open 6am–8pm. US insurance can be found here.
- All the relevant vehicle documentation can be obtained at the Mexican Customs Post, 21km (13km) south of Nogales. However, be sure to have the necessary documents with you before you reach this point.

Ciudad Juárez

- The crossing from El Paso, Texas to Ciuddad Juárez is simple, with minimal border formalities required.
- If arriving on foot, you can take a bus in El Paso from outside Gate 9 of the Greyhound terminal for $9. The driver should wait for you at the border as the relevant immigration process is carried out.
- You are automatically given 30 days to stay in Mexico, unless you ask for longer at the immigration office.

Northeast Mexico

- There are five main crossings in this area and the major roads all converge at the Mexican city of Monterrey. The relevant documentation is required at every one.

- Nuevo Laredo is the most important Mexican town in the area and borders with Laredo on the US side.
- East of Nuevo Laredo is the crossing between McAllen in the US and Reynosa in Mexico.
- The crossing between Brownsville in the US and Matamoros in Mexico is quick and easy. It is possible to get a visa from the Mexican Consulate in Brownsville and permission is normally granted for six months at the immigration office at the border.

The border crossing between Mexico and Belize at Chetumal

- Northwest of Nuevo Laredo, there is a crossing between Eagle Pass in the US and Piedras Negras in Mexico, and Del Rio in the US and Ciudad Acuna in Mexico.

GUATEMALA

Guatemala has three major border-crossing points with Mexico.

Ciudad Cuauhtémoc

- Open Monday to Friday, 8am–4pm and Saturday to Sunday, 9am–2pm. Remember that Mexico is one hour ahead of Guatemala.
- Tourist cards and visas can be obtained at the border, but you may only be granted 15 days. Extensions can be obtained in Oaxaca and Mexico City.
- The process is slightly longer for those entering Mexico with a vehicle. At the crossing, your vehicle will be fumigated ($7.25) and you should get a receipt for this. If you are re-entering Mexico, the documents from any prior entry will also be checked here.
- About 4km (2.5 miles) after the crossing, you must go to the Migración office where a tourist card and visa can be obtained or your existing visa checked.
- Finally, head to the Banjército to get the relevant vehicle papers you will need and windshield sticker.

Talismán

- This is a 24-hour border crossing, 8km (5 miles) from Tapachula. The Mexican customs office is very close to its Guatemalan counterpart.
- You must pay an exit tax of $0.45 and there is a throng of children pushing to help you through the formalities–pay just one of them $2 to $3 to keep the others away.
- Be extremely careful at the toilet at the crossing–hold-ups and muggings have been reported here.
- If entering Mexico by vehicle, ensure that you have the necessary documents. These are issued at the Garuda de Aduana on Route 200 out of Tapachula. If you need to make photocopies, do so in Tapachula as there are no other facilities closer to the border.
- The procedures at this crossing are said to be difficult, so patience is required.

Ciudad Hidalgo

- This crossing, south of Tapachula, is reputed to be the easiest and most efficient of the three from Guatemala. It is open 24 hours.
- Mexican immigration is close to the town plaza at the start of the bridge across the Río Suchiate.
- There is a small charge to cross the bridge to Mexico.

BELIZE

- The only major crossing is between Santa Elena in Belize and Chetumal in Mexico, which are connected via a bridge over the Río Hondo.
- It is open 24 hours and can often get incredibly busy with an influx of Belizeans heading into Mexico on shopping trips.
- An exit tax of $13.75 is charged, but the formalities are generally relaxed.
- Mexican tourist cards of 30 days can be obtained at the border. These can be extended by going to immigration in Cancún.
- If you need a visa, go to the Mexican Embassy in Belize City.

By Sea

CRUISE SHIPS

Cruise ships from around the world regularly stop at many of Mexico's ports–both on the Pacific and the Gulf of Mexico. Destinations such as Acapulco, Cancún, Cabo San Lucas, Cozumel, Ensenada, Ixtapa-Zihuatantejo and Puerto Vallarta are popular with cruise operators. For specific schedules, itineraries and entry requirements it is best to contact travel agents or try out websites such as www.cruiseweb.com/ or www.mexicoexpo.com/pages/h_cruise.html. **See also page 42.**

GETTING AROUND

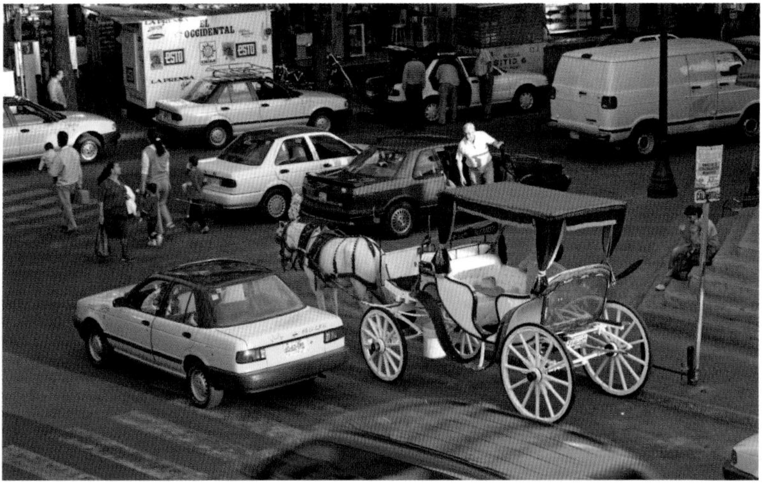

A mixture of modern and traditional transportation in the city of Guadalajara

Mexico is a vast country but getting around can be relatively painless and straightforward, providing you are realistic, plan carefully and remain patient. Unless you have unlimited time, transport will be an issue at some point in your trip. While Mexico does have a good bus system and adequate highways, the country's vast distances mean you could find yourself on a bus for days just to get from one side of the country to the other. It is often better to spend a little more and take an internal flight. If you want to explore the hidden areas of Mexico you will almost definitely need your own vehicle.

TRAVEL INFORMATION

- The main means of travel is via road, whether this be on a bus or in a private vehicle. Although the national bus system can be confusing, the fact remains that there will almost always be a bus from where you are to where you want to go. Most companies offer a varying degree of comfort and this is certainly something that should be considered, as the price will vary markedly.
- If touring through difficult, mountainous terrain on a long bus journey do not necessarily expect to arrive according to the schedule.
- Many bus journeys can take more than several hours and so food and drink breaks are often part of the itinerary. While these come as a welcome relief to all, care must be taken when buying anything to eat or drink. Stick to whatever the locals choose and be ready to leave as soon as the driver has finished.
- Safety on buses is fine, providing you look after your belongings and are sensible with the route you take.
- Touring by car is a feasible means of getting around Mexico. It is often only with your own transport that some of the more inaccessible and untouched areas can be visited.
- Mexico has both toll and free highways—while the toll roads are expensive, they do cut journey times significantly.
- The free highways and other roads may be in a state of disrepair so be prepared; however, the routes they take are often interesting as they lead through small villages and towns.
- If driving into the major cities of Mexico, be prepared for the ultimate challenge as congestion can make progress very difficult.
- Car crime is a real threat all over Mexico and the relevant precautions should always be adhered to. However, most hotels provide private parking facilities to ensure that your car will remain safe.
- Apart from a couple of train routes that are more geared up to sightseeing (▷ 49 and 159), Mexico does not offer any form of integrated rail network, so this method of travel is not really an option.
- Domestic air coverage is good throughout Mexico, with most medium-sized towns being accessible with internal flights. Although prices are high compared to bus travel, the amount of time saved with a flight may well make flying the best option.
- The two major domestic flight operators are Mexicana and AeroMéxico.

Getting Around in Mexico City

Mexico City is one of the largest capital cities in the world. Getting around it can be relatively simple or incredibly taxing, depending on the method of transportation you choose. The metro is cheap, clean, efficient and the most convenient form of public transportation as most of the city's sights are within walking distance of a station. The alternatives are bus and taxi, which are not only affected by the city's notorious congestion, but also add to the chronic pollution problems.

BUS

- The buses have now been consolidated into one system which is simple—all odd-numbered buses run from north to south, while all even-numbered buses run from east to west.
- Mexico City also has four long-distance terminals that broadly correspond with the points of the compass—Norte, Sur, Oriente, Poniente (North, South, East, West).
- It is often easier to identify the bus you want by the route and destination displayed in the windshield, rather than by the number of the bus itself.
- For all large buses, there is a standard charge of $0.20–$0.40, which must be paid in exact change.
- Coverage of the city by the bus routes is extensive, with 60 direct routes and 48 feeder (SARO) routes currently in operation.
- Be wary of thieves and pickpockets on some routes, particularly those in the tourist areas such as along Reforma and Juárez.
- One of the most useful buses for visitors is the No. 76, which leads from Uruguay along Reforma beside Chapultepec Park. Unfortunately the thieves know this too, so be extra vigilant when on this route.
- In addition to the standard buses, there are trolley buses in operation that charge just $0.20 per ticket.

METRO

- This is undoubtedly the best way of getting around the city. The French-built system is efficient and modern and is particularly useful at times when pollution is at its worst.
- The trains themselves are fast, regular, clean and quiet. However, they do get crowded at rush hour (approximately 7.30am until 10am and 5pm until 7pm), and only two pieces of medium-sized luggage are normally allowed.
- As with the buses, watch out for pickpockets and thieves, especially at Pino Suárez, Hidalgo and Autobuses del Norte.
- In total, there are nine lines in service, leading all over the city. They are color-coded in the stations and on maps for ease of use. Maps are available throughout the city and among the best are the Atlas de Carreteras ($1.65) and the Guía práctica del Metro ($9).
- At Insurgentes station (on the Pink Line 1) there is a metro information service and there are many other information kiosks in most of the interchange stations.
- Use of the metro costs a standard $0.20 per ride and it is recommended that you buy a number of tickets in order to avoid queuing at a later date.

PINO SUAREZ 1 2

Sign (above) for a Mexico City metro station (right)

Trolley bus in front of the National Palace (below)

ON THE MOVE

MEXICO CITY METRO MAP

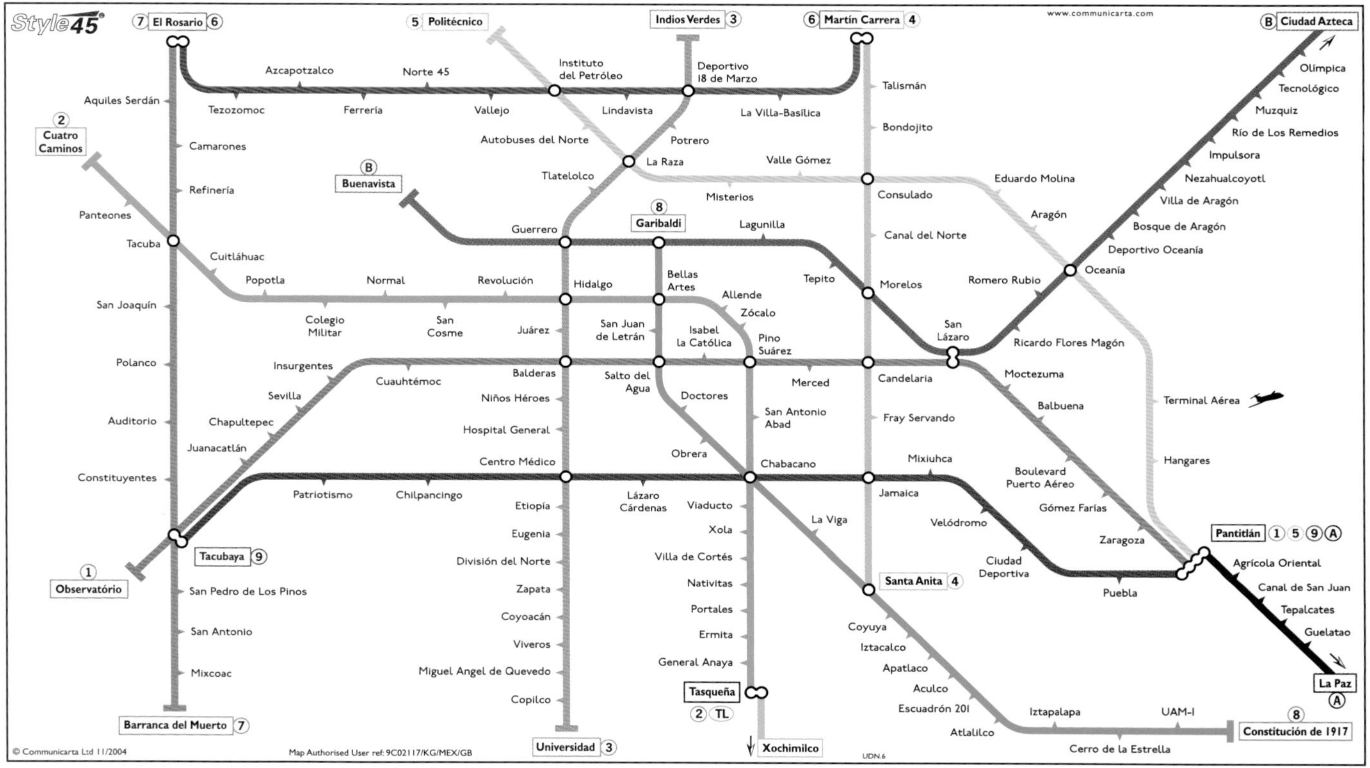

www.communicarta.com

© Communicarta Ltd 11/2004

Map Authorised User ref: 9C02117KG/MEX/GB

UDN6

- Lines 1, 2, 3 and A run from 5am until 12.30am Monday to Friday, 6am until 1.30am on Saturday and from 7am until 12.30am on Sunday and holidays.
- All the other lines open one hour later during the week, but operate the same times on weekends and also during holidays.

Mexico City's ubiquitous taxis (above and left)

TAXI

There are several different types of taxi operating within Mexico City and visitors should be aware of the dangers of using others than those listed below as muggings and robberies often occur.

- Turismo taxis are by far the most expensive (sometimes as much as three times more than regular taxis) and can usually be found outside the most expensive hotels and major tourist sites. While these should generally be avoided, most drivers speak a little English and could be useful in the event of an emergency or a quick dash to the airport.
- Sitio taxis have fixed stands throughout the city and at the airport. They are cheaper than the Turismo taxis, but still cost a little more than ordinary cabs. However, they are safer—you pay at a booth before entering the taxi. Prices vary depending on the distance; generally about $4.60 for up to 4km (2.5 miles).
- Taxis on unfixed routes are the ones that can be hailed at any time. They are usually VW Beetles, or Nissans and other such Japanese cars, but can be clearly identified by their distinctive paintwork. Currently they are green, but are due to be changed to white with a broad red horizontal band. There are also yellow cars, but these are in the process of being phased out and so should not be used.
- The basic tariff is $0.45, with an additional $0.05 for each 250m (273 yards) or 45 seconds traveled. The price increases by 20 percent between 10pm and 6am. Make sure that the meter is turned on and set at the basic tariff when you enter the taxi.
- You can bargain for a fixed price before setting off and you may have to do this, as some drivers may refuse to use their meter after 6pm.
- It is common to find that taxi drivers do not actually know of the street that you want—if this happens, try to give the name of the intersection of two streets to make it easier.
- Unless special help has been given (for example carrying heavy bags), no tip is necessary.
- Solo visitors, and especially women, should take great care when using taxis. If possible, take only the official Sitio taxis from your hotel. It has also been recommended by the tourist police in Mexico City that you make a note of registration and taxi numbers before getting in.

DRIVING

Driving your own vehicle in Mexico City is not to be recommended—the congestion is a huge issue, and getting anywhere in the city can take hours. A far better option is to find a hotel with parking facilities and leave your vehicle there to explore the city on the public transportation system.

However, if you are intent on using your car then you must be aware of the pollution-related restrictions (*día sin auto hoy no circula*) that are in place throughout the week. These correspond to the last digit of your vehicle's numberplate and mean that your vehicle is not allowed on the street at all on the following days:

Monday (numbers 5 and 6)
Tuesday (numbers 7 and 8)
Wednesday (numbers 3 and 4)
Thursday (numbers 1 and 2)
Friday (numbers 9 and 0)

This system only runs on weekends if pollution levels are extremely bad. If this is the case then all even numbers and 0 are banned on Saturday, while all odd numbers are banned on Sunday.

This should not apply to foreign registered vehicles.

Ferries and Trains

Travel around Mexico is restricted largely to the air and road, though there are still some areas on the coast where ferry transport is a possibility, particularly Baja California and the Caribbean Coast. The rail network is virtually non-existent today but a couple of journeys remain popular.

FERRY

There are three major ferry routes in the Baja California area—La Paz to Mazatlán, La Paz to Topolobampo and Santa Rosalía to Guaymas. All of these are car and passenger ferries and therefore convenient for anyone using their own vehicle. The operators offer various options for the long journey, from standard seating to a private cabin; prices vary accordingly.

Tickets for the long-haul services in Baja California can be bought at the terminal on the day of travel or at the company office in the middle of town if you want to reserve a place in advance. For these journeys, you are expected to be at the pier at least three hours before departure time.

It is important to remember that you must have a valid tourist card and, if driving your own vehicle, you must make sure that it has a valid permit. Be prepared for delays, particularly from September on, as the chances of bad weather are increased. Essentially, keep your timescale flexible.

On the Caribbean Coast there are regular, quick services linking the area around Cancún with Isla Mujeres and Cozumel. They are good for both day trips and longer stays.

For the shorter crossings on the Caribbean coast tickets can be bought at the terminal or pier from which the service departs. No advance reservations are needed as the operators run frequent services throughout the day.

TRAIN

There are very few passenger train services running in Mexico today. Although research has shown that most trains will still take passengers, the reality is that they seldom depart or arrive on time, making this an incredibly unreliable method of transportation. In fact, you are likely to reach your destination more through good luck than planning.

Although Mexico does not have an effective passenger rail network, two world-famous train rides continue to prosper.

Chihuahua al Pacifico

- The Chihuahua al Pacifico train journey goes from Chihuahua to Los Mochis. It is known for its spectacular descent through the Copper Canyon (▷ 159).
- For the best views, sit on the left side going to Los Mochis, and the right side on the way back.
- Such a famous railway line attracts a large volume of people—you will have to book seats in advance at busy times. For more information and reservations, tel 01-800-122-4373, www.ferromex.com.mx or www.chepe.com.mx.
- There are two services—*Primera* and *Económica*. Be sure to take your own drinking water, food and toilet paper on both.
- The trains depart early (6am) and often end up at least 1 hour behind schedule.

The Ferromex train in the Copper Canyon

- For the full trip expect to pay $96 for the *Primera* service and roughly half for the *Económica*.

Tequila Express

- This is an easy and convenient way of visiting Tequila from Guadalajara.
- For information, see www.tequilaexpress.com.mx or tel (33) 38 80 90 99. Book tickets through tour operators in Guadalajara.
- Departs 10am and returns 8pm; $60 for adults, $32 for children.

FERRY ROUTES

ROUTE	JOURNEY TIME	OPERATIONAL DETAILS
La Paz to Mazatlán	*19 hours	Daily at 4pm. Prices: $60 to $220 (one way) Sematur (tel 01-800-718-9531; www.ferrysematur.com.mx)
La Paz to Topolobampo	*7 hours	Monday–Friday at 4pm, Sunday–Friday at noon. Prices: $65 and over Baja Ferries (tel 01-800-122-1414; www.bajaferries.com.mx)
Santa Rosalía to Guaymas	*9 hours	Tuesday, Friday, Sunday at 8pm. Prices: $60 (foot passenger) to $185 (with own vehicle). Santa Rosalía Ferries (tel 01-615 152 12 46; www.ferrysantarosalia.com)
Cancún to Isla Mujeres	30 minutes	9 times per day between 9am and 4.45pm. Prices: $12.50 (return)
Puerto Juárez to Isla Mujeres	30–45 minutes	3 ferries operating every 30 minutes between 6am and 11.30pm, car ferry 5 times per day. Prices: $3.80, $7–$8 with car.

*Approximate journey times

Domestic Flights

The domestic flight network in Mexico is extensive as many towns and cities have modern airports. However, while air travel within the country is efficient and safe, tickets are more expensive than in many other Latin American countries. This is because of the lack of competition within the market created by the bankruptcy of Taesa in early 2000. Currently, the two main airlines are AeroMéxico and Mexicana. While there are other domestic airlines, their routes and schedules are limited. Mexico City is the hub for all domestic air travel and you may find that you have to go via here in order to get somewhere else—this not only adds to the cost, but also to the time taken up by travel.

BUYING TICKETS

- As competition slowly filters back into the Mexican air industry, ticket prices are gradually falling. The market is still dominated by the two big airlines who fly all over Mexico, but there are smaller airlines with schedules for some of the more popular routes. Where this is the case, prices will invariably be cheaper.
- As a general rule, it will be difficult to find out schedules and prices of the airlines unless they serve the particular town or city where you are based. Most travel agents should be able to help on this front, as can the internet.
- If you intend to fly frequently on your trip to Mexico, it may be worth considering the option of an air pass. Both Mexicana and AeroMéxico offer this service.
- Air passes can only be obtained by those arriving on transatlantic flights and have to be bought prior to visiting Mexico.
- Prices vary from between $50–$400 per coupon, but extra can be purchased and reservations are flexible. For more information, check the relevant websites.

MAIN DOMESTIC CARRIERS

AeroMéxico (www.aeromexico.com), one of the two major national airlines. It has regular flights to most domestic destinations, as well as many services throughout the world.

Mexicana (www.mexicana.com), the second major domestic airline. This offers very similar destinations as AeroMéxico, both domestically and internationally.

Aerolitoral (www.aerolitoral.com), a subsidiary airline of AeroMéxico. It offers mainly charter flights to several destinations from its main hubs of Monterrey, Guadalajara and Chihuahua.

Aviacsa (www.aviacsa.com), an independent operator with destinations in Mexico, the US, Central and South America.

LUGGAGE ALLOWANCE

This information is taken from the allowances issued by AeroMéxico. It may not be the same for the other domestic operators—double check before you fly.

25kg (55 pounds) in coach class.
30kg (66 pounds) in premier class.
Hand luggage allowance is one piece weighing no more than 12kg (26 pounds), in addition to a briefcase, handbag or laptop.

DOMESTIC FLIGHTS AND PRICES

Although Mexico has a large number of provincial airports, it is not always easy to fly direct between them. Mexico City is the hub of the entire system and you will often find that you will have to go via here in order to get your next destination. Below is a list of the prices and times of flights from Mexico City to the major towns and cities elsewhere in Mexico, the prices quoted are for an adult return trip in high season with AeroMéxico.
Mexico City to Acapulco: 1 hour, $350, non-stop.
Mexico City to Cancún: 1 hour 55 minutes, $344, non-stop.
Mexico City to Guadalajara: 1 hour 10 minutes, $326, non-stop.
Mexico City to Monterrey: 1 hour 30 minutes, $333, non-stop.
Mexico City to Tijuana: 3 hours

30 minutes, $410, non-stop. Mexico City to Oaxaca: 55 minutes, $327, non-stop.

- Apart from charter flights, the majority of flights between towns will go via Mexico City.
- Different airlines will offer various routes and you may be able to find direct flights from certain locations that no others have.
- For up-to-date information check operator websites and telephone numbers as well as asking local travel agents, who should be able to provide information on any special offers being given by the airlines.
- If you want to fly from one town to another, rather than travel by road, it is worth checking to see whether you can do this direct, as the time difference between a bus journey and a flight may not be all that much and the prices of the buses may be much lower.

ROUTES

- Monterrey to Cancún: There is no direct flight available and the journey will take a minimum of 5 hours.
- Guadalajara to Monterrey: There are direct flights available at certain times during the day with a travel time of around 1 hour 15 minutes. If there is a connection in Mexico City the travel time will increase to 4 hours 30 minutes.
- Tijuana to Acapulco: Once again it is not possible to fly direct on both legs of the journey; at least one part will have a connection in Mexico City. If flying direct, the journey should take 3 hours 40 minutes, while the total time if connecting at Mexico City is 7 hours 40 minutes.
- Cancún to Oaxaca: The total journey time with a connection at Mexico City is 5 hours.
- Puerto Vallarta to Ciudad del Carmen: There is no direct flight for this route; the connection in Mexico City makes the journey 8 hours 10 minutes.

NATIONAL AIRLINE CARRIER ROUTES

	AEROMEXICO	MEXICANA	AEROLITORAL	AVIACSA
Acapulco	✔	✔	✔	✔
Aguascalientes	✔	✔	✔	
Campeche	✔			
Cancún	✔	✔		✔
Chihuahua	✔	✔	✔	
Ciudad del Carmen	✔	✔	✔	
Ciudad Juárez	✔	✔	✔	
Ciudad Victoria	✔	✔		
Colima	✔	✔		
Cozumel		✔		
Culiacan	✔	✔	✔	
Durango	✔	✔	✔	
Guadalajara	✔	✔	✔	✔
Hermosillo	✔	✔	✔	✔
Huatulco	✔	✔		
Ixtap	✔	✔		
Jalapa	✔	✔		
La Paz	✔	✔	✔	
Lazaro Cardenas	✔	✔		
León	✔	✔		✔
Los Cabos	✔	✔		
Los Mochis	✔	✔	✔	
Manzanillo		✔	✔	
Matamoros	✔	✔	✔	
Mazatlán	✔	✔		
Mérida	✔	✔		✔
Mexicali	✔	✔	✔	✔
Mexico City	✔	✔	✔	
Minatitlan	✔	✔		
Monclova	✔		✔	
Monterrey	✔	✔	✔	✔
Morelia	✔	✔		✔
Oaxaca	✔	✔		✔
Piedras Negras	✔	✔	✔	
Poza Rica	✔	v	✔	
Puerto Vallarta	✔	✔	✔	
Querétaro	✔	✔	✔	
Reynosa	✔	✔	✔	
Salina Cruz	✔	✔		
Saltillo		✔		
San Jose del Cabo		✔		
San Luis Potosí	✔	✔	✔	
Tampico		✔	✔	
Tapachula	✔	✔		✔
Tepic	✔	✔		
Tijuana	✔	✔	✔	✔
Torreon	✔	✔	✔	
Tuxtla Gutiérrez	✔	✔		✔
Uruapan	✔	✔		
Veracruz	✔	✔	✔	
Villahermosa	✔	✔	✔	✔
Zacatecas	✔	✔		
Zihuatanejo		✔	✔	

National Bus Network

Mexico's domestic bus network is efficient and much cheaper than air travel. While the journey can take a significant amount of time, travel by bus is a good option if you are not on a tight schedule. One of the main problems is trying to find exactly where the bus you want leaves from. In most towns and cities there is a central terminal, although in others there are two terminals according to first- and second-class travel, and there is sometimes even a division according to the different companies operating. As with most things in Mexico, the capital is the central hub for all bus travel—you can get anywhere from here—though most towns and cities operate services to other towns and cities in the region. Comfort and safety on buses can be an issue, but should not detract from using them as a reliable option.

BUS SERVICES

- Recent upgrades of Mexican buses have left them for the most part organized, clean and prompt.
- If you are planning to cover a long distance the full range of services is likely to be available, but this will probably not be the case if you are going between two small towns or villages.
- The distances involved in long-distance bus travel are huge, and so buses of all classes will make food and comfort stops.
- You can travel in absolute luxury or in second class, and the prices often reflect this. At the top end of the market are the luxury services, which compete with airlines for comfort.
- Luxury buses offer an exceptional level of comfort and service, but this does add between 35 to 40 percent onto the price of regular first-class buses.
- First-class buses are probably the best means of road travel—they are a reliable and fairly economical means of covering large distances in relative comfort. All offer air-conditioning, toilets, videos etc.
- Second-class buses are really only suitable for shorter journeys. They are often in a state of disrepair and travel along poorly maintained routes, which makes for a bumpy and uncomfortable ride, particularly as they are often the most crowded.

USEFUL TIPS

- Try to sit at the front of a bus on long journeys—by the time of arrival they can get smelly.
- Bring warm clothing if the bus has air-conditioning—it can get very cold.
- If visiting the Yucatán Peninsula always try to book in advance, especially at holiday times.
- Be aware of the busiest times of the year when seats are hard to come by—these tend to be school holidays, August and the 15 days leading up to New Year.

BUYING TICKETS

- Some of the more organized bus companies now have computerized systems, so reservations can be made on certain journeys.
- There are many different bus companies, so prices do vary. The best means of comparing these is to go to the bus terminal itself and shop around—prices, classes and timetables should be posted at the company office in the terminal itself.

BUS COMPANIES

BUS COMPANY	AREAS SERVED	CONTACT DETAILS
ADO	the Yucután, the southeast, the Gulf and northeast Mexico	01-800-702-8000 www.ado.com.mx.
Cristóbal Colón	south of Mexico City	01-800-702-8000 www.cristobalcolon.com.mx.
ETN	northeast of Mexico City	01-800-715-5519 www.etn.com.mx.
Estrella de Oro	southwest of Mexico City	(55) 55 49 85 20 www.estrelladeoro.com.mx.
Flecha Amarilla	Central Mexico	01-800-375-7587 www.flecha-amarilla.com
Grupo Estrella	runs services through several companies all over Mexico	01-800-507-550 www.estrellablanca.com.mx.
Omnibus de México	north of Mexico City	01-800-849-0208 www.omnibusdemexico.com.mx.
Primera Plus	mid-central to southern Mexico	(55) 55 67 71 76 www.primeraplus.com.mx.
UNO	north of Mexico City	01-800-702-8000 www.uno.com.mx.

SERVICES FROM MEXICO CITY			
DESTINATION	**COMPANIES**	**JOURNEY TIME**	**TERMINAL**
Acapulco	Estrella de Oro, Turistar, Futura	5–6 hours	Sur
Aguascalientes	ETN, Fletcha Amarilla	6 hours	Norte
Cancún	ADO	24 hours	Sur
Chihuahua	Transportes Chihuahenses, Omnibus de México	20 hours	Norte
Cuernavaca	Pullman de Morelos	1 hour 30 minutes	Sur
Guanajuato	ETN, Primera Plus	5 hours	Norte
Guadalajara	ETN, Primera Plus, Futura, Fletcha Amarilla	7 hours	Norte, Poniente
Huatulco	Cristobal Colon, Fletcha Roja	14 hours	Sur, Oriente
La Paz (via Mazatlán)	Futura, ABC (serves Baja California)	17 hours to Mazatlán, 19 hours ferry to La Paz	Norte
Manzanillo	ETN, UNO	12 hours	Norte
Mazatlán	Futura, Transportes del Pacifico	17 hours	Norte
Monterrey	Estrella Blanca, Futura	12 hours	Norte
Oaxaca	UNO, Cristobal Colon, ADO	7 hours	Oriente, Sur
Puerto Vallarta	Futura	12–14 hours	Norte
Querétaro	ETN, Primera Plus, Futura, Omnibus de México, Fletcha Amarilla	3 hours	Norte
San Luis Potosí	ETN, Primera Plus, Futura, Omnibus de México, Fletcha Amarilla	10–11 hours	Norte
Veracruz	ADO, UNO	5–6 hours	Oriente
Zacatecas	Omnibus de México	7–8 hours	Norte

- Once you have paid for your ticket, be aware that most companies expect luggage to be checked in at least 30 minutes before departure time.
- Some companies offer as much as a 50 percent discount to those with international student cards, especially during holiday periods.
- Refunds are often given for cancellations as long as they are given at least three hours notice before departure time.
- For up-to-the-minute information and the opportunity to purchase tickets for certain routes, the website www.magic-bus.com.mx is very useful.

LONG-DISTANCE TRAVEL FROM MEXICO CITY

Mexico City is the main departure and arrival point for all services. Due to the sheer scale of the operation there are four bus terminals, each serving a different region of the country.

Terminal del Norte: this serves northern Mexico, as well as the US border. There are good facilities here including a *casa de cambio* and cafés.

Terminal del Sur: this serves the Cuernavaca, Acapulco, Oaxaca and Zihuatanejo areas. This terminal can get extremely busy and it is best to reserve tickets in advance.

Terminal Poniente: this serves all locations in the west of Mexico.

Terminal Oriente: this serves southeast Mexico (including Yucatán and Oaxaca) and has a tourist information office among other facilities.

Mexico City Airport: although not a designated terminal, it has very convenient services to Puebla, Toluca, Cuernavaca and Querétaro.

SAFETY ON BUSES

Bus travel in Mexico is basically a safe means of travel. However, there are some points to bear in mind before you leave.

- If possible avoid using buses at night, especially in the states of Guerrero, Oaxaca, Veracruz and Chiapas. Highway robbery is an issue, but journeying by day and trying to keep to the toll roads helps to avoid this problem.
- If you have luggage that needs to be stowed on board, be sure to watch it onto the bus and always keep the receipt if you are given one.
- Try to avoid buses where your luggage is stowed on the roof (this usually occurs in outlying areas) as this leaves you open to theft, especially at night.
- Always clip or lock your smaller bags to the luggage rack when inside the bus.

Driving

Driving in Mexico is a suitable option for travel, providing the correct planning and precautions are taken. In recent years great efforts have been made to upgrade the road network—a number of well-maintained interstate highways now link the main towns and cities. While these charge fees, the contrast with the lower quality, older roads is noticeable and journey times can be significantly shorter. Driving can be an excellent way to see the country's more inaccessible areas, but it is important to be aware of Mexico's distinct driving culture. It is vital to have the correct documents and to be conscious of some of the potential dangers involved. Driving is on the right.

DOCUMENTATION

It is illegal to drive without the correct documents and the police may not be as liberal as you are used to. There should be no problem, however, as long as you remember always to have copies of the following:

- Valid vehicle permit; this is required whether it's a rental car or your own
- Driver's license
- Passport
- Rental car agreement (if applicable)
- Current car registration card (original) and a copy of the proof of ownership (title papers)
- Valid tourist card
- Proof of insurance

SPEED LIMITS

Interstate highways: 110kph (68mph)
Open country: 70kph (43mph)
Built-up areas: 40kph (25mph)

TOLL ROADS

- Toll roads are called *cuota*; they generally work out at about 1 peso ($0.10) per kilometer. The network of these roads is now quite extensive, but they are expensive—between $5 and $14 or more for routes that bypass the middle of cities.

DRIVING DISTANCES

	Acapulco de Juárez	Cancún	Chihuahua	Ciudad de México	Ciudad Juárez	Guadalajara	Guaymas	La Paz	Matamoros	Mazatlán	Mérida	Monterrey	Oaxaca	Querétaro	San Luis Potosí	Tampico	Tapachula	Tijuana	Veracruz	Villahermosa
Cancún	2061																			
Chihuahua	1857	3260																		
Ciudad de México	329	1732	1419																	
Ciudad Juárez	2125	3528	377	1796																
Guadalajara	850	2253	1120	521	1497															
Guaymas	2147	3550	747	1818	681	1297														
La Paz	4623	6026	2951	4294	2571	3773	2476													
Matamoros	1328	2445	1223	999	1600	1029	1970	4129												
Mazatlán	1367	2770	1008	1038	1385	517	780	3256	1311											
Mérida	1739	322	2829	1410	3206	1931	3228	5704	2123	2448										
Monterrey	1334	2451	903	1005	1280	759	1650	3809	320	991	2129									
Oaxaca	671	1550	1914	495	2291	1016	2313	4789	1387	1533	1228	1393								
Querétaro	542	1945	1206	213	1583	416	1713	4157	884	933	1623	736	708							
San Luis Potosí	744	2147	1004	415	1381	347	1578	3955	682	798	1825	534	910	202						
Tampico	840	1921	1405	475	1782	748	1979	4356	524	1199	1599	530	637	556	401					
Tapachula	1101	1614	2535	1116	2912	1637	2934	5410	1829	2154	1292	1835	677	1329	1531	1305				
Tijuana	2822	4554	1479	2822	1099	2301	1004	1472	2657	1784	4232	2337	3317	2685	2483	2884	3938			
Veracruz	778	1425	1868	449	2245	970	2267	4743	1020	1487	1103	1026	367	662	864	496	809	3271		
Villahermosa	1123	938	2213	794	2590	1315	2612	5088	1507	1832	616	1513	612	1007	1209	983	676	3616	487	
Zacatecas	939	2342	809	610	1186	311	1383	3760	768	603	2020	448	1105	397	195	596	1726	2288	1059	1404

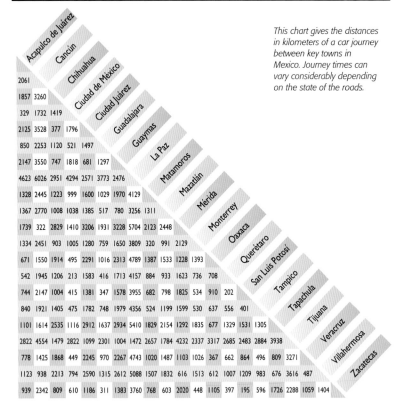

This chart gives the distances in kilometers of a car journey between key towns in Mexico. Journey times can vary considerably depending on the state of the roads.

MEXICO'S ROAD NETWORK

Tijuana
Mexicali
Nogales
Ciudad Juárez
USA
Hermosillo
Chihuahua
Guaymas
Piedras Negras
Santa Rosalía
Nuevo Laredo
Los Mochis
Monterrey
Matamoros
La Paz
Durango
Ciudad Victoria
Mazatlán
Zacatecas
San Luis Potosí
Tampico
Aguascalientes
Puerto Vallarta
Guanajuato
San Miguel de Allende
Querétaro
Mérida
Cancún
Cozumel
Guadalajara
CIUDAD DE MÉXICO
Campeche
Colima
Morelia
Veracruz
Chetumal
Islas Revilla Gigedo
Cuernavaca
Puebla
Villahermosa
Taxco
Palenque
Oaxaca
BH
Acapulco de Juárez
San Cristóbal de las Casas
Tapachula
GCA
HN
ES

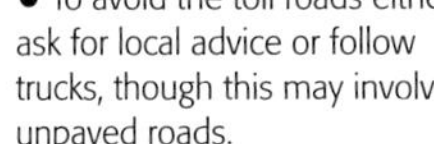

- The high cost of these roads makes them too expensive for many Mexicans, so they are often empty and fast.
- To avoid the toll roads either ask for local advice or follow trucks, though this may involve unpaved roads.
- The free roads are often fine, and have much more interesting scenery.

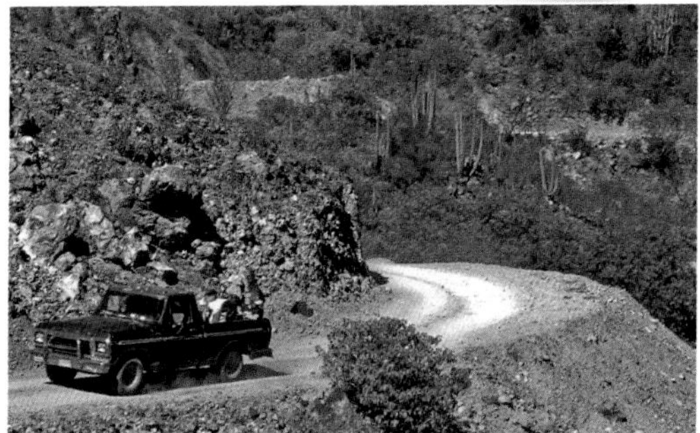

Typical canyon road in the state of Chihuahua

OVERTAKING AND JUNCTIONS

- Mexican drivers have very different procedures when overtaking or meeting oncoming traffic. Be careful in these situations as you may be taken by surprise.
- Road procedures also vary from town to town and state to state, so make sure you acquaint yourself with the local rules to avoid problems.
- When two vehicles converge or when a vehicle is stuck behind a slower one, the driver who flashes his lights first has the right of way.
- If a bus or truck wants to turn across the road you are on, you must give way if that vehicle flashes its lights—in doing this it is effectively claiming right of way.
- At crossroads where there are no traffic lights, the vehicle that comes to a complete stop first has the right of way over everyone else.

BREAKDOWNS

- If your vehicle breaks down on a highway, give warning to other drivers, either with a warning triangle or red cloth attached to your car. If you don't have these, lay branches some distance in front of and behind your car.
- The Mexican Tourist Department offers a free assistance service called the *Angeles Verdes* (Green Angels). They patrol the main roads, often speak English, carry fuel, offer first aid, towing, tourist information and can make minor repairs if required. The service is free; free hotline number (tel 01-800-903-9200).

ACCIDENTS

- It is important not to leave your vehicle if you are in an accident.
- Inform your insurance company immediately. Always carry your insurance policy identification card.
- If the parties cannot agree on whose fault the accident was, or if minor bodily injury occurs, the vehicles may be impounded until the case is resolved.

MEXICAN ROAD SIGNS

Parking Okay

No Parking

No Parking Section Ends Here

Speed Limit

Inspection Area

Stay Right

Stop

Yield (Give Way)

Railroad Crossing

Detour

Speed Bumps

All of Mexico's Pemex gas stations are government-owned

- If there is a more serious injury, you may be confined to a hotel or hospital until the claim has been settled.
- Call the operator (02) and ask to be connected to Mexico City to call a helpline for road accidents; tel (55) 56 84 97 15 or (55) 56 84 97 61.

FUEL

- All fuel is unleaded and all stations are owned by Petróleos Mexicanos (PEMEX).
- Prices are uniform throughout the country—currently $0.70 per liter.
- There are two types of petrol—*Magna* is the cheaper (in the green pumps), while *Premium* is more expensive (in the red pumps).
- Fuel stations are not self-service—specify how much you want (in fuel or price) and make sure the meter is set at zero. A small tip is often expected.

WARNINGS

- If you have any work done to your vehicle in Mexico, try to supervise and keep records of everything, and where it was carried out.
- Do not interact with police (especially in financial terms), but be sure to watch any proceedings closely.
- If you are stopped for something you know you didn't do, do not pay an on-the-spot fine. Instead, demand to see the chief at the tourist police headquarters.
- All cars must display a number plate on both the front and the back.
- If your car breaks down and is irreparable, it must be donated to the Mexican people through the Secretaría de Hacienda.

Be wary of drug searches, especially on the west coast. If this happens, bear the following precautions in mind:

- Keep copies of medicinal prescriptions and medicine in the original containers.
- Keep evidence of all conditions requiring medication with a hypodermic syringe or emergency treatment.
- Never take any packages from other people or take hitchhikers across the borders.

City Transportation

Public transportation in Mexico's towns and cities is varied but effective. In Mexico City, Monterrey and Guadalajara, the metro is one of the easiest and cheapest ways of getting around. Elsewhere, various types of buses offer a sometimes complex, but extensive coverage at very reasonable prices. Every town and city has numerous taxis and in a large city these can often be the most effective means of getting from A to B. Public transportation is normally very safe, but take precautions to ensure that this remains the case.

BUSES

- Most tourist offices will be able to give you information on the best routes and buses to take to your destination; if this is not the case then ask the bus driver.
- As in Mexico City, the destination of a particular bus should be marked on the front of the windshield—double check before getting on.
- Prices vary from town to town, but most bus travel will be a fixed fare, regardless of how far you are going on a particular route. Ask a local or a bus driver to find out—in Guadalajara, for example, the regular price is $0.35; in Oaxaca it is $0.45.
- In some of the bigger towns and cities, be prepared for an uncomfortable journey as the buses are often packed, especially at peak times. As on long-distance buses, be extra vigilant with your belongings.

COLECTIVOS, COMBIS AND PESEROS

- These are essentially minibuses that have a capacity of about 14 people and operate along set lines in much the same way that buses do.
- They are less expensive than taxis and usually less crowded than buses.
- It is possible to flag down a *colectivo* if you are not at the start of the route; tell the driver where you are intending to go before getting on, just to be sure you have the correct one.
- Prices vary normally, depending on how far you travel. While they are more expensive than the buses, the journey is significantly faster and generally more comfortable.

TAXI

- There are numerous taxis in every town and city throughout Mexico.
- Outside Mexico City, taxi colors vary, so check what the official marks are. It is generally safe to hail an official taxi from anywhere other than Mexico City.
- Although all taxis should have a meter, it is sometimes a good idea to fix a price before getting in.
- *Sitio* taxis around airports and bus terminals are a safe form of transportation where you pay at a booth or kiosk before getting in.
- If you are not familiar with the town or city that you are in, arrange a taxi through your hotel—it may be more expensive than regular taxis, but is safer.
- No tipping is required unless the driver has given an extra service such as carrying heavy luggage to a hotel or airport terminal.

CYCLING

- Cycling can be a good way of getting around towns and cities, although in bigger places the busy and polluted roads are not always particularly safe or convenient.
- In the busiest places a rear-view mirror is a recommended safety precaution.
- Cycling is particularly popular in Baja California and there are bicycle repair and rental shops in towns such as La Paz.
- The main cities have bicycle repair shops, but in the smaller places you are unlikely to find much more than the basics such as spokes, tires and inner tubes.
- If repairs need to be made, be wary of mechanics who get quickly to work rather than admit that they do not really know what they are doing.

Typical transport in Tehuantepec

Visitors with a Disability

Mexico is constantly improving its accessibility for visitors with disabilities. The major cities and resorts such as Cancún and Acapulco have many hotels which should be able to cater for most needs. However, outside of these areas, the facilities are generally not adequate for independent disabled travel. One of the best ways to visit the country is with a specially organized tour group, of which there are many—through these you do not have to stay confined within a resort.

BY TRAIN

Train travel is virtually impossible for anyone with a disability. This is the case everywhere, including Mexico City metro, where only a few of the stations have ramps and elevators for wheelchair users, as well as special assistance for the visually impaired. Even at stations with ramps, at busy times this may not be a good option for travel around the city.

The Chihuahua–Los Mochis railway journey does have some disabled access, although it may not be suitable for all. People are generally willing to offer assistance on and off the trains. For more information, check the operator's website.

BY AIR

Most, if not all, airports in Mexico are accessible for wheelchair users. If you do not see the necessary facilities (such as an elevator), do not be afraid to ask for assistance. To be sure that your destination will be accessible for you, check with the relevant airline before starting your journey.

BY BUS

Very few, if any, town buses have wheelchair access. A better option is to use the official taxis. Long-distance buses are much more amenable to disabled travel. Although they may not have specific access for wheelchairs, there is a lot of space inside and members of staff should be more than willing to help if you ask.

BY FERRY

The relatively new ships operated by Baja Ferries between La Paz, Mazatlán and Topolobampo have access for wheelchair users. Ramps, elevators and escalators on the vessel ensure that the journey is a comfortable one. It is still worth, however, enquiring at a travel agent shop or on the pier itself before you travel.

AROUND TOWN

Much of Mexico remains particularly difficult for visitors with disabilities. Away from the major resort towns, such as Cancún, sidewalks (pavements) are rarely ramped and are often uneven or broken. In some places it is unlikely that there will be handrails on the stairwells. However, this should not necessarily prevent you from visiting the sights around town. Many people hire taxi drivers who are more than willing to help those with mobility problems to visit the sights for an extended period of time.

SPECIALIST TOUR OPERATORS

Specialist tour operators are often the best means of visiting Mexico with a disability. Among the best are:

- Directions Unlimited, 123 Green Lane, Bedford Hills, NY 10507, tel 800-533-5343. Specializes in tours for visitors with disabilities from the US. Can organize group and individual tours.

- Disability Action Group, 2 Annadale Avenue, Belfast BT7 3JH, Northern Ireland, tel 01232-491011; www.disabilityaction.org. Information about access for disabled British visitors.

- Disabled Persons' Assembly, PO Box 27-524, Wellington 6035, New Zealand, tel 04-801-9100, gen@dpa.org.nz; www.dpa.org.nz. Has lists of tour operators and travel agencies catering to visitors with disabilities.

USEFUL INFORMATION SOURCES FOR VISITORS WITH DISABILITIES

The tourist board is not overly helpful in finding out how accessible particular destinations and sites are in Mexico, so the best thing is to contact either a disability organization or travel agent for further information.

www.makoa.org has a vast number of resource links for people with disabilities, including information on travel; look under Travel and Recreation Resources.

www.geocities.com/Paris/1502/ is a Global Access website which is very useful for visitors with disabilities. There is information on Mexico, although it focuses largely on Cancún and Puerto Vallarta.

UK: RADAR, 12 City Forum, 250 City Road, London, EC1V 8AF (tel +44 (0)20 7250 3222; www.radar.org.uk).

US: SATH, 347 5th Avenue, Suite 610, New York City, NY 10016 (tel +1 212/447-7284; www.sath.org).

Canada: The Easter Seals Society, 1185 Eglinton Avenue, Suite 800, Toronto, ON M3C 3C6 (tel +1 800/668-6252; www.easterseals.org).

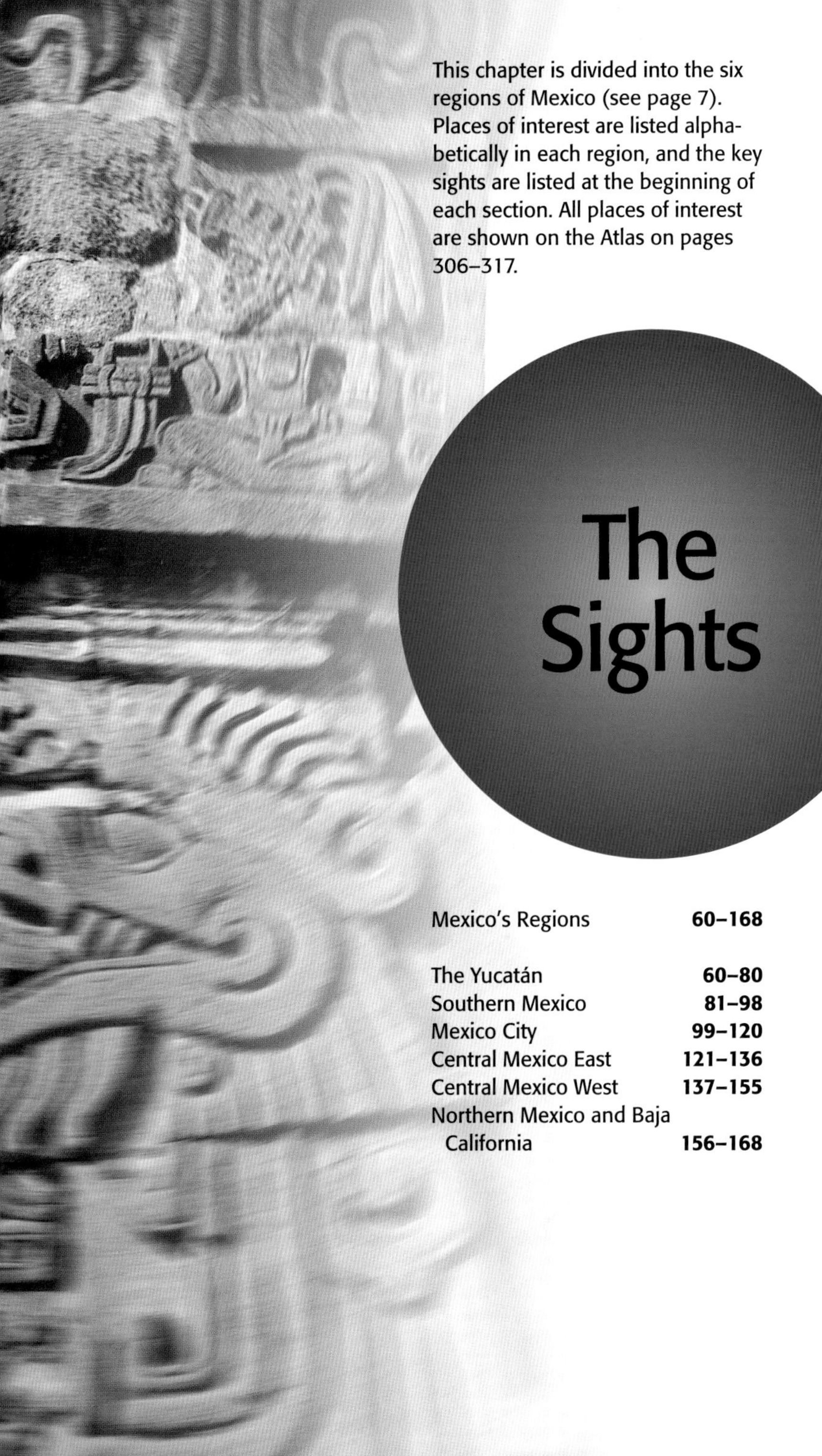

This chapter is divided into the six regions of Mexico (see page 7). Places of interest are listed alphabetically in each region, and the key sights are listed at the beginning of each section. All places of interest are shown on the Atlas on pages 306–317.

The Sights

Mexico's Regions	**60–168**
The Yucatán	**60–80**
Southern Mexico	**81–98**
Mexico City	**99–120**
Central Mexico East	**121–136**
Central Mexico West	**137–155**
Northern Mexico and Baja California	**156–168**

THE YUCATÁN

The Yucatán Peninsula—the land of Maya temples and pyramids and Caribbean beach resorts—includes the states of Campeche, Quintana Roo and Yucatán. The warm turquoise sea of the Riviera Maya, fringed with white-sand beaches and palm groves, is second to none, while the archaeological sites of Chichén Itzá, Uxmal and Tulúm, among many others, invite exploration, as do the area's ecological reserves.

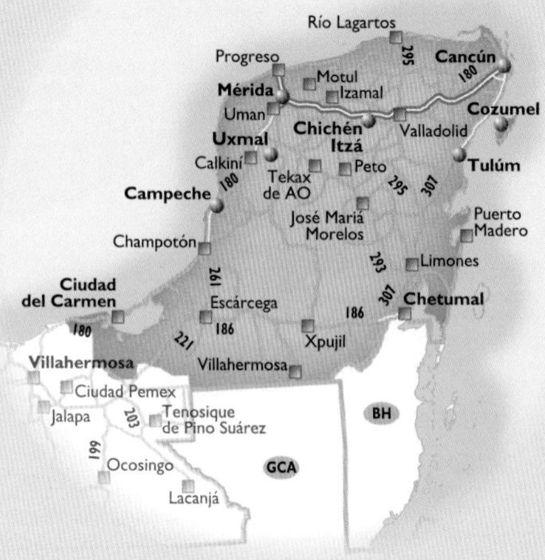

MAJOR SIGHTS

Campeche	**62**
Cancún	**63**
Chichén Itzá	**64–67**
Cozumel	**68–69**
Mérida	**73**
Tulúm	**75**
Uxmal	**78–79**

The sandy beach at Akumal, the "place of the turtles"

The waters around Akumal teem with marine life

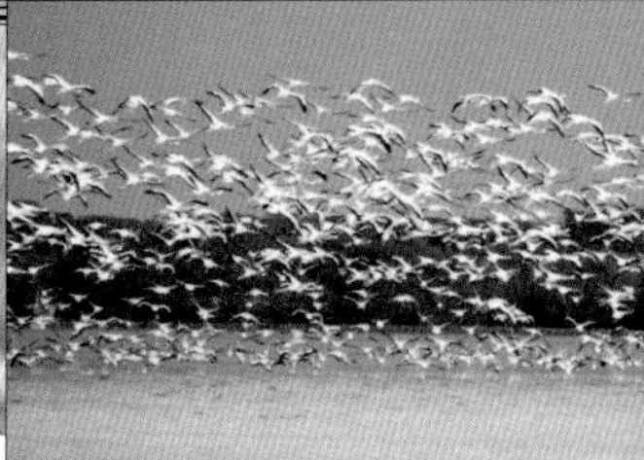
Celestún is famous for its colony of pink flamingos

AKUMAL

317 S8 Buses from Cancún, Playa del Carmen and Tulúm
www.mayayucatan.com

Akumal sits on a gorgeous stretch of coastline, with pristine beaches, azure sea and magical *cenotes* (natural sinkholes). Aside from its laid-back ambience, which makes a pleasing contrast to Cancún and Playa del Carmen, the resort's main attraction is its excellent swimming and snorkeling, with exquisite coral and a series of caves. Divers swarm to the underwater world, marveling at the many species of coral and series of caves separated by canyons beyond the coral wall.

Akumal, meaning "the place of the turtles," is so named because of the turtles that used to come ashore here to lay their eggs. These days numbers are declining as building development increases.

Head north of Akumal, passing through Half Moon Bay, to reach the stunning Ya Kul lagoon (daily 8–5), another popular snorkeling destination.

BECÁN

317 R9 • 15km (9.5 miles) west of Xpujil Daily 8–5 $3

Becán, meaning "path of the serpent," is an important Maya site in the Río Bec style, characterized by heavy masonry towers simulating pyramids and temples, usually found in pairs. Built in the Late Classic period (AD600–900), it was the political, religious and administrative capital of the Río Bec zone.

The site is surrounded by a moat, now dry, which is believed to be one of the oldest defense systems in Mesoamerica. Seven entrance gates cross the moat to the city. The buildings are a strange combination of decorative towers and fake temples, as well as structures used as shrines and palaces. The twin towers are set on a pyramid-shaped base supporting a cluster of buildings that seem to have been used for a variety of functions: religious, administrative and residential.

CALAKMUL

317 R9 • 213km (132 miles) southeast of Campeche, 60km (37 miles) off main Escárcega–Chetumal road
Daily 8–5 $3 Buses from Campeche and Xpujil Agencies in Chetumal offer tour packages (two people minimum)
www.calakmul.org

Calakmul, within the Reserva de la Biósfera Calakmul, is one of the largest archaeological sites in Mesoamerica; it is also the biggest of the Maya cities, with about 10,000 buildings—many of them unexcavated. The city was discovered in 1931 by American explorer Cyrus Longworth Lundell (1907–93), who christened it "the city of two adjacent mounds."

In the middle of the site is the Gran Plaza, overlooked by a pyramid whose base covers 2ha (5 acres). One of the buildings grouped around the Gran Plaza is believed—due to its curious shape and location—to have been designed for astronomical observation. The Gran Acrópolis, the largest of all the structures, is divided into two sections: Plaza Norte, with its ball court, was used for ceremonies; Plaza Sur was used for public activities. Within the reserve there are more than 800 plant species, and wildlife includes pumas, deer and howler monkeys.

CAMPECHE

See page 62.

CANCÚN

See page 63.

CELESTÚN

316 Q8 • 90km (60 miles) west of Mérida Buses from Mérida
www.mexonline.com/celestun

The Reserva de la Biósfera Celestún, on the spit of land separating the Río Esperanza estuary from the Bahía de Campeche, on the west coast of Yucatán, was created to protect thousands of migratory waterfowl. The area's major attraction is North America's sole colony of pink flamingos. Pelicans, fish, crabs and shrimps also inhabit the lagoons, and manatees, toucans and crocodiles can sometimes be glimpsed in the quieter waterways. There are more than 234 species of mammal, including spider monkeys, ocelots, jaguars and sea turtles. The reserve's springs and freshwater pools are good for swimming.

Celestún town is a small, dusty fishing resort, although the long beach, with little shade, is relatively clean with clear water ideal for swimming. Along the beach fishing boats bristle with *jimbas*—cane poles used for catching octopuses. Boat trips to view the wildlife can be arranged at the river bridge 1km (half a mile) back along the Mérida road.

Flamingo from Celestún

THE SIGHTS

CAMPECHE

An ideal base from which to explore the archaeological sites of Campeche state, Campeche is one of Mexico's most engaging cities, renowned for its colonial architecture.

It was here in 1517 that the Spanish, under Francisco Hernández de Córdoba, first disembarked on Mexican soil. Infamous bands of buccaneers constantly raided the port and in 1663 they slaughtered the city's inhabitants. Over the next five years, the Spanish settlement was fortified with a series of formidable bulwarks and *baluartes (*bastions), some of which now house museums. If the heart of the city is the shady *zócalo* (main square), with its small central pagoda, the soul is the *malecón* (seafront promenade), destroyed by a hurricane in 1996, but since rebuilt and now a handsome promenade.

WALKING THE CIRCUITO BALUARTES

Begin at the *zócalo*, where the Franciscan Catedral de la Concepción (1540–1705) stands. Inside is the *Santo Entierro* (Holy Burial), a sculpture of Christ on a mahogany sarcophagus with silver trim. Right in front of the *zócalo* is the Baluarte de la Soledad, the central bulwark of the city walls, now housing the Museo de la Cultura Maya (Tue–Sat 9–2, 4–8, Sun 9–1), which displays Maya stelae (carved upright stones) and sculpture. Walking westward, you will pass the Palacio de Gobierno and the Congreso. Next on the *circuito* is the Templo de San José, on Calle 10, a baroque church with a tiled facade, followed by the Baluarte de Santa Rosa, now the visitor information office. Then comes Baluarte de San Juan, from which a large chunk of the old city wall still extends and connects with Puerta de la Tierra, where a *Luz y Sonido* (Light and Sound) show takes place (Tue, Fri and Sat 10.30pm). A short detour north takes you to the Casa de Teniente del Rey (King's Lieutenant's House), which houses the Museo Regional de Campeche (Calle 59, Tue–Sat 8–2, 5–8, Sun 9–1). This museum charts the history of Campeche state since Maya times. The *circuito* then leads past the Baluarte de San Francisco and the market, just outside the line of the city walls, then down to the northwest tip of the old city. Here the Baluarte de Santiago has been turned into a walled garden, the Jardín Botánico Xmuch'Haltun.

Don't miss The Fuerte de San Miguel, on the *malecón*, southwest of the city, houses the archaeological museum (Tue–Sat 9–8, Sun 9–1), which has a well-documented display of pre-Columbian exhibits.

RATINGS

Cultural interest	●●●●
Historic interest	●●●●
Photo stops	●●●●
Walkability	●●●

BASICS

316 Q8

Avenida Ruíz Cortines s/n, Plaza Moch-Couoh, tel (981) 811 92 55

Buses from Mérida

www.campeche.gob.mx
Excellent background information on archaeological sites in Campeche state.

TIPS

- Campeche's streets in the Old Town are numbered rather than named. Even numbers run north/south, beginning at Calle 8 near the *malecón*, east to Calle 18 inside the walls; odd numbers run east (inland) from Calle 51 in the north to Calle 65 in the south.
- Take the 45-minute Centro Histórico tour. A regular tram runs from the main plaza daily 9–1 and 5–8, and you can just hop on and off.
- Buses marked "Circuito Baluartes" provide a regular service around the perimeter of town.

The Templo de San José (top)

Exhibition of typical Campechan interiors in the zócalo *(inset)*

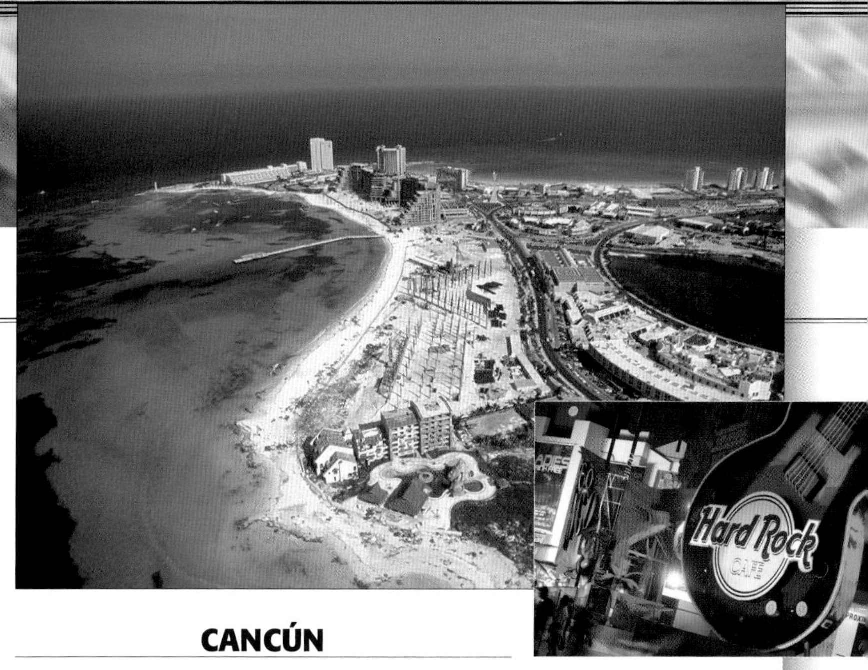

CANCÚN

Cancún is Mexico's party capital, delivering round-the-clock entertainment. It lies close to the ancient wonders of the Maya world and the natural beauty of the Riviera Maya.

Cancún, a beachside metropolis with little authentic Mexican flavor and yet the number-one visitor destination in Mexico, is loved and loathed in equal measure. The 25km (16-mile) Hotel Zone, set on a narrow strip of land in the shape of a number seven alongside the coast, is an ultra-modern boulevard, with five-star hotels, high-tech nightclubs, high-class shopping malls, and branches of McDonald's, Burger King and Planet Hollywood. The main avenue is Tulúm, formerly the highway running through the city; now it is the location of the handicraft market, the main shops, banks and the municipal tourist office. There are restaurants here, too, but the better ones are along Avenida Yaxchilán, which is also the main focus for nightlife. Cancún City—a modern sprawl that evolved from temporary shacks housing the thousands of workers in the Hotel Zone—has little to attract visitors.

THE BEACH AND BEYOND

With pale white sand stretching for 19km (12 miles), a turquoise sea, coral gardens, lagoons and mystical *cenotes* (natural sinkholes), watersports enthusiasts flock to Cancún. The diving is world class, reefs have visibility of 24m (80ft) and there are many dive schools offering PADI courses. The panoply of watersports operators and all-inclusive resorts has facilities for windsurfing, jetskis and waterskiing. With waters teeming with dorado, grouper and billfish, game fishing is big, and Cancún plays host to several international fishing tournaments; March to July is the high season.

Late-afternoon shopping is another major recreational activity, and along the strip numerous malls overflow with designer labels, perfume emporiums, jewelry stores and Mexican handicrafts. Prices here are higher than anywhere else in Mexico. Cancún's diversity extends to gastronomy and nightlife, with top-class international restaurants, tassel-shaking cabarets and all manner of live musical performances ranging from Cuban jazz quartets to rapper artists such as 50 Cent.

The sights and natural wonders beyond Cancún offer much greater reward. You can rent a jeep and cruise the Riviera Maya as far as Tulúm (▷ 75), taking in the archaeological site of Cobá and the more tranquil beach of Akumal (▷ 61).

RATINGS

Good for food	◕ ◕ ◕ ◕
Nightlife	◕ ◕ ◕ ◕
Outdoor pursuits	◕ ◕ ◕ ◕
Shopping	◕ ◕ ◕ ◕

BASICS

317 S7

Avenida Cobá s/n, tel (998) 884 65 31 (Mon–Fri 9–2, 4–7)

Buses ply the Hotel Zone strip heading into the middle of town

Cancún airport, 16km (10 miles) south

www.cancunmx.com
The official government website for Quintana Roo state.

TIP

- **Taxis are inexpensive and abundant. The flat rate within central Cancún is $1–$1.50; to the Hotel Zone $3.**

Aerial view of Cancún's hotel strip along the beach (top)

The Hard Rock Café is the place to party (inset)

Chichén Itzá

Iconic, majestic and harmonious, Chichén Itzá is one of the most spectacular Maya sites, adorned with exquisite sculptures and tributes to its mighty gods, a fascinating insight into the astrological and mathematical genius of the Maya.

RATINGS	
Cultural interest	● ● ● ● ●
Good for kids	● ● ● ●
Historic interest	● ● ● ●
Photo stops	● ● ● ● ●

BASICS

317 R8

Highway 180

(985) 851 01 37/851 01 24

Daily 8–5

$8, Sun $3.50, child (under 13) free. You are given a yellow band to wear so that you may leave and re-enter as often as you like on day of entry

Guides charge $40 for 1.5-hour tours

Drinks and snacks at entrance (expensive), at the *cenote* and on the path to Old Chichén

At the visitor center and on the path to Old Chichén

$1

Visitor center at entrance has a restaurant, free cinema (short film in English at noon and 4pm), museum, shops, exchange facilities and luggage deposit (free)

Chac Mool (top)

Stone carving of an eagle (above); Temple of the Thousand Columns (above middle); carving on the Skull Wall (above right)

Images of Chac, the rain god, adorn the temples (right)

SEEING CHICHÉN ITZÁ

Chichén Itzá is Mexico's most-visited Maya sight. The giant stepped pyramid of Kukulkán, or El Castillo, dominates the site, watched over by Chac Mool (or Chaac Mool), a reclining statue once used to receive sacrificial offerings. Frequent buses and tours connect the coastal resorts and the nearby city of Valladolid to the east. It requires at least one day to do the site justice.

HIGHLIGHTS

EL CASTILLO (PIRÁMIDE DE KUKULKÁN)

Interior pyramid 11–3 and 4–5, closed if raining

The Castle is one of the Maya world's most impressive structures. Also known as the Pyramid of Kukulkán—the "feathered serpent", the greatest of the Maya gods—it rises majestically to a height of 30m (98ft) and dominates the buildings in the northern half of the site. Four flights of stairs, each with 91 steps, lead up to the final platform—making a total of 365 steps, corresponding to the number of days in the solar calendar. The head of a plumed, open-mouthed serpent decorates the base of the pyramid. There is also an interior ascent of 61 steep, very narrow steps leading to a chamber lit by electricity. The red-painted jaguar that probably served as the throne of the high priest burns bright, with its jade eyes and flint fangs. The northwest side of the pyramid is oriented toward the sacred *cenote* (▷ 66), where Kukulkán would come to receive tributes. The castle, together with the Platform of Venus and the *sacbé* (white road), represented the religious and political power of the Itzá people. *Sacbeob*, known as white roads, because they were built of limestone and surfaced with cement, were sacred Maya paths, thought to have been used for ceremonial purposes or as transportation routes.

One of the best times, and also the busiest, to view El Castillo is on the morning and afternoon of the spring (March 21) and autumn (September 21) equinoxes, when the alignment of the sun's shadow casts a snake-shaped shadow on the steps of the Castle. To the ancient Maya, this image represented Kukulkán. The phenomenon was also an expression of the divine spirit of Maya cosmology, an allegory of the earth's renewal with the changing of the seasons; the spring and autumn equinoxes heralded the arrival of the crop planting and harvesting seasons.

The famous reclining Chac Mool (right) and detail of a carved serpent's head (inset) on the Temple of the Warriors

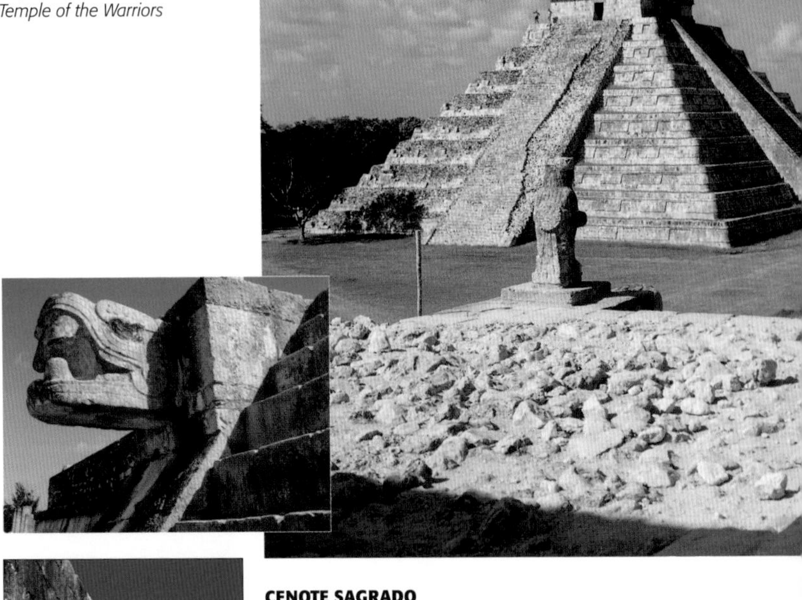

MORE TO SEE

JUEGO DE PELOTA

Northwest of El Castillo is the largest ball court in Mesoamerica, and one of the oldest structures on the site; it is estimated to have been constructed around AD864. For the Maya, the ball game was of great ritualistic importance (▷ 29) and at Chichén Itzá it involved attempting to throw the ball through one of the two rings (see above) protruding from the towering walls. The court has almost perfect acoustics—someone talking normally in front of the north temple can be heard at a distance of 150m (165 yards).

CENOTE SAGRADO

Running north of El Castillo is the *sacbé* leading to the Cenote Sagrado (Sacred Well), dedicated to the rain god Chac. Women and children, animals and valuable propitiatory objects of all kinds, were thrown into its deep blue cavern as sacrifices. It was first dredged between 1904 and 1907, when a vast quantity of pottery, jade, copper and gold objects was found. In 1962 it was explored again, and some 4,000 further pieces were recovered, including beads, polished jade, lumps of copal resin, small bells, a statuette of rubber latex, another of wood and a quantity of animal and human bones. Another well, the Cenote de Xtoloc, to the south of El Castillo, was probably used as a water supply.

TEMPLO DE LOS GUERREROS

To the east of El Castillo is the Temple of the Warriors, with its famous reclining Chac Mool statue at the entrance to the two enclosures. Chac Mool was a messenger to the gods and the ancient Maya would place offerings on his stomach. The temple is richly decorated with motifs representing the military elite to whom the temple was dedicated. The pyramidal platform has now been closed off to avoid erosion. Inside are vivid carvings of plumed serpents, warriors and priests. Next to it is the Mil Columnas (Thousand Columns Group), so called for its procession of pillars with intricate relief carvings.

CHICHÉN VIEJO

About 500m (550 yards) from the main clearing are the buildings of the earlier city, Old Chichén. El Caracol (Snail), or the Observatory, is included in this group, so named because of its interior spiral stairway, which resembles a snail's shell, and its astrological associations. Above the doors of the observation tower carvings represent the rain god Chac. The structure's windows are aligned with the cardinal points in order to make astrological calculations. So incredibly sophisticated were the Maya systems that they are believed to have predicted solar eclipses occurring between the seventh and 24th centuries.

Next to El Caracol is the Casa de las Monjas, or Nunnery, which has two patios in the Puuc architectural style. The upper facade is stunning—a latticework of glyphs and sculpted masks of the gods. A 30-minute walk to the right of Las Monjas leads to the Templo de los Tres Dinteles (Temple of the Three Lintels).

HEADS YOU WIN, OR LOSE

In the ball court, at eye-level, a relief shows the decapitation of the winning captain, one of the most significant and powerful examples of Maya art. At one time historians thought it was the losing team that was sacrificed, yet the latest theories suggest it was the captain of the winning side, as his success made him a fitting tribute to the gods.

Losers—or winners—paid the ultimate price for their sport

BACKGROUND

Chichén Itzá was built in the Late Classic period and once covered 25sq km (10sq miles); the administrative, cultural and religious focus—occupied by priests and ruling elite—was concentrated in an area of 6sq km (2sq miles). The Itzáes, who settled here in the ninth century, were descended from the Putun or Chontal Maya. By the end of the 10th century the city was more or less abandoned, and although it was re-established in the 11th to 12th centuries it is not known by whom. Whoever the people were, a comparison of some of the architecture with that of Tula, north of Mexico City, indicates they were heavily influenced by the Toltecs of central Mexico. Despite the site's decline, its potent majesty continued down the years to such an extent that Spanish conqueror Francisco Montejo (1479–1549) considered making it his capital.

SITE PLAN

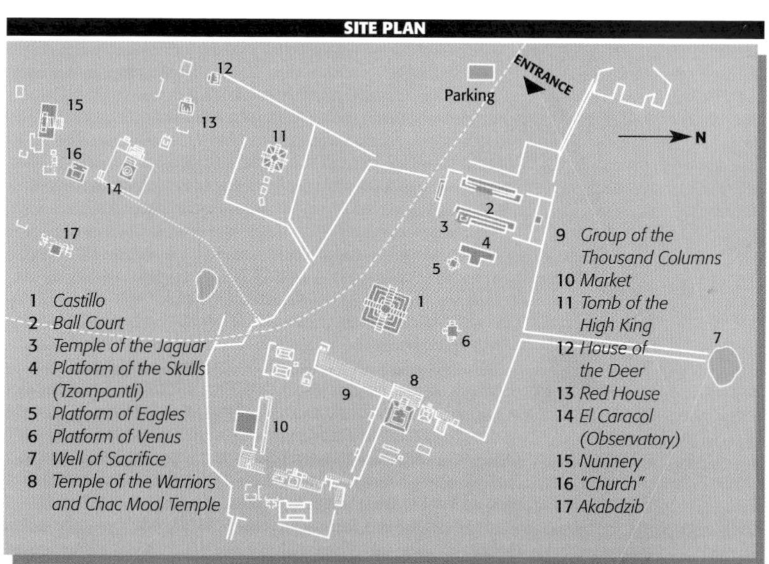

Cozumel

Mexico's largest Caribbean island and one of the world's most popular diving destinations also teems with wildlife and birdlife, as well as some small archaeological sites of interest.

RATINGS

Cultural interest	●●●
Natural attractions	●●●●
Watersports and activities	●●●●●

BASICS

317 S8

Altos Plaza de Sol, Colonia Centro, tel (987) 869 02 11/12 (Mon–Fri 8.30–4.30)

Ferries from Playa del Carmen

www.islacozumel.com.mx/
The official government site for the island. Good information on all aspects of Cozumel.

TIP

• There are no local buses, but Cozumel town is small enough to explore on foot. To get around the island, take an organized tour or a taxi; otherwise, rent a jeep, moped or bicycle.

Black marlin (top)

Chankanab is idea for snorkeling (above and inset opposite)

SEEING COZUMEL

The island of Cozumel, encircled by more than 25 reef formations, is a fabulous diving site. At the northern end, the archaeological site of San Gervasio, with a temple dedicated to Ixchel, goddess of fertility, is unmissable. San Miguel de Cozumel, the only town, has little character—due mainly to the construction of a US air base during World War II. The best public beaches are some way from San Miguel town. (Note that some roads are suitable only for 4WDs.)

A circuit of the island on paved roads is easily done in a day. Head due east out of San Miguel (take the continuation of Avenida Juárez). Make the detour to San Gervasio then carry on to the Caribbean coast at Mescalito's restaurant. Here, turn left for the northern tip (road unsuitable for ordinary vehicles), or right for the south, passing Punta Morena, Chen Río, Punta Chiqueros (restaurant, bathing), El Mirador (a low viewpoint with sea-worn rocks) and Paradise Cove. Here, the paved road heads west, while an unpaved road continues south to Punta Celarain, where there is an old lighthouse.

HIGHLIGHTS

ARCHAEOLOGICAL SITES

There are some 32 archaeological sites on Cozumel; those on the east coast are mostly single structures (thought to have been lookouts or navigational aids). The easiest to see are the restored ruins of the Maya-Toltec period at San Gervasio (daily 7–5) in the north—7km (4 miles) from Cozumel town, then 6km (10 miles) to the left up a paved road, toll $1. Guides are on hand, or you can buy a self-guiding booklet at the *librería* (bookstore) on the square in San Miguel, or at the flea market. It is an interesting site, quite spread out, with *sacbeob* (sacred white roads) between the groups of buildings. There are no large structures, but it has a pleasant plaza and an arch, and pigment can be seen in places. It is also a great place to listen to birdsong and watch for butterflies, lizards, land crabs and insects.

BEACHES

In the north of the island the beaches are sandy and wide. South of San Miguel, they tend to be narrow and rocky. The east (Caribbean) coast is rockier, but very picturesque; swimming and diving on the unprotected side is dangerous due to strong undercurrents. The only safe place to swim is the sheltered bay at Chen Río. Punta Morena is a good surf beach with reasonable accommodation and seafood.

MUSEO DE LA ISLA COZUMEL

Avenida Rafael Melger, between Calle 4 and Calle 5 Norte 987 214 34
Daily 9–5 $3.50

The Museo de la Isla Cozumel on the waterfront provides a well-laid-out history of the island from pre-Columbian times to the arrival of Juan de Grijalva and Hernán Cortés in the 16th century, with engaging anecdotes revealing the seminal moments in Cozumel's history. Displays also present the island's flora and fauna. There is a good bookshop, an art gallery, a library, an auditorium and a rooftop restaurant with excellent food and views.

PUNTA CELARAIN

Parque Punta Sur: ☎ (987) 872 09 14

The ecological park of Parque Punta Sur covers a variety of natural landscapes including lagoons and mangrove jungles. A snorkel center has opened here too, and there is a viewing platform. On the road north, opposite the turn-off to El Cedral, is a sign to Restaurante Mac y Cía, an excellent fish restaurant on a lovely beach; it is popular with dive groups for lunch. Next is Playa San Francisco, and a few kilometers beyond that the former Holiday Inn, the last big hotel south of San Miguel. Just beyond this is Parque Chankanaab (daily 8–4), a lagoon behind the beach (9km/6 miles from San Miguel). Now a national park, it has a botanical garden with local and imported plants, a rather artificial "Maya Area," swimming (ideal for families with young children), snorkeling, swimming with dolphins, dive shops, lockers, souvenirs and good—but expensive—restaurants.

BACKGROUND

Cozumel was settled by the Maya as early as AD300 and went on to become a major seaport for Mayan trade between Veracruz and Honduras. The Maya successfully resisted Spanish attempts to colonize the Yucatán Peninsula until 1519, when Hernán Cortés arrived with his men and destroyed many of the island's temples, marking the start of the bitter struggle to control the peninsula. Following Cortés' departure, the island was struck by a smallpox epidemic and the population rapidly decreased to under 300 by 1570. Thirty years later it was abandoned.

Pirates used Cozumel as a base during the 17th century, and in 1848 settlers from the mainland fled here to escape the bloodthirsty reprisals of the Maya, who were wreaking revenge for the many atrocities perpetrated against them by the Spanish. In 1961, French explorer Jacques Cousteau arrived, and when he discovered that the surrounding waters possessed some of the best scuba diving sites in the world, this quiet little fishing community developed into the major diving destination it is today.

MORE TO SEE

EL CEDRAL

✉ 3km (5 miles) from the main island road

El Cedral is a two-room temple, overgrown with trees, in the middle of the village of the same name. Behind it is a ruin, and next to it a modern church with a green-and-white facade. In the village are large, permanent shelters where agricultural shows are held, rugs are sold and locals pose with *iguanas doradas* (golden iguanas) so visitors can take photographs.

BILLFISH

Cozumel hosts an annual international billfish tournament at the end of April/beginning of May which attracts fishermen from all over the world; the salt fishing is excellent, with abundant swordfish, marlin and tuna.

A deep-sea fishing boat off Cozumel (top)

A pelican, a common sight around Chetumal

The climb up Nohuch Mul, Cobá, rewards with fabulous views

Dzibilchaltún's Temple of the Seven Dolls

CHETUMAL

317 S9 Avenida 5 de Mayo, tel (983) 835 05 00 (Mon–Fri 8.30–4) Buses from Valladolid www.corozal.com

Visitors en route to Belize and Guatemala often use Chetumal, the state capital of Quintana Roo, as a stopover. It is also a good base to explore the ruins of the Río Bec group in Campeche state—Xpujil, Becán and Chicanná. Though attractions are thin on the ground, this small Mexican city has a more authentic feel than most of the other towns on the Riviera Maya. The avenues are broad and busy, and those at its heart are lined with huge stores selling inexpensive imported goods.

The Museo de la Cultura Maya on Avenida Héroes de Chapultepec (Tue–Thu and Sun 9–7, Fri–Sat 9–8) has good models of sites and touch-screen computers explaining the Maya calendar and glyphs. Although there are few original Maya pieces, it gives an excellent overview of Maya culture. Chetumal Bay has been designated a Natural Protected Area for manatees.

CHICANNÁ

317 R9 • 12km (7 miles) west of Xpujil Daily 8–5 $2 Agencies in Chetumal offer day tours to Chicanná, Xpujil and Becán

Chicanná, meaning "house of the serpent's mouth," is named after its most outstanding feature—the dramatic entrance to one of the temples in the shape of a monster's mouth with fangs jutting over the lintel and lining the access stairway. Many of the structures have intricate baroque carvings in the Chenes style.

Chicanná is considered to have been a small residential base for the rulers of the ancient regional capital of Becán. It was occupied during the Late Preclassic period; the final stages of activity at the site have been dated to the Post Classic era. Consistent with the Río Bec style, there are numerous representations of Itzamná, the Maya god of creation.

CHICHÉN ITZÁ

See pages 64–67.

COBÁ

317 S8 • 40km (25 miles) inland from Tulúm (998) 883 36 71 Daily 7–6 $3.50 Buses from Valladolid Bilingual tours $1.50, outside the entrance to the site

The great appeal of the little-excavated archaeological site of Cobá is its jungle setting and lakes. An important Maya city in the eighth and ninth centuries AD, with a population estimated to have been between 40,000 and 50,000, Cobá was abandoned for unknown reasons. The urban extension of Cobá is put at some 70sq km (27sq miles).

An unusual feature is the network of *sacbeob* (sacred white roads). More than 40 of these sacred roads pass through the site, some local, some of great length—such as the 100km (62-mile) road to Yaxuná in Yucatán state.

Lago Macanxoc, within the site, has many turtles and fish, and is a good bird-watching area. Toucans may be seen very early in the day, and greenish-blue and brown mot-mots in the early morning. Both Lago Macanxoc and Lago Cobá, as well as their surrounding forest, can be seen from the summit of the Iglesia, at 24m (78ft) the second tallest structure at Cobá.

There are three other groups of buildings to visit: the Macanxoc Group, about 1.5km (1 mile) from the Cobá Group; Las Pinturas, 1km (half a mile) north-east of Macanxoc, with a temple and the remains of other buildings that had columns in their construction; and the Nohoch Mul Group, at least another kilometer from Las Pinturas. Nohoch Mul has the tallest pyramid in the northern Yucatán (42m/138ft), a magnificent structure providing superb views of the jungle on all sides. A good way to explore the ruins and jungle is to rent a bicycle, or tricycle and driver, at the entrance to the Cobá Group.

COZUMEL

See pages 68–69.

DZIBILCHALTÚN

317 R8 • 14km (9 miles) north of Mérida Daily 8–5 $6 VW *combis* leave from Calle 69, between 62 and 64 in Parque San Juan, every 1 or 2 hours between 5am and 7pm, stopping at the ruins en route to Chablekal Site map available from museum by ticket office

The Maya city of Dzibilchaltún includes more than 8,000 structures. The site (in two halves, connected by a *sacbé*) was founded as early as 1000BC; it was occupied for thousands of years but reached its peak between AD600 and 1000. The most important building is the Templo de Las Siete Muñecas (Temple of Seven Dolls), named after the seven clay dolls buried within it. These can now be seen in the site museum. The structure is aligned with the four cardinal points and there is a show here each year for the spring and autumn equinoxes on March 21 and September 21. At the west end is the ceremonial hub with temples, houses and a large plaza with an austere, open chapel.

Nearby is Cenote Xlacah, 44m (144ft) deep. You can swim in the clear water (take a mask and snorkel as it is full of fascinating

Stucco mask on Edzná's Temple of the Stone Masks

The most impressive structures at Edzná are clustered around the central Gran Plaza

fish). A nature trail, lined with indigenous trees, all labelled, starts halfway between the temple and the *cenote*, rejoining the *sacbé* halfway along.

EDZNÁ

317 R9 • 61km (38 miles) southeast of Campeche Tue–Sun 8–5 $3.50 Tourist bus from Campeche town wall Daily tours from Viajes Programados, Calle 59, Edificio Belmar, in Campeche

Edzná, meaning "house of grimaces" or "house of the Itzáes" and built in a tranquil valley, was a huge Maya ceremonial base. Occupied from about 600BC to around AD800 or 900, it was constructed in the simple Chenes style like Chicanná, but mixed with Puuc, Classical and other influences. The focal point is the magnificent Templo de los Cinco Pisos (Temple of the Five Levels), a stepped pyramid with four levels of living quarters for the priests and a shrine and altar at the top; 65 steep steps lead up from the Central Plaza. Opposite is the Paal U'na (Temple of the Moon). Excavations are being carried out on the scores of lesser temples, but most of Edzná's original sprawl remains hidden under thick vegetation.

Imagination is needed to picture the network of irrigation canals and holding basins built by the Maya along the valley below sea level. Some of the site's stelae remain in position (two large stone faces with squinting eyes are covered by a thatched shelter); others can be seen in various Campeche museums. There is also a good example of a *sacbé* (white road). In July (the exact date varies), a Maya ceremony to Chac is held here to encourage or to celebrate the arrival of the rains, as appropriate.

EK-BALAM

317 S8 • 25km (16 miles) north of Valladolid Daily 8–5 $3 *Colectivos* to Temozón, from where you can bicycle the remaining 12km (7 miles) to the ruins

Ek-Balam ("Black Jaguar") is surrounded by traditional Maya villages. A series of temples, sacrificial altars and residential buildings is grouped around a central plaza, elaborately finished with carved sculptures or polychrome stucco; the most impressive of these is a gruesome mask with protruding fangs on the main facade of the acropolis, which appears to be a monster, and winged idols believed to be angels, imagery unique to Ek-Balam.

Occupied from 300BC, this site formed the hub of the Tah kingdom that dominated the eastern Yucatán state. It flourished during the Late Classic period, reaching its zenith around AD600 to 1200. The acropolis is the second-largest standing pyramid in the state of Yucatán after the Kinich Kakmó pyramid in Izamal (▷ 72), with richly carved stucco and a series of interconnecting passageways. The site's most important discovery was the tomb of the ruler Ukit Kan Lel Tok, containing valuable objects such as jewelry and weapons.

GRUTAS DE BALANKANCHÉ

317 S8 • 6km (4 miles) east of Chichén Itzá Daily 9–5 (allow about 45 minutes for the 300m/984ft descent) $4.70 Buses from Chichén Itzá and Pisté-Balankanché Guided tours in English at 11, 1 and 3

The Balankanché Caves lay hidden until Humberto Gómez, a tour guide from Chichén Itzá, discovered them in 1959. In addition to being extraordinarily beautiful, with a tangible sense of mysticism, the caves are of significant archaeological importance. Close to the entrance, dripping stalactite formations cluster around a gigantic stalagmite, 7m (23ft) tall, that resembles a ceiba tree, the sacred tree of the Maya. Inside, a variety of ceremonial objects, believed to be offerings to the rain god Tlaloc (the Aztec equivalent of Chac), were discovered. Within the same echoing chamber is the Balam Throne, a sacred altar. The museum houses a collection of ceremonial objects including pots and *metates* (grinding stones). It is very damp and hot within the caves, but there are lovely gardens outside. There is a *son et lumière* show, but it is rather poor.

ISLA HOLBOX

317 S7 Buses to Chiquilá for boats three times daily, and direct from Tizimín

Isla Holbox lies just off the northern tip of the Yucatán Peninsula, a world apart from the resorts of Cancún and Playa del Carmen, with long stretches of dazzling pink-tinged sand glistening with mother-of-pearl shells shelving to an emerald ocean.

In the small fishing village founded in 1847, dusty streets dotted with painted wooden houses and palm-thatched *palapa* (thatched) restaurants are home to an eclectic population. The best way to explore the island is by golf cart or moped. Local fishermen run eco-tours where you can swim and snorkel alongside sharks and barracuda; though very few nasty occurrences have been reported, extreme caution is advised. There are five uninhabited islands beyond Holbox, including the bird-watching paradise of Isla de Pajaros (Bird Island).

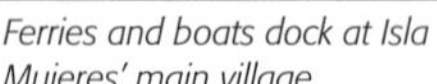
Ferries and boats dock at Isla Mujeres' main village

Detail of a carving in Kohunlich's Pyramid of the Masks

The Convento de San Antonio de Padua, Izamal

ISLA MUJERES

317 S7 Avenida Rueda Medina 130, tel (998) 877 03 07; Mon–Fri 9–9, Sat 9–2 Ferry from Cancún www.isla-mujeres.net

Just a 20-minute ferry trip from Cancún, Isla Mujeres (Island of Women) is a refreshing antidote to the urban sprawl of the big resorts and the hurly-burly of package tourism. The town is strictly low-rise, with brightly painted buildings giving it the feel of a Caribbean island. The island's laws prohibit any building higher than three floors, and US franchises are not allowed to open branches here. There are several good beaches on the northwest coast, 5 minutes' walk from the town. Laid-back restaurants and nightspots with live music are plentiful. Away from the town, at the south of the island, is El Garrafón, a national park established to protect the coral reef (▷ 182).

A 15-minute walk from El Garrafón will take you to the only known Maya shrine to a female deity: Ixchel, goddess of the moon and fertility. At the heart of the island are the curious remains of a pirate's domain, Casa de Mundaca (▷ 209).

IZAMAL

317 R8 Daily 8–5 Buses from Mérida

Izamal is known as the "golden city" for its colonial heart, entirely painted in rich yellow. Once a major Classic religious site said to be founded by Itzamná, the god of creation who sometimes appeared as a priest, 20 Maya structures have been identified—several of them on Calle 27. Izamal became one of the hubs from which the Spanish attempted to Christianize the Maya. Fray Diego de Landa, the historian of the Spanish Conquest of Mérida, founded the huge Franciscan convent and church—Convento de San Antonio de Padua. Constructed on top of a Maya pyramid, it was begun in 1549 and has the second largest atrium in the world. The surrounding stone walls are embellished with carvings of Maya origin. In 1993 the throne was built for the Pope's visit. The image of the Inmaculada Virgen de la Concepción in the church was made the Reina de Yucatán (Queen of Yucatán) in 1949, and the patron saint of the state in 1970.

Just a couple of blocks away are the ruins of a great mausoleum known as the Pirámide Kinich Kakmó. At 195m (640ft) long, 173m (567ft) wide and 36m (118ft) high it is the fifth-highest pyramid in Mexico.

Don't miss From the top of the Kinich Kakmó pyramid there is an excellent view of the town and surrounding *henequén* (sisal) and citrus plantations.

KOHUNLICH

317 R9 • 61km (38 miles) west of Chetumal 8–5 Buses and *colectivos* from Chetumal Many agencies in Chetumal (▷ 70) offer tours

A local Mayan discovered the ruins of Kohunlich in 1967. Kohunlich means "cahoon ridge": a *cahoon* is the Belizian name for a type of palm, and these soaring trees line the pathways around the site. The ruins' most outstanding feature is the Pirámide de los Mascarones (Pyramid of the Masks), flanked by striking masks carved in stucco. Tinged with red, each mask is more than 2m (8ft) tall. Iconic and enigmatic, they are believed to be a representation of gods, or Kohunlich's ruling elite, yet their true identification eludes archaeologists and historians. This peaceful, isolated site, built during the Early Classic period, doesn't receive the same number of visitors as the sites farther north.

LAGUNA BACALAR

317 S9 • 37km (23 miles) north of Chetumal Buses from Chetumal

Close to the border with Belize is the Laguna Bacalar, a crystal-clear freshwater lagoon, 42km (26 miles) long and 2km (1.2 miles) wide. It is one of Mexico's largest and most mesmerizing lakes, also known as the Laguna de Siete Colores for its different shades of greens and blues. The lake teems with fish and waterbirds, and on the lakeshore the birdlife is resplendent. If you are lucky, you may see rare giant tropical otters, as well as monkeys and toucans. Activities include kayaking, mountain biking, swimming and skin-diving.

Overlooking the lake is the wooden Spanish fort of San Felipe, believed to have been built around 1729 by the Spanish to defend the area from English pirates and smugglers (there is a plaque praying for protection from the British). British ships roamed the islands and reefs, looting Spanish galleons laden with gold on their way from Peru to Cuba. There are many old shipwrecks on the reef and around the Banco Chinchorro, 50km (31 miles) out in the Caribbean.

The village of Bacalar is a subdued town, which goes about its business seemingly oblivious to the trickle of largely Mexican visitors. There is a dock for swimming north of the plaza, with a restaurant and disco next to it. About 3km (2 miles) north of the village is the startlingly clear Cenote Azul, 90m (295ft) deep, which teems with fish and invites swimming and snorkeling.

MÉRIDA

Mérida is a convenient base for exploring the archaeological sites on the Puuc and Convent routes. Its backstreets are dotted with colonial buildings, and there's plenty of lively bustle.

The capital of Yucatán state and its colonial heart is Mérida, a frenetic, tightly packed city full of buildings in varying states of repair, from the grandiose to the dilapidated. Originally a large Maya city called Tihó, it was conquered by Francisco de Montejo on January 6 1542. He dismantled the Maya pyramids and used the stone as the foundations for the Catedral San Ildefonso (1556–98).

ZÓCALO

The city revolves around the large, shady *zócalo* (Plaza Mayor), site of the Catedral San Ildefonso. Completed in 1598 it is the oldest cathedral in Latin America and has a fine baroque facade. Inside is the Cristo de las Ampollas (Christ of the Blisters), a statue carved from a tree that burned for a whole night after being hit by lightning without showing any damage at all. To the left of the cathedral is the 19th-century neoclassical Palacio de Gobierno (Government Palace), with its collection of enormous murals by Campeche artist Fernando Castro Pacheco (1918–66), which can be viewed daily until 8pm. Casa de Montejo, on the south side of the plaza, now a branch of the Banamex bank, is a 16th-century palace built by the city's founder. Away from the main plaza along Calle 60 is Parque Hidalgo, a tree-filled square bordering the 17th-century Iglesia de Jesús. A little farther along Calle 60 is the early 20th-century Teatro Peón Contreras, with a neoclassical facade, marble staircase and Italian frescoes.

MUSEUMS

Museo de Antropología e Historia ✉ Paseo de Montejo 485 ☎ (999) 923 05 57 ⏲ Tue–Sat 8–8, Sun 8–2; Museo Macay ✉ Calle 60 ☎ (999) 924 52 33 ⏲ Wed–Mon 10–5.30; Museo de la Canción Yucateca ✉ Calle 63 ☎ (999) 923 72 24 ⏲ Tue–Sun 9–5; Pinacoteca Juan Gamboa Guzmán ✉ Calle 59 ☎ (999) 924 52 33 ⏲ Tue–Sat 8–8, Sun 8–2

The Museo de Antropología e Historia in Palacio Cantón has an excellent collection of original Maya objects from various sites in Yucatán, including jade jewelry dredged from *cenotes* and deformed skulls with sharpened teeth. Museo Macay, on the main plaza, has a permanent exhibition of Yucatecan artists. The Museo de la Canción Yucateca has an exhibition of objects and instruments relating to the history of music in the region. The Pinacoteca Juan Gamboa Guzmán is a gallery showing classic and contemporary painting and sculpture.

RATINGS

Cultural interest	●●●
Specialist shopping	●●●
Walkability	●●●

TIPS

- During July and August Mérida is subject to heavy rains during the afternoon—as well as being very hot.
- Mérida is renowned for the quality of its hammocks (▷ 171) and Panama hats.

BASICS

317 R8

Teatro Peón Contreras, Calle 60 and 57 (just off Parque Hidalgo), tel (999) 924 92 90; Mon–Fri 8am–9pm, Sat and Sun 8–8

Mérida airport, 8km (5 miles) south

Restoring the impressive artwork in Mérida's neoclassical Palacio de Gobierno (top)

The facade of Catedral San Ildefonso, Latin America's oldest cathedral (inset)

Fun for all the family on the beach at Playa del Carmen

The leaning tower at Puerto Morelos, victim of a hurricane

Coconut milk makes a refreshing drink on a hot day

PLAYA DEL CARMEN

317 S8 Avenida Juárez and Avenida 15, tel (984) 873 28 04; Mon–Sat 9–8, Sun 9–5 Buses from Cancún

A 50-minute drive south of Cancún, the former fishing village of Playa, as it is locally known, has developed rapidly to become a major visitor resort. The beach is dazzling white, with clear shallow water, and the vast number of diving and watersports schools create a youthful, energetic beach culture. Activities include yoga, massage, salsa classes and Spanish lessons. Because of its good transportation links, many visitors choose Playa as a base for trips to the archaeological sites of Tulúm and Cobá, Cozumel and the less developed beaches of the Riviera Maya.

While Playa has not had the high-rise treatment of Cancún, the beach area is still very commercialized and international. The focal point is the pedestrianized Avenida 5, one block from and parallel with the beach, which funnels south to a new, classy mall. This busy strip is punctuated with TGI Fridays, Hemingway-themed *palapa* (thatched) restaurants, sports bars, international restaurants, cafés, designer-label outlets and souvenir shops with a hard sell.

PUERTO MORELOS

317 S8 Buses from Playa del Carmen to Cancún stop on the main highway turn-off close to Puerto Morelos, where taxis are available Cancún airport 18km (11 miles) north

The quiet, unspoilt fishing village of Puerto Morelos, with pristine, uncrowded beaches and good diving and snorkeling opportunities, is a low-key place to relax for a few days, or stop over en route to larger towns farther south, such as Playa del Carmen. The village is little more than a large plaza right on the waterfront with a couple of streets running off it, but there is a good supply of hotels and restaurants. If on arrival at Cancún airport you don't wish to spend the night in the city, you could get a taxi directly to Puerto Morelos. This is also the place to catch the car ferry to the island of Cozumel. The Sinaltur office on the plaza offers snorkeling and kayak, birdwatching and fishing trips.

RESERVA DE LA BIÓSFERA SIAN KA'AN

317 S8 • 3km (2 miles) south of Tulúm Los Amigos de Sian Ka'an, Plaza América, Avenida Cobá 5, 3rd floor, suites 48–50, Cancún, tel (884) 95 83; 9–3, 6–8 Don't try to get there independently without a car. It is possible to drive into the reserve from Tulúm village as far as Punta Allen; beyond that you need a launch

Declared a UNESCO World Heritage Site, Sian Ka'an, meaning "he who is born beneath the sun," lies south of Tulum and covers 4,500sq km (1,755sq miles) of the Quintana Roo coast down to the Punta Allen peninsula. While independent travel is difficult, the rewards are great. The opportunities for spotting wildlife and birdlife in the reserve are excellent, and the vast area is also studded with more than 20 unrestored Maya ruins, all the more mystical and powerful for their primordial setting. About one-third of the reserve is tropical forest, one-third savannah and mangrove and one-third coastal and marine habitat—including 110km (68 miles) of barrier reef, the second-largest reef in the world. Mammals include jaguars, pumas, ocelots and other big cats, monkeys, tapirs, peccaries, manatees and deer; turtles nest on the beaches; and there are crocodiles, plus a wide variety of land and aquatic birds.

The small community of Punta Allen at the tip of the peninsula makes it's living mostly by lobster fishing, using traditional Maya methods. There are one or two small hotels and restaurants here, but you'll need provisions for the drive down.

RÍO LAGARTOS

317 S7 • 100km (62 miles) north of Valladolid

This attractive little fishing village on the north coast of Yucatán state is the focal point for boat rides through the biosphere reserve, which contains thousands of pink flamingos as well as many other species of bird. Boat trips to the flamingo reserve can be arranged by walking down to the harbor, where you'll receive many offers from boatmen.

The largest colony of flamingos is near Las Coloradas (15km/ 9 miles away), recognizable by a large salt mound on the horizon—make sure your boatman takes you there rather than to the smaller groups of birds along the river (▷ 184). Fifteen minutes' walk east from the Río Lagartos harbor is an *ojo de agua*, a pool of sulphurous water for bathing, supplied by an underground *cenote*.

Keel-billed toucan

Tulúm's fabulous clifftop location (also pages 76–77)

TULÚM

The 12th-century Maya-Toltec ruins of Tulúm, with its city walls of gleaming white stone, overlooking the dazzling turquoise waters of the Caribbean, are one of the Yucatán's most visited sites.

317 S8 • 130km (80 miles) south from Cancún toward Chetumal Daily 8–5 Avenida Cobá s/n, Cancún, tel (998) 884 65 31 Buses from Valladolid. Frequent buses ply the coast from Cancún to Chetumal, stopping at Tulúm en route There is a visitor complex at the entrance to the ruins

RATINGS	
Cultural interest	●●●●●
Historic interest	●●●●●
Photo stops	●●●●●

Perched on craggy coastal cliffs, Tulúm was once an important trading port whose fortress was still occupied when the Spanish arrived in 1518. Although this relatively small site does not rank among the greats, today the walled ruins have become a magnet for sun-worshippers and archaeological enthusiasts alike.

TEMPLO DEL DIOS DESCENDENTE

The Templo del Dios Descendente (Temple of the Descending God) is named after the upside-down stucco figure carved over its entrance. The significance of this god is unclear, although he may have symbolized rain or the setting sun (Cozumel was the home of the rising sun), or have been the Bee God, Ah Mucen Cab, an important deity in the region. Similar images can be seen on the other buildings.

EL CASTILLO

El Castillo is the main structure on the site, fronted by serpent columns, which were built in several stages. It commands a view of both the sea and the forested Quintana Roo lowlands stretching westwards. All its main openings face west, as do most, but not all, of the doorways at Tulúm. The majority of the main structures are roped off so that you cannot climb the Castillo, nor get close to the surviving frescoes, especially on the Templo de los Frescos (Temple of the Frescoes). The facade of the palace is decorated with carved reliefs of the descending god (see above).

Don't miss Right in the middle of the site is a small beach cove—most visitors come prepared with bathing suits. There are also quieter beaches nearby, which require a relatively easy clamber down the cliffs. In the Tulúm area there are more than 50 *cenotes*, with opportunities for cave diving (▷ 174).

Traditional clothes stall in the local market at Valladolid

UXMAL

See pages 78–79.

VALLADOLID

317 S8 East side of *zócalo*, tel (985) 856 18 65 (Mon–Sat 9–8, Sun 9–1)
www.chichen.com.mx/valladolid

Roughly halfway between Mérida and Cancún is Valladolid, a relaxed, vibrant little town with some fine colonial architecture; it has experienced a steady increase in visitors due to its proximity to Chichén Itzá. The heart of town is the leafy central plaza, with a fountain that is illuminated in the evening. Here, elderly *Vallisoletanos* take siestas beneath the trees, young couples share ice cream and in the evening dance to the brass bands which often play from 8pm. The Franciscan cathedral dominates the plaza, honey-gold in the late-afternoon light. There is a slightly medieval feel to the city, with some of the streets tapering off into mud tracks. Valladolid's location makes it an ideal place to settle for a few days while exploring the ruins of Chichén Itzá, Cobá, Tulúm, the fishing village of Río Lagartos and the three beautiful *cenotes* in the area. With its excellent-value hotels and a welcoming, low-key atmoshpere, it is a much more appealing base than Mérida.

Iglesia de Santa Ana, one block east of the plaza on Calle 41, has a small town museum (daily 9–9) with a lovely courtyard garden. It shows the history of rural Yucatán and has exhibits from the ruins of Ek-Balam (▷ 71). A 10-minute walk east from the plaza, on calles 36 and 39, is Cenote Zací (daily 8–6), where you can swim (except when there is algae in the water). There is a restaurant and lighted promenades. For other *cenotes* in the area see pages 174–175.

Uxmal

One of the most important Maya sites in Mexico, with outstandingly intricate stone carvings and mosaics, Uxmal encapsulates the purity and beauty of the Puuc style.

RATINGS	
Cultural interest	●●●●●
Good for kids	●●●●
Historic interest	●●●●●
Photo stops	●●●●●

BASICS

317 R8
8–5
$8, $3.50 on Sun
$40 per 1.5-hour tour
Expensive café in the visitor center
In the visitor center
$1 for the day
Son et lumière shows in Spanish 8pm in summer, 7pm in winter

TIPS

- A visit to Uxmal makes a grand end to the Puuc route tour (▷ 212–213), and sunset is the perfect time to view the site in its full glory.
- Views of the whole site can be had from the top of the fifth temple, reached via the eastern staircase.

Carved stone turtle (top)

View from the Grand Pyramid towards the ruins of the Nunnery, Pyramid of the Magician and House of the Turtles (above)

SEEING UXMAL

Uxmal means "that which was thrice built" or "place of abundant harvest." The site dates back to the Preclassic era, although the majority of its 150 or so structures were built during the Late Classic period and final stages of the Classic period. Maya cities in this region are characterized by the quadrangular layout of the buildings—set on raised platforms, with a plain lower section and a richly embellished upper section—and a man-made underground water-storage system. Representations of the rain god Chac, who was believed to have been supremely important due to the area's low rainfall, are omnipresent.

HIGHLIGHTS

CASA DEL ADIVINO (PYRAMID OF THE MAGICIAN)

This oval-shaped pyramid is set on a large rectangular base; rather than "thrice built," there is evidence that five stages of building were used in its construction. This is one of the most enigmatic Maya structures, and many myths surround its creation. According to one legend, the god Itzamná is supposed to have built the pyramid in one night, without any assistance. It is 38m (125ft) tall, with steep staircases leading to two temples at the top. The Fangs of Chac and fine stone latticework mark the doorways. The ancient city of Uxmal was constructed in strict accordance to the position of the planets, and the western stairway of the Pyramid of the Magician aligns with the setting sun at the summer solstice (June 21). Sacrificial rituals at Uxmal were carried out from this pyramid—the priest would rip out the beating heart of the living victim before tossing the body down the staircase.

CASA DE LAS MONJAS

The Nunnery has four low buildings set around a large courtyard. It was named by the Spanish, who thought the 74 rooms resembled convent cells. Chac, the rain god, is represented with fine masks arranged vertically on the corners of the buildings. The northern building, the oldest and most ambitious, is the purest representation of the Puuc style, while the east building is decorated with double-headed serpents and intricate latticework on its cornices. Plumed serpents adorn the facade of the west building.

PALACIO DEL GOBERNADOR

The House of the Governor is considered to be one of the most outstanding buildings in Mesoamerica. Its facade was constructed with more than 20,000 stones. Above the central entrance is an elaborate trapezoidal motif, with a string of Chac masks interwoven into a flowing, undulating, serpent-like shape extending to the facade's two corners. The stately two-headed jaguar throne in front of the structure suggests the building had a royal or administrative function.

CASA DE LAS TORTUGAS

Compared with many buildings at Uxmal, the House of the Turtles is rather sober. It is named for the carved turtles on the upper cornice; below, a short row of tightly packed columns resemble the Maya *palapas*—houses made of sticks with thatched roofs, still used today.

EL PALOMAR

The Dovecote is the oldest (AD700–800) and most damaged of the buildings at Uxmal, and in many ways sits rather incongruously with the Puuc style. What remains is still impressive: a long, low platform of wide columns topped with clusters of roof combs, whose serrated appearance bears a similarity to dovecotes.

BACKGROUND

At its peak, Uxmal was one of the largest of the Maya cities, with a population of around 25,000. Its rulers probably also governed nearby Kabah, Labná and Sayil (▷ 212–213). Much of the city's prosperity came from the fertility of the soil, and sophisticated engineering techniques meant that rainwater could be collected in *chultunes*, or cisterns. Unlike at Chichén Itzá, there were no *cenotes* to provide a water supply. With the growth of Chichén Itzá under Toltec rule, Uxmal declined in power and prosperity and was finally allied with nearby Mayapán in the Late Post Classic period. The buildings were abandoned for reasons unknown in the 10th century, and may have come under the Toltec influence.

Pyramid of the Magician (top and inset)

Detail on the Nunnery (middle right) and one of the carved masks of the rain god, Chac, on the Pyramid of the Magician (above)

Swimming with the dolphins at Xcaret, an incredible experience

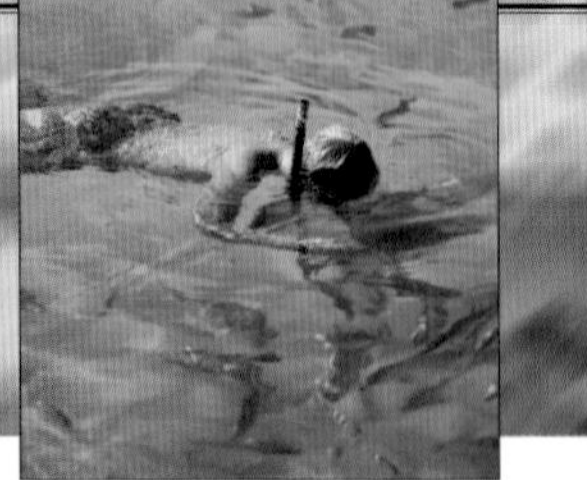

The clear, semi-freshwater lagoon of the ecological reserve at Xel-Há, full of tropical fish, is a snorkeler's delight

XCALAK

317 S9 Private launch from Chetumal *Colectivos* from Chetumal

Xcalak, at the tip of Quintana Roo, across the bay from Chetumal, is a curious blend of Mexican and Belizean culture that appeals to those in search of a remote, rugged, Caribbean landscape with good facilities for outdoor activities. The area is famous for its excellent fishing and the scuba diving is highly rated. The village itself has very little in the way of visitor infrastructure, with just a few shops selling beer and basic supplies, and one small restaurant serving Mexican food.

Fishing for amberjack or Jack Cravalle

A few kilometres north of Xcalak, Hotel Villa Caracol rents comfortable (though expensive) *cabañas* (huts) and provides sportfishing and diving facilities. Trips can be arranged from Villa Caracol to the fabulous Banco Chinchorro, an unspoiled island which has a large offshore coral reef 26km (16 miles) offshore and a graveyard of shipwrecks spanning centuries, or to San Pedro in Belize. In the village you may be able to rent a boat to explore Chetumal Bay and Banco Chinchorro. Do not try to walk from Xcalak along the coast to San Pedro; the route is virtually impassable.

XCARET

317 S8 • 72km (445 miles) south of Cancún (998) 883 31 43 Daily 8.30am–10pm Adult $46.55, child $23.75. Additional charges for activities 1km (half mile) walk from entrance to Xcaret. Alternatively take a taxi, or a tour from Playa del Carmen or Cancún. You can also walk along the beach from Playa del Carmen; it takes 3 hours **www**.xcaret.net

Xcaret, south along Route 307 from Cancún, is promoted as an eco-archaeological Maya theme park. Geared towards daytrippers from the Riviera resorts, it is either a glossy, multimedia sprint though the nature, culture and traditions of the Maya, or an overpriced, tasteless, tacky theme park—depending on your point of view. Originally a port called Polé, the ancient Maya site of Xcaret was the departure point for voyages to Cozumel. Attractions include an underground river winding through *cenotes*, caves and tunnels lit by natural light shafts, a dolphin enclosure with interactive dolphin programs, a butterfly pavilion, a bird sanctuary, horseback-riding and bicycling. Many visitors come here for the glitzy evening show "Xcaret by night," a gala performance that includes a re-enactment of a pre-Hispanic ball game, and traditional music and dance performances.

XEL-HÁ

317 S8 • 10km (6 miles) north of Tulúm (984) 875 60 00 Daily 9–6 (closing times vary) Weekdays: adult $30, child $16. Weekends: adult $24, child $12. Additional charges for activities Buses from Cancún, Playa del Carmen and Tulúm **www**.xelha.com.mx

Meaning "where the water flows," the national park of Xel-Há, on the Riviera Maya, surrounds a small bay with a beautiful clear lagoon. Here you can snorkel (arrive as early as possible to see the fish, as the lagoon is full of visitors throughout most of the day), swim in *cenotes*, snuba dive (without tanks) or visit the dolphin enclosure, spa, or "hammock island." Of the land-based activities, the highlight is the marvelous "path of conscience" through the jungle, which leads to one of the lagoon bays. The path is lined with sculptures and anecdotes relating to nature. Across the road from the park are the Xel-Há ruins, also known as Los Basadres.

XPUJIL

317 R9 • 100km (62 miles) west of Chetumal Daily 8–5 $2.50

The tiny village of Xpujil, on the Chetumal–Escárcega highway, is convenient for the three sets of ruins in this area—Xpujil, Becán (▷ 61) and Chicanná (▷ 70). It has two hotels and a couple of shops.

Xpujil is a small site constructed in the Río Bec style, which is characterized by heavy masonry towers simulating pyramids and temples, usually found rising in pairs at the ends of elongated buildings. The main building has an unusual set of three towers with rounded corners and steps that are too steep to climb, suggesting they may have been purely decorative. On the facade, on either side of the main entrance, are the open jaws of an enormous reptile in profile, possibly representing Itzamná, the Maya god of creation. Xpujil's main period of activity was AD500 to 750; it began to go into decline around 1100. It can be very peaceful and quiet here in the early morning, compared with the throng of visitor activity at the more accessible sites such as Chichén Itzá and Uxmal.

SOUTHERN MEXICO

The world-famous beach resort of Acapulco is high on the list of top-class destinations in Mexico's southern states. The magnificient colonial city of Oaxaca, at the heart of the Valley of Oaxaca, is surrounded by fascinating craft villages and the archaeological sites of Monte Albán and Mitla, while further east, deep in the rain forest of Chiapas, lies Palenque.

MAJOR SIGHTS

Acapulco	**82**
Monte Albán	**86–87**
Oaxaca	**88–91**
Palenque	**92–95**
San Cristóbal de las Casas	**96**

ACAPULCO

Mexico's premier beach playground has a spectacular setting, backed by the high mountains of the Sierra Madre del Sur.

Acapulco, wrapped around the 11km (7-mile) curve of Acapulco Bay, is the archetypal package holiday resort—unashamedly loud and brash, with high-rise hotels, trendy restaurants and swanky shops rubbing shoulders with heaving nightclubs, golf courses, tour touts and street vendors. Some 380km (240 miles) from Mexico City, it thrived during colonial times as the nearest Pacific port to the capital. From the moment the first Spanish galleon set sail for Manila in 1565, its fate was sealed as the terminal for the prosperous new trade route with the East, but its fortunes changed after Independence. The arrival of the international airport in the 1950s halted the decline and Acapulco quickly became the "in" place for Hollywood stars, who flocked here during the 1960s to party in their exclusive homes, before the happening scene moved to the other side of the country.

THE BEACHES

Acapulco's main attractions are its golden beaches, particularly playas Hornos, Hornitos, Condesa and, on the eastern side of the bay, Playa Icacos. Beside the latter is the CICI marineland amusement park (daily 10–6) with a pool with wave machine, a water slide and arena with performing dolphins and sea lions. On the southern shore of the Peninsula de la Playas, at the western end of the bay, are playas Caleta and Caletilla, whose calm (but murky) waters make them popular with families with small children. Playa Angosta, in a tiny, sheltered cove on the western side of the peninsula, is a 20-minute walk from the *zócalo*. Some 10km (6 miles) northwest of Acapulco is Pie de la Cuesta, a long narrow spit separating the booming ocean surf from the mangroves and palms of Laguna Coyuca.

FUERTE DE SAN DIEGO

Away from the beach life is Fuerte de San Diego (Tue–Sun 9.30–6.30), where the last battle for Mexican Independence was fought. It has been transformed into an attractive museum recalling the history of Mexico, and of Acapulco in particular.

Don't miss The cliff divers at La Quebrada plunge 40m (131ft) into the water below, timing their dives to coincide with the incoming waves (daily at 1pm, 7.15pm, 8.15pm, 9.15pm and 10.15pm).

RATINGS

Activities	●●●●
Good for kids	●●●
Photo stops	●●●●

BASICS

314 K10

Costera Miguel Alemán 4455, tel (744) 434 01 70/484 44 16/484 24 23

Aeropuerto Alvarez Internacional (ACA), 23km (14 miles) east

www.sectur.guerrero.gob.mx
Lively site with pictures, music and good links to other sites.

TIPS

- **The most useful bus route runs the full length of Costera Miguel Alemán, linking the older part of town to the beaches and hotels. Bus stops on the main thoroughfare are numbered, so find out which number you need to get off at**
- **Though a beach resort, you'll need to lose the shorts and sandals and dress to impress if you want to sample the city's legendary nightlife.**

Acapulco is justly famous for its beaches, cliff divers and nightlife

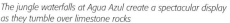

The jungle waterfalls at Agua Azul create a spectacular display as they tumble over limestone rocks

Bonampak's stunning murals have stood the test of time

AGUA AZUL

316 Q10 • 35km (21 miles) south of Palenque Carretera 199 to Ocosingo 01 55 53 29 09 95 ext 7002, Misol-Ha ext 7006 Daily 8–5 $1 x 2 per person (*caseta* at entrance to town and at the falls means you pay twice) Travel agencies in Palenque and many of the hotels offer tours to Agua Azul, including a visit to the waterfall at Misol-Há, 22km (14 miles) from Palenque *Colectivos* from Avenida Hidalgo and Calle Allende in Palenque for Agua Azul and Misol-Há

This series of stunning jungle waterfalls and rapids runs through the lush valleys of the Sierra Madre. You can follow a path on the left of the rapids for 7km (4 miles), with superb views and secluded areas for picnics. Swimming is good—the water is clear and blue during fine weather, muddy brown in bad—but stick to the roped areas; the various graves on the steep path alongside the rapids testify to the dangers. Watch out for the Liquidizer, a particularly dangerous area of white foaming water. Even in the designated areas the currents are ferocious, and you must beware of hidden tree trunks. The main swimming area at Agua Azul—its name means "blue water"—is surrounded with restaurants and local children selling fruit.

Misol-Há, north of Agua Azul, is a waterfall 40m (130 feet) high. A narrow path winds behind the falls, allowing you to stand behind the immense curtain of water. You can swim here also, and there are simple facilities and restaurants.

Warning: Military checks occasionally take place between Palenque and San Cristóbal de las Casas. If you are stopped at night, turn off the car engine and lights and switch on the inside light. Always have your passport handy.

BONAMPAK

316 Q10 • 176km (109 miles) southeast of Palenque Tue–Sun 10–5 Officially free, but ecological restrictions mean that you must leave you car some distance from the gate, from where a bus will take you to the site Buses from Palenque Flights from Palenque to Bonampak and Yaxchilán Tour operators from Palenque offer a 13-hour day trip to Bonampak and Yaxchilán (▷ 98)

Bonampak was built in the Late Classic period on the Río Lacanjá, a tributary of the Río Usumacinta. It is famous for its realistic murals in the Templo de las Pinturas (Temple of Paintings), dated AD800, which tell the story of a battle and the bloody aftermath involving sacrificial torture and execution of prisoners. Painted on the walls, vaulted ceilings and benches of the temple's three rooms, the murals also describe the rituals surrounding the presentation at court of the future ruler. The people participating were mainly the ruling elite, and a strict hierarchy was observed whereby minor nobility attended eminent lords. In Room 1, the celebration opens with the young prince, clothed in white robes, being presented to an assembly of lords. The king, dressed simply, watches from his throne, while lords in sumptuous clothing and jewelry and musicians line up for a procession. The right of the heir to accede to the throne and the need to take captives to be sacrificed in his honor is depicted in the paintings of Room 2. Here, a ferocious battle is in progress in which the ruler, Chaan Muan, shining heroically, proves his right to the throne. Then, on a stepped structure, Chaan Muan oversees the torture and mutilation of the captives; one victim has clearly been decapitated, his head resting on a bed of leaves. The paintings that cover the walls of Room 3 appear to celebrate these sacrifices in an exuberant display of music and dance.

CAÑON DEL SUMIDERO

316 P10 • 10km (6 miles) north of Tuxtla Gutiérrez Parque Ecoturístico Cañon del Sumidero (961) 602 85 00 10–4.30 Adult $16, child (5–12) $8 Tours from San Cristóbal, including a boat trip *Colectivos* from San Cristóbal
www.sumidero.com

From Tuxtla Gutiérrez, a drive through spectacular scenery leads to the rim of the 1,000m-deep (3,280ft) Sumidero Canyon, now a national park. During the Spanish Conquest indigenous warriors, unable to endure the subjugation, hurled themselves off the edge. Myriad trails wind through lush vegetation with orchids, cascading waterfalls and crystalline rivers. Frolicking monkeys and cavorting birdlife are more or less guaranteed, while the promise of jaguars and pumas is usually unfulfilled. In addition to hiking, swimming and lazing in hammocks, the park offers many adventure activities, including kayaking and cycle rides. The animal hospital is particularly popular with children.

About 15km (9 miles) beyond the national park, the colonial town of Chiapa del Corzo is the embarkation point for boat trips to the canyon (▷ 186), but it's worth allowing a couple of hours to explore the town, which was a Preclassic and Proto-Classic Maya site and shares features with early Maya sites in Guatemala. The ruins are behind the Nestlé plant. Other sights of interest include the fine 16th-century Moorish-influenced fountain and the 16th-century Iglesia de Santo Domingo, which has an engraved altar of solid silver.

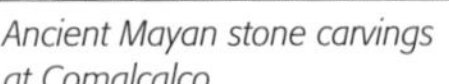

Ancient Mayan stone carvings at Comalcalco

The long sandy beach at the modern resort of Ixtapa

Mitla's church is surrounded by a fence of cacti

COMALCALCO

316 P9 • 52km (32 miles) northwest of Villahermosa Tue–Sun 10–5 $3 Buses from Villahermosa www.comalcalco.gob.mx

In pre-Hispanic times the ancient city of Comalcalco wore the mantle of the most important political capital in Tabasco. Comalcalco in Nahuatl means "place of the earthenware pans," and, unlike other Maya sites, its palaces and pyramids were built of fired bricks rather than stone. The city was populated by the Chontal or Putun people, who were noted for their trading. The archaeological zone includes a ceremonial area built during the Preclassic period, the North Plaza complex and the Great Acropolis. The axis of Temple I, which forms part of the North Plaza, is aligned with the setting sun. At the entrance to the site, a museum houses many of the treasures unearthed during excavations, including fragments of intricate stucco decoration that would once have covered the entire base of the temple, and clay figurines symbolizing Maya society.

HUATULCO

315 M11 Sedetur, Boulevard Benito Juárez, near the golf course, Tangolunda, tel (958) 581 01 77 www.baysofhuatulco.com.mx

East along the coastal road from Pochutla is Huatulco, a meticulously engineered and environmentally aware international vacation resort. The complex is surrounded by a forest reserve and nine splendid bays. Golf, swimming pools, nightlife, international and Mexican cuisine, beaches, watersports, excursions into the forest and tours of archaeological sites are all available. The complex encompasses several interconnected towns and development areas. Tangolunda is set aside for large luxury hotels and resorts, with a golf course, the most expensive restaurants, souvenir shops and nightlife. Chahué, on the next bay west, has a town park with a spa and a beach club, a marina and a few hotels.

Some 6km (4 miles) west of Tangolunda is Santa Cruz Huatulco, once an ancient Zapotec settlement and Mexico's most important Pacific port during the 16th century (later abandoned). Tour boats leave from its marina, which has facilities for visiting yachts, hotels, restaurants, shops and a few luxury homes. There is an attractive open-air chapel by the beach, the Capilla de la Santa Cruz, and a well-groomed park. La Crucecita, 2km (1 mile) inland, is the hub of the Huatulco complex, with the more economical hotels, restaurants and shops.

IXTAPA-ZIHUATANEJO

313 J10 Ixtapa shopping plaza, tel (755) 553 19 67; Palacio Municipal, Zihuantanejo www.ixtapa-zihuatanejo.com

The two resorts of Ixtapa and Zihuatanejo are promoted as a package even though they are 7km (4 miles) apart and totally different in character. Ixtapa is a popular modern resort, with its fashionable hotels, restaurants, bars, discos, shopping complex, golf courses, yacht marina and beaches.

The beautiful, laid-back fishing port of Zihuatanejo, on the other hand, makes a welcome change from high-rise Ixtapa, and still retains much of its Mexican village charm. There is a handicraft market by the church, some beachside cafés and a small Museo Arqueológico on Avenida 5 de Mayo. The Plaza de Toros, at the entrance to town, hosts seasonal *corridas* (bullfights).

LAGUNAS DE MONTEBELLO

316 Q11 (963) 240 47 8–5 $3 (charge for vehicle) *Combis* or buses from Comitán

From Comitán de Dominguez you can reach this exhilarating region of more than 50 lakes, lagoons and caves, which became a national park in 1959. One group of lakes is known as the Lagunas de Siete Colores—due to oxides in the water and refracted light, they take on wonderful hues ranging from deep emerald, turquoise and violet to steely gray. The national park has more than 7,000 pine groves, forests of oak and a jungle with orchids. Five of the lakes are accessible by paved road; you must hike to the others (not recommended in the rainy season). The most attractive are Agua Tinta and Bosque Azul. Buses go as far as Laguna Bosque Azul, a one-hour journey. It is also possible to camp in the park.

MITLA

315 M10 • 42km (26 miles) from Oaxaca (951) 568 03 16 Daily 8–5 $2.70 Buses from Oaxaca Half-day tours to Tule, Tlacolula and Mitla from Oaxaca agencies

Mitla is one of the foremost sites in the state of Oaxaca and remarkable for its ornate stonework, considered by many archaeologists to be without peer. Inhabited in the Classic period, Mitla reached its zenith in the Post Classic period and was still inhabited when the Spanish arrived. There are five groups of buildings, of which the most notable is the Grupo de las Columnas (Group of Columns), in the eastern part of the site. Here, the principal elements are the Salón de las Columnas (Hall of Columns) and the Patio de las Grecas (Hall of Mosaics), notable

Admiring the geometric stone mosaics at the ancient Zapotec site of Mitla, southeast of Oaxaca

Bringing home the daily catch at Puerto Escondido

for its geometric stone mosaics. In the north and east of the complex are tombs where Zapotec priests and kings were buried.

In the village of Mitla, near the square, is a lively tourist market and the Museo Frissell de Art Zapoteca, with a good collection of pre-Hispanic ceramics.

MONTE ALBÁN

See pages 86–87.

OAXACA

See pages 88–91.

PALENQUE

See pages 92–95.

PUERTO ANGEL

315 M11 Huatulco airport, 32km (20 miles) east, Puerto Escondido airport, 90km (56 miles) west

From Pochutla, a pretty road winds south through hilly forest country before dropping to the sea at Puerto Angel. This low-key fishing port lies above a flask-shaped bay, and the central beach is an ideal spot from which to watch the activity of the small dock. Unfortunately the turquoise water is polluted. Nearby is Playa del Panteón, a small beach in a lovely setting, but crowded in season. There are cleaner and more tranquil beaches east of town, including Estacahuite (beware of strong currents and sharp coral).

Some 4km (2.5 miles) west of Puerto Angel is Zipolite, one of Mexico's few nudist beaches. It has gained a reputation for drugs and violence, although things are improving. The steeply shelved beach has dangerous undercurrents, especially near the rocks at the east end.

Another 3km (2 miles) west is San Agustinillo, a long, pretty beach with safe swimming at the west end; surfing is best near the middle. About 1km (half a mile) west again is Mazunte, the least-developed major beach. Nude bathing is prohibited; the safest swimming is at either end of the bay. At the east end of Mazunte is the Centro Mexicano de la Tortuga (▷ 188).

Hammocks for sale

PUERTO ESCONDIDO

315 M11 Sedetur, Avenida Juárez, at the entrance to Playa Bacocho, tel (954) 582 01 75; Mon–Fri 9–5, Sat 10–1 Buses from Oaxaca

Reached via a corkscrew mountain drive on the pacific coast of Oaxaca state, Puerto Escondido has been transformed from a sleepy fishing village into one of the most popular destinations in southern Mexico. With stunning beaches, world-class surfing and a relaxed alternative lifestyle, its appeal is obvious. Hotels, restaurants and cultural complexes cater to surfers, yoga gurus and independent visitors. Daily rituals revolve around the beach, contemplating glorious sunsets. At night, restaurants serve up feasts of fresh shrimp and seared tuna to the sound of chilled-out music or the lapping of the waves. Experienced surfers make the pilgrimage to Playa Zicatela, the premier Mexico surfing scene. Playa Principal, abutting El Adoquín pedestrian mall, has the calmest water, but is not very clean. A few fishermen still bring in the catch of the day here. Playa Manzanillo and Puerto Angelito share the Bahía Puerto Angelito and are an easy 15-minute walk away; they are pretty, with reasonably safe swimming, but rather commercial. The state tourist police now patrol both the main beach and tourist areas.

Safety is an important issue in and around Puerto Escondido. Never walk on any beach at night, even in groups.

RESERVA DE LA BIÓSFERA EL TRIUNFO

316 P11 Park entrance about 184km (115 miles) south of Tuxtla Gutiérrez via Angel Albino Corzo (961) 612 36 63 (Institute of Natural History, Tuxtla) Daily 8–5

In the Sierra Madre, the Triunfo Biosphere Reserve is one of the most pristine and diverse wildlife regions in the country. Most importantly, it protects Mexico's only cloud forest, 2,750m (9,000ft) above the Pacific coast. The main hiking route into the forest runs from Jaltenango (reached by bus from Tuxtla) to Mapastepec on the coastal highway. It's about 29km (18 miles) from Jaltenango to Finca Prusia; then follow a good mule track for 3 hours to the El Triunfo camp (1,650m/5,410ft).

Endemic species of wildlife include the rare azure-rumped tanager and the horned guan, birds found only here and across the border in the nearby mountains of Guatemala. Other birds and animals include the quetzal, harpy eagle, jaguar, tapir and white-lipped peccary.

Turn left in the clearing for the route down to Tres de Mayo, 25km (16 miles) away; this is an easy descent of 5 hours to a pedestrian suspension bridge on the dirt road to Loma Bonita. From here, take a pick-up to Mapastepec.

Monte Albán

Enigmatic and compelling, the ancient capital of the Zapotecs has a legacy of sophisticated architecture and fascinating iconography, with temples, tombs, plazas and ball courts revealing Zapotec culture at its zenith.

THE SIGHTS

RATINGS

Archaeological interest	●●●●●
Cultural interest	●●●●●
Historic interest	●●●●●
Photo stops	●●●●●

BASICS

315 M10

(951) 516 12 15

8–6

$3.80

Several buses depart from Hotel Trébol, one block south of the *zócalo* in Oaxaca. Autobuses Turísticos (tourist buses) depart from Hotel Rivera del Angel, Calle Mina 518

$12 per hour for an official guide. Non-official guides hang around the site. Beware of overcharging and check their credentials

Informative literature and videos in several languages

Café in museum complex serves pricey snacks and better-value lunches

In museum complex

Five minutes' walk from site

www.oaxaca.gob.mx
Spanish only.

One of the many treasures excavated from Tomb 7 (top)

Intriguing bas-reliefs of Los Danzantes (The Dancers; above and inset opposite)

SEEING MONTE ALBÁN

Monte Albán lies 10km (6 miles) west of Oaxaca, on a hilltop dominating the valley, and is easily reached by car or public transportation. Restoration was carried out between 1992 and 1994, when a museum and visitor center were built. Walls, terraces, pyramids, tombs, staircases and sculptures reveal the Zapotecs' cultural achievements and monumental architecture. The Gran Plaza, 400m (1,312ft) up a steep mountain, without immediate access to water or arable land, is the focal point.

HIGHLIGHTS

GRAN PLAZA

The main plaza may have been the site of the marketplace, but this theory is undermined by the back-breaking hill and the restricted access. It would also seem ideal for religious ceremonies and rituals, but the absence of religious iconography contradicts this interpretation. The imagery at Monte Albán is almost exclusively militaristic, with allusions to tortured prisoners and captured settlements. The Gran Plaza is delineated north and south by the two largest structures in the city, which have been interpreted as palace and/or public building (Plataforma Norte/North Platform) and temple (Plataforma Sur/South platform). Apart from these, the ball court and arrow-shaped building in front of the South Platform, there are 14 other structures—six along the west side, three in the middle and five along the east side.

EDIFICIO DE LOS DANZANTES

One structure, known as the Edificio de los Danzantes (Building of the Dancers), to the west of the Gran Plaza, has bas-reliefs, glyphs and calendar signs (probably fifth century BC). The intriguing, strangely shaped figures that give the building its name are possibly dancing, but their symbolism is unclear.

BALL COURT

The ball court is east of the Gran Plaza, marked by two structures at the sides of the rectangular base, with slanting walls. The western side is covered with a sculpture representing a grasshopper.

BEYOND THE GRAN PLAZA

From AD450 to AD600, Monte Albán had 14 districts beyond the confines of the Gran Plaza: theories suggest that each of the 14 structures within the Main Plaza corresponded with one of the districts outside. Each pertained to a distinct ethnic group or polity, brought together to create a pan-regional confederacy. The arrow-shaped structure functioned as a military showcase; it also has astronomical connotations.

THE CONFEDERACY

The presence of a number of structures on or bordering the Main Plaza that housed representatives of various ethnic groups supports the theory that Monte Albán came into being as the site of a confederacy or league, and its neutral position, unrelated to any single polity,

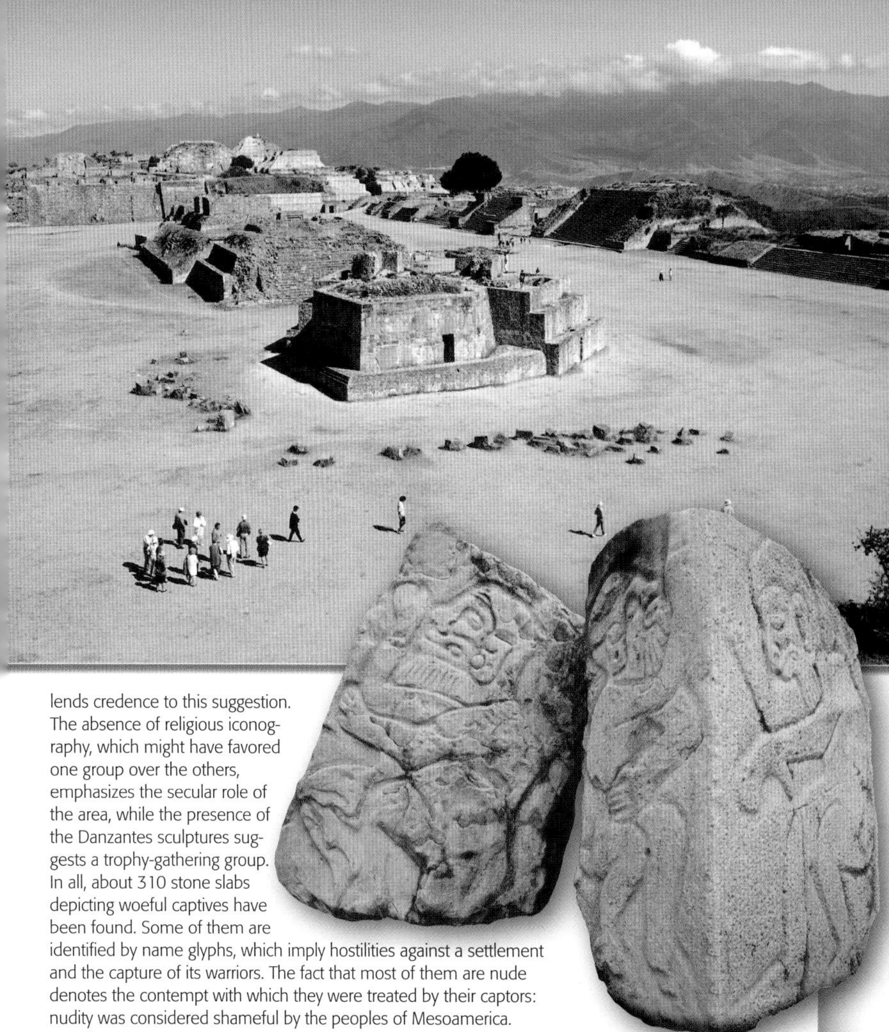

lends credence to this suggestion. The absence of religious iconography, which might have favored one group over the others, emphasizes the secular role of the area, while the presence of the Danzantes sculptures suggests a trophy-gathering group. In all, about 310 stone slabs depicting woeful captives have been found. Some of them are identified by name glyphs, which imply hostilities against a settlement and the capture of its warriors. The fact that most of them are nude denotes the contempt with which they were treated by their captors: nudity was considered shameful by the peoples of Mesoamerica.

Looking down over Monte Albán's Gran Plaza (top)

THE COLLAPSE

Monte Albán reached its maximum size around AD600, with a population of between 15,000 and 30,000. Shortly after that date, the city changed dramatically in form and function. The population shrank by nearly 82 percent, the Gran Plaza was abandoned, and most people moved nearer the valley floor, but behind protective walls. The abandonment of the Gran Plaza was a direct result of the collapse of the political institution focused there. This collapse has been seen as a consequence of the fact that, early in the seventh century, Teotihuacán was already showing signs of decadence. Gaining momentum, the decadence led to the massive abandonment of that great centre. It is unlikely to have been coincidental that the Gran Plaza at Monte Albán was abandoned around this time.

BACKGROUND

Monte Albán was one of the first cities in Mesoamerica and one of the most populous. It was founded around 500BC and flourished until AD750, exerting considerable political and economic control over the other communities in the central valley of Oaxaca and surrounding mountains. Although it had been developing a policy of offense and capture as early as 200BC, the expansion of the city really gained impetus with the growth of Teotihuacán (▷ 132–134).

TIPS

- To allow more time at the ruins (3 hours minimum is recommended), take the tourist bus to Monte Albán, then walk the 4km (2.5 miles) downhill to Colonia Monte Albán and get a city bus back from there.
- The Centro Cultural Santo Domingo in Oaxaca (▷ 90) houses the contents of Tomb 7 and presents the rise and fall of Monte Albán.
- The place is radiant at sunset, but permission is needed to stay that late (take a torch/flashlight).

SAN
MAYOR
SAN
PEDRO
DIVINO PASTOR
PABLO

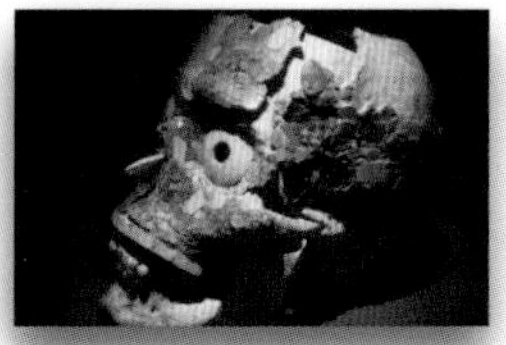

Oaxaca

Oaxaca is a graceful blend of pre-Columbian and colonial influences, with the finest baroque church in Mexico, a crop of engaging museums and galleries, ebullient feast days, kaleidoscopic markets and the curious complexities of *Oaxaqueña* cuisine.

RATINGS	
Cultural interest	●●●●●
Excursions	●●●●●
Historic interest	●●●●
Traditional arts and crafts	●●●●●
Walkability	●●●●

BASICS

☎ 315 M10 (also walk page 217)
ℹ Sedetur, Independencia 607, tel (951) 516 07 17; daily 8–8
✈ Aeropuerto Xoxocotlán (OAX), 9km (6 miles) south

www.oaxaca.gob.mx
Spanish only.

TIPS

- To get an insight into Oaxaca's history and culture before you begin exploring the city and archaeological sites in the area, visit the Museo de las Culturas de Oaxaca.
- Women should be aware of *gavacheros*, local young men who hang around the *zócalo* picking up foreign women and seeking favors.

Exhibit from the Museo Rufino Tamayo (top)

Iglesia de Santo Domingo (above and left); selling flowers in Benito Juárez market (above middle); balloon-seller in Plaza de Oaxaca (above right)

SEEING OAXACA

Oaxaca is the cosmopolitan capital of the state of Oaxaca. Declared a UNESCO World Heritage Site in 1987, this relatively compact city, blessed with an average temperature of 22°C (72°F) is best explored on foot. It is one of Mexico's most handsome cities, and at every turn breezy patios and majestic stone buildings reveal its importance during the colonial period, while the vibrant markets displaying local crafts and regional delicacies, traditional *Guelaguetza* folk dances and feast days (▷ 189) point to its indigenous roots. The highlights for those with little time include the animated *zócalo* (main square), the sublime Iglesia de Santo Domingo and monastery, the hypnotic Mercado Abasto, and the mystical Monte Albán archaeological site (▷ 86–87) overlooking the town. The major sights are concentrated around the *zócalo* or along Calle Macedonio Alcalá, a cobbled pedestrian mall that joins the square with the Iglesia de Santo Domingo. Avenida Independencia is the main street running east–west; the most photogenic part of the old city lies to the north, and the commercial area, housing the cheaper hotels, to the south. Avenida Independencia is also a dividing line for the north–south streets, which change names here.

HIGHLIGHTS

ZÓCALO

The *zócalo* is the heart of town. Oaxacan life ebbs and flows through its leafy central park, along its arcades and beneath shady porticos lined with open-air cafés and restaurants. Around the ornate central bandstand men have their shoes shined while munching on *chapulines* (deep-fried grasshoppers) and, in the shade of giant laurel trees, vendors offer charms to prevent the loss of the soul. The square has a perpetual carnival air, with gaudy helium balloons bobbing over romantic fountains, pearly-pink cotton candy (candyfloss) stands and live music. Political demonstrations are often held opposite the graceful arcades of the Palácio de Gobierno (Government Palace), which occupies the south side of the square and contains two fine murals painted by Arturo García Bustos in 1980. The 17th-century cathedral (daily 7am–8pm) has a fine baroque facade and an antique pipe organ. In front, scattered among the laurels and shocking-pink bougainvillea, stands sell everything from cloth dyed with purple snails to fruit sherbets. In the evening music and dance events provide great free entertainment.

Pre-Columbian figure in the Museo Rufino Tamayo (below)

Typical black-clay pottery from Oaxaca (bottom)

IGLESIA DE SANTO DOMINGO

✉ Calle Macedonia Alcalá and Gurrión 🖐 Daily 7–1, 5–8 ? Flash photography not allowed

Four blocks from the *zócalo* is Oaxaca's unmissable sight—the Franciscan church of Santo Domingo with its adjoining monastery, now the Centro Cultural de Santo Domingo (see below). The church is considered one of the best examples of baroque style in Mexico, possibly the western world. When English novelist Aldous Huxley visited in 1933, he enthused that it was "one of the most extravagantly beautiful churches in the world." Elaborately carved by the Dominicans in 1608, it underwent extensive refurbishment in the 1950s that revealed wonderful ceilings and walls 9m (30ft) thick and ablaze with gold leaf. The church is dominated by a three-level gilded altar, and a spectacular polychrome bas-relief on the ceiling above the entrance reveals the family tree of Santo Domingo de Guzmán, founder of the order.

CENTRO CULTURAL SANTO DOMINGO

✉ Calle Macedonia Alcalá and Gurrión ☎ (951) 516 29 91 ⏲ Tue–Sun 10–8 🖐 $3.80 ? Flash photography not allowed. Jardín Etnobotánico ☎ (951) 516 76 15

Housed in the former convent of Santo Domingo, the cultural complex includes the Museo de las Culturas de Oaxaca, Biblioteca Francisco Burgoa, Jardín Etnobotánico and a bookstore. Construction of the convent started in 1575 and Dominican friars occupied the convent from 1608 to 1812. Subsequently the Mexican army occupied it until 1972, when it became the regional museum.

Exhibits in the museum's14 galleries are well displayed, with detailed explanations in Spanish (audiovisual tours available in English). The history of Oaxaca from pre-Hispanic times to the contemporary period is presented through an archaeological collection and includes spectacular riches found in Tomb 7 of Monte Albán (▷ 86–87). There are also displays of different aspects of Oaxacan culture such as crafts, cooking and traditional medicine, as well as temporary exhibits, often including the work of contemporary Mexican artists.

The Biblioteca Francisco Burgoa (admission included) houses a collection of 24,000 volumes dating from 1484. There are temporary exhibits and the library is open to scholars for research.

The Jardín Etnobotánico preserves southern Mexico's native plants. Species include the agaves used to make *mezcal*, *pulque* and tequila and plants used in folk medicine.

BASÍLICA DE LA SOLEDAD

✉ Avenida Independencia 107 ⏲ Daily 7–10. Museo Religioso de la Soledad ⏲ Mon–Sun 8–2, 4–7

The massive 17th-century Basílica de la Soledad has fine colonial ironwork and sculpture. Construction began on the site of the hermitage to San Sebastián in 1582, but was halted until 1682 because of earthquakes. The building was consecrated in 1690 and the convent was finished in 1697. Sculptures include an exquisite Virgen de la Soledad, which at one time was endowed with a crown of pure gold and embellished with some 600 glittering diamonds. The interior of the basilica is lavishly gilded, and the plaques on the walls are painted like cross-sections of polished stone. The Museo Religioso de la Soledad at the back of the church has a display of religious objects.

MARKETS

⏲ Daily 7am–8pm

The markets and varied crafts of Oaxaca are among the foremost attractions of the region. There are four main markets, all of which are worth a visit; polite bargaining is the rule everywhere. The Mercado de Abastos, also known as the Central de Abastos, at the corner of Periférico and Las Casas, is the largest in Oaxaca and the second-

MORE TO SEE

CERRO DE FORTÍN

Planetarium: ☎ (951) 51 475 00 ⏲ Shows Mon–Sat 12.30 and 7pm, Sun 12.30pm, 6pm and 7pm

There are grand views of the city from the hilltop of Cerro de Fortín, northwest of the center. Here you'll find the *Guelaguetza* amphitheater, a monument to Juárez, an observatory and a planetarium. Take a taxi, as the route is deserted and muggings have been reported on the trails.

MUSEO RUFINO TAMAYO

✉ Avenida Morelos 503 ☎ (951) 516 47 50 ⏲ Mon, Wed–Sat 10–2, 4–7, Sun 10–3 🖐 $1.50

This museum contains an outstanding display of pre-Columbian objects dating from 1250BC to AD1100, donated by the Oaxacan abstract painter and muralist Rufino Tamayo. The rooms devoted to the Olmecs, Totonacs and Maya are exceptional.

largest craft market in Mexico after Toluca; it's a cacophony of sights, sounds and aromas, busiest on Saturdays and not to be missed. Prices here tend to be lower than in the smaller markets. In the middle of town is the Mercado 20 de Noviembre (Calle Aldama, on the corner of 20 de Noviembre), with clean stands selling prepared foods, including barbequed *tasajo* (dried beef), cheese and sweet breads. To the rear of the market on Mina and 20 de Noviembre, a deep chocolatey aroma fills the air from the numerous chocolate mills, including Mayordomo (▷ 187). Next door to the Mercado 20 de Noviembre, the larger Mercado Benito Juárez sells household goods, fruits, vegetables, crafts and regional products such as *quesillo* (string cheese), bread and chocolate. Mercado Artesanal (Zaragoza and J. P. García) has a good selection of crafts.

BACKGROUND

Nomadic tribes, related to the Olmecs, are believed to have first inhabited Oaxaca's central valleys more than 10,000 years ago. The period 700BC to 300BC witnessed the construction of the spectacular Monte Albán (▷ 86–87), which reached its zenith between AD500 and AD750 to become the leading Zapotec base. By AD800 the city had been abandoned, for reasons unknown. As Zapotec culture declined, Mixtec culture began to flourish and conquest by the Aztecs in 1486 added to the complex mosaic of cultures encountered by the Spaniards. In 1529 the Spaniards erected a city—the Villa de Antequera—that rapidly developed a more Spanish character. It was only in 1872 that it was named Oaxaca, a word from the Nahuatl Huaxyacac language meaning "in the nose of the gourds." Alonso García Bravo, architect of Mexico City and Veracruz, and one of Spain's most esteemed town planners, was commissioned to design the city. He began by creating the Plaza Central or *zócalo*, then built the cathedral over a former Aztec burial site. On the other side of the square, municipal buildings provided the basis for civil power, establishing a harmonious balance between the sacred and the secular. The city flourished during the Viceroyalty as Oaxaca's sheep farms, sugar cane and gold and silver mines produced more wealth. Today, Oaxaca has the largest indigenous population (around 1,209,000) in Mexico, speaking more than 150 dialects.

Benito Juárez market is the place to go for Oaxacan crafts and delicacies

MORE TO SEE

MUSEO DE ARTE CONTEMPORÁNEO (MACO)

✉ Calle Macedonio Alcalá 202 ☎ (951) 514 22 28 🕐 Wed–Mon 10.30–8 🎫 $1

This late 17th-century house with a stone facade, also known as the House of Cortés, has a permanent exhibition of Oaxacan artists, including Rufino Tamayo, Francisco Gutiérrez and Rodolfo Nieto. International exhibits have featured modern art ranging from sculptures by Francisco Zuñiga to traditional African sculptures and pop art. There is also a library and a café.

MUSEO DE SITIO CASA DE JUÁREZ

✉ Cabrera García Vigil 609 ☎ (951) 516 18 60 🕐 Tue–Sat 10–7, Sun 10–5 🎫 $3

Benito Juárez (1806–72) lived here from the age of 12. The museum provides an atmospheric homage to Mexico's most revered president and has an engaging display of his possessions, historical documents and some bookbinding tools (he was once apprenticed to a bookbinder).

Palenque

Suffused in mystery, Palenque is a fine example of a Maya sanctuary of the Classic period, eerily atmospheric amid wild jungle, and hailed as the most beautiful of all the Maya ruins in Mexico.

RATINGS

Cultural interest	●●●●●
Good for kids	●●●●
Historic interest	●●●●●
Photo stops	●●●●●

BASICS

316 Q10

Avenida Juárez, esq Abásalo, tel (916) 345 03 56 (Mon–Sat 9–9, Sun 9–1)

Daily 8–5

$3.80

Minibuses from Palenque town

Multilingual guides, $35 for 1.5 to 2 hours; ask at the ticket office

Expensive restaurant at museum on way back to town. Vendors outside gates

Near ticket office and on site

Free parking outside main entrance

www.palenquemx.com
English site under construction.

TIP

- There have been reports of criminals hiding in the jungle and occasional muggings in out-of-the-way places. Leave valuables at your hotel to minimize any loss.

Detail from stone carvings (top and opposite)
Temple of the Inscriptions (above); Temple of the Foliated Cross (above middle); the Palace (above right)

SEEING PALENQUE

Palenque has a mystical charm that enchants archaeologists, historians and visitors alike. From Palenque town, minivans run every 10 minutes along the 7km (4-mile) road to the ruins, where there are handicraft stands and an information booth where guided tours can be organized.

Two rulers, Pakal the Great and his son Chan Bahlum, immortalized their divine ancestry and military accomplishments here in a mesmerizing series of palaces, temples, glyphs and stucco. At the heart of the site is the Palacio, a group of buildings arranged around four patios to which a tower was later added, the Templo de las Inscripciones (Temple of the Inscriptions), which rises above the tomb of Pakal.

HIGHLIGHTS

EL PALACIO

The Palace stands in the middle of the site on an artificial platform over 100m (328ft) long and 9m (30ft) high. When Chan Bahlum's younger brother, Kan Xul, became king he devoted himself to enlarging the palace and built the four-floor tower in memory of their dead father. The top of the tower is almost on a level with Pakal's mortuary temple, and on the winter solstice (December 21) the sun, viewed from here, sets directly above his crypt. Large windows where Maya astronomers could observe and chart movement of the planets pierce the walls of the tower. Kan Xul reigned for 18 years before being captured and probably sacrificed by the rulers of Toniná, to the south.

TEMPLO DE LAS INSCRIPCIONES

The Temple of the Inscriptions, along with Temples XII and XIII, lies to the southwest of the Palacio group and is one of the few Maya pyramids to have a burial chamber incorporated at the time of its construction. It was erected to cover the crypt in which Pakal the Great, the founder of the first ruling dynasty of Palenque, was buried. Discovered in 1952 by Alberto Ruz Lhuillier, the burial chamber measured 7m (23ft) long, 7m (23ft) high and 3.75m (12ft) across, an incredible achievement considering the weight of the huge pyramid pressing down upon it. According to the inscriptions, Lord Pakal was born in AD603 and died in 684. Inside, Ruz Lhuillier discovered his

THE SARCOPHAGUS LID

Pakal's sarcophagus is fashioned out of a solid piece of rock, with a carved limestone slab covering it. Every element in the imagery of the lid is consistent with Maya iconography. The central image is that of Pakal falling back into the fleshless jaws of the earth monster who will transport him to Xibalba, the realm of the dead. A cruciform world-tree rises above the mouth to the underworld. The long inscription around the edge of the lid includes a number of dates and personal names that record a dynastic sequence covering almost the whole of the seventh and eight centuries. Although the imagery of the sarcophagus lid refers to Pakal's fall into Xibalba, the location of the tower of the palace ensures that he will not remain there. The sun, setting over the crypt on the winter solstice, will have to do battle with the Nine Lords of the Night before re-emerging triumphantly in the east. Pakal, who awaits the sun at the point where the final battle had been fought, will accompany the sun as he re-emerges from Xibalba in the east.

bones adorned with jade ornamentation. Around the burial chamber various stucco figures depict the Bolontikú—the Nine Lords of the Night—from Maya mythology. A narrow tube was built alongside the stairs, presumably to give Pakal spiritual access to the outside world. Pakal also left a record of his forebears in the inscriptions. These three great tablets contain one of the longest texts of any Maya monument. There are 620 glyph blocks; they tell of Pakal's ancestors, astronomical events, and an astonishing projection into the distant future (AD4772). One of the last inscriptions reveals that, 132 days after Pakal's death, his son, Chan Bahlum, ascended to power as the new ruler of Palenque.

TEMPLE XIII

In 1994 a secret passageway was unearthed alongside the Temple of the Inscriptions, which led to an underground temple with three rooms. In the middle room were the remains of a woman within a stone coffin. While the coffin bore no inscriptions, archaeologists have concluded that the woman was of royal lineage, and she was christened the "Red Queen" because her remains were covered in cinnabar (mercury sulfide).

GRUPO DE LA CRUZ

To the extreme southeast of the middle of the site lie the temples of the Group of the Cross, which include the Templo del Sol (Temple of the Sun), with detailed relief carvings. The three temples in this group all have dramatic roof combs, originally believed to have a religious significance, although traces of roof combs have been found on buildings now known to have been purely residential. Human and mythological time come together in the inscriptions of these temples. In each tableau carved on the tablets at the back of the temples, Chan Bahlum, the new ruler, receives the regalia of office from his father, Pakal, now in the underworld and shown much smaller than his living son. The shrines in the three temples are dedicated to the Palenque Triad, a sacred trinity linked to the ruling dynasty of the city,

A panoramic view of Palenque takes in many of the key buildings

whose genealogy is explained in the inscriptions. They were certainly long-lived: the parents of the triad were born in 3122BC or 3121BC and the children were born on October 19, October 23, and November 6, 2360BC. It has been shown that these were dates of extraordinary astronomical phenomena: the gods were intimately related to heavenly bodies and events. On each set of balustrades, Chan Bahlum began his text with the birth of the patron god of each temple. On the left side of the stairs he recorded the time between the birth of the god and the dedication of the temple. Thus, mythological time and contemporary time were fused.

MUSEUM

Tue–Sun 10–5

Many of the stucco carvings retrieved from the site are displayed at the site museum on the way back to town, as well as pieces of jade jewelry, funerary urns and ceramics.

PALENQUE TOWN

Palenque town's sole purpose is to cater to visitors heading for the archaeological site nearby. There is plenty of accommodation for every budget, with dozens of inexpensive *posadas* (inns) around the middle of town, and a new visitor *barrio* (district), La Cañada, with more expensive hotels, restaurants and bars. Palenque is also a convenient place to stop en route to the southern Chiapan towns of San Cristóbal and Tuxtla Gutiérrez. Visitors coming to Palenque from Mérida, Campeche and other cities in the Yucatán Peninsula will find it much hotter here, particularly in June, July and August.

BACKGROUND

Palenque grew from a small agricultural village at the height of the Classic period to one of the most important cities in the pre-Hispanic world. Usumacinta, the alluvial plain to the north, provided Palenque's inhabitants with the resources to construct this majestic city. From about the fourth century AD, during the reign of Pakal the Great, the city rapidly rose to the first rank of Maya states. The duration of Pakal's reign is still a bone of contention among Maya scholars because the remains found in his sarcophagus do not appear to be those of an 81-year-old man—the age implied by the texts in the Temple of the Inscriptions.

SITE PLAN

1 *Mirador*
2 *Temple of the Foliated Cross*
3 *Temple of the Cross*
4 *Temple of the Sun*
5 *Temple of the Lion*
6 *Temple of the Inscriptions*
7 *Temple XIII*
8 *Temple of the Skull*
9 *Palace*
10 *Temple XI*
11 *Temple X*
12 *Temple of the Count*
13 *North Group*
14 *Ball Court*
15 *Encampment*
16 *Queen Baths*
17 *Otolum Aqueduct*
18 *Temple XIV*
19 *Temple XX*
20 *Temple XXI*
21 *Temple XXII*
22 *Temple XVII*

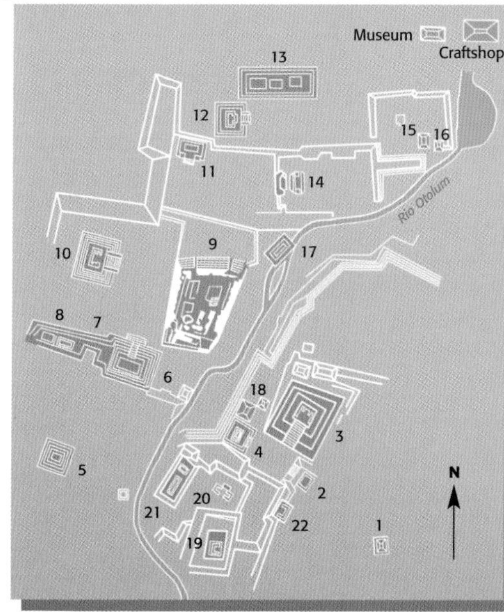

THE SIGHTS

RATINGS

Architectural interest	● ● ● ●
Arts and crafts	● ● ● ●
Cultural interest	● ● ● ● ●
Walkability	● ● ● ● ●

BASICS

316 P10

Delegacíon Regional de Turismo, Hidalgo 1-B, tel (967) 678 65 70; Mon–Sat 8–8, Sun 9–2

San Cristóbal airport, 15km (9 miles) north

www.turismochiapas.gob.mx
Spanish only.

TIPS

- San Cristóbal has a mild climate compared to Palenque and Tuxtla Gutiérrez. During June, July and August it is warm and sunny in the morning, while in the afternoon it tends to rain heavily, with a sharp drop in temperature, rising again in the evening.
- If you are coming from San Cristóbal to Palenque by car you can use the new 210km (130-mile) paved road; avoid nighttime journeys because of the risk of armed robberies.
- If you don't take an organized tour to the nearby villages it is advisable to travel with a guide; contact Na Bolom (tel (967) 678 14 18; see right).
- Don't take cameras to the villages as photography is seen as invasive and profiteering.

San Cristóbal's market beside the church of Santo Domingo

SAN CRISTÓBAL DE LAS CASAS

San Cristóbal's fascinating blend of colonial architecture and indigenous culture, eclectic restaurants and lively bars and cafés make this an ideal base to explore Chiapas.

In the town's main square, Plaza 31 de Marzo, is the neoclassical Palacio Municipal, dating from 1885, and a gazebo built during the era of Porfirio Díaz (▷ 36). Nearby stands the 16th-century Catedral de San Cristóbal, painted in earthy yellow, brown and white, with a baroque pulpit added in the 17th century. It is flanked by the Iglesia de San Nicolás, which dates from 1613. The 16th-century Casa de la Sirena (Avenida Insurgentes 1), now the Hotel Santa Clara, is a rare example of colonial residential architecture. North, along Avenida 20 de Noviembre, is the Iglesia y Ex-Convento de Santo Domingo, by far the most dramatic building in the city, with an elaborate baroque facade in molded mortar, especially striking when viewed in the late afternoon sun. See Drive 4 (▷ 214–215) for the indigenous villages around San Cristóbal.

INDIGENOUS CULTURE

Twenty-one indigenous groups live in San Cristóbal and they form an important part of the town's atmosphere—each district is distinguished by it own dress and handicrafts. The main market is in front of the Iglesia de Santo Domingo, with dozens of stands selling traditional textiles, handmade dolls, wooden toys and jewelry. The cultural center Na Bolom (Mon–Fri 9.30–1.30, 4.30–7), at Avenida Vicente Guerrero 33, is an excellent resource on all aspects of indigenous culture. It was founded in 1951 by the Danish archeologist Frans Blom and his wife, Swiss photographer Gertrudis Duby. After the death of Frans in 1963 Gertrudis continued campaigning for the conservation of the Lacandón area. Since her death in 1993, at the age of 92, the center has continued to function as a non-profit organization dedicated to conserving the Chiapan environment and helping the Lacandón people. Knowledgeable volunteers conduct tours and provide fascinating anecdotes about the life of the Bloms and their friends.

The Museo de Los Altos, in the Ex-Convento de Santo Domingo (Tue–Sun 10–5), at Avenida 20 de Noviembre, charts the history of San Cristóbal, with an emphasis on the plight of the indigenous people. The Centro de Desarrollo de la Medicina Maya (Mon–Fri 9–2, 4–6), at Avenida Salomón González Blanco 10, has a herb garden with detailed displays on the use of some of the medicinal plants.

One of the many traditional Chiapanecan dress styles

The impressive facade of Tuxtla Gutiérrez' San Marcos Cathedral

Detail of a Cabeza Olmeca (Olmec Head) from La Venta

TEHUANTEPEC

315 N11 Sedetur, Carretera Transístmica 7, 2nd floor, tel (971) 715 12 36

Santo Domingo Tehuantepec, to give it its full name, is a vibrant town that conserves the region's indigenous roots. Robust Zapotec matrons in bright dresses stand in the back of motorized tricycles known as *motocarros*. Life moves slowly here, focused on the plaza, which has arcades on one side and a market next to it. Many churches with attractive white buildings were built here during the early colonial period. Houses are low, in white or pastel shades. The Río Tehuantepec runs two blocks from the plaza.

The Casa de la Cultura (Mon–Fri 10–4) is housed in the 16th-century Dominican former convent Rey Cosijopi. Although it's quite run down, original frescoes can be seen on some of the walls. There is a library and simple exhibits of regional history, archaeology and costume. Ask the caretaker to open it up.

The Museo Casa de la Señora Juana C. Romero (Mon–Fri 10–4) is a chalet built entirely with materials brought from France; Romero's great-granddaughter lives there today, and you can ask for permission to visit the house.

TUXTEPEC

315 M10 Cámara Nacional de Comercio Serytour, Libertad esq Allende, opposite Parque Juárez; Mon–Fri 9–2, 5–8, Sat 9–1 Buses from Córdoba, Mexico City, Veracruz and Oaxaca

The large commercial city of San Juan Bautista Tuxtepec on the border of Veracruz and Oaxaca states is the natural place to overnight if you are journeying between the two. It's tranquil and unpretentious, and prices here are lower than in other parts of Oaxaca. Avenida Independencia, the main commercial avenue, runs along the riverfront. Here you will find a bustling market selling piles of ripe tropical fruits, vegetables and coriander placed incongruously between bleeping alarm clocks, plastic hair adornments, cheap T-shirts and sacks of chilies. Shops selling electronic goods blare out *Veracruzana* rhythms and Caribbean salsa, while local women in traditional Oaxacan dress negotiate the traffic-clogged streets. Sleepy Parque Benito Juárez, the main plaza, with its ample Palacio Municipal to the south and a modern cathedral to the east, comes alive in the evenings when families and cotton candy (candyfloss) vendors jostle for space. Farther west is Parque Hidalgo, with a statue of the father of Mexico's independence.

TUXTLA GUTIÉRREZ

316 P10 Boulevard Belisario Domínguez 950, Plaza Instituciones, tel (961) 602 52 98; Mon–Fri 9–9, Sat 9–8, Sun 9–7 *Colectivos* to the zoo from Mercado, Calle 1a Ote Sur and Calle 7 Sur Ote www.turismochiapas.gob.mx

The capital of Chiapas state is a busy, shabby city with several points of interest for the visitor. The main sights are a long way from the middle of town and are too far to walk. In the Parque Madero at the east end of Tuxtla is the Museo Regional de Chiapas on Calzada de los Hombres Ilustres 885 (Tue–Sun 9–4), with a fine collection of Maya objects, an auditorium and a library.

Some 3km (2 miles) south of town up a long hill is the superb Zoológico Miguel Álvarez del Toro (Tue–Sun 9–5.30), founded by Dr. Miguel Alvarez del Toro, who died in 1996. His aim was to provide a free zoo for the children and indigenous people of the area. Many of the animals are kept in open areas rather than cages. Take mosquito repellent with you.

LA VENTA

316 P10 • 120km (74 miles) west of Villahermosa

The almost impenetrable forest of La Venta was once the hub of the ancient Olmec culture. An expedition of archaeologists in 1925 found huge sculptured human and animal figures, urns and altars. When the discovery of oil in the 1950s threatened the destruction of the monuments, poet Carlos Pellicer established the Parque Nacional de La Venta, also called the Museo Nacional de la Venta, on Boulevard Adolfo Ruiz Cortines, around 3km (2 miles) from central Villahermosa (daily 8–4). Thirty-three exhibits lie scattered in small clearings. The huge heads, one of them weighing 20 tons, were created by the Olmecs, a culture that flourished between about 1150BC and 150BC. Exposure to the elements has damaged certain figures but to see them in natural surroundings is an experience you should not miss.

A group of children and their teachers on a school outing to Parque La Venta, 3km (2 miles) from Villahermosa

The complex site of Yagul, meaning "old tree or stick"

VILLAHERMOSA

316 P10 Esq Calle 13, Avenida de los Ríos, tel (993) 316 36 33; Mon–Fri 8–8
www.tabasco.gob.mx

Villahermosa, the capital of Tabasco state, stands on the Río Grijalva. It is a busy, prosperous city, with a warren of modern, colonial-style pedestrian malls throughout the central area. Visitors from Chiapas will find it more expensive, hotter and more humid. A few minutes' walk from the middle of town, southwest along the river bank, is the Centro de Investigaciones de las Culturas Olmecas (CICOM), a new modern complex with a large public library, an expensive restaurant, airline offices and souvenir shops.

The Museo Regional de Antropología Carlos Pellicer (Tue–Sun 9–7), covering three floors, has well laid-out displays of Maya and Olmec objects. Two other museums worth visiting are the Museo de Cultura Popular, at Calle Zaragoza 810 (Tue–Sun 9–8), and the Museo de Historia de Tabasco, at Avenida 27 de Febrero esq Juárez (Tue–Sun 9–8, Sun 10–5). On the corner of Avenida Pino Suárez and Bastar Zozaya is the Mercado Pino Suárez, where every nook and cranny is taken up with goods of all sorts (▷ 189).

Day trips from Villahermosa can be made to Parque Yumká, 16km (10 miles) east, a 108ha (266-acre) safari park with three major habitats—jungle, savannah and lagoon. Visitors can walk through rain forest or take boat tours through each zone (▷ 189).

Within reach of Villahermosa is the ancient site of La Venta (▷ 97), one of Tabasco's most notable attractions.

YAGUL

315 M10 • 36km (22 miles) southeast of Oaxaca, just off Route 190 to Mitla (951) 516 01 23 Daily 8–5 $2.70 Buses to Mitla from Oaxaca; ask to get off at the paved turn-off to Yagul, 1km (half a mile) uphill to the site Guided tours in English on Tue, arranged by Oaxaca travel agencies

Yagul is an outstandingly picturesque archaeological site. Serene, ghostly and absorbing, it is often described as the most moving of Oaxaca's ruins, with its acropolis majestically overlooking the Oaxaca Valley. It was a large Zapotec and later Mixtec religious base that flourished following the decline of Monte Albán (▷ 86–87). The city enjoyed a renaissance just prior to the arrival of the Spanish. Yagul's labyrinthine structures bear striking similarities to those of Monte Albán, and the Palacio de los Seis Patios (Palace of the Six Patios) also resembles the Salón de las Columnas (Hall of Columns) at Mitla (▷ 84–85). The ball court, set in a landscape punctuated by candelabra cactus and agave, is said to be the second largest found in Mesoamerica; it is also one of the most perfect discovered to date. If you take the path behind the ruins (the last part is steep) there are fine tombs and a superb view from the hill.

YAXCHILÁN

316 Q10 Carretera 307, direction of Escudo Jaguar, 1-hour (*lancha*) boat trip to Yaxchilán Daily 9–4 $3.50 per person 1-hour boat journey from Echeverría. Be there before 9am to meet other visitors wanting to share a boat Flights from Palenque to Bonampak and Yaxchilán, in a light plane for 5 people

Southeast of Palenque is Yaxchilán, one of the least accessible but most rewarding of the Maya sites. Built along a terrace and hills above the Río Usumacinta, it is reached by a combination of car and boat. The site is spectacular, as much for its position amid luxuriant vegetation saturated with the sounds of birds, insects and howler monkeys, as for the exquisite inscriptions on its buildings. Yaxchilán developed from a small agricultural village to become one of the most outstanding Maya bases in the region. With the rise of Cráneo-Mahkina II to the throne in AD526, it became the regional capital. The temples are ornately decorated with stucco and stone and the lintels are carved with scenes of ceremonies and conquests.

La Venta's giant basalt Olmec heads remain a mystery

MEXICO CITY

Beyond its pollution, poverty, overcrowding and myriad problems, Mexico City is a fascinating place to explore. Finding your way around can be frustrating at times, but this vibrant, stimulating megalopolis rewards those who persist. The city's Museum of Anthropology is one of the finest in the world, putting Mexico's complex history and civilizations into perspective.

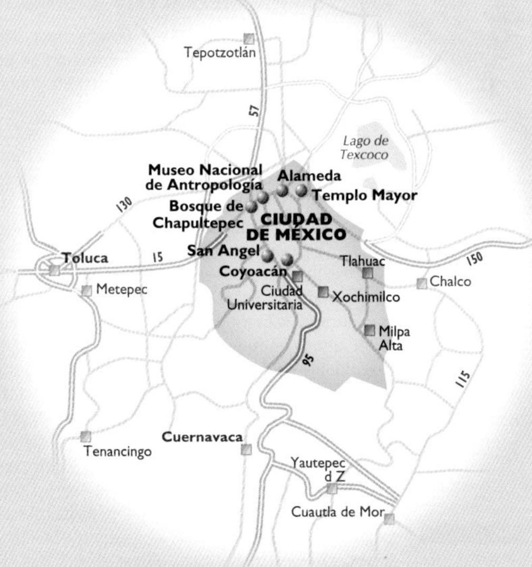

MAJOR SIGHTS

Alameda	**104**
Bosque de Chapultepec	**105**
Coyoacán	**106**
Museo Nacional de Antropología	**108–111**
San Angel	**117**
Templo Mayor	**118–119**

Mexico City

314 L9 Zona Rosa: 54 Calle Amberes with Calle Londres, tel (55) 55 25 93 80; daily 9–7. The Ministry of Tourism (SECTUR), Avenida Presidente Masaryk 172, Polanco, tel (55) 52 50 01 23; Mon–Fri 8–5, Sat 10–3
Benito Juárez Airport, 13km (8 miles) east of Mexico City (tel (55) 55 71 36 00
www.mexicocity.com.mx • A comprehensive site covering all aspects of the city, including its history

View over Mexico City's business district (top)

Getting into the swing at a dancing exhibition (above)

SEEING MEXICO CITY (CIUDAD DE MÉXICO)

Mexico City, one of the world's most densely populated urban areas, is home to more than 24 million people; shanty towns in the city's outskirts continue to mushroom, with up to 1,000 immigrants said to arrive from the countryside every day. At 2,400m (7,872ft) above sea level, and built on a former lake bed surrounded by volcanoes, its physical location is not exactly ideal: earthquakes plague the city, buildings are prone to sinking into the soggy earth and the ring of mountains traps all the traffic fumes, forming a cloud of pollution that hangs over the capital. However, the city's lure is irresistible: it is frenetic and bustling, elegant and sophisticated, vibrant and bright. Above all, it is alive, and for the visitor, utterly enthralling and totally bewildering. It is also unavoidable, and even if you do not enjoy exploring big cities, Mexico's capital is so much a part of the soul of the country that you should try to spend at least a couple of days here to soak up the atmosphere and see some of the major sights.

Mexico City's hub is undisputedly the *zócalo*, the huge main square. Once the spiritual heart of the Aztec city Tenochtitlán, then of colonial New Spain, it maintains its role as political and religious nucleus of both city and country. Still largely colonial and surrounded by the city's oldest streets, it is elegant and chic heading west, down calles 5 de Mayo, Tacuba and Madero, and somewhat run-down and neglected towards the east and southeast, down calles Corregidora and Venustiano Carranza. Both areas are fascinating to explore; the boutiques and restaurants of the former are replaced by the street vendors and endlessly chaotic stands exuding exotic smells of the latter.

West of the *zócalo* is the Alameda, the small park that marks the extent of the original colonial city. Much of this area was destroyed in the tragic 1985 earthquake and new, modern buildings spring up every year. Both the metro stations of Bellas Artes to the east and Hidalgo to the west serve this area. Farther west still, the area around the Monumento a la Revolución and the train station is where many of the cheaper hotels and eateries are. From here, heading southwest down Paseo de la Reforma, you reach the Bosque de Chapultepec, where the murmur of traffic seems very distant as you wander past boating lakes and mature trees. To the east, at the junction of Paseo de la Reforma with Avenida Insurgentes, lies the Zona Rosa, with its expensive hotels and bohemian chic. To the south, the district of Condesa

TIPS

- The bus network is great for getting along the main arteries of Paseo de la Reforma and Avenida Insurgentes.
- To reach more distant locations, go by metro. Buy a few tickets at a time to save queuing.
- Mexico City is referred to by Mexicans either as México or El DF—the Distrito Federal (Federal District).
- Take the same precautions you would in any large city: leave valuables in the hotel safe, don't carry lots of cash on you, don't wear conspicuous watches or jewelry, and don't carry an expensive camera openly.

has become the fashionable and trendy place to eat, drink and be seen, while the more refined Polanco, north of Chapultepec, is home to the city's real wealth and finest shops and restaurants.

As well as the central areas around the *zócalo* and Alameda, Mexico City has many historically and culturally interesting suburbs and districts, all easily reached by public transportation. Avenida Insurgentes is one of the most important arteries, running south down to the characterful, bohemian *barrios* (suburbs) of San Angel and Coyoacán, with their leafy, sunlit cobbled streets, pavement cafés, museums and galleries. Farther south is the Ciudad Universitaria (University City) and the waterways and canals of Xochimilco.

Day of the Dead exhibits (above)

BACKGROUND

When Hernán Cortés arrived in Tenochtitlán in 1519 he found a highly developed city of about 300,000 people. It was built across several islands linked by a sophisticated system of causeways crisscrossing the spectacular, mountain-ringed Texcoco Lake. The Aztecs settled here in the mid-1300s and by the time of the Conquest were rulers of an empire stretching to the far reaches of the country and as far south as Guatemala.

Believing that Cortés was the pale-skinned god Quetzalcóatl returning from the sea as predicted, Moctezuma II, the Aztec emperor, invited the Spanish to the city. In return, he was imprisoned and killed, and eventually, after a three-month siege in 1521, the Spanish conquered Tenochtitlán. The city was almost completely destroyed and the Spanish began the construction of the capital of New Spain, building their cathedrals and palaces with the stones of the ancient temples they destroyed. The lake was drained, filled in and built over. The new colonial city grew despite the soft earth and the many earthquakes.

Museo Frida Kahlo (above); Siqueiros mural, Chapultepec Park (below)

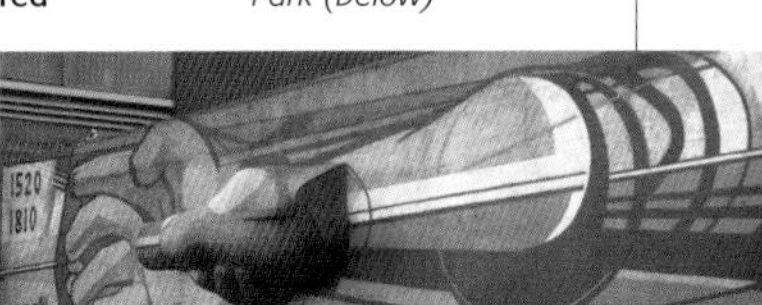

Between the late 1870s and 1911, during the Porfirio Díaz dictatorship, the avenues and boulevards connecting the suburbs were laid out, and a surge of new development and building saw the expansion of public transport systems. By the time of the Revolution in 1910, Mexico City's population had reached 400,000. During the ensuing, turbulent years, thousands of dispossessed country dwellers fled to find refuge and better lives in the capital. In just three decades, the population quadrupled. Shanty towns multiplied and the city expanded dramatically. The construction of the metro, completed in the 1970s, relieved the increasing transport problems. The government has also tried, with only moderate success, to attract industry and investment away from the capital. At the same time, New York-style crime-fighting methods have been imported to deal with a wave of kidnappings and petty crimes. For all its flaws, however, this huge city continues as the motor and heart of Mexico.

Olmec head (above); modern sculpture (below)

Stone of Coyolxauhqui, Templo Mayor

DON'T MISS

A performance by the **Ballet Folclórico** (▷ 192), a spectacular show of Mexican dance, music and song.
The **Zócalo**, the gloriously chaotic, pulsating heart heart of this vast country (▷ 120).

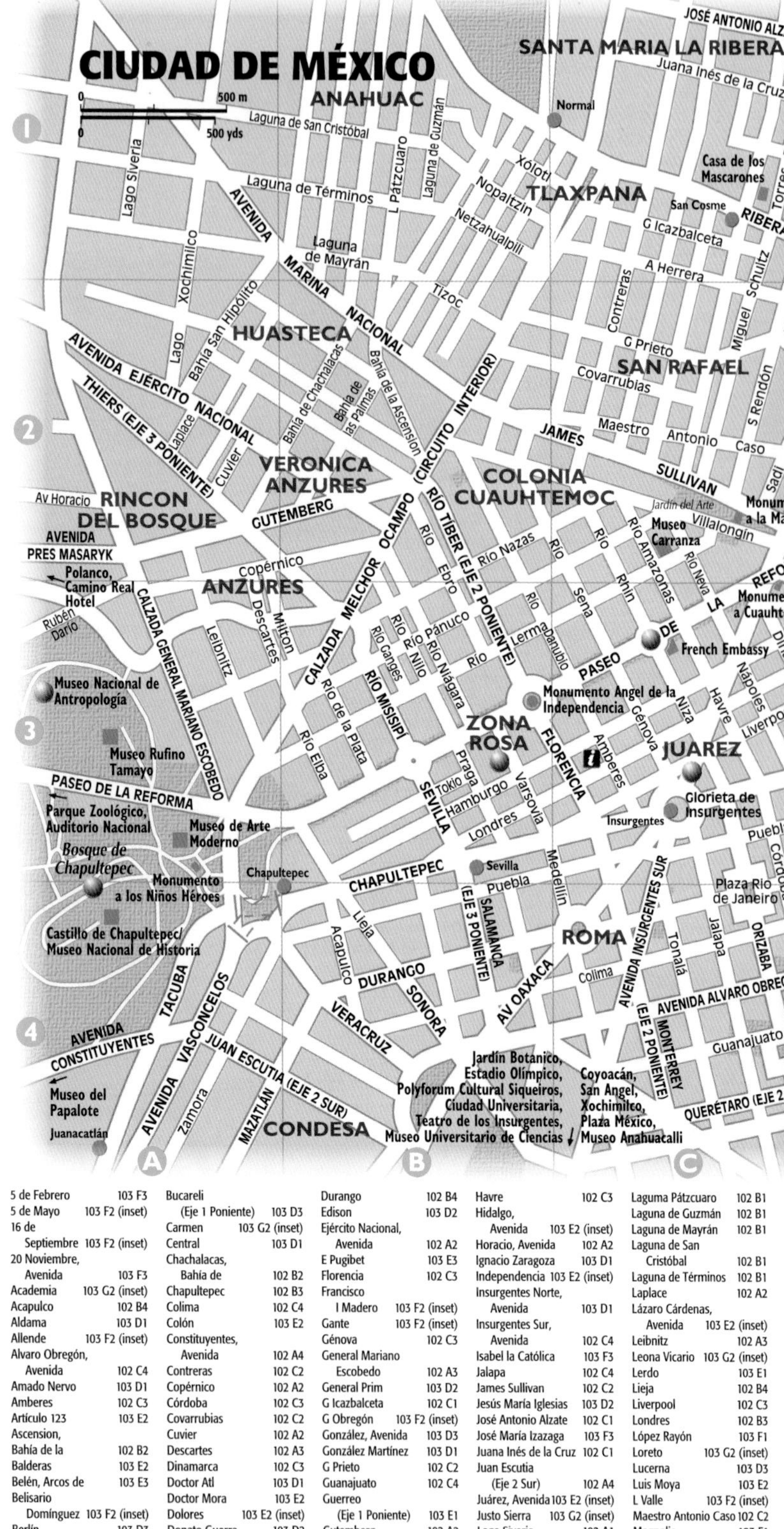

5 de Febrero 103 F3
5 de Mayo 103 F2 (inset)
16 de Septiembre 103 F2 (inset)
20 Noviembre, Avenida 103 F3
Academia 103 G2 (inset)
Acapulco 102 B4
Aldama 103 D1
Allende 103 F2 (inset)
Alvaro Obregón, Avenida 102 C4
Amado Nervo 103 D1
Amberes 102 C3
Artículo 123 103 E2
Ascension, Bahía de la 102 B2
Balderas 103 E2
Belén, Arcos de 103 E3
Belisario Domínguez 103 F2 (inset)
Berlín 103 D3
Bolívar 103 F3
Bucareli (Eje 1 Poniente) 103 D3
Carmen 103 G2 (inset)
Central 103 D1
Chachalacas, Bahía de 102 B2
Chapultepec 102 B3
Colima 102 C4
Colón 103 E2
Constituyentes, Avenida 102 A4
Contreras 102 C2
Copérnico 102 A2
Córdoba 102 C3
Covarrubias 102 C2
Cuvier 102 A2
Descartes 102 A3
Dinamarca 102 C3
Doctor Atl 103 D1
Doctor Mora 103 E2
Dolores 103 E2 (inset)
Donato Guerra 103 D2
Donceles 103 F2 (inset)
Durango 102 B4
Edison 103 D2
Ejército Nacional, Avenida 102 A2
E Pugibet 103 E3
Florencia 102 C3
Francisco I Madero 103 F2 (inset)
Gante 103 F2 (inset)
Génova 102 C3
General Mariano Escobedo 102 A3
General Prim 103 D2
G Icazbalceta 102 C1
G Obregón 103 F2 (inset)
González, Avenida 103 D3
González Martínez 103 D1
G Prieto 102 C2
Guanajuato 102 C4
Guerreo (Eje 1 Poniente) 103 E1
Gutemberg 102 A2
Hamburgo 102 B3
Havre 102 C3
Hidalgo, Avenida 103 E2 (inset)
Horacio, Avenida 102 A2
Ignacio Zaragoza 103 D1
Independencia 103 E2 (inset)
Insurgentes Norte, Avenida 103 D1
Insurgentes Sur, Avenida 102 C4
Isabel la Católica 103 F3
Jalapa 102 C4
James Sullivan 102 C2
Jesús María Iglesias 103 D2
José Antonio Alzate 102 C1
José María Izazaga 103 F3
Juana Inés de la Cruz 102 C1
Juan Escutia (Eje 2 Sur) 102 A4
Juárez, Avenida 103 E2 (inset)
Justo Sierra 103 G2 (inset)
Lago Siveria 102 A1
Lago Xochimilco 102 A2
Laguma Pátzcuaro 102 B1
Laguna de Guzmán 102 B1
Laguna de Mayrán 102 B1
Laguna de San Cristóbal 102 B1
Laguna de Términos 102 B1
Laplace 102 A2
Lázaro Cárdenas, Avenida 103 E2 (inset)
Leibnitz 102 A3
Leona Vicario 103 G2 (inset)
Lerdo 103 E1
Lieja 102 B4
Liverpool 102 C3
Londres 102 B3
López Rayón 103 F1
Loreto 103 G2 (inset)
Lucerna 103 D3
Luis Moya 103 E2
L Valle 103 F2 (inset)
Maestro Antonio Caso 102 C2
Magnolia 103 E1
Margil 103 G2 (inset)

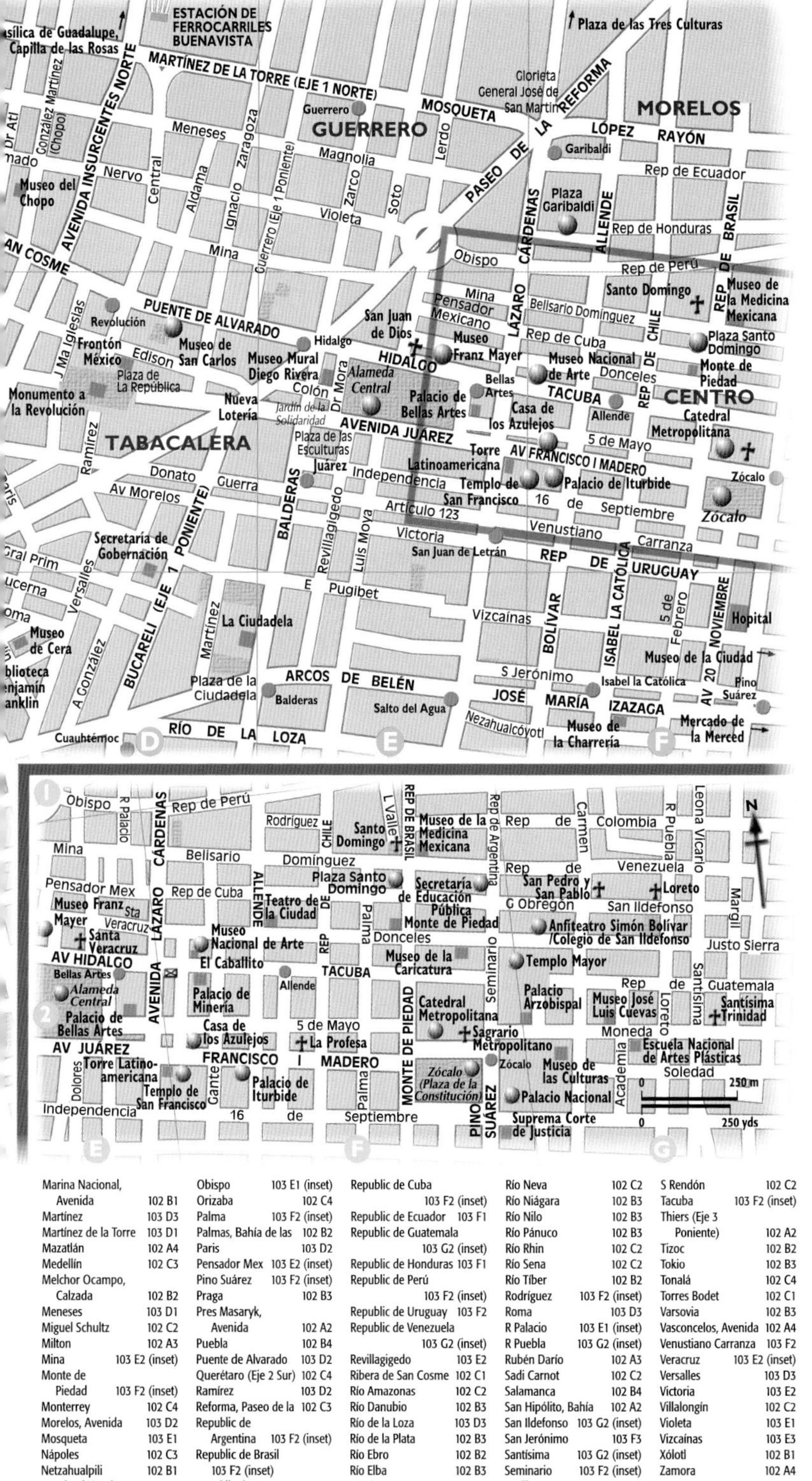

Marina Nacional, Avenida 102 B1
Martínez 103 D3
Martínez de la Torre 103 D1
Mazatlán 102 A4
Medellín 102 C3
Melchor Ocampo, Calzada 102 B2
Meneses 103 D1
Miguel Schultz 102 C2
Milton 102 A3
Mina 103 E2 (inset)
Monte de Piedad 103 F2 (inset)
Monterrey 102 C4
Morelos, Avenida 103 D2
Mosqueta 103 E1
Nápoles 102 C3
Netzahualpili 102 B1
Nezahualcóyotl 103 E3
Niza 102 C3
Nopaltzin 102 B1
Oaxaca, Avenida 102 B4
Obispo 103 E1 (inset)
Orizaba 102 C4
Palma 103 F2 (inset)
Palmas, Bahía de las 102 B2
Paris 103 D2
Pensador Mex 103 E2 (inset)
Pino Suárez 103 F2 (inset)
Praga 102 B3
Pres Masaryk, Avenida 102 A2
Puebla 102 B4
Puente de Alvarado 103 D2
Querétaro (Eje 2 Sur) 102 C4
Ramírez 103 D2
Reforma, Paseo de la 102 C3
Republic de Argentina 103 F2 (inset)
Republic de Brasil 103 F2 (inset)
Republic de Chile 103 F2 (inset)
Republic de Colombia 103 G2 (inset)
Republic de Cuba 103 F2 (inset)
Republic de Ecuador 103 F1
Republic de Guatemala 103 G2 (inset)
Republic de Honduras 103 F1
Republic de Perú 103 F2 (inset)
Republic de Uruguay 103 F2
Republic de Venezuela 103 G2 (inset)
Revillagigedo 103 E2
Ribera de San Cosme 102 C1
Río Amazonas 102 C2
Río Danubio 102 B3
Río de la Loza 103 D3
Río de la Plata 102 B3
Río Ebro 102 B2
Río Elba 102 B3
Río Ganges 102 B3
Río Lerma 102 B3
Río Misisipí 102 B3
Río Nazas 102 B2
Río Neva 102 C2
Río Niágara 102 B3
Río Nilo 102 B3
Río Pánuco 102 B3
Río Rhin 102 C2
Río Sena 102 C2
Río Tíber 102 B2
Rodríguez 103 F2 (inset)
Roma 103 D3
R Palacio 103 E1 (inset)
R Puebla 103 G2 (inset)
Rubén Darío 102 A3
Sadi Carnot 102 C2
Salamanca 102 B4
San Hipólito, Bahía 102 A2
San Ildefonso 103 G2 (inset)
San Jerónimo 103 F3
Santísima 103 G2 (inset)
Seminario 103 F2 (inset)
Sevilla 102 B3
Soledad 103 G2 (inset)
Sonora 102 B4
Soto 103 E1
S Rendón 102 C2
Tacuba 103 F2 (inset)
Thiers (Eje 3 Poniente) 102 A2
Tizoc 102 B2
Tokio 102 B3
Tonalá 102 C4
Torres Bodet 102 C1
Varsovia 102 B3
Vasconcelos, Avenida 102 A4
Venustiano Carranza 103 F2
Veracruz 103 E2 (inset)
Versalles 103 D3
Victoria 103 E2
Villalongín 102 C2
Violeta 103 E1
Vizcaínas 103 E3
Xólotl 102 B1
Zamora 102 A4
Zarco 103 E1

The Palacio de Bellas Artes, designed by Adamo Boari

ALAMEDA

An attractive park with fountains and heroic statues under the shade of eucalypti, cypresses and ragged palms, Alameda is overlooked by the Palacio de Bellas Artes—an art deco gem and home to the Ballet Folclórico de Mexico.

103 E2 (E2 inset) Bellas Artes

RATINGS	
Cultural interest	●●●●●
Historic interest	●●●
Photo stops	●●●
Walkability	●●●●●

The Alameda park has served several functions in its long history—from Aztec market, to execution ground for the Spanish Inquisition, to temporary camp for US soldiers in the late 1840s. Its heyday was in the 19th century when all social classes mingled here for their Sunday stroll. Badly affected by the 1985 earthquake, the surrounding area is being transformed by new building work.

LANDMARKS

Flanking the eastern side of the park is the Palacio de Bellas Artes (Mon–Sat 11–7, Sun 9–7), which was completely refurbished in 1994 to celebrate its diamond jubilee. A large, flamboyant art deco building, it houses a museum, theater, cafeteria, excellent bookshop on the arts (▷ 191) and a museum with old and contemporary paintings, prints, sculptures and handicrafts. The building also contains frescoes by Rivera, Orozco, Tamayo and Siqueiros. On the top floor a museum of architecture details the building's history. Perhaps the most remarkable thing about the theater is its glass curtain designed by Tiffany, but this can only be seen during performances, either by the Ballet Folclórico de México or the many operas and orchestral concerts that are staged here (▷ 192).

Across the road at the southeast corner of the park is the Torre Latinoamericana (daily 9am–10pm), which has a viewing platform with telescopes on the 44th floor. On the south side is the Juárez Hemiciclo, a white marble monument inaugurated in 1910 to honor president Benito Juárez. Opposite, the colonial Iglesia de Corpus Christi is used to display and sell folk arts and crafts. Farther west a sunken section of the pavement shelters the Plaza de las Esculturas (1998), which is filled with 19th-century sculptures.

Diego Rivera's huge mural, *Sueño de una Tarde Dominical en la Alameda Central*, was removed from the earthquake-damaged Hotel del Prado on Avenida Juárez in 1985. It now occupies its own purpose-built museum, the Museo Mural Diego Rivera (Tue–Sun 10–6) at the west end of the Alameda. One of Rivera's finest works, it presents a pageant of Mexican history from the Conquest up to the 1940s.

The old Basilica de Guadalupe (above) and the Virgin (below)

BASÍLICA DE GUADALUPE

Off 103 D1 Plaza de las Américas (55) 55 77 60 22 Daily 6am–8pm La Villa Basílica

Buses marked La Villa travel north along Paseo de la Reforma through the suburbs of Mexico City to the Basilica of Guadalupe, the most venerated shrine in Mexico. It was here, in December 1531, that the Virgin appeared to Juan Diego and imprinted her portrait on his cloak (▷ 33). A basilica was built on the site in 1533, growing to become the huge baroque structure you see today. At the back, a museum (Tue–Sun 10–6) is stacked with religious art and some curious 19th-century votive offerings. A new basilica was built in 1976 and it is here that Juan Diego's cloak, set in gold, is now housed. To see it, step onto the moving walkway behind the altar. (Note: shorts are not permitted in the basilica.) From the plaza you can walk up Cerro de Tepeyac past numerous chapels to the Capilla de las Rosas, with fine views on a clear day. On December 12 thousands of people assemble here to celebrate the anniversary of the Virgin's appearance (▷ 169).

BOSQUE DE CHAPULTEPEC

Bosque de Chapultepec is the lungs of the city, a vast green park with boating lakes, botanical gardens and shady picnic spots, and is home to some of the city's finest museums.

This beautiful green space, with its thousands of *ahuehuete* trees (so sacred to the Aztecs), covers 646ha (1,600 acres) and has enough to keep you occupied for a couple of days. Sunday is the liveliest time to go, when families and daytrippers throng to the zoo (▷ 195) and museums (which are free for nationals on Sundays). However, it can get very crowded, so expect a wait at some sights.

EAST TO WEST

Paseo de la Reforma runs east to west along the top of the park, connecting it to the middle of the city. On entering the park from the eastern gate, you will pass the large, six-columned Monumento a los Niños Héroes, commemorating the young soldiers who defended the castle (Castillo) of Chapultepec (then a military academy) against the 1847 American occupation. Behind the monument is Chapultepec Hill, visible from afar, with the imposing Castillo perched on top giving a view over the Valley of Mexico from its balconies. It now houses the Museo Nacional de Historia (Tue–Sun, 9–4.15), but its opulent rooms were once used by Emperor Maximilian and Empress Carlota during their brief reign in the 1860s. There is an impressive mural by David Siqueiros (1896–1974), *From the Dictatorship of Porfirio Díaz to the Revolution*, in Sala XIII, near the entrance, and a notable one by Juan O'Gorman (1905–1982) on the theme of Independence.

Just south of Paseo de la Reforma is the Museo de Arte Moderno (Tue–Sun, 10–6), where José-Clemente Orozco (1883–1949), Siqueiros and Diego Rivera (1886–1957) are well represented in the excellent permanent collection of modern Mexican art. World-class temporary exhibitions are also regularly staged. There is a good bookshop, gift shop and an open-air cafeteria behind the first building.

North of here is the Museo Rufino Tamayo (Tue-Sun 10–6), with a fine collection of works by this Modernist painter (1899–1991), as well as his private collection of European and American 20th-century art, including works by Henry Moore, Francis Bacon and Picasso.

Next door is the world-famous Museo Nacional de Antropología (▷ 108–111).

Don't miss The view from Chapultepec Castle over the city is worth the climb up the hill.

RATINGS

Cultural interest	●●●●
Good for kids	●●●●●
Walkability	●●●●

BASICS

102 A3

Free

Chapultepec

In the museums; public toilets at the foot of the Chapultepec Hill

The park is dotted with food stands selling hamburgers, *quesadillas* and cotton candy (candyfloss), and there is an open-air café in the Museu de Arte Moderno

TIP

• The Auditorio Nacional, one of the city's most important concert halls, is in Chapultepec Park at Paseo de la Reforma 50 (tel (55) 52 80 92 43). Free classical music concerts are given on Sunday at noon by the Bellas Artes Chamber Orchestra; arrive early for a seat.

Enjoying a day out in Chapultepec Park (top)

Monumento a los Niños Héroes in front of the Castillo (inset)

Decorated facade of the Mudejar-style House of Tiles

THE SIGHTS

CASA DE LOS AZULEJOS

103 F2 (F2 inset) Avenida Madero 4 (55) 55 12 13 31 Daily 7am–1am Free Bellas Artes

Blue-and-white 18th-century Puebla tiles cover the front of the 16th-century Casa de los Azulejos (House of Tiles). They were made in 1653 in a factory managed by Dominican friars. Occupied by the Zapatista army during the Revolution, the house is now one of the Sanborn chain of restaurants. The central courtyard (the main dining room) has Moorish arches, stone pillars and an ornamental fountain. On the far side of the courtyard a stone staircase leads to the wooden balconies above. José Clemente Orozco's fresco, *Omniscienda (Omniscience)*, on the inside stairwell, dates from 1925.

CATEDRAL METROPOLITANA

103 F2 (F2 inset) Plaza de la Constitución (55) 55 10 04 40 7.30am–8pm Free Zócalo

This immense cathedral, which dominates the *zócalo*, is the largest and oldest in Latin America. It was first built soon after the Conquest, and completed in 1525, four years later, using stones taken from the Aztec Temple of Huitzilópochtli (Templo Mayor) nearby. The structure you see today dates from 1573. Guided visits take you up to the bell tower to see the largest of the bells, Santa Maria de Guadalupe, weighing 13 tons. Like many of the city's heavy colonial buildings, the cathedral is sinking into the soft lake bed below and a lengthy schedule of work is under way to build new foundations. The tilt is quite obvious. However, for the first time in years, the interior is free of scaffolding and the immensity of the building can be

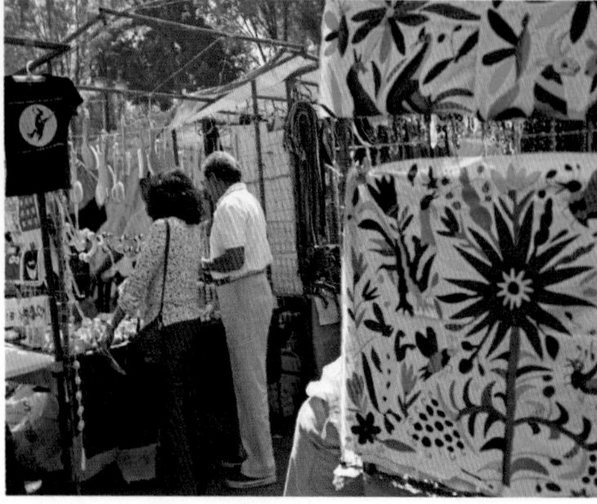

Wooden crafts and textiles at Coyoacán's lively Sunday market

COYOACÁN

Coyoacán is one of the most culturally dynamic areas of Mexico City, packed with cultural centers that come alive at weekends.

Off 102 C4 Viveros, Miguel Ángel Quevedo, General Anaya

RATINGS	
Cultural interest	●●●●
Good for food	●●●●●
Historic interest	●●●●
Value for money	●●●●

This charming district south of the historic heart is where Hernán Cortés had his headquarters during the battle for Tenochtitlán in 1521. It is also one of the most beautiful and best-preserved parts of the city, with scores of fine old buildings (▷ 222). If coming from metro Viveros or Miguel Angel de Quevedo, it is worth approaching via the elegant, tree-lined Avenida Francisco Sosa, said to be the first urban street laid in Spanish America. Halfway between Avenida Universidad and the Jardín Centenario is pretty Plaza Santa Catarina, where on Sundays, after 1pm, people gather to tell stories (all welcome).

The studio of Frida Kahlo, one of Mexico's greatest artists

A 10-minute walk from here will take you the Jardín Centenario, formerly the atrium of a Franciscan monastery, and now home to the lively Sunday crafts market. Overlooking the garden is the bulky 16th-century Iglesia de San Juan Bautista (Mon–Sat 8–1, 5–8.30, Sun 8–8.30), with a magnificent interior. Directly to the northeast lies the pretty Plaza Hidalgo, with the Palacio de Cortés, built on the site of Cortés's original house. Just off Plaza Hidalgo, half a block up Avenida Hidalgo, is the Museo Nacional de Culturas Populares (Tue–Thu 10–6, Fri–Sun 10–8), which hosts excellent folkloric exhibitions and a schedule of films, dance and concerts. Another top-quality cultural complex is the Foro Cultural de Coyoacán (▷ 193) on Calle Allende, half a block north of the Plaza Hidalgo.

Admirers of Frida Kahlo should visit the Museo Frida Kahlo (▷ 223), northeast of the Plaza Hidalgo. Two rooms are preserved as they were when Kahlo and her husband Diego Rivera lived there, while the rest contain Kahlo's wonderful collection of traditional costumes and folk art, as well as her wheelchair and several paintings.

In the same direction at Calle Río Churubusco 410 is the Casa de León Trotsky (▷ 223).

The Catedral Metropolitana dominates the Zócalo

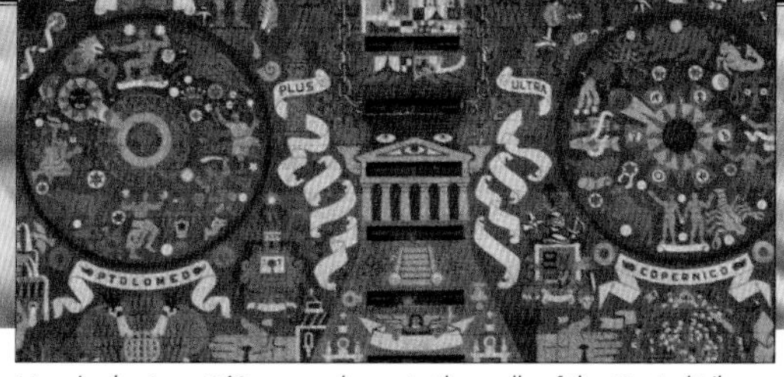

Mosaics by Juan O'Gorman decorate the walls of the Central Library in the Ciudad Universitaria

fully appreciated. The most attractive feature is the enormous gilt Retablo de los Reyes behind the main altar, built between 1718 and 1737, depicting European monarchs.

Next door is the beautiful 18th-century church of El Sagrario, which has a fine Churrigueresque facade decorated with sculpted saints and a gilt interior.

CIUDAD UNIVERSITARIA

Off 102 C4 Free Copilco (then 20-min walk) or Universidad (then 30-min walk) Bus marked CU along Eje Lázaro Cárdenas or bus 17, marked Tlalpan
www.unam.mx

The city university, 18km (11 miles) south from central Mexico City, via Avenida Insurgentes Sur on the road towards Cuernavaca, was founded in 1551 and has occupied a number of sites. The present-day campus was built between 1950 and 1955 and is one of the largest universities in the world with 300,000 students. The most notable building is the 10-floor Biblioteca Central (Central Library), its outside walls iridescent with a mosaic mural by Juan O'Gorman telling the story of scientific knowledge, from Aztec astronomy to molecular theory. The nearby Rectoría building is covered with vast, semi-sculptured murals by David Alfaro Siqueiros.

Also in this area of the campus is the Museo Universitario de Ciencias y Arte (MUCA), with a wide-ranging collection including traditional masks from all over Mexico, as well as exhibitions on contemporary art and culture. Beyond this, the grassy Plaza Mayor marks the beginning of the enormous grounds of the main campus. Across the highway is the massive Estadio Olímpico (Olympic Stadium), used in the 1968 Olympic Games and 1986 World Cup, but now closed and fairly run-down. Close by is the Jardín Botánico, with a cactus collection, jungle plants and arboretum.

Farther south on Avenida Insurgentes is a cultural complex including the Sala Nezahualcóyotl (where concerts are held), the Teatro Juan Ruiz de Alarcón and a bookshop.

COLEGIO DE SAN ILDEFONSO

103 G2 (inset) Calle Justo Sierra 16 (55) 57 02 25 94 ext 223 Tue–Sun 10–6 (box office closes 5.30) $3.50 (free on Tue) Zócalo
www.sanildefonso.org.mx

The former Colegio de San Ildefonso is home to some interesting murals by José Clemente Orozco and Diego Rivera, among others. Built in 1749 in splendid baroque style as the Jesuit School of San Ildefonso, it then became the Escuela Nacional Preparatoria, before being converted into one of the city's most important temporary exhibition spaces. Don't miss the Orozco murals—*The Trench* (ground floor) and the *The Aristocrats* (first floor). In the Anfiteatro Bolívar look out for Rivera's *Creation* (1922), and by the stairs between the first and second floors, Fernando Leal's evocative *The Fiesta of Lord of Chalma*, both in excellent condition. A pleasant first-floor cafeteria under the colonnades of the principal courtyard serves snacks and good cappuccino.

Modern steel sculpture at the Ciudad Universitaria

INSURGENTES

102 C3 Buses from Plaza de la República marked Insurgentes Sur

Heading out of the city along Avenida Insurgentes towards the suburbs of San Angel and Coyoacán there are several sites worth looking for. The Polyforum Cultural Siqueiros (daily 10–6), nowadays used as a convention hall, is covered on the outside by striking murals. Inside the ovoid dome is a gigantic mural by Siqueiros. A little farther south and along Avenida San Antonio is the Plaza México, the largest bullring in the world (▷ 194). Continuing south at the corner with Calle Mercaderes is the Teatros de los Insurgentes, with its curved facade, designed by Diego Rivera, sporting a gigantic pair of hands holding a mask.

Diego Rivera's murals on the Teatro de los Insurgentes

Museo Nacional de Antropología

One of the most comprehensive anthropological museums in the world.

Section of an Aztec Tzompantli or wall of skulls

Carved basalt Olmec figure, nicknamed The Wrestler

Detail from a Zapotec temple from the state of Oaxaca

RATINGS	
Cultural interest	●●●●●
Historic interest	●●●●●
Value for money	●●●●

BASICS

102 A3

Paseo de la Reforma and Calzada Gandhi, Chapultepec Park

(55) 55 53 63 81/55 53 63 86/ 55 53 19 02

Tue–Sat 9–7

$3.50 except Sun (free, and very crowded; arrive early)

Chapultepec, Auditorio or any *colectivo* along Reforma marked Auditorio

Guided tours in English or Spanish Tue–Sat 9.30–5.30, free, with minimum of 5 people. Audioguide available in English, $5.50

English and Spanish books, plus some in French and German, and guides to Mexican ruins including maps. Guide books of the museum ($5.50)

Next to museum

In the entrance hall

On-site cafeteria good but pricey

Permission required to photograph (no tripod or flash allowed) $1; $5 for video camera

www.mexicocity.com.mx/musantro.html Good information in Spanish.

The Stone of the Fifth Sun or Aztec Calendar (opposite)

SEEING MUSEO NACIONAL DE ANTROPOLOGÍA

This huge museum in the northern part of Bosque de Chapultepec (▷ 105) is a work of art in itself and contains an awesome collection of pre-Hispanic finds. Ranged around a central courtyard, it is shaded by a gigantic concrete mushroom, with an area of 4,200sq m (45,192sq ft)—the world's largest concrete and steel expanse supported by a single pillar, sculpted by José Chávez Morado. Water, symbolizing eternal life, cascades down around this pillar, on which scenes from Mexico's history are carved. The two-floor building has a facade 350m (1,148ft) long. All of the ground-floor exhibition rooms can be reached from the central patio.

On the right as you enter the courtyard are the first rooms, an excellent introduction to anthropology and to Mesoamerican prehistory. Some rooms have outdoor areas with sculptures, reconstructions of houses and other exhibits. A walk counterclockwise will lead you in and out of the various rooms and allow you to take restful breaks.

The upper floor is devoted to indigenous cultures today, with fabulous collections of clothing, masks, pottery, musical instruments, items from domestic life, and much more. Because of the enormous number of exhibits to see and information to digest, allow at least two days to do justice to the museum. Floor plans are available at the ticket booth. (Note that most of the labelling is in Spanish.)

HIGHLIGHTS

GROUND FLOOR

PRECLÁSICO

The first cultures (Preclassic) of the Valley of México are covered in this room, spanning the years 2300BC to AD100. The miniature female figurines are of particular note, dating from 1700BC to 1300BC. The Tlatilco burial site, reconstructed exactly as it would have been found when excavated, contains the lovely acrobat figure that was found in the grave of a shaman, hinting at the existence of mysterious religious rites.

TLALOC?

The large exhibit (almost 9m/30ft tall and weighing 167 tons), just outside the main entrance, was found near San Miguel, close to the town of Texcoco, and thought to be the image of Tlaloc, the Aztec rain god. Latests theories indicate it might possibly be his sister, Chalchiuhtlicue, the water goddess (immediately below).

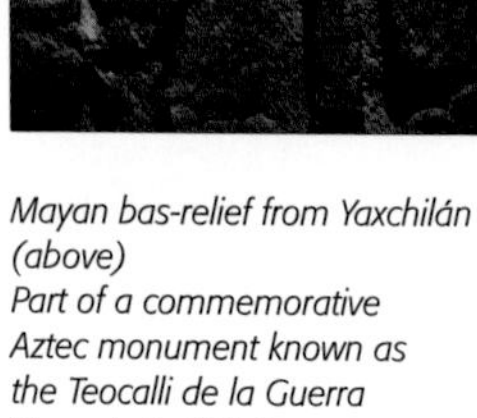

Mayan bas-relief from Yaxchilán (above)
Part of a commemorative Aztec monument known as the Teocalli de la Guerra Sagrada (middle)

TEOTIHUACÁN

Displayed here are some of the most important objects found at this site (▷ 132–134), the first great city of the Valley of Mexico. It is immediately obvious that the craftsmanship has become more sophisticated. The stunning turquoise, obsidian and shell-covered stone burial mask as well as the complex incense pot representing Xochipilli (the god of flowers) stand out, among other exquisite pieces. Of particular note is the massive full-scale reconstruction of part of the Temple of Quetzalcóatl.

TOLTEC

With pieces from several Toltec cities, most notably Xochitécatl and Tula, this room covers the years between AD750 and 1200. From Tula come the Atlantes of Tula—stone sculptures of warriors with their arms pointing down—as does the Chac Mool from Chichén Itzá, a reclining figure with a receptacle on its stomach for sacrificial offerings. From Xochicalco (▷ 131), near Cuernavaca, come the weighty stone columns; note the intricately carved column depicting Tlaloc, god of water, with his characteristically long tongue.

MÉXICA

The Aztec room, displaying stunning objects from perhaps the most bewitching of pre-Hispanic cultures, is the highlight of the museum. Greeting you at the entrance is the Ocelotl-Cuauhxicalli, a jaguar baring its teeth with a hollow in its back for the placing of sacrificial human hearts. The huge statue of Coatlicue, goddess of the earth, shows her wearing a necklace of hands and hearts and a skirt of serpents under which her eagle claw feet protrude. The undisputed focal point is the 24-ton Piedra del Sol (Sun Stone), also known popularly though not accurately as the Aztec Calendar, the epitome of the cosmological and mathematical knowledge of the people of pre-Hispanic America. This vision of the Aztec universe was found by early colonists, reburied, then rediscovered in 1790. In the middle is the sun god, Tonatiuh, with his tongue shaped like a sacrificial knife.

OAXACA

This room is dedicated to the Zapotec and Mixtec cultures from the Oaxaca Valley, with most pieces coming from Monte Albán (▷ 86–87), a site first developed by the Zapotecs but taken over by the Mixtecs. Look out for the Zapotec jade bat god and the jaguar motif pottery, as well as the rare Mixtec musical instruments, including a flute made from a human femur.

GOLFO DE MÉXICO

Covering the modern-day regions of Tuxtla, Veracruz and Tabasco, the Gulf Coast room is dedicated to Olmec civilization, a sophisticated culture that preceded Teotihuacán. The colossal heads are the highlights here, noted for their mysteriously African features. But look out, too, for the handsome sculpture of the *hombre barbado*, or the wrestler, a wonderfully evocative piece.

MAYA

Next comes the room dedicated to Maya culture, whose influence at its apogee between AD300 and 900 spread as far as modern-day Costa Rica. The undisputed highlight of this, one of the better rooms on this side of the museum, is the sunken reproduction of the tomb of Pakal from the Temple of the Inscriptions at Palenque (▷ 92–95), which also includes the spectacular jade death mask of the king.

NORTE (NORTH) AND OCCIDENTE (WEST)

The primarily agricultural cultures of the north and west of Mexico have generally bequeathed a less impressive historical legacy. However, these rooms have an interesting reconstruction of adobe houses from Paquimé (Casas Grandes; see page 160) in Chihuahua state, as well as some pottery from Chicomoztoc—the desert site which some historians believe is where the Aztecs originated.

BACKGROUND

The crowning glory of Chapultepec Park, the Museo Nacional de Antropología is not only famed for its vast collection of pre-Hispanic objects, but also for the building's design. The brainchild of architect Pedro Ramírez Vásquez, built in just 19 months between 1963 and 1964, the museum dervies its inspiration from Mexico's ancient archaeological sites. Covering around 44,000sq m (473,600sq ft), over a third of which is outdoors, this is a vast archaeological treasure trove. The collection itself began to be amassed in the late 19th century, with many further additions over the years.

GALLERY GUIDE

Upper floor: ethnography section, counterclockwise from right to left:

A: Indigenous peoples of Mexico
B: Gran Nayar
C: Purépecha
D: Los Otomainos
E: Puebla
F: Oaxaca
G: The Gulf of Mexico
H: Lowland Mayans
I: Highland Mayans
J: The Northeast
K: Nahuas

Ground floor: counterclockwise from the first room on the right:

A: Introduction to Anthropology
B: Cultures of Mesoamerica
C: Origins
D: Preclassic
E: Teotihuacán
F: Toltec
G: México
H: Oaxaca
I: Gulf of Mexico
J: Maya
K: Western cultures
L: Northern cultures

FLOOR PLAN

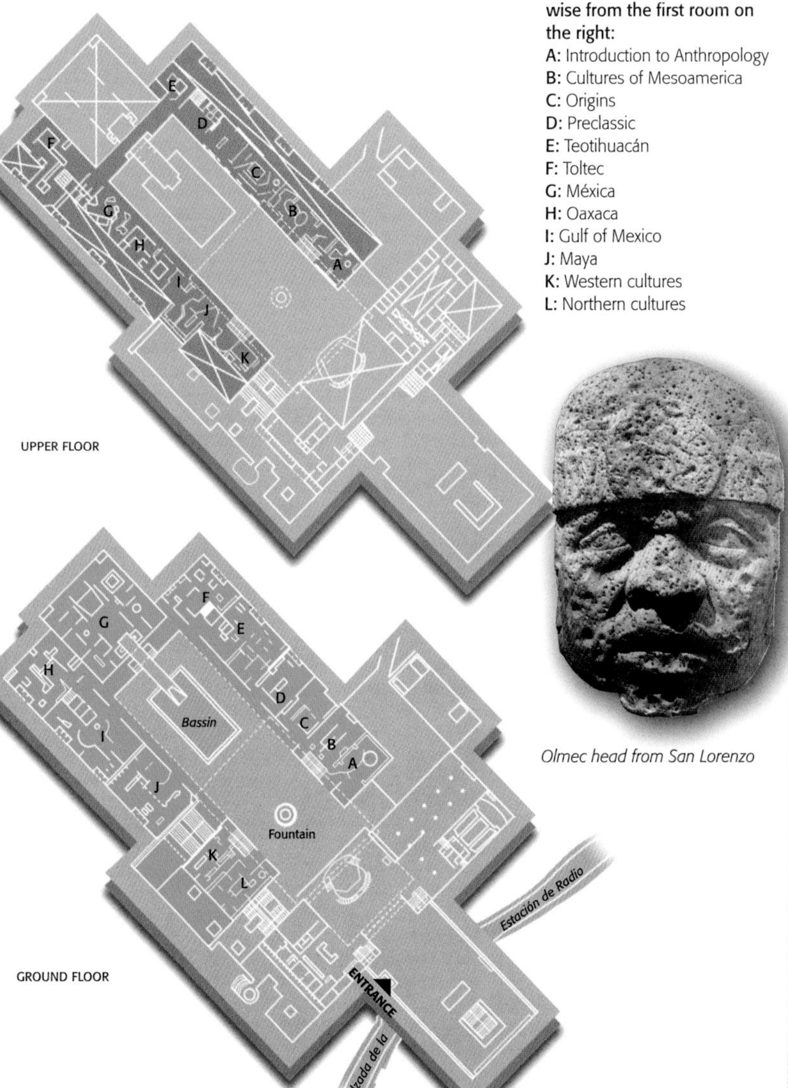

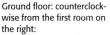

Olmec head from San Lorenzo

The Mercado de la Merced is a shopper's paradise

Museo Anahuacalli's dramatic setting on the edge of Coyoácan

The Museo Franz Mayer occupies a former hospital

MERCADO DE LA MERCED

Off 103 F3 Calle Rosario Puerta 4, between calles Santa Escuela and General Anaya Daily 7–7

This giant indoor market, considered the largest market in the Americas, spills out over several blocks in a riot of commercial activity. It sells everything from fresh market produce to shoes and cheap nylon clothes. Wander south of the *zócalo* and east along Calle República de El Salvador past tiny alleyways crammed with stands and bustling with street vendors.

Exhibit from the Museo Anahuacalli

MUSEO ANAHUACALLI

Off 102 C4 Calle Museo 150 (55) 56 17 43 10/56 77 29 84 Tue–Sun 10–6 $3, with student card $2, free Sun, free with ticket to Frida Kahlo Museum in Coyoacán (and vice versa) *Combi* 29 from the Taxqueña metro to Estadio Azteca Bus marked División del Norte from outside Salto del Agua metro

Museo Anahuacalli, also known as the Diego Rivera Museum, was built by the painter to house his large collection of pre-Hispanic sculptures and pottery. The extraordinary pseudo-Mayan tomb, in the shape of a pyramid, was begun in 1933 and finished in 1963, after Rivera's death. It contains a web of small, gloomy passageways opening into rooms through angled, flat-topped Mayan arches. The first floor is a huge art studio displaying some of Rivera's sketches. There are splendid views from the rooftop.

MUSEO DE ARTE CARRILLO-GIL

Off 102 C4 (San Angel) Avenida Revolución 1608, San Angel (55) 55 50 12 54 Tue–Sun 10–6 $3 www.macg.inba.gob.mx

This excellent modern museum-houses the private art collection of Álvaro Carrillo-Gil (1899–1974). The renovated museum lies north of San Angel's Plaza Jacinto, 10 minutes' walk up Avenida Revolución. The collection, amassed from the 1930s to 1960s, is dominated by paintings by José Clemente Orozco (174), David Alfaro Siqueiros (47) and Diego Rivera (27, mainly of his Cubist period), as well as Carrillo-Gil's own paintings. There are also works by Rodin, Picasso and Klee, along with changing exhibitions of Mexican contemporary art. A central ramp links the building's three floors. There is also a fine selection of 17th- and 18th-century Japanese Ukiyo-e (woodblock prints).

MUSEO DE LA CIUDAD DE MÉXICO

Off 103 F3 Avenida Pino Suárez 30 (55) 55 22 99 36/55 42 00 83 Tue–Sun 10–6 Free Pino Suárez www.arts-history.mx

Occupying a splendid 18th-century colonial residence, the Museo de la Ciudad, founded in 1964, showcases the city's cultural past and present through temporary exhibitions, educational courses and permanent exhibits such as photographs detailing the construction of the metro system and minor pre-Hispanic and colonial objects. The building consists of two magnificent courtyards built of grey stone and embellished with elaborate cornices. Note also the fine wooden doors. Upstairs there is a chapel built in 1778 and a music room. In the attic is the studio of Joaquín Clausell (1866–1935), a journalist, painter and caricaturist who was exiled in Paris during the Porfirio Díaz dictatorship. His political sketches line the staircase leading up to the attic, and there are copies of the controversial *El Demócrata* newspaper, which he edited. He often hosted meetings of the leading intellectuals and artists of the day in this studio. There is an excellent bookshop at the museum's entrance and on the other side of the road a memorial marks the spot where Hernán Cortés is supposed to have first met the Aztec ruler Moctezuma II.

MUSEO FRANZ MAYER

103 E2 Avenida Hidalgo 45, Plaza de la Santa Veracruz (55) 55 18 22 66 Tue–Sun 10–5, Wed 10–7 $3, $1.50 with student card ($0.50 if only visiting the cloister), free Tue Bellas Artes, Hidalgo www.franzmayer.org.mx

On the northern side of the Alameda two churches flank the Jardín Morelos: Santa Veracruz, built in 1730 and heavily tilting to one side, and San Juan de Dios, with its richly carved baroque exterior and unusual red hexagonal stone slabs. A former hospital is attached to the latter, and it is here that the fabulous collection of applied art belonging to the Franz Mayer Museum is housed. Mayer, a financier who arrived in Mexico from Germany in 1905, was also an avid collector of Mexican crafts and decorative arts. As well as Mexican glass, silver, clocks, furniture, textiles

The elegant, neoclassical Museo de San Carlos

Discover the fun side of learning at the Museo del Papalote

A statue of Carlos IV of Spain fronts the National Art Museum

and a fine collection of Talavera ceramics from Puebla, there are European paintings from the 14th to 20th centuries and a library with rare first editions. Note the Mexican 17th-century paintings inlaid with mother-of-pearl and the fine painted screen from the same period, depicting a view over Mexico City. The cloister behind San Juan de Dios, attached to the museum, is now a pleasant café.

MUSEO NACIONAL DE ANTROPLOGÍA

See pages 108–111.

MUSEO NACIONAL DE ARTE

103 F2 (F2 inset) Calle Tacuba 8 (55) 55 12 99 08/55 21 73 20 Tue–Sun 10.30–5.30 $3; free on Sun Bellas Artes
www.cnca.gob.mx/cnca/buena/inba/subbellas/museos/munal/index.html

An equestrian statue of Charles IV of Spain, once in the *zócalo*, marks the main entrance to the National Art Museum, built in 1904 and designed by Italian architect Silvio Contri: Inside are magnificent staircases made by the Florentine firm Pignone. Magnificently refurbished in 2003, the museum houses a large collection of Mexican paintings, drawings, sculptures and ceramics from the 16th century to 1950. It's best to start on the second floor in order to keep to chronological order. There are more than 100 paintings by José Maria Velasco (1840–1912), Diego Rivera's teacher—look out for his landscapes in Room 22. Other highlights include the 19th-century photography on the second floor, and the miniature portraits by Hermenegildo Bustos (1832–1907) in Room 23. There are also works by Rivera, Orozco, Siqueiros, Rufino Tamayo and Tina Modotti.

MUSEO DEL PAPALOTE

Off 102 A4 Avenida Constituyentes 268, Bosque de Chapultepec (55) 52 37 17 00/17 81 Mon–Fri 9–1, 2–6, Sat–Sun 10–2, 3–7, also Thu 7–11pm $6, IMAX extra Constituyentes

This delightful museum, specially designed for children, is an excellent place for them to have fun while learning about the human body, communications and the world we live in. It is full of hands-on, interactive exhibits, including a stomach-churning flight simulation 565km (350 miles) above earth.

MUSEO DE SAN CARLOS

103 D2 Puente de Alvarado 50 (55) 55 66 80 25 Wed–Mon 10–6 $2 (free on Mon) Revolución, Hidalgo
www.mnsancarlos.inba.gob.mx

The Museo de San Carlos has a wide-ranging collection of 17th- and 18th-century European paintings and stages temporary exhibitions. Housed in a fine neoclassical 19th-century palace, its permanent collection is displayed in first-floor galleries around an oval courtyard and contains works by Ingres and Rubens. Look for *Mujeres Bretones a la Orilla del Mar (Women from Brittany on the Sea Shore)* by Manuel Benedito Y Vives (1875–1963), in the first gallery.

During its lifetime the building has served as a residence to Mexican dictator Santa Anna, a school and a cigarette factory. The pretty garden directly behind the museum is dedicated to Latin America's revolutionary Left, with busts of Che Guevara and Cuban student leader Julio Antonio Mella, who was assassinated in Mexico City in 1929.

The Museo del Papalote's tower

PALACIO DE ITURBIDE

103 F2 (F2 inset) Avenida Madero 17 (55) 55 52 25 02 81 Tue–Sun 9–6 Free Bellas Artes
www.arts-history.mx

Next to the Convento San Francisco is the beautifully restored Iturbide Palace, now owned by Mexico's national bank, Banamex. It was built between 1779 and 1784 for the Conde de Valparaíso, and ranks among the city's most elegant baroque buildings. At the time of construction the interior courtyard would have been the most sumptuous in the area, with graceful arches and columns adorned with elaborate masonry. From 1821 to 1823 the palace was the home of the Emperor Agustín de Iturbide, a royalist general who, during the struggle for Independence, changed sides, throwing in his lot with the rebels led by Vicente Guerrero. In 1821 he signed a treaty acknowledging Mexican independence with the last Spanish viceroy and in 1822 declared himself emperor, only to be forced to abdicate a year later, and executed the year after that. It now hosts temporary art exhibitions.

Looking out over the Palacio Nacional on the Zócalo

The broad, leafy sweep of Paseo de la Reforma

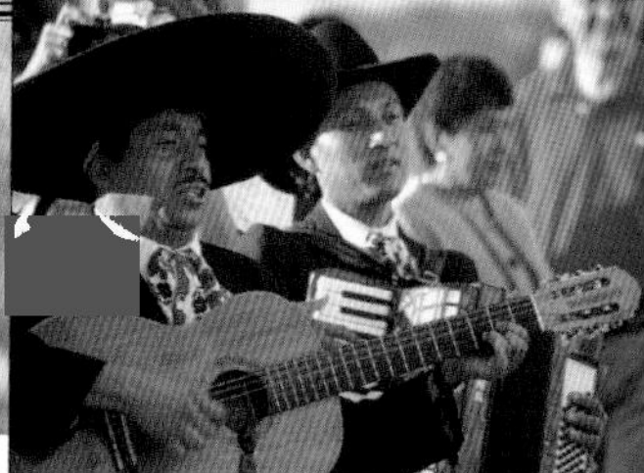
Plaza Garibaldi is famous for its wandering mariachi *bands*

PALACIO NACIONAL

103 F2 (inset) Plaza de la Constitución (55) 91 58 12 59 Daily 9.30–7 Free. Some form of ID is essential to enter the building Zócalo

The National Palace takes up the whole of the eastern side of the *zócalo*. Built on the site of the Palace of Moctezuma at the time of the Conquest, it has been rebuilt and added to many times over the centuries; President Calles added the third tier of arches around the central patio in the 1920s. Over the central door hangs the Liberty Bell, rung every year at 11pm on September 15 by the President to commemorate Mexican independence. Inside, a series of Diego Rivera murals, begun in 1929, are among the artist's finest. The enormous work covering the staircase is a sweeping panorama of Mexican history, *México a Través de los Siglos*. The right-hand panel depicts pre-Hispanic Mexico with a highly idealized vision of life in Tenochtitlán. The large central panel, finished in 1935, relates Mexican history from the Conquest in 1521 through war and oppression, invasion, independence and revolution. Almost every figure of consequence through the ages appears here: note Padre Hidalgo waving the banner of Independence and Benito Juárez with his Constitution. The left-hand panel is known as *El Mundo de Hoy y de Mañana* (*The World Today and Tomorrow*). Along the first floor frescoes depicts daily life in Aztec Tenochtitlán.

The central panel of Diego Rivera's mural of Mexican history in the Palacio Nacional (left)
The golden angel crowning the Independence Monument (right)

PASEO DE LA REFORMA

102 C3 Any bus from Chapultepec or from the western end of the Alameda marked Paseo de la Reforma

Cutting across the city diagonally from the Bucareli roundabout to the Bosque de Chapultepec is the wide, tree-lined Paseo de la Reforma, laid out by Emperor Maximilian during the 1860s to emulate the fashionable French 19th-century boulevards. It is lined with fine mansions, banks and offices, luxury hotels and chic boutiques. During the Porfirio Díaz dictatorship a series of monuments relating to key moments in the country's history was added: first (from north to south) is a statue of Christopher Columbus at Glorieta Colón; next, at the crossing with Avenida Insurgentes, is Cuauhtémoc, the last Aztec emperor; and finally, at the intersection with calles Tiber and Florencia, a marble column—45m (148ft) high and supporting a golden winged Victory—representing Independence, inaugurated in 1910 and known as "El Angel." One block north of Paseo de la Reforma, on Calle Rio Lerma 35, is the Museo Carranza (Tue–Sun 9–5), a 1908 mansion once home to Presidente Venustiano Carranza, author of the 1917 Constitution. It is now a museum about his life and the 1910 Revolution.

PLAZA GARIBALDI

103 F1 Garibaldi

Go to Plaza Garibaldi on a Friday or Saturday night, when up to 200 *mariachis* in their traditional costume of sombrero, tight silver-embroidered trousers, pistol and sarape blanket will serenade you (for a fee!). The whole square throbs with life, although it would be wise to keep a close eye on your belongings in the crowds. Should you find yourself here during the day wander east down Calle Honduras and browse the overwhelming range of bridal shops and stands selling bouquets, garlands and all possible other wedding accessories.

PLAZA SANTO DOMINGO

103 F2 Allende

Two blocks north of the cathedral is a small plaza surrounded by fine colonial buildings. There is the Antigua Aduana (former customs house) on the east side; the Portales de Santo Domingo on the west side, where public scribes and owners of hand-operated printing presses still carry on their business; the Convento de Santo Domingo (1737), in Mexican baroque, on the north side; and the old Edificio de la Inquisición, where the tribunals of the Inquisition were held, at the northeast corner. The latter is now the Museo de la Medicina Mexicana (daily 10–6; closed during university holidays), housing, among other exhibits, an entire room dedicated to skin diseases—strictly for those with a strong stomach.

View across the Plaza de las Tres Culturas

The iconic Camino Real Hotel, designed by Ricardo Legorreta

The Templo de San Francisco's highly decorated altar

PLAZA DE LAS TRES CULTURAS

Off 103 F1 ✉ Eje Central Lázaro Cárdenas, Esq. Flores Magón ☎ Zona Arqueológica Tlatelolco (55) 55 83 02 95 ⏲ Daily 8–6 Free; donations encouraged Tlatelolco

Lázaro Cárdenas leads to Santa María la Redonda, at the end of which is Plaza Santiago de Tlatelolco, the city's oldest plaza after the *zócalo* and one that holds great symbolism for Mexicans. The square is now known as the Plaza de las Tres Culturas since it shows elements of Aztec, colonial and modern architecture. It was here that the Aztecs held their main market, and on it, in 1524, the Franciscans built a huge church and convent using the stones of the Aztec temples. What's left of the market and ceremonial area has been restored and is open to the public.

Mexico's modern era is represented by the massive, multifloor Nonoalco-Tlatelolco public housing scheme (heavily damaged in the 1985 earthquake) and the Mexican Foreign Ministry looming over the ruins. A plaque sums up Tlatelolco's significance in the Mexican psyche: "On 13 August 1521, Tlatelolco, heroically defended by Cuauhtémoc, fell to Hernán Cortés. It was neither a triumph nor a defeat, but the painful birth of the *mestizo* race that is Mexico today." The poignancy is reinforced by a memorial to the massacre of October 1968, in which many students were killed in clashes with police.

POLANCO

Off 102 A2 ? *Colectivos* marked Horacio from metro Chapultepec or Polanco

North of the Bosque de Chapultepec lies the trendy area known as Polanco, laid out in a grid pattern. The area is one of the most chic districts in the city, and includes the striking Camino Real Hotel (▷ 272), worth a walk-in visit. Also here are exclusive private residences, commercial art galleries, fashion stores and expensive restaurants—collectively a monument to the consumer society. One glaring example of this is the huge Palacio de Hierro department store at the corner of calles Molière and Homero. There is little of cultural value with the exception of the Sala de Arte Siqueiros, on Tres Picos 29 (Tue–Sun 10–6) and a couple of unremarkable modern churches.

The instantly recognizable triangular-shaped Palacio de Hierro department store

SECRETARÍA DE EDUCACIÓN PÚBLICA

103 F2 (inset) ✉ Entrance on Avenida Argentina 28 ☎ (55) 53 28 10 97 ⏲ Mon–Fri 9–6 Zócalo

The Ministry of Education, three blocks north of the *zócalo*, was built in 1922. Among frescoes by different artists are some by Diego Rivera; they illustrate the lives and sufferings of the common people as well as satirizing the rich. Look out for *Día de los Muertos (Day of the Dead)* on the ground floor (far left in the second courtyard) and, on the first floor, *El Pan Nuestro (Our Daily Bread)*, showing the poor at supper, in contrast to *El Banquete de Wall Street (The Wall Street Banquet)* and *La Cena del Capitalista (The Capitalist's Supper)*. A passageway connects the Secretaría with the courtyards of the older Ex-Aduana de Santo Domingo (Mon–Fri 9–6), where there is a striking Siqueiros mural, *Patriots and Parricides*.

TEMPLO MAYOR

See pages 118–119.

TEMPLO DE SAN FRANCISCO

103 F2 (F2 inset) ✉ Avenida Madero ☎ (55) 55 18 46 90 ⏲ Daily 7am–8pm Free Bellas Artes

Opposite the Casa de los Azulejos is the Templo de San Francisco, founded in 1525 by the "Apostles of Mexico," the first 12 Franciscans to reach the country. By far the most important church in colonial days, Mass here was attended by the viceroys themselves, including Hernán Cortés. For 200 years the monastery was plagued by earthquakes, modifications and demolitions and the church we see now dates from the rebuilding that took place in 1716.

SAN ANGEL

This suburb of plazas, narrow cobbled streets and attractive colonial mansions is home to the Bazar Sábado, a splendid Saturday folk art and curiosity market.

RATINGS	
Cultural interest	●●●●
Specialist shopping	●●●●
Value for money	●●
Walkability	●●●

BASICS

Off 102 C4

Bus from Chapultepec Park

Miguel Angel de Quevedo

Villa Obregón, popularly known as San Angel, lies 13km (9 miles) southwest of central Mexico City, with its narrow, cobbled streets, many old homes, huge trees and the charm of an era now largely past. Most of the distinguished architecture in the area is from the 19th century. Many visitors come for the Saturday Bazar Sábado, but the area has plenty to offer on other days. Look out for the triple domes of the Iglesia del Carmen, covered with painted tiles, and the domes of the former Convento del Carmen, now the Museo Colonial del Carmen (Tue–Sun 10–4.45), which houses 17th- and 18th-century furniture and paintings. In the crypt, several mummified bodies are displayed in glass-topped cases. Opposite, on Calle Revolución, is the Centro Cultural San Angel, which stages exhibitions, concerts and lectures (for information tel (55) 56 16 12 54). See also the beautifully furnished and preserved old Casa del Risco (Tue–Sun 10–5), near the Bazar Sábado, on Callejón de la Amargura, former home of Mexican intellectual and politician Don Isidro Fabela (1882–1964).

Also worth a visit is the Iglesia de San Jacinto (access in the southeast corner of Plaza San Jacinto), first built in 1596 when this area was an outlying village known as Tenanitla. Don't miss the immaculate walled garden behind the church, a popular spot for wedding photos. The Museo Estudio Diego Rivera (Tue–Sun 10–6) at Avenida Altavista y Calle Diego Rivera, opposite the San Angel Inn (▷ 255) is where Rivera and Kahlo lived and worked. Actually two houses joined by an overhead walkway, the innovative design is the work of Juan O'Gorman. It's worth remembering just how daring his use of concrete and stark angular lines would have been in this traditional district in the early 1930s. The museum contains several works by Rivera, as well as belongings and memorabilia, although as you ascend the narrow spiral staircase and pass through the diminutive rooms it's slightly difficult to imagine the larger than life Rivera fitting in here. Until, that is, you reach his wonderfully well-appointed studio, any artist's dream.

The Museo Estudio Diego Rivera, where the artist once lived with Frida Kahlo

Art for sale in San Angel (top)

One of San Angel's delightful colonial-style houses (inset)

Don't miss Look for the peculiar fountain made from mother-of-pearl, old plates and broken vases in the patio of the Casa del Risco.

Templo Mayor

The Templo Mayor was the spiritual and ceremonial heart of Tenochtitlán, former capital of the Aztec Empire. Its fascinating and informative museum has reconstructions of how Tenochtitlán would have looked at its height.

Detail of stone serpent (top)
View across the site (above)

RATINGS

Cultural interest	●●●●
Historic interest	●●●●●
Photo stops	●●●

BASICS

103 G2 (inset)
Calle Seminario 4 and Calle Moneda, entrance in northeast corner of the *zócalo*
(55) 55 42 47 84
Tue–Sun 9–5
Museum and temple $3.50, students free with ISIC. $3.00 to use video camera
Zócalo
Guided tours in Spanish Tue–Fri 9.30, 11.30, 2.30, 4.30, Sat 9.30, 11.30, reservation necessary. In English Tue–Sat 10 and midday (not always available—call first)
Bookshop in museum
In basement of museum
Drinks and snacks

TIPS

- Pass by in the evening when the pyramid is flood-lit.
- Leave plenty of time for the museum: it is just as interesting as the ruins.

SEEING TEMPLO MAYOR

To the eastern side of the cathedral lie the partially excavated foundations of the greatest temple of Tenochtitlán, capital of the Aztecs. The entrance to the site is on Calle Seminario. Once inside, the fixed route takes you along raised metal platforms and walkways from which you can view the ruins. Leave enough time for the museum at the end of the circuit (entered on the same ticket), as it helps put in context what you have seen. As well as reconstructions of life in Tenochtitlán, the museum contains many beautiful sculptures found during excavations.

The layout of the museum's eight rooms aims to reproduce symbolically the Templo Mayor's two-part structure: start by ascending the right-hand side of the building through Rooms 1 to 4, dedicated to Huitzilopochtli (god of war), then descend the left-hand side through Rooms 5 to 8, dedicated to Tlaloc (god of rain). The rooms cover all aspects of life in Tenochtitlán, from the Aztec religion, war and sacrifice to trade and agriculture.

HIGHLIGHTS

ETAPA IV (ARCHAEOLOGICAL SITE)

The different stages of construction have been categorized into *etapas* (stages) to identify from which era each building belongs. Due to the Aztec practice of building a new temple every 52 years at the completion of their calendar cycle, seven have been identified piled on top of each other. Note here the small platform with four serpent heads, dating from 1486 to 1502, that would have marked the foot of one of the two wide staircases that led to the sanctuaries on top. The enormous undulating serpents at the north and south corners of this platform still retain traces of their original red, blue and yellow, and date from the temple's second expansion between 1469 and 1481.

THE COYOLXAUHQUI DISC (MUSEUM VESTIBULE)

The museum's central feature is the find that sparked off excavations—the vast, circular disc, weighing about 8 tons and depicting the dismembered body of Coyolxauhqui, who was killed by her brother Huitzilopochtli. According to Aztec myth, Coyolxauhqui's mother became miraculously pregnant. Desperately ashamed, Coyolxauhqui vowed to kill her mother to restore honor. But before she could, her brother Huitzilopochtli jumped out of his mother's womb fully grown and armed and cut his sister to pieces in revenge, before throwing her down a mountain. Thus Coyolxauhqui is always portrayed dismembered and lying at the foot of the Temple of Huitzilopochtli.

THE TZOMPANTLI (THE VESTIBULE)

The spectacular replica of a *tzompantli* (wall of skulls) is on your right as you enter the vestibule. Although the structure has been rebuilt to demonstrate the structure of an Aztec *tzompantli* and is not the temple's original, the skulls themselves were found on the site during the

excavations, which have been in place since 1978. All Aztec temples included a *tzompantli*, where the skulls of sacrificed victims were traditionally placed.

One of the huge stone eagle warriors (above); display of old pottery (inset left); the Tzompantli (Wall of Skulls; inset right)

THE TEOTIHUACÁN MASK (ROOM 3)

This striking dark green stone mask with its beady black eyes and one earring is one of many such masks originating from Teotihuacán. These pieces impressed the Aztecs with their expressive features and superb craftsmanship. The mask is beautifully inlaid with obisidian and shells.

THE OLMEC MASK (ROOM 3)

Similarly, this unique mask, 3,000 years old and originating from the Olmec area of coastal Veracruz, was found in one of the most sacred inner rooms of the temple. The Aztecs recognized its artistic significance and certainly would have venerated such a precious and ancient object.

BACKGROUND

Although it was known that Tenochtitlán's ceremonial fulcrum lay under central Mexico City, it was believed that the Templo Mayor, or Teocalli, lay directly beneath the cathedral. However, in 1978 workmen discovered an enormous stone disk depicting the goddess of the moon, Coyolxauhqui, in the northeastern corner of the *zócalo*. Further exploration revealed the hidden foundations of Teocalli. The existing buildings were cleared and excavations begun. In 1987, the adjoining museum was opened to house the sculptures and reliefs found in the main pyramid of Tenochtitlán. The building, in the middle of the city's colonial heart, was designed by the architect Pedro Ramírez Vazquez to be as discreet as possible. According to the Spanish chroniclers who arrived in the city with Hernán Cortés, the grandeur of the entire sacred complex with its gleaming white stucco pyramids and frescoes depicting great battles was overwhelming. What you see here are the bare foundations, so it can only be imagined how great this temple would have looked at the height of the empire.

MUSEUM GUIDE

Room 1: The archaeological excavations of the temple: an explanation of the process used to excavate the Templo Mayor.
Room 2: War and Sacrifice: an insight into the importance of war during the growth of the Aztec Empire, and the role of sacrifice.
Room 3: Trade and tax systems: information on the peoples conquered by the Aztecs and how trading relationships developed after war.
Room 4: Huitzilopochtli, god of war. Of note are the huge stone eagle warriors.
Room 5: Tlaloc, god of rain.
Room 6: Flora and fauna of Tenochtitlán: animals the Aztecs would have been familiar with.
Room 7: Agricultural methods: includes a model of how the Aztec market would have looked.
Room 8: Arrival of the Spanish: this room focuses on the fall of Tenochtitlán and displays exhibits found on the site from the colonial era as well as later Aztec pieces.

Brightly decorated boats glide along Xochimilco's canals laden with people and musicians

The Catedral Metropolitana dominates the historic heart of Mexico City

XOCHIMILCO

Off 102 C4 Official tariffs operate, although prices actually depend on your ability to negotiate. A small punt seats 12 and generally costs $12 an hour Take a bus or *colectivo* (any heading south down Avenida Insurgentes), or the metro to Tasqueña, and from there get the *tren ligero* to Xochimilco at the end of the line There are seven *embarcaderos* (landing stages) in the town, the largest of which are Fernando Celada and Nuevo Nativitas

Xochimilco—"the place where flowers grow" in Nahuatl—lies 28km (17 miles) southeast of central Mexico City. It is an extraordinary network of canals and islands, and an important supplier of market produce and flowers to the capital. This is the one place where it is still possible to envisage the ancient city as it was: built on islands in the lake interconnected by causeways, with a floating commercial life against a vibrant backdrop. In order to make the lake fertile, the Aztecs developed a form of agriculture using *chinampas*, "floating gardens," formed by mud and reeds. Nowadays Xochimilco is famed for its carnival-like atmosphere on Sundays, when brightly painted punt-like boats laden with hundreds of daytrippers from the capital jostle along the waterways amid a riot of color and music. As you glide down canals past luxuriant gardens, smaller boats carrying anything from fruit and jewelry to entire *mariachi* bands will sell their wares, or music, for a fee. In Xochimilco town, the Saturday market still sells plump, succulent fruit and a profusion of flowers, as it has done for centuries.

On the main square is the town's indisputable architectural jewel, the Iglesia de San Bernardino de Siena. Begun in 1535 and completed in 1595, it contains a magnificent Renaissance altarpiece, one of the oldest and best preserved in the Americas. Its convent, built by the Franciscans in 1585, has finely detailed masonry.

ZÓCALO

103 F2 (F2 inset) Zócalo

The vast main square, whose official name is Plaza de la Constitución, is the city's political and religious heart. Its name comes from the monument to independence that was supposed to stand in the middle of the square. However, as General Santa Anna only got as far as erecting the statue's base, the square became known popularly as "the plinth"—the *zócalo*. On the north side sits the cathedral (▷ 106) and to the east is the Palacio Nacional (▷ 115). Opposite are the Portales de los Mercaderes (Arcades of the Merchants), where small shops and businesses have traded since 1524. Opposite the cathedral is the Monte de Piedad, a government-run pawn shop (Mon–Fri 8.30–6, Sat 8.30–1) in a 16th-century building supposedly used by Moctezuma II.

There is a continuous stream of entertainment: groups performing pre-Hispanic spectacles in costume dance to the pounding of drums while buskers and street vendors vie for attention. It is the place to hold official ceremonies and celebrations, demonstrations and marches. Activists use the central space as a campsite, displaying banners facing the Palacio Nacional. The ceremonial lowering of the enormous flag in the middle of the square takes place daily at 6pm accompanied by much pomp and circumstance. It is raised again at 6am.

Conchero dancer entertains people in the Zócalo

ZONA ROSA

102 B3 Between Paseo de la Reforma and Avenida Chapultepec Sevilla, Insurgentes, Cuauhtémoc

In the politically charged late 1960s an area of the Juárez district came to be known as the Pink Zone, a part of town that was bohemian and hedonistic and saw itself as non-political and non-partisan—neither red nor white. The area, halfway between Chapultepec and the historic heart, continues to support an impressive range of restaurants, nightclubs, hotels and bars. Although it lost ground to Polanco after the 1985 earthquake, it has in recent times seen something of a revival, with new shops, internet cafés and European-style streetside restaurants opening up. While the area has no obvious visitor attractions, it's ideal for eating out and bar-hopping—and its size means you can easily negotiate it on foot. Multilingual tourist police patrol the streets but at night it's advisable to travel by taxi.

CENTRAL MEXICO EAST

From the lofty, snow-capped heights of Popocatéptl to the tropical, palm-fringed coast of Veracruz, Central Mexico's eastern region offers rich historical pickings that include the spectacular pre-Hispanic site of El Tajín, steeped in mystery, and the magnificent baroque churches and convents of colonial Taxco and Puebla. Lush vegetation and traditional witchcraft distinguish the less visited region of southern Veracruz state.

MAJOR SIGHTS

Cuernavaca	124
Puebla	126–127
El Tajín	129
Taxco	130
Teotihuacán	132–134
Veracruz	135
Xalapa	136

Illuminated caves in Cacahuamilpa National Park

Cacaxtla's spectacular murals were discovered as recently as 1975 by tomb robbers

THE SIGHTS

ACTOPAN

314 L8 Buses from Pachuca and Tula
www.actopan.com

The 16th-century town of Actopan is set in the verdant Valle del Mezquital. Its Otomí name means "fertile lands." For visitors, however, Actopan's wealth lies in its beautifully preserved old core: Narrow, cobbled streets cluster around the *zócalo* and come alive on Wednesdays when the traditional *tianguis* (market stands) sell regional products—textiles, hats, fruit—as they have done for 400 years. Founded in 1548, the fine Augustinian ex-Convento de San Nicolás Tolentino (Tue–Sun 9–5) houses a religious art museum within its cloisters; there is an unusual open chapel beside the main church.

From Actopan, a 56km (35-mile) branch road runs to one of Mexico's great archaeological sites: Tula (▷ 153), capital of the Toltecs.

BARRANCA DE METLAC

315 M9 Take Highway 150 out of Orizaba towards Córdoba

The road east from Puebla to Veracuz is one of the loveliest drives in Mexico. As the *altiplano* (high plateau) gradually recedes behind you, the road descends into a lush and fertile coffee-producing area. The exuberant vegetation is best appreciated from the bridge, 130m (426ft) above the river, which crosses the dramatic Barranca de Metlac, 8km (5 miles) from Orizaba on the road to Fortín de las Flores. The steep banks plunge down to the torrent below in a cascade of luxuriant vegetation, flame trees and hummingbirds.

CACAHUAMILPA

314 L9 Daily 10–5 $4 including a 2-hour tour Minibuses from Taxco Take Highway 166 out of Taxco and turn right at the Cacahuamilpa sign

The road to Ixtapan de la Sal from Cacahuamilpa passes by the Grutas de Cacahuamilpa, known locally as "Las Grutas." These are some of the largest caves in North America and a major visitor attraction. From the vast cave entrance a slippery path (walking sticks available at the entrance for $1) winds its way down through eerie cathedral-like halls punctuated by 75-million-year-old columns and elaborate stalactite and stalagmite formations. At its highest point the ceiling is 70m (230ft) above the cave floor, while at its deepest there are 180m (590ft) of solid rock above you. Guides take you on a 2km (1.2-mile) circuit, lighting the chambers to reveal their full majesty and pointing out fanciful shapes in the spectacular rock formations. It is more fun to visualize your own figures, which you can do as you make your own way back to the entrance.

CACAXTLA

314 L9 Daily 9–5.30 $3.50 (includes access to Xochitécatl) Buses from Puebla to just beyond Nativitas, where a sign on the right points to San Miguel del Milagro and Cacaxtla From Puebla take Highway 119 towards Tlaxcala. At Zacatelco, turn off onto the minor road marked Nativitas and Cacaxtla

A remarkable series of pre-Columbian frescoes depicting battle scenes with giant eagle and elaborately costumed jaguar warriors can be seen at the ruins of Cacaxtla on a hilltop near San Miguel del Milagro, between Texmelucan and Tlaxcala. The colors are still sharp and some of the figures are larger than life size. Occupied by the Olmec-Xicalanca civilization between AD400 and 1200, Cacaxtla was a thriving market town (its name means "place of the woven market baskets") that maintained strong trade links with the Gulf civilizations. Many obsidian knives, ceramic pots from El Tajín and shells from the Gulf were found during excavations and are displayed in the site museum. A huge roof covering the entire pyramid base protects the paintings from the elements.

From Cacaxtla, the pyramid at Xochitécatl 3km (2 miles) away is clearly visible, perched impressively on a hill and accessible only on foot. An exclusively ceremonial site, Xochitécatl is considerably older than Cacaxtla; the Pirámide de la Serpiente was built in 700BC. Following an eruption by Popocatépetl in AD100 the site was abandoned, then reoccupied from AD500 to 950. Don't miss the unusual spiral pyramid dedicated to the cult of Ehécatl, god of wind.

Detail of an Olmec jaguar head found at Cacaxtla

Tourist boats tied up along the shores of Lake Catemaco

Las Chimeneas at the Totonac site of Cempoala

The Iglesia de Nuestra Señora de los Remedios, Cholula

CATEMACO

315 N9 Buses from Veracruz and San Andrés Tuxtla
www.catemaco.com.mx

Picturesque Catemaco is set on the western shore of the enchanting mountain-ringed Lake Catemaco and is a famous focal point for traditional witchcraft and spiritual purification rites. Although something of a tourist attraction nowadays, the cult is still taken seriously and all manner of *brujos* (witches), warlocks, wizards and sorcerers live in the area. Calm pervades the town, whose dusty streets only stretch about six blocks inland from the lakeshore. One of the highlights is a boat trip on the lake (boat owners along the lakeside charge $30–$35 per boat and stop at all the major sites). You will visit the shrine to the Virgin del Carmen, set in a tiny grotto where the Virgin appeared, and stop at the Isla de los Monos, home to a colony of macaque monkeys introduced from Thailand for the University of Veracruz.

About 7km (4 miles) round the northern shore of the lake, on the road to Coyamé, is the Reserva Ecológica Nanciyaga, which offers walks in the surrounding rain forest, and *temazcal* treatments consisting of steaming patchouli-scented baths, vigorous massages and a vegetarian meal. Nanciyaga's lush, tropical setting was used to film the movie *Medicine Man* (1992), starring Sean Connery.

CEMPOALA

315 M9 Daily 9–6 $1.40
Buses from Veracruz to Cardel, then a local bus to Cempoala

The ruins of Cempoala (Zempoala) are an inspiring archaeological site set in lush vegetation and sugar cane plantations. Watered by the Río Chachelacas and only 8km (5 miles) from the Gulf coast, the city was founded by the Totonacs in approximately AD1200. In April 1519 at the invitation of Cempoala's chief, Xicomecoatl, the newly disembarked Hernán Cortés visited, then promptly conquered the city and forced its inhabitants to became the Spaniards' allies against the fierce Aztecs. Arriving in Cempoala, Cortés' troops reported brilliant temples covered in shells, stucco work that shone like silver and an ordered city of 30,000 inhabitants, comparable to Seville in Spain at the time.

There is a small museum with findings from the site, including a female stone figure surrounded by obsidian knives found in the Templo de la Muerte. Don't miss the Templo de las Caritas, once decorated with rows of little carved heads and now partially hidden by tall sugar cane, to the right of the main site.

CHOLULA

314 L9 Buses from Puebla
www.puebla.com.mx

Now effectively a suburb of Puebla, when Cortés arrived in 1519 Cholula was a thriving ceremonial settlement with 100,000 inhabitants and 400 temples grouped round the Gran Pirámide de Tepanapa (daily 10–5). When razing the shrines, Cortés vowed to build a chapel for each one destroyed, hence the rather surprising number of churches, around 70. Entering town you can't miss the 16th-century Iglesia de Nuestra Señora de los Remedios (▷ 224) atop its great pyramid, with a fine view of Cholula's many spires and domes, and the snow-capped, majestic Popocatépetl (▷ 125). The pyramid, now overgrown and ruined, has 8km (5 miles) of excavated tunnels. About 1km (half a mile) of tunnel is open to the public, giving an idea of the layers that were superimposed over 10 centuries to create the structure. The museum near the tunnel entrance has a copy of the 60m (197ft) Mural de los Bebedores (The Drinkers), depicting a pulque-drinking ritual, found inside the tunnels. The Franciscan fortress church of San Gabriel is on the *zócalo*; next to it is the Capilla Real, modeled on the great mosque of Córdoba in Spain.

COATEPEC

315 M9 Buses from Xalapa (Jalapa). For the Cascada de Texolo take the bus from Los Sauces marked Xico and get off at the entrance to the village. You will then have to walk 3km (2 miles) down a paved road through coffee plantations

Coatepec, an enchanting place to spend an afternoon, is reached along a lush and winding highway. It is famous for its fruit liqueurs and orchids, and is also an important base for the surrounding coffee haciendas; the whole town is infused with the sweet scents of roasting coffee beans, vanilla and freshly baked bread—still delivered by bicycle to the town's residences. The pretty *zócalo* bristles with cotton candy (candyfloss) sellers picking their way through the palms, flowers and snoozing old men, while the surrounding streets appear to end at the foot of the captivating, snow-capped Pico de Orizaba (▷ 125), in whose shadow the town sits.

Around 19km (11 miles) southwest of Coatepec is the 40m (132ft) Cascado de Texolo, a lovely place for a cold swim, bird-watching and walking. Many of the scenes in the movie *Romancing the Stone* (1984) were filmed here.

CUERNAVACA

Colonial Cuernavaca, with its year-long warm and sunny climate, is a weekend resort for the capital's elite, who fuel the city's buzzing cultural and intellectual life.

Cuernavaca's proximity to Mexico City, its warm climate and attractive provinciality have made it a prime spot for escaping the metropolis. Already popular as a resort with the Aztec elite long before it was conquered by Cortés, the tradition continues today with the ultra-modern high-walled homes of wealthy *capitalinos*. Its Nahuatl name of Cuauhnáhuac, meaning "adjacent to the tree," was soon corrupted by the Spanish to Cuernavaca (cow horn). The remarkably plain Catedral de la Asunción (daily 8–2, 4–7), on Calle Hidalgo, three blocks west of the Plaza de Armas, was founded in 1529. Note the fine 17th-century murals depicting the martyrdom of the Mexican saint San Felipe de Jesús on his journey to Asia. By the cathedral entrance stands the small Iglesia de Tercera Orden, built in 1529, whose facade carved by Indian craftsmen contains a small figure said to be one of the only two known statues of Cortés in Mexico.

MUSEUMS

The Palacio de Cortés at the eastern end of the tree-shaded *zócalo* is now the Museo de Historia Cuauhnáhuac (Tue–Sun 9–6), exhibiting local archaeological finds such as the remains of a mammoth and articles from Xochicalco (▷ 131); note the lovely seated stone sculpture of the goddess Diosa Xochiquetzal and colonial art and weaponry. Cortés built the palace in 1531 for his second wife, Doña Juana de Zuniga.

Next to the cathedral on Calle Nezahualcoyotl 4 is the Museo Robert Brady (Tue–Sun 10–6) housing a fabulous collection of paintings by, among others, Diego Rivera, Frida Kahlo and Paul Klee, as well as colonial furniture, textiles, pre-Hispanic objects and African art belonging to Brady, an American artist, who lived here until his death in 1986. The house, a former 16th-century convent, is grouped around a delightful pool and garden.

The 18th-century Jardín Borda (Tue–Sun 10–5.30) on Calle Morelos 103 was much loved by Emperor Maximilian and his wife, Carlota. Inspired by Granda's Generalife in Spain, these enchanting formal gardens are guarded by two fine watchtowers called *chocolateros*. According to legend, it was customary to sip a cup of afternoon chocolate in the tower while admiring the scenery.

RATINGS

Cultural interest	●●●●
Historic interest	●●●●
Walkability	●●●●

BASICS

314 L9

Avenida Morelos Sur 187, tel (777) 314 38 72; Mon–Fri 8am–9pm, Sat–Sun 10–4

Buses from Mexico City

Good bookshop

From central Mexico City, follow Avenida Insurgentes Sur south, past Ciudad Universitaria, and then take Highway 95D

www.cuernavaca.gob.mx
www.morelostravel.com
Excellent, English-language websites with up-to-date information on what's on, cultural events, language schools.

TIPS

- Sunday morning Mass in the cathedral at 11am is accompanied by a mariachi band.
- The café in the Jardin Borda is an ideal place to take a break, with tables by an immaculate lawn and trickling fountain.
- The Diego Rivera murals in the Palacio de Cortés depict Mexican history from Conquest to Revolution and focus on the revolutionary Emiliano Zapata.

The courtyard of the cathedral (above left)

Painting of a battle scene in the Palacio de Cortés (above right)

Enjoying a meal under the arcades in Córdoba

While seismic activity continues Popocatépetl remains off limits

Colorful houses straggle up the hillside in Pachuca

CÓRDOBA

315 M9 Avenida 3 and Calle 1, tel (271) 717 17 00; Mon–Fri 10–2, 4.30–7 Buses from Mexico City, Puebla, Veracruz and Orizaba www.cordoba.com.mx

Highway 150 from Puebla to Veracruz passes through this pleasant colonial city in the rich coffee-producing valley of the Río Seco. Founded in 1618 by 30 families, its leafy and elegant Plaza de Armas is arcaded on three sides and lined with cafés where you can taste the delicious local brew. The Portal de Zevallo on the north side is where the last Spanish viceroy, Don Juan O'Donojú, signed the Treaty of Córdoba with General Iturbide in 1821, acknowledging Mexican independence from Spanish colonial rule. On the east side is the Catedral de la Immaculada Concepción. The Museo de la Ciudad at Calle 3 No. 303 (daily 9–1, 4–8) has interesting Totonac and Olmec pieces.

ORIZABA

315 M9 Basement of Palacio Municipal, Avenida Colón Poniente 230; tel (272) 726 58 61; Mon–Fri 8–2 Buses from Puebla and Veracruz www.orizaba.veracruz.gob.mx

Orizaba was once the much-loved resort of Emperor Maximilian, but lost most of its charm in the 1973 earthquake when the bullring and many 19th-century buildings were lost. Although the town is now heavily industrialized—Cervecería Moctezuma has brewed its beer here since 1896—its setting at the foot of the majestic volcano Pico de Orizaba (or Citlaltépec), at 5,760m (18,898ft), is unrivalled. Sites of interest in town are clustered around the *zócalo*. On the north side is the many-domed Iglesia San Miguel, finished in 1729; at the daily market nearby, women in traditional dress sell local produce. On the staircase of the Palacio Municipal (daily 8am–10pm), on the other side of the river, is a mural by José Clemente Orozco (1926). The ex-Palacio Municipal (now a café) on the *zócalo* is a rather odd cast-iron pavilion brought piece by piece from France after the famous 19th-century Paris Exhibition.

Bells on display in Córdoba

PACHUCA

314 L8 Avenida Revolución 1300, tel (771) 718 44 89; Mon–Fri 10–5, Sat–Sun 10–1 Buses from Mexico City www.hidalgo.gob.mx

Pachuca de Soto, capital of Hidalgo state, is one of the oldest silver-mining towns in Mexico. The Aztecs, the Spaniards and more recently the English all mined here, leaving the hills honeycombed with old workings and terraced with tailings. Although Pachuca is largely modern there are a number of colonial mansions dotted along its narrow, steep and crooked streets. The Plaza de la Independencia is dominated by the huge Reloj Monumental, a neoclassical clock tower built just before the Revolution, in 1910, with four marble figures representing Liberty, the Constitution, Reform and Independence. The Museo de la Fotografía (Tue–Sun 10–6), in the cloister of the former Convento de San Francisco on Arista y Hidalgo, is the principal museum of note. It has a fascinating section on the history of photographic techniques and a superlative archive of early Mexican photography, including pictures by Agustín Casasola (1874–1938), who documented the Revolution. The Museo de la Minería (Wed–Sun 10–2, 3–6) at Calle Mina 110 has an interesting display on the history of mining in Pachuca.

POPOCATÉPETL AND IZTACCÍHUATL

314 L9 www.cenapred.unam.mx/mvolcan.html

The snow-capped, volcanic peaks of Popocatépetl (Popo), 5,452m (17,888ft) and Iztaccíhuatl, 5,286m (17,343ft), rise majestically to the east of the capital en route to Puebla. Their names recall the tragic legend of the beautiful princess Ixtaccíhuatl (White Lady) who, believing her lover Popocatépetl (Smoking Mountain) had been killed in battle, poisoned herself in grief. When the warrior returned alive he laid her body on the mountain and jumped into its crater. The three summits of Iztaccíhuatl are the head, breasts and knees of the princess. In 2000, Popocatépetl had its largest eruption for 500 years. Smoke and ash rose to a height of more than 10km (6 miles). For the foreseeable future it will not be possible to climb, or get close to, Popo.

Puebla

Puebla is one of Mexico's oldest and most historically important cities, home to a multitude of magnificent baroque churches, Churrigueresque facades and sparkling tiled domes.

Talavera-tiled balcony (top)
Decorated pots and plates for sale (above)

RATINGS	
Cultural interest	●●●
Good for food	●●●●●
Historic interest	●●●●
Specialist shopping	●●●●

BASICS

314 L9

Calle 5 Oriente 3, Avenida Juárez, tel (222) 246 20 44; Mon–Sat 10–7, Sun 10–1

Aeropuerto Hermanos Serdán; mostly domestic flights

www.turismopuebla.com.mx
Up-to-date information on museum opening times, hotel rates, weather and transport. In Spanish.

TIPS

- Churches close at varying and constantly changing times, but most shut for lunch between 1 and 4pm.
- *Chiles en nogada* is a must. One of Mexico's most delicious and patriotic dishes (its colors are those of the national flag), it is only made between July and September when the *nuez de castilla* (nuts), a crucial ingredient, are harvested.
- Pick up the fortnightly *Andanzas* magazine which lists cultural events in the city.

SEEING PUEBLA

Nowadays Puebla de los Angeles, "the city of the angels," is largely industrial and in parts very modern, but the colonial heart is small enough to walk around quite easily. Most of the city's sites of interest are concentrated in the middle around the *zócalo*. The gridded streets are numbered in a complex system and called Poniente (west), Oriente (east), Norte (north) or Sur (south), depending on their location in relation to the *zócalo*; it's worth getting hold of a map. The city is well served by a comprehensive bus and *colectivo* system for sights farther out of the old heart.

HIGHLIGHTS

ZÓCALO

Dominating the lively, arcaded *zócalo* is the city's bulky grey Catedral de la Inmaculada Concepción, the second-largest cathedral in the country and rather more impressive inside than out. Notable for its marble floors, onyx and marble statuary and stunning gold-leaf altarpiece, it was begun in 1575 and completed in the middle of the following century when Bishop Juan de Palafox y Mendoza injected a large portion of his inheritance into the project. He also partly funded the 74m (243ft) towers.

To the right of the cathedral on Calle 5 Oriente 5 is the Biblioteca Palafoxiana (Tue–Sun 10–4.30), the library founded by Bishop Palafox, who donated his 6,000-volume collection in 1646. It now contains 46,000 antique volumes, as well as the city's Casa de la Cultura, which hosts regular art exhibitions and concert recitals. Two blocks south of the cathedral is the Patio de los Azulejos, (Mon–Fri 9–5), at Calle 3 Sur 110, with a tiny entrance on Avenida 16 de Septiembre. The former almshouses for retired priests have fabulous tiled facades, a fine example of these *mestizo* craftsmen's skill.

CHURCHES

Many of Puebla's numerous churches—about 60 in all—have domes that sparkle with the glazed Talavera tiles for which the city is famous, and exuberant baroque interiors. The magnificent Capilla del Rosario (Rosary Chapel), inside the Iglesia de Santo Domingo at Calle 5 de Mayo 407, displays a beauty of style and lavishness of form that served as a model and inspiration for all later baroque in Mexico. Both the chapel and the altar of the main church are covered in very detailed gold leaf. Note the strong indigenous Indian influence in Puebla's baroque architecture, which can also be seen in the churches of Tonantzintla and Acatepec (▷ 224). Two lovely churches excelling in baroque plasterwork and Talavera tiles are those of San Cristóbal, Calle 4 Norte and Calle 6 Oriente, built in 1687 with modern Churrigueresque towers and Tonantzintla-like plasterwork inside; and the 18th-century San José, Calle 2 Norte and Calle 18 Oriente, with a tiled facade and decorated walls around the main doors and

beautiful altarpieces inside. One of the oldest local churches is San Francisco at Avenida 14 Oriente 1009, with a glorious tiled facade and a mummified saint in its side chapel.

MUSEO AMPARO

✉ Calle 2 Sur 708 🕐 Wed–Mon 10–6

This is Puebla's most outstanding museum, modern and well laid out, with exhibits spread over two colonial buildings with tranquil patios. Although far smaller than the anthropology museums of Mexico City and Xalapa (Jalapa), the museum owns one of the most comprehensive and well-presented pre-Hispanic collections in Mexico. The glass reproduction of a *tzompantli* (wall of skulls) with alternating Totonac and Olmec heads is an impressive introduction. Olmec art is well documented here, with an enormous and mysterious huge stone head for which this culture is famed. Some colonial painting and furniture is also on display. There are excellent audiovisual explanations in several languages, although you will need to rent the headsets.

BACKGROUND

Founded in 1531, Puebla was constructed on an entirely new site, unusual in this part of the country, where the Spanish used pre-Hispanic sites on which to build their towns. According to some sources, friar Julián Garcés saw angels in a dream indicating where the city should be built. More likely, the Spanish were keen to make a break from the powerful ancient sites of Cholula and Tlaxcala. The city prospered due to its location en route from the rich mines of the highlands to the port of Veracruz. Further wealth was generated from the manufacture of Talavera tiles and ceramics, a skill brought to Puebla by artisans from Talavera de la Reina in Spain. The tiles, an outstanding element of Puebla's architecture, are used extensively on the colonial buildings and inside the cloisters and closed interior patios across the city.

MORE TO SEE

MUSEO DE SANTA MÓNICA

✉ Avenida 18 Poniente 103

🕐 Tue–Sun 10–4.30

The museum is housed in a former 17th-century convent where generations of nuns remained in secret after the reform laws of 1857 made the convent illegal. The secret entrances have been preserved, as has the concealed screen between the nuns' hidden chapel and the main, still-operating church below.

EX-CONVENTO DE SANTA ROSA

✉ Avenida 3 Norte 1203 🕐 Tue–Sun 10–4.30

Santa Rosa has a priceless collection of 16th-century yellow Talavera tiles on the walls and ceilings of its kitchen, where, legend has it, the nuns invented the famous *mole poblano* (▷ 256). The highlights are the rooms full of the crafts produced in the state of Puebla.

MUSEO DE LA REVOLUCIÓN MEXICANA

✉ Avenida 6 Oriente 206 🕐 Tue–Sun 10–4.30

The house of Aquiles Serdán (1876–1910), a revolutionary leader whose assassination here proved to be one of the most important events leading up to the fall of Porfirio Díaz, is preserved as it was during his lifetime and displays some interesting photos and paraphernalia associated with the Revolution.

The vaulted nave of Iglesia de Santa Maria, Tonantzintla (main)

Multicolored blankets in the Parián market (above left)

The Iglesia de Santo Domingo houses the Capilla del Rosario (above right)

The busy main plaza in San Andrés Tuxtla

A huge carved Olmec head at Santiago Tuxtla

Traditional blankets and linen for sale in the market at Tepoztlán

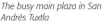

SAN ANDRÉS TUXTLA

315 N9 Secretaría de Relaciones Exteriores, Palacio Municipal, on the *zócalo*; Mon–Fri 10–2, 4–7 Buses from Catemaco, Tuxtepec and Veracruz
www.sanandrestuxtla.gob.mx

The larger of the two Tuxtlas on the road to Catemaco, San Andrés Tuxtla is a warren of narrow, winding streets. The bustling daily market is well stocked with Oaxacan foods such at *totopos* (fried tortilla chips with cheese) and *tamales de elote* (crispy tortillas, spicy meat and cakes of maize flour steamed in leaves), tropical fruits and medicinal herbs.

The town is surrounded by tobacco plantations, and is famed for its cigar trade; a visit to a cigar factory is a must. The most central factory, founded in 1830, is Santa Clara (Mon–Fri 9–1, 3–7, Sun 9–11) on Calle 5 de Febrero 10. The 30 or so factory workers welcome visitors and allow you to observe the production process, from the selection of dried leaves to the hand-rolling of the *puros* (cigars). You can even have a go at it yourself and there's a small shop on site with excellent prices.

SANTIAGO TUXTLA

315 N9 Buses from Veracruz, San Andrés Tuxtla and Catemaco
www.santiagotuxtla.gob.mx

This small, pleasant, colonial town set along the river enjoys a cool climate 1,700m (5,578ft) above the Gulf coast in the attractive volcanic area of Los Tuxtlas, known as the Switzerland of Mexico for its mountains and perennially green vegetation. The area was the heartland of the Olmec civilization that flourished between 1500BC and 600BC. In the middle of the *zócalo* is the town's chief attraction—the largest of the 16 known Olmec heads, carved in solid stone, measuring 3.4m (11ft) high and 1.5m (5ft) wide. Thought to represent a dead person due to its closed eyes, drooping mouth and stylized headpiece, it has the characteristically flattened nose and thick lips common to all the Olmec heads, which, some theorists believe, raise questions of the possible presence of, or contact with, Negroid peoples in the Americas. Also on the *zócalo* is the Museo Tuxtleco (Mon–Sat 9–6, Sun 9–3), displaying among other things local Olmec and Totonac objects used in traditional witchcraft *(brujería)*, the first sugar-cane press used in Mexico and another Olmec stone head.

TAMPICO

311 L7 Calle 20 de Noviembre 218, tel 212 26 68; Mon–Sat 9–7 The bus station is 10km (6 miles) out of town. Buses from San Luis Potosí and Veracruz
www.tamaulipas.gob.mx

The busy port town of Tampico, on the tropical Gulf of Mexico, was founded in 1522 by Gonzalo de Sandoval, sacked by pirates in the 17th century and refounded in 1823. Oil was discovered here in 1901, marking the beginning of a new era of wealth and prosperity based on the huge refinery at Río Pánuco.

Despite new construction, Tampico retains an air of faded grandeur with its ramshackle, peeling colonial buildings laced with wrought-iron verandas and wooden-slatted windows. Caribbean in atmosphere, the animated Plaza de la Libertad springs to life in the sweltering evenings when local *jarocho* musicians and dancers perform in the elegant Victorian bandstand. A more sedate area is the Plaza de Armas, with the Catedral Santa Iglesia, whose clock comes from England and altar from Carrara in Italy, and the art nouveau former Palacio Municipal, now a bank.

TAXCO

See page 130.

TEOTIHUACÁN

See pages 132–134.

TEPOZTLÁN

314 L9 Buses from Cuernavaca and Mexico City

Scenic Tepoztlán lies at the foot of the spectacular Parque Nacional El Tepozteco, ringed by volcanoes and perched between rocky crags. Until recently an isolated rural village, its picturesque, steep cobbled streets with plodding, heavily laden donkeys are now lined with fashionable crafts boutiques and pretty cafés, attracting daytrippers from Cuernavaca at weekends. On the western side of the *zócalo* a crowded outdoor market sells fresh produce and crafts. Opposite, a gated entrance and overgrown churchyard lead to the remarkable 16th-century church and ex-convent of María de la Natividad (Tue–Sun 10–5). It was built by the Dominican order in 1580, occupied by French soldiers under Emperor Maximilian between 1864 and 1867 and again by revolutionaries in 1910. The interior patios are decorated with restored frescoes.

Don't miss The small Tepozteco pyramid (daily 10–4.30) high up in the mountains above the town was built around 1130 and is dedicated to the god of *pulque* (a drink made of fermented maguey cactus). It is a strenuous 2km (1.2-mile) climb uphill from the end of Avenida Tepozteco, but spectacular views make the effort worthwhile.

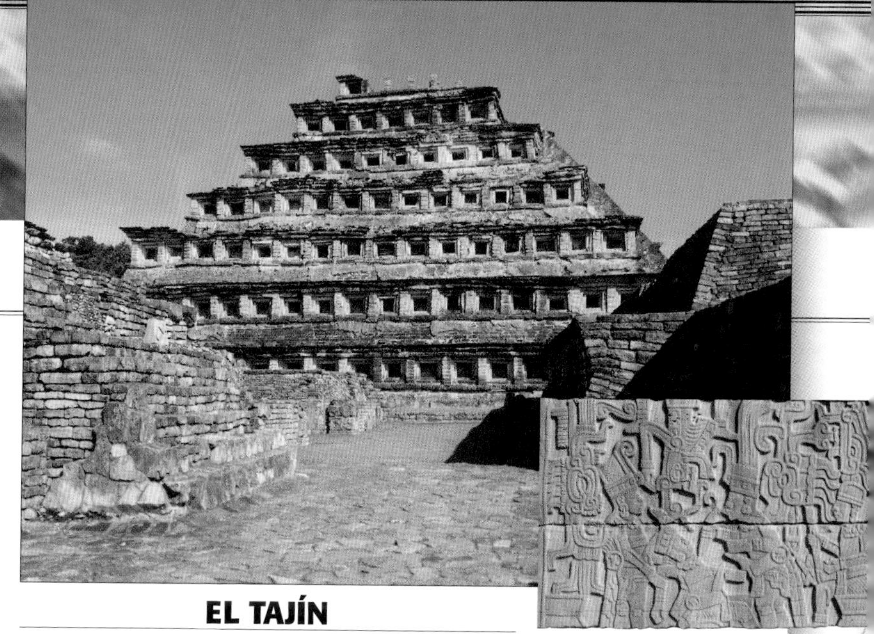

EL TAJÍN

The most impressive archaeological site on the Gulf coast, El Tajín has a rich body of iconography telling of the interplay between humans and the gods, and the dignified sacrifice of warriors and ball players.

The great city of El Tajín ("thunderbolt" in Totonac) is one of the most enigmatic archaeological sites in Mexico. At its zenith in about AD600 it would have covered 1,050ha (2,595 acres), but by the time of the Conquest it had been completely forgotten, only to be rediscovered in 1785. Little is understood about El Tajín; no one even knows who built it. Some suggest the Huastecs, others the Totonacs. Its date of construction is less contested. The important structures were built between AD300 and AD900, with a surge of energy around AD600 when Teotihuacán and Monte Albán were being abandoned.

MAIN BUILDINGS

In the most important of the 17 ball courts, the Juega de Pelota Sur (South Ball Court), the bas-relief tableaux along the walls provide a fascinating glimpse into the philosophy that underpinned the ball game (▷ 29), including a portrait of a decapitated player—his head by his feet with the death god, Mictlantecuhtli, at his side—demonstrating an important association with human sacrifice. The obsession with the ball game suggests that the city was an immense academy where young men were trained in its skills and rules.

The Pirámide de los Nichos, one of the most famous structures at El Tajín, is punctuated by 365 niches, which would have originally been painted deep red on a black background. Their purpose is unknown; perhaps they held offerings, one for each day of the year. The pyramid is crowned with a sanctuary lined with engraved panels, one of which shows a cacao plant bearing fruit. Cacao was of great commercial value to the people of the area and there is some evidence that the rulers of El Tajín controlled its cultivation in the zones surrounding the site.

TAJÍN CHICO

The structures on this artificially tiered natural hill above the main site are thought to have been elite residences and administrative buildings. The Edificio de las Columnas was the special domain of the ruler, 13 Rabbit, who governed at the city's zenith.

RATINGS

Good for food	●●
Historical interest	●●●●●
Photo stops	●●●●

BASICS

315 M8

Daily 8–6

$3.50, free with student card, $3 for use of video camera

Buses from Papantla and Poza Rica

Guides at the entrance charge $14 for a 75-min tour. Limited written information on site

Small pamphlets in Spanish for $0.80. Buy a guidebook in the Anthropology Museum, Mexico City, $6

Open at 10am

In the entrance hall

TIPS

- Arrive when the site opens at 8am; the air is cool, the grass dewy and parrots squawk in the palms.
- Papantla and Tuxpán are much more pleasant places to overnight than nearby Poza Rica.
- The Voladores de Papantla (flying dancers) perform at El Tajín daily during high season, weekends in low season (▷ 23).

Pyramid of the Niches (top)

Detail of a carved panel (inset)

One of the flying dancers (left)

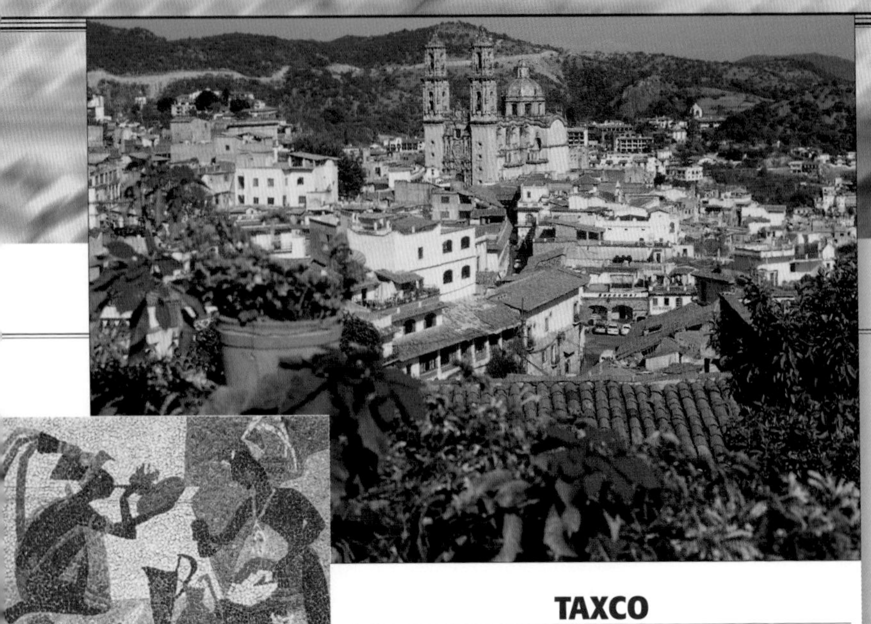

TAXCO

The colonial town of Taxco, distinguished for its remarkable silver jewelry, clings to its steep hill.

RATINGS	
Photo stops	●●●●●
Specialist shopping	●●●●●
Walkability	●●●●

BASICS

314 K9

Avenida de los Plateros 1, tel (762) 622 22 74; Mon–Fri 8–3, Sat 9–11am

Buses from Mexico City

www.guerrero.gob.mx
Helpful information on cultural events and transport updates. In Spanish.

TIPS

- Taxco is a small town and, although hilly and cobbled, it is best experienced on foot.
- If you are buying silver, make sure it is genuine: check for the hallmark sterling or .925.
- To reach Ixcateopan de Cuauhtémoc, take the road north out of Taxco towards Teloloapan. *Combis* leave from the Estrella de Oro bus station in Taxco every 30 minutes.

View across the rooftops of Taxco (top)

Stone mosaic in the Museo Guillermo Spratling depicting silversmiths at work (inset)

Mexico's most famous silver town is a warren of whitewashed, terra-cotta-tiled houses lining the steep and twisting cobbled streets that climb up the hillside to the Plaza Borda. French immigrant José de la Borda became fabulously rich after discovering the San Ignacio vein in the 18th century and he founded the town as you see it today, spending a fortune on building Iglesia de Santa Prisca. Although no longer mined in large quantities, silver—in the shape of jewelry—remains the town's main livelihood and literally hundreds of silver shops (*platerías*) cater to visitors.

AROUND TOWN

The plaza is dominated by the magnificent, baroque, rose-hued Iglesia de Santa Prisca, whose twin towers soar above everything except the mountains. Built between 1751 and 1759, its interior is a dazzling display of Churrigueresque altarpieces with paintings by Miguel Cabrera (1695–1768), with scenes from the life of the Virgin behind the altar. The Museo de Arte Virreinal (Tue–Sat 10–3.30, Sun 10–2.30) on Calle J Ruiz de Alarcón 12 is housed in the Casa Humboldt, named after the renowned German explorer Baron von Humboldt (1769–1859), who stayed here once in 1801. Exhibits include superb religious art and ecclesiastical objects from Santa Prisca as well as some interesting background on Taxco's importance on the trade route from Acapulco.

The Museo Guillermo Spratling (Tue–Sun 9–3), behind Santa Prisca at Calle Porfirio Delgado 1, contains the personal collection of pre-Hispanic memorabilia belonging to this American architect and writer. Spratling arrived in Taxco in 1929 to set up a jewelry workshop, and his designs in silver helped bring the city to world recognition.

There are superb views from the Teleférico (cable car; daily 8–7) to Monte Taxco, reached by walking 2km (1.2 miles) up Calle Benito Juárez to the northern end of town.

IXCATEOPAN DE CUAUHTÉMOC

Some 45km (28 miles) from Taxco is the pretty village of Ixcateopan de Cuauhtémoc. Most of the buildings, and even the cobblestones, are made of marble. A statue commemorating Cuauhtémoc, the last Aztec emperor, stands at the entrance to the village, his birthplace. His skeleton is said to rest in the glass-covered tomb in the 16th-century Iglesia de Santa Maria de la Asunción, now a museum.

Musicians serenading diners in Tlacotalpan

The Church of San José in Tlaxcala

Carving on the Pyramid of the Plumed Serpent, Xochicalco

TEOTIHUACÁN

See pages 132–134.

TLACOTALPAN

315 N9 (southwest of Cuernavaca) *Zócalo*, tel (288) 884 21 51; daily 9–3, 5–7 Buses from Veracruz via Alvarado, or direct from Santiago Tuxtla, San Andrés Tuxtla, Tuxtepec

Small, quiet Tlacotalpan lies on the Río Papaloapan, about 15km (9 miles) from Alvarado on the spectacular road inland to Tuxtepec and Oaxaca. Picturesque, secluded and very laid-back, the town has a distinctly Caribbean feel, its low houses fronted by stuccoed columns and arches painted in pastel shades. Large French windows with wrought-iron grilles reveal cool, dark interiors, heavy 19th-century furniture, rocking chairs and white linen curtains that float in the welcome breeze from whirring fans. There are two churches on the *zócalo*, the Parroquía de San Cristóbal (daily 8–7) on the west side and the Capilla de la Candelaria (daily 7am–8pm) on the north side. Opposite, on Calle Manuel Allegre, the Museo Salvador Ferrando (daily 10–8) contains some interesting local 19th-century paintings and furniture.

TLAXCALA

314 L9 Avenida Juárez y Landizábal, tel (246) 462 00 27; Mon–Fri 9–6, Sat–Sun 10–6 Buses from Puebla, Mexico City

The quaint town of Tlaxcala, with its simple buildings washed in pinks and yellows, is the capital of the state of the same name, where wealthy ranchers breed fighting bulls but the landless peasantry is still poor. The Palacio de Gobierno (daily 7–6), which takes up one side of the main square, has some vivid murals inside painted by Desiderio Hernández Xochitiotzin (born 1922) depicting the indigenous history of Tlaxcala. On the intersection of Calle Mariano Sanchez with Calle 1 de Mayo is the Museo de Artes y Tradiciones Populares (Tue–Sun 10–5), where Otomí people demonstrate traditional arts such as embroidery, weaving, cooking and *pulque*-making (a cactus-based liquor). You can't miss the twin white towers of the Basílica de Ocotlán (daily 7–7), perched on a hill overlooking Tlaxcala—walk up Avenida Guridi y Alcocer for 1km (0.5 mile). Its facade of lozenge-shaped vermilion bricks frames the white stucco portal, while the Churrigueresque interior is covered with gold leaf.

The ruined pyramid of Xicoténcatl, at San Estaban de Tizatlán, 5km (3 miles) outside Tlaxcala, has two sacrifical altars with original color frescoes preserved under glass.

VERACRUZ

See page 135.

XALAPA

See page 136.

XOCHICALCO

314 L9 (southwest of Cuernavaca) Daily 10–5 $3; extra $3 for video cameras Buses from Cuernavaca

The name of this pre-Hispanic hilltop site means "place of the flower house," although the surrounding hills are now dry and barren. No matter—the views are spectacular. This city and ceremonial hub, discovered in 1770, was one of the principal settlements of Mexico's central plain, occupying a strategic site on the north–south trade route. Its heyday occurred from AD650 to AD900, after which it was abandoned mysteriously. The city's elaborate defensive features suggest, however, that it had enemies: archaeologists have discovered a complex system of doors and tunnels within the city walls. At its highest point is the Pirámidé de Quetzalcóatl (Pyramid of the Plumed Serpent), faced with andesite slabs which fit together invisibly without mortar. The friezes depict skeletal jaguars and figures of a serpent. The site also has two impressive ball courts, as well as numerous minor temples and living quarters. About 500m (550 yards) from the ruins down the hill an innovative new museum is housed in hexagonal rooms. Look out for the remnants of the original piping system that ensured dampness would not deteriorate the friezes on the buildings. There are also some interesting photographs depicting the temples in a severe state of disrepair, taken by Hungarian Pál Rosti, who visited the site in 1856.

The site is large and requires at least 2–3 hours to do it justice.

Bas-reliefs of Maya figures decorate the Pyramid of the Plumed Serpent at Xochicalco

Teotihuacán

The site has some of the most remarkable relics of an ancient civilization in the world, including the massive Pyramid of the Sun, and was home to a mysterious people who existed at the same time as the Roman Empire.

RATINGS	
Cultural interest	●●●●●
Photo stops	●●●●●
Walkability	●●●

BASICS

314 L9

Daily 7–6; if entrance near bus stop is not open at 7am, try entrance near Pyramid of the Moon. Museum daily 9–6; entrance included on ticket

$3.50; extra $3 for video cameras; $2 parking fee. *Son et lumière* display $4 per person.

Buses from Mexico City, Terminal del Norte, usually Gate 8. Note that the site is more generally known as Pirámides rather than Teotihuacán

Official guidebook ($1.75) gives a useful route to follow. Students give free guided tours on weekends

At exits and at museum

http://archaeology.la.asu.edu/teo/
Excellent information on the site, including recent excavation reports.

Carving of Quetzalcóatl (top)

View from the Pyramid of the Moon (above left)

Carving of a plumed butterfly or quetzalpapálotl (above middle)

Painted wall plaster on display in the museum (above right)

Pyramid of Quetzalcóatl (left)

SEEING TEOTIHUACÁN

Allow at least two to three hours to see the site properly—longer if you're really interested. Arrive early before the vast numbers of wandering vendors and tour groups, who descend around 11am.

The site can be roughly divided into three distinct areas of interest connected by the 4km-long (2.5-mile) Avenida de los Muertos (Avenue of the Dead). At the southern end is La Ciudadela, in the middle section is the Pirámide del Sol and the museum, and at the northern end is the Pirámide de la Luna, surrounded by some smaller temples. To the west lie the mostly unexcavated sites of Tetitla, Atetelco, Zacuala and Yayahuala.

HIGHLIGHTS

LA CIUDADELA

This enormous square, dominated by the impressive Templo de Quetzalcóatl on its east side, was mistakenly thought to be the site of a fortress (*ciudadela*) by the Spanish. At Teotihuacán it was common practice to build on top of existing temples, creating overlapping structures akin to an onion—each layer represented a different era. Underneath the newest of the temples archaeologists have found an earlier pyramid with decoration that is unique to the site. Lining the staircase are huge carved heads of the much-revered feathered serpent, as well as Tlaloc, the beady-eyed rain god. You can still make out traces of pigment—remember that the rather dour pyramids you see today would once have been brightly painted.

PIRÁMIDE DEL SOL AND AROUND

Following the Avenue of the Dead north, you will reach the Pyramid of the Sun, the tallest pyramid on the site and the third largest in the world, measuring 65m (213ft) high and 213sq m (2,292sq ft) at its base. The sides are terraced, and wide stairs lead to the summit. The pyramid was heavily restored between 1905 and 1910 in time for Mexico's centennial independence celebrations: controversial archaeologist Leopoldo Batres (1852–1926) has been blamed for taking the top off the pyramid and removing the original 4m (13ft) covering of stone and stucco. What you see now are the jutting stones on the sloping sides that would have held in place decorative panels, known as the *talud-tablero* technique. Underneath the pyramid, and not

MORE TO SEE

On the west side of the site, between Gates 1 and 2, are four minor sites that are rarely visited: Tetitla, a walled complex with fine frescoes and paintings; Atetelco with its three tiny temples and excellent murals; and the abandoned sites of Zacuala and Yayahuala.

open to the public, is a system of natural caves discovered in 1971; some historians believe this may have been the most important point of the whole city—a sacred womb or site of an ancient underground spring. Nowadays, the pyramid's spiritual cast is most obvious on the spring equinox on March 21, when sun-worshippers flock here to see the sun's alignment with the west face of the pyramid.

Just south of the Pyramid of the Sun is the site museum, surrounded by a sculpture garden. As well as an excellent model of old Teotihuacán, the museum has many fascinating objects including masks, ceramics and larger sculptures of deities—all well displayed.

Wall markings in the Palace of Quetzalpapálotl

PIRÁMIDE DE LA LUNA

Smaller than the Pyramid of the Sun, but built on higher ground, the Pyramid of the Moon is at the northernmost end of the Avenue of the Dead. You approach it through the Plaza de la Luna. The climb to the summit is hard, though it's worth getting at least as far as the first platform—48 steep steps—for wonderful views down the Avenue of the Dead. Excavations carried out in 2001 have uncovered numerous remains of sacrificial victims towards the middle of the pyramid, throwing into doubt earlier theories that human sacrifice wasn't a feature of life at Teotihuacán.

PALACIO DE QUETZALPAPÁLOTL

To the west of the Pyramid of the Moon is the Palace of the Precious Butterfly, where the priests serving the sanctuaries of the moon lived. The area has been restored, together with its columned patio—note especially the obsidian inlet in the highly decorated carved pillars. Following the path left of the palace and through a warren of chambers thought to have been the living quarters of priests, you will find the Palacio de los Jaguares (Jaguars' Palace). Impressive murals of cat-like creatures are displayed under protective shelters. Continue through a narrow tunnel to the right and you will emerge in the Temple of the Feathered Shells, with shells, flowers and green parrots decorating the base of an earlier temple.

The grisly skeletons of sacrificial victims

MUSEO DE LA PINTURA MURAL TEOTIHUACANA

Exiting from Gate 3 behind the Jaguars' Palace, cross the parking area and the road to reach the excellent Museum of Teotihuacán's murals (opening hours same as site; price included in site admission). From the road a 350m (1,150ft) path leads past unexcavated temples covered in cacti to the museum, which houses around 40 murals from the site. Jaguars, shells and maguey, as well as figures of Tlaloc and Quetzalcóatl, appear again and again in the multihued paintings.

TIPS

- Take water and food—most shops (overpriced) are limited to the west side of the site.
- If you're short of time, the best place to start is the Pyramid of the Moon (Gate 3), the area of most interest.
- The simplest way to visit Teotihuacán is on an organized tour, though an early departure from Mexico City doesn't mean you'll arrive at the site early, since tours tend to stop off at the Basilica de Guadalupe and a souvenir shop en route. Mexbus offers day trips, which include pick-up and return from central hotels, a stop at the Basílica , English-speaking guide and lunch for $23; leaving 7am, returning 4.30pm (tel (55) 55 22 48 20).

BACKGROUND

Teotihuacán is thought to date from around 300BC to AD750, with its heyday between AD450 and 650. Much of the city and the identity of its creators remains a mystery. Some archaeologists have suggested an ecological disaster—soil exhaustion or desertification of the surrounding area after years of deforestation—to explain the city's collapse. Even the name Teotihuacán is something of a misnomer; it was the Aztecs who gave the city the name by which we now know it: "the place where men become gods." Equally, the Avenue of the Dead was named mistakenly by the Aztecs, who thought it was lined with the burial chambers of Teotihuacán's rulers. It does appear, however, that the city housed some 200,000 people at its apogee, spread over an area of around 20sq km (8sq miles), making it the sixth largest city in the world at the time. Excavations show that the ceremonial hub you see today was surrounded by areas occupied by artisans, workmen, merchants and representatives of those crafts and professions that contribute to a functioning city.

There is certainly no doubting the city's influence—research indicates that an individual from Teotihuacán arrived at Copán in Honduras and usurped the power of the rightful ruler, extending the influence of Teotihuacán throughout the Maya region.

VERACRUZ

The tropical town of Veracruz exudes Caribbean style and rhythm. Languid evenings in the *zócalo* are enlivened by marimba players and couples dancing the romantic *danzón*.

On Good Friday, in 1519, Hernán Cortés and his troops disembarked at Isla de los Sacrificios on the Gulf Coast of Mexico and founded the town of Villa Rica de la Veracruz. In fact, this first settlement was a few kilometers to the north; the present site was established in 1598. For 400 years Veracruz was the setting for all manner of military defeats, foreign occupations and heroic deeds. Basically, it is a Caribbean city; its culture (called *jarocho*) is a fusion of Andalucian and African elements, reflected in its Afro-Mexican ethnicity, music—featuring marimbas, flutes and harps—and dance. This is one of the country's most enjoyable places to sit back, relax and be entertained.

COLONIAL VERACRUZ

The heart of the city is the Plaza de Armas. White-paved, palm-fringed and studded with attractive cast-iron lampstands and benches, it is watched over by the Palacio Municipal, cathedral and several hotels in colonial buildings. The floodlit plaza comes alive during the sultry evenings with a crush of dancers and marimba players. Two blocks east of the plaza, the *malecón* (seafront) also bristles with activity at nighttime, and you can often catch street performers and fire-eaters entertaining the crowds.

The city's main historic attraction is the fortress of San Juan de Ulúa (Tue–Sun 10–4.30), joined by a causeway to the mainland. For 300 years the fortifications failed to deter buccaneers and a series of foreign invasions, and in 1825 the Spanish made their final stand here. Later, it became a political prison where Mexico's "Robin Hood," Chucho el Roto, was imprisoned, and Benito Juárez established his constitutional government in exile between 1858 and 1861.

The Baluarte de Santiago (Tue–Sun 10–4.30), at Avenida 16 de Septiembre, is one of nine forts that once formed part of the city walls. Built in 1635, it now contains a small pre-Hispanic gold collection recovered from a shipwreck. The Museo de la Ciudad (Tue–Sun 10–6), at Calle Zaragoza 397, traces the history of Veracruz from the Conquest to 1910 and displays some lovely Olmec sculptures, as well as interesting information on the trans-Atlantic slave trade.

Boca del Río, once a small fishing village a short drive east along the coast, is now a developed area of beach hotels, bars and restaurants.

Don't miss Enjoy the local *julep* drink—made with dark rum, vermouth, sugar and mint—in the *portales* of the plaza, while you listen to the sound of marimbas.

RATINGS

Cultural interest	●●●●●
Good for kids	●●●●
Historic interest	●●●●●
Outdoor pursuits	●●●

BASICS

315 M9

Palacio Municipal, Plaza de Armas, tel (229) 989 88 00; Mon–Sat 8–8, Sun 10–6

Buses from Mexico City, Xalapa, Puebla. The bus terminals are 4km (2.5 miles) from the middle of town, on Avenida Díaz Mirón

www.veracruz-puerto.gob.mx/turismo/ Suggestions on rafting, diving and general information on adventure tourism companies. In Spanish.

TIPS

- **Veracruz' beaches leave much to be desired. The beach at Mocambo is the best, but the sand can be dirty.**
- **It is generally hot and humid in Veracruz, however, between July and September the region can be plagued by heavy rains and from October to January the beaches and *malecón* tend to be empty, and many resorts close.**

Musicians entertaining people in Plaza de Armas (top)

Replica of the Marigalante*, at rest in the harbor (inset)*

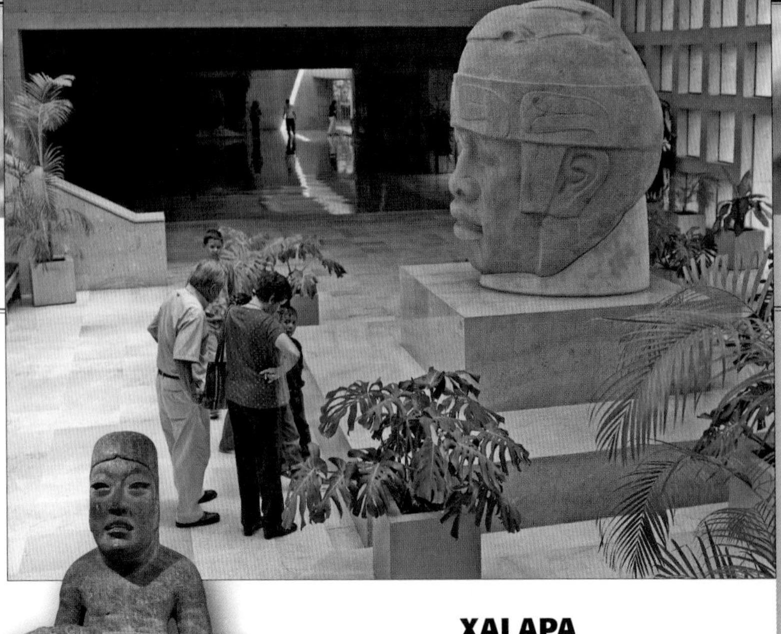

XALAPA

Xalapa (Jalapa), capital of Veracruz state since 1885 and home to the university—a hub of great creativity, energy and cultural flair—is surrounded by rich vegetation in the shadow of the 4,282m (14,049ft) peak of Cofre de Perote.

RATINGS	
Cultural interest	●●●●●
Historic interest	●●●
Outdoor pursuits	●●●●
Walkability	●●●

BASICS

315 M9

Boulevard Cristóbal Colon 5, tel (228) 812 85 00; Mon–Sat 9–5, Sun 10–2

Buses from Mexico City, Puebla, Veracruz

www.xalapa.net/sitios/xalapa.htm
Information on restaurants, hotels, museums and transport. In Spanish.

TIPS

- Watch out for the daily downpour that usually occurs at the end of the afternoon.
- Pick up the monthly cultural magazine *La Agorera* from the arts center, Agora de la Ciudad, Parque Juárez.
- Put the ruins of El Tajín into greater context by visiting the Anthropology Museum first.

Giant Olmec head (top) and El Señor de las Limas *(inset) in the Museo de Antropología*

Set in the lush, coffee-producing area of Mexico, the inland capital of Veracruz state enjoys a warm and damp climate. Walled gardens, stone houses and steep, cobbled streets overflow with flowers, and early mornings in the Parque Juárez ring to the sound of birdsong. Interspersed between colonial buildings are flamboyant, Gothic-style, 19th-century mansions, while surrounding the old heart is the modern town with its wide, congested avenues. Around Parque Juárez note the 18th-century cathedral with its sloping floor and the Palacio de Gobierno with murals by the Chilean artist José Chavez Morado (1909–2002).

MUSEUMS

In the northern suburbs of Xalapa, on the road out to Mexico City, is the outstanding Museo de Antropología (Tue–Sun 9–5), displaying a remarkable collection of treasures from the Olmec, Totonac and Huastec coastal cultures. Inaugurated in 1986 and considered the best anthropology museum in the country after Mexico City's for its scale and quality, it provides a superb, comprehensive introduction to the Gulf Coast civilizations, the highlight being its splendid Olmec stone sculptures. The 1.5m-wide (5ft) carved basalt heads from San Lorenzo are up to 1,000 years old, and each one has a different expression as well as the characteristically flat nose. Note the exquisite jade masks from 900BC and the lovely *El Señor de las Limas*, a stone sculpture of a priest sitting cross-legged holding a limp child in his arms. Look for the Xipetotec standing stone figure with flayed skin representing the victim of a sacrificial rite and, less gruesome, the adorable little toys from central Veracruz—dogs on wheels and smiling clay figurines on swings.

An exceedingly pleasant retreat from the bustle of the city is the Hacienda Casa de Santa Anna (Tue–Sun 10–5), 10km (6 miles) outside Xalapa on the road to Veracruz. This colonial hacienda was built by Juan Lencero, a soldier who arrived in Mexico with Hernán Cortés. It later became the residence of general and president Antonio López de Santa Anna, and today is a well-preserved example of a 19th-century house with original furniture and lovely grounds.

CENTRAL MEXICO WEST

This region encompasses a wide range of attractions. The rugged Bajío, studded with colonial silver towns, is steeped in the heroism and tragedy of Mexican history. West of here lie the states of Jalisco, Nayarit and Michoacán, where strongly indigenous traditions mix with Spanish colonialism. Here, too, is the country's second city, Guadalajara, and then there's the Pacific Coast with its idyllic beaches.

MAJOR SIGHTS

Aguascalientes	**138**
Guadalajara	**141**
Guanajuato	**142–144**
Morelia	**146–147**
Querétaro	**148**
San Miguel de Allende	**149**
Zacatecas	**154–155**

A boat moves through the calm waters of Barra de Navidad

AGUASCALIENTES

Aguascalientes hosts the annual San Marcos National Fair, one of Mexico's biggest cultural festivals, and is home to the excellent José Guadalupe Posada Museum.

RATINGS	
Cultural interest	●●●●
Specialist shopping	●●●
Value for money	●●●

TIP

• With more than 1.5 million visitors, the *Feria Nacional de San Marcos* is Mexico's biggest fair (▷ 203). Booking a hotel room in advance is essential, and if rodeo and ranchero country music isn't your thing then the city is best avoided altogether from mid-April to early May.

313 J7
Manuel M. Ponce 134, Barrio de San Marcos, tel (449) 915 11 55
Aguascalientes airport, 21km (13 miles) south
www.aguascalientes.gob.mx

Founded in 1575, Aguascalientes is capital of the state of the same name. It owes its name, "hot waters," to the mineral springs once abundant here. Nowadays Spanish heritage jostles for space with modern shopping malls, but there are some pretty parks.

AROUND THE PLAZA

Most of the city's visitor attractions lie on or near Plaza de la Patria, dominated by a soaring, fluted column on top of which rests an eagle poised to kill a snake. On the south side is the Palacio de Gobierno (Mon–Fri 8–6, Sat 8–2), begun in 1665, with a splendid interior courtyard decorated with vivid murals by Chilean artist Osvaldo Barra Cunningham (1922–99).

On the west side of the plaza is the cathedral (Mon–9–5, Sun 8–7), built on the site of a hermitage used by workers heading for the silver mines to the north, and finished in 1738. To the south of the cathedral is the Teatro Morelos, where in 1914 the revolutionary factions led by Pancho Villa, Emiliano Zapata and Venustiano Carranza met to find common ground. The meeting ended in failure. About 10 blocks south is the Museo José Guadalupe Posada (Tue–Sun 11–6), hosting a small display of his prints and original engravings. Born in Aguascalientes, Posada (1852–1913) has near legendary status in Mexican art (▷ 37).

East of Plaza de la Patria on Zaragoza 505 is the neoclassical Museo de Aguascalientes (Tue–Sun 11–6), home to a collection of contemporary art, including paintings by Saturnino Herrán (1887–1919) and José Clemente Orozco (1883–1949). Next door is the Iglesia de San Antonio, inaugurated in 1908, with a baroque facade in faded yellow.

Mural by Osvaldo Barra Cunningham in the Palacio de Gobierno (top), with its two tiers of pillared arches (above)

BARRA DE NAVIDAD AND SAN PATRICIO MELAQUE

313 H9 Jalisco 67, tel (315) 355 51 00; Mon–Fri 9–5, Sat–Sun 10–6
Buses from Manzanillo, Guadalajara, Puerto Vallarta
www.barradenavidad.com

Towards the southern end of the 450km (280-mile) stretch of coastline between Puerto Vallarta and Manzanillo known as La Costa Alegre, the villages of Barra de Navidad and Melaque are small, laid-back resorts at either end of Bahía de Navidad (Christmas Bay), famous for its calm waters. Although there is creeping commercialization, both villages feel much more down to earth than many of the purpose-built resorts along La Costa. Melaque is better for shopping, while Barra de Navidad has more hotels and restaurants, as well as a footnote in history proudly marked by a monument in the main square—it was from here that Spanish ships set out in 1564 to conquer the Philippines. Local buses shuttle back and forth between the two villages, or you can walk along the beach.

CELAYA

314 K8 Casa del Diezmo, Juárez 204, tel (461) 612 74 76; Mon–Fri 9–5, Sat 10–1 Buses from Mexico City, Aguascalientes, Querétaro and intermittent services to Morelia, Guadalajara, San Luís Potosí

Celaya is famous for its confectionery—especially *cajeta* (below), a sweet caramel

Boats for rent on the shores of Laguna de Chapala, Mexico's largest lake, with its backdrop of mountains

Facade of the Church of Our Lady of Sorrows, Dolores Hidalgo

spread, available on practically every street corner, which according to purists is better when made with goat's milk *(leche de cabra)*—and its churches, most of them built by Francisco Eduardo Tresguerras (1759–1833), a native of the town. His masterpiece is considered to be the neoclassical Templo del Carmen (daily 10–1, 3–6) with its fine yellow-tiled dome. Just outside the main door on Calle Madero is his mausoleum. Tresguerras also rebuilt much of the huge Convento de San Francisco (daily 9–4), with an imperious courtyard surrounded by handsome confessional boxes. Outside the monastery stands a monument called the Torre Hidráulica, or *bola de agua* (ball of water), as it's popularly known. It marks the centenary of Mexico's independence from Spain and has become the symbol of the city. Nowadays Celaya is an industrial city based on food processing and chemicals.

CHAPALA

313 J8 · Madero 407 above the Sol de Chapala liquor store; tel (376) 765 31 41 or toll-free long distance only (01 800) 363 22 00; Mon–Fri 9–7, Sat 9–1 · Buses from Guadalajara www.chapalareview.com

Chapala, on the northern shore of Laguna de Chapala, Mexico's largest lake, is a resort town with gorgeous lake views and a reliably agreeable climate. It is for this reason that "Lakeside," as it's often called, is home to one of the world's largest communities of expatriate Americans and Canadians. As a result, the town and its surroundings have good sporting facilities, plenty of hotels and restaurants and handsome private residences—the village of Chula Vista on the way towards Ajijic is known by locals as the "Beverly Hills" of Lakeside. In Chapala, boat trips around the lake or to the Isla de los Alacranes are available at the pier at the end of Calle Madero ($22 per person). Here you can pick up fried *charales*, a local delicacy similar to whitebait.

CHICOMOSTOC

313 J7 • 48km (30 miles) southwest of Zacatecas · Site and museum: daily 10–5 · Buses from Zacatecas

Chicomostoc (also known as La Quemada) is an archaeological site on Highway 70. Mystery surrounds the identity of the people who inhabited this citadel, but the most popular theory suggests that this was the site of Las Siete Cuevas (The Seven Caves). According to legend it was a stopping point in the wanderings of the Méxica tribes before they went on to found Tenochtitlán. The Palacio de las Once Columnas (Palace of the Eleven Columns) is Chicomostoc's outstanding structure, and the museum contains a good scale model of the site. But it is its location on a rocky outcrop that makes the trip worthwhile—the views are breathtaking.

COLIMA

313 H9 · Palacio de Gobierno, Avenida Hidalgo 96, tel (312) 312 43 60; Mon–Fri 9–8, Sat 10–2 www.visitacolima.com.mx

This clean and attractive state capital, dubbed the "city of palms," has recovered remarkably quickly from a large earthquake that killed at least 25 people and damaged many buildings in January 2003. The town's focal point is the verdant Jardín de Libertad, dominated by the late 19th-century cathedral (daily 7.30–4). Next door is the neoclassical Palacio de Gobierno (Mon–Fri 9–5, Sat 10–1), home to a mural painted in 1953 by local artist Chávez Carrillo that pays homage to Father Miguel Hidalgo (see below). On the southern side of the square lies the Museo Regional de Historia (Tue–Sat 9–6, Sun 5–10pm), with an impressive collection of pre-Hispanic ceramics from La Campana and El Chanal.

North of Jardín de Libertad is the Andador Constitución, a pedestrian street lined with stands selling crafts. There is also a DIF state-run artisan's shop (▷ 200). Walking east along Colima's main drag, Avenida Madero, you will pass two more tranquil plazas, the Jardín Torres Quintero and the Parque Núñez.

Farther afield, at Calzada Pedro Galván in the Casa de Cultura complex, is the interesting Museo de las Culturas de Occidente María Ahumada (Tue–Sun 9–7), with a huge display of pre-Hispanic figurines.

DOLORES HIDALGO

314 K8 · Main square, tel (418) 182 11 64; Mon–Sat 10–7 · Buses from San Miguel de Allende, Guanajuato, Mexico City

It was in Dolores Hidalgo that local priest Don Miguel Hidalgo y Costilla tolled the church bells to mark the beginning of the uprising against Spanish rule in 1810 (▷ 35). Nowadays the town is a tranquil place with a lovely main square, dominated by a statue of Hidalgo. The town attracts a steady stream of mainly Mexican visitors who come to visit the shrine-like Museo Casa Hidalgo (Tue–Sun 10–5) on Calle Morelos and Avenida Hidalgo, two blocks south of the main square, as well as the famous Iglesia de Nuestra Señora de los Dolores, built between 1712 and 1778 (daily 6–9pm). Confusion surrounds the fate of the bell rung by Hidalgo—it either hangs

The late baroque Church of Our Lady of Sorrows, Dolores Hidalgo

Dome of the Chapel of Napoles in the convent of Guadalupe

Relaxing in one of the Roman tiled baths in Ixtapan de la Sal

in the Palacio Nacional in Mexico City or was melted down for arms. Whatever the case, the bells you see are not the originals. What Dolores Hidalgo can claim as its own, however, is its extraordinary tradition of homemade ice cream, available at stands all around the Jardín.

GUADALUPE

313 J7 · Buses from Zacatecas

Now really a suburb of Zacatecas, Guadalupe is a dusty little place whose chief attraction is the Convento de Guadalupe (daily 8–5). From here the colonization and evangelization of Mexico's northern tribes took place. The convent was also an orphanage and children's hospice. Nowadays it has an excellent Museo de Arte Religioso (daily 10–4.30) with some fascinating colonial-era paintings by local *mestizo* artists depicting traditional biblical scenes in a way that makes quite clear their antipathy towards Spanish rule.

GUANAJUATO

See pages 142–144.

Statue of Father Hidalgo, arm outstretched, in Dolores Hidalgo

GUAYABITOS

312 G8 · At the entrance to town just off Highway 200; official opening hours daily 10–1, 2–5, but often shut in the afternoons · Puerto Vallarta airport 42km (26 miles) to south, Tepic airport further north
www.guayabitos.com

Just off Highway 200 is Guayabitos, a languid little resort popular with Mexican families who want to avoid the bustle of the nearby resort of Puerto Vallarta. Guayabitos is much cheaper than Puerto Vallarta and built on a different scale entirely—in fact there's really very little to the place except a street lined with hotels, restaurants and shops selling inflatable plastic toys. The beach is pleasant and the sea calm, although in high season it can get very crowded. Many of the hotels have swimming pools overlooking the beach and there is a good selection of bungalows in the more peaceful, southern end of town. Whale-watching tours run from December to March.

IXTAPAN DE LA SAL

314 K9 · Buses from Mexico City, Toluca, Taxco, Coatepec and Cuernavaca

Ixtapan de la Sal is a pleasant leisure resort with medicinal hot springs, surrounded by attractive pine forests on Route 55. In the middle of this quiet, whitewashed town is the municipal spa (daily 7–6), refurbished in 2004 and equipped with thermal and mud baths, hydro-massage facilities, individual changing rooms and masseurs. It's very pleasant, particularly in the mornings before midday, but can get crowded during school holidays.

For those after a more exclusive experience, the Parque Los Trece Lagos spa is set in private grounds at the edge of town, with its own train and numerous idyllic picnic spots. Private baths cost $10 for admission only—everything else is extra. There is also an Olympic-size swimming pool, rowing facilities and a 150m-long (492ft) water slide (prohibited to those over 40 years old).

Alternatively, try the Hotel Ixtapan Spa on Boulevard San Román, which offers total pampering—including aromatherapy, Thai and Swedish massages, facials and "detox" packages, as well as three tennis courts and an 18-hole golf course.

IXTLÁN DEL RÍO

313 H8 · Los Toriles: daily 9–6 · Buses from Tequila, Guadalajara and Tepic · To reach Los Toriles by car from Ixtlán del Río, pass the Cristo Rey bullring on your right before turning left at the sign and over the railway tracks into the site

Ixtlán del Rio is an unremarkable small town with an agricultural economy. The chief reason for stopping here is to visit the ruins of Los Toriles, a Toltec ceremonial base on a warm, windswept plain 2km (1.2 miles) out of town on Highway 15. The archaeological remains open to the public cover around 8ha (20 acres) and include 15 structures, representing the key ceremonial hub of the original 50ha (123-acre) settlement.

The city enjoyed its heyday from around AD750 to 900. Its most significant structure is the Temple to Quetzalcóatl, noted for its unusual circular shape and cruciform windows. It is topped by two small pyramids thought to commemorate the sun and moon, though archaeologists believe the site was dedicated to the god of wind. There is a caretaker and some faded explanatory notes dotted around the site, but no real facilities.

Orozco's mural in the Palacio de Gobierno (top left)
The Independence Bell (top right)
Mercado de la Libertad (above)

GUADALAJARA

Mexico's second city, home to masterpieces by muralist José Clemente Orozco, is full of graceful colonial arcades, or *portales*, which flank the old plazas and shaded parks. It also has some of the region's best craft shopping.

AROUND THE CATHEDRAL

The heart of the city is Plaza de Armas. On its north side is the cathedral, built in a medley of styles—its two spires were replaced after an 1818 earthquake destroyed the originals, and the dome dates from 1875. On the east side of the plaza in elegantly severe baroque style is the Palacio de Gobierno, which houses a striking Orozco mural depicting the looming figure of Independence hero Miguel Hidalgo.

East of the cathedral is the Plaza de la Liberación, overlooked by the Teatro Degollado, where Guadalajara's famous Ballet Folclórico dance company perform (▷ 200). On the square's north side is the Museo Regional de Guadalajara (Tue–Sat 9–5.30, Sun 9–4), with a superb prehistoric section and one of the finest displays of 17th- to 18th-century colonial art in Mexico.

PLAZA TAPATÍA AND SOUTH

Heading east behind the theater brings you to the modern Plaza Tapatía, lined with huge department stores. At its eastern end is the Instituto Cultural Cabañas (Tue–Sat 10.15–5.45, Sun 10.15–2), an elegant neoclassical cultural center with excellent temporary exhibitions. It displays 53 Orozco murals depicting key events in Mexican history. South of here is the vast, covered Mercado Libertad (market), known locally as San Juan de Dios (▷ 200).

GUADALAJARA'S SUBURBS

In the northwestern part of the city is the Basilica of Zapopán, which houses a much-venerated image of the Virgin of Zapopán above the main altar. Next door is an excellent museum of Huichol indigenous art (Mon–Sat 9.30–1.15, 3–5.45).

About 7km (4 miles) southeast of the city is the attractive suburb of Tlaquepaque, worth a visit for its numerous arts and crafts shops (▷ 200). And for attractive outside bars and a Sunday afternoon mariachi serenade, there's no better place than the Parián, next to Jardín Hidalgo, Tlaquepaque's main square.

RATINGS	
Cultural interest	●●●●
Good for kids	●●●●
Historic interest	●●●
Specialist shopping	●●●●

BASICS

313 H8

Morelos 102, Plaza Tapatía, tel (333) 668 16 02; Mon–Fri 9–8, Sat–Sun 10–2

Bus terminal 10km (6 miles) from central Guadalajara

Aeropuerto Internacional Miguel Hidalgo, 20km (12 miles) south of city

www.guadalajara.gob.mx
Spanish only.

TIPS

- Tonalá, 15km (9 miles) southwest of Guadalajara on the road to Mexico City, is noted for its Sunday and Thursday markets (▷ 200).
- *El Público* newspaper has a good entertainment supplement, *Ocio*, every Friday, with music, film and art listings for the week ahead. There is also an English-language monthly listings paper, *Guadalajara Weekly*, from tourist offices.
- The old bus station, south of the central area, serves towns within 100km (62 miles) of the city. mainly with second-class buses. To get to Zapopán take a blue TUR bus from Calle Alcade ($0.50).

Guanajuato

For centuries Guanajuato was the wealthiest city in Mexico, seemingly hewn out of the rock. Today it is full of twisting, narrow alleyways, magnificent colonial mansions, baroque and neoclassical churches and hidden squares.

RATINGS	
Cultural interest	●●●●●
Good for food	●●●●
Photo stops	●●●●●
Walkability	●●●●

BASICS

314 K8

Plaza de la Paz 14, tel (473) 732 76 22; Mon–Fri 9–7.30, Sat 10–5, Sun 10–2

Buses from Mexico City, León

Aeropuerto del Bajío 40km (25 miles) west

www.guanajuato.gob.mx
Excellent information on the city.

SEEING GUANAJUATO

Nestled in a narrow gorge amid wild, striking scenery, Guanajuato emerges from the hills as a patchwork of colonial buildings that tumble down the steep hillside, the roofs appearing to be suspended from the floor of the building above. It was declared a UNESCO World Heritage Site in 1988, and has been spared industrial development—there are no traffic lights or neon signs. The Guanajuato River, which cuts through the city, has now been covered and underground streets opened up to relieve the stress of traffic in the narrow streets above—an unusual, often confusing system. The polluted subterranean Avenida Miguel Hidalgo passes directly underneath the Avenida Juárez, which runs straight through the heart of the city. Almost everything of interest is either along here or just off it, down one of the steep, winding *callejones* (alleyways). The only way to see the city is on foot; wander around and lose yourself in the warren of cobbled streets where you will inevitably stumble upon a charming *plazuela*, ornate fountain or one of the many baroque churches.

Looking down over the city of Guanajuato, with its church spires and colorful houses (right)

The Jardín de la Unión (inset left)

The bearded face of Don Quixote stands out amid the complex carvings on the unusual Cervantes Monument (above)

HIGHLIGHTS

JARDÍN DE LA UNIÓN

The city's triangular *zócalo*, the Jardín de la Unión, is dominated by the neoclassical Teatro Juárez (Tue–Sun 9–2, 5–8), inaugurated in 1903 by Porfírio Díaz, with Doric columns and a sumptuous art nouveau interior—all red velvet, gilt fittings and crystal chandeliers. Next door is the 17th-century Iglesia de San Diego, with a stunning rococo facade. After a huge flood in 1780 the level of the streets was raised and in the gap between the church and the theater you can look down onto the original level of the street, where much of the original church foundations lie. The Iglesia de la Compañía, built in 1734 by the Jesuits, with a stunning, pinkish-grey baroque facade, is behind the *zócalo*. Clear glass in the dome lights up the solemn interior and reveals one of the finest Churrigueresque gilt retablos in the country. Note the unusual red-brick ceiling at the entrance to the church.

On Plaza de la Paz, directly to the east of the Jardín de la Unión, is the yellow and ocher Basílica de Nuestra Señora de Guanajuato, with a dazzling gold interior draped with glass chandeliers and an ornately painted vaulted ceiling and dome. The wooden Virgin, seated among silver and jewels, was given to the city in 1557 by King Philip II of Spain in gratitude for the enormous wealth that was pouring into his country from the city's mines. According to legend, on arrival in Mexico the Virgin was already 800 years old, having survived centuries of Moorish occupation hidden in a cave in Andalucía.

ALHÓNDIGA DE GRANADITAS

☒ Avenida Juárez ⓔ Tue–Sat 10–2, 4–6, Sun 10–3

The massive Alhóndiga de Granaditas was built originally as a granary, then later turned into a fortress, and is now the most important of Guanajuato's museums, with items from the pre-Columbian and

TIPS

• Although there is a lot to see in Guanajuato, many of the interesting places are along and around Avenida Juárez and can be visited on foot in a day or two.

• *Las callejóneadas* are a tradition whereby students don black capes and wander down *callejones* (alleyways) singing and drinking flasks of wine. The groups gather daily at 4pm on Jardín de la Unión, and the public can join in.

MORE TO SEE

CALLEJÓN DEL BESO

The Alley of the Kiss, directly behind the Plaza de los Angeles, is so narrow that, according to legend, two lovers kept apart by their families were able to exchange kisses from opposite balconies.

MORE TO SEE

MUSEO DE LAS MOMIAS

✉ Panteón Municipal ⓘ Daily 9–6

The most unusual museum in the city is the Museo de las Momias, where glass cases display more than 100 naturally mummified bodies (see below) exhumed from the local cemetery. Some of the leathery bodies are over a century old. Their mouths gape from skin contraction; one is a pregnant woman and, it is claimed, one is the smallest mummy in the world.

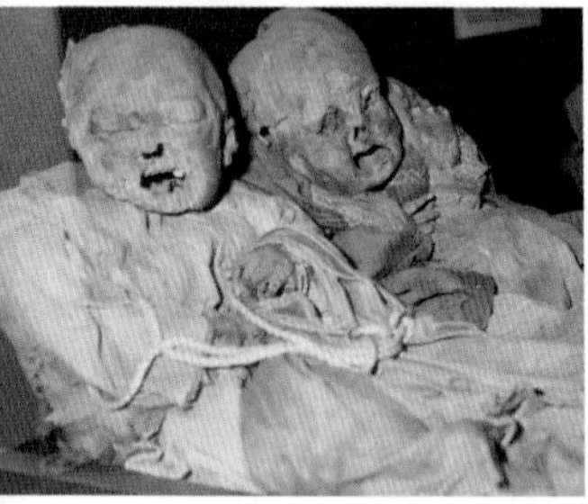

EL PÍPILA MONUMENT

Funicular: ⓘ Mon–Fri 8am–10pm, Sat 9am–10pm, Sun 10–9

Directly over the city, crowning the hill of Hormiguero, the Pípila monument (see above) gives fabulous views of Guanajuato, especially just before sunset when the sun disappears behind the gorge, turning the city pink. Proud and fearless, the statue of El Pípila represents the city's independence hero (see Alhóndiga de Granaditas, page 143). The stirring inscription below El Pípila reads, "there are still other Alhóndigas to burn down." To get there, either take the funicular from Calle Constancia, directly behind the Teatro Juárez, or walk up the steep cobbled stairway, Callejón del Calvário, off Calle Sopeña, past picturesque terraces.

colonial periods. It was the scene of one of the Independence movement's earliest and bloodiest battles. After the Cry of Independence *(El grito)* went up in Dolores Hidalgo, Father Miguel Hidalgo marched on the city, forcing the outnumbered Spanish to retreat into the Alhóndiga. A young miner, Juan José de los Reyes Martínez, known as "El Pípila," volunteered to crawl to the doors, protected from Spanish bullets by a stone slab on his back, and set fire to the entrances. He died in the attempt, and thus begun the wanton slaughter of Spanish soldiers and royalist prisoners. Later when Hidalgo was himself caught and executed, along with three other leaders in Chihuahua, their severed heads were fixed, in revenge, at the four corners of the Alhóndiga, where they remained for 10 years. The hooks are still there on the outside walls.

MUSEO ICONOGRÁFICO DEL QUIJOTE

✉ Calle Manuel Doblado 1 ⓘ Tue–Sat 10–6.30, Sun 10–2.30

This small museum consists of a collection of paintings and drawings—including a Picasso drawing and a couple of Salvador Dalí paintings, as well as sculptures, busts, miniatures, medals, pipes and trinkets devoted entirely to Don Quixote (▷ 203).

MUSEO DIEGO RIVERA

✉ Calle Pocitos 47 ⓘ Tue–Sat 10–6.30, Sun 10–2.30

Diego Rivera (1886–1957) was born at Calle Pocitos 47, now the Museo Diego Rivera housing a permanent collection of 90 of his paintings. The Rivera family lived on the ground floor, where the artist's bed and other household objects are displayed.

MUSEO DEL PUEBLO

✉ Calle Pocitos 7 ⓘ Tue–Sat, 10–6, Sun 10–2.30)

Opposite the university is the home of the Marqués de San Juan de Rayas, one of the city's notoriously wealthy silver barons. Now displaying an assorted collection of local art, the museum's highlight is the room covered in murals by José Chávez Morado (1909–2002), one of the most important Mexican muralists of the present day.

IGLESIA DE LA VALENCIANA

The splendid Iglesia de La Valenciana (daily 7–7) is 5km (3 miles) out of town on the road to Dolores Hidalgo. Built between 1765 and 1788 for the workers of the Valenciana silver mine, it opened in 1548 and was for hundreds of years the richest in the world. Behind the elaborate facade carved in pink *cantera* stone, the church is a profusion of Churrigueresque gilt, with three huge gold-painted wooden altarpieces and a wooden pulpit of sinuous design.

About 400m (440 yards) down a dusty path to the left of the church is the mine (daily 9–8), still functioning though on a much reduced scale. Guides are on hand to show you around the workings, nowadays little more than some rusting machinery and decayed buildings. To the left of the church is the Casa del Conde de la Valenciana (▷ 201), a stunning colonial hacienda. Formerly the mining company's headquarters, it is now an attractive craft shop with a pleasant café in the courtyard.

BACKGROUND

The city's name derives from the Tarascan word Quanax-Huato, "place of frogs," and they are much in evidence—in stone sculpture, on T-shirts and as souvenir gifts. The nomadic Chichimec people inhabited this region before the Conquest and continued to invade the town long after it was founded in 1570. Decreed a city in 1741 by King Philip V of Spain, for centuries Guanajuato was the wealthiest city in Mexico, its mines producing silver and gold in staggering quantities, enriching both the city and the Spanish Crown. Today, Guanajuato is above all a cultural and university city. The *Festival Cervantino* (▷ 203) is the largest cultural event in the country and an important showcase for alternative and contemporary dramatic arts. Guanajuato's most famous son at present is Mexico's first non-PRI president, Vicente Fox.

León, with its fountains (above) and statues (below), is a delightful place to spend a relaxing morning or afternoon

Manzanillo, "swordfish capital of the world," has a busy harbor

LEÓN

313 J8 Adolfo López Mateos 1511, tel (477) 763 44 01; Mon–Fri 9–2, 4–5 Buses from Mexico City, Guanajuato, Querétaro, Aguascalientes Del Bajio International airport (also serving Guanajuato), 20km (12 miles) www.leon-mexico.com

Set in the fertile plain of the Gómez River, León is one of Mexico's fastest-growing cities. Much of the outskirts are taken up by light manufacturing industries and agrobusiness. The good news is that León is the place to pick up top-quality leather goods and shoes at rock-bottom prices; you'll find the best bargains around the bus station.

In the middle of town, the pedestrianized Plaza Fundadores is dominated by the Jesuit-built cathedral, completed in 1837, and the Palacio Municipal, with a fine clock tower said to have been built as a result of a winning lottery ticket bought by a local doctor. Also on the main square is the Casa de Cultura, which hosts contemporary art exhibitions (check notice boards in doorways for current events). Just three blocks away at Madero 721 is the unusual Templo Expiatorio (Thu–Tue 10–12), a soaring Gothic church begun in 1921 and only finished in 2000. In addition to striking modern stained-glass windows, there is an interesting crypt (Fri–Sun 10–1) at the left-hand side of the main entrance. Farther afield at Boulevard Francisco Villa 202 is the Explora Science Museum (▷ 201), with its giant IMAX screen and old steam engines.

MALINALCO

314 L9 10–5 $3 Buses from Mexico City

Perched above the attractive town of Malinalco are the remarkable partly excavated ruins of the same name. The site (reached by more than 400 steps) is on the Cerro do los Ídolos and, although small, offers spectacular views. The undisputed highlight is the temple carved from a single monolithic rock, thought to have served as a ritual base for the jaguar and eagle orders of the Aztec warrior class. Particularly impressive is the entrance to the temple, which takes the form of a menacing snake. According to legend, Malinalxochtle, sister of the supreme god of the Aztecs, Huitzilopochtli, argued with her brother and left to settle in the area around what is today Malinalco. The Aztecs built the site in 1501, having subdued the Malinalcans in 1476.

Also worth visiting is the Augustinian Templo y Ex-Convento del Divino Salvador (1540), in the middle of town. Behind an attractive plateresque facade and nave with a patterned ceiling, the convent has interesting two-floor cloisters painted with elaborate frescoes. The streets surrounding the church are particularly busy on Wednesday, market day—a good time to pick up locally made breads and fruit liqueurs at the stands in the main square.

MANZANILLO

313 H9 Boulevard Miguel de la Madrid 1294, tel (314) 333 13 80; Mon–Fri 9–3 Buses from Colima, Guadalajara, Mexico City Playa de Oro airport 13km (8 miles) from central Manzanillo
www.manzanillo.com.mx

Spread along the twin bays of Santiago and Manzanillo, the city and working port of Manzanillo enjoys an undeniably picturesque setting. It's a sprawling place, difficult to get around without a car, though the middle has a certain shabby charm, the beaches are attractive and the tropical climate is pleasant all year round. But it is for anglers, above all, that Manzanillo is paradise. This is the swordfish capital of the world, as well as a good place to catch marlin and tuna. Keen golfers will also find first-class facilities (▷ 201).

MEXCALTITÁN

312 G7 • Santiago Ixcuintla is 65km (40 miles) north of Tepic on Highway 15. From here take a bus or shared taxi to the Batanga quay 45km (28 miles) away Boats from Batanga (15 min)

According to local folklore, the island of Mexcaltitán ("in the house of the moon" in Nahuatl) is where, in 1091, the Aztecs began their journey south, eventually founding Tenochtitlán in 1325. It is a wonderfully picturesque place, an oval-shaped island sitting in a lagoon measuring 6km (4 miles) by 3km (2 miles). Just 350m (1,148ft) in diameter, the island doesn't take long to wander around; the main building of note is the 19th-century Templo Parroquial del Señor de la Ascensión on the pretty main square. In the rainy season (June to August) many of the streets are flooded and locals paddle around in canoes—hence the epithet "the Venice of Mexico."

Morelia's cathedral (above) and Church of Guadalupe (left)

Ferry boats ply between Pátzcuaro and Janitzio Island

MORELIA

The attractive city of Morelia, birthplace of Independence hero José María Morelos y Pavón, has a historic heart built of rose-tinted stone.

314 K9
Palacio Clavijero (south end), Calle Nigromante 79, tel (443) 312 80 81; Mon–Fri 8–8, Sat and Sun 9–7
Buses from Salamanca, Uruapan, Zamora, Mexico City Airport 27km (17 miles) north
www.morelia.mx

RATINGS	
Cultural interest	●●●●
Historic interest	●●●●●
Specialist shopping	●●●●
Walkability	●●●

Morelia, capital of Michoacán state, is a city with grand colonial buildings, courtyards and shady plazas. Founded in 1541 and formerly called Vallodolid, it changed its name to Morelia in 1828. The cathedral, completed in 1744 in sober baroque with a fine facade and two towers said to be the tallest of all Mexico's church towers, is set between the city's two main plazas, the Plaza de Armas and the Plaza Melchor Ocampo. Opposite the cathedral is the Palacio de Gobierno (Mon–Fri 8–5), adorned with murals depicting key episodes in Mexican history. To the east is the most ornate church in the city, Guadalupe (also known as San Diego).

AROUND PALACIO CLAVIJERO

Two blocks west of the cathedral is the Palacio Clavijero, with the Mercado de Dulces y Artesanías (▷ 201) alongside. On the corner of calles Madero and Nigromante is the Colegio de San Nicolás de Hidalgo, the second oldest institute of higher education in the Americas. Two blocks north is the tree-lined Jardín de las Rosas, overlooked by the Museo del Estado (Mon–Fri 9–8, Sat and Sun 9–2, 4–7), whose eclectic collection includes traditional Tarascan looms, textiles and pottery, a typical Day of the Dead altar (▷ 24) and a reconstructed 19th-century apothecary.

SOUTH OF THE CATHEDRAL

One block from the Plaza de Armas down Calle Abasolo is the Mercado Hidalgo with scores of local eateries under the arcades. On Calle Corregidora, next to the 16th-century Templo de los Agustinos, is the Casa Natal de Morelos (Mon–Fri 9–8, Sat and Sun 9–7), where the local independence hero was born in 1765, the exact spot marked by a plain monument and flag. The house Morelos bought for his sister in 1801 on the corner of calles Morelos Sur and Saldaña is now the Museo Casa de Morelos (daily 9–7). As well as exhibits on the guerilla priest's life, the background to the War of Independence is put in context.

PÁTZCUARO

313 J9 West side of the Plaza Quiroga under Portales Hidalgo, tel (434) 342 12 14; Mon–Fri 9–3, variable in afternoon, usually 5–7, Sat 10–1
Buses from Mexico City, Morelia, Uruapan

Above Lake Pátzcuaro (▷ 230), the town of Pátzcuaro is one of the most picturesque in Mexico, with narrow cobbled streets and houses with deep overhanging eaves. As well as the attractive main square, highlights include fine murals of local history by Juan O'Gorman in the Biblioteca (Mon–Fri 9–2, 4–7) on the Plaza Gertrudis Bocanegra. East from here along Calle La Paz is the Basílica de Nuestra Señora de la Salud (daily 8–4, Sun until 7), containing a much-revered figure of Our Lady of Health. Also worth visiting is the Museo de Artes Populares (Tue–Sat 9–7, Sun 9–3), a regional handicrafts museum on Calle Enseñanza.

The island of Janitzio, with its giant statue of Morelos, rises sharply from the middle of Lake Pátzcuaro.

PUERTO VALLARTA

312 G8 Local 18, Zona Comercial Hotel Canto del Sol, tel (322) 224 11 75; Mon–Fri 9–2, 4–7, Sat 9–1
Aeropuerto Internacional Ordaz, 6km (4 miles) north
www.visitpuertovallarta.com

Puerto Vallarta is a highly commercialized resort, with all the trappings of any US or European city, including Burger Kings, glitzy nightclubs and chain hotels. On the plus side, the town stretches along the beautiful Banderas Bay, where you can often see dolphins cavorting in the waters.

Playa Los Muertos is probably the best beach in town, but beware the undertow. There is an attractive old core with steep cobbled lanes that rise above the

Guardian angel of fishermen on Puerto Vallarta's malecón

city: here, at Calle Zaragoza 445, film stars Richard Burton and Elizabeth Taylor had their love nest (Mon–Sat 9–6). There is plenty to do in the surrounding area, from hiking and mountain-biking to watersports.

QUIROGA

313 J9 Buses from Pátzcuaro, Guadalajara, Morelia

The inhabitants of Quiroga voted in 1852 to rename their town (then called Cocupao) after Bishop Vasco de Quiroga, who was responsible for most of the Spanish building in the area and for teaching the Purépecha people the various crafts they still practice: work in wool, leather, copper, ceramics and cane. The chief reason to visiti is the craft market, at its best on Sunday when locals from the surrounding villages sell their wares.

RESERVA ECOLOGICA EL CAMPANARIO

314 K9 Daily 9–6 $2, plus tip for compulsory guide Buses from Zitácuaro to Ocampo, then local bus to parking area below reserve (15-min walk to reserve) Angangueo and Zitácuaro cater to butterfly-watchers. Alternatively, arrange transport from Mexico City (4 hours away)

This ecological reserve, above the village of El Rosario, is the gateway to one of the natural wonders of the world: the wintering ground of the monarch butterfly (▷ 16). The best time to visit is January and February when huge clusters of them hang from branches. When warm air blows through the reserve they rise en masse in swirling red clouds. The reserve is at a high altitude and you will need to walk a few kilometers to see the butterflies. Warm clothes and sensible shoes are essential.

Querétaro's Church of Santa Rosa de Viterbo

QUERÉTARO

The elegant and wealthy city of Querétaro has superb colonial mansions and some of the country's finest ecclesiastical architecture.

314 K8
Calle Pasteur Norte 4, tel (442) 121 412; daily 9–8
Main bus station 6km (4 miles) southeast of central Querétaro. Buses from Mexico City
www.queretaro.mx

RATINGS	
Good for food	●●●●
Historic interest	●●●
Walkability	●●●●

This modern industrial city retains a well-preserved historic core with fine plazas linked by narrow, cobbled streets and elegant mansions. Founded in 1531, it served as the site where Father Hidalgo and his fellow conspirators plotted their 1810 rising. On discovering that the *Corregidor* (Mayor) had learned of their intentions, his wife, Doña Josefa Ortiz de Dominguez, now known as La Corregidora, got word to Hidalgo that their plans for revolt had been discovered, despite being locked up in a room by her husband. Hidalgo immediately gave the cry *("El grito")* for Independence. It was here, too, that Emperor Maximilian surrendered after defeat, was tried and then shot on June 19 1867, on the Cerro de las Campanas (the Hill of Bells), west of the city.

MAIN SIGHTS

Queretero's main square is the Jardín Zénea, dominated by the Iglesia de San Francisco. The adjoining monastery now houses the Museo Regional (Tue–Sun 10–6), with exhibits on the Independence movement and objects relating to the imprisonment and death of Emperor Maximilian. To the southeast is the smaller Jardín Corregidora, surrounded by cafés. The 16th-century Convento de la Santa Cruz (Tue–Sat 9–2, 4–6, Sun 9–4), on Calle Independencia, was founded by the Franciscans in 1683. In 1867 during the final weeks of his reign, Emperor Maximilian was imprisoned here to await execution. Guided tours take you to see the famous *árbol de la cruz*, a tree whose thorns grow in the shape of a perfect cross. There are lovely views of the 18th-century aqueduct (right) with a series of elegant arches from behind the convent. The Teatro de la República, on Calle Hidalgo, is where Maximilian and his generals were tried, and where the Constitution of 1917 (still in force) was drafted.

SAN MIGUEL DE ALLENDE

This colonial gem on a steep hillside facing the broad sweep of the Río Laja has numerous boutiques, restaurants and an active cultural scene—thanks to its expatriate community.

Known simply as San Miguel until 1826, when the town was renamed in memory of the independence hero born here, San Miguel de Allende is a wonderfully picturesque town of colonial mansions, pretty patios and cobbled lanes. It also has a large non-Mexican community, due partly to the art school established here in the 1930s by US artist Stirling Dickinson. In summer, the town buzzes with students from the many Spanish-language schools.

JARDÍN PRINCIPAL

Social life revolves around the Jardín Principal. Around it are the colonial Palacio Municipal (1736) and on the south side the striking Parroquía (daily 9–7), whose neo-Gothic facade was added in the late 19th century. On the corner of Calle Allende and Calle Umaran is the Casa de Don Ignacio de Allende (Tue–Sun 10–3), a small museum focusing on Allende's role in the independence movement.

AROUND TOWN

Five minutes' walk to the north through cobbled streets is the Plaza Cívica, in the middle of which stands a fine monument to General Ignacio Allende. A couple of blocks farther is the good crafts market (daily 11–6). West of the main square lies the Centro Cultural "El Nigromante", also known as the Escuela de Bellas Artes (Tue–Sun 10–6). It houses excellent temporary exhibitions along with murals by David Alfaro Siqueiros.

Heading south down Calle San Antonio is the Instituto Allende, once a Carmelite convent and private residence of the impressively named Don Tomás de la Canal y Bueno de Baeza, and now a cultural center offering language classes, tours and summer courses, from jewelry-making to art therapy. It is also a good source of information on homestays and apartments or rooms for rent. One steep block up from the shady Parque Juárez at the southern end of town is El Chorro, the site of the original spring upon which the town was founded, and where you can see pretty outdoor washing tubs still used today.

RATINGS	
Cultural interest	●●●●●
Good for food	●●●●
Specialist shopping	●●●●
Walkability	●●●●

BASICS

314 K8

Jardín Principal, next to the church, tel (415) 152 65 65; daily 9–6

Buses from Guanajuato, Querétaro

Aeropuerto del Bajío at Silao near León, 56km (35 miles) southwest

www.sanmigueldeallende.gob.mx
Spanish only.

The Churrigueresque Church of San Francisco, near the Plaza Civico (top)

Holy Week in San Miguel de Allende (inset)

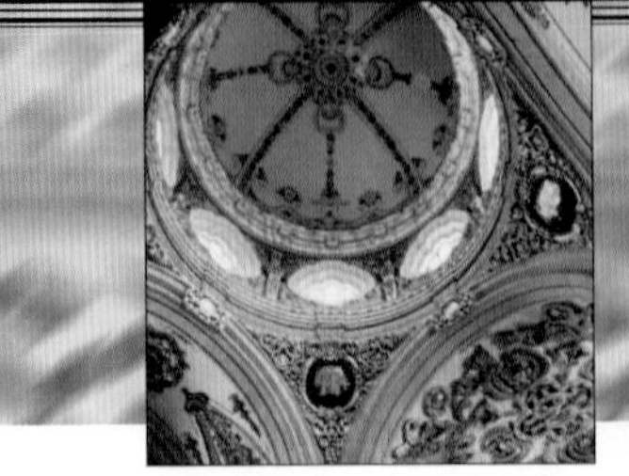

The ceiling of San Luis Potosí's Capilla de Aranzazú

The village of Tapalpa makes a pleasant day trip from Guadalajara (above); an exhibit from San Luis Potosí's Mask Museum (below)

THE SIGHTS

SAN BLAS

312 G8 Casa del Gobierno, Zócalo, tel (323) 285 02 21; Mon–Fri 9–3 Buses from Guadalajara, Tepic, Porto Vallarta

This old colonial port is nowadays a chilled-out holiday resort, popular with surfers attracted by the legend of the world's longest surfable wave (1.7km/1 mile) which hits this coast between May and October. The town's past is reflected in the old customs house, now a cultural center (Tue–Sun 11–6), towards the waterfront. On the hill overlooking San Blas are the ruins of the Contaduría (daily 10–4), the former tax revenue office, together with the Iglesia de la Marinera. Both are worth visiting for the views—but beware the mosquitoes. Since Hurricane Kena hit in 2002 authorities have done much to improve facilities, especially at El Borrego beach. The best beaches, however, are outside town: Playa Los Cocos, 16km (10 miles) to the south, is the most beautiful, and is deserted during the week. Local agencies organize eco-tourism trips and rent out surfboards (▷ 202).

SAN LUIS POTOSÍ

310 K7 Obregón 6, tel (444) 812 99 06, half a block west of Plaza de los Fundadores Buses from Tampico, Mexico City, León, Zacatecas www.slp.gob.mx

Originally founded in 1592 as a Franciscan mission, San Luis developed into a rich mining town after the Spanish discovered deposits of gold and silver in the surrounding hills. Despite the city's largely industrial sprawl, the historic heart retains its colonial charm: pedestrianized cobbled streets interspersed with church domes and tiled mansions are set around the stately Jardín Hidalgo, dominated by the cathedral, whose exterior is crafted from pink *cantera* stone and flanked by ornately carved bell towers. Opposite is the Palacio de Gobierno, which Benito Juárez occupied in 1863 when San Luis became his temporary capital. The most beautiful of the city's churches is the Templo del Carmen on the square of the same name, with

its vivid tiled dome, fine pulpit and striking gold-leaf retablos. Behind the palms and fountain of the lovely Plaza San Francisco is the Museo Regional Potosino (Tue–Sat 10–7, Sun 10–5), with an excellent collection of pre-Hispanic items, mainly from the Huastec culture. On the upper floor is the magnificent baroque Capilla de Aranzazú, executed in a flourish of Churrigueresque. **Don't miss** The Museo de la Máscara, at Calle Villerías 2 (Tue–Fri 10–2, 4–6, Sat–Sun 10–2), has reputedly the most diverse collection of masks in Mexico, some dating from pre-Hispanic times.

TAPALPA

313 H8 Buses from Guadalajara

Tapalpa, a pretty village popular as a weekend retreat, is on a winding road that offers spectacular views. At over 2,000m (6,560ft) above sea level and set amid attractive pine forests, it has something of an alpine feel to it and is frequented by extreme-sports enthusiasts, in particular hang-gliders. Cobbled lanes, fountains and ornamental lamps in the colonnades make Tapalpa an appealing place to wander around. Look out for the Templo de la Merced (Tue–Sun 10–4) and its restored gold-leaf retablo. On Sundays there is a lively local market around the Jardín Principal. The local brew, called *Ponche*, is made out of seasonal fruits including guava, pomegranate or tamarind with cinnamon sticks and a shot of alcoholic spirit, usually *mezcal*, and can be a boon on chilly evenings.

TEPIC

313 H8 Avenida México , tel (311) 214 80 71; daily 9–8 Buses from San Blas, Guadalajara

Capital of Nayarit state, Tepic was founded in 1531 at the foot of the extinct volcano of Sangagüey. The Plaza Principal is dominated by the cathedral (daily 8–1, 3–7), with two fine Gothic towers and a wedding-cake interior decorated in creamy primrose and gold. Outside during the day numerous stands sell Huichol crafts, including bags (carried only by men) and bright beadwork. Five blocks north along Avenida México is the Plaza Constituyentes, overlooked by the handsome pink Palacio de Gobierno adorned with two unusual corner towers. The Museo Regional (Mon–Fri 9–7 Sat 9–3) on Avenida Mexico is worth a look for its collection of Toltec objects and Huichol crafts. The Casa de Amado Nervo at Calle Zacatecas Norte 281 (Mon–Fri 10–2, Sat 10–1) has an exhibition dedicated to Nervo (1870–1919), the local-born modernist poet.

Pottery, such as this unusual frog design (left), is for sale in Tequisquiapan's market, near the Church of Santa Maria (middle)

Toluca's cathedral, on the south side of Plaza de los Mártires

TEPOTZOTLÁN

314 L9 Buses from Mexico City

In the town of Tepotzotlán (not to be confused with Tepoztlán near Cuernavaca), just off the road to Querétaro, is the splendid former Jesuit church and convent of San Francisco Javier, which houses the Museo Nacional del Virreinato (Tue–Sun 10–5). As well as a striking Churrigueresque facade, the church interior, with its five gold-leaf retablos, is breathtaking. The Camarín de la Virgen is a veritable feast for the eyes—an octagonal chamber bedecked with highly elaborate floor-to-ceiling baroque carvings. The convent, built around attractive patios and backing onto a lovely walled garden, is something of an anticlimax by comparison, but comes to life just before Christmas, when nativity plays are performed here.

TEQUILA

313 H8 Booth in front of Iglesia de Purísima Concepción; daily 11–7 Buses from Guadalajara Tequila Express www.tequilaexpress.com.mx

Approaching Tequila you will see field upon field of blue agave, the raw material used to make the famous Mexican drink. In pre-Conquest times, the Indians used the agave sap to brew a mildly alcoholic drink, *pulque*, still drunk today. The Spaniards, wanting something more refined and stronger, developed *mezcal* and set up distilleries to produce what later became tequila. The first of these was established in 1795 by royal decree and is still in existence today: La Rojena, the distillery of José Cuervo, at the end of Sixto Gorjón. A tour includes a video on the history of the drink and the firm, a look at the tequila-making process, a tasting and an opportunity to visit the shop (hour-long tours Mon–Fri every hour from 10–4, Sat 10–3, Sun noon–1pm). Tequila Sauza, dating from 1873 and found on the main square, runs hourly tours (Mon–Sat 10–1). Also worth a visit is the Museo Nacional de Tequila (Tue–Sun 10–5) illustrating the history and evolution of both town and drink.

TEQUISQUIAPAN

314 K8 Plaza Principal, tel (414) 273 02 95; daily 9–3, 5–7 Bus station 4km (3 miles) from middle of town. Buses from San Juan del Río, Querétaro

The picturesque town of Tequisquiapan, in the southwest of Querétaro state, is at the geographical midpoint of the country. Its other claim to fame is as a center for thermal baths, making it a popular vacation destination with Mexican families. Bathing can be arranged by your hotel or by local tour agencies (▷ 203). The central Plaza Cívica is surrounded by colonnades and dominated by the neoclassical Parroquía de Santa María. Local crafts including basketware and pottery are for sale at the market at Calle Ezequiel Montes and Calle Carrizal.

The blue maguey (agave), used to make tequila

TOLUCA

314 K9 Calle Urawa 100, Puerta 110, Col. Izcalli, tel (722) 219 19 51 Buses from Mexico City, Guadalajara

At 2,680m (8,793ft), Toluca is the highest city in Mexico and capital of the state of the same name. Named after the god Toltzin, meaning "he who leans his head" in Nahuatl, Toluca is nowadays an industrial powerhouse whose outskirts dwarf its colonial heart. The spacious Plaza de los Mártires is at the city's heart, overlooked by the somewhat gloomy Palacio Nacional and the enormous cathedral, begun in 1870 but not finished until 1978. Next door is the Iglesia de Veracruz (Tue–Sat 9–2, 4–7, Sun 8–5), which houses a black Christ. Northeast of the main square lies the Plaza Garibay, whose highlight is the splendid Jardín Botánico Cosmovitral (Tue–Sun 10–6), a former market that in 1980 was reopened as a botanical garden. If possible, visit on a sunny day when the light is streaming through the stained-glass windows. Toluca's real claim to fame, however, is its Friday market, said to be the biggest in the country. Unfortunately, it's increasingly being taken over by cheap junk, but still attracts crowds from Mexico City. The market takes place around the bus station, making non-market-related travel to or through Toluca on Fridays inadvisable.

The gigantic Atlantes figures at Tula (also below)

Celebrating a religious festival in Valle de Bravo

San Juan Parangaricútiro's church lies buried in lava

TULA DE ALLENDE

314 L8 • 84km (53 miles) northwest of Mexico City Tue–Sun 10–5 $3 weekdays, half-price for ISIC holders; $3 extra for video cameras Buses from Mexico City, Querétaro, Guanajuato, León

A half-day excursion from Mexico City can be made easily to Tula de Allende, thought to be the most important Toltec site in Mexico, whose apogee was between AD900 and AD1200. The site covers 17sq km (6.5sq miles), but the most interesting parts are in a compact area. There are two ball courts, several pyramids in varying states of disrepair and some interesting friezes. What has made Tula famous, however, are the four huge *Atlantes*—5m-high (16ft) warrior-pillars in black basalt—on top of the main pyramid. Note the butterfly emblem on the warriors' chests—Toltec warriors venerated Izpapalotl, the obsidian butterfly, as their protector in battle. These figures would have originally supported a roof above the pyramid. Around the bottom of this pyramid, under a corrugated plastic shelter, are impressive friezes of skulls being devoured by a rattlesnake. There are good views from the site, and the *Atlantes* look their best casting long shadows in the late afternoon sunshine.

URUAPAN

313 J9 Carranza 44, tel (452) 524 71 99; daily 9–7 Buses from Pátzcuaro, Angahuan, Morelia

Uruapan means "place where flowers are beautiful" in Purepecha. Nowadays the thriving agricultural economy around town is avocados, and Uruapan is known as the "world capital of the avocado." Its reputation for handmade lacquerwork has also put it on the map (▷ 203). The attractive *zócalo* is at the heart of town, and on its east side is Uruapan's oldest building, the pretty, arcaded Huatápera. This former hospital, built by town founder Fray Juan de San Miguel in the 16th century, is now an interesting ceramics and crafts museum (Tue–Sun 9.30–1.30, 3.30–6) and a good place to visit before you purchase lacquerware. To the left of the Huatápera is the Casa de la Cultura (Mon–Sun 9–8), which houses temporary exhibitions, as well as a good display on the history of Uruapan. Behind here is the bustling Mercado de Antojitos with numerous food stands selling local delicacies such as tamarind *atole*, a thick sweet warming drink, or *uchepos*, steamed pancakes served with pork and tomato. Four blocks west of the *zócalo* up Calle Independencia is the entrance to the Parque Nacional (daily 8–6), an attractive park with many paths, streams and waterfalls.

VALLE DE BRAVO

314 K9 Buses from Toluca, Mexico City and Zitácuaro

The resort of Valle de Bravo, on a branch road of Highway 134, is a charming old town on the edge of an attractive artificial lake. Set in a mountainous area with a temperate climate, it receives many weekenders from the capital who own second homes in the area. This weekend influx means that the town has some excellent restaurants and swanky boutiques—although many are closed during the week. The pleasant outdoor eateries on Callejón El Arco are testament to the town's unpretentiousness, and the yellow and cream buildings, red-tiled roofs and cobbled streets make for a charming atmosphere. Down by the lake, canoeing, sailing and fishing are on offer.

VOLCÁN PARICUTÍN

313 J9 Buses from Uruapan

Rarely do volcanologists get to watch the birth, growth and death of a volcano, but the Volcán Paricutín provided such an opportunity. It started erupting on February 20 1943, spewed lava for almost three years, then died down by 1952 into a quiet, grey mountain (460m/1,509ft), surrounded by a sea of cold lava. The church tower of San Juan Parangaricútiro, a buried Indian village thrusting up through the lava, is a truly fantastic sight.

It can be reached on an organized tour from the little village of Angahuan, with horses and guide included.

ZACATECAS

See pages 154–155.

The stained-glass ceiling at the Jardín Botánico Cosmovitral, Toluca (opposite; see page 151)

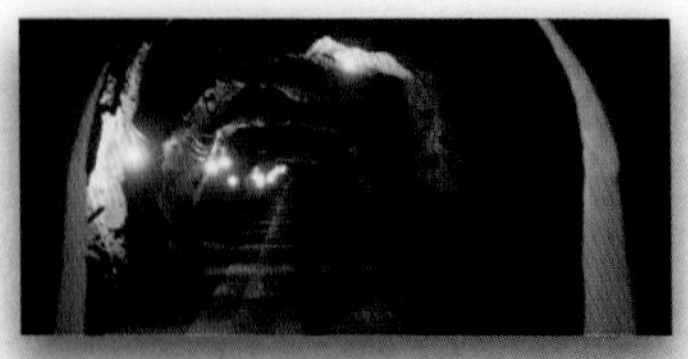

Zacatecas

Built on the fabulous wealth of its silver mines, Zacatecas is a delightful and uncommercialized colonial city. The cathedral, with its sublime façade, is one of the most extraordinary examples of Mexican baroque.

SEEING ZACATECAS

Zacatecas sits in the middle of a rugged wilderness of *nopal* cacti and scrub 610km (380 miles) north of Mexico City. But the city is anything but frontierlike. Its colonial core is remarkably compact and its principal attractions are easy to see on foot. Avenida Hidalgo is the main street, running north–south, either side of which you'll find almost everything of interest. Cerro de la Bufa, overlooking the town, is helpfully linked to the middle of town by a Swiss-built cable car.

RATINGS

Cultural interest	●●●●
Historic interest	●●●●●
Photo stops	●●●●●
Walkability	●●●●

BASICS

313 J7

Avenida Hidalgo 403, 2nd floor, tel (492) 924 03 93; Mon–Sat 10–5

Buses from Ciudad Juárez, Tijuana, Saltillo and Mexico City via Aguascalientes, Leon and Querétaro

Aeropuerto La Calera, 27km (17 miles) north

www.turismozacatecas.gob.mx
Spanish only website.

TIP

- **The city orchestra gives free concerts every Wednesday at 6pm in the Plazuela Goitia. Farther down Avenida Hidalgo you'll find a weekend book market under the arcades.**

The train tunnel leading into the heart of Mina El Edén (top)

Mural on display in the Palacio de Gobierno (above)

HIGHLIGHTS

AROUND THE CATHEDRAL

The city's spectacular pink-tinted Catedral Basílica Menor (1730–52), with its detailed baroque facade, dominates the Plaza de Armas. This is flanked by the 18th-century Palacio de Gobierno, with a modern mural (1970) by Antonio Pintor Rodríguez showing the history of Zacatecas. Opposite, on Avenida Hidalgo, is the Casa de la Mala Noche (House of the Bad Night). According to legend, its owner, Manuel de Rétegui, was a near-bankrupt mine owner who spent his last *peso* to feed a beggar. He passed a sleepless night (hence the name), only to be roused from his gloom by his foreman, who had come to tell his boss of a miraculous discovery of a rich vein of silver, making them millionaires overnight. South of the cathedral is the handsome 19th-century arcaded Mercado González Ortega (▷ 203). Its south side opens onto the stepped Plazuela Goitia, overlooked by the Teatro Calderón, where young Zacatecanos rendezvous in the evenings.

MUSEUMS OF THE CORONEL BROTHERS

Pedro (1921–1985) and Rafael (born 1933) Coronel, two locally born brothers, both collectors and artists in their own right, each have an excellent museum that houses their collections. The Museo Pedro Coronel (Fri–Wed 10–5), on Plaza Santo Domingo, one block north of the cathedral, has a remarkable collection of European and modern art, including works by Goya, Hogarth, Miró, Tàpies and Picasso, as well as folk art from Mexico and around the world (take a guide to make the most of the collections). The Museo Rafael Coronel (Thu–Tue 10–5), in the ex-Convento de San Francisco, has a vast collection of masks and puppets, as well as an attractive garden.

CERRO DE LA BUFA

Meaning "pig bladder" in Spanish Aragonese, La Bufa is a rocky crag that dominates the city, giving breathtaking views for miles around. Here you will find three gigantic revolutionary statues, the most famous being a burly Pancho Villa astride his horse. The Museo Toma de Zacatecas (Museum of the Taking of Zacatecas; daily 10–4.30) has relics of the battle that took place here in 1914. Next door is a pretty church, El Santuario de la Virgen del Patrocinio, dedicated to the city's patron. Directly behind is the station for the cable car or *teleférico* (10–6; cancelled when windy).

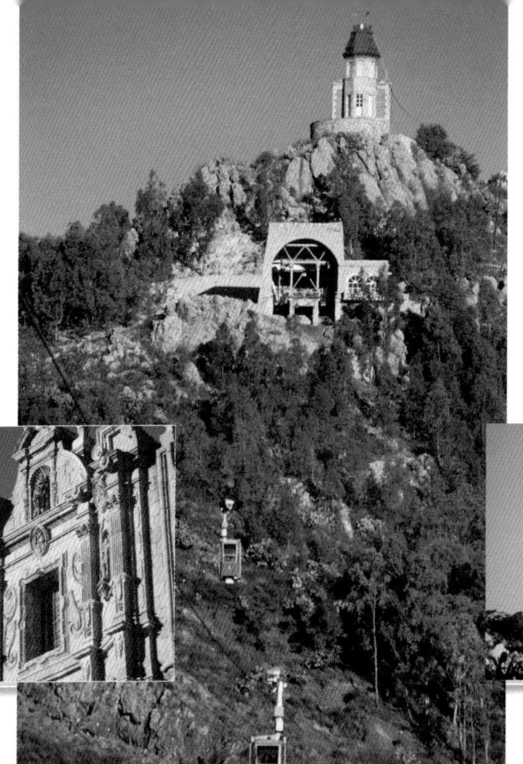

The teleférico, *going up the Cerro de la Bufa (left)*
The baroque Church of Santo Domingo, the richest in Zacatecas (left inset)
Statue of Pancho Villa (below)

MINA EL EDÉN

✉ Antonio Dovali off Avenida Torreón 🕐 Daily 10–6

The El Edén mine makes for an interesting visit, whether you see it on a guided tour by day or as a chance to dance the night away in the mine's disco (▷ 203). To reach the mine, take Avenida Hidalgo south, turn right on Avenida Juárez, and continue along the left side of the tree-lined Calle Alameda until you reach the enormous yellow IMSS hospital. The mine entrance is just behind here. Whichever way you see it, you'll take a train 500m (1,640ft) into the heart of a mine where work first began in 1586, finally ending in 1960. The guided tour proceeds on foot for another 320m (1,050ft), passing hanging bridges, tortuously narrow tunnels and an altar to the Santo Niño de Atocha, emerging an hour later at the cable-car station for the trip up to La Bufa. Take warm clothing as it gets pretty chilly down there.

BACKGROUND

The name Zacatecas means "the place rich in long grass" in Nahuatl. The area was also rich in silver, and the fabulous deposits found by the Spanish quickly led to the city's official founding in 1546. The city prospered during the colonial era and by the beginning of the 17th century was producing a fifth of the world's silver supplies.

After Independence, with silver production on the wane, Zacatecas sought greater local autonomy, putting the state into conflict with the federal government. In 1835 a local militia was routed by General Santa Anna's forces in nearby Guadalupe. Santa Anna separated the city of Aguascalientes from Zacatecas, depriving the state of rich agricultural terrain and sowing seeds of bitterness that still exist today. In 1914, during the Revolution, Zacatecas was the stage for a key battle between the irregular forces of Pancho Villa and the troops of usurper president Victoriano Huerta, ending in an unlikely victory for Villa.

MORE TO SEE

MUSEO FRANCISCO GOITIA

✉ Enrique Estrada 102 ☎ 922 0211
🕐 Tue–Sun 10–5

Ten minutes' walk south down Avenida Hidalgo from the cathedral, Hidalgo becomes Calle González Ortega and opens onto the pretty Parque Enrique Estrada and the town's old aqueduct. On the west side of the small park is the Museo Francisco Goitia, housed in what was once the governor's mansion. The museum has changing displays of modern Mexican art, but its main attractions are the paintings of small-town poverty in Mexico by local artist Francisco Goitia (1882–1960), a radical rural teacher and one-time follower of Pancho Villa.

MAKE A DAY OF IT

About 7km (4 miles) behind Cerro de la Bufa, continuing on the road towards Saltillo just after the Pemex gas station, is the town of Veta Grande on the site of an old mine. The church perched on the hilltop against the rugged backdrop of plains and mountains is an impressive sight—particularly in the early morning, when the scene looks almost biblical.

NORTHERN MEXICO AND BAJA CALIFORNIA

Northern Mexico, a region of arid desert, high plains, rugged mountains and spectacular canyons, stretches from the Gulf of Mexico in the east to the Gulf of California in the west. Further west, between the Pacific Ocean and the Mar de Cortés is a narrow finger of land, Baja California, an area of rugged sierra and desert.

THE SIGHTS

MAJOR SIGHTS

Barranca del Cobre	**158–159**
Monterrey	**165**
Tijuana	**168**

Sunset over the desert in Baja California

The vast expanse of the beach at Bahía Kino, named for the Jesuit missionary and explorer Eusebio Kino (1644–1711)

ALAMOS

308 F4 Calle Juárez 6, tel (647) 428 04 50; Mon–Fri 9–1, 2–5 Buses from Navajoa Airports at Los Mochis (south) and Ciudad Obregon (northwest)
www.alamosmexico.com

Inland from Navojoa on the northwest coast, the colonial town of Alamos is now a national monument. Although the area was explored by the Spanish in the 1530s, development did not begin for another 100 years, when the Jesuits built a mission where the Iglesia de la Purísma Concepción now stands on the main plaza. In 1683 silver mines were discovered near the village of Aduana, 3km (2 miles) west, and the population began to rise—the photogenic old mine site near the village of Minas Nuevas can be visited. By the end of the 18th century, silver production reached its peak and Alamos was the world's greatest producer, but by 1909 nearly all the mines had closed.

Most of the sights of interest are within easy walking distance of the Plaza de Armas. The Museo Costumbrista de Sonora (Wed–Sun 9–6) has a collection of items related to colonial life in Alamos and the history of mining in the area, with good explanations. At the end of January the Ortiz de Tirado Music festival takes place, an annual extravaganza in memory of Dr. Alfonso Ortiz Tirado (1893–1960), also known as "Mexico's Pavarotti."

BAHÍA DE LOS ANGELES

307 C3

Since the 1940s the Bay of Angels has drawn a devout following of marine biologists and sportfishing enthusiasts, including the American novelist John Steinbeck. One of the major draws is the area's whale population, including sperm, orca and humpback. In July and August you can hear the whales breathe as you stand on shore. Easier to spot, however, are the thousands of dolphins that gather in the bay from June to December, and the large colonies of seals. A boat and guide can be rented for around $100 a day.

The bay, sheltered by the forbidding slopes of Isla Ángel de la Guarda (Baja's largest island and now a nature reserve), is also a haven for boating, although the winds can be tricky for kayaks and small craft. Note that facilities in town are limited and the water supply is inadequate.

In the town (also called Bahía de los Angeles) there is a small but interesting museum, the Museo de Naturaleza y Cultura (Tue–Sat 9–noon, 2–5), with good information on mining techniques used in the region, as well as shells, fossils and a selection of arts and crafts produced by the Cochimi Indians.

BAHÍA KINO

307 D3 Buses from Hermosillo

Bahía Kino is an attractive bay with azure waters, refreshing breezes and deserted beaches during the week. Pleasant public beaches provide a good balance between relaxation and adventure activities, with swimming, diving and sailing. The main attraction is sportfishing in the new Kino Nuevo area, a "winter gringoland" of condos, trailer parks and a couple of expensive waterfront hotels.

On Avenida Mar de Cortés, the Museo de los Seris (Tue–Sun 9–1, 2–5) has exhibits about the Seri people, who used to live across El Canal del Infiernillo (Little Hell Strait) on the mountainous Isla Tiburón (Shark Island (▷ 163). Now occupying a settlement at nearby Punta Chueca, the Seri go into Bahía Kino on weekends to sell their ironwood animal sculptures and traditional basketware. The old part of town—the fishing village of Bahía Kino—is more somnolent and down-at-heel.

BAHÍA MAGDALENA

306 D6 (inset) Road west from Ciudad Constitución (57km/35 miles) ends at San Carlos

"Mag Bay" is considered the finest natural harbor between San Francisco and Acapulco and provides the best boating on Baja's Pacific coast. The coastline is protected by two long, thin islands—Isla Magdalena and Isla Santa Margarita—and small craft can explore the mangrove-fringed inlets where bird and marine life flourishes. Naturalists flock to the bay to view the gray whales that come here in the winter season. One of the best places to view them is at Punta Entrada, at the southern tip of Isla Santa Margarita. Fishing is excellent in the area, and a clutch of restaurants serves excellent fish and seafood. On the narrow south end of Isla Magdalena is Puerto Magdalena, a sedate lobstering village.

From January to March gray whales can be seen at Puerto Adolfo López Mateos farther north, where you can choose from a wide number of water-based activities such as kayaking, swimming, fishing and diving.

Resident of Bahía Magdalena

The red-brick Mission of Satevo at Batopilas

BARRANCA DEL COBRE

Rugged, untamed and beautiful, the Barranca del Cobre is one of Mexico's unmissable experiences on one of the world's greatest railway journeys.

308 F4 Misión in Creel (parish church, opposite main plaza); Mon–Sat 9–1, 3–6, Sun 9–1 Buses from Chihuahua to Creel, then from Creel to Batopilas

RATINGS	
Activities	●●●●
Cultural interest	●●●●
Nature and wildlife	●●●●●

Daily trains leave Chihuahua and Los Mochis between 6am and 7am, arriving around 8pm or 9pm. Delays are common. One-way ticket US$115 www.coppercanyon-mexico.com

The Barranca del Cobre, or Copper Canyon, is one of a series of canyons that forms part of the Sierra Madre, more commonly known as the Sierra Tarahumara. Five times deeper and one-and-a-half times wider than the Grand Canyon, it is one of Mexico's most amazing sights.

THE RAILWAY

The Copper Canyon was first made accessible to visitors in 1961 with the opening of the Chihuahua al Pacífico Railway between Chihuahua in the north and Los Mochis on the coast. The journey is one of majestic beauty. The descent to the coast south of Creel passes through 86 tunnels and crosses 37 bridges, and is considered the most spectacular part of the trip. The best time to visit the canyons is from July to September; while there may be short bursts of rain in later summer, the weather is warm and the Sierra is at its most vibrant.

THE COPPER CANYON TOWNS

Creel, north of the Copper Canyon, is the commercial hub of the Tarahumara region, and a good starting point for reaching several of the canyons. It is named for Enrique Creel (1854–1931), governor of Chihuahua state in 1907, who initiated the building of the railway and planned to improve the lives of the Tarahumara people by establishing a colony here. His statue stands in the central square, just below the railway.

Batopilas, 120km (74 miles) south of Creel, is a former silver-mining town—quiet, palm-fringed and subtropical, hemmed in by the swirling jade-green river of the same name and the cactus-studded canyon walls. It is an excellent base for walking and is within easy reach of the Urique Canyon. Hotel Divisadero Barrancas, in El Divisadero, perches precariously on the edge of the cliffs, with breathtaking views of the Urique Canyon.

The distinctive arch of El Arco, at the very tip of Cabo San Lucas

CABO SAN LUCAS

306 E7 (inset) Calle Madero, by the marina Bus from La Paz www.allaboutcabo.com

Cabo San Lucas has grown from a sleepy fishing village immortalized as a "small boy's dreams of pirates" in John Steinbeck's 1940 novel *Log from the Sea of Cortez*, to a bustling, expensive international resort with a permanent population of 8,500. There are trailer parks, cafés and restaurants, condominiums, gift shops, discos and a marina to cater to the increasing flood of Americans who come for the world-famous sportfishing or to find a retirement paradise.

Spanish explorer Francisco de Ulloa first rounded and named the cape in 1539 and the sheltered bay became a watering point for the treasure ships from the East; pirates rested here too. Now, Cabo San Lucas is on the cruise ship itinerary. A popular attraction is the government-sponsored regional arts center (daily 9–6) at the cruise-liner dock.

Ringed by pounding surf, columns of fluted rock enclose Lover's Beach (be careful if walking along the beach as huge waves sweep away several visitors each year), a romantic, sandy cove with views out to the seal colonies on offshore islets.

At the very tip of Cabo is the distinctive natural arch, El Arco; you can rent a boat to see it close up, but care is required because of the strong riptides. At the harbor entrance a pinnacle, Pelican Rock, is home to vast shoals of tropical fish; it's an ideal place for snorkeling and scuba diving, and glass-bottomed boats can be rented at the waterside.

The Chihuahua al Pacifico Railway (inset) is dwarfed by the Copper Canyon (opposite)

The partially restored ruins of Casas Grandes

The dramatic Cascada de Basaseáchic

The ornate facade of the cathedral in Chihuahua

CASAS GRANDES

308 F2 (636) 692 41 40 Sun–Tue 10–5 $3.50 Buses from Chihuahua

Just a couple of hours' drive south of the US border is the most important archaeological site in northern Mexico—Casas Grandes, or Paquimé. A maze of multilevel adobe buildings, Casas Grandes was once a thriving community (probably a trading base) with more than 3,000 inhabitants. The city reached its peak between 1210 and 1261, before being destroyed by fire in 1340. Its commercial influence is said to have reached as far as Colorado in the north and into southern Mexico. Today, significant archaeological reconstruction is under way and the site is well maintained, although few buildings are more than one floor high: The niches that held the beams of the upper floors are still visible in some structures. A water system, also visible, carried hot water from thermal springs to the north, and acted as drainage. You can see a ball court and various plazas among the buildings. The Museo de las Culturas del Norte includes a scale model of Paquimé and examples of the distinctive local pottery which is made in the nearby village of Mata Ortiz, copying the original patterns, either black on black or beige with intricate red and gray designs..

CASCADA DE BASASEÁCHIC

308 F4 Top of the falls is 3km (2 miles) from town (2km/1.2 miles by dirt road, 1km/0.5 mile by signed trail)

In the state of Chihuahua, the spectacular Basaseáchic waterfall, at 311m (1,020ft), is the highest single-jump waterfall in North America and one of the country's natural wonders. Its scale and power are overwhelming. A paved road leads 1.5km (1 mile) to a parking area where you will find taco stands and a *mirador* (lookout point). From here, a path leads to the top of the falls and continues steeply to the turquoise pool at the bottom (it's best to swim in the morning when the sun still strikes the pool). Two-thirds of the way to the bottom is the Mirador Ventana, offering the best viewpoint of the falls. From here a path leads to the top of the falls and continues steeply—hiking is difficult here, so take a tour from Creel. The best time to visit the falls is between July and September.

CHIHUAHUA

308 G3 Avenida Libertad and Calle 13, Edificio Agustín Melgar 1300, tel (614) 429 33 00; Mon–Fri 9–7, Sat–Sun 10–5 Bus terminal is 8km (5 miles) southeast of town. Buses from Cuidad Juaréz, Creel www.chihuahua.gob.mx

Chihuahua City, capital of the state of Chihuahua and hub of a silver-mining and cattle-rearing area, is 375km (233 miles) from the US border. A modern and rather run-down industrial sprawl, it lacks immediate appeal but it has strong historical connections, especially with the Mexican Revolution, and several engaging museums. Pancho Villa operated in the surrounding countryside, and once captured the city by disguising his men as peasants going to market. There are also associations with the last days of independence hero Hidalgo.

One of the main attractions is the Quinta Luz (1914), Calle 10 No. 3014, where Pancho Villa lived with his official wife, Luz Corral, and which now houses the Museo Histórico de la Revolución Mexicana (daily 9–1, 3–7). Exhibits include many old photographs, the car in which Villa was assassinated (looking like a Swiss cheese from all the bullet holes) and his death mask. The Museo Regional (Tue–Sun 9–1, 4–7), in the former mansion Quinta Gameros on Paseo Bolívar, has interesting exhibits and fine art nouveau rooms, including the dining room, the child's room which features Little Red Riding Hood scenes, the bathroom—with frogs playing among reeds—and an exhibition of Paquimé ceramics (see Casas Grandes), as well as temporary exhibitions.

The old tower of the Capilla Real, where Hidalgo awaited his execution in 1811, is in the Palacio Federal (Libertad y Guerrero). Worth closer inspection is the Catedral Metropolitana on Plaza Constitución, begun in 1717 and finished in 1789. The interior is mostly unadorned, with square columns, glass chandeliers and a carved altarpiece.

Summer temperatures often reach 40°C (104°F), but be prepared for ice at night as early as November.

CUAUHTÉMOC

308 G3

Cuauhtémoc is known for the 20 or so Mennonite villages *(campos menonitas)* which surround the town. Having fled from Europe in search of religious freedom in the early 20th century, almost 20,000 Mennonites from Belgium, Holland and Germany arrived in Mexico. The president during that time, Álvaro Obregón, established an agreement with the Mennonites that they could enjoy total liberty providing they worked the land. Many of the villages' inhabitants are blond, blue-eyed and speak old German; they can be seen in

Kayaking on Laguna de San Ignacio

The village of Villa de Oeste, near Durango, has become a popular location for filming Hollywood Westerns

town (also in Chihuahua and Nuevo Casas Grandes) wearing their distinctive bib overalls and straw hats or long dresses and bonnets, and selling their cheese and vegetables or buying supplies. There is a small but engaging Mennonite Museum (at Rubio km2.5, tel 625 582 1382) that re-creates the living conditions and lifestyle of the first immigrants, and you may be able to organize a visit to a cheese factory.

DESIERTO VIZCAÍNO

306 C4 You will need your own transport to explore the Vizcaíno desert

The road from Guerrero Negro crosses the peninsula to San Francisquito overlooking the Gulf of California (77k/48 miles). These minor Bajan roads require high-clearance, preferably 4WD, vehicles carrying adequate equipment and supplies, water and fuel. A new gravel road from Bahía de Los Angeles (135km/84 miles) gives easier road access than from El Arco, 64km (40 miles) east of Guerrero Negro, and opens up untouched stretches of the Gulf coast. Southeast of El Arco is Misión de Santa Gertrudis (1752), some of whose stone ruins have been restored.

Some 2.5 million hectares (6.2 million acres) of the Desierto Vizcaíno are protected by the Reserva de la Biósfera El Vizcaíno, located south of the state border of Baja California Sur between the Gulf of California on the east and the Pacific Ocean on the west. Encompassed by the reserve are the desert, the Vizcaína Peninsula, Scammon's Lagoon (Laguna Ojo de Liebre; ▷ 164), Las Tres Vírgenes volcano, the Laguna de San Ignacio and several offshore islands.

The Vizcaíno Peninsula, which thrusts into the Pacific south of Guerrero Negro, is one the remotest parts of Baja. Although part of the Vizcaíno Desert, the scenery of the peninsula is varied and interesting and there is an abundance of wildlife, including lynx and the endangered Cedros mule deer; isolated fishing camps dot the silent coast of beautiful coves and untrodden beaches which provides a remote watersport haven for divers, surfers and fishermen. Until recently only the most hardy ventured into the region; now an improved dry-weather road cuts west through the peninsula to Bahía Tortugas and the rugged headland of Punta Eugenia. It leaves Highway 1 70km (43 miles) beyond Guerrero Negro at the Vizcaíno Junction.

DURANGO

313 H6 Calle Florida 1106, 2nd Floor, Col. Barrio del Calvario, tel (618) 811 21 39; Mon–Fri 9–1, 2–6 Buses from Chihuahua, Mexico City

Victoria de Durango , capital of Durango state, was founded in 1563. Although the city has been modernized, it retains many graceful old buildings, including 18th-century Churrigueresque Casa del Conde de Suchil—now a bank—on Calle 5 de Febrero; the French-style Teatro Ricardo Castro, staging operatic, orchestral and dance productions; and the baroque cathedral (1695). A small Cinema Museum on Calle 16 de Septiembre (Tue–Sat 10–7.30, Sun 11–6.30), has a good collection of Mexican film posters, plus old cameras. To buy leather goods try Mercado Gómez Palacio, on Calle Pasteur between Avenida 20 de Noviembre and Calle 5 de Febrero. Parque Guadiana at the western edge of town, with its huge eucalyptus trees, is a pleasant place to relax. There are good views over the city from the hill called Cerro de Los Remedios, from which many flights of steps lead up to a chapel.

Halfway between Durango and Zacatecas to the southeast is Sombrerete, a pretty, colonial silver-mining town, which once rivalled Zacatecas at the height of its prosperity toward the end of the 17th century. Worth visiting is the partially restored Franciscan convent San Mateo (1567).

Some 7km (4 miles) north of the Durango road and 12km (7 miles) before Sombrerete, is the Sierra de los Organos (Valley of the Giants), now a national park. It is named after the organ-like basaltic columns which are supposed to resemble organ pipes.

Desert cactus

Huge cruise liners frequently dock in the seaport of Ensenada

Dramatically illuminated rock formations, Grutas de García

Twin spires looking over the town of Guaymas

EL FUERTE

308 F5 First-class trains leave Los Mochis at 6am and arrive at train station, 10km (6 miles) from the town, around 7.25am; taxi to town $4 per person

Founded in 1564, El Fuerte was of great strategic importance to the Spanish in their aspirations to lay claim to and settle Arizona and New Mexico, and was a key trading base for the abundant gold and silver which came from the nearby mines. Tranquil and low key, the town has interesting colonial architecture at its heart, an attractive plaza, cobblestone streets and several good restaurants. The Museo de El Fuerte (daily 9–8) is housed in a reconstruction of the fort (from which the town takes it name) which was built by the Spanish in the 17th century to fortify the city against attacks from local Indians.

El Fuerte is the first stop after Los Mochis on the Chihuahua al Pacifico railway.

ENSENADA

306 B1 Boulevard Costero 147, tel (646) 172 30 22; Mon–Fri 8–5, Sat–Sun 10–3 Buses from Tijuana, Mexicali, La Paz
www.ensenada.tourism.com

Ensenada—Baja's leading seaport—on the northern shore of the Bahía de Todos Santos, is a popular place for weekenders from San Diego in the US. While most visitors head out to the attractions of nearby Estero beach, a couple of good museums in the town are worth seeking out. The Museo Histórico Regional (Tue–Sun 10–5), near Calle 1, has an ethnographic collection on peoples of Mesoamerica and temporary exhibits that focus on seminal historical events and themes. The Museo de Historia de Ensenada, Centro Social Cívico y Cultural Riviera, Boulevard Costero (Mon–Sat 9–2, 3–5, Sun 10–4) relates the history of Baja, detailing episodes which range from Amerindian history through an engaging series of ceramics, weapons, letters and photographs, to the arrival of Catholic missionaries (information in Spanish and English).

While a tourist village atmosphere prevails at the heart of town, there is a lively and very American nightclub/bar zone at its northern edge. A few small, rustic restaurants and a good fish market can be found on the harbor fringe. Beyond the waterfront the town is more commercial with little of interest for visitors.

The blue waters of the bay are home to dolphins and there are seasonal whale-watching trips (December–March) and bay and coastal excursions available from the Sportfishing Pier on Boulevard Costero.

The Bodega de Santo Tomás, Avenida Miramar 666, between Calle 6 and Calle 7, is Mexico's premier winery, dating back to 1888 (tours 11am, 1pm, 3pm).

GRUTAS DE GARCÍA

310 K5 Salida a Garcí (818) 347 15 99 9–5 Buses from Monterrey Tours from Monterrey

About 45km (28 miles) west of Monterrey, off the road to Saltillo, are the Grutas de García. They were formed more than 50 million years ago and are said to be Mexico's largest cave network. Guided tours, lasting around two hours, follow a 2.5km (4-mile) route through 16 enormous caves dripping with stalagmites and stalactites. The caves are reached via a turn-of-the-20th-century cable car which leaves from the parking area, where there is a recreational complex, including a swimming pool.

GUAYMAS

307 E4 Calle 19 and Avenida 6, tel (622) 226 03 13; Mon–Fri 9–3 Buses from Hermosillo

The port of Guaymas sits on a lovely bay backed by desert mountains and its main attraction is the excellent deep-sea fishing and gourmet seafood. Miramar Beach, on Bocachibampo Bay—its blue sea sprinkled with green islets—is the town's resort area. The 18th-century Iglesia de San Fernando is worth a visit; so too is the 17th-century Iglesia de San José de Guaymas, outside the town. The port area also has some buildings of note, including the Templo del Sagrado Corazón de Jesús, the Banco de Sonora, the Palacio Municipal (1899), the Ortiz Barracks and the Antigua Carcel Municipal (old Municipal Prison) constructed in 1900.

About 15km (9 miles) north of Guaymas is Bahía San Carlos. Above the bay a twin-peaked hill, the Tetas de Cabra, is a significant landmark. There is good fishing—marlin, tuna, snapper, wahoo—at San Carlos, with an international tournament held each July.

GUERRERO NEGRO

306 C4 Boulevard Zapata 15701, tel (615) 157 01 00; daily 10–2, 4–6 Buses from Tijuana

The shallow lagoons that surround Guerrero are some of the best places in Baja for whale-watching, especially during the mating season between January and March. Many local tour operators arrange trips on *pangas* (small fishing boats unique to Baja), with lunch on Isla Arena included. The town is the headquarters of Exportadora de Sal, the world's largest salt-producing firm, and salt is transported by barge to a deepwater port on Isla

View over the marina at Guaymas

Stone portal on Plaza de los Tres Pueblos, Hermosillo

Typical countryside around Hidalgo del Parral

Cedros. From there, ore carriers take it to the US, Canada and Japan. Permits which enable you to tour the facility are available from Exportadora.

HERMOSILLO

307 E3 Palacio de Gobierno, ground floor, tel (662) 172 964; Mon–Fri 9–1, 2–6, Sat–Sun 10–1, 2–4 Buses from Nogales, Agua Prieta, Tijuana, Mazatlán, Kino Nuevo

Capital of Sonora state, Hermosillo is a modern city, resort and heart of a rich orchard area. Reminders of an illustrious colonial past can be found around the central Plaza Zaragoza: The imposing neo-classical Catedral de la Asunción (1779) has a baroque dome and three naves; the Palacio de Gobierno, with intricately carved pillars and pediment, stands amid landscaped gardens; and the old traditional quarter lies a few blocks southeast of the plaza, where attractive houses and narrow streets wind around the base of Cerro de la Campana, which has fine views of the city. On the eastern slope of the hill is the Museo Regional de Sonora (Tue–Sat 10–5.30, Sun 10–3.30), with exhibits on Sonora's history and geology. Not far north of downtown (Calle Rosales and Transversal) is Ciudad Universitaria (University City), whose modern buildings of Mexican architecture blend effectively with Moorish and mission influences. The main building contains a large library auditorium and interesting museum (daily 9–1, closed holidays). Many of the town's year-round fine arts and cultural events are open to visitors (details available at the tourist office).

Don't miss About 2km (1.2 miles) south of Plaza Zaragoza, near the Periférico Sur, is the Centro Ecológico de Sonora (Wed–Sun), a botanical garden and zoo with endemic species of plants and animals, including the rare Mexican gray wolf.

HIDALGO DEL PARRAL

308 G4 No tourist office but you can get information from Cámara de Comercio, Colegio 28, tel (627) 200 18 Buses from Durango, Zacatecas

Hidalgo del Parral's history is split between its mining heritage (lead, copper and silver were produced here for more than 350 years) and Pancho Villa's assassination in 1923. Parral (as it's generally called) is a compact city withshaded plazas, bridges over the often dry, Río del Parral, and several churches. In 1629 Juan Rangel de Viezma discovered La Negrita, the first mine in the area. Now known as La Prieta, it overlooks the city from the top of Cerro la Prieta. The mine owners were very generous benefactors to the city and left a legacy of many handsome buildings. Plaza Baca has a statue called *El Buscador de Ilusiones (The Dream Seeker)*, a naked man panning for gold. The cathedral is on this square, and on the opposite side is the Templo San Juan de Dios, with an exuberant altarpiece painted gold. Across the road from the cathedral is the former Hotel Hidalgo (not in use), built in 1905 by mine owner Pedro Alvarado and given to Pancho Villa in the 1920s. Continuing on Calle Mercaderes, before the bridge, is Casa Griensen, now the Colegio Angloamericano Isaac Newton. Griensen, a German, married Alvarado's sister. Behind this house is Casa Alvarado (privately owned), built at the beginning of the 20th century. Its limestone facade is carved with human faces and animals. Across the bridge at the end of Calle Mercaderes is the site of Villa's death, on the corner of Plaza Juárez. Also worth seeing is the facade of the Teatro Hidalgo on Plazuela Indpendencia.

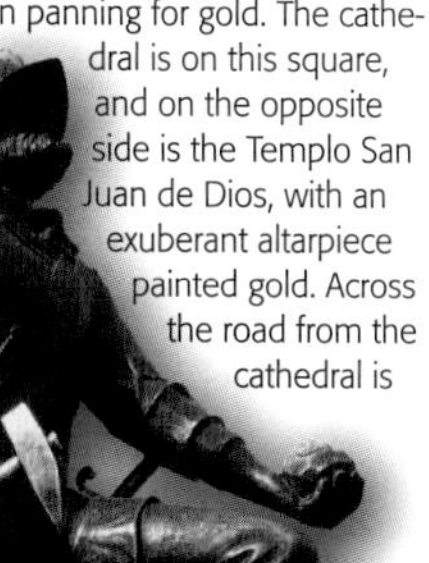

ISLA TIBURÓN

307 D3 Information on boat trips to the island from Seri government on main street in Kino Viejo, tel (662) 242 05 57

Offshore from Bahía Kino (▷ 157), which draws the crowds for its lovely beaches, is the nature reserve of Isla Tiburón (Shark Island). Mexico's largest island is the ancestral home of the Seri, one of the indigenous cultures of North America. The Seri are no longer allowed to live on the island, which was protected as a reserve in 1963, but the Seri government organizes boat trips to Tiburón and the Seri people still fish the surrounding waters as part of their livelihood. A population of bighorn sheep and mule deer roam the mountain ranges, and there are birds such as peregrine falcons, frigates and boobies. The waters around the island are excellent for scuba diving, with depths of 50m (165ft) or more common at the southern end.

Juan Rangel de Viezma, founder of Hidalgo del Parral

This sculpture of a whale's tail lies at the entrance to La Paz

Pelicans feeding offshore from Loreto, a popular destination with fishing enthusiasts

LAGUNA OJO DE LIEBRE

306 C4 Unless you are going on an organized tour, you will need your own transportation. The access road for Laguna Ojo de Liebre branches off Highway 1, 8km (5 miles) east of the junction. Whale signs lead the way to the park; the road is sandy in places, so drive with care

Laguna Ojo de Liebre is also known as Scammon's Lagoon, after the whaling captain Charles Melville Scammon who came here in 1857. Its shores are part of the Parque Natural de la Ballena Gris, where California gray whales mate and give birth between the end of December and February. Most leave by the beginning of April, but some stay as late as May or June. They can be seen cavorting and sounding from the old salt wharf 10km (6 miles) northwest of Guerrero Negro on the Estero San José (estuary), or from a designated whale-watching area with an observation tower on the shore of Scammon's Lagoon, some 37km (23 miles) south of town.

LA PAZ

306 E6 (inset) Carretera al Norte Km 5.5, tel (612) 124 01 00; Mon–Fri 8–3, Sat 9–1, 2–3; till 7pm high season Ferries to Mazatlán and Topolobampo

La Paz, capital of Baja California Sur, is a relaxed modern city at the southern end of Bahía La Paz. First impressions certainly inspire you to move on fairly promptly, but though the ever-expanding outskirts are an ugly sprawl, the heart of the city still has touches of colonial grace, and the duty-free shopping can kill a few hours while waiting for the next ferry. The one real sight, other than the beaches, is the Museo Antropológico de Baja California Sur (Mon–Fri 8–6, Sat 9–2), at Avenida Ignacio Altamirano and Calle 5 de Mayo (four blocks east of the plaza), with a small but admirable display of anthropology, history and prehistory, folklore and geology.

There are many beaches around La Paz, the most popular of which are on the Pichilingüe Peninsula. Heading northeast of town to the ferry terminal at Pichilingüe you'll pass Palmira, Coromuel, El Caimancito and Tesoro, most of which have basic facilities and restaurants. There are buses to the ferry terminal from the bus station at Paseo Álvaro Obregón and Avenida Independencia.

LORETO

307 D5 (306 D5 inset) City Hall, Calle Madero, tel (613) 135 04 11; Mon–Fri 9–3

Tucked in between the slopes of the Sierra Giganta and the offshore Isla del Carmen, Loreto has gone through something of a tourist revival, with the development of southern Baja as a whole and its attraction for fishing enthusiasts, who come here to enjoy some of the best fishing in Baja California. Loreto is also one of the most historic places in Baja, and was the first capital of the Californias. Spanish settlement of the peninsula began here with Father Juan María Salvatierra's founding of the Misión de Nuestra Señora de Loreto on October 25 1697. The mission church, on the *zócalo*, is the largest structure in town and perhaps the best restored of all the Baja California mission buildings. The museum (Tue–Sun 9–1, 1.45–6) beside the church is worth a visit for its displays on the missions and Bajan history.

Some 8km (5 miles) south of Loreto is the proposed super-resort of Nopoló, which was tipped to rival the developments at Cancún, Ixtapa and Huatulco. An international airport, streets and electricity were all installed, then things slowed down as money was diverted elsewhere. Now, the development looks rather forlorn, though some construction is still going on.

LOS MOCHIS

308 F5 Buses from Mexico City, Guadalajara, Tres Estrellas de Oro, Ciudad Obregón, Tijuana, Mazatlán, Tres Estrellas de Oro, Tepic Airport Federal, 6.5km (4 miles) north

Los Mochis, 25km (16 miles) from the coast in the state of Sinaloa, is the departure point for the Chihuahua al Pacífico Railway (see Barranca del Cobre, ▷ 159) which links the coast with the Sierra Tarahumara. Among the attractions here is the wonderful music, courtesy of the mariachis, who roam the lively nightspots and bars.

The city was founded in 1904 around a sugar mill built by the American Benjamin Johnson. The name is derived either from a local word meaning "hill like a turtle," or possibly from *mocho*, meaning one-armed, perhaps after a cowboy who was thus mutilated. Johnson's wife was responsible for building the Iglesia de Sagrado Corazón. A stairway leads up the hillside behind La Pérgola, a pleasant public park near the city reservoir, for an excellent view of Los Mochis.

MAZATLÁN

312 G6 Edificio Banrural, Piso 4, Camarón Sábalo s/n, tel (669) 916 51 60; Mon–Fri 8–5 Buses from most major cities west and north of the capital Aeropuerto General Rafael Buelna (MZT), 19km (12 miles) south www.mazcity.com.mx

Mazatlán, the largest Mexican port on the Pacific Ocean, spreads along a peninsula at

Monumento a la vida *(life)* on Paseo Claussen, Mazatlán

the foot of the Sierra Madre. With its stunning backdrop, golden beaches, excellent fishing and warm winters, its popularity has been increasing, gradually transforming the area from a laid-back visitors' haven to a smarter, more polished resort.

Approaching Mazatlán by sea from Baja shows the city at its most impressive—two pyramid-shaped hills, one with a lighthouse on top, the other the peninsula of Isla de la Piedra (Rock Island), guard the harbor entrance. The old part of town is around Plaza Machado, on Calle Carnaval—far and away the most interesting part of the city. Half a block from the plaza is the restored Teatro Ángela Peralta, the 17th-century opera house. The Acuario Mazatlán (Aquarium, daily 9.30–6), on Avenida de los Deportes III, just off the beach, includes sharks and blindfish. The Museo Arqueológico de Mazatlán (Mon–Sat 10–6, Sun 10–3), Calle Sixto Osuna 115, has exhibits on the state of Sinaloa. The Zona Dorada (Golden Zone) is a developed tourist area, with corresponding prices, including the beaches of Gaviotas, Los Sábalos, Escondida, Delfín, Cerritos, Cangrejo and Brujas (north of Playa Brujas is a rocky area which is good for snorkeling). From Olas Altas, the promenade curves northward around the bay, first as Paseo Claussen, then Avenida del Mar, which leads to Avenida Camarón Sábalo in the Zona Dorada. The sunsets are superb seen from this side of the peninsula; at this time of day high-divers can be seen and the fishermen return to the north beach. Mazatlán is also renowned for its Carnaval in February/March (⊳ 206), one of Mexico's best known.

The Faro del Comercio (above); clock tower monument (below)

MONTERREY

Monterrey has a thriving university, ebullient nightlife, diverse gastronomy, eclectic shopping and some of the finest museums in the country.

RATINGS	
Activities	●●●●
Cultural interest	●●●●
Nature and wildlife	●●●●●

310 K5 Edificio Kalos, Zaragoza 1300 Sur, tel (81) 8340 1080/8344 4343; Tue–Sun 10–5 (sometimes closed at lunchtime) Several major bus routes converge at Monterrey, connecting it to the rest of Mexico and to Nuevo Laredo, Reynosa and Matamoros on the US border Aeropuerto Internacional General Mariano Escobedo (MTY), 24km (15 miles) east

Monterrey, capital of Nuevo León state and the third-largest city in Mexico, is dominated by Cerro de la Silla (Saddle Hill) from the east. Despite being one of Mexico's major industrial players, it is worth visiting for its fine museums.

The city's heart lies just north of the Río Santa Catarina. Plaza Zaragoza, Plaza 5 de Mayo, Explanada de los Héroes and Parque Hundido link with the Gran Plaza to the south to form the Macro Plaza, claimed to be the biggest civic square in the world. It runs north–south and is nine blocks long by two blocks wide; its focal point is the Faro del Comercio, a rust-red 70m (230ft) obelisk designed by Luis Barragán (1902–88). To the east of the Faro is the 18th-century cathedral, badly damaged in the war against the US between 1846 and 1847. The older area, to the east of the cathedral, is the Barrio Antiguo.

HISTORY AND ART

The Museo de Historia Mexicana (Tue–Fri 10–7, Sat–Sun 10–4) off the north end of the plaza is an excellent interactive museum, which reveals the history of Mexico from pre-Columbian times through to the modern era, highlighting the first great achievements in art, architecture and scientific knowledge of the Mesoamerican cultures. The Museo de Arte Contemporaneo de Monterrey (MARCO), Calle Zua Zua (Wed and Sun 11–9, other days 11–7; closed Mon) is a superb modern art gallery. The permanent collection brings together the most influential Mexican artists including Frida Kahlo, Diego Rivera and Rufino Tamayo, alongside important contemporary Latin American and international artists.

Northern Mexico has a diverse range of cacti

La Purisíma Concepción church in Real de Catorce

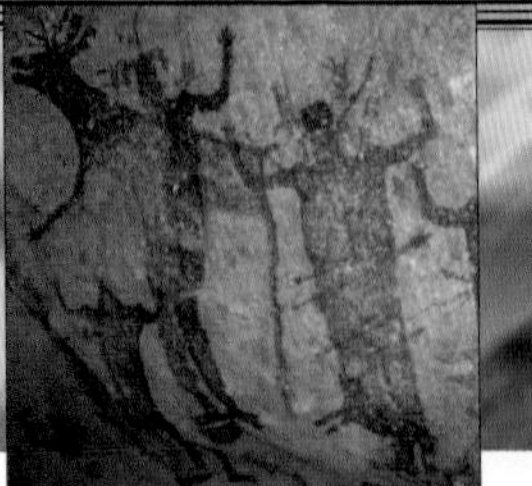
Prehistoric drawings in the caves at Las Flechas, near San Ignacio

THE SIGHTS

MULEGÉ

307 D4 Buses to the south do not leave at scheduled times, ask in town as everyone knows when they come through

Mulegé is a real oasis; a tranquil retreat outside of the spring break, and an increasingly popular hideaway for retirees from the US and Canada. There are lovely beaches, good diving, snorkeling and boating in the Bahía Concepción. The old Federal territorial prison (La Cananea), a short walk from the heart of town, has been converted into the Museo Mulegé (Mon–Fri 9–1). It became known as the "prison without doors" because the inmates were allowed out during the day to work in the town. Just upstream from the highway bridge on the south side of the river is the Misión de Santa Rosalía de Mulegé (▷ 236), founded by the Jesuits in 1705. Above the mission there is a good lookout point over the town and its sea of palm trees. Facing the other way there is a fine view at sunset over the inland *mesas*. There are no banks in Mulegé, but you can change dollars, so make sure you come with cash.

PARQUE NACIONAL SIERRA DE SAN PEDRO MÁRTIR

306 B2 Main entrance at La Corona de Abajo From Highway 1 follow signs for the Observatorio

The serrated peaks of the Cordillera's highest mountain range rise dramatically from the Sierra de San Pedro Mártir National Park. The highest peak in Baja, Picacho del Diablo (Devil's Summit) stands at 3,078m (10,096ft). A hiker's paradise, the park is crisscrossed by trails revealing an ethereal landscape of deep canyons where cascading waterfalls and petroglyphs provide wilderness adventure. The flora and fauna vary according to altitude and range from pine, yucca and sagebrush to sugar pine and the endemic San Mártir cypress, and provide a lush contrast to the barren beauty of so much of the Baja peninsula. Myriad trails afford wonderful views of the canyons and there are many hikes across open meadows to more challenging boulder-strewn rivers. From the observatory, which crowns the Cerro de la Cúpula, 22km (14 miles) from the main park entrance, a trail leads to the Cañon del Diablo, the deepest canyon in the park.

REAL DE CATORCE

310 K6 Calle Lanza, at Casa de la Moneda

High in the Sierra Madre Oriental is Real de Catorce, one of Mexico's most interesting old silver-mining towns. Founded in 1772, it clusters around the sides of a valley with the river 1,000m (3,280ft) below. At its height in the late 19th century the town had a population of around 40,000, but because of falling silver prices after World War II hundreds of people left and many of the buildings became derelict. However, with increasing tourism and the reopening of a silver mine, the one-time ghost town is reviving.

The first church to be built was the Iglesia de Virgen del Guadalupe (1779), a little way out of town. Lovely ceiling paintings remain, as well as the black coffin used for the Mass of the *Cuerpo Presente*. Many of the images from this church were moved to the Iglesia de San Francisco (1817). Here the floor is made of wooden panels, which can be lifted to see the catacombs below. In a room to one side of the main altar are retablos, touchingly simple paintings on tin given as votive offerings to the saint for his intercession.

Guided tours are available from the Casa de la Moneda (the former mint where you can now see silversmiths at work), in front of the cathedral; they include the *palenque*—an eight-sided cockfighting arena built in 1863, which seated 500 to 600 people (this is otherwise closed to the public).

SAN FELIPE

306 C2 Avenida Mar de Cortés y Manzanillo, opposite Motel El Capitán, tel (686) 577 11 55; Tue–Sun 9–2, 4–6 Highway 5 heads south from Mexicali to San Felipe. After passing Río Hardy and Laguna Salada (Km 72)—a vast, dry, alkali flat unless turned into a muddy morass by rare falls of rain—the road continues to San Felipe. When floods close the road across the Laguna Salada use Highway 3 from Ensenada

San Felipe is a tranquil fishing and shrimping port on the Gulf of California with a population of about 25,000. Long a destination for devoted sportfishermen and a weekend retreat for Americans, it has burgeoned into an easy-going beach resort with a clutch of budget trailer parks and activities ranging from kayaking to golf. Or you can just stroll along the wide stretches of sand, contemplating the stunning sunsets.

San Felipe is protected from desert winds by the coastal mountains and is unbearably hot during the summer, but in winter the climate is perfect. There is a good view of the wide sandy beach from the Virgin of Guadalupe shrine near the lighthouse. *Día de la Marina* (Navy Day) is celebrated on June 1 with a carnival, street dancing and boat races.

The beautiful mission church at San Ignacio

The rocky coastline between San José del Cabo and Los Arcos

Store in the old copper mining town of Santa Rosalia

SAN IGNACIO

307 D4

The oasis of San Ignacio comes as a blessed relief after the arid landscape of the Desierto Vizcaíno (▷ 161). It's a very attractive stop on the way south, with its thatched roofs and pastel shades. Here the Jesuits built a mission in 1728 and planted the ancestors of the town's date palm groves. The beautifully preserved mission church, completed by the Dominicans in 1786 and one of the finest examples of colonial architecture in all Baja California, stands on the square.

In the barren hills to the north and south of the town are countless caves, many of which are decorated with ancient human and animal designs left by Baja's original inhabitants. These still defy reliable dating, or full understanding, and to reach most of them requires a trek by mule over tortuous trails. The easiest to visit are those near San Francisco de la Sierra, 45km (28 miles) north of San Ignacio: a guide is required by law. Tours can be arranged through most hotels and agencies in town, but they are expensive. The cave at the Cuesta del Palmarito, 5km (3 miles) east of Rancho Santa Marta (50km/31 miles) northwest of San Ignacio), is filled with designs of humans with uplifted arms, in brown and black; a jeep and guide (if you can find one) are required. The same hotels and agencies will also arrange whale-watching tours to Laguna San Ignacio, one of the best whale-viewing sites in Baja.

Playing with a whale at Laguna de San Ignacio

SAN JOSÉ DEL CABO

306 E7 (inset) Plaza Mijares and Calle Zaragoza, tel (624) 142 29 60 Buses from La Paz, Cabo San Lucas Los Cabos international airport, 13km (8 miles) north

Founded in 1730 by the Jesuits, San José del Cabo is now essentially a modern town divided into two districts: the Americanized resort sector, with swanky condos, golf courses, fine restaurants and new Fonatur development on the beach, and the northern downtown zone, with government offices and businesses near Parque Mijares. The main attraction is the relaxed atmosphere and more traditional and low-key Mexican way of life than in Cabo San Lucas (▷ 159).

The chief reference point is the main square, Plaza Mijares. From here narrow streets lined with restored adobe buildings meander into tranquil leafy enclaves. The attractive church on the square was built in 1940 on the final site of the mission of 1730; a tile mosaic over the entrance depicts the murder of Padre Tamaral by rebellious Indians in 1734. This area has become increasingly chichi, with small galleries and cosmopolitan coffee shops and boutiques. Most of the top hotels are west of San José along the beaches or nearby *estero* (estuary), although the Fonatur development blocks access to much of the beach near town. The best are Playa Nuevo Sol and Playa California, about 3km (2 miles) from downtown.

SAN QUINTÍN

306 B2 The coast of San Quintín is virtually impossible to explore without your own transport Buses between Tijuana and Lázara Cárdenas

San Quintín's appeal lies in its proximity to the beach areas of Santa María to the south, where there are excellent conditions for inshore fishing. Several operators in town can organize fishing trips. Brigades of dedicated clam diggers can be also seen along Playa Santa María. Good point breaks at Cabo San Quintín ensure a lively surf scene, despite the area's inaccessibility, and there is scuba diving; conditions for underwater photography are excellent.

SANTA ROSALIA

307 D4

Santa Rosalia, 38km (24 miles) north of Mulegé, was built by the French El Boleo Copper Company in the 1880s and laid out in neat rows of wood-framed houses, many with broad verandas, which today give the town its distinctively un-Mexican appearance. Most of the mining ceased in 1953, though the smelter, several smokestacks and much of the original mining operation can be seen north of town. There is a small museum off Calle Francisco with historic exhibits of mining and smelting. The cast-iron church of Santa Barbara, a block north of the main plaza, was built for the 1889 Paris's World Exposition from a design by Gustave Eiffel. It was then shipped to Baja. A car ferry service operates between Santa Rosalia and Guaymas from the small harbor.

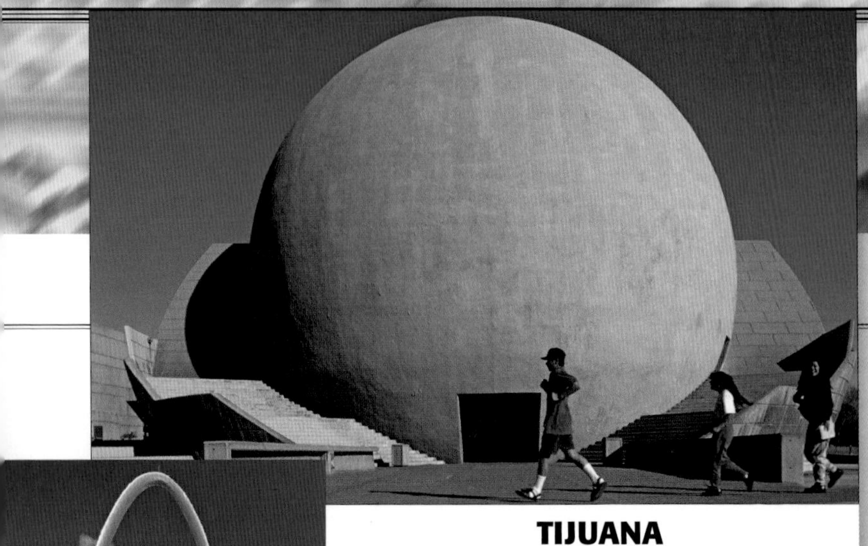

TIJUANA

The border town of Tijuana, the former playground for America's thirsty exiles from the prohibition years, is now driven by tourism, with the lure of inexpensive goods.

More than 40 million people cross the border annually, fueling Tijuana's claim to be "the world's most-visited city": This is the front-line between the US and Mexico, where the two face up to each other in pleasure and politics. Often criticized as not being the "real Mexico," it is nevertheless a historic and impassioned place.

Tijuana came to prominence during the 1920s Prohibition in the US, when Hollywood stars and other Americans flocked to the sleazy bars and enterprising nightlife of Tijuana and Mexicali, both at that time little more than large villages. Today, tourism is the major industry. Although countless bars and nightclubs still vie for the visitor's dollar, it is duty-free bargains, horse-racing and inexpensive English-speaking dentists that attract many visitors. It is your last, or first, opportunity to buy craftwork drawn in from all around Mexico, but remember that this border area is much more expensive than places farther south, and on weekends prices are hiked up even higher. The main drag, Avenida Revolución, runs directly south from the tourist kiosk on the edge of the red-light district and is awash with bars, restaurants and souvenir shops (usually open 10–9), and is generally regarded as one of the world's most popular streets for shopping.

RATINGS	
Cultural interest	●●
Nightlife	●●●
Shopping	●●●●

BASICS

306 B1

Paseo de los Héroes 10289, 4th floor, tel (664) 634 63 30; Mon–Fri 10–7

Bus station 5km (3 miles) southeast of town

TIJUANA SIGHTS

The Centro Cultural Tijuana, a spectacular building designed by Pedro Ramírez Vázquez, on Paseo de los Héroes at Mina (Tue–Sun 10–8), contains the excellent Museo de las Identidades Mexicanas, which makes visitors aware in no uncertain terms that they are in Mexico. Visit the small Museo de Cera de Tijuana (Wax Museum; daily 10–7.30) on Calle 1 y Madero to see historical figures and movie stars ranging from Pancho Villa to Marilyn Monroe and Michael Jackson. There are also handicraft shops, a restaurant, concert hall and the ultra-modern spherical Omnimax Theater, where films are shown on a 180-degree screen.

The Jai Alai Palace (Palacio Frontón), downtown at Avenida Revolución and Calle 7, is one of the oldest venues of this sport in Mexico. This fast and furious game is probably the fastest sport in the world, with ball speeds exceeding 160km (100mph); spectators can bet on each game.

Tijuana has two bullrings: the Plaza de Toros Monumental at Playas de Tijuana is the only one in the world built on the sea shore. El Toreo bullring is 3km (2 miles) east of downtown on Bulevar Agua Caliente; *corridas* (bullfights) alternate between the two venues between May and September. The bulls are killed at the end of the fight so this is not for the squeamish.

The unmissable Tijuana Cultural Center (top)

The giant arch at the Mexitlán Theme Park, where you can see 150 scale models of pre-Hispanic and colonial sites (above)

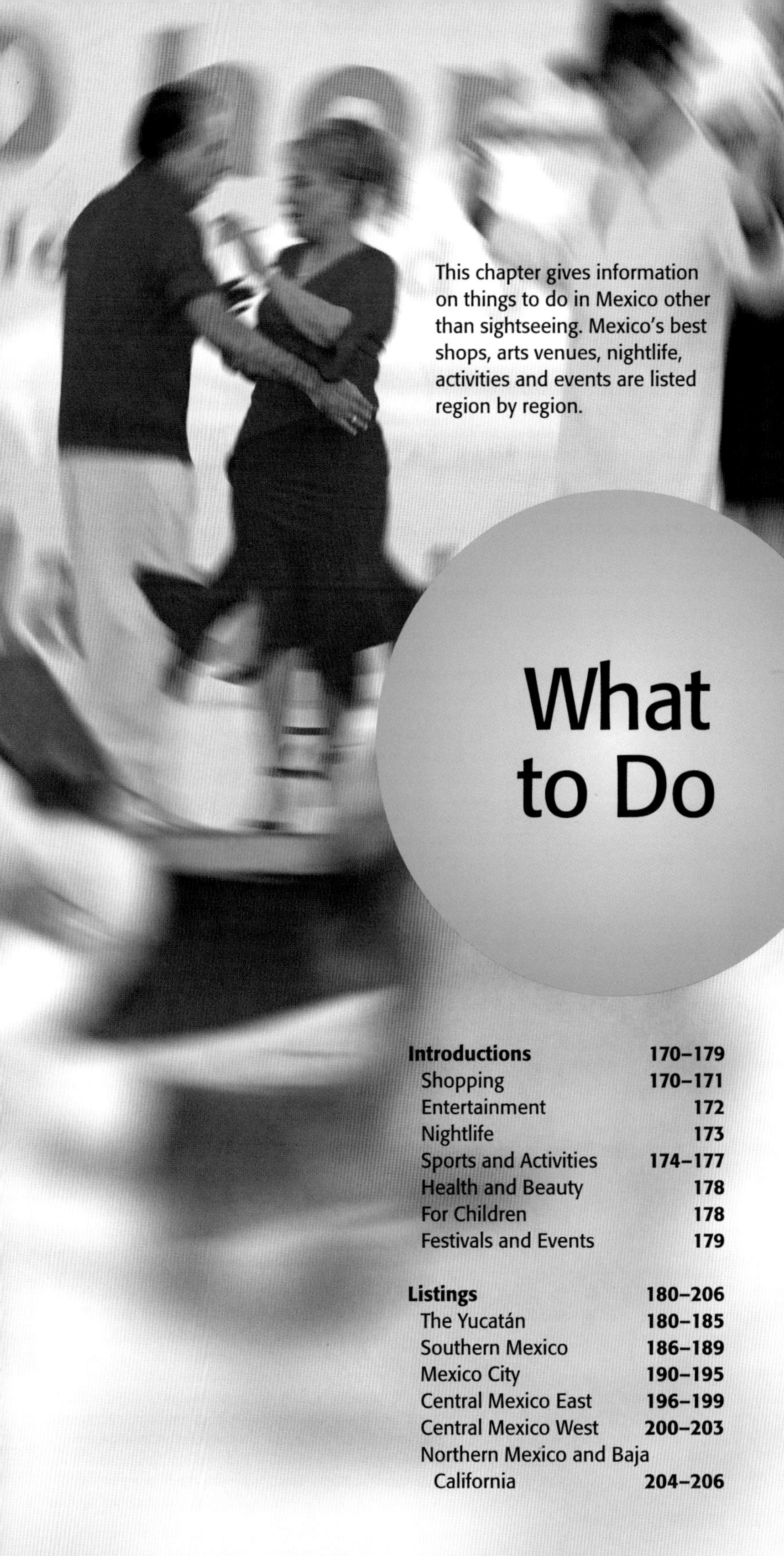

This chapter gives information on things to do in Mexico other than sightseeing. Mexico's best shops, arts venues, nightlife, activities and events are listed region by region.

What to Do

Introductions 170–179
Shopping 170–171
Entertainment 172
Nightlife 173
Sports and Activities 174–177
Health and Beauty 178
For Children 178
Festivals and Events 179

Listings 180–206
The Yucatán 180–185
Southern Mexico 186–189
Mexico City 190–195
Central Mexico East 196–199
Central Mexico West 200–203
Northern Mexico and Baja California 204–206

SHOPPING

Mexico has taken to the shopping mall in a big way. These shiny, air-conditioned temples of retail therapy now grace every self-respecting large town and city. A highlight of any visit to Mexico, however, is to wander around the busy markets and *artesanía* (handicrafts) shops that appear with unerring regularity up and down the country, offering not only a mind-boggling variety of wonderful folk art, but also an exotic assault on the senses.

DEPARTMENT STORES

Mexico's big name is Sanborn's, with branches in all the major towns and cities. It sells a huge range of gifts, DVDs, video games and CDs, electrical goods, jewelry, cosmetics, books, chocolates and sweets. It also has good in-store restaurants (▷ 253).

A fine display of textiles for sale in Oaxaca

MARKETS

Every Mexican town has a weekly market (*mercado*), when people from the surrounding countryside come to buy and sell their wares. Mostly it's food and everyday household items, but many have a section devoted to *artesanía*, while larger towns may even have a separate crafts market. Bargaining is usually the order of the day and there are often some good deals to be had, but it's a good idea to shop around first and check up on the value of certain items. When haggling, be courteous and good natured, and bear in mind that, by First World standards, usually only a small amount of money is involved.

CRAFT SHOPS

It is usually cheaper to buy crafts away from the capital or major visitor areas, but not everyone has the time to visit the villages where the *artesanía* is still made.

Almost everything can be found in Mexico City, and most regional capitals have a Casa de las Artesanías with exhibitions, and sometimes sales, of local craftwork. You'll also come across FONART shops in the main towns and cities. These are run by a government agency and are designed to promote and preserve *artesanía* and artesans. Though relatively expensive, they always stock a wide range of excellent quality goods. The main advantage of buying your souvenirs in more established shops—other than sheer convenience—is that they will often ship items home for you, thus saving a huge amount of bureaucratic hassle.

OPENING HOURS

Opening hours are flexible and vary according to the region, city, town and type of shop. Small shops tend to close for a few hours around lunch, from around 1 or 2pm to 4 or 5pm. Climate is also a factor and in hotter areas, such as the Gulf coast and Yucatán, shops tend to close for longer in the heat of the day and stay open later in the evening. In larger towns and resorts, most shops open from 9am till around 8 or 9pm.

PAYMENT

Credit cards are acceptable in larger stores and boutiques in the main visitor hubs, though smaller shops and markets will only accept local currency. In more popular resorts such as Acapulco and Cancún it is just as easy to pay in US dollars and even dollar traveler's checks. Larger chains charge a sales tax of between 12 and 15 percent, depending on which state they are in.

Traditional Oaxacan black clay pottery

WHAT TO BUY

Artesanía

Artesanía is an art form and a craft skill, lending functional, everyday items an inherent beauty and profound religious meaning. Each town has its own particular special crafts. Traditional indigenous communities the length and breadth of Mexico congregate in colonial towns such as Oaxaca, Pátzcuaro, San Cristóbal and Uruapan to ply their wares, and these visitor hotspots are good places to see the superb range of products on offer, from *huipiles* (sleeveless blouses) to hammocks, from silverware to scary masks.

Ceramics
Ceramics are an excellent buy and can be seen at roadside stands, local markets or retailers in the main towns and resorts. One of the best examples is the Patambán pottery found in Michoacán and on sale in Uruapan. Also outstanding is the *bandera* pottery of Tonalá (Jalisco), decorated in the Mexican national colors. One of the most typical forms is the famous *árboles de vida* (trees of life) from Metepec (▷ 24). Guanajuato is famous for its Majolica pottery, and Puebla, one of the country's main bases for ceramics, for its decorative tiles.

Oaxaca is renowned for its decorative arts

Jewelry
For silver and gold work, known as *orfebrería*, look in Taxco and the markets in Mexico City. Jade jewelry is made in Michoacán, while semiprecious stones such as onyx, obsidian, amethyst and turquoise are found in Oaxaca, Puebla, Guerrero, Zacatecas and Querétaro. Beware of mistaking the cheapish pretty jewelry called *alpaca*, an alloy of copper, zinc and nickel, for the genuine stuff. By law, real silver, defined as 0.925 pure, must be stamped somewhere on the item with the number 925, unless the item is very small, in which case a certificate is provided instead.

Lacquerware
Olinalá is the focus of inspiration for *laca* (lacquerware) in Guerrero and its influence spreads to other towns such as Temalacacingo, 20km (12.5 miles) away, while the Sunday market in Chilapa is a good place to shop. Things to look out for include large chests, boxes, furniture, toys and gourds shaped into fruit and animal figures. Michoacán has the most elaborate lacquerwork, while Pátzcuaro and Uruapan are also good places.

Leatherwork
Leather goods can be bought in northern Mexico, particularly in the ranching towns of Durango and Zacatecas, and also in Central Mexico. Jackets, belts, boots and shoes are all good value, though make sure you road test the footwear as the quality is usually inferior to that found in Spain or Italy.

Masks
Masks are a vital component of Mexican festivals and make excellent souvenirs. They come in all shapes and forms, from animals such as eagles and monkeys, to papier-mâché skulls used for the *Día de los Muertos* (Day of the Dead) celebrations (▷ 24). Good places to seek out masks are the markets in Paracho, in Michoacán, and throughout Tlaxcala state, where you can find the wooden "old man" masks with white face, tiny moustache and crystal eyes peering out from behind huge eyelashes. At Papantla (Veracruz), black wooden masks stir up African spirits in magic rituals.

Textiles
Weaving and textile design go back a long way in Mexico. Many woven items are on sale in the markets, from *sarapes* (ponchos) and *morrales* (shoulder bags) to wall hangings, rugs and bedspreads, which are found around Oaxaca state. Synthetic materials are often used too, so make sure you know what you're getting before you buy.

Ponchos come in two distinctive types: the *sarape*, which is a long garment, and the *jorongo*, which is shorter. They are found all over Mexico but the former is worn especially in the Valle de Oaxaca, where it is made in Santa Ana del Valle and Teotitlán del Valle, and in San Luis Potosí.

Hammocks are another excellent buy and the best place to look is Mérida in the Yucatán peninsula. Different materials are used for making hammocks. Sisal is very strong, light and durable, but rather scratchy and uncomfortable, while cotton is soft, flexible and comfortable, though it doesn't last as long. The surest way to judge a good hammock is by weight: 1,500g (3.3 pounds) is a fine item, under 1kg (2.2 pounds) is junk. Also, the finer and thinner the strands of material, the more strands there will be, and the more comfortable the hammock. The best hammocks are the so-called 3-ply, but they are difficult to find. There are four sizes: single *(sencilla)*, double *(doble)*, matrimonial and family; buy at least a matrimonial for comfort.

An assortment of bright string hammocks

ENTERTAINMENT

Away from the hectic calendar of festivals that testify to Mexico's hedonistic tendencies, the cities and main resorts provide a year-round schedule of good times for local people and visitors alike. Mexico City, in particular, is a hotbed of cultural activity, with classical music concerts and performances of ballet and opera by touring companies, while university cities such as Xalapa are cultural centers in their own right, with art-house cinemas and lively student bars and clubs.

CINEMA

Mexicans are avid cinema-goers and popular movies are inevitably sold out. Latest releases arrive very soon after showing in the US, often before their European debut, and are always shown in their original language, with Spanish subtitles—except in the case of children's movies.

Poster at the Palacio de Bellas Artes, Mexico City

As in Europe and North America, the huge multiplex cinemas dominate. The largest chain is Cinemex, which you'll find in all the main towns and cities. You can buy tickets on its website, www.cinemex.com.

Art-house cinemas, showing independent releases, are prevalent in the capital and large cities, as well as university towns such as Xalapa.

A night out at the cinema is relatively inexpensive, with prices ranging from $3–$4, and Wednesday nights are half-price in the capital. Complete listings are given in *Tiempo Libre* magazine (see Listings, below).

CLASSICAL MUSIC, DANCE AND OPERA

The big cities, especially the capital, are the best places to hear good classical music concerts, or to see operatic and ballet performances by touring companies. One event particularly worth seeing in Mexico City is the Ballet Folklórico (▷ 192). Aimed at the tourist market, this distillation of various traditional folk dances may be more like a Broadway or West End show than an authentic indigenous experience, but is a good night out nevertheless. Guadalajara also hosts its own impressive version, as well as a schedule of theater and dance. Away from the main cities, the best chance of seeing traditional forms of dance is at one of the myriad festivals that take place throughout the country.

LIVE MUSIC

It's difficult to avoid hearing live music, be it in on the street, at the beach, on the plaza or in a club. The main sources of this pervasive soundtrack are, of course, the *mariachi* bands (▷ 23), those groups of strolling Mexican minstrels who seem to magically appear, as if from nowhere, every time you sit down. Plaza Garibaldi in Mexico City has always been a good place to hear *mariachi*, as well as other types of Mexican music such as *norteño* (a kind of Tex-Mex country) and marimba, but it gets very busy late at night and may prove a daunting experience for more sensitive visitors. Other types of Latin music, particularly Cuban, can also be heard in bars and clubs up and down the country.

The alternative rock scene is thriving, most notably *rock en español* (▷ 19), which can be heard in the capital as well as the other larger cities. Details of gigs are given in *Tiempo Libre* (see below).

A flamenco performance in a club in Mexico City

THEATER

Mexican theater can be rather heavy going unless you're a fluent Spanish speaker. Many of the country's finest theaters, however, double up as music or dance venues and it is worth checking these out, if only to see their grand interiors.

LISTINGS

Details of events in Mexico City can be found in *Tiempo Libre* (www.tiempolibre.com.mx) on sale at most newsstands every Thursday, costing $1. Elsewhere, the local newspapers, tourist offices and hotel concierges are excellent sources of information.

NIGHTLIFE

Mexico City enjoys a vibrant nightlife, which starts late and usually continues till sunrise. Away from the capital, Guadalajara and the Caribbean and Pacific beach resorts such as Veracruz, Cancún and Acapulco are always buzzing after dark. The popularity of nightclubs and bars changes, and places come and go continually, so check out the latest scene before making plans. Tijuana's proximity to the US border has made it enormously popular with Americans who come to party.

BARS AND NIGHTCLUBS

Places for drinking alcohol in Mexico run the whole gamut, from rough-and-ready *cantinas* to plush hotel cigar bars. Mexican *cantinas* are, of course, legendary. They are no place for shrinking violets, but an eye-opening introduction to the country's macho culture, where shots of tequila may be accompanied by shots of a different sort. These are not really the place to go for a family night out. *Cantinas* are traditionally men-only affairs, though accompanied women may be tolerated.

Pulquerías are also working-class male preserves, where *pulque*, a thick, astringent and fairly weak fermented drink made from the maguey cactus, is drunk in copious quantities.

Further up the scale, much of Mexico's socializing goes on in restaurants, bars, cafés and lounges, as well as "pubs," a more recent feature on the country's drinking landscape. Often based around some theme (such as Irish), pubs are very much aimed at visitors and young Mexicans out to enjoy themselves.

Nighttime scene outside Barbarroja's in Acapulco

Nightclubs come in all shapes and sizes and range from huge *über*-clubs with several dance floors on different levels to smaller, more intimate places where you might actually be able to hold a conversation.

Mexico City and the large resorts such as Acapulco, Cancún, Puerto Vallarta and Veracruz have the broadest range and you can choose to suit your own musical preference, be it techno, house, hip-hop or Cuban groove. Many of the classiest places in the capital are in the more salubrious suburbs such as Zona Rosa, Condesa, Polanco and San Angel.

GAY AND LESBIAN

There are gay bars and clubs in the large cities such as the capital, Guadalajara, Monterrey and Veracruz, major resorts and in the towns along the US border. The lesbian scene is less developed but nevertheless exists and is growing.

In terms of attitudes towards gay and lesbian visitors, machismo and religion are deeply entrenched and prejudice is all-pervasive. This means that discretion is the order of the day, particularly in rural areas, where even holding hands can offend.

Most bars have televisions tuned into the sports channels

OPENING HOURS

It's difficult to generalize about opening times in Mexico. Bars tend to stay open until around 1 or 2am, but opening times are flexible and vary considerably from place to place, depending on the night in question, or how busy the place is.

Clubs generally don't get going until the wee small hours and most young Mexicans don't leave until dawn. Many places charge a cover of $10–$20, though women are usually allowed in free.

Nightlife in more rural areas will obviously start earlier and finish earlier.

SPORTS AND ACTIVITIES

In a way, Mexico has always been synonymous with sports, from that famous leap of Bob Beaman in the long jump at the Mexico City Olympics in 1968 to the movie reel of young Turks leaping from the cliffs at Acapulco into the crashing waves far below.

Mexico's massive coastline of reefs and swells and expanse of mountain ranges cut by long rivers make it very well suited to outdoor adventure. The Caribbean offers superb diving off the Quintana Roo coastline, particularly off Isla Mujeres and Isla Cozumel. Even if you're not diving the water is crystal clear, warm and impossibly blue, and the beaches refreshingly quiet. On the other side of the country is the wild Pacific with its giant rollers, a must for natural surfers and goofies alike who schlep down here in their droves to catch those waves in places like Puerto Escondido, Oaxaca state, and the length of Baja California.

ADVENTURE TOURISM

The adventure tourism organization in Mexico City, Associación Mexicana de Turismo de Aventura y Ecoturismo (AMTAVE), Insurgentes Sur 1981-251, Colonia Guadalupe Inn, Mexico DF, can provide a list of reputable operators for all the activities listed here and their website, www.amtave.org, is also in English.

BASEBALL

Professional baseball *(beisbol)*, though not on a par with wrestling or soccer, commands quite a following. The season runs from April to August, with the top teams going forward to represent Mexico, along with the champions of Dominican Republic, Puerto Rico and Venezuela, in the Serie del Caribe, held in February.

BULLFIGHTING

Bullfighting is an integral part of Mexican life. Whatever your views, it is rooted in tradition and deeply symbolic. Mexico's *toreros* (matadors) have a reputation for being particularly brave (or foolish) and are in demand in Spain. Unless you are vehemently opposed, it is worth attending a *corrida de toros* (bullfight) to experience this national obsession. Mexico City's Plaza México is the largest bullring in the world, where *corridas* take place on Sundays at 4pm from October to April. Prices are low ($3–$5) if you're happy to sit on the concrete sun *(sol)* terraces, but more expensive (up to $48) for a seat in the shade *(sombra)*. Posters—an art form in themselves—around town advertise forthcoming events.

Bullfighting is still a popular form of entertainment in Mexico

Snorkeling in the crystal clear waters round Cozumel

CANYONING

Canyoning, or canyoneering, is the practice of climbing up and down waterfalls, swimming through rivers and scrambling through caves and over huge rocks. Two of the best locations for this infant sport are the Cañadas de Cotlamani, near Jalcomulco in Veracruz, and Cumbres de Monterrey National Park.

CAVING

Caving, or speleology, in Mexico is more than just going down into deep dark holes. Sometimes it is a sport more closely related to canyoning, as there are some excellent underground river scrambles. The best of these is probably the 8km-long (5-mile) Chontalcuatlán, a part of the Cacahuamilpa cave system near Taxco. Other possibilities are in Cuetzalan, near Puebla. Beside the Matacanes River circuit in Nuevo León, near Monterrey (see Canyoning above) there are some large caves—the Grutas de La Tierrosa, La Cebolla and Pterodáctilo. The biggest cave systems are in Chiapas, especially around Tuxtla Gutiérrez.

CENOTE DIVING

There are over 50 *cenotes* (natural sinkholes) on the Yucatán peninsula, accessible from Ruta 307 and often well

marked. *Cenote* diving has become very popular in recent years. However, it is a specialized sport and can be very dangerous: Unless you have a cave-diving qualification, you must be accompanied by a qualified dive master. A cave-diving course involves over 12 hours of lectures and a minimum of 14 cave dives using double tanks, costing around $600. Some of the best *cenotes* are "Carwash," on the Cobá road, good even for beginners, with excellent visibility; and "Dos Ojos," just off Ruta 307 south of Puerto Aventuras, the second largest underground cave system in the world. It has a possible link

Golf has become a major attraction in Mexico

to the Nohoch Nah Chich, the most famous *cenote* and part of a subterranean system recorded as the world's largest, with more than 50km (31 miles) of surveyed passageways connected to the sea.

CLIMBING

The main climbing region is in the highlands, with several peaks over 5,000m (16,400ft). The big glaciated volcanoes are within relatively easy reach of Mexico City. Although there are few technical routes, crampons, an ice axe and occasionally rope are required for safe ascents. The season is October to May. Now that Popocatépetl (5,452m/17,888ft) and Colima Volcano (3,842m/12,605ft) are sporadically erupting, the two remaining high-altitude challenges are Pico de Orizaba, Citlatépetl (5,760m/18,897ft), Mexico's highest volcano, and Iztaccíhuatl (5,286m/17,343ft), which offers the best technical climbing. Two good acclimatization climbs are Cofre de Perote (Nouhcampatépetl, 4,282m/14,049ft) and Nevado de Toluca (Xinantécatl, 4,583m/15,036ft).

DIVING

There's good diving off most of Mexico's coastline but two regions, Quintana Roo and Baja California, at opposite ends of the country, stand out. Cozumel, in Quintana Roo, has some of the best diving in the world and there are marine parks at Chankanaab and at Palancar Reef, with numerous caves and gullies and a horseshoe-shaped diving arena.

Southern Baja is warmer than the north but it is still advisable to wear a wetsuit, not least to protect from skin-irritating hydroza organisms.

A diving organization, the Club de Exploraciones y Deportes Acuáticos de México (CEDAM), is based in Puerto Aventuras.

GOLF

Some of Mexico's best golf courses are attached to hotels. Check out information on www.worldgolf.com/golfdestinations/mexico

HIKING AND WALKING

Mexico's national parks were set up a long time ago primarily to provide green recreation areas for city dwellers. In Chiapas, El Triunfo Biosphere Reserve protects Mexico's only cloud forest, on the mountains (up to 2,750m/9,020ft) above the Pacific coast. The main hiking route runs from Jaltenango (reached by bus from Tuxtla) to Mapastepec on the coastal highway. Groups need to book in advance through the state's Institute of Natural History, on Calzada de Hombres de la Revolución, by the botanical garden and Regional Museum (Apartido 391, Tuxtla 29000; tel (961) 612 36 63).

Another excellent area for hiking is the Copper Canyon. Creel is the best base, but an excellent trek is from Batópilas to Urique—three days in the heart of the Barranca, through Tarahumara lands. The best hiking within easy reach of a major city is around Monterrey, particularly in the Cumbres de Monterrey National Park.

The Instituto Geográfico Militar sells topographical

Scuba diving lesson in a swimming pool in Cancún

maps, scale 1:100,000 or 1:50,000. The physical features shown on these are usually accurate; the trails and place-names less so. National park offices also sell maps.

Trekking should not be approached casually. Even if you only plan to be out a couple of hours you should have comfortable, safe footwear (which can cope with the wet) and a daypack.

JAI ALAI

Also known as *frontón* or *pelota*, this fast-paced Basque game is played with a curved scoop attached to the player's hand, which is used to propel the ball against a large wall at

high speed, rather like squash. This isn't so much a spectator sport, however, as a way to win, or lose, money on bets.

ROCK CLIMBING

This is an increasingly popular sport for Mexicans and there is very good climbing in most parts of the country. On the outskirts of the capital there are two convenient natural high-rises above the smog: the cliffs at Magdalena Contreras to the southwest and at Naucalpan to the northwest. Going north of the capital, 70km (43 miles) east of Querétaro, is the Peñón de Bernal, the world's largest monolith after Ayer's Rock in Australia. The north face route is 400m (1,312ft) in elevation. You have to go much farther north, to Monterrey, for the best rock in Mexico. Near the small town of Hidalgo is the Potrero Chico big wall, 650m (2,132ft) of limestone nirvana.

Contact the Club Alpino Mexicano, AC Coahuila 40, Espuina Córdoba, Colonia Roma, México DF; tel (55) 55 74 96 83, www.clubalpinomexicano.com.mx, for more details and advice.

Kayaking in the warm waters of the Sea of Cortés

RODEOS

Charrerías, as they are known in Mexico, take place mostly in northern towns and cities and are lively events, notable as much for their glitz and glitter as the horsemanship of the various competitors. In Baja *charrerías* are held most weekends from May to September.

SEA KAYAKING

This requires no special prior expertise and you can usually take off on your own in quiet waters for day trips. The warm waters of the Sea of Cortés off Baja California Sur are kayak heaven. Isla Espirítu Santo and Isla Partida are easily accessible from La Paz, and whether in or out of your kayak you can experience a fine display of stingrays, sea lions, dolphins, porpoises and occasionally gray whales and hammerheads. Farther up the coast, Loreto is another good base for hiring gear and at Bahía Coyote, near Santispac, on the mainland side of the larger and more encompassing Bahía Concepción, there are many small islands you can explore in a day on calm waters. The Baja Sea Kayak Association is based in La Paz. The simplest kayaks are more like rafts and have no open compartments, so there's no need to worry about flooding. Agencies will assess your experience when renting out more advanced equipment or basic equipment for longer periods.

SOCCER

Bullfighting may be an obsession but soccer, or football *(fútbol),* is by far the most popular spectator sport in Mexico. The biggest club teams are those from the capital, particularly América and Necaxa, who both play their home games at the Estadio Azteca (Aztec Stadium), and Guadalajara. Perhaps the biggest game in the soccer calendar is América (Mexico City) versus Chivas (Guadalajara), which fills the 114,000-seat Aztec Stadium. The university team, Pumas UNAM, who play their games at the Estadio Olimpico in Mexico City are also a strong side, as are Cruz Azul, also based in the capital. Games are played on Sunday afternoons during the season, from August to May, and tickets are normally easy to come by at the ground; the exceptions are the big games and local derbies. Check the local newspapers for details.

Though Mexico has failed to emulate its South American counterparts in winning the World Cup, it has hosted the competition twice, in 1970 and 1986.

Sport fishing off Cabo San Lucas, the marlin capital of the world

SPORT FISHING

Some of the best fishing is in the Sea of Cortés, particularly off La Paz, around Islas Espíritu Santo and Cerralvo, from Loreto, and off the Buena Vista resort (which has boats), near Los Barriles, 60km (37 miles) south of the Baja Sur capital. Here the high season for many species such as marlin, swordfish, sailfish, roosterfish, dorado, cabrilla and wahoo is May to September. For sierra, it is November to January, and yellowtail from March to May. There are international competitions in July and August and one in March dedicated to catching yellowtail. Tampico, in the Gulf of Mexico, is the focus

for competition fishing for robalo (April), marlin (June) and sábalo (July and August).

SURFING
You can experience some of the world's most exhilarating surfing along Mexico's Pacific coast. Highlights are the huge Hawaiian-size surf that pounds the Baja shoreline and the renowned Mexican Pipeline at Puerto Escondido. There are many possibilities, from developed beaches to remote bays accessible only by 4WD vehicles. Many can be found at the estuaries of rivers where sandbars are deposited and points are formed. San Blas, in Nayarit state, is an excellent learning base. The waves are normally not too big and there are few rocks or dangerous currents. Surfing is best between July and October.

WHITEWATER RAFTING
The variety in Mexico's rafting rivers creates all types of opportunities. The attraction is not just the run but the trek or rappel to the start and the moments between rapids, drifting in deep canyons beneath hanging tropical forests, some of which contain lesser-known and quite inaccessible ruins. For sheer thrills, many of the best rivers are in the middle of the country.

The most popular is the Río Antigua/Pescados in Veracruz. The upper stretch, the Antigua, has some good learning rapids (Grade II running into Grade III), but, if you have more than one day, the Pescados (the lower Antigua), closer to Jalcomulco, can give a bigger adrenalin rush, with some Grade IV whitewater. The biggest rushes in the country, however, are on the Barranca Grande and at Cañón Azul, where there is excellent Grade V water.

Rafting in Chiapas covers the spectrum from sedate floats on rivers such as the Lacan-Há through the Lacandón jungle to Grade IV/V rapids on the Río Jataté, which gathers force where the Lacan Tum enters it and gradually diminishes in strength as it nears the Río Usumacinta.

The season for whitewater rafting is generally July to September in the middle of the country, when rivers are fuller, but in Chiapas, January and February are better because the climate is cooler.

WILDLIFE-WATCHING
Mexico has an immense range of flora and fauna and presents spectacular wildlife-watching opportunities. The wetland lagoons and rainforest sites provide some of the most vibrant birdlife. For the novice, the resplendent quetzal, with its flamboyant tail feather, is an essential sighting. In Chiapas, El Triunfo Biosphere Reserve (▷ 85) protects many endemic species, including the rare azure-rumped tanager. Other wildlife includes the harpy eagle, jaguar, tapir and white-lipped peccary. It is also well worth visiting the Río Lagartos (▷ 74) and Río Celestún (▷ 61) reserves on the north and west coasts of Yucatán, well known for their flamingos. The Mapimí Biosphere Reserve, to the east of Ceballos, on the Gómez Palacio–Ciudad Jiménez highway, is home to giant turtles, now in enclosures at the Laboratory of the Desert.

In Baja California, the Sea of Cortés is one of the world's richest marine feeding grounds and in many places you can see hammerheads, whales and dolphins—if you go at the right time. The best time to watch for California gray whales is between December and February, but you can see them as late as May or June in some spots.

For information on national parks and biosphere reserves, contact the Instituto Nacional de Ecología I Periférico 5000, Colonia Insurgentes Cuicuilco, CP 04530, Delegación Coyoacán, México DF; www.ine.gob.mx. Other conservation organizations include Naturalia I Apdo Postal 21541, 04021 México DF, tel (55) 56 74 66 78, and Pronatura, Asociación Mexicano por la Conservación de la Naturaleza, Aspérgulas No. 22, Colonia San Clemente, CP 01740, México DF, tel (55) 56 35 50 54, www.pronatura.org.mx. Both of these websites are in Spanish only.

Storks feature among the large number of birds in Mexico

WRESTLING
Wrestling—*lucha libre*—is a hugely popular spectator sport, second only to soccer. Imported originally from the US, it has evolved into a fast-flowing sport with its own complex rules and up to eight or even ten grapplers (*luchadores*) in the ring at the same time. The most important Mexican ingredient, however, is the use of masks to conceal the participants' identities. Fights can be seen in Mexico City at the Arena Coliseo, Calle Republica de Peru 73 (Mertro Allende) and Arena México, Río de la Loza 94, Colonia Doctores (Metro Balderas) on Fridays.

HEALTH AND BEAUTY

Spas *(balnearios)* have a long tradition in the country and were used by the nobles of the great pre-Hispanic dynasties.

The Mexican version is not the five-star beauty farm that American or British visitors will be accustomed to, but a far more rustic equivalent, often comprising a series of hot mineral baths of increasing temperatures and pretty basic changing facilities. More exclusive options are available, however, to cater for wealthy vacationers from the capital as well as foreign visitors.

Cuernavaca, in Morelos, is well known for its thermal springs, around which resort spas have developed, and there are also excellent spa resorts at Puerto Vallarta, San José del Cabo in Baja Sur, and at Punta Mita, Bahía de Banderas in Nyarit state. For more details, visit www.spasdirectory.com.

Beauty salons in Mexico are not hard to find, so any visitor needing an emergency manicure or pedicure will not have far to look.

FOR CHILDREN

Mexicans love children and touring with your family can bring you into closer contact with local people. Officials tend to be friendlier where children are concerned and teaching your child a little Spanish goes a long way. Moreover, even thieves and pickpockets seem to have some of the traditional respect for families and may leave you alone because of it.

One drawback for families touring in Mexico is that the anti-smoking movement has yet to reach the country, so restaurants and hotel lobbies can be smokier than you are used to.

FAMILY ATTRACTIONS

Swimming pools with slides, wave machines and cascades are all popular for family fun and can be found on both the Caribbean and Pacific coasts. Museums in Mexico, particularly in the capital, have also caught on to the vogue for interactivity, encouraging children to touch, push, prod and poke to get the most out of them. Zoos and aquariums are also easy to find in most cities and resorts for an introduction to Mexican wildlife.

TAKING CARE

- Excessive heat and sun can be damaging and uncomfortable, so ensure children drink enough water and are well protected from the sun with high-factor sunscreen, a T-shirt and a sun hat.
- To counter the risk of rabies, keep children away from animals and consider giving them a rabies vaccination before your trip.
- Take extra care with drinking water and food. Diarrhea can be dangerous for children, and it is a good idea to carry rehydration salts just in case.

TRAVEL TIPS

- For an overview of touring with children look at www.babygoes2.com.
- Overland travel in Latin America can involve a lot of time waiting for public transportation, so make sure you pack enough toys, books and things to amuse them.
- Food can be a problem if the children are not adaptable. It is easier to take snacks, drinks, bread and so forth with you on longer trips than to rely on rest stops where the chili-dominated food may not be to their liking.
- On long-distance buses children generally pay half or reduced fares. For shorter trips it is cheaper, if less comfortable, to seat small children on your knee. Often there are spare seats which children can occupy after tickets have been collected.
- In city and local excursion buses, small children do not generally pay a fare, but are not entitled to a seat when paying customers are standing. On sightseeing tours you should always bargain for a family rate—often children can go free. Note that children going free on long excursions are not always covered by the operator's travel insurance.
- When flying, check the child's baggage allowance, which is sometimes are as low as 7kg (15 pounds).
- Many hotels offer family rates. If charges are per person, you can insist that two children will occupy one bed, counting as one tariff. If rates are per bed, the same applies. In either case you can almost always get a reduced rate at cheaper hotels.
- In the better hotels in more commercial resorts, it is quite common for children under 10 or 12 years to stay for no extra charge, as long as they are sharing your room.

FESTIVALS AND EVENTS

Fiestas are a fundamental part of life for most Mexicans, taking place the length and breadth of the country and with such frequency that it would be hard to miss one, even during the briefest of stays. They come in all shapes and sizes, from the fast and furious Veracruz Carnival to the more sedate Blessing of Pets in Mexico City (mid-January). Some are highly Catholicized, while others incorporate Spanish colonial themes into predominantly ancient pagan rituals.

Celebrating in Oaxaca (left); Dance of the Old Man, Tzintzuntzán (middle); Day of the Dead (right)

MAIN NATIONAL FESTIVALS

Carnival

One of the biggest and most riotous celebrations is Carnival, which takes place a week before Lent, in February or early March. It is a time for indulgence and excess before the hardships of Lent and is celebrated with parades, eating and dancing, most spectacularly in La Paz, Mazatlán and Veracruz. It builds up to a wild climax on the last day, Mardi Gras.

Easter

Another great time to be in Mexico is during Easter week. Thousands gather in towns all over the country for processions and Passion plays. In places like Mexico City's Ixtapalapa suburb, millions hit the streets to watch an annual crucifixion. Besides the main regional bases there are renowned parades in small towns, among them Valle de Allende near Hidalgo de Parral and Huaynamota, up in the mountains above Tepic.

Día de la Marina

June 1 is Navy Day, when coastal towns re-enact navy battles with fireworks.

Día de la Independencia

September 16, Independence Day, has regional festivities and parades up and down the country, the most impressive being those in Mexico City.

Día de los Muertos

Between October 31 and November 2, all over Mexico, rural cemeteries come alive as villagers set up all-night vigils to entertain returning souls. These celebrations, known as *Día de los Muertos* (Day of the Dead), are a fascinating spectacle. The ground blazes with candles and orange and red cempasúchil flowers, while the air is scented with copal (resin). Two of the best places to witness it are the island of Janitzio and the village of Tzintzuntzán, both on Lake Pátzcuaro. In the cities, the *calavera*, or dancing skeleton, reigns over altars decorated with flowers, tissue paper cut into delicate shapes, food offerings and sugar skulls.

La Virgen de Guadalupe

Another important national celebration is held in honor of Our Lady of Guadalupe, on December 12. The pilgrimage of thousands to the Basílica de Guadalupe, in Mexico City, the most venerated shrine in Mexico (▷ 104), is the most impressive example, but there are big celebrations in Tuxtla Gutiérrez and San Cristóbal de las Casas.

Navidad

During the nine days before Christmas, groups of people go asking for shelter *(posada)*, as did Joseph and Mary, and are invited into different homes. This culminates on the night of December 24 with *calendas*, a parade of floats representing scenes from the birth of Christ; every church prepares a float honoring their patron saint.

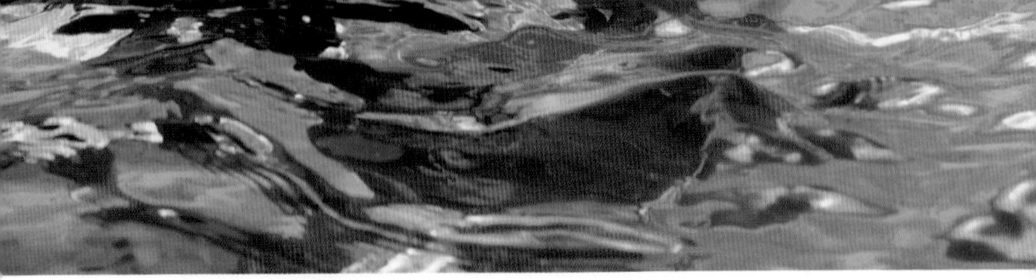

THE YUCATÁN

The best shopping locations in the Yucatán are Playa del Carmen, Cancún, Cozumel and Mérida. Cancún is the number-one entertainment spot, with the greatest selection of bars and clubs, though Playa del Carmen is a happening place, with plenty of options.

KEY TO SYMBOLS

- Shopping
- Entertainment
- Nightlife
- Sports
- Activities
- Health and Beauty
- For Children

BECAL

PANAMA HATS

Becal is known for its Panama hats, called *jipis* (pronounced "hippies") and ubiquitous throughout the Yucatán. Many of the town's families have workshops in cool, damp, backyard underground caves—necessary for keeping the shredded leaves of the *jipijapa* palm, from which the hats are made, moist and pliable. Most vendors will give visitors a tour of their workshop, but they are quite zealous in their sales pitches. Prices are better for *jipis* and other locally woven items (cigarette cases, shoes, belts) in the market than in the shops near the plaza.

CAMPECHE

ALAMEDA PARK

Calle 57 (south end), Campeche

There are plenty of bargains at the main market in Alameda Park. You can find excellent, inexpensive Panama hats (*jipis*), finely and tightly woven so that they retain their shape even when crushed into your luggage (within reason). Note, though, that they are cheaper at source if you buy them in Becal (see left).

Daily

CASA DE ARTESANÍA TULSULNA

Calle 10 No. 333, Campeche

Tel (981) 690 98

In general, handicrafts in Campeche are less expensive than in Mérida. Occupying a colonial house, this shop sells intricately embroidered regional dresses and blouses, hats, jewelry, baskets and weavings.

Mon–Fri 9–8, Sat–Sun 10–2

CANCÚN

HANDICRAFT MARKET

Avenida Tulúm, Cancún

Avenida Tulúm, near the market in the middle of town, is a huge network of stands, all selling exactly the same merchandise: silver jewelry from Taxco, ceramic Maya figurines, hammocks, jade chess sets. Prices are hiked up to the limit, so bargain hard—most vendors expect to get half what they first ask for.

Daily 8am–10pm

LA ISLA

Boulevard Kukulcán Km 12.5, Cancún

Tel (998) 883 50 25

www.gocancun.com

Just opposite the Sheraton Hotel, this partly outdoor mall is one of the more pleasurable shopping experiences in the Hotel Zone. You'll find Zara, Ralph Lauren, Mexican handicrafts stores, familiar US brands, coffee shops and a food court. On the upper level there is a multiplex cinema.

Daily 10–10

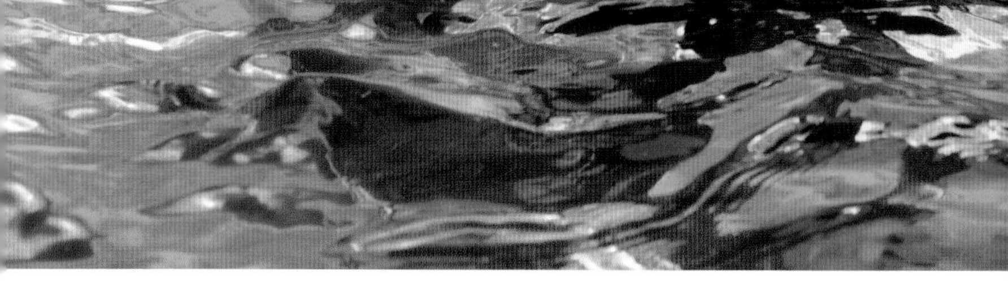

PLAZA KUKULCÁN

Boulevard Kukulcán Km 13, Cancún
Tel (998) 885 22 00
www.kukulcanplaza.com.mx

Kukulcán is one of the main US-style malls in the Hotel Zone, with more than 200 shops. They mostly cater to a younger market, with beach and surf labels, diving equipment, restaurants, a bowling alley and video games. The prices are high for most things, including souvenirs.

Daily 10–10

COCO BONGO

Boulevard Kukulcán Km 9.5, Cancún
Tel (998) 885 05 92

Coco Bongo is a nightlife mega-complex, a three-level club with myriad bars and improvised dance floor spaces populated largely by a crowd of energetic young Americans.

Disco from 10pm

ROOTS BAR

Avenida Tulipanes 26, Cancún
Tel (998) 884 24 37

Roots Bar is one of the sleeker venues in downtown Cancún, with jazz, flamenco, blues, rock and pop. It usually gets into full swing by 10pm. If it all gets a bit much, you can head to the nearby Parque de las Palapas, where there are usually free evening concerts.

Mon–Sat 9pm–1 or 2am

AQUAWORLD

Boulevard Kukulcán Km 15.2, Cancún
Tel (998) 848 83 27
www.aquaworld.com.mx

A variety of water sports can be organized on the beaches along the Hotel Zone. Aquaworld, Cancún's "water kingdom," offers "jungle" tours, parasailing, introductory scuba-diving courses and advanced certification, waterskiing and windsurfing. You can also rent waverunners, jetskis and kayaks. Take a dinner cruise to round off the day.

Daily 6.30am–10pm

ECO-PARK KANTÚN CHÍ

Carretera Cancún–Tulúm Km 266.5
Tel (984) 873 00 21
www.kantunchi.com

Within easy reach of Cancún, and a popular day trip, this lush ecological park in the heart of the Riviera Maya has an atmospheric network of underground caves packed with stalactites and stalagmites which you can explore, and a series of impressive *cenotes* (natural sinkholes) where you can swim. Tours include guides and snorkeling equipment. There is also a small zoo.

Daily 9–5

Park: $10 adult, $5 child. Cave: $35 adult and child over 8 years

Getting ready to jetski from the beach at Cancún

TRES RIOS

Carretera Cancún-Tulúm Km 54
Tel (998) 887 80 77
www.tres-rios.com

Many operators in Cancún offer a visit to this beautiful reserve, 35km (22 miles) south of Cancún airport. There is *cenote*-diving, kayaking, bicycle tours along jungle paths, horseback-riding on the beach and snorkeling. Or simply take it easy and chill out in one of the hammocks.

Daily 9–5

Package with transportation $45, child (5–12) $22; all-inclusive package $68, child $31. Children under 5 free

COZUMEL

DEEP BLUE

A R Salas 200, Avenida 10 Sur, Cozumel
Tel (987) 872 56 53
www.deepbluecozumel.com

This is the best of the smaller diving schools in Cozumel, offering personalized support with a maximum of eight people per small boat. Matt and Deborah, an English/Colombian couple, run the school. All PADI and NAUI certifications.

Open Water Diver $360; 3- to 5-day dive packages $171–$285; cavern and *cenote*-diving, including two dives, transport and lunch $140

PUNTA SUR ECOLOGICAL RESERVE

27km (17 miles) from downtown San Miguel on the Costera Sur (coastal highway), Cozumel
Tel (987) 872 29 40

This national eco-tourism development occupies the southern tip of the island, with a variety of natural landscapes including lagoons and mangrove jungles. A snorkel base has opened here as well as a viewing platform, and there is a Mayan ruin in the shape of a shell, El Caracol, which is believed to have been used as a lighthouse. There are four boat rides a day on the Columbia lagoon. You can arrange a round-trip taxi service from San Miguel

Daily 9–5

$10

ISLA MUJERES

AVENIDA HIDALGO

Isla Mujeres

This main avenue is lined with souvenir shops, most of them selling similar things: ceramic and clay Maya figurines and masks, hammocks, blankets and silver jewelry from Taxco. Bargaining is obligatory—try and get the desired item for half the original asking price, which is what the vendors expect to receive.

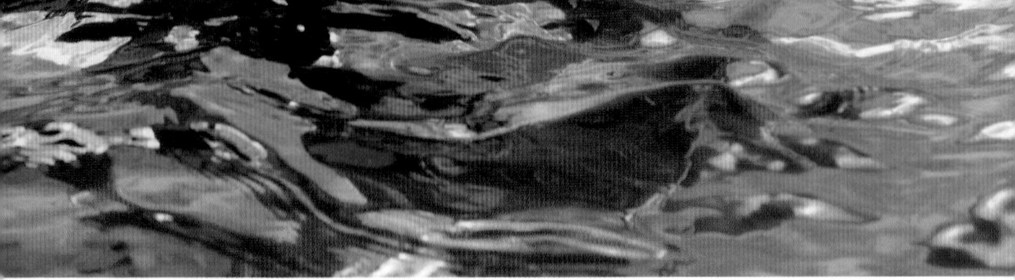

COSMIC COSAS

Calle Matamoros 82, Isla Mujeres
Tel (998) 876 34 95

This is a very friendly, US-run bookstore with new and used books bought, sold and exchanged, mostly beach-read novels and a few out-of-date guidebooks. There are also CDs for sale, an internet café and a dog-adoption notice board. This is a good place to meet fellow visitors.

Mon–Sat 9am–10pm

BUHOS

Cabañas Maria del Mar
Avenida Carlos Larzo, 1, Isla Mujeres
Tel (998) 877 01 79

This almost legendary beach bar-restaurant, in an idyllic Caribbean setting, is fun and lively, with great music, tasty food ranging from *fajitas* to lobster, and a wide repertoire of cocktails and beer. A sunset cocktail here is a must.

Daily 7am–9pm

FAYNES

Avenida Hidalgo, Isla Mujeres

Faynes, popular with a younger crowd, is a large, open-air bar-restaurant on two levels. It serves great food, from Tex-Mex to Caribbean-style seafood, accompanied by a buoyant Latin soundtrack. The welcoming, gregarious atmosphere makes it a good spot for a beer or a cocktail. Happy hour is between 10 and 11pm, with pitchers of margarita for 50 pesos.

Daily till late

LA PEÑA

Avenida Guerrero, Centro, Isla Mujeres
Tel (998) 845 73 84

Close to the main square, the breezy roof terrace here is a perfect place to relax to laid-back music until 10pm with an industrial-strength cocktail. There is a good mix of people and the staff are welcoming. Plans are afoot to open a courtyard restaurant and movie lounge.

Daily 7.30pm–around 3am

BAHÍA

Avenida Rueda Medina 166, Isla Mujeres
Tel (998) 877 03 40

Snorkeling trips depart from the ferry dock daily between 10 and 11am. They include two hours snorkeling and lunch, returning at 2.30pm.

$150 per person

CORAL SCUBA DIVE CENTER

Avenida Matamoros 13-A, Isla Mujeres
Tel (998) 877 07 63
www.coralscubadivecenter.com

This is the only dive school on the island affiliated with PADI; it has over 20 years' experience, bilingual staff, and more than 50 local dive sites, including reef, adventure, coral gardens or the Ultra Freeze shipwreck options.

Daily 9am–10pm

Introductory course $59; two-tank dive $60; two-tank reef dive $39; eight-dive package $154; snorkel trips $22. Equipment rental, an additional $15

Snorkeling in the warm waters around Isla Mujeres

EL GARRAFÓN

Punta Sur, Isla Mujeres
Tel (998) 877 11 00
www.garrafon.com

This ecological recreational park (▷ 72) offers day passes, which include snorkeling in the shallow reef next to the shore, a visit to the Maya ruin and Caribbean village, and the use of the pool and hammocks. In addition, all-inclusive packages comprise lockers, towels, snorkel equipment and unlimited food and drink at the restaurants and open bar. Additional activities, such as bungee jumping and snuba-diving (scuba-diving without a tank), are available at extra cost. The reef is 320m (1,050ft) long, extending some 12m (39ft) from shore, with a maximum depth of 3m (10ft).

Daily 9–5.30

Day passes $15, child $8; all-inclusive packages $44

ISLA CONTOY EXPRESS TOUR

Avenida Rueda Medina, Abasolo and Matamoros, Isla Mujeres
Tel (998) 877 13 67

Boat trips on board the *Caribbean Express* leave Isla Mujeres at 8.30am, arriving at Isla Contoy at 10am, following snorkeling on the reef. A lunch of Yucatán fish is served before returning at 2.30pm.

Daily

Adult $60, child (6–11) $50

PLAYA PARAÍSO

Isla Mujeres

This lovely stretch of beach, just a 30-minute walk from El Garrafón (▷ 72), close to the tip of Punta Sur, has been transformed into an expensive mini-resort for Cancún daytrippers.

RICARDO GAITÁN

Contoy Pier, Avenida Rueda Medina, Isla Mujeres
Tel (998) 877 13 63

Ricardo Gaitán is the specialist guide for birdwatching tours to Isla Contoy, 30km (19 miles) north of Isla Mujeres. Knowledgeable and professionally run trips include snorkeling on Ixlache reef, fishing and a barbecued fish lunch. Tours of the island are provided by wardens and visiting scientists.

Daily, leaving 9am, returning 5pm

$40

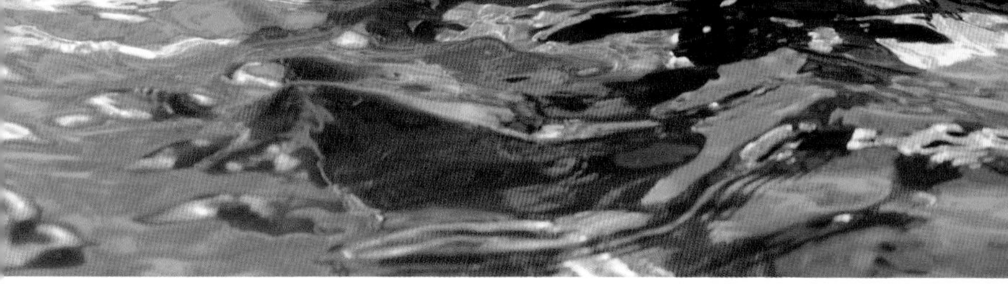

SEA HAWK
Zazil-Ha (behind Hotel Na-Balam), Isla Mujeres
Tel (998) 877 02 96
Sea Hawk specializes in scuba-diving and snorkeling, with certified PADI instructors. There are various reefs for diving and snorkeling around the island, as well as a sunken cross specially placed in deep water for divers to explore. Snorkeling and fishing trips are also available.
Daily 9–8
Two-tank dive $50; introductory course, including shallow dive $75

MÉRIDA

CASA DE LAS ARTESANÍAS
Calle 63 No. 503A, Mérida
Tel (999) 928 66 76
One of the best, but most expensive, places to buy handicrafts in Mérida is in this former monastery. The quality is high in finely embroidered *huipiles*, textiles, hammocks, pottery and jewelry. Local art exhibitions are often held in the courtyard gallery.
Mon–Sat 9–8, Sun 9–2

MAIN MARKET
Corner of Calle 56 and Calle 57, Mérida
Here you'll find good leather *huaraches* (sandals) and excellent cowboy boots for men and women.
Daily from 5am

MERCADO DE ARTESANÍAS
Calle 67, between 56 and 58, Mérida
Many well-made handicrafts are on sale here, as well as good postcards, but prices are high and the salespeople are pushy.
Daily 9–5

ZOCÁLO
Mérida
Many of the souvenir shops dotted in the streets around the plaza specialize in hammocks. They also sell silver jewelry from Taxco, Panama hats, *guayabera* shirts, *huaraches*, baskets and Maya figurines. Always bargain hard; the salesmen are pushy.

TEATRO PEÓN CONTRERAS
Calle 60 with 57, Mérida
This theater first opened its doors in 1908 and is considered one of the best in Mexico, acclaimed for its classical ballet performances. The stage is grandiose and there is a wonderful marble staircase. Visiting politicians and celebrities have included former US president Bill Clinton. There is a bookshop and exhibitions are held regularly.
Shows at 9pm
Tickets $4

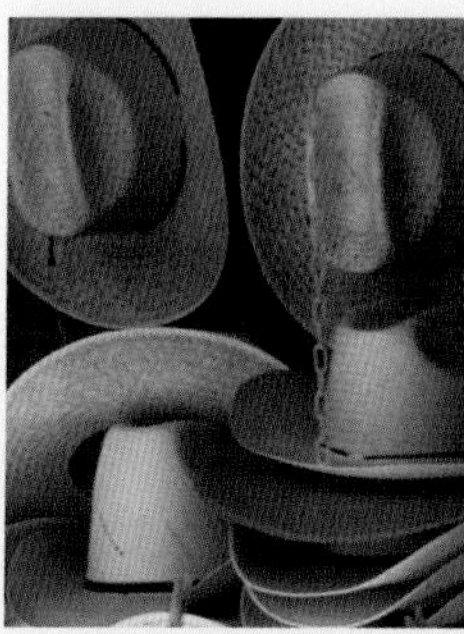
Panama hats are a very popular buy in Mérida

PANCHOS
Calle 59, between Calle 60 and Calle 62, Mérida
Tel (999) 923 09 42
Although this bar-restaurant is very touristy, it has live music every night, and the lovely patio, with candles, fairylights and infectious merriment make it a popular early-evening stop-off.
Daily 6pm–2am

PLAYA DEL CARMEN

BLUE PARROT INN
Calle 12 at the beach, Playa del Carmen
Tel (984) 873 00 83
www.blueparrot.com
This is the best nightspot in Playa, with an excellent bar with swing seats, a dance floor, and tables right on the beach. Each night delivers a different theme or spectacle; from Best Beach Body contests to the Sunday night Retro Dance party, Tuesday night Extreme Beach party, and weekend Sundown to Sunrise dance party. Cocktails cost about $4.50–$6, but there's a happy hour from 5 to 8pm.
Daily midday–4am

BOURBON STREET
Avenida 5, between Calle 6 and Calle 8, Playa del Carmen
Tel (984) 803 30 22
A mellow, Deep South vibe, live Louisiana blues, and jazz and rock (nightly from 9pm) are on offer at this streetside bar. It's a good place to prop up the bar and meet people, chat to the friendly staff or owner. In addition to draft beer and good cocktails, piquant Cajun food is served.
Daily 10am–2am

SEÑOR FROG'S
Centro Commercial Plaza Marina, Playa del Carmen
Tel (984) 873 09 31
Right on the beach with its own marina, volleyball court and beach club, the brash and loud Señor Frog's is one of the most popular drinking holes in the area. Entertainment ranges from monthly music festivals to nightly DJs and titillating contests.
Daily 10am–last person leaves

ABYSS
Blue Parrot Inn, Calle 12, Playa del Carmen
Tel (984) 873 21 64
www.abyssdiveshop.com
On the beach next to the Blue Parrot, this diving school run by fully PADI-certified American instructor David Tomlinson has a good reputation.
PADI courses $350; one-tank dive $38; one-day introductory course $74; two-tank *cenote* trip $100; one-tank night dive $45

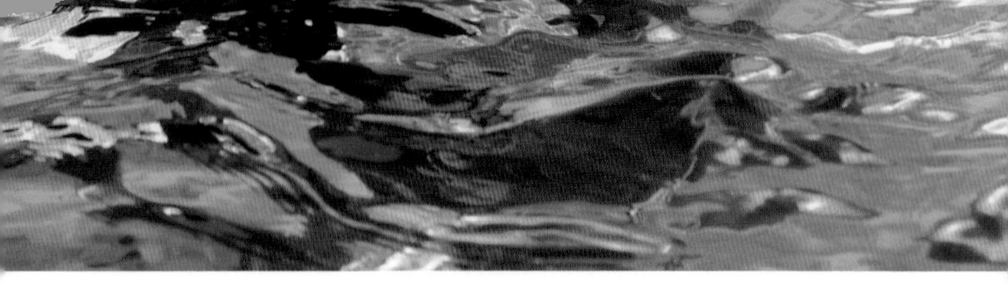

WHAT TO DO

✪IKARUS

Avenida 5, Calle 16, Playa del Carmen
Tel (984) 803 20 68
www.ikaruskiteboarding.com

This was the first kitesurfing company in Mexico to follow Professional Air Sport Association standards. Classes are held at Puerto Morelos—halfway between Cancún and Playa del Carmen—or Tulúm. Students can obtain Level 1 pilot certification.

$65 per hour

✪SKYDIVE PLAYA

Playa Marina Loc 32, Playa del Carmen
Tel (984) 873 01 92
www.skydive.com.mx

For an extreme adrenalin rush, try the skydiving courses or tandem dives available here, with amazing views, soft beach landings, and lots of freefall time. An introductory orientation course is given before each dive. Skydive is a member of the Parachute Association, with licensed instructors.

Daily 9–8
$200 for tandem dive with certified instructor

✪TANK-HA DIVE CENTER

Avenida 5, between Calle 8 and Calle 10, Playa del Carmen
Tel (984) 873 03 02/879 34 27
www.tankha.com

You will find experienced, qualified, multilingual instructors at this very professional, long-established company. It offers snorkeling and diving for all levels, along with PADI and advanced courses up to Divemaster.

Office open daily 8am–10pm
PADI open-water course $350 (includes DAN medical insurance), one-tank dive $40, two-tank dive Cozumel $120 (including transport from Playa), two-tank *cenote* dives $100

PROGRESO

MUNDO MARINO

Calle 80, Progreso
Tel (969) 915 13 80

Luis Cámara, the friendly owner of this souvenir shop, once caught a great white shark, and many shark-related and other marine souvenirs are on sale.

Mon–Fri 9–8, Sat 10–2

PUERTO MORELOS

✪LA PALAPA DE FÉLIX

SM1 MZ 14, Lote 8, Puerto Morelos
Tel (998) 884 23 16

The marina in Puerto Morelos offers activities within the national park such as tailor-made excursions and boat trips. The snorkeling here is excellent, and there are fishing trips and visits to nearby *cenotes* (sinkholes)

Daily 8–2
Park tour $65 (including lunch)

Río Lagartos is famous for its flocks of flamingos

RÍO LAGARTOS

✪BIRD-WATCHING

Early-morning boat trips (2.5–4 hours) can be arranged in the fishing village of Río Lagartos to see the flamingos. Check before going whether the flamingos are there; they usually nest during May and June and stay through July till August (although salt mining is disturbing their habitat).

$35 in an 8- to 9-seater boat (fix the price before embarking)

TICUL

HUIPILES

Ticul, 80km (50 miles) south of Mérida, is a small, pleasant little village known for its *huipiles*—the embroidered white dresses worn by older Maya women. You can buy them in Mérida, but the prices and quality of those in Ticul are much better. Look out for them on Calle 23.

TULÚM

✪AKTUN DIVE CENTER

PO Box 119, Tulúm
Tel (984) 871 23 11
www.aktundive.com

Aktun is 1km (half a mile) out of Tulúm on the main road. Gunnar Wagner runs it with his wife, Lina. They offer cave and cavern-diving courses, open-water diving and jungle-camp dive expeditions.

Cave-diving courses $350; fun dives from $80

✪AQUATECH DIVE CENTRE

Villas de Rosa, Akumal, Tulúm
Tel (984) 875 90 20
www.cenotes.com

Open-water and cavern diving programs, snorkeling, sport fishing and underwater photography are all available at this dive school. The resort is 105km (65 miles) south of Cancún.

Packages can be arranged which include accommodation in beachfront condos ($120 per night). A one-tank dive costs $40

✪HIDDEN WORLD'S CENOTES

Dos Ojos Caverns, just off Route 307, south of Puerto Aventuras, Tulúm
Tel (984) 877 85 35
www.hiddenworlds.com.mx

Located at Dos Ojos, this is the second-largest underground cave system in the world, and has a possible link to the Nohoch Nah Chich, part of a subterranean system recorded as the world's largest, with more than 50km (31 miles) of surveyed passageways connected to the sea. Trips can be organized for first-time snorkelers as well as underwater vetreans.

Snorkeling from $40; diving trips from $50

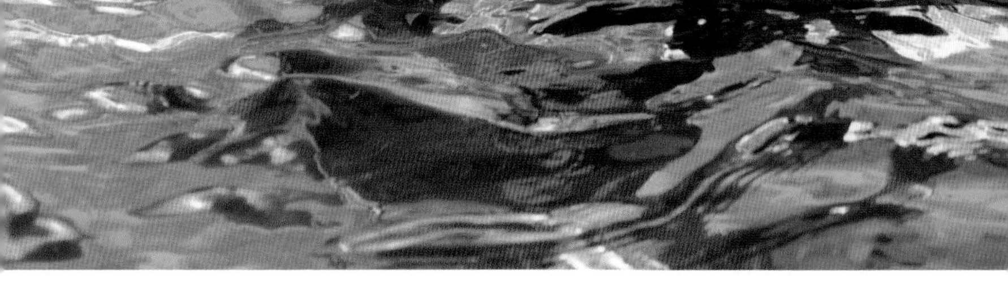

MIKE MADDEN'S CEDAM DIVE CENTERS

PO Box 1, Puerto Aventuras, Tulúm
Tel (984) 873 51 29

This specialist dive school offers a cave-diving course that involves more than 12 hours of lectures and a minimum of 14 cave dives using double tanks. Some of the best *cenotes* (natural sinkholes) are in the Tulúm area, including the colorfully named "Carwash," on the Cobá road, which is also suitable for beginners, and has excellent visibility.

Accompanied dives start at around $60; cave-diving course from around $600

VALLADOLID

ZÓCALO

Valladolid

Valladolid's lovely, and safe, main square with its illuminated central fountain, colonial feel, food stands and handicrafts stalls is frequently the venue for live musical entertainment in the early evening, ranging from jazz quartets to salsa and merengue. Sprightly dancing, gregarious chatter, ice cream and spirited *joie de vivre* are the usual accompaniments.

ANTONIO "NEGRO" AGUILAR

Calle 44 No. 195, Valladolid

Something of a local celebrity, Antonio Aguilar was a baseball champion in the 1950s and '60s, playing for the Leones de Yucatán and the Washington Senators. Now semi-retired, he runs a shop selling sports equipment and renting out bicycles. Recommended bicycling routes are to the Cenote X-Kekén (see above right) and Ek-Balam (▷ 71) archaeological ruins, north of Valladolid. Antonio will draw you a map of the best route and advise you on what to take.

Daily 9–7
$2 for 3 hours

CENOTE X-KEKÉN

7km (4 miles) southwest of Valladolid

More commonly known as Dzitnup, this beautiful, underground, cathedral-like *cenote,* just 7km (4 miles) from Valladolid, is stunningly lit with electric lights—the only natural light source being a tiny hole in the cavernous ceiling dripping with stalactites. Swimming is excellent, the water is cool, clear and refreshing (although reportedly a little dirty at times) and bats flit around overhead. Exploratory walks can also be made through the many tunnels leading off the *cenote*, for which you will need a flashlight. Be careful as the steps can be very slippery. Also be prepared to be swamped with children offering to take you round the *cenote*. Almost directly across the road from X-Kekén is Cenote Samula, generally quieter and less crowded.

Daily 8–6
$1.20
Colectivos leave hourly from the front of Hotel María Guadalupe at Calle 44, between Calle 39 and Calle 41; they return until 6pm, after which you will have to get a taxi back to Valladolid. You can also take any bus heading west to the turn-off (it's then a further 2km/1.2-mile walk) or rent a taxi or bicycle

CENOTE ZACÍ

Calle 36, between Calle 37 and Calle 39, Valladolid
Tel (985) 62 107

Right in the middle of town, just several blocks from the main plaza, this artificially lit, open-air *cenote* has good swimming, although it is sometimes closed due to algae in the water. There is a popular thatched-roof restaurant with an excellent view over the *cenote* and good food, lighted promenades and a mini-zoo.

Daily 8–6
$1. Half price for children

WHAT TO DO

FESTIVALS AND EVENTS

FEBRUARY

MÉRIDA CARNIVAL

Week before Ash Wednesday
Mérida

During this week Mérida erupts with floats, dancers in regional costume, music, dancing around the plaza and children dressed in animal suits. There are parades starting from the Monument to the Flag on Paseo Montejo heading south to Parque San Juan in downtown, with the route lined with stands selling regional snacks. Local and international musicians perform at concerts.

MARCH AND SEPTEMBER

FIESTAS DEL EQUINOXIO

March 21 and September 21
Chichén Itzá

Twice a year, on the morning and afternoon of the spring and fall equinoxes, the alignment of the sun casts a serpentine-shaped shadow on the steps of El Castillo at Chichén Itzá which gradually moves down to meet a serpent's head carved at the base. Expect large crowds on these days, and make hotel reservations well in advance if you are considering staying.

MAY

CANCÚN JAZZ FESTIVAL

Memorial Day weekend
Cancún

Jazz lovers descend on Cancún to savor a host of top jazz musicians from around the world who come to take part in free nightly concerts which are held throughout the city towards the end of May.

SOUTHERN MEXICO

The villages around Oaxaca and San Cristóbal de las Casa are magnets for visitors looking for typical handicrafts—black clay pottery, rugs, textiles and leather goods. Acapulco, more famous for its nightlife than its beaches, parties 24 hours a day.

KEY TO SYMBOLS

- **Shopping**
- **Entertainment**
- **Nightlife**
- **Sports**
- **Activities**
- **Health and Beauty**
- **For Children**

ACAPULCO

BABY'O

Costera Miguel Alemán, Acapulco
Tel (744) 484 74 74

This small, intimate dance venue is a welcome antidote to the crop of superclubs that make up the city's late-night scene. Everything from techno to hip-hop is played to a largely 20-something crowd.

Daily 10pm–5am
Cover charge $5–$17 for women, $10–$28 for men

BENITO JUÁREZ

TOURIST YÚ Ù

Comité de Ecoturismo de Benito Juárez, Benito Juárez
Tel (954)599 94 or (951) 609 84 (Sedetur)

Tourist Yú ù is a Government-run eco-tourism project where you can stay in rustic cabins in the mountains and experience traditional Oaxacan village life. Activities include trout fishing hiking, cycling and horseback-riding. The scenery is idyllic, with cascading waterfalls and brooks crisscrossing lushly carpeted valleys.

$10 per person camping, $30 *cabaña*

CHIAPA DEL CORZO

PARQUE ECOTURÍSTICO CAÑON DEL SUMIDERO, SA DE CV

Chiapa del Corzo
Tel (961) 602 85 00
www.sumidero.com

The boat trip from Chiapa del Corzo to Cañon del Sumidero has magnificent views of the canyon, the Cueva de Silencio, the Cueva de los Colores, and cliffs 600m (1,968ft) high, including the Arból de Navidad with its waterfall. The tour ends as the canyon opens out into the valley with a series of magical waterfalls (▷ 83).

40-minute boat trip into the Sumidero Canyon $7 per person for 2 hours, boats leave when full; $65 to rent a boat for a private group. Transfer *en lancha* from the park, $12, leaves 10, 11, 12 and 1, returns 4.30 and 5

HUATULCO

BOAT TRIPS

Travel agencies offer full-day boat tours to see the different bays, with stops for swimming, snorkeling and a meal; there are catamarans, sailboats, yachts and small launches. Trips can also be arranged at the Santa Cruz marina directly with the boatmen; they will probably speak only Spanish. Some of the bays can also be reached by land, and there are tours on all-terrain quad bikes *(cuatrimotos)*.

Full-day boat tours $18–$30 per person

HIKING

In the Huatulco area, the mountains of the Sierra Madre del Sur drop from the highest point in the state of Oaxaca (3,750m/12,300ft) to the sea. There are ample opportunities for day hiking. In the hills north of Huatulco a number of coffee plantations can be

visited, which include a meal with traditional dishes at the farm and bathing in freshwater springs or waterfalls.
$45 per person

OAXACA

AMATE BOOKS
Calle Macedonio Alcalá 307, Oaxaca
Tel (951) 516 68 60
This has the best selection of English-language books in Oaxaca, with a good choice of Latin-American literature and archaeology books, coffee-table books, including glossy art volumes featuring Mexican artists Rufino Tamayo and Frida Kahlo, guides to Oaxaca, post-cards, CDs and magazines.
Mon–Sat 10–9, Sun 2–7

ARTE MEXICANO DE ANTEQUERA
Calle Macedonia Alcalá 407, Oaxaca
Tel (951) 516 32 55
Here you can see a small but significant collection of art-works from some of Oaxaca's leading contemporary artists, including Ixrrael Montes.
Mon–Sat 10–2, 4–8

CHOCOLATE MAYORDOMO
Calle Mina and 20 de Noviembre, Oaxaca
Tel (951) 516 33 09
The smell of cacao permeates the air around the Mayordomo mill, which grinds cacao beans, almond, sugar and cinnamon into a paste for making delicious hot chocolate. The ubiquitous outlets also sell Oaxacan *mole* (▷ 243) and delicious organic coffee.
Daily 7am–9pm

LA MANO MÁGICA
Calle Macedonia Alcalá 203, Oaxaca
Tel (951) 516 42 75
Contemporary art and high-quality *artesanía* draw many collectors to La Mano Mágica. The wool and silk tapestries feature the creations of one of Oaxaca's most renowned weavers, Arnulfo Mendoza. Behind the shop in the colonial patio you can watch tapestries being woven. Mano Mágica also organizes cultural tours to the surrounding villages, and cooking classes in Teotitlán del Valle on the first and third Friday of the month (8.30–3, $70 including transport for class with Reyna Mendoza, and lunch).
Daily 10.30–2.30, 3.30–7

MUJERES ARTESANAS DE LAS REGIONES DE OAXACA
Calle 5 de Mayo 204, Oaxaca
Tel (951) 516 06 70
MARO was founded by a group of women to preserve the traditional methods of regional handicrafts, which have been threatened by increasing industrialization and mass production. There is a good selection of top-quality textiles, ceramics, *alejibres* (animals carved in copal wood then brightly painted) and embroidered dresses.
Daily 9–8

Dancers wearing traditional Oaxacan costume

EL RINCÓN DEL LIBRO
Jardín de la Soledad 1, Oaxaca
Tel (951) 516 44 08
This small bookstore, in the leafy and lively garden that encircles the Basílica de La Soledad, has a limited selection of art and archaeology books, Latin-American and international literature, and travel guides (in Spanish). The major draw is the relaxing colonial setting, great café and internet access.
Daily 9–9 (café), 10–9 (shop)

SEDETUR
Calle Murguia 206, Oaxaca
Tel (951) 4 77 33
For the highest-quality rug collection, visit this shop selling crafts; the profits go to the artisans and the prices are good.
Daily 9–8

CAMINO REAL
Calle 5 de Mayo 300, Oaxaca
Tel (951) 516 06 11
www.caminoreal.com
The Hotel Camino Real is the setting for the Gualaguateza spectacles—smaller-scale versions of the exuberant folk traditions of the various cultural groups in the region.
Show Fri 7.30pm
$30 (includes buffet dinner)

NOUVEAU
Avenida Garcia Vigil 205, Oaxaca
Tel (951) 603 33
This modern, cosmopolitan bar with a lounge-style mezzanine level serves very good light snacks during the day, including bagels with smoked salmon and cream cheese, and becomes an upbeat bar at night. Modern art adorns the clean, neutral walls, but while the seating designs may look good, they are uncomfortable. The very friendly staff serve decent cocktails, sangria and vodka redbulls, alongside the full tequila repertoire.
Mon–Sat 10am–11pm

SOL Y LUNA
Calle Reforma 502, Oaxaca
Tel (951) 514 80 69
This is one of the top spots in Oaxaca for Latin music, with a welcoming vibe. The music kicks off after 9.30pm with excellent salsa and merengue, tango and flamenco. Food is also served.
Daily 6.30pm–1.30am, closed Sun
Cover $5

BICICLETAS BRAVO

Avenida García Vigil 409C, Oaxaca
Tel (951) 516 09 53
www.bikeoaxaca.com

Here you can rent new aluminum-frame bicycles with front suspension. Photocopied sections of topographic maps are also available on request. Guided mountain bicycling trips, rated from "easy" to "technically challenging"—all with great itineraries—are a wonderful way to see the surrounding countryside.

Mon–Sat 10–1, 3–6, Sun 11–4
Minimum two people, $28 each; make reservations at least one day before

PEDRO MARTÍNEZ ADVENTURE TOURS

Calle Aldama 415, Oaxaca
Tel (951) 514 59 35
www.bicicletaspedromartinez.com

Pedro Martinez offers a variety of personally tailored trips, from day-long tours, which take in the artisan villages, to tours of two days or longer, which combine hiking and cycling through the diverse landscapes of the sierra. The service is very professional with brand-name equipment, 4x4 ground support and English-speaking guides on request.

4-day tours from $350

TIERRAVENTURA

Abasolo 217, Oaxaca
Tel (951) 501 13 63

This eco-tourism organization aims to promote sustainable tourism and runs adventure trips and cultural excursions to the indigenous villages, Sierra Mixteca, the mountains and the Oaxaca coast. Personalized tours range from one day to several weeks; themes include horseback-riding, shamanism, hikes and traditional Indian medicine.

Mon–Sat 10–2, 5–7
1-day tour $55–$77; 2-day tour $68–$135; 4-day tour $362

PUERTO ANGEL

CENTRO MEXICANO DE LA TORTUGA

East end of Mazunte beach, Puerto Angel

This organization studies sea turtles and works to conserve these endangered species, as well as educate visitors and locals. You can see many species in viewing tanks. A trail leads from the west end of the beach to Punta Cometa, a spit of land with lovely views of the thundering breakers below and spectacular sunsets.

Tue–Sat 10–4.30, Sun 10–2.30
$2, child (under 12) $1
Guided tours in Spanish and English

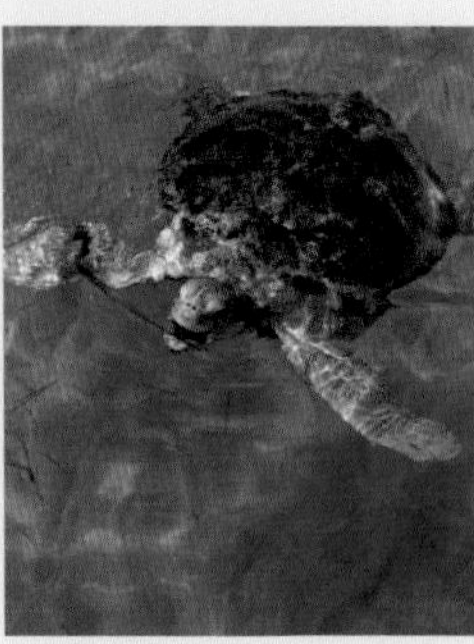

A turtle swimming in the waters off Puerto Angel

SAN ANTONIO ARRAZOLA

WOODCARVINGS

10km (6 miles) southwest of Oaxaca

San Antonio Arrazola is another town where *alejibres* are sold by artisans.

SAN BARTOLO COYOTEPEC

POTTERY

12km (7.5 miles) southeast of Oaxaca

San Bartolo Coyotepec is known for its black pottery. Doña Rosa de Nieto accidentally discovered the technique for the black-glazed ceramics in the 1930s and her family continues the tradition, as do many other potters in town.

SAN CRISTÓBAL DE LAS CASAS

LA CASA DEL JADE

Museo Mesoamericano de Jade, Avenida 16 de Septiembre 16, San Cristóbal de las Casas
Tel (967) 678 25 57

Informative tours reveal the beauty and significance of jade, the treasured symbol of life. The museum has a collection of replicas and jade jewelry from the Toltec, Zapotec and Olmec cultures, including re-creations of King Pakal's tomb (▷ 92–95). You can visit the workshop and watch the craftsmen at work.

Daily noon–8

LA GALERIA

Avenida Hidalgo 3, San Cristóbal de las Casas
Tel (967) 678 15 57

Kiki Suárez works with a variety of mediums and her gallery-shop exhibits a fresh and vital collection of copperprint etchings, watercolors, collages and sculptures.

Daily 9–9

LAS VELAS

Francisco Madero 14, San Cristóbal de las Casas
Tel (967) 678 04 17

Just one block from the *zócalo* is one of the town's most popular hangouts with live music every night. Happy hour is from 8pm–midnight, with searing cocktails and glasses of beer. Live music ranging from reggae to blues, Latin jazz and salsa continues until the early hours. With an upbeat, friendly atmosphere, it's a great place to meet people and dance.

Daily 8pm–4am

LAS GRUTAS DE SAN CRISTÓBAL

Km 94, San Cristóbal de las Casas

Horses can be rented at Las Grutas, 10km (6 miles) southeast of San Cristóbal, for a five-hour ride (guide extra) through the surrounding forest.

Daily 9–6
Horse-riding $13

NA BOLOM

Avenida Vicente Guerrero 33 CP 29220, San Cristóbal de las Casas
Tel (967) 678 14 18
www.ecosur.mx/nabolom/

Na Bolom (▷ 96) runs various conservation projects staffed by volunteers who are given help with accommodation and a daily food allowance. Contact Allison Motto for further information. Na Bolom also run tours (Tuesday–Sunday) to San Juan Chamula and San Lorenzo Zinacantán ($10 per person).

Daily 10–6

SAN MARTÍN TILCAJETE

WOODCARVINGS

21km (13 miles) from Oaxaca

San Martín Tilcajete, 1km (half a mile) west of the main road, is the center for the production of *alejibres*—animal carvings. They often have a look of the supernatural about them.

SAN TOMÁS JALIEZA

TEXTILES

24km (15 miles) south of Oaxaca

Santo Tomás Jalieza is the center for cotton and wool textiles produced with backstrap looms and natural dyes in the surrounding villages. Friday is market day.

TEOTITLÁN DEL VALLE

WEAVING

32km (20 miles) east of Oaxaca

The best prices for weavings are at the stores along the road as you come into the town of Teotitlán del Valle, but they may be even cheaper in Oaxaca where competition is stronger. Make sure you know whether you are getting all wool or a mixture, and check the quality. A well-made rug will not ripple when unfolded on the floor. Every Monday, from 7am, visitors can buy food as well as local arts and crafts at the market.

VENTANILLA

TOURS

Some 2km (1.2 miles) west of Mazunte is a signed turn-off for Ventanilla. It is 1.5km (1 mile) from here to the village and visitor center where local residents run tours, combining a rowboat ride through mangroves for up to 10 people, a visit to a crocodile farm and a walk on the beach. Horseback-riding tours along the beach are also available. Those wishing to spend the night can camp or stay with a family. Simple meals are available in the village. Guides speak Spanish only.

Tour $4 per person

Chamula weaving from San Cristóbal de las Casas

VILLAHERMOSA

MERCADO PINO SUÁREZ

Corner of Avenida Pino Suárez and Calle Bastar Zozaya, Villahermosa

Every nook and cranny of the Mercado Pino Suárez is crammed with goods, from barbecued *pejelagarto* (pike-like fish) to cowboy hats, fabrics, spices and dead chickens en route to the pot. The local drink, *pozol*, a somewhat acquired taste, is believed to cure a hangover. You can watch it being made as the *pozoleros* grind the hominy into a thick dough then mix it with cacao and water.

Daily 9–7

PARQUE YUMKÁ

Camino Yumka, Ejido dos Montes, Villahermosa
Tel (993) 356 01 07

Parque Yumká is an easy day trip from Villahermosa. This safari park containing 108ha (265 acres) of jungle, savannah and lagoon is a "zoo without cages," offering walking, trolley and boat tours of each habitat. While the ecological park promotes the diversity of the region's indigenous flora and fauna, there are also animals from Asia and Africa.

Daily 9–4

$4. Most tour agencies offer round trips for about $8

WHAT TO DO

FESTIVALS AND EVENTS

JULY

GUELAGUETZA

The two Mondays following July 16 (unless July 18, anniversary of death of Benito Juárez, falls on a Monday, then it's the following two Mondays)
Oaxaca
www.oaxacalive.com/guelaguetza.htm

This spectacular carnival is when Oaxaca's many different cultural groups come together in one place. The main event is a grand folk dance show that takes place at the Gualaguetza stadium on the slopes of Cerra del Fortín, on the first Monday morning. The most important festival, *Los Lunes del Cerro*, is held on the second Monday. Performances begin at 9am and end around 1pm. Tickets are available from the Sedetur office on Calle Murguía 206 and cost $35.

DECEMBER

LA NOCHE DE RÁBANOS (NIGHT OF THE RADISHES)

See page 23.

MEXICO CITY

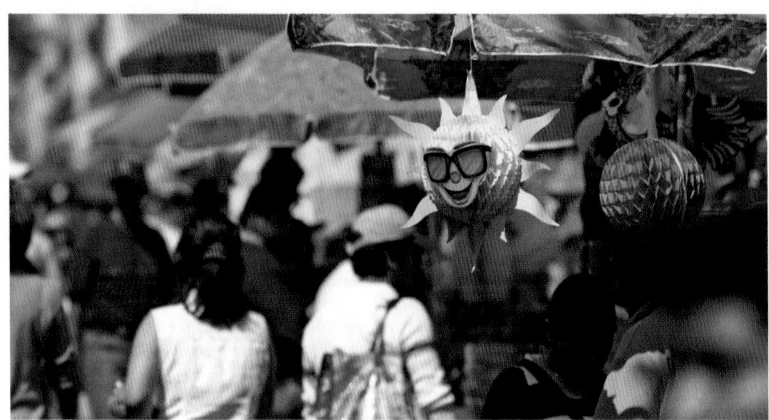

Mexico City is great for shopping, whether you're looking for something specific, such as arts and crafts, jewelry and glass, or just wandering through the fascinating *mercados* (markets). Entertainment ranges from the performing arts (opera, ballet, theater) to a vibrant club and music scene via the traditional mariachi bands on the Plaza de Garibaldi.

KEY TO SYMBOLS

- Shopping
- Entertainment
- Nightlife
- Sports
- Activities
- Health and Beauty
- For Children

SHOPPING

ARTS AND CRAFTS

ARTESANÍAS DEL CENTRO
Calle Palma Norte 506-F
Tel (55) 55 12 04 47
You can always find an interesting buy in this curious little establishment crammed with paintings, scented candles, silver crosses, images of the Virgin Mary, clocks and even the odd José Guadalupe Posada-style skeleton.
Mon–Sat 10–8
Allende

LA CIUDADELA
Calle Balderas 95
If you missed out on a purchase somewhere else on your trip, you will most likely find it again here. Selling crafts from all regions of the country, La Ciudadela comprises row upon row of pottery, jewelry and indigenous clothes stands. Prices are not much higher than in the provinces, but bargaining won't get you far.
Mon–Sat 11–7, Sun 11–5
Balderas

FONART (FONDO NACIONAL PARA EL FOMENTO DE LAS ARTESANÍAS)
Avenida Júarez 89
Tel (55) 55 21 01 71
www.fonart.gob.mx
The best quality textiles, pottery and silver from all over Mexico are sold in this lovely crafts shop on the west side of the Alameda. Founded in 1974, FONART aims to rescue, promote and diffuse the traditional crafts of all the Mexican states and peoples. The products are fairly traded and the organization is well worth supporting. Prices are high, but the quality merits them.
Mon–Sun 10–7
Hidalgo

PLAZA DEL ÁNGEL
Entrances on Calle Hamburgo 150 and Calle Londres 161
A delightful Victorian-style gallery between Florencia and Amberes, Plaza del Ángel offers around 20 antiques shops filled with furniture, bric-à-brac, art and Mexican crafts all under one roof—perfect for easy browsing. On Saturdays it turns into a lively street fair.
Individual shops tend to keep their own hours, but most are open Mon–Fri 11–7 and Sat and Sun noon–4, with some closing on Mon
Insurgentes

BOOKS, MUSIC AND STATIONERY

THE AMERICAN BOOKSTORE
Boulevard 23, between Calle Madero and Calle 16 de Septiembre
Tel (55) 55 12 03 06
This is Mexico City's oldest English-language bookshop and by far the best place to pick up vacation reading.
Mon–Sat 10–7
Allende, Zócalo

COLECCIÓN BELLAS ARTES MÚSICA
Lobby of the Palacio de Bellas Artes, Avenida Hidalgo
Tel (55) 55 10 15 98/55 12 25 93
This is one of the best places in the country to buy Mexican classical and traditional music, including an excellent collection of Manuel Ponce piano music as well as a comprehensive selection of western classican music and jazz. The staff are well informed and can recommend the best records of Mexican music.
Tue–Sun 11–7 (later on performance nights)
Bellas Artes

GANDHI BELLAS ARTES
Avenida Juárez 4
Tel (55) 55 10 42 31
A very popular and well-stocked bookshop with branches around the city. The Bellas Artes branch has the widest range of English-language books. Also very good for CDs, videos, guides and maps.
Mon–Sat 10–9, Sun 11–8
Bellas Artes

LIBRERÍA E IMPRESOS DE PAPEL SAMA
Calle Florencia 57PB
Tel (55) 55 25 06 47/52 08 31 25
You'll find a comprehensive range of up-to-date international newspapers, from the US and Europe, in this Zona Rosa bookshop—although they don't come cheap.
Mon–Fri 7am–9pm, Sat–Sun 8–6
Insurgentes

LIBROS Y ARTE
Palacio de Bellas Artes, Avenida Hidalgo
Tel (55) 55 21 97 60
This excellent chain of literary and art bookshops has its largest branch in the Palacio de Bellas Artes, with a large selection of books on Mexican art and anthropology, also posters, videos, children's books and tourist guides.
Mon 11–7, Tue–Sat 10–9, Sun 9–9
Bellas Artes

DEPARTMENT STORES

PALACIO DEL HIERRO
Calle Moliere 222, Polanco
Tel (55) 52 83 72 00
This huge chrome-and-glass structure at the junction of Molière with Homero houses a decent selection of global designer brands including the expensive but ever fragrant Crabtree & Evelyn toiletries. There's also a very good food hall.
Mon–Sat 11–9, Sun 11–8
Polanco

SEARS
Avenida Juárez 4
Tel (55) 55 30 72 12
A good starting point for virtually anything you might need, Sears is a western-style department store selling everything from perfume and lingerie to designer clothes, electronic equipment and household goods. Prices tend to be on a par with those of Europe and the US.
Mon–Thu 11–10.30, Fri–Sun 11–9
Bellas Artes

SUBURBIA
Calle San Juan de Letrán, between Calle 16 de Septiembre and Calle Carranza
Tel (55) 55 42 90 30
Cutting-edge fashion this may not be, but you can find some very reasonable bargains at this enormous Mexican superstore laden with clothes for men, women and children, as well as toys, accessories and household goods. It tends to be understaffed, so don't expect lightning service at the cash register.
Mon–Thu 10–8, Fri–Sat 10–9, Sun 10–6
San Juan de Letrán

FOOD AND DRINK

BRIQUETTE AU CHOCOLAT
Calle Fernando Montes de Oca 81C, corner with Calle Yautepec
Tel (55) 52 11 02 76
This Parisian-style chocolatier in the Condesa district stocks a divine range of exquisitely presented sweets and chocolates, both European and Mexican. Superbly made gift boxes are available. Try the almond Olives de Provence.
Mon–Fri 10–6, Sat 10–2
Juanacatlan

DULCERIA DE CELAYA
Avenida 5 de Mayo, 39
Tel (55) 55 21 17 87
Founded in 1874, this little pastry shop displays its traditional Mexican sweets in glass cabinets in an elaborate belle époque interior. The specialty is Rompope, a sweet concoction made of milk, sugar, egg yolk and cinnamon that you add to rum. Among the other mouthwatering delicacies are limes stuffed with coconut, *turrones* and *suspiros meringues*—fluffy meringue puffs.
Mon–Sun 10.30–7.30
Allende, Zócalo

Outside the Dulceria de Celaya pastry shop

JEWELRY AND SILVER

ARTE EN PLATA
Calle Londres 162
Tel (55) 55 11 14 22
In addition to a good selection of jewelry in both modern and traditional designs, this is a good place to shop for amethyst, onyx, tiger eye and lapis lazuli.
Mon–Sat 10–9
Insurgentes

DANIEL ESPINOSA JEWELRY
Calle Tamaulipas 72, Condesa
Tel (55) 52 11 39 94
Top-quality jewelry from one of Mexico's most highly acclaimed young designers is showcased here. Espinosa has exhibited his work in the US and Europe. Expect to pay high prices for the original designs and fine workmanship.
Mon–Sat 10–6
Juanacatlan

TALLERES DE LOS BALLESTEROS
Calle Presidente Masarik 126
Tel (55) 55 45 41 09/55 45 16 66
www.ballesteros.net
Come here for excellent quality, top-end jewelry and tableware, in both modern and traditional designs. There's another branch of the shop in Zona Rosa at Amberes 24.
Mon–Sat 10–7
Polanco

WHAT TO DO

MARKETS

COYOACÁN CRAFTS MARKET
Plaza Hidalgo
Sundays are packed in Coyoacán when the suburb comes to life and the hippie crafts market takes over the Plaza Hidalgo. Mexican embroidered clothing, rain-sticks, jewelry, sandals, incense and candles can be found here, to the accompaniment of music. Food stands line the sides of the Jardin Centenario and the cafés and restaurants spill out onto the sidewalk (pavement). Finding a table can be tricky so book in advance.
Sun 10–7
Viveros

LAGUNILLA
Calle Rayon, two blocks north of Plaza Garibaldi
This open area of *tianguis* (stands) laden with antiques, books and bric-à-brac rivals La Merced in size and diversity. It is a great place to wander on a Sunday when the atmosphere is festive and bargains are snapped up with panache and much shouting.
Daily 10–7
Plaza Garibaldi

MERCADO DE LA MERCED
Izazaga San Pablo and Calle Eje 1 Ote
The metro Merced exit takes you straight up into the heart of this enormous warren of stands, one of the largest and liveliest markets in Latin America. Almost anything you can think of and a lot more besides can be bought here, although fruit and vegetables are the principal produce. As if the indoor area were not vast enough, the market has spilled out into the surrounding streets for several blocks in each direction, but here it becomes seedier with little other than cheap clothes, shoes and nylon flowers.
Daily 6–6
Merced

Working in the daily Mercado de la Merced

SAN ANGEL BAZAR
Plaza San Jacinto, San Angel
This is a very popular open-air crafts market, relaxed and friendly despite the crowds and traffic chaos. In addition to the usual items from across the country you can find some original jewelry, textiles and Talavera pottery at good prices, and the beautiful location in the heart of San Angel makes this a great way to spend your Saturday. Trendy and popular bars and cafés line the sides of the plaza. Parking is difficult.
Sat 10–6
Miguel Angel de Quevedo

PERFUME

ESSENCIAS Y PERFUMES EUROPEOS
Calle Tacuba 54 and 72
Tel (55) 55 10 13 66/55 12 18 72
An immensely popular perfume factory whose walls are lined with plastic bottles, this shop creates exact replicas of the famous designer brands at a fraction of the price. Find Coco Chanel, Calvin Klein, Nina Ricci and Lancôme, among many others.
Mon–Sat 10–7
Allende

PERFUMERÍA EDELWEISS
Boulevard 14, between Avenida 5 de Mayo and Calle Tacuba
Tel (55) 55 12 08 48
A tiny old-fashioned perfumery with bottles displayed from floor to ceiling in mahogany and glass cabinets, Edelweiss stocks all the famous brands at excellent discount prices.
Mon–Sat 10–7
Allende

SHOPPING MALL

PARQUE ALAMEDA
Avenida Juárez
Next door to the Sheraton Alameda, this glittering new shopping mall houses coffee shops and expensive perfumeries and sports shops.
Daily 8–9 (shop times vary)
Hidalgo, Juárez

ENTERTAINMENT

BALLET

BALLET FOLCLÓRICO DE MÉXICO
Palacio de Bellas Artes, Avenida Hidalgo
Tel (55) 55 12 36 33
www.balletamalia.com.mx
A performance by the Ballet Folclórico in its home theater (an attraction in itself with its dazzling interior and glittering

jeweled stage curtain) is a must. This long-standing, world-famous company puts on spectacular shows of elaborately choreographed Mexican dances interspersed with traditional music and song. Peasant dances may be a trifle glamorized and costumes more at home in the West End than in Mexican villages, but the overall spectacle is dazzling.
Performances usually Sun at 9.30am and 8.30pm, Wed at 8.30pm
Tickets from $20
Bellas Artes

CINEMAS

CINEARTE
Plaza del Ángel, Londres 161, Zona Rosa
Tel (55) 52 08 40 44
www.contempocinema.com
This small art cinema is hidden away on the first floor of the gallery Plaza del Ángel. It has two modern cinemas, digital sound, a café, a bar and parking. Wednesdays are half price.
Insurgentes

CINEMEX CASA DE ARTE
Plaza Masaryk, Calle Anatole France 120, Polanco
Tel (55) 52 57 69 69
www.cinemex.com
This is an exclusive cinema showing foreign-language and art films, with a café, bar and valet parking.
Polanco

CINETECA NACIONAL
Avenida Mexico Coyoacán 389
Tel (55) 12 53 93 00
www.cinetecanacional.net
Home to cinema festivals and regular screenings of art-house movies, the Cineteca often shows English-language films.
Coyoacán

CONTEMPORARY LIVE MUSIC

HOSTERÍA DEL BOHEMIO
Avenida Hidalgo 107
Tel (55) 55 12 83 28
Guests here, in the interior patio of the ex-San Hipolito convent, are treated to live jazz and *nueva trova* from the shadows of the candlelit tables around the patio. Coffee, cakes, savory snacks and beer are on the menu.
Daily 5pm–1am
Hidalgo

SALA MANUEL PONCE
Palacio de Bellas Artes, Avenida Hidalgo
Tel (55) 55 29 93 20
The pick of the city's jazz is here, in this smaller concert hall in the Palacio de Bellas Artes, along with Cuban music and visiting world-music groups. Check the monthly schedule with the box office (open from noon) and buy tickets in advance, as the venue is very popular.
Bellas Artes

The facade of the Teatro de los Insurgentes, Coyoacán

SALA NEZAHUALCOYOTL
Ciudad Universitaria
Tel 56 65 07 09/56 22 71 25
Some of the world's leading musicians as well as local and student performers appear at this excellent recital hall within the UNAM campus.
Tickets usually from $8
Copilco

CULTURAL CENTERS

CENTRO NACIONAL DE LAS ARTES
Calle Río Churrubusco with Calle Canal de Miramontes
Tel (55) 55 49 48 39
This is one of the most important cultural centers in the city, comprising theaters, concert exhibition halls and 10 cinemas. The city's Orquesta Sinfónica Carlos Chávez often plays here, as do visiting string quartets and solo recitalists.
Daily 11–10
General Anaya

FORO CULTURAL COYOACÁN
Calle Allende 36
Tel (55) 55 54 07 38
Tucked behind Coyoacán's Casa de Cortés, this lively cultural center, full name Foro Cultural Coyoacanese Hugo Argüelles, has a dynamic schedule of events that includes theater, dance and concerts—from Beatles cover groups to string quartets. There are discounts for students, and there's a good café on site.
Daily 11–10

THEATER

TEATRO DE LA CUIDAD
Calle Donceles 36
Tel (55) 55 18 49 23
The Opera de México and Orquesta Sinfónica often give performances in this beautiful theater just next door to the Museo Nacional de Arte.
Bellas Artes, Allende

TEATRO DE LOS INSURGENTES
Avenida Insurgentes
Tel (55) 55 25 90 00 (Ticketmaster)
This modern and rather rundown theater hosts musicals, pantomimes and popular shows, mostly in Spanish although occasionally a visiting theater group from Europe or the US will perform here.
Box office open Tue–Sun 10–6
Any bus heading south down Avenida Insurgentes

NIGHTLIFE

BARS AND CLUBS

BAR COLMILLO
Calle Versalles 52
Tel (55) 55 92 61 14
Firmly established as a landmark on the international DJ map, Bar Colmillo keeps the dance floor heaving with a mix of Asian dub, hip hop and

psychedelic trance, while the groovy Upstairs Lounge, with armchairs and ambient tunes, offers respite for the weary.
Wed–Sat 10.30am–4am
Cover from $8
Cuauhtemoc

BARRACUDA
Calle Nueva León 4-A, Condesa
Tel (55) 52 11 94 80
You could be forgiven for thinking you are in London or New York in this swanky post-modern bar, attracting the city's rich, beautiful and wealthy. The *mojitos* are superb and the service impeccable.
Wed–Sun 7pm–2am
Chilpancingo

WHAT TO DO

CAFEÍNA
Calle Nueva León 73, Condesa
Tel (55) 52 12 00 90
Monday evenings are especially spirited in this trendy bar, when lovers of Brazilian music can drink excellent *caipirinhas* to the sweet tones of MPB and samba. There is a dance floor, which gets packed, and live music every evening.
Daily 9pm–2am
Chilpancingo

HOOKAH LOUNGE
Calle Campeche 284, Condesa
Tel (55) 52 64 62 75
This super-chilled-out bar in the city's hippest district is reminiscent of scenes from *A Thousand and One Nights*. You can relax here, sprawl out on sumptuous cushions, smoke a bubble pipe with honey tobacco and eat delicious Arabic mezze.
Thu–Sun 7pm–2am
Chilpancingo

MAMA RUMBA
Plaza San Jacinto 23, San Ángel
Tel (55) 55 50 80 99
Decked out in patriotic red, blue and white Cuban flag tablecloths and vibrating to the rhythms of merengue and salsa, this is one of the best-known and best-loved Cuban bars in town. Quality live music every night, a spacious dance floor and a restaurant serving spiced-up Cuban cuisine are all on the menu.
Bar Thu–Sat 9pm–4am, Restaurant Thu–Sun 1–11
$2.50 entrance fee after 10pm
Any bus heading south down Avenida Insugentes, or walk/taxi from metro Miguel Ángel de Quevedo

PUNTO Y APARTE
Calle Amberes, 62
Tel (55) 55 33 54 42
www.cabaretito.com
Hidden away on the first floor, up a cramped and crooked staircase, this lively and intimate gay bar has a cabaret every evening from 9pm, a good selection of wines and good-value snacks and pasta dishes.
Daily 2pm–1am
Insurgentes

Mexico City's bullring is the largest in the world

T-GALLERY
Calle Saltillo 39
Tel (55) 52 11 12 22
Groovy acid jazz is played live every evening in this bar packed with an eclectic mix of antiques and odds and ends—all for sale, incidentally. Arrive early to get a private room with velvet sofas or you may find yourself perching on the stairs with the crowds.
Mon–Sat 10pm–2am
Chilpancingo

CAFÉS AND CANTINAS

CANTINA EL CENTENARIO
Calle Vicente Suárez 42, Condesa
Tel (55) 55 53 44 54
Here is a Mexican cantina at its best—pass through the saloon doors into a noisy den of happy revelers knocking back tequilas and munching on nachos. Service is strictly no frills, and the *michelada* (beer with ice, lime juice and salt) will put hair on your chest.
Mon–Wed 10am–11.30pm, Thu–Sat 10am–12.30am
Junancatlan, Chilpancingo

MAMBO CAFÉ
Avenida Insurgentes Sur 644
Tel (55) 55 23 94 52
Excellent groups from Puerto Rico, Cuba and the Dominican Republic play in this café that oozes Caribbean spirit. Dancers are flashy and confident and competitions are sometimes held. However, don't let this put you off; the atmosphere is welcoming and every generation, race and social class enjoy dancing here.
Wed–Sun 9pm–2am
Any bus heading south down Avenida Insurgentes

YUPPIES SPORTS BAR
Calle Genova 34, with Calle Hamburgo
Tel (55) 55 33 09 19
Television screens showing 24-hour sporting events dominate this huge pub-style bar. The menu includes Tex-Mex tacos, chicken wings, pizza and nachos. Popular with visitors.
Daily 1pm–2am (Sat and Sun until 3am)
Insurgentes

SPORTS AND ACTIVITIES

BULLFIGHTING

PLAZA MÉXICO
Calle Augusto Rodin No. 241
Tel (55) 56 11 44 13
www.lamexico.com
Mexico's bullfighting season runs from October to April (▷ 174). Bullfights usually start at 4pm on Sundays at this

47,000-capacity bullring, the world's largest. Seats are usually available the day of the fight, and on sunny days it's worth paying more to sit in the shade. Cushions can be rented.
$3–$48
Buses heading south down Avenida Insurgentes pass outside it

GOLF

CHAPULTEPEC GOLF CLUB
Tel (55) 55 89 14 08
www.golfchapultepec.com.mx
Day passes for golf clubs in Mexico City can be difficult to come by, with rules requiring that you attend with an existing member. This challenging 18-hole course (par 72) with a pleasant clubhouse is the easiest place to get a game.

HORSE RACING

HIPÓDROMO DE LAS AMÉRICAS
Avenida Industria Militar, Colonia Lomas de Sotelo
Tel (55) 53 25 90 00
The full gamut of Mexican society gathers under one roof for Mexico City's weekly races. For the most exclusive experience, the Turf Club is the place to base yourself, but wherever you are there are always plenty of bookies on hand, eager for you to part with your cash.
Sat and Sun 3pm
Entry from $2
Buses marked Hipodromo heading west on Avenida Reforma

RODEO

RANCHO DEL CHARRO
Avenida de los Constituyentes 500, Bosque de Chapultepec
Tel (55) 52 77 87 06
www.nacionaldecharros.com
This is the place to see exciting rodeo action, including remarkable feats of horsemanship and showy pageantry. Mariachi bands add to the atmosphere.
Shows usually held at 11am on Sun
Chapultepec

SOCCER

ESTADIO AZTECA
Calzada de Tlalpan 3465
Tel (55) 54 87 31 26
www.ticketmaster.com.mx (tickets)
Home to the capital's biggest soccer club, América, Estadio Azteca is the vast stadium where the World Cup finals of 1970 and 1986 were held. Guided tours on the hour every hour from 10–3.
Tasqueña, then bus 26 towards Xochimilco

HEALTH AND BEAUTY

ENRIQUE BRICKER
Calle Londres 136-A
Tel (55) 52 08 17 63
This trendy beauty salon offers reliable quality cuts without an appointment, as well as tanning and reviving facials.
Mon–Sat 10.30–10.30
Insurgentes

FOR CHILDREN

PAPALOTE MUSEUM
See page 113.

PARQUE ZOOLÓGICO CHAPULTEPEC
Bosque de Chapultepec
The city's zoo at the western end of the lake occupies a large section of Chapultepec Park and is home to more than 2,000 animals from five continents. The landscape desert, tropical and temperate forests, and the animals seem well cared for. The ocelots and spider monkeys are highlights, as are the pandas. The zoo is popular with families and can be overcrowded at weekends.
Tue–Sun 9–4
Free
Chapultepec

PISTA DE HIELO SAN JERÓNIMO
Avenida Contreras 300
Tel (55) 56 83 19 29
This well-kept and spacious indoor ice-skating arena toward the south of the city has two cafés on site.
Tue–Thu 11–3, 5–7.30, Fri 11–9, Sat–Sun 11–8
$5.50 unlimited time
Metro to Universidad then taxi

FESTIVALS AND EVENTS

JANUARY

FEAST OF SAN ANTONIO ABAD
January 17
The Blessing of the Animals takes place at the church of Santiago Tlatelolco on Plaza de las Tres Culturas, San Juan Bautista Church in Coyoacán and the Church of San Fernando, north of Juárez and Reforma. Pets and livestock are decorated with flowers and ribbons and blessed in the church.

SEPTEMBER

EL GRITO DE INDEPENDENCIA (THE CRY OF INDEPENDENCE)
September 15–16
Palacio Nacional, Zócalo
This fiesta commemorates Mexican independence from Spain, or more specifically, the day Father Hidalgo irang the bell of his small church n Dolores Hidalgo calling on his parishioners to fight for liberty. Every year at 11pm on September 15, the President stands on the balcony of the National Palace and shouts "Viva México" several times while the crowd below replies "Viva," and the great bell hanging over the entrance is rung. On the last shout, fireworks shatter the sky and the party continues all night.

DECEMBER

FIESTA DE NUESTRA SEÑORA DE GUADALUPE
See page 179.

CENTRAL MEXICO EAST

Silver jewelry from Taxco and Talavera dinnerware from Puebla are two of the traditional crafts to look out for in this region. Veracruz's Carnaval is one of the best celebrations of this festvial in the whole of Mexico.

KEY TO SYMBOLS
- Shopping
- Entertainment
- Nightlife
- Sports
- Activities
- Health and Beauty
- For Children

COATEPEC

DENICIA ARTESANÍAS
Calle Lerdo 3, Local 4 and 5, Coatepec
Tel (228) 816 81 63
This pretty shop just off the *zócalo* specializes in local Veracruzana crafts such as wooden boxes and handmade paper. It also sells local coffee beans and interesting coffee liqueurs, which you can taste before buying. No Amex cards.
Daily 10.30–9

LA EUROPEA
Calle 5 de Mayo 5, Coatepec
Tel (228) 816 71 87
One block from the *zócalo*, La Europea is stuffed with first-rate tents, rucksacks, bicycling and fishing gear, binoculars, camping, hiking and kayaking equipment—virtually anything you could possibly need for adventure and eco-tourism trips.
Mon–Sat 10.30–3, 5–7

CUERNAVACA

CENTRO COMERCIAL LAS CAMPANAS
Calle Comonfort 2, Cuernavaca
Tel (777) 314 34 45
Browsers and bargain hunters will find this fantastic bric-à-brac and craft shop a dream, full of Guatemalan *huipil* shawls, local pottery, furniture, old records and secondhand clothing. Cash only.
Daily 10–2, 4–8

LIBROS Y ARTE
Palacio de Cortés, Boulevard Juárez 100, Cuernavaca
Tel (777) 312 99 33
The Cuernvaca outlet of this nationwide chain specializes in guidebooks, hardbacks covering all aspects of the art, history and anthropology of Mexico, English-language books, art postcards and posters.
Tue–Sun, 11–8

LOS AMATES DE AXOCHIAPAN
Axochiapan, Carretera Ahuaxtl –Teotlalco, Cuernavaca
Tel (735) 351 03 55
This spa, off Highway 160 between Cuernavaca and Puebla, consists of two thermal sulphuric pools rich in calcium and iron and naturally heated to 30°C (86°F), changing rooms, a restaurant, children's games and gardens, and is one of the most pleasant, although most remote, spas in Morelos state.
Daily 9–6
Take the Cuatla–Izucar de Matamoros highway. At the Amayuca junction, turn right towards Tepalcingo

AQUA SPLASH
Carretera Tequesquitengo-Jojutla, Km 4.5, Cuernavaca
Tel (734) 343 34 24
www.aquasplash.com.mx
With 13 pools, 8 water slides, children's pools and games, wave machines, restaurants, gardens for picnics and parking, this excellent, modern and well-run water theme park is well worth inserting into your

itinerary, and is easily reached by car from Cuernvaca. It gets very crowded on weekends.

Daily 8–6

From Cuernavaca take Highway 95 towards Acapulco, pass the tollbooth at Alpuyeca, then leave the highway and take minor road towards Tequesquitengo. Turn right onto the road to Jojutla and park entrance is 4km (2.5 miles) from the turn-off

PUEBLA

BARRIO DEL ARTISTA

Calle 6 Oriente with Calle 6 Norte, Puebla

The cobbled Plazuela del Torno, now surrounded by artists' studios open to the public, owes its name to the spinning wheels that traditionally occupied the square. By day it is a relaxing area to wander around and check out the artists' work, while most evenings there is live jazz.

Daily 10–6

CAMOTERÍA EL LIRIO

Calle 6 Oriente 204, Puebla
Tel (222) 232 23 66

Halfway along Santa Clara Street, lined with shops selling local cakes and sweets in honor of the Santa Clara nuns who were famed for their candies, is Sara Martinez's sweet shop. A huge gilt mirror towers over an old-fashioned glass cabinet displaying mouth-watering cakes made from ground nuts and almonds, cherries filled with almond paste, glazed fruit sticks and *tortitas* de Santa Clara—cream tarts. Cash only.

Daily 10.30–8

CARLOS OLEA MUEBLES Y ANTIGUEDADES

Calle 6 Sur No. 506, Puebla
Tel (222) 242 11 55

This high-ceilinged colonial house at the hub of the antiques shops surrounding the Plazuela de los Sapos is stuffed with rustic and antique furniture, rugs, lamps, paintings and religious statues. Even for those not looking to make a purchase, it is worth popping into this rambling building to browse the sheer quantity of quirky objects. No Amex cards.

Mon–Fri 10–2, 4–7, Sat–Sun 10.30–6

MERCADO DE ARTESANÍAS "EL PARIÁN"

Calle 2 Oriente with Calle 6 Norte, Puebla

Occupying the ancient Plaza San Roque, the market's mass of craft stands specialize in Talavera ceramics at excellent prices, embroidered blouses, glass, local sweets, onyx and much more.

Daily 10–7.30

Highly decorative pots are produced in Puebla

TALAVERA URIARTE

Calle 4 Poniente 911, Puebla
Tel (222) 232 15 98
www.uriartetalavera.com.mx

Founded in 1824, this is one of the most prestigious Talavera factories in Puebla, allowing visitors to observe every stage in the pottery-making process from the shaping of the clay and firing of the plates and tiles to the application of the intricate blue-and-white patterns. The interior patio is beautifully tiled and displays the factory shop's wares: superb ceramics and pottery at high prices.

Mon–Fri 9–6.30, Sat 10–6.30, Sun 11–6

TEATRO PRINCIPAL

Calle 6 Norte with Calle 8 Oriente, Puebla
Tel (222) 232 60 85

Inaugurated in 1760, this is the oldest still-operating theater in the Americas, hosting ballets, musicals, plays and symphony concerts. You can visit he plush interior outside performance times.

Open for visits daily 10–4.30

Tickets from $7

LAS BRUJAS

Calle 3 Oriente 407, Puebla
Tel (222) 864 46 69

This trendy café serves excellent espressos and ice-cold beer, and often hosts student theater performances, live jazz, wine tastings and tarot readings. Student discounts with card.

Mon–Sat 10am–10.30pm

CAFÉ RENTOY

Calle 8 Norte 602, Puebla
Tel (222) 246 44 59

This well-liked groovy café and wine bar on the northeast corner of the Barrio del Artista square serves a wide range of cocktails. The bohemian clientele often spill out on to the cobbled *plazuela*, where live musicians perform jazz, Cuban *son* and *trova* every evening from 6 to 8pm and midnight to 2am. There's jazz on Sundays from 3pm.

Daily 8–3

MUSEO DE HISTORIA NATURAL

Centro Cívico 5 de Mayo, Cerro de Guadalupe, Puebla

Animal skeletons and life-size model dinosaurs are highlights of this interactive museum, often full of primary school groups. The Planetarium next door has IMAX screens showing films all day on Saturdays and Sundays.

Tue–Sun 10–4.30

$4

Ruta 72 marked "centro cívico" from Boulevard de los Héroes del 5 de Mayo, three blocks east of the *zócalo*

WHAT TO DO

TAXCO

LAPIDARIO BARRERA

Calle Juan Ruiz de Alarcón 3, Local 2, Taxco
Tel (762) 622 87 08
Designers Salvador Barrera and Lorena Chávez sell their individual creations in this small shop two blocks from the Plaza Borda. Particularly notable is their Mata Ortíz line of silver jewelry that incorporates pottery, inspired by traditional designs from this town in northern Chihuahua.
Daily 9–7

LUNA COLECTION

Plaza Borda 1, Taxco
Tel (762) 622 64 47
The interior of Luna Colection resembles a mysterious Aladdin's cave with sparkling precious stones on display. You'll find lovely handmade silver pieces at good prices.
Daily 9–7

TEPOZTLÁN

SANTA FE

Avendia Revolución 24, Tepoztlán
Tel (739) 395 27 97
This boutique sells embroidered dresses, silver jewelry and unusual pots made from dried orange peel, all handmade in town.
Sat–Sun 11–7, Mon–Fri times vary; phone ahead and the shop will open

VERACRUZ

LIBROS Y ARTE

Callejón Portal de Miranda 9, Veracruz
Tel (229) 932 69 43
One of a chain, this is an excellent place to browse for travel, art and history books. It's also useful for English books and guidebooks, and there's a section for children's games, puzzles and books, plus a selection of crafts and posters.
Mon–Sat 10–7.45, Sun 1–7.45

EL MAYAB

Calle Zaragoza 78, corner with Zamora, Veracruz
Tel (229) 932 14 35
This faded, very old-fashioned shop is stuffed with Cuban *guayaberas* in every style and shade imaginable. The simplest start at $30. Helpful staff can offer useful advice.
Mon–Sat 10–2, 5–9, Sun 10–2

PLATERÍA MARQUEZ

Callejón Trigueros 39-A, between calles M. Molina and Aquiles Serdán, Veracruz
Tel (229) 926 56 53
Silver, gold jewelry and precious stones, as well as some rather incongruous beachwear, are on sale in this boutique in a tiny *plazuela* at the end of Portales Miranda, southeast of the *zócalo*. Some original pieces can be found. No credit cards.
Mon–Sat 10–2, 4–8

Musicians serenading diners outside a bar in Veracruz

PLAZA DE ARTESANÍAS

Calle Serdan with Calle Landero and Cos, Veracruz
This large, enclosed market is the best place for buying Cuban *guayaberas*, traditional *huarache* ponchos, hammocks, souvenirs, regional sweets and flip-flops. No credit cards.
Daily 9am–10pm

ZÓCALO

Veracruz
The *zócalo* makes a perfect setting for the languid open-air *danzón* dance session, backed by the sweet sounds of the local band consisting of guitar, violins, flute, double bass and *guiro* (percussion instrument). This stately, elegant Caribbean dance originated in Cuba and reached Mexico at the beginning of the 20th century.
Daily from 7pm

KACHIMBA

Boulevard M. Avila Camacho, with Médico Militar, Boca del Río, Veracruz
Tel (229) 927 19 80
This is the place to dance salsa, in the suburb of Boca del Río, 6km (4 miles) from the city.
Thu–Sun 8pm–2am
Entrance $3

EL PALACIO

Calle Miguel Lerdo 127, Veracruz
Tel (229) 932 24 10
On the *zócalo* under the arched northern side, El Palacio comes alive every evening. A great place to sit and watch couples dancing *danzón* on the square, listen to the marimba players and soak up the Caribbean atmosphere of a Veracruzana night. Try the local tipple—*julep*—made from dark rum, mint and sugar, or the *el torito* with peanut liqueur. No Amex cards.
Daily noon–4am

EL RINCÓN DE LA TROVA

Plazuela de la Lagunilla, Veracruz
Hidden away down a dark, cobbled passageway off Calle Serdán, which emerges onto a pretty square, this rambling old house opens in the evenings with live Afro-Cuban *son* and salsa. Informal, it attracts a mix of people; the bar serves mainly rum. Cash only.
Tue–Sat 7pm–2am

ALBERCA OLÍMPICA

Mocamco beach, behind the Hotel Mocambo on Avenida Adolfo Ruiz Cortínez, Veracruz
If the beach doesn't tempt you, try this large, clean pool right on the beach, within a complex that has a children's pool, changing facilities and shower, lounge chairs and toilets.
Winter 9–5; summer 10–6
$6

MEXICO VERDE
Veracruz
Tel (228) 812 01 34 (Xalapa)
www.mexicoverde.com
This reliable, well-run and ecologically conscious adventure holiday company offers hikes to waterfalls and crystalline natural pools, rappelling (abseiling) down 85m-high (279ft) rock faces and rafting down the River Pescado through 18 Class III and IV rapids, as well as child-friendly adventures for the family.
Mon–Fri 10–1, 4–7.30, Sat 10–1
1 day to 5 days from $100 to $420

ACUARIO
Boulevard M. Avila Camacho, Veracruz
www.acuariodeveracruz.com
This modern aquarium with 25 spacious pools is well worth visiting. Its star attractions are the sharks, barracudas and rays.
Mon–Thu 10–7, Fri–Sun 10–7.30
Adult $5, child $2.50

PARQUE RECREATIVO REINO MÁGICO
Avenida Salvador Díaz Mirón with Calzada Armada de México, Veracruz
The Magic Kingdom Theme Park has a swimming pool with water slide, an Indian village with tepees, a cowboy town with horseback-riding, mini golf, soccer pitches, roller-blading and bicycles for rent.
Tue–Sun 10–6
Adult $7, child (3–10) $5, under 3 free

XALAPA

EL GIRASOL
Callejón del Diamante 6-6, Xalapa, tel (228) 818 01 45
Xalapeõs Ilustres 22, Xalapa, tel (228) 841 41 98
Crafts from all over Mexico are sold at good prices in these beautiful *artesanía* shops. You'll find ceramics, embroidered dresses and blouses, silver jewelry, candles, glass and furniture. No Amex cards.
Mon–Sat 10–2, 4–8, Sun 12–2

EL AGORA DE LA CIUDAD
Parque Juárez, Xalapa
Tel (228) 818 57 30
This cultural center buzzes with students attracted by the art and foreign films on show in the small, modern cinema. There is a café on site.
Showings Tue–Sun 4.30pm, 7pm, 9.30pm, Sat and Sun noon
Tickets from $1.50

TEATRO DEL ESTADO
Avenida M. Avila Camacho with Calle de la Llave, Xalapa
Tel (228) 817 31 10
The city is justly proud of this ultramodern theater/concert hall which has a reputation for attracting the best performers and shows in the country. Regular dance and theater performances are hosted here, as well as free off-season concerts (Jun–Aug).
Box office daily from 3pm
Tickets start at around $5

LOS MOLINOS
Calle Ursulo Galván 57, Xalapa
This very popular restaurant-bar draws Xalapa's hip student population and serves a wide selection of spirits at cheap prices. It throbs to the beat of live rock and *trova* music on Fridays and Saturdays. No credit cards.
Mon–Sat 8pm–1am

AVENTURAS SIN LÍMITE
Calle Emilio Carranza 58, Xalapa
Tel (228) 817 76 09
Try this well-reputed adventure tourism company for horseback riding, rafting, hiking and rappelling (abseiling) around Jalcomulco, only 40 minutes from Xalapa. Food and equipment are included in the price and the guides speak English.
Daily 9–7
Day trips from $35

FESTIVALS AND EVENTS

FEBRUARY

DÍA DE LA MEXICANIDAD
February 22–23
Ixcateopan de Cuauhtémoc
The anniversary of the death of Cuauhtémoc, the last Aztec ruler, is celebrated in his birthplace, the village of Ixcateopan 20km (12 miles) from Taxco. Runners come from Mexico City via Taxco carrying a torch representing the identity of the Mexican people. Aztec dancers in traditional costume and plumed headdresses come from all over Mexico to dance all night and most of the following day.

FEBRUARY/MARCH

CARNAVAL
Starting second Tuesday before Ash Wednesday
Veracruz
This is the largest Carnaval in Latin America outside Brazil. The night parades are spectacular shows of water, light and music. For seven days, the fantastically decorated *carros alegóricos* (floats), carrying scantily clad women shaking to Latin American rhythms, present a feast of color and sparkle and attract millions of visitors. The opening ceremony on the *zócalo* is the "Quema del mal humor," the burning of bad moods, then everyone can proceed to dance and sing to the music.

JULY/AUGUST

FERIA DE SANTIAGO APOSTOL
Last week of July
Santiago Tuxtla
These festivities celebrate Santiago (St. James the Apostle), the town's patron saint. Processions, rodeos, horse-racing, street theater and dancing take place over five consecutive days.

WHAT TO DO

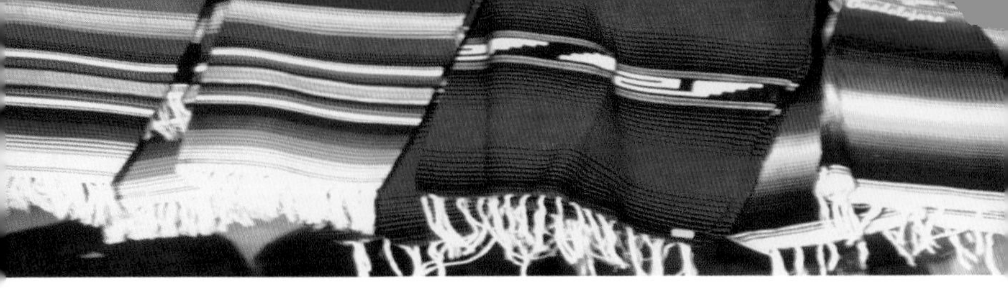

CENTRAL MEXICO WEST

The handicrafts and decorative arts in Guadalajara are some of the best in the country. Puerto Vallarta has become a base for excursions and special interest trips, including ornithology and whale-watching, with good hiking, watersports and diving opportunities.

KEY TO SYMBOLS
- Shopping
- Entertainment
- Nightlife
- Sports
- Activities
- Health and Beauty
- For Children

COLIMA

DIF ARTESANÍA

Calle Andador Constitución 12, Colima

Handsome wooden musical instruments, clay figurines, masks and ceramics are on sale at this great-value state-run crafts shop on Andador Constitución, leading north from Colima's main square.

Mon–Sat 10–2, 5–8, Sun 10–2

GUADALAJARA

ANTIGUA DE MEXICO

Avenida Independencia 255, Tlaquepaque, Guadalajara

Tel (33) 363 534 02

This is a wonderful antiques emporium with antique furniture, custom-made stonework and sublime articles for the home—an interior design fan's heaven. Unfortunately, quality doesn't come cheap. Shipping is possible on request.

Mon–Fri 10–2, 3–7, Sat 10–6

HUICHOL MUSEUM SHOP

By the main entrance to Basilica of Zapopan, Guadalajara

Attached to the Huichol Museum, this is one of the best places to buy crafts made by the Huichol people of Jalisco and Nayarit. Exquisite bead bowls and yarn paintings are on offer, and staff will explain the symbolism of each piece. All works are left unfinished, as the Huichol believe only God can achieve perfection. Cash only.

Mon–Sat 9.30–1.15, 3–5.45

MERCADO LIBERTAD OR SAN JUAN DE DIOS

South of Plaza Tapatía, Guadalajara

This vast covered market houses a panoply of local goods, ranging from Paracho guitars, cowboy hats, *huarache* sandals and good food on the first floor—try the *birria* (goat meat). The east end of the market is better for local crafts.

Daily 10–6

TONALÁ MARKET

Tonalá, 15km (9 miles) southwest of Guadalajara

At the Sunday and Thursday street markets you can find great bargains in pottery, glass and ceramics. The market is held on the central avenue, where buses from Guadalajara stop.

Thu and Sun

BALLET FOLCLÓRICO DE GUADALAJARA

Teatro Degollado, Calle Degollado

Tel (33) 361 54 9 22

This superb dance troupe performs every Sunday at 10am in the Teatro Degollado. Their repertoire includes memorable renditions of pre-Hispanic and regional dances.

$14 or $19—book in advance

LA MAESTRANZA

Maestranza 179, Guadalajara

Tel (33) 361 358 78

Bullfighting's the theme in this bar five minutes south of the Plaza de Armas. Arrive early for a seat—the place is heaving on weekends.

Tue–Sun 1pm–3am

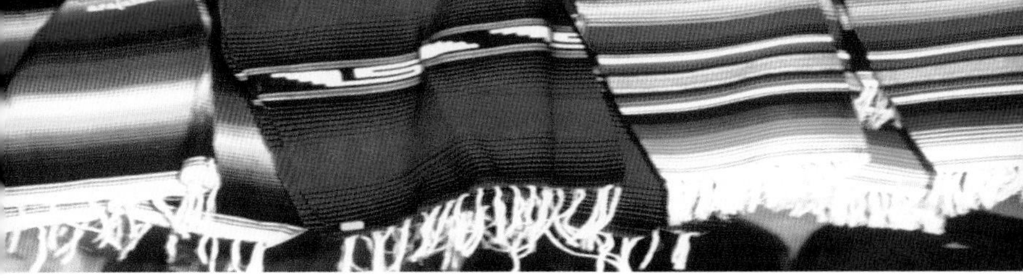

LIENZO CHARRO DE JALISCO

Calle Dr. Michell 572, Guadalajara

Authentic Mexican rodeo, including wild mare riding and team bull riding, takes place here every Sunday at midday.

$5 entrance

Head south on Avenida Independencia, turning left at third roundabout

ZOOLÓGICO GUADALAJARA

Paseo del Zoológico 600, Parque Natural Huentitán, Guadalajara

Tel (33) 367 444 88

www.zooguadalajara.com.mx

Guadalajara's internationally acclaimed zoo has 2,000 animals. New exhibits include "Safari Masai Mara," where animals are free to roam.

Wed–Sun 10–6 (daily only during school holidays)

$3.50

Take Calzada Independencia Norte and turn right after ring road (Periférico Norte) at Paseo del Zoológico

GUADALUPE

SARAPES DE GUADALUPE

Avenida Colegio Militar 117, Guadalupe

This gem of a workshop sells fabulous handmade *sarape* rugs and ponchos. Eusebio Salas Ramírez has been working here for more than 65 years, and is happy to show visitors the antique wooden looms they still use.

Mon–Sat 8–6

GUANAJUATO

CASA DEL CONDE DE LA VALENCIANA

Plazuela de Valenciana, Guanajuato

Tel (473) 732 25 50

Right opposite the Templo de San Cayetano de Valenciana on the road to Dolores Hidalgo, this delightful antiques emporium consists of several large rooms of tasteful furniture. The locally made tin and copper lamps are particularly fine. No Amex cards.

Mon–Sat 10.30–6

Take the road 4km (2.5 miles) out of Guanajuato towards Dolores Hidalgo

MERCADO HIDALGO

Avenida Juárez, main entrance opposite Calle Mendizabal, Guanajuato

You can't miss the enormous iron-framed building housing this crafts market. Local specialties include basketware and embroidered dresses, flowers and *charamusca*—a confection of melted twisted brown or white sugar, usually with peanuts or coconut.

Daily 7am–9pm

LEÓN

ANTROPÍA

Calle Niebla 202, León

Tel (477) 773 92 99

Live acts—from Pablo Milanés covers to Afro-Peruvian rhythms—can be seen and heard at trendy Antropía, north of central León in the Jardines del Moral district between López Mateos and Insurgentes. Excellent cocktails and dips.

Daily 7pm–1am, Fri–Sat until 3am

Leopards at Guadalajara's modern zoo

EXPLORA SCIENCE MUSEUM

Boulevard Francisco Villa 202, La Martinica, León

Tel (477) 711 67 11

This is a great interactive science museum for kids with the added attraction of an IMAX screen. In the gardens there are two handsome old steam engines.

Tue–Fri 9–6, Sat–Sun 10–7

MANZANILLO

GOLF LAS HADAS

Avenida Los Riscos and Vista Hermosa, Peninsula de Santiago, Manzanillo

Tel (314) 331 01 01

Condé Nast voted this 18-hole Roy Dye-designed course one of the most scenic golf courses in the world—the 18th hole is spectacular. There's a laid-back clubhouse too.

$80 per day includes shared golf car

MORELIA

LA ANTIGUA VALLADOLID

Calle Galeana 82, Morelia

This secondhand bookshop one block west of the Plaza de Armas has a good selection of pocket Spanish-English dictionaries, as well as books in English, French and German. And the cappuccino in the café isn't bad either. Cash only.

Mon–Sat 10am–10.30pm

MERCADO DE DULCES

East side of Calle Valentín Gómez Farías, next to Palacio Clavijero, Morelia

Morelia's block-long, arcaded Mercado de Dulces, alongside the Palácio Clavijero, overflows with stands selling local Michoacánense sweets—cloyingly sweet for some tastes, but worth sampling nevertheless. Try the guava paste rolls, sugar-cane drinks and tamarind balls dusted with chili powder.

Daily 10–6, but most stands tend to keep their own hours

LAS MERCEDES

Calle Madero 185, corner with Calle Valentín Gómez Farias, Morelia

Tel (443) 313 15 55

Directly opposite the Mercado de Dulces, Las Mercedes is an epicurean interior design shop that blends traditional crafts from the region—including fine Cocucha pots—with modern designs. Knowledgeable staff will help you pick your way through the kitchenware, Talavera ceramics and furniture (including pigskin chairs) on the large shop floor.

Mon–Sat 10–9, Sun 10–6

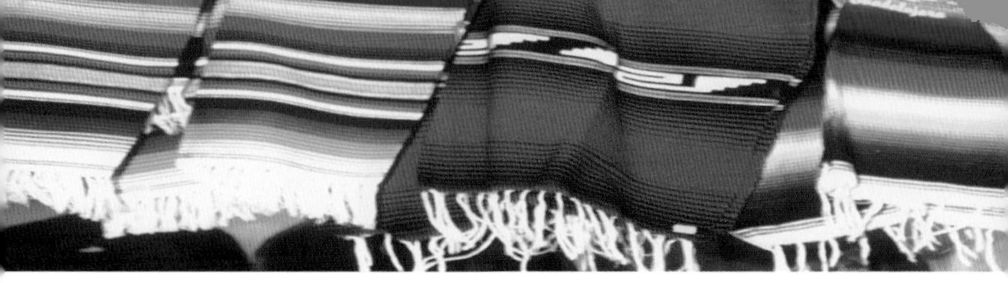

EL RINCÓN DE LOS SENTIDOS

Calle Madero 485, Morelia
Tel (443) 317 59 74
This is a great place to catch soulful live *trova* music (Thu–Sat from 8pm) in a pretty courtyard decked out with cool modern sculptures, paintings and photographs.
Sun–Wed 10–12, Thu–Sat 10am–2am

PÁTZCUARO

CASA DE LOS ONCE PATIOS, PÁTZCUARO

Between Calle Lerin and Calle Coss
Don't leave Pátzcuaro without wandering through the craft shops in this warren of courtyards. You'll find lacquerware, religious art, clay pottery and musical instruments of the highest quality—but not cheap.
Daily 10–7, but most stores keep their own hours

LA CASA DEL FUEGO

Portal Pueblito No. 1, Pátzcuaro
Tel (434) 342 66 77
This splendid colonial mansion across from the basilica has been converted into a fun bar with live music on Friday and Saturday nights (starts 8pm). Different rooms have different atmospheres, but all are decorated with modern art and painted in outlandish shades.
Wed–Thu 3–11, Fri–Sat 1–11

PUERTO VALLARTA

ORIGENES

Calle Zaragoza 160, Puerto Vallarta
Tel (322) 223 14 55
Less than one block north of the main square is this stylish interior-design boutique that stocks well-made furniture, basketware and ornaments, including original candles and lamps. Great for special gifts.
Daily 10–10

CLUB CHRISTINE

Krystal Vallarta Hotel, Avenida de las Garzas, Puerto Vallarta
Tel (332) 224 02 02
This is the resort's top nightspot playing the latest techno and house hits. The light show and decor are spectacular and it's always crowded.
Tue–Sun from 10pm
Cover charge $15 includes first drink

ECORIDEMEX

Calle Miramar 382, Puerto Vallarta
Tel (332) 222 79 12
Mountain biking in the mountainous jungle of the Sierra Madre around Puerto Vallarta is what this friendly tour company offers. There are a variety of different excursions, from relaxed to seriously strenuous, all with an English-speaking guide. The office is two blocks behind the cathedral.
Mon–Sat 10–6

An intricate lacquer plate, Casa de los Once Patios, Pátzcuaro

VALLARTA ADVENTURES

Paseo Las Palmas 39A, Nuevo Vallarta, Puerto Vallarta
www.vallarta-adventures.com
Swimming with dolphins, whale-watching, snorkeling and sailing are organized by this, one of Puerto Vallarta's most established tour operators, with small groups and good safety. It's best to book online or by phone. The visit to the "authentic" Huichol village is best avoided.

VENUS MASSAGE

Aquiles Serdán 220, Puerto Vallarta
Tel (332) 223 27 14
Pamper yourself with a massage (Swedish, Turkish or with aromatherapy oils), hot stone therapy and facials at this great health complex, next to Hotel Molino de Agua. Masseurs will also visit your hotel.
Daily 10–7

SUPER GO-KARTS

Crucero Las Juntas, on the road to Tepic, Puerto Vallarta
Tel (332) 290 06 63
Opposite the airport, this is a great place to race to your heart's content. The track is good and safety precautions (including helmets) are top-notch. No driver's license is required. Also on site you'll find mini-golf, a children's maze and open-air bowling.
Daily 2–10

QUERÉTARO

DOÑA URRACA SPA

Calle 5 de Mayo 117, Querétaro
Tel (442) 238 54 00
www.donaurraca.com.mx
This luxurious spa has views over the whole city. Choose from the Jacuzzi, the gym, massages, facials or a sauna; you'll come out feeling reinvigorated—even your wallet will have lost weight.
Daily 8–6

SAN BLAS

STONERS SURF CAMP

Playa El Borrego, San Blas
Don't be put off by the name—this is an efficiently run surfing school at the beginning of Playa El Borrego. Run by friendly former Mexican champion surfer José Manuel "Pompis" Cano, it rents out boards, bicycles and gives surfing classes. They can arrange canoe trips too.

SAN MIGUEL DE ALLENDE

CLANDESTINO

Calle Zacateros 19, San Miguel de Allende
Tel (415) 152 16 23
Three blocks south of the Escuela de Bellas Artes, before the Insituto Allende, you'll find this cool crafts and antiques

shop filled with local *artesanía* and fabrics, as well as items from Guatemala.
Mon, Wed–Sat 11–7; Sun 12–5

7TH HEAVEN
Calle Diez de Sollano 18, San Miguel de Allende
Tel (415) 124 46 77
Attentive service and original jewelry, hats, clothes and gifts await you in this fashionable boutique two blocks from the *zócalo*. Jewelry can be made to order. Prices are high but the quality of goods and a tranquil ambience make it worth the extra pesos. No Amex cards. Traveler's checks accepted.
Mon–Sat 10–8, Sun 11–3

ASHTANGA YOGA
Calle Mesones 101, San Miguel de Allende
Tel (415) 154 61 37
Classes in English with instructor Fabienne Gauthier are the attraction of this relaxing yoga center. Ask about out-of-town yoga retreats.
Classes at 10am on weekdays, with special classes for beginners at 4pm on Tue and Thu. No appointment needed

TEQUISQUIAPAN

TURISMO ALTERNATIVO
Andador Comercial Vista Hermosa, local 1, Tequisquiapan
Tel (414) 226 71 86
This local tour company opposite the bus station offers great half-day guided tours in English that take in local spas, haciendas, thermal pools, geysers and an opal mine.
Daily 10–6

URUAPAN

EL ARTE TARASCO
Calle Culver City 32, Uruapan
This is one of the best shops for exquisite handmade lacquerware, at the top of Calle Independencia opposite the entrance to the Parque Nacional. There's also a workshop where you can watch the painstaking process of layered painting taking place.
Daily 9–2, 3–7

CASA DE LAS ARTESANÍAS DE MICHOACÁN
Calzada Fray Juan de San Miguel 129, Uruapan
Tel (452) 312 08 48
Crafts from around Michoacán state are sold here. Traditional lacquerware and pottery share space with superb examples of modern design, including silk scarves, as well as *changunga,* a potent fruit liqueur, local sweets and all-natural macadamia nut perfume.
Mon–Fri 10–7, Sat and Sun 10–6

VALLE DE BRAVO

ZELÁMPAGO CLUB LOUNGE
Calle Joaquín Arcadio Pagaza 316, Valle de Bravo
Tel (726) 262 49 46
Recline amid Moroccan splendor in this bar perched above Calle Pagaza. Soul and acid jazz are on the playlist, and there's a gas heater (as well as good cocktails) to warm you on chilly evenings.
Fri–Sat 8pm–2am

SALON SPA DE VALLE
Calle Nicolás Bravo 402, Valle de Bravo
Tel (726) 262 4919
Raymundo González is building himself a reputation as a great stylist, offering professional service at his trendy hair salon. Good facials and a relaxing massage are also available.
Tue–Sat 10–6

ZACATECAS

GONZÁLEZ ORTEGA MARKET
Avenida Hidalgo, between the cathedral and Plazuela Goitia, Zacatecas
Built in the late 19th century, this richly ornamented arcade houses 10 classy boutiques—an excellent place to pick up Zacatecan silver, Huichol crafts, leather goods, antiques and handmade sweets.
Mon–Fri 9–6, Sat 10–3 (shops have individual opening times)

MINA EL EDÉN
Cerro Grillo, Zacatecas
Tel (492) 922 30 02
A small train takes you the 450m (490 yards) or so to the entrance of this unusual disco buried in the depths of the "Del Grillo" hill (▷ 155). It is comfortably decked out around a circular dance floor, and has rocky walls, waiter service and international and Mexican hits on the playlist.
Thu–Sat 9pm–2am
Cover charge $7

FESTIVALS AND EVENTS

APRIL/MAY

FERIA DE SAN MARCOS
Last week April to first week May
Aguascalientes
www.feriadesanmarcos.com
Originally an agricultural fair, this two-week event has mushroomed into a vibrant cultural festival with dancing, bullfights, a rodeo, craft exhibtions, beauty pageants, mariachi bands and live music.

OCTOBER

CERVANTINO FESTIVAL
Starts first week October
Guanajuato
The International Cervantino Festival draws around 150,000 visitors each year for a feast of recitals, concerts, plays, dance and opera in a variety of locations around town to commemorate the Spanish writer Miguel de Cervantes.

FIESTA DE LA VIRGEN DE ZAPOPÁN
October 12
Guadalajara
This is when the revered Virgin returns from her annual pilgrimage of all the churches of Guadalajara. More than 150,000 people accompany her on the final leg of her journey back to the basilica in Guadalajara.

NORTHERN MEXICO AND BAJA CALIFORNIA

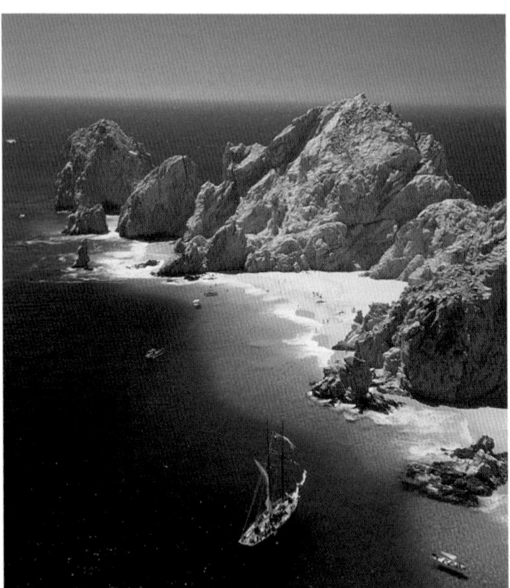

KEY TO SYMBOLS
- Shopping
- Entertainment
- Nightlife
- Sports
- Activities
- Health and Beauty
- For Children

Baja's Tijuana–Ensenada corridor attracts the majority of visitors, while Cabo San Lucas and San José del Cabo (Los Cabos) in Baja California Sur are a magnet for serious divers, golfers and sports fishers. The Tarahumara from the highlands of northern Mexico sell their traditional crafts in the region, particularly in Chihuahua and Creel.

CABO SAN LUCAS

BAJA CANTINA

Marina, L-M Dock, Cabo San Lucas
Tel (642) 143 15 91
Baja Cantina is one of the busiest spots, with a laid-back, holiday vibe. The dockside bar with a large-screen sports TV packs in the local gringo residents, who enjoy the all-day happy hour specials. There is a highly regarded restaurant where anglers can have their catch prepared to their liking.
Daily 7am–1am

CABO WABO CANTINA

Calle Lázaro Cárdenas and Calle Guerrero, Cabo San Lucas
Tel (624) 143 11 98
The lively Cabo Wabo has been a veritable gringo hotspot since it opened in the late 1980s. Owned by rock and roll star Sammy Hagar, it has an unpretentious and upbeat atmosphere, with live music most weekends during winter, including Mexican and international bands playing everything from rock and pop to Latin.
Club open 7pm–2am; restaurant serves decent meals 11–11

EL SQUID ROE

Boulevard Marina, Plaza Bonita, Cabo San Lucas
Tel (642) 143 06 55
www.elsquidroe.com
Wallflowers should retreat in haste; hot and raw, the Squid Roe is where anything well and truly goes. The dance floor, surrounded by a three-tier people-watcher's heaven, is the focal point. By 11pm gyrating hipsters are packed into every nook and cranny, with music ranging from hard core dance and garage to more light-hearted rock and pop. Dinner is served until 11.30.
Daily 8pm–4am

SOLMAR FLEET

Boulevard Marina, Cabo San Lucas
Tel (624) 143 06 46
www.solmar.com
A variety of fishing cruises is offered, from short excursions in *pangas* (small boats) beginning at $35 to more luxurious sportfishing cruisers at $350–$650 for serious anglers interested in catching marlin, dorado, tuna and wahoo. Prices include rent of cruiser, on-board captain, live-bait tank, international premium tackle and fighting chairs.
Daily 9–4

CHIHUAHUA

CASA DE LAS ARTESANÍAS DEL ESTADO DE CHIHUAHUA

Avenida Niños Heroes 1101, Chihuahua
Tel (614) 437 12 92
There are many good *artesanía* shops in Chihuahua that sell everything from silver jewelry to weavings, musical instruments and more mass-produced items. The best collection of Tarahumara crafts can be found here with an eclectic selection of ceramics, baskets and furniture. Prices are generally very fair in Chihuahua, so bargaining is unnecessary.
Daily 10–6

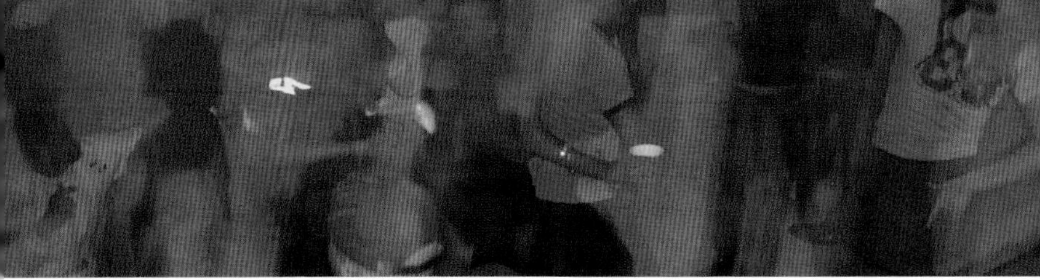

CREEL

MISIÓN TARAHUMARA

Parroquia, opposite the plaza, Creel
Tel (635) 456 00 97

Creel is the commercial hub of the Tarahumara region and throughout the town there are several souvenir shops selling Tarahumara weavings, musical instruments, pine-needle baskets and more. The Misión also sells maps of the region and guides which detail the Barrancas del Cobre (Copper Canyon) train journey (▷ 159). The *National Parks of Northwest Mexico* guide is on sale and another recommended read is *Tarahumara of the Sierra Madre* by John Kennedy (published by AHM).

Mon–Sat 9–1, 3–6, Sun 9–1

EXPEDICIONES UMARIKE

Avenida Ferrocarril s/n, north of tracks west of Plaza, PO Box 61, Creel
Tel/fax: (635) 456 02 48
www.umarike.com.mx

The professionally run Expediciones Umarike organizes high-quality adventurous pursuits in the Copper Canyon, including customized mountain biking and hiking to remote regions, rock-climbing, exploring colonial mining towns and thrilling rides across spectacular landscapes with 1,830m (6,000ft) descents. Guides speak both Spanish and English.

Trips range from 4 to 8 days and cost $520 and $975 respectively

ENSENADA

HUSSONG'S CANTINA

Avenida Ruíz 113, Ensenada
Tel (646) 178 32 10

Hugely popular, Hussong's Cantina is one of the liveliest spots in town. Earthy, raw and lively, the vibe often tips from light-hearted ebullience to frenzied revelry. Locals and visitors alike lap up the meandering *mariachi* soundtrack often punctuated with *ranchera*. Recommended for one drink at least.

LORETO

ARTURO'S SPORTFISHING FLEET

Loreto
Tel (613) 135 07 66
www.arturosport.com

Arturo's offers a multitude of marine activities from snorkeling in the waters around Coronado to fishing and scuba diving in the Loreto Bay Marine Park. Trips explore the bay's five islands where you dive among rainbow fish, Cortez angel fish and surgeon fish and a variety of other marine species. Dives are suitable for all levels of experience.

Trips leave daily at 9am
Day rates $115–$250

Traditional pine-needle baskets from the Tarahumara region

MAZATLÁN

THE FIESTA MEXICANA

Playa Mazatlán Hotel, Playa las Gaviotas, Mazatlán
Tel (669) 989 05 55

One of the longest-standing dinner fiesta shows in the country, this regional extravaganza is great entertainment for all the family. Live music, dancing, vibrant costumes, mariachis, fire throwing, magic shows, Mexican wedding and hat parties and plenty of audience participation; not for the shy.

Every Saturday 7pm–10.30pm
Show ticket $28, includes an all-you-can-eat buffet

PLAZA DE TOROS MONUMENTAL

The bullfighting season runs from December to April and events are held at the Plaza de Toros Monumental, Calzada Rafael Buelna.

Tickets $30–$40

LA PAZ

KUMUTÚ

Calle Domínguez 1245, La Paz
Tel (612) 122 24 71

This excellent shop is a labor of love for owners Marta and Aldo, who sell and eulogize over their bright collection of regional products, from travel literature to wildlife guides, local food, wine and delicacies, ceramics, textiles and maps. There is also small café, which sells coffee, tea, homemade cakes and sandwiches.

Daily 10–7

EL TEATRO DE LA CIUDAD

Avenida Navarro, La Paz
Tel (612) 125 04 86

El Teatro de la Ciudad is the cultural heart of La Paz and has a lively repertoire of performances ranging from classical music to theater, symphonies, ballet and experimental dance. The majority of performances are by local and Mexican artists, but there are occasional shows of international prestige and critical recognition.

Depends on performance

ROSARITO

MERCADO DE LAS ARTESANÍAS

Boulevard Juárez 306, Rosarito

While Baja is certainly not renowned for being a shopping Shangri-la, Rosarito tends to provide a greater selection of goods than most towns, in terms of handicrafts and more upscale household items. The artisans' market has a good selection of rather predictable souvenirs, ranging from hand-painted ceramics to tequila and sombreros.

Daily 10–6

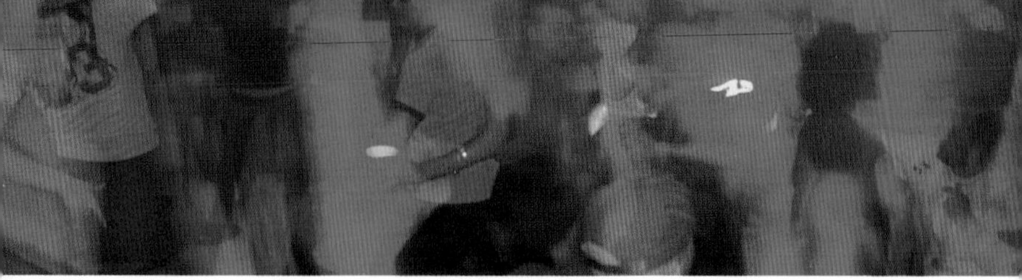

WHAT TO DO

FESTIVAL PLAZA

Boulevard Juárez 1207, Rosarito
Tel (661) 612 29 50
This popular youthful hotel is a party playground with over seven theme bars to choose from with such offerings as karaoke and El Museo Cantina, live music on weekends and a quite catatonic range of tequila. The "amphitheater" in the hotel's main plaza showcases up-and-coming and established rock, pop and *folclórico* acts.

PAPAS AND BEER

Boulevard Juárez, Rosarito
Tel (661) 612 04 44
Due to its proximity to the US, hip young southern Californians flock across the border to Rosarito to take advantage of the 18-year legal drinking age. One of the most popular drinking dens is Papas and Beer, a block north of the Rosarito Beach Hotel. It has taken the concept of a beach bar and let it fly. A college campus spirit prevails, complete with all the requisite fun and frolics. Beyond the unbridled devotion to drinking and partying, there are also dancing stages and a volleyball court.
Daily 3pm–2am

SERGIO'S SPORTFISHING CENTER

Malecon, Rosarito
Tel (646) 178 21 85
www.sergios-sportfishing.com
Sergio's offers daily group boat excursions to Todos Santos from 7am to 3pm for around $40 per person. Private boat charter services are also available, from *pangas* (small fishing boats) at $200 to a clipper sleeping up to 36 passengers for $3,300 (cheaper rates available Monday to Friday). Bonito, yellowfin tuna, albacore, barracuda, rockfish and bass are reliable catches.

SAN JOSÉ DEL CABO

GORDO BANKS PANGAS

Box 140, La Playa, San José del Cabo
Tel (624) 142 11 47
www.gordobanks.com
The Gordo Banks, close to the entrance to the Sea of Cortés, support a rich variety of marine life including yellowfin, dorado, marlin and sailfish. Fishing excursions in *pangas* leave at 6.30am and include a bilingual guide and all fishing equipment, $180–$220, based on a six-hour trip and three anglers.

TIJUANA

PLAZA DEL ZAPATO

Paseo de los Héroes, opposite Plaza Río shopping mall, Tijuana
There are more than 40 shoe shops under one roof here selling everything from men's brogues to women's strappy sandals. Most styles are leather, but the swiftly turned-out production line means that you should think in terms of disposable fashion rather than lasting classic staples.
Daily 9–7

FESTIVALS AND EVENTS

FEBRUARY/MARCH

LA PAZ CARNIVAL

Before Lent
La Paz
This Pre-Lenten Mardi Gras (carnival) is becoming one of Mexico's finest. The *malecón* (waterfront) is converted into a swirling mass of dancing, games, restaurants and stands, and the street parade is highly entertaining.

MAZATLÁN CARNIVAL

Mazatlán is renowned for its carnival extravaganzas with a spectacular array of parades, costumes, *mariachis*, live concerts, food and drink and general revelry. The hub of activity is Olas Altas *malecón* coastal boulevard, and festivities reach their climax on the eve of Ash Wednesday. Reserve rooms in advance.

APRIL

ROSARITO TO ENSENADA BICYCLE RIDE

www.rosaritoensenada.com (register online, $30 to participate)
This 81km (50-mile) ride across rural countryside is one of the world's largest cycling events, with as many as 10,000 competitors. Rated as moderately difficult, it's a great experience although you need to have a reasonably high level of fitness. Finishing time varies between 2 and 4 hours.

JULY

CABO SAN LUCAS JAZZ FESTIVAL

Last week July
Cabo San Lucas
www.loscabosguide.com
Big-name jazz artists perform on one of Cabo's most beautiful beaches—Sunset Beach—beneath a dazzling display of fireworks.

NOVEMBER

BAJA 1000 DESERT RACE

Ensenada
Tel (818) 225-8402 in US
Competitors race over 1,600km (992 miles) along the length of the Baja Peninsula. The race begins in Ensenada and ends in La Paz and any vehicle can be entered, ranging from a motorbike to a 2CV to a 10-ton truck—the only prerequisite being that you don't mind if it gets totally trashed. The road surfaces are hazardous to say the least and competitors see the event as a test of endurance.

Out and About

This chapter describes 11 driving tours and 4 walks that explore Mexico's scenic countryside, outstanding coastal areas, archaeological sites and major cities. The location of each walk and drive is marked on the map on page 208, where you will also find the key to individual maps.

Drives and Walks 209–237
Organized Tours 238

LOCATION OF WALKS AND DRIVES

Tijuana
Mexicali
Nogales
Ciudad Juárez
USA
Hermosillo
Chihuahua
Piedras Negras
Santa Rosalía
Nuevo Laredo
Loreto
Los Mochis
Monterrey
Matamoros
La Paz
Durango
Ciudad Victoria
Mazatlán
Zacatecas
San Luis Potosí
Tampico
Aguascalientes
Puerto Vallarta
Guanajuato
San Miguel de Allende
Querétaro
Guadalajara
Morelia
CIUDAD DE MÉXICO
Colima
Cuernavaca
Puebla
Veracruz
Taxco
Islas Revilla Gigedo
Acapulco de Juárez
Oaxaca
Cancún
Mérida
Cozumel
Campeche
Chetumal
Villahermosa
Palenque
San Cristóbal de las Casas
BH
Tapachula
GCA
HN
ES

KEY TO THIS MAP

- Drive
- Capital City
- Walk
- City / Town

1. Drive
Isla Mujeres (p. 209)

2. Drive
The Riviera Maya (p. 210–211)

3. Drive
The Convent & Puuc Routes Highlights (p. 212–213)

4. Drive
Indigenous Villages Near San Cristóbal (p. 214–215)

5. Walk
Oaxaca City (p. 216–217)

6. Drive
Craft Villages Around Oaxaca (p. 218–219)

7. Walk
Exploring Mexico City's Centro Histórico (p. 220–221)

8. Walk
San Angel and Coyaoacán (p. 222–223)

9. Drive
The Churches of Puebla (p. 224–225)

10. Drive
The Missions of The Sierra Gorda (p. 226–227)

11. Drive
Silver Towns of the Bajío (p. 228–229)

12. Drive
Around Lago de Pátzcuaro (p. 230–231)

13. Walk
On the Edge of the Copper Canyon (p. 232–233)

14. Drive
Cave Paintings and a Mountain Mission (p. 234–235)

15. Drive
The Sea of Cortés: Loreto to Mulegé (p. 236–237)

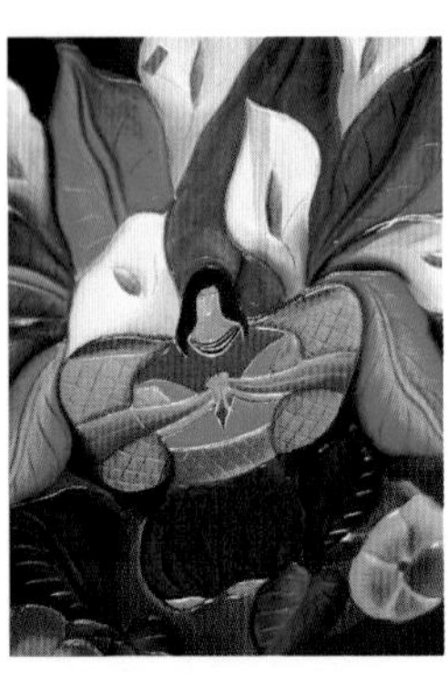

Woodwork from Pátzcuaro

A boat at rest near the beach at Isla Mujeres

GENERAL INFORMATION

Before setting out on any of the walks or drives, it is advisable to buy a detailed map of the area. Seek full advice on any travel outside San Cristóbal de las Casas. Visitors are strongly warned not to wander around on their own, especially in the hills surrounding the town, as they could risk assault (▷ 214).

KEY TO ROUTE MAPS IN THIS CHAPTER

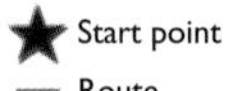

- Start point
- Route
- Alternative route
- Route direction
- Walk start point on drive
- Featured sight along route
- Place of interest in Sights section
- Other place of interest

1. DRIVE

ISLA MUJERES

Pristine white coral sands and azure sea provide the perfect antidote to the brash urban sprawl of Cancún.

THE DRIVE

Distance: 22km (14 miles)
Allow: 1 day
Start/end: El Muelle Pier

HOW TO GET THERE

Ferries leave from Puerto Juárez in Cancún every 30 minutes beween 6am and 11.30pm, $3.80 each way.

On leaving the ferry terminal, on El Muelle Pier, turn right and after two blocks you will come to Rentador Gomar, one of the places where you can rent a golf cart/moped, the best way to get around. From Gomar, take the first left along Calle Nicolas Bravo, heading inland. After two blocks you reach the main square.

1 Plaza Municipal, with its central pagoda, is overlooked by Iglesia de La Concepción and flanked with a baseball court, ice-cream parlors, the main supermarket and a children's merry-go-round. The square is at its most vibrant on Sunday evenings when families from across the island set up stands selling tacos, regional delicacies and handicrafts.

Head one block toward the waterfront, turn left onto Calle Guerrero, then right after one more block onto Calle Madero, which brings you to the sea. Park your golf cart or moped and walk out on to the main promenade of the shore.

2 This windward stretch of coast is wild and rugged and off-limits to swimmers. You can take a 15-minute detour south along the coastal promenade where there are hotels, bars and streets lined with painted clapboard houses.

Continue north along the coast (about a 10-minute walk) to the most beautiful beach on the island.

3 Playa del Norte is the archetypal Caribbean beach: glimmering turquoise sea, a wide stretch of fine white sand, palms and an infectiously mellow vibe. The sea is shallow for over 90m (300ft) and there is good snorkeling. The blazing scarlet sunsets here are spectacular.

Walk along the beach toward the lighthouse. Just before reaching it, leave the beach and turn left onto Calle López Mateos. Some 100m (110 yards) along the street, on the left-hand side, is the cemetery.

4 Here, amid tombs decorated with funerary sculptures, angels and flowers, is the grave of slave trader/pirate Fermín Mundaca, whose tale of unrequited love is legendary on La Isla. Ask a local to point it out to you. Mundaca built Vista Alegre (see below) for the young girl he loved, but she rejected him and he died, broken-hearted, in Mérida.

Leave the cemetery and turn right immediately onto Hidalgo, the town's main avenue. Continue to Calle Madero and turn left here to collect your golf cart or moped, then return to Avenida Rueda de Medina and head south. The road continues to the Punta Sur, passing the naval base, airport and Miraflores and Cañatol districts, before arriving at Playa Paraíso and Playa Lancheros, just south of Laguna Makax.

5 Playa Paraíso is an expensive mini-resort for Cancún daytrippers. Playa Lancheros is another lovely stretch of beach and recreation center.

From Playa Lancheros, the main highway (known as the Corredor Panorámico) hugs the coast as it heads south. In between chic apartment buildings, luxury hotels and spas there are fleeting glimpses of the sea, with the high-rise beach metropolis of Cancún on the horizon. The road ends at El Garrafón.

6 This snorkeling center, 8km (5 miles) from the town, has been developed into a recreational resort in the style of Xcaret (▷ 80) on the mainland.

A 15-minute walk from here takes you to the tip of the island and the ruins of a Maya shrine, Santuario Maya a la Diosa Ixchel—unique in being dedicated to a female deity.

7 There is a cultural center near the shrine, with large sculptures by several international artists. The views from the lighthouse are stunning.

Return to the highway and head north. In the middle of the island, southeast of the lagoon, a dirt road leads off the main highway to Casa de Mundaca, home of the pirate Fermín Mundaca.

8 A big arch gate marks its entrance. Paths have been laid out among the trees, but all that remains of the estate (Vista Alegre) are one small building and a circular garden with raised beds, a well and a gateway. Look for the poignant carving on the garden side of the gate, *La entrada de La Trigueña* (La Trigueña was the girl's nickname).

From Casa de Mundaca, head north to Avenida Rueda Medina—Laguna Makax is on your left. It's a 10-minute ride back to El Muelle Pier.

TOURIST INFORMATION

Avenida Rueda Medina 130, Cancún
✉ (998) 877 03 07
www.puntaislaguion-mujeres.com.mx, www.isla-mujeres.net

PLACES TO VISIT

Casa de Mundaca
Daily 9–5

WHERE TO EAT

Bistro Francés
(▷ 245)
Lonchería La Lomita
(▷ 245)

THE RIVIERA MAYA

A warm turquoise sea, white sands and palm groves stretch from Cancún south to Tulúm. Threaded between exclusive palaces, commercial recreational parks and the archaeological sites of the Ruta Maya, a less trodden path of traditional fishing villages, virgin beaches and exotic wildlife awaits discovery.

THE DRIVE

Distance: 285km (177 miles)
Allow: 1 day
Start: Cancún airport
End: Cancún

The Riviera Maya officially begins at Cancún and continues south along the four-lane Highway 307 to Tulúm. Each turn-off is well marked. The first stop, 20km (12 miles) from the airport, is Puerto Morelos.

❶ Puerto Morelos (▷ 74) is the oldest fishing village on the Riviera and remains charming and unspoiled. You can park close to the village and walk along deserted stretches of beach or go snorkeling. A 1km (0.6-mile) path south from Puerto Morelos leads to Jardín Botánico Dr. Alfredo Barrera Marin, with exotic species of flora and fauna in tropical rain forest.

From Puerto Morelos, return to Highway 307, passing Playa Paraiso and Punta Maroma, two of the best beaches along the coast. Continue south for 14km (9 miles) and at Km 54 take the turning for Tres Ríos.

❷ Tres Ríos is one of the Riviera Maya's less commercial eco-parks, with more than 100 species of animal in lush sub-tropical jungle with myriad trails. There is a 1.6km (1-mile) stretch of silky sand beach where you can horseback-ride, snorkel and swim in *cenotes*. For relaxation, there are lots of hammocks and places to drink and eat.

Return to Highway 307; 23km (14 miles) from Tres Ríos is Playa del Carmen.

❸ Playa del Carmen (▷ 74) has metamorphosed from a subdued fishing village into a beach party hotspot. Along the main thoroughfare, Avenida 5, US franchises nudge up against souvenir shops, designer-label stores, tequila bars, spas and all-you-can-eat buffets where waiters brandish multilingual menus; it's a hard sell, essentially catering to a sun-and-fun tourist market. For a more genuine Mexican atmosphere, take a stroll along Avenida Juárez, or to find a less crowded stretch of beach, walk along Avenida 5 north as far as Calle 12, then turn onto the beach and continue north for 40 minutes along Playa de Cocos, where several beach bars provide wonderful vantage points.

A 3-hour walk south from Playa del Carmen, or a 20-minute drive south along Highway 307, brings you to the ancient Maya site of Xcaret.

❹ Xcaret (▷ 80), the former port of Polé, has been transformed into a Maya Disneyland aimed at Cancún daytrippers. However, the surroundings are glorious, with turquoise waters, powdered-sand beaches and mysterious jungle trails.

Continue south along Highway 307 for 29km (18 miles) to Akumal. Look for the turn-off to the resort on the right-hand side of the road, signposted Club Akumal Caribe Villas.

❺ Akumal (▷ 61) is an exclusive resort that has seen much development, but despite the proliferation of complexes it has a relaxed ambience. You can walk north from Akumal for 3km (2 miles) to the Ya Kul lagoon (daily 8–5), another excellent snorkeling spot.

Return to Highway 307 and in 1km (0.6 mile), on the right-hand side of the road, is a green sign for Aktun Chen, another of the Maya Riviera's eco-parks. Turn onto this unpaved road to the park, in 3km (2 miles).

❻ Aktun Chen, meaning "cave with an underground river inside," lies in more than 400ha (988 acres) of rain forest. There are three caves with a *cenote* 12m (39ft) deep. The stalactites and stalagmites, formed more than 5 million years ago, are spectacularly illuminated. Guided tours last 1.5 hours.

Continue south on Highway 307 for another 5km (3 miles) to Xcacel, reached by a dirt road from the main highway (watch out for the steep drop from the highway) that eventually leads to a chained gate—pay the security guard 20 pesos.

❼ Xcacel is a superb beach and one of Mexico's most important sites for nesting sea turtles, with deep sands and minimal reef. Behind the beach are more than 362ha (893 acres) of jungle, mangrove swamps, dunes and beaches. The area was a federal reserve until 1992, when the property was bought by a hotel chain for $2.5 million. Controversy has since raged over the construction of a luxury resort. There is a wonderful *cenote*; turn right onto the beach, head south to a jungle trail and in 5 minutes you'll reach it. During the turtles' nesting season, the beach is strictly off limits from 6pm.

About 21km (13 miles) south from Xcacel is Tulúm (▷ 75).

❽ The ruins lie 4km (2.5 miles) north of Tulúm village, and are well signposted from

Relaxing on the beach at Akumal (above)

Turtle swimming off the shores of Isla Mujeres (below)

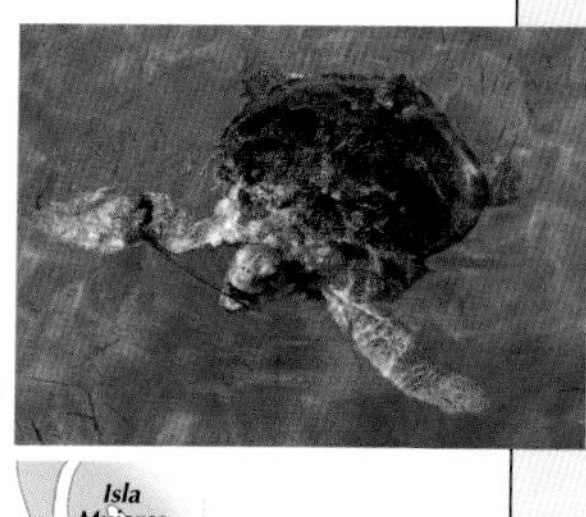

S7
Porvenir
Chiquilá
Isla Mujeres
Puerto Juárez
Cancún
Yucatán
Buenaventura
Kantunil Kin
180
Leona Vicario
El Rey
Tixcancal
Popolnah
Vicente Guerrero
307
0 10 km
0 6 miles
El Cedral
El Ident
Puerto Morelos
S8
X-Can
Tres Ríos
T8
Tres Reyes
Isla del Cozumel
Playa del Carmen
Xcaret
Chemax
Paamul
Cobá
Cozumel
Akumal
Aktun Chen
Xcacel
Cedral
Xel-Há
P N de Quintana Roo
Punta Celarain
Tulúm
307
Reserva de la Biósfera Sian Ka'an
Chunyaxché
Boca Paila

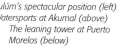

Tulúm's spectacular position (left)
Watersports at Akumal (above)
The leaning tower at Puerto Morelos (below)

Highway 307. Parking is just off Highway 307, in an area known as El Crucero.

From Tulúm, it is 136km (84 miles) back to Cancún. An optional detour, if time permits, or if you plan to stay overnight in Tulúm, is to head inland for 47km (29 miles) to Cobá (▷ 70).

TOURIST INFORMATION

Avenida Cobá and Avenida Bonampak, Cancún
☎ (998) 884 65 31

WHERE TO EAT

Media Luna, Playa del Carmen
(▷ 246)

WHERE TO STAY

Cabañas Copal, Tulúm
(▷ 268)

WHEN TO GO

If you are staying in Cancún or Tulúm make reservations in advance as it's crowded at Christmas, *Semana Santa* and national holidays.

THE CONVENT & PUUC ROUTES HIGHLIGHTS

The Puuc and Convent routes, in the central west of Yucatán state, are dotted with Maya villages, ancient ruins, convents and *cenotes* (sinkholes).

THE DRIVE

Distance: 264km (164 miles)
Allow: 1 day
Start/end: Mérida

Get an early start from Mérida, aiming to be on the Periférico to Route 18 (signs say Kanasín, not Ruta 18) by 7.30am. Follow the signs to Acancéh, where on the main plaza you will find a Grand Pyramid, a colonial church and a modern church. Continue south on Route 18 for 8km (5 miles) to Tecoh.

❶ Tecoh has an ornate church and convent dedicated to the Virgin of the Assumption. There are carved stones around the altar. Both church and convent stand at the base of a large Maya pyramid.

From Tecoh, continue on Route 18 and pass through the small village of Telchaquillo, which has a *cenote* in the plaza. In 4km (2.5 miles), a turn-off to the right brings you to the Maya ruins of Mayapán.

❷ Considered the last great Maya capital, Mayapán is a walled city with 4,000 mounds, six of which are in varying stages of restoration. There are murals depicting death and war, painted in the style of the codices of the Post Classic period, and sculpture in stucco. Mayapán once formed a triple alliance along with Uxmal (▷ 78–79) and Chichén Itzá (▷ 64–67).

Return to Route 18 and continue for another 22km (14 miles) to Tekit, a large village containing the Iglesia de San Antonio de Padua. The next village, Mama, 8km (5 miles) farther, has the oldest church on the route and is famous for its ornate altar and bell-domed roof. In 9km (6 miles) is Chumayel, where the legendary Maya document *Chilam Balam* was found. Another 12km (7 miles) on is Maní, the most important stop on this route.

❸ At Maní you will find a large church, convent and museum with good multilingual explanations. It was here that Fray Diego de Landa (1524–79), the Bishop of Yucatán, ordered important Maya documents and objects to be burned during an intense period of Franciscan conversion of the Maya people to Christianity.

From Maní head west to the town of Ticul, which is on both the Convent and Puuc routes.

❹ Ticul is known for its *huipiles*, the embroidered white dresses worn by older Maya women (prices and quality here are much better than in Mérida) and for producing the area's ubiquitous red-clay planter pots and leather shoes.

About 16km (10 miles) southeast of Ticul, on Route 184, is the town of Oxkutzcab, with a large market on one side of the plaza and a 15th-century church on the other. The area around Ticul and Oxkutzcab is intensively farmed with citrus fruits, papayas and mangoes. Around 6km (4 miles) southwest of Oxkutzcab are the caves at Loltún.

❺ The Grutas de Loltún extend for 8km (5 miles) along illuminated pathways. Excavations in the Huechil cave revealed animal remains, including mammoth and bison, and there are relief carvings, petroglyphs and murals.

From Loltún, continue 30km (19 miles) southwest to Labná.

❻ Once a city of 1,500 to 2,500 inhabitants, Labná has an unusual monumental arch. Most Maya arches are purely structural, but this one was constructed for aesthetic purposes, clearly meant to be seen from afar. The two facades on either side of the arch differ greatly in their decoration; the western one is decorated with delicate latticework and stone carving imitating the wood or palm-frond roofs of Maya huts. Across the eastern facade, a line of zigzag carvings is believed to represent the feathered serpent, a potent symbol in Maya mythology. The palace also has some 70 *chultunes* (water cisterns).

Continue for another 9km (6 miles) to the ruins of Xlapak, which have not been as extensively restored as the others in this region. After 13km (8 miles) from this turning is Sayil, or the Place of the Ants.

❼ Sayil, dating from AD800 to 1000, has many areas still under reconstruction, including the ball court and *mirador* (lookout point). Stelae (inscribed stone slabs) are displayed near the entrance. In its day, the three-tier palace included 90 bathrooms for some 350 people. A broad mask with huge fangs forms the central motif on the upper part of the facade.

From Sayil, turn right at the intersection after approximately 5km (3 miles)—the route is well marked—to the Classic Puuc site of Kabah.

❽ Kabah is renowned for its Palacio de los Mascarones (Palace of the Masks). Its structures, most notably the Temple of the Sun, were built on artificial platforms, making them distinct from other Maya buildings. The facade has the image of Chac (God of Rain) mesmerically repeated 260 times, the number of days in the Almanac Year. The central chamber is entered via a huge Chac mask whose curling snout forms the doorstep.

Some 37km (23 miles) north, along Route 261, is Uxmal ❾ (▷ 78–79). From here it is 74km (46 miles) along Route 261 back to Mérida.

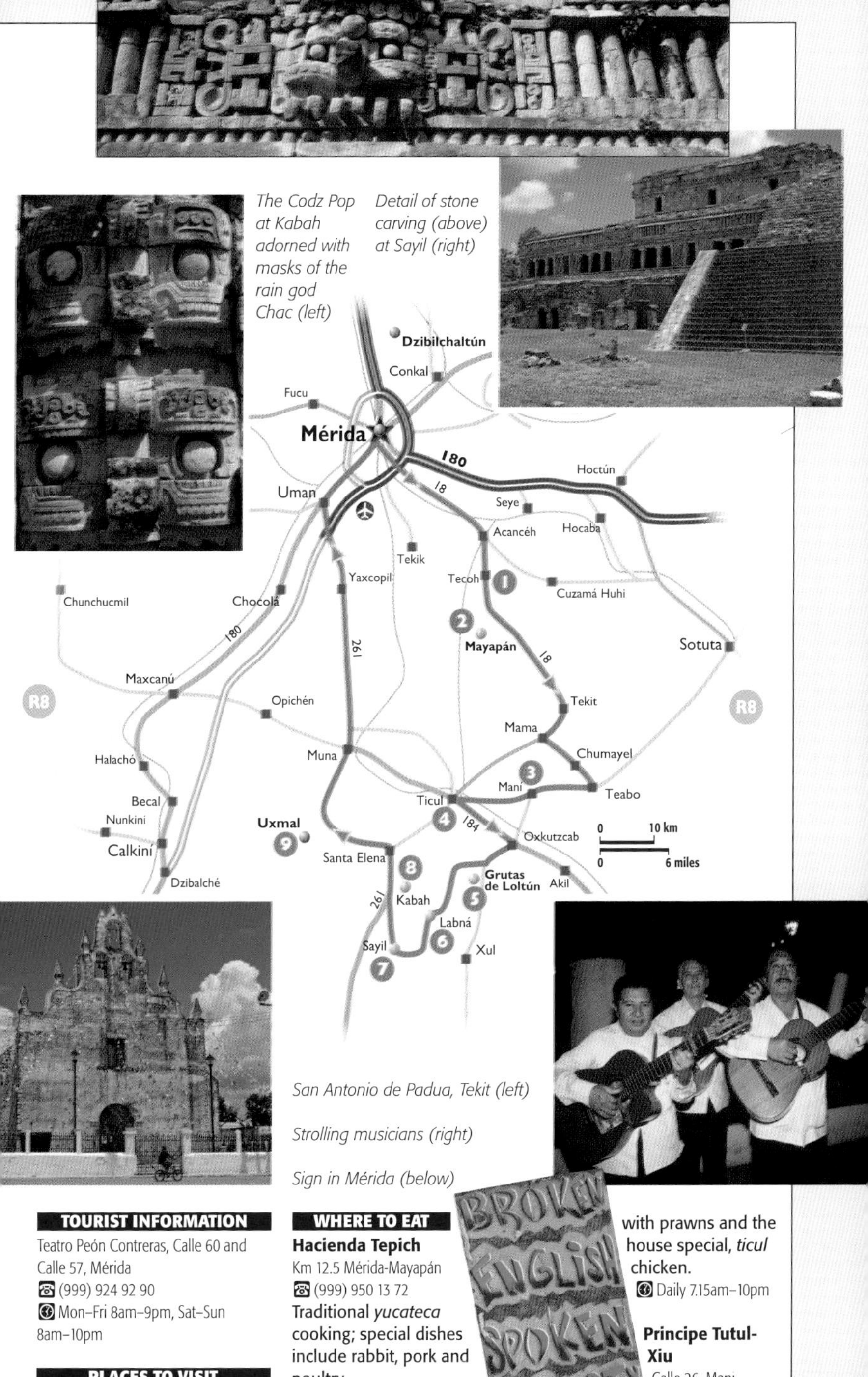

The Codz Pop at Kabah adorned with masks of the rain god Chac (left)

Detail of stone carving (above) at Sayil (right)

San Antonio de Padua, Tekit (left)

Strolling musicians (right)

Sign in Mérida (below)

TOURIST INFORMATION

Teatro Peón Contreras, Calle 60 and Calle 57, Mérida
☎ (999) 924 92 90
Mon–Fri 8am–9pm, Sat–Sun 8am–10pm

PLACES TO VISIT

Grutas de Loltún
Tours Tue–Sun 9.30, 11, 12.30 and 2
$3

Labná, Xlapak, Sayil, Kabah
Daily 8–5
$5

WHERE TO EAT

Hacienda Tepich
Km 12.5 Mérida-Mayapán
☎ (999) 950 13 72
Traditional *yucateca* cooking; special dishes include rabbit, pork and poultry.

Hacienda Uxmal
Km 78 Carreterra-Campeche
☎ (997) 976 20 12
Generous portions of excellent regional and international cooking, including avocado with prawns and the house special, *ticul* chicken.
Daily 7.15am–10pm

Principe Tutul-Xiu
Calle 26, Manı
Tel (999) 798 40 86
Rustic decoration, with a menu featuring *chiles rellenos* (stuffed chilies) and *poc-chuc* (barbecued pork).
Daily 11–7

INDIGENOUS VILLAGES NEAR SAN CRISTÓBAL

San Cristóbal de las Casas provides the ideal base for half-day or full-day excursions to the area's indigenous villages. Steeped in ancestral traditions, potent mysticism and bloody revolution, they provide powerful insights into the lost world of Chiapas.

THE DRIVE

Distance: 280km (174 miles) total distance to visit all towns
Allow: one half day per excursion
Start/end: San Cristóbal de las Casas

Excursion 1
To Zinacantán and San Juan Chamula

Leave San Cristóbal (▷ 96) on the San Juan Chamula road and head west for 5km (3 miles) until the road forks. Take the left fork and continue for a further 5km (3 miles) to Zinacantán.

❶ Zinacantán in the Tzotzil language means "place of the bats," referring to the abundance of bats in the area and the discovery of a stone in the form of a bat, which later became a titular god. Before the arrival of the Aztecs, Zinacantán was an important commercial hub and considered the capital of the Tzotziles. The main gathering place is around the church; the roof was destroyed by fire ($0.40 charged for entering church, official ticket from tourist office next door; photography inside is strictly prohibited). Annual festival days here are January 6, January 19–22 and August 7–11; visitors are welcome.

The Tzotzil village of San Juan Chamula lies 12km (7 miles) northwest of San Cristóbal de las Casas. From Zinacantán take the left fork north, instead of turning onto the San Cristóbal road.

❷ The painted church in San Juan Chamula is particularly beautiful. To visit it you will need to obtain a permit ($1) from the village tourist office on the square, and remember photographing inside the church is strictly forbidden. Some Indians believe cameras steal their souls, and photographing their church is stealing the soul of God. There are no pews or formal services: family groups sit or kneel on the floor, chanting, with candles burning in memory of their loved ones. A food market is held on Sundays, and there are many permanent handicraft stands on the way up the small hill southwest of the village. Take heed of signs saying that it is dangerous to walk in the area.

Decorative belts, San Cristóbal

Return to San Cristóbal the way you came.

Excursion 2
To Tenejapa

Head northeast from San Cristóbal de las Casas for 28km (17 miles), a journey of approximately one hour and 15 minutes, to reach the little-visited village of Tenejapa.

❸ Tenejapa is especially worth visiting on a Thursday for its traditional fruit and vegetable market and a clutch of other stands. You can buy excellent woven items from the weavers' cooperative near the church. There is a fine collection of old textiles in the regional ethnographic museum adjoining the handicraft shop. The cooperative can also arrange weaving classes.

Excursion 3
To Amatenango del Valle

From San Cristóbal de las Casas, head south on the Pan-American Highway through roads lined with cornfields to Amatenango del Valle in the Teocicca Valley.

❹ Amatenango del Valle is a Tzeltal village with around 7,400 inhabitants. The women make and fire pottery in their yards in strict accordance to traditional ways by building a fire around the pieces, rather than using a kiln.

Excursion 4
To Ocosingo and Toniná

Ocosingo (often written as Ococingo) lies 58km (35 miles) northeast of San Cristóbal de las Casas. Follow the route to Palenque, a scenic two-hour drive along a paved serpentine road.

❺ Ocosingo, nestling in one of Mexico's most beautiful valleys, is a largely Tzeltal village with a local airport, a lively market and several hotels. It was one of the cells of fighting in the uprising in January 1994. The town makes a good base for visiting the Maya ruins of Toniná, about 12km (7 miles) southeast.

The road is unpaved but marked with signs once you leave Ocosingo. Beside the road is a marsh, frequented by thousands of swallows in January.

❻ Toniná is the perfect place to enjoy the countryside and Maya architecture in peace and quiet. The huge pyramid complex, with seven stone platforms creating a man-made hill, is 10m (33ft) higher than the Temple of the Sun at Teotihuacán and is the tallest pyramidal structure in the Maya world. The stelae (engraved slabs) take diverse forms, as do the wall panels; some are in styles and of subjects unknown at any other Maya site. In December 1990 the well-preserved Mural of the Four Swans was discovered on the sixth level.

From Toniná it is around 86km (53 miles) back to San Cristóbal de las Casas.

Market day in Ocosingo (above and bottom left)

The church in San Juan Chamula

Colorful house in San Cristóbal

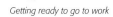

Getting ready to go to work

TOURIST INFORMATION

Municipal office

Palacio Municipal, San Cristóbal de las Casas

☎ (967) 678 06 65

🕐 Mon–Sat 8–8, Sun 9–2

San Cristóbal de las Casas Delegacíon Regional de Turismo

Hidalgo 1-B, San Cristóbal de las Casas

☎ (967) 678 65 70

🕐 Mon–Sat 8am–10pm, Sun 9–2

WHERE TO EAT

There are few eating options in the villages. Tours arranged by Na Bolom include lunch in Zinacantán. San Cristóbal de las Casas has good restaurants and cafés (▷ 250–251).

Casa de Pan

Calle Dr. Navarro 10, San Cristóbal de las Casas

☎ (967) 678 58 95

🕐 Tue–Sun 8am–11pm

Paloma

Avenida Miguel Hidalgo 3, San Cristóbal de las Casas

☎ (967) 678 15 47

🕐 Daily 9am–11pm

WHERE TO STAY

Na Bolom

(▷ 271)

Posada El Paraíso

(▷ 271)

TIPS

- It is best not to take cameras to villages as photographing is seen as invasive and profiteering. There are good postcards and photographs on sale.
- During the rainy season (May to October), heavy flooding can result in the roads being impassable.

OAXACA CITY

From the serenity of colonial churches and romantic patios to the exuberance of lively street markets and festivals, a walk through Oaxaca reveals a cultural maelstrom.

THE WALK

Distance: 5km (3 miles)
Allow: 3 hours
Start/end: *Zócalo*

Begin at the *zócalo*, the heart of Oaxaca (▷ 88–91), with the Palacio de Gobierno behind you, and head north to the Alameda de León, where you will find the 17th-century cathedral on the right.

❶ The cathedral has a fine baroque facade. Construction began in 1535, but the building was not consecrated until 1733, after being damaged on several occasions by earthquakes. The 14 side chapels contain many examples of 18th-century sacred art.

From the cathedral, head north across the Alameda, passing through craft stands and food carts, to Calle Macedonio Alcalá, a cobbled pedestrian walkway.

❷ Along Macedonio Alcalá are many colonial buildings with swirling wrought-iron balconies. Archways and ornate doorways lead to leafy patios, craft shops, museums, art galleries, gourmet restaurants and cafés.

At No. 202 is one of the finest museums in Oaxaca.

❸ Housed in a late 17th-century mansion with a stone facade, the Museo de Arte Contemporáneo de Oaxaca presents contemporary art works from renowned Oaxacan artists, including Rufino Tamayo (1899–1991). The building is a perfect example of Spanish colonial architecture, with rooms fanning out from three interior courtyards.

On the next block you can make a short detour by turning right onto Calle Murguia. This brings you to one of Mexico's most renowned hotels, the Camino Real (▷ 270), housed in the former Convento de Santo Catalina. Two blocks south at Calle 5 de Mayo and Avenida Independencia is the Teatro Macedonio Alcalá.

❹ The elegant belle époque Macedonio Alcalá theater dates back to the mid-19th century, with a reproduction Louis XV entrance and white marble staircase. Regular performances are held here, (currently closed for restoration).

Return along Avenida Independencia to Calle Macedonio Alcalá and walk four blocks north, passing a line of oil canvases displayed on Avenida Abasolo, to reach the Iglesia de Santo Domingo.

❺ With the construction of the Iglesia de Santo Domingo, Mexican baroque reaches its apogee, with walls emblazoned with gold and polychrome bas-relief. The adjoining monastery houses the Centro Cultural Santo Domingo (▷ 90), which includes the unmissable Museo de las Culturas de Oaxaca, Jardín Etnobotánico, the Biblioteca Francisco Burgoa and Hemeroteca (newspaper library).

Continue north, passing the Instituto de Artes Gráficas de Oaxaca (IAGO) on your left after one block, to reach Calle Cosijopi, where there is a small, peaceful garden. Take a left turn in one block to Calle García Vigil, where, you will see the remains of an aqueduct and an area referred to as the Arcos de Xochimilco.

❻ The Arcos de Xochimilco is a picturesque district of cobbled passageways draped in jacaranda, with closet-sized *taco* cafés, romantic fountains, gigantic cacti and ornate street lanterns. The aqueduct once brought water from San Felipe del Agua to the city.

After exploring the area take Calle García Vigil south, passing the Museo Casa de Juárez, then continue south for four blocks to Avenida Morelos. Turn right and walk a block and a half to the Museo Rufino Tamayo.

❼ This museum has an outstanding display of pre-Columbian objects dating from 1250BC to AD1100, donated by the Oaxacan painter Rufino Tamayo in 1974.

At the next left, turn onto Calle Tinoco y Palacios, and in one block again the Iglesia de San Felipe Neri, with its elaborate altars, which brings you to Avenida Independencia, the busier, commercial part of the city. Turn right and walk two-and-a-half blocks. Steps lead up to the Jardín de la Soledad that surrounds the monumental Basílica de la Soledad (▷ 90).

❽ This massive 17th-century building houses a much-revered statue of the Virgin. Don't miss the small museum at the back.

Walk back along Avenida Independencia towards the cathedral for three-and-a-half blocks, then turn right onto Calle 20 de Noviembre and head south for four blocks. Between two of Oaxaca's markets, Mercado Benito Juárez and Mercado 20 de Noviembre, is the Iglesia de San Juan de Dios.

❾ Inside the Iglesia de San Juan de Dios are Indian paintings of the Conquistadors arriving in Oaxaca in 1629 and an anti-Catholic uprising in 1700. This was the first church to be built in Oaxaca, and was originally dedicated to Santa Catalina Mártir.

Turn left one block after the church onto Calle Mina and continue for two blocks, left into Calle Bustamante for two blocks, right into Calle Colón and first left into Calle Armenta y Lopez.

(Along Mina a deep chocolate aroma emanates from the many chocolate mills in the area.) Turn left onto Armenta y Lopez and head in the direction of the *zócalo* and the Iglesia de San Agustín.

⑩ The church of San Agustín has an intricate facade, with a Guerrero bas-relief of St. Augustine holding the City of God above adoring monks.

From the church, turn left and it's just one block west to the *zócalo*.

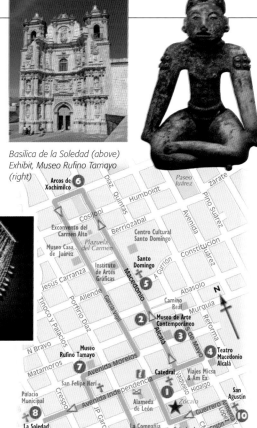

Basilica de la Soledad (above) Exhibit, Museo Rufino Tamayo (right)

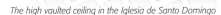

Treasure from Monte Albán's Tomb 7, Museo Rufino Tamayo

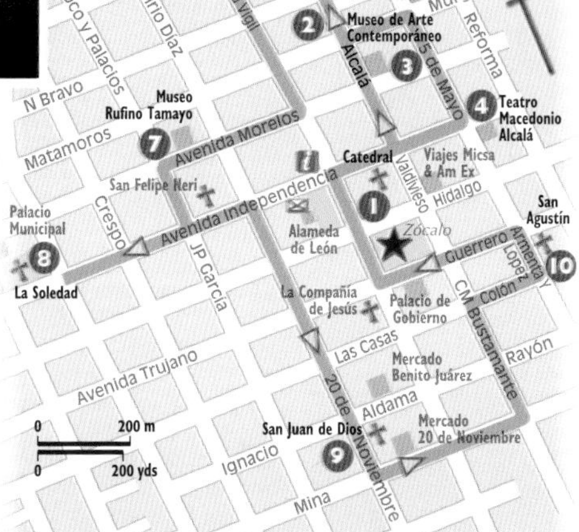

The high vaulted ceiling in the Iglesia de Santo Domingo

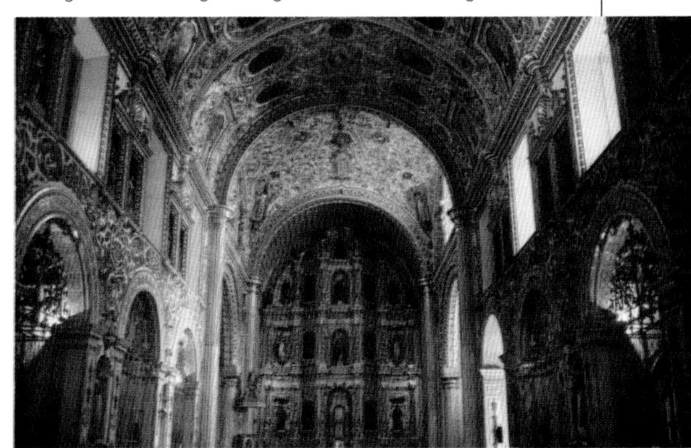

TOURIST INFORMATION

Visitor information
Sedatur, Avenida Independencia 607
☎ (951) 516 01 23
Daily 8–8

PLACES TO VISIT

Museo de Arte Contemporáneo de Oaxaca
Calle Macedonio Alcalá 202
☎ (951) 514 22 28
Wed–Mon 10.30–8

Iglesia de Santo Domingo
Calle Macedonio Alcalá
Daily 7–1, 5–8

Museo de las Culturas de Oaxaca
Calle Macedonio Alcalá
☎ (951) 516 29 91
Tue–Sun 10–8
$3.60

Jardín Etnobotánico
Calle Gurrion and Calle Reforma
☎ (951) 516 76 15
1-hour guided tours in Spanish at 1pm and 6pm, in English Tue, Thu, Sat at 11am and 4pm; sign up in advance

Biblioteca Francisco Burgoa and Hemeroteca
Calle Macedonio Alcalá
☎ (951) 516 29 91
Mon–Fri, 9–8, Sat 9–5

Museo Rufino Tamayo
Avenida Morelos 503
Mon, Wed–Sat 10–2, 4–7, Sun 10–3

WHERE TO EAT

María Bonita
(▷ 249)

CRAFT VILLAGES AROUND OAXACA

Beyond the city of Oaxaca you'll find ghostly ancient ruins, Zapotec villages steeped in mysticism, hypnotic craft markets and a dramatic landscape with cascading waterfalls and abundant wildlife.

THE DRIVE

Distance: 126km (78 miles)
Allow: 1 day
Start/end: Oaxaca

Leave Oaxaca (▷ 88–91) on the main highway, Route 190, heading east. The road is poorly paved in parts with potholes and risk of occasional flooding. Continue for 12km (7 miles) until you reach a sign on the right to El Tule.

❶ El Tule has what is thought to be the world's largest tree, a *savino* (*Taxodium mucronatum*), estimated at 2,000 years old. On the left, near the basilica as you drive into town, it stands 40m (131ft) high, 42m (138ft) around the base, weighs an estimated 550 tons, and is watered by an elaborate pipe system. El Tule also has a market with good food on sale at Guerrero 4-A.

Continue east along Route 190 for 5km (3 miles) to San Jerónimo Tlacochahuaya, which has a 16th-century church with plateresque rococo altarpieces and vivid Indian murals. Upstairs, in the cloisters to the rear, there is an ornate organ. Continue along the highway for another 3km (2 miles) to Dainzú. Take the turn-off on the right, shortly after the Km 20 sign, then follow the unpaved road for approximately 1.5km (1 mile).

❷ Secluded and peaceful, the labyrinthine archaeological site of Dainzú flourished alongside Monte Albán (▷ 86–87), reaching its apogee around AD350. The site is significant for its elaborate depictions of ball players wearing feline masks and gloves, and for the superlative jaguar carvings on Structure G.

Return to Route 190 and after around 7km (4 miles) turn left at Km 27, where a paved road leads to Teotitlán del Valle (4km/2.5 miles).

❸ The name Teotitlán comes from a Nahuatl word imeaning "place of the gods," and the village's 4,500 inhabitants call themselves *beeni xiguiee*, "charmed/magic people," who believe that they are descended from the clouds. Bright wall-hangings and *tapetes* (rugs) are woven with subjects ranging from pre-Columbian scenes to reproductions of paintings by famous artists such as Diego Rivera and Rufino Tamayo. There is a daily artisans' market near the 16th-century church, and the Museo Comunitario.

From Teotitlán you can make an optional detour involving a one-hour hike north through stunning scenery to the town of Benito Juárez, one of the highest points of the valley.

❹ At Benito Juárez in the Sierra Norte, soaring aromatic pine forests and cascading waterfalls teem with flora and fauna. Hike, or rent a mountain bike from Tourist Yú ù (▷ 186), near the turn-off from Route 190 and head to El Mirador (3,050m/10,007ft) for spectacular views of the Tlacolula Valley.

Return to Route 190 and continue for approximately 8km (5 miles) to the village of Tlacolula.

❺ Tlacolula has one of the oldest Sunday markets in Mesoamerica; a scintillating array of traditional crafts lines the main street and surrounds the church, which is similar in style to the Iglesia de Santo Domingo in Oaxaca, with intricate white and gold stucco, lots of mirrors, silver altar rails and sculptures of martyrs in gruesome detail. Two beheaded saints guard the door to the main nave. The town is renowned for its *mezcal* liquor preparation, with more than 24 varieties.

About 3km (2 miles) north of Tlacolula is the peaceful Zapotec village of Santa Ana del Valle.

❻ Santa Ana del Valle is one of the best places to buy quality weavings, and has an important rug market. There is an 18th-century baroque temple and a small but engaging community museum with displays revealing the seminal events of the Mexican Revolution and ancient textile techniques; ask any villager to point you toward the keyholder.

Return to Route 190 and continue east for 7km (4 miles) to the turn-off north for Yagul.

❼ Yagul (▷ 98) is one of the most intimate and ethereal ancient sites in the region, with an acropolis gloriously poised overlooking the Oaxaca Valley.

From Yagul, return to Route 190 and in 5km (3 miles) you'll reach a paved road, which branches left and leads to Mitla (4km/2.5 miles).

❽ Mitla (▷ 84–85) flourished during the Post Classic period (AD750–1521) and is renowned for its majestic stonework mosaics. In the town, you can visit the Museo Frissell de Arte Zapoteca, in the former Posada La Sorpresa—whose famous visitors included English novelist D. H. Lawrence—which has a collection of Indian arts and crafts.

From Mitla, drive for 12km (7 miles) to San Pedro Ayutla. Take the diversion for San Lorenzo Albarrades and in 8km (5 miles) is San Isidro Roaguía, where you will find the stunning Hierve el Agua waterfalls.

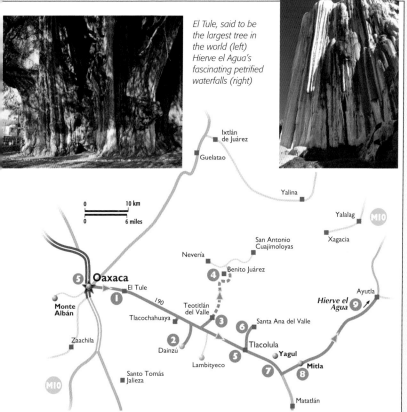

El Tule, said to be the largest tree in the world (left)
Hierve el Agua's fascinating petrified waterfalls (right)

0 10 km
0 6 miles
Ixtlán de Juárez
Guelatao
Yalina
Yalalag
M10
Xagacia
San Antonio Cuajimoloyas
Nevería
Benito Juárez
4
5
Oaxaca
El Tule
1
190
Ayutla
Hierve el Agua
9
Monte Albán
Teotitlán del Valle
Tlacochahuaya
3
6
Santa Ana del Valle
2
Zaachila
Dainzú
Tlacolula
Yagul
5
Lambityeco
7
Mitla
8
Santo Tomás Jalieza
M10
Matatlán

Textiles and rugs are a specialty of Oaxaca's craft villages (left and below)
The Zapotec site of Yagul (right)

9 Hierve el Agua is a series of petrified waterfalls created by the water's high mineral concentration. The most spectacular fall plummets 30m (98ft). Once a sacred site for the Zapotecs, the falls were used 2,400 years ago by early inhabitants who constructed wells for terraced crops. A 2km (1.2-mile) pathway leads to El Anfiteatro, a lookout point with dizzying views of the valley.

Return to Route 190 and retrace your route to Oaxaca.

TOURIST INFORMATION

Sedatur, Avenida Independencia 607, Oaxaca
☎ (915) 516 01 23 Daily 8–8

PLACES TO VISIT

Museo Comunitario
Teotitlán del Valle
☎ (524) 41 43
Tue–Sun 10–6

Museo Frissell de Art Zapoteca
Mitla
☎ (956) 801 74 Thu–Tue 10–5

Pensamiento Mezcal
Route 190, km 32, Tlacolula
☎ (956) 200 17
One of the *mezcal* factories on Route 190 that offers tours of the production process.

WHERE TO EAT

El Descanso
Avenida Juárez 51, Teotitlán del Valle
☎ (951) 524 41 52
A pleasant modern restaurant serving good local cuisine.
Daily 10–11

El Centeotl
Domicio Conocido, Yagul
☎ (951) 661 86
Rather expensive, but one of the finest restaurants for traditional *cocina oaxaqueña*.
Daily 11–7

EXPLORING MEXICO CITY'S CENTRO HISTÓRICO

The heart of Mexico City, with its Aztec, colonial and modern architecture, is a lively mix of ancient and modern—layered and packed together in a fascinating profusion of urban life.

THE WALK

Distance: 1.6km (1 mile)
Allow: 3–4 hours
Start/end: Plaza de la Constitición (Zócalo), Mexico City

HOW TO GET THERE

Take Line 2 of the metro to the Zócalo stop.

If you're an early riser, start with breakfast at the rooftop terrace restaurant of the Majestic Hotel (▷ 273) and look out across the spectacular view of the huge Zócalo. The main square of the city has much to delay the curious, with the cathedral on the north side and the Palacio Nacional to the east.

Leave the square at the north-east corner, heading east down Calle Moneda.

❶ Cobbled Calle Moneda is crisscrossed with old streets packed with the noise and trade of a street market and fringed by the Palacio Arzobispal, the Palacio Nacional (▷ 115) and the Museo de las Culturas.

After three blocks, just past Iglesia de Santa Ines, a left turn up Calle Academia leads to the Museo José Luis Cuevas.

❷ Housed in the cloister of a former convent, the Museo José Luis Cuevas has exhibits of the erotic works of the artist. A huge bronze, La Giganta, dominates the central patio.

After two blocks you reach the richly carved facade and fine towers of the 17th-century Iglesia de La Santísima Trinidad. On leaving the church turn right for two blocks, then left down Calle de Mixcalco to arrive at the southern side of the Plaza de Loreto after one block.

❸ The Plaza de Loreto is an attractive square with a fountain in the middle. The Iglesia de Santa Teresa la Nueva looks on from the east, while from the north, the Iglesia de Loreto is a fine example of primitive neoclassicism.

Conchero dancer in the Zócalo

Continuing west on Calle de Mixcalco, now called 2a Calle del Maestro Justo Sierra, your stroll takes in the Sociedad Mexicana de Geografía y Estadística (Mexican Society for Geography and Statistics) on the left, the Antigua Colegio de San Ildefonso (No. 16) on the right, and back on the left a superb view—albeit somewhat obscured by railings—of architecture spanning the centuries, with the Templo Mayor in the foreground and the cathedral in the distance. With your back to the monumental architecture, turn right up República de Argentina—you're in the home of the pirate CD now and the competing sounds of salsa, merengue, house and hip hop are bewildering. After two blocks turn left along República de Venezuela to reach Plaza Santo Domingo.

❹ On entering the plaza, immediately to your left is the Secretaría de Educación Pública (SEP), home to a bonanza of Rivera murals. To your right is the Edificio de la Inquisición, now housing the Museo de la Medicina Mexicana (▷ 115), which describes the history of Mexican medicine. On the west side of the plaza, printers hand-print invitations to weddings and family occasions. The Mexican baroque Convento de Santo Domingo overlooks the busy plaza of artists and workers.

After exploring the square, continue down Belisario Dominguez. If you're in need of refreshment, drop in at the Hosteria Santo Domingo (No. 72), Mexico City's oldest restaurant. Turn left at República de Chile, heading south for three blocks, then turn right onto Calle Tacuba.

❺ Now in a more traditional retail part of the city, you pass Metro Allende and, shortly on the right, Café Tacuba, the popular haunt of Mexico's lunch crowd. Farther on, to the right, is the Museo Nacional de Arte (▷ 113), which faces the late 18th-century Palacio de Minería.

One block west is the magnificent Post Office, its gilding sparkling in the midday sun, and then you reach the Alameda (▷ 104).

❻ This large city park with overgrown trees is the best place for a quiet moment in the sprawling, magnificent metropolis. Once the site of an Aztec market, the name Alameda comes from the *álamaos* or poplar trees planted in the square in the 16th century by Viceroy Luis de Velasco. On the eastern side is the art nouveau facade of the Palacio de Bellas Artes, and to the southeast is the 44-floor Torre Latinoamericana, a survivor of countless earthquakes since its completion in 1956.

Leave the Alameda at the south-east corner and head east along Calle Francisco Madero. Turn left at the first small street, Condesa

Market stalls outside the Cathedral

The tiled facade of the Casa de los Azulejos

Marconi, pausing to pop into the ornate Casa de los Azulejos (▷ 106), decorated with Talavera tiles. Continue north and turn right on Calle 5 de Mayo, looking in on Bar La Opera, at the first intersection with Calle Filomeno Mata, where Pancho Villa blasted a hole through the ceiling before being assassinated in 1923. A couple of blocks farther east along Calle 5 de Mayo are the divine handmade sweet creations of Dulcería de Celaya (▷ 191), which you can nibble at on your return to the Zócalo.

Charles IV of Spain outside the Museo Nacional de Arte (left)
Tiles, Café de Tacuba (bottom)

TOURIST INFORMATION

Northwest corner of the Zócalo

WHERE TO EAT

Café Tacuba
(▷ 252)

Casa de los Azulejos
(▷ 106)

Hosteria Santo Domingo
Belisario Dominguez 72
☎ (55) 55 10 14 34
Fine traditional dining; or just pop in for a snack.
Mon–Sat 9am–10.30pm, Sun 9–6

Majestic Hotel
(▷ 273)

Sushi Roll
(▷ 255)

PLACES TO VISIT

If you plan to visit any of the places of interest on the walk you will need proof of ID with a photograph—a photocopy will often be sufficient.

Museo Nacional de las Culturas
Calle Moneda 13
Tue-Sun 10–5
Free

Museo José Luis Cuevas
Calle Academia 13
Tue–Sun, 10–5.30
$1, free Sun

Museo de la Medicina Mexicana
Republica de Brasil 33
☎ (55) 29 75 42
Daily 10–6, closed during university holidays
Free

Torre Latinoamericana
Corner of Calle Madero
Daily 11–11
$4.50

SAN ANGEL AND COYOACÁN

The figures of Frida Kahlo, Diego Rivera and Hernando Cortés stand tall in Mexican history. They each called the southern suburb of Coyoacán home, and a walk through the area takes in the city's past, from colonial times to post-revolutionary Mexico.

THE WALK

Distance: 7km (4.5 miles)
Allow: 3–4 hours
Start: Museo Estudio Diego Rivera
End: Plaza Hidalgo or Plaza de la Conchita

HOW TO GET THERE

Take a taxi from Miguel Angel de Quevedo (Line 3) or Barranca del Muerto to reach Museo Estudio Diego Rivera.

From this Modernist museum (⊳ 117), built by the Mexican functionalist architect Juan O'Gorman for the two artists, walk up to the San Angel Inn and, looking straight ahead, take Lazcano, spurring off the main road diagonally. Continue ahead and turn right at the end of the road down Calle de Reina, a pleasant cobbled street with balconies festooned with flowers. Turn left along Calle del General Aureliano Rivera, then take the second right to Plaza San Jacinto.

❶ Plaza San Jacinto is a whirlwind of activity, especially at the Bazar del Sábado, a great place to pick up souvenirs and handicrafts, or have a bite to eat or a drink. Just off the plaza is the 16th-century Iglesia de San Jacinto, and to the north the 18th-century Casa del Risco with its peaceful courtyards.

Continue round the plaza and leave from the southeastern corner, heading down Calle del Dr. Gálvez, a short road of just 50m (55 yards) that meets the busy Avenida Revolución. Cross over here and turn left. Continue for about 200m (220 yards), then look for a gap in the stone wall through an arched doorway that leads to the church and the Museo Colonial del Carmen.

❷ This 17th-century former Carmelite monastery is now a museum housing colonial furniture and art.

Turn right out of the courtyard, cross the first road and take the right fork, cutting the corner to turn right onto Avenida La Paz.

Museo Colonial del Carmen

Pass several restaurants before reaching Avenida Insurgentes Sur. Cross over and cut through the Parque de la Bombilla, taking the left fork after the Monumento a General Alvaro Obregón.

❸ This memorial commemorates the assassination of the Mexican president in 1928 during the Cristero Revolt.

Head out of the park behind the monument and turn right at the cobbled street (away from the main road) and in 20m (22 yards) turn left, before the guarded checkpoint, towards Plaza Federico Gamboa, across Calle Chimalistac.

❹ The small, shaded Plaza Federico Gamboa hides the 17th-century chapel of San Sebastián Mártir, which has a fine baroque altarpiece. The square is home to artists and writers, including Gabriel Garcia Marquez (born 1928).

Continue through the plaza, turn left at the Intersection with Callejon San Angelo, then cross over Miguel Angel de Quevedo to join Calle Allende before turning right onto Avenida Arenal which, on crossing Avenida Universidad, becomes Avenida Francisco Sosa.

❺ To the side of a small bridge crossing Avenida Río Magdelena is the 17th-century Capilla de San Antonio Panzacola, at the end of Avenida Francisco Sosa, one of the oldest streets in Latin America, lined with balconies hung with flowers, and ornate doorways and arches.

Continue east and at Calle Salvador Novo turn right for a quick visit to the Museo Nacional de la Acuarela. Back on Avenida Francisco Sosa, the road heads west, passing the shady Plaza Santa Catarina before arriving at Jardín Centenario—the heart of Coyoacán.

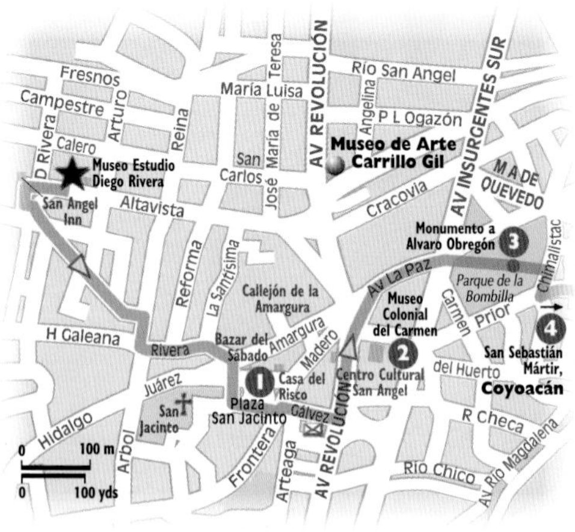

6 The garden and nearby Plaza Hidalgo to the east form one of the city's great meeting places. Architecturally the tone is set by the 18th-century Palacio de Cortés to the north, and to the southwest by the bold exterior of the 16th-century Templo de San Juan Bautista, ornately decorated with frescoes and gilded altars. On any day of the week the plaza hums and stirs, stepping up a notch on weekends when all of Mexico appears to stroll through the street fairs, enjoying live music and street performers.

From here, head to the eastern side of Plaza Hidalgo and turn left down Calle Allende. Passing between Parque Allende and the market.

7 In six blocks you will reach the Museo Frida Kahlo, the long-time home of Mexico's best-known artist.

Allende and passing the Museo Frida Kahlo again to return to the Plaza Hidalgo. A short extension down Calle Higuera leads to the Plaza de la Conchita.

9 Overlooking Plaza de la Conchita is the exquisite facade of the Iglesia de la Conchita, and to the southwest the Casa de La Malinche, the home of the mistress of Spanish conquistador Hernán Cortés (▷ 32).

TOURIST INFORMATION

Avenida Revolución at Madero
☎ (55) 56 16 20 97

WHERE TO EAT

La Guadalupana
Calle Higuera 14
☎ (55) 55 54 62 53
A traditional Mexican *cantina* dating from 1932. Few airs and graces, and not to everyone's taste, but worth popping in for a drink.
🕐 Mon–Sat 11–11, Sun 11–6

San Angel Inn
Calle Diego Rivera 50
☎ (55) 56 16 05 37
Top-class dining in the former Carmelite monastery.
🕐 Mon–Sat 12.30–3am, Sun 1–9.30

PLACES TO VISIT

Casa del Risco
Plaza San Jacinto 15
☎ (55) 56 16 27 11
🕐 Daily 10–5
✋ Free

Museo Colonial del Carmen
Avenida Revolución 4 and 6
☎ (55) 55 16 15 04
🕐 Tue–Sun 10–5 ✋ $3.20

Casa de León Trotsky
Calle Río Churubusco 410
☎ (55) 55 54 06 87
🕐 Tue–Sun 10–5
✋ $3

Museo Frida Kahlo
Londres 247
☎ (55) 55 54 59 99
🕐 Tue–Sun 10–6 ✋ $3

Museo Frida Kahlo, Coyoacán

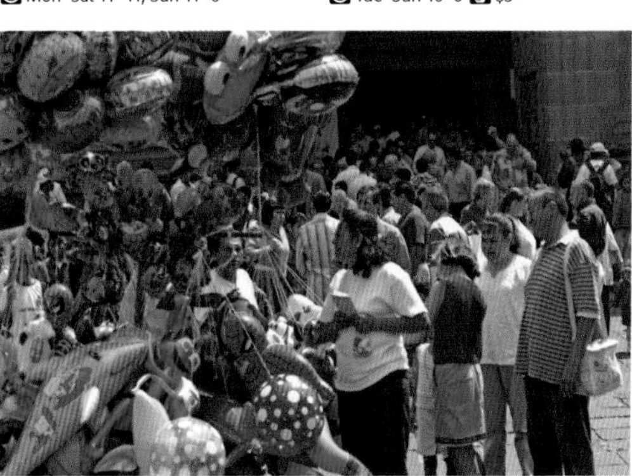

Coyoacán comes to life on the weekend with a lively market

If you're tiring, head back down the street to Jardín Centenario. But a short trip left out of the museum, taking the third left up Calle Morelos for three blocks, leads to Casa de León Trotsky.

8 The exiled Russian revolutionary made his home here in 1937, where he was eventually murdered in 1940. You can see the bullet holes of a previous attempt on his life and in the high-walled garden is the tomb where his ashes are laid.

Leave the Trotsky Museum, turn right and continue straight ahead, taking the third left down Calle

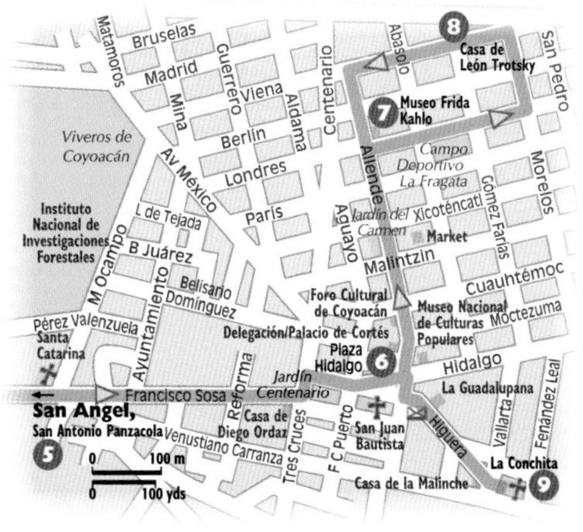

9. DRIVE

THE CHURCHES OF PUEBLA

From the stunning Capilla del Rosario in the heart of Puebla, to exquisite marvels in tiny, dusty villages scattered around the city, this drive takes in some of the most spectacular examples of baroque architecture in Mexico.

THE DRIVE

Distance: 60km (37 miles)
Allow: 5 hours
Start/end: Puebla

Start in the *zócalo*, heart of the city of Puebla (⊳ 126–127).

❶ The great Catedral de la Inmaculada Concepción (⊳ 126) sits at the southwest corner, facing Calle 16 de Septiembre. Although the grey exterior walls are unremarkable, the interior has wonderful marble and onyx statuary. Mestizo artist Manuel Tolsa designed the gold-leaf altarpiece in 1797.

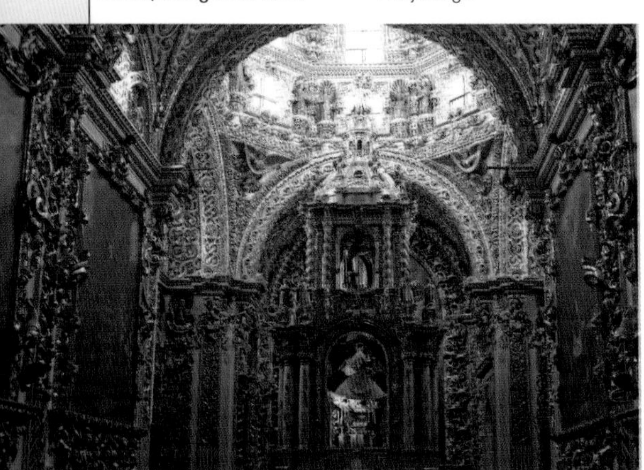

The magnificent Rosary Chapel in the Church of Santo Domingo

Turn right out of the cathedral and walk up Calle 16 de Septiembre. Beyond the *zócalo*, the street becomes pedestrianized. After three-and-a-half blocks you will cross Calle 4 Oriente. On the northeast corner is the Iglesia de Santo Domingo.

❷ Inside the church, the Capilla del Rosario, on the left-hand side, is an extraordinarily lavish display of gold leaf and baroque flounces. Completed in 1659, the decorative stucco work here provided the inspiration for all later baroque art and architecture in Mexico.

From central Puebla, follow Avenida Reforma west. After 2km (1 mile) it becomes Prolongación Reforma. On leaving the city it becomes Carretera Federal Mexico-Puebla, passing through Cholula. The views of Popocatépetl and Ixtaccíhuatl are stunning on the left-hand side. After 16km (10 miles), you will come to the town of Huejotzingo.

❸ In Huejotzingo, Avenida Carlos Zetina borders the eastern side of the *zócalo*. Halfway along is the Convento Franciscano, set back on the right-hand side. The second oldest church and monastery in Mexico, it was begun by the first Franciscans to arrive in the country in 1529 and finished in 1570. Note the Moorish *mudejar* influences in the fortress-like exterior and stonework around the door frame. Inside the church is one of the only remaining original 16th-century altarpieces in the country. The monastery has a lovely walled garden and cloisters.

Return to Cholula on the same road—Carretera Federal Mexico-Puebla—which becomes Calle 12 Poniente in town. At the *zócalo*, turn right, following the sign "Zona archaeológico."

❹ Sitting atop the ancient pyramid of Cholula (⊳ 123) is the small, beautiful Iglesia de Nuestra Señora de los Remedios, a riot of white, cream and gold stucco decoration that glitters in the light from the clear glass windows in the dome. Originally built by the Spanish in 1594, the church was destroyed by an earthquake in the mid-19th century and rebuilt between 1864 and 1874 in neoclassical style.

From the *zócalo*, follow Boulevard Miguel Alemán south, which becomes Carretera Cholula-Tonanzintla. After 3km (2 miles) is the tiny village of Tonantzintla.

❺ In Tonantzintla, turn right off Avenida Hidalgo, where the road curves to the left, onto Avenida Hombres Ilustres. Park and walk two blocks west to the pedestrianized main square. Here the ornate tower of the exquisite church, built in the first half of the 18th century, features figurines clothed in blue and green, while the tiled dome glitters in blue and yellow. The Moorish-style arched doorway is surrounded by terra cotta and blue-and-white star-shaped tiles. Inside, look for the gold-leaf angels' dark, indigenous faces, the tropical fruit, maize and children wearing feathers that are surrounded by whipped-up, white swirls edged with gold. The Virgin above the altar sits in the middle of this splendor in her own pillared pavilion, surrounded by flowers and more angels that emerge from the swirls of white.

Return to the Carretera Cholula-Tonantzintla and continue in the same direction—towards Puebla—for 1km (0.5 mile), passing the Panteón la Puríssima, a large cemetery, on your left, until you reach San Francisco Acatepec.

❻ On entering San Francisco Acatepec, directly ahead of you is the village's 17th-century baroque church of San Francisco. The wonderfully tiled, mosaic and polychrome facade, a feast of detail, is constructed from local Talavera glazed ceramics. The density and brilliance of the interior shimmers with gold leaf, and the ornate altarpiece appears to flow seamlessly into the decorations of the dome and side chapels. Within the four arches of the dome there are figures of the four Apostles: St. Mark with a lion; St. Matthew with an angel; St. Luke with a bull; and St. John with an eagle.

Nuestra Señora de los Remedios at Cholula (below)

TOURIST INFORMATION

Calle 5 Oriente No. 3, Puebla
☎ (222) 246 20 44
Mon–Sat 10–7, Sun 10–1

PLACES TO VISIT

Convento Franciscano de San Miguel de Huejotzingo
Plazuela Fr. Juan de Alameda
☎ (222) 276 02 28
Daily 10–5
$3

PLACES TO EAT

El Convento
Plazuela Fr. Juan de Alameda, Huejotzingo
☎ (222) 610 86

On the tiny square just off the *zócalo* in Huejotzingo, this is an excellent option for good-value Mexican fare.
Daily 9–7

Cholula
Cholula's *zócalo* is full of cafés and restaurants. Try Los Jarrones (Portal Guerrero 4, tel (224) 247 10 98; daily 8am–11pm), with a sunny terrace fronting the square.

The Church of Santa Maria de Tonantzintla (top and above left)
Church of San Francisco, Acatepec (above right)
Inside the Church of San Miguel in Huejotzingo (below)

Continue on the same road towards Puebla. After crossing the Anillo Periférico, the road becomes the Carretera a Atlixco. Continue through the suburbs of Puebla, where the road becomes Boulevard Atlixco, until you reach Avenida Juárez. Turn right onto Juárez and follow this road for 1km (half a mile) to the *zócalo*.

THE MISSIONS OF THE SIERRA GORDA

The drive to and over the Sierra Gorda is spectacular, crawling over big-country scenery to reach the five missions founded by Fray Junípero Serra in the 18th century. En route the huge Bernal monolithic outcrop provides a useful break in a long, dramatic and enjoyable drive known as the route of 700 curves.

THE DRIVE

Distance: 540km (335 miles)
Allow: 2–3 days
Start/end: Querétaro

Note: The road is in good condition and the journey is safe.

Leave Querétaro (▷ 148) on Highway 57, heading south. At Km 15 look for the sign and road feeding off on the left to Peña de Bernal. At Km 36 the monolithic outcrop of Bernal appears.

❶ Bernal is the third largest outcrop of its type in the world after Sugar Loaf Mountain in Brazil and the Rock of Gibraltar in southern Europe. It's worth a stop to wander around the pleasant colonial heart of the town and to scramble on the lower slopes of the rock.

Back on the road, the curves begin gently at first, increasing as the road climbs through the first of many passes to reveal a spectacular view of the flats of San Pablo below. At Km 56 a fuel station marks the road off to the right to Jalpan. Climbing out of the valley, you can see the spectacular silhouette of Bernal in the distance. There's a viewpoint with a parking spot after Km 62 and again at Km 63.

Again the road sneaks through a pass, opening up to reveal the small village of Higuerillas below. Shortly after the roads from San Juan del Río (Highway 120) and Bernal merge, there is a police checkpoint. There is nothing to worry about if you're polite and explain your plans (*Voy/Vamos a ver los misiones*—I/We're going to see the missions).

The road continues to rise and fall with the dramatic desert landscape, picking a route through the scrubby cactus and passing isolated buildings such as the Puerta del Cielo (Gateway to Heaven). As it climbs, it inches towards the bulbous massif of the Sierra Gorda. Soon after Cuesta Colorada, Bernal is visible again on the horizon. By Maguey Verde, trees have replaced the cactus as the higher altitude brings lower temperatures and increased moisture.

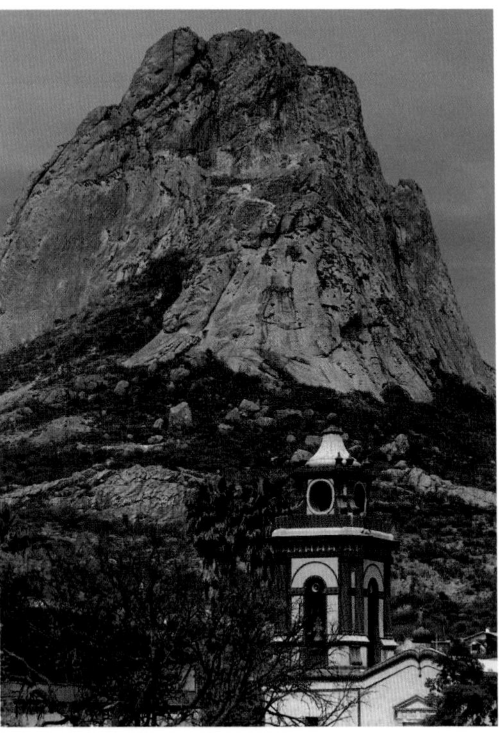

Peña de Bernal towers above the little village of Bernal

The road clings to the mountainside as it drops through the maze of valleys, passing through small towns and villages, including Pinal de Amoles and Ahuacatlán, before finally arriving in Jalpan at around Km 175.

❷ This may be a good opportunity to stop for the night. The Jalpan mission was the first to be built by Fray Junípero Serra, and served as the model for the four other missions in the region. It dates from 1751 to 1758 and is considered to be one of the best examples of baroque architecture in the New World.

From Jalpan head northwest to Concá along Highway 69—the intersection marked by the Mexican flag. The route rides the contours of the broad valley, eventually crossing and climbing the valley of the Río Santa Maria. Gentle hills fringe this valley, hiding the harsh desert landscape to the west. Turn left at Km 35 next to Restaurant La Palapa. At the end of the cobbled drive, continue for one block and turn right, following the road until you arrive at the Misión de Concá.

❸ Misión de Concá is simpler and less ornate than the mission at Jalpan; in fact it is the smallest church in the Sierra Gorda. There are images of maize and vegetables above the entrance adorning the orange facade.

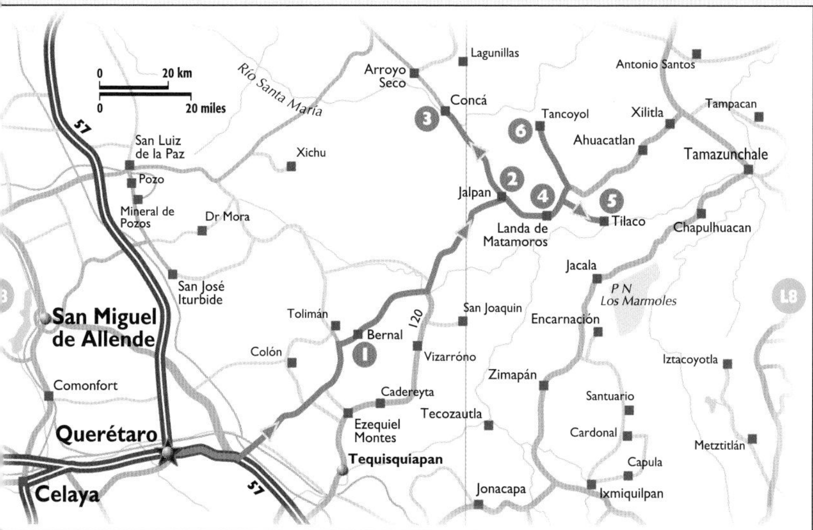

Misión de Landa de Matamoros

The intricate facade of the Misión de Tilaco

Returning along the same route to Jalpan, turn left at the Mexican flag onto Highway 120; from here, it's 22km (14 miles) to Misión de Landa de Matamoros. It's a gentle climb to the pass, with a fairly quick drop immediately after to the town and a signposted turn to the left.

❹ Misión de Landa de Matamoros was the last of the missions to be built and is the best preserved. It has a small community museum with items that demonstrate the use of agriculture in the region. Carved saints decorate the elaborate facade.

Head out of the village the way you came. After 10.5km (7 miles) is La Lagunita. Here take the right turn to Misión de Tilaco.

❺ Above the wide door of the Misión de Tilaco there are sculptures of St. Joseph and the Virgin, with angels above flying towards a garden.

The road heads west, climbing rapidly and revealing the plateau of Tilaco below, 16km (10 miles) from La Lagunita. Head back to Highway 120 and turn right. In 4km (2.5 miles) you'll reach the left turn to Misión de Tancoyol.

❻ Although all five missions clearly share the same style, Misión de Tancoyol, dedicated to Our Lady of the Light, is the simplest of the designs.

The return journey is less complex. Follow Highway 120 for 220km (136 miles), at which point it joins Highway 57.

Continue on this road back to Querétaro.

TOURIST INFORMATION

Plaza de Armas, Querétaro
☎ (442) 212 14 12
🕐 Mon–Fri 8–8, Sat–Sun 9–8

WHERE TO EAT

There are several good hotels with restaurants in Bernal and around the main plaza in Jalpan, and along Highway 120 on the way back to Querétaro.

WHERE TO STAY

Hacienda Misión Concá
Highway 69, 1km (0.5 mile) south of the turn-off for the mission
☎ (441) 296 02 55

Hacienda Misión Jalpan
Downtown Jalpan
☎ (441) 296 02 55

11. DRIVE

SILVER TOWNS OF THE BAJÍO

This easy drive passes through pleasant scenery, visiting some of the colonial jewels of the historic Bajío region

THE DRIVE

Distance: approximately 135km (84 miles)
Allow: 1–2 days. An easy one-day trip, but make it two if you want more time to sightsee in San Miguel de Allende
Start/end: Guanajuato

Guanajuato (▷ 142–144) is the natural place to start and end a driving tour of the Bajío. Once you are familiar with the town's warren-like tunnels, it's an entertaining city to drive around, although parking is always difficult. Head out of town through the Túnel Santa Fé under Cason del Quijo. At the first traffic circle (roundabout) take the turn almost straight ahead, marked La Valenciana. At the second traffic circle turn right. Climb out of Guanajuato, twisting past San Javier (to your right), to reach the Iglesia de la Valenciana.

❶ The Iglesia de La Valenciana, the splendid Churrigueresque church in Valenciana (▷ 144), was built for the workers of the nearby mine, once the richest in the world. A short distance down the hill the Hacienda del Cochera draws in passing visitors with the Museo de las Momias—a rather morbid display of mummies in positions of torture.

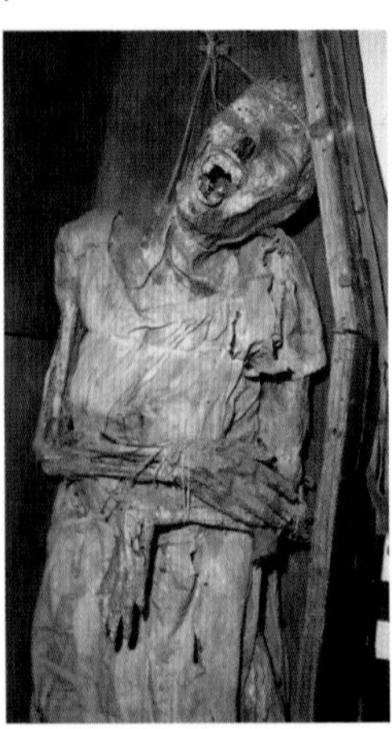

Exhibit, Museo de las Momias

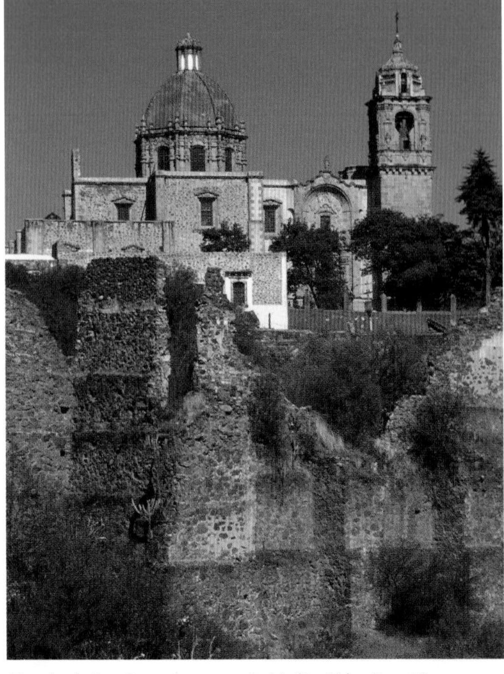

Templo de San Cayetano towers behind La Valenciana Mine

Continue climbing out of the valley of Guanajuato, the road twisting and turning to Santa Rosa.

❷ At Santa Rosa you can stop for a drink or breakfast and enjoy the splendid view across the forest.

The road continues to climb out of the valley, eventually reaching the open plains before hitting the outer suburbs of Dolores Hidalgo. At Km 39 turn left at the traffic circle, heading north into the middle of Dolores Hidalgo. After the bridge, take the fourth right turn, Calle Ithacan, marked by a collection of blue signs saying, among other things, Centro Historical. Continue straight ahead for several blocks and on reaching the Plaza Principal pull up. There is a small parking charge.

❸ Dolores Hidalgo (▷ 139) is the home of the Mexican Independence movement, where the local priest Miguel Hidalgo rang the church bells issuing the famous call to arms, *El Grito* (The Cry), on September 16 1810. The revolt failed, Hidalgo was executed and Mexico waited a further 11 years to achieve independence from Spain.

Leave the plaza and return to the traffic circle—as you drive back up the road you'll pass many ceramics stores selling all manner of items from the appalling to the offensive. There are, however, some fine items among the junk, including Talavera tiles. Head straight on for about 3km (2 miles), turning left to San Miguel de Allende. Go straight across at the first intersection, then take the right fork at Km 10.7, marked San Miguel de Allende. The road drops into the town on Calle Hidalgo. Look for the road names—once you've reached Avenida Insurgentes you're a

A statue of local priest Miguel Hidalgo stands in the Plaza Principal in Dolores Hidalgo

couple of blocks from the plaza so look for a parking spot.

❹ San Miguel de Allende (⊳ 149) is a colonial town with cobbled streets and fine old mansion houses. It makes a convenient base for exploring the temples and churches of the region, and also has several good restaurants, so take your pick and stop for lunch before exploring the plaza. If you are staying the night in San Miguel, park carefully and watch for time limits. Ask at your hotel.

Leave San Miguel de Allende where Calle Hidalgo meets the Plaza Allende and turn right, then take the second left down Avenida Zacatecas. Take the right turn for Guanajuato from the plaza in San Miguel.

❺ Passing by the southern shoreline of Presa Ignacio Allende (dam), the road winds through cactus and grassy scrubland, with the lumpy massif of the hills around and Guanajuato appearing in the distant west.

At Km 37 turn right toward Guanajuato and León, and follow the road to Guanajuato. At the first traffic circle (roundabout), marked Guanajuato Centro, go straight through. Peel off right at Km 72.6, with a sign for Guanajuato, and you will soon enter a short tunnel, then another at Km 74.2, followed by a stretch of speed humps. From here on *ayudantes* (helpers) appear at the side of the street offering parking and other services. A feeder lane comes in from the left; move to the left lane marked Guadalajara Centro. The road is cobbled from here onwards as you pass over one traffic circle with a statue of miners and another (barely noticeable) one. Get in the middle lane and go straight ahead at the traffic circle before bearing right and heading into the tunnels of Guanajuato.

Dolores Hidalgo is renowned for its ceramics (above and left)

Nighttime view of San Miguel de Allende's cathedral (below)

TOURIST INFORMATION

Plaza de la Paz 14, Guanajuato
☎ 738 11 40
🕒 Daily 9–7

WHERE TO EAT

Ciao Bella
Guanajuato
(⊳ 260)

Mesón de San José
Calle Mesones between Colegio and Presa, San Miguel de Allende
A secret spot hidden in a small courtyard of cobbled stone, with a good mix of *enchiladas* and *quesadillas,* blended with international dishes, and a children's menu. There's something for everyone.
🕒 Daily 8am–10pm

12. DRIVE

AROUND LAGO DE PÁTZCUARO

This drive takes you around Lake Pátzcuaro, through the Tarascan Indian villages on its shores where the way of life has hardly changed.

THE DRIVE

Distance: 99km (61 miles)
Allow: 8 hours
Start/end: Pátzcuaro

Begin the drive at the northern edge of Pátzcuaro (▷ 147). Turn north on Highway 14 at the signs to Quiroga. After passing several small roadside handicraft stands and motels, the road climbs a small hill to a lookout point with a view of the lake. After 11km (7 miles) a sign appears on the east side of the road for the turn-off to the archaeological site of Tzintzuntzán.

❶ The cluster of restored structures at Tzintzuntzán, the first capital of the Purépecha Empire, includes an unusual round temple and five pyramid-shaped temples. About 40,000 Purépecha lived around the lake when the Spaniards arrived in the 16th century.

The road continues through the town.

❷ In the town of Tzintzuntzán, a daily market (busiest from Friday to Sunday) sprawls along the west side of the road in front of a 16th-century restored Franciscan monastery; pilgrims often walk on their knees to reach the church. Woodcarvers work in shops and stands on the east side of the road. Local crafts include straw ornaments and green-and-blue ceramics.

From Tzintzuntzán the road continues for 7km (4 miles) past lake views, churches and rural homes to Quiroga (▷ 148).

❸ An important commercial and ceremonial base since pre-Hispanic times, Quiroga is known for its plaza lined with stands selling local delicacies, including fragrant *carnitas* (roasted pork). Visitors stop here for *carnitas* tacos, bowls of *pozole* (hominy stew) and *menudo* (tripe soup).

Head west from Quiroga for 8.5km (5 miles), following signs south to Parque Chupícuaro.

❹ Wooded Parque Chupícuaro is on the edge of Lake Pátzcuaro. The park has lavatories and picnic tables, and is popular with families who picnic on food they've picked up in Quiroga.

Continue 26km (16 miles) southwest of the park to Erongarícuaro.

❺ This small lakeside town, formerly important for textiles, is known for its woodworkers. Families linger all day at Campestre Alemán, just south of town, where the restaurant fronts a lake stocked with trout and has boat rentals, apple and pear trees providing shade, and a large playground.

About 2 miles (3km) south of Eronarícuaro is Tocuaro.

❻ This tiny town is home to several excellent mask-makers, many of whom will open their studios to visitors. Among the best artists is Gustavo Horta Horta, whose gallery is called Puerta del Sol. It's on the north side of the main street near the entrance to town; no phone.

Continue southeast for 14km (8.5 miles) to the outskirts of Pátzcuaro to complete the drive. If you wish to extend the drive, turn south at the intersection with Highway 41, which becomes Highway 120 about 10km (6 miles) south of Pátzcuaro, to reach Santa Clara del Cobre.

❼ The streets of Santa Clara del Cobre town are lined with shops selling gleaming copper pots, bowls, platters and jewelry. At the Museo del Cobre, workmen pound out patterns on flaming hot sheets of copper beside large fires; their skill and endurance are impressive.

Return to Pátzcuaro by driving north on Highway 120 for 15 miles (24 km).

TOURIST INFORMATION

Calle Buenavista 7, Pátzcuaro
☎ (434) 342 12 14
Mon–Fri 9–3, 5–7, Sat 9–12

WHEN TO GO

If you intend visiting Pátzcuaro during the Day of the Dead celebrations (Nov 1–2), make reservations for accommodations well in advance.

PLACES TO VISIT

Museo del Cobre
Calle Morelos at Piño Suárez
Tue–Sun 10–3, 5–7
50 cents

Tzintzuntzán archaeological site
Tue–Sun 9–4
$3.50, free on Sun

WHERE TO EAT

Campestre Alemán
Carretera a Pátzcuaro, Km 14
☎ (434) 344 00 06
Smoked trout is served as an appetizer, main course and in soup here; other specials include Hungarian goulash, beef, rabbit, and apple strudel. No credit cards.
Daily 1–7

Los Escudos Portal Hidalgo 73
Plaza Vasco de Quiroga, Pátzcuaro
☎ (434) 342 13 13
Daily 11–7
An excellent place to try *sopa*

Janitizio Island in the middle of Lake Pátzcuaro

Market stalls in Quiroga (above) and Pátzcuaro (below)

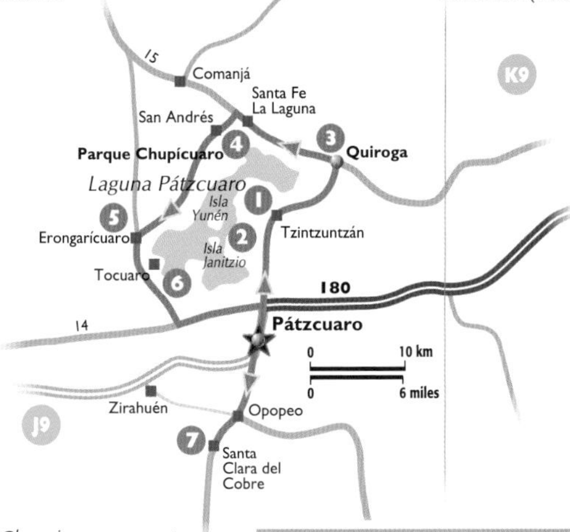

15
Comanjá
Santa Fe La Laguna
San Andrés
Parque Chupícuaro
Quiroga
Laguna Pátzcuaro
Isla Yunén
Erongarícuaro
Tzintzuntzán
Isla Janitzio
Tocuaro
180
14
Pátzcuaro
0 10 km
0 6 miles
Zirahuén
Opopeo
Santa Clara del Cobre
K9
J9

Boats moored along the shores of Lake Pátzcuaro (below)

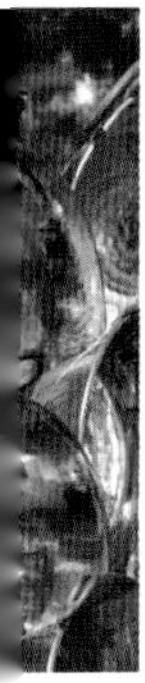

Gleaming copper pots (left) and carved wooden handicrafts (below) for sale in Quiroga

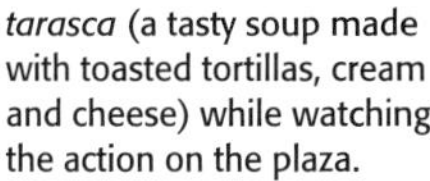

tarasca (a tasty soup made with toasted tortillas, cream and cheese) while watching the action on the plaza.

WHERE TO STAY

Mansión de los Sueños
Calle Ibarra 15, Pátzcuaro
☎ (434) 342 57 08
www.prismas.com.mx
As much a museum as hotel, this faithfully restored 17th-century home has 11 rooms decorated with handcrafted furnishings; art from the region fills the courtyards and gardens. The restaurant serves excellent regional cuisine.
$165–$200

Hotel Mansión Iturbide
Portal Morelos 96, Plaza Vasco de Quiroga, Pátzcuaro
☎ (434) 342 03 68
www.mexonline.com/iturbe/htm
This colonial-era mansion turned hotel has 12 rooms, all nonsmoking. Some face the plaza, others the courtyard with a fireplace and avocado trees. Viejo Gaucho restaurant serves *queso fundido* (melted cheese with tortillas), pizza and other snacks and has live music Tuesday to Sunday nights.
$80–$100

Hotel Misión
San Manuel Portal Aldama 12, Plaza Vasco de Quiroga, Pátzcuaro
☎ (434) 342 10 50
Rooms at the front of this converted colonial-era mansion have tiny wrought-iron balconies and views of the plaza; those at the back are larger. The best choice of restaurants is the outdoor café serving robust coffee and homemade *pan dulce* (sweet bread).
$40–$80

13. WALK

ON THE EDGE OF THE COPPER CANYON

This walk skirts the edge of the Urique Canyon, one of a series of dramatic gorges that make up the Barrancas del Cobre, passing through pine forests and three lookout points.

THE WALK

Distance: 2.5km (1.5 miles)
Allow: 3 hours
Start/end: Hotel Divisadero Barrancas

HOW TO GET THERE

Visitors to El Divisadero usually arrive on Ferrocarril Chihuahua al Pacifico (tel (614) 439 72 10, www.chepe.com.mx), more commonly known as the Copper Canyon train, which runs 653km (405 miles) between Los Mochis, on the Pacific Coast, to Chihuahua city. El Divisadero can also be reached by car via Highway 127 from Creel, which connects with Highway 16 from Chihuahua.

Urique is the deepest canyon in Mexico. El Divisadero sits some 2,392m (7,847ft) above sea level and provides extraordinary vistas into and across the canyon. The Tarahumara, who have remained one of Mexico's most traditional indigenous cultures, live in caves and small settlements in and around the canyon. Tarahumara women sit alongside the train tracks, hotels and lookout points at Divisadero, selling carved wooden dolls, hand-woven baskets, belts woven on back-strap looms and rustic pottery. Carry a bottle of water and snacks, as there are no restaurants along the route. A market next to the train station sells sodas, water and food and vendors along the stairway to the station sell *tacos*, *burritos*, *quesadillas* and other hot snacks.

❶ Begin your walk at the parking area at the Hotel Divisadero Barrancas, across a dirt road from El Divisadero train station. Head southeast on the dirt road, walking past a large dirt field where Tarahumara dancers often perform for tour groups. If you see people assembling there, wait around for the show.

Continue on the dirt road until you see a sign and fence for Hotel Barrancas on the west side of the road. Cross through the fence (there is an old, rickety gate, but this is not used) and turn south on the dirt trail alongside the edge of the canyon. Carry on for about 125m (140 yards) to cross a dirt airstrip that is occasionally used by private planes. Continue to the Mirador Elefante, a fenced-in lookout point at the edge of the canyon.

❷ From the viewpoint, look south to the rock formation that resembles an elephant and north to the Hotel Divisadero Barrancas—seemingly suspended over the canyon. Vendors selling local crafts gather here, but the selection is better farther on.

Stay to the right side of the fence as you continue to the next lookout, Divisadero Escalera.

❸ A narrow ladder is set in a crevice in the rocks below the lookout point. The Tarahumara use it to get to and from their homes in the canyon. The women climb up or down barefoot, carrying a large plastic bag stuffed with their wares on their heads. Tarahumara is a Spanish corruption of the indigenous word *Raramuri*, meaning "running people." They are extraordinarily fleet of foot, running long distances through the canyon chasing deer until the animals are exhausted and easy to capture.

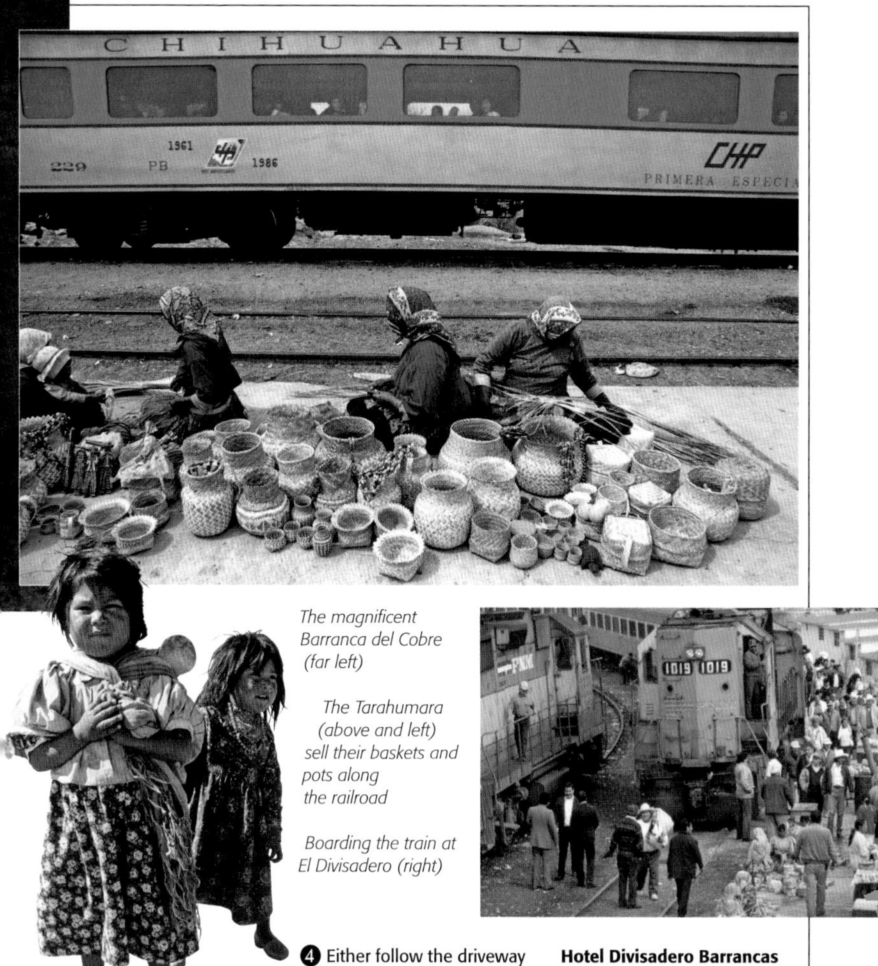

The magnificent Barranca del Cobre (far left)

The Tarahumara (above and left) sell their baskets and pots along the railroad

Boarding the train at El Divisadero (right)

Unless you're exceptionally dexterous and strong, resist the urge to descend the perilous ladder. Again, women have their crafts on display for sale here.

From Divisadero Escalera walk southeast to reach the Piedra Volada (Balancing Rock), the most popular attraction in the area. A large stone hangs over the canyon, looking as if it's about to topple at any moment. Brave souls climb it and balance as the rock tips from side to side. The selection of crafts for sale at this point is of better quality than at the others. The beaded belts and wristbands are especially attractive. There are restrooms and trash cans here.

❹ Either follow the driveway west to the main dirt road or backtrack along the trail you came along to the Hotel Divisadero Barrancas.

If you wish to continue, turn south at the road that runs along the edge of the canyon and follow it to the Hotel Posada Mirador for lunch, then return the same way to the Hotel Divisadero Barrancas.

WHERE TO EAT AND STAY

Hotel Posada Mirador
El Divisadero, Los Mochis
☎ (668) 818 70 46
www.mexicoscoppercanyon.com
Perched on the rim of the canyon, this lodge has 51 rooms, most with fireplaces and canyon views. It's popular with group tours. Meals are served in a dining room with log ceilings; food is average.
From $160, including meals

Hotel Divisadero Barrancas
El Divisadero
☎ (614) 415 11 99
www.hoteldivisadero.com.mx
Right across the road from the train station, the hotel has 52 rooms; most have fireplaces and some have canyon views.
$140–$210, including meals

Hotel Mansión Tarahumara
El Divisadero
☎ (614) 415 47 21
www.mansiontarahumara.com
The turreted towers seem a bit out of place in the pine forest but the heated indoor pool, sauna and steam room feel good after a long hike.
From $150, including meals

WHEN TO GO

The best times to visit are September to November and March to June. It snows in Divisadero from December to February.

CAVE PAINTINGS AND A MOUNTAIN MISSION

One of the most dramatic drives in Baja, this route takes in stunning views of the sea from high in the mountains. On the way you'll pass a small cluster of prehistoric petroglyphs (cave paintings) and an 18th-century mission church.

THE DRIVE

Distance: 74km (46 miles)
Allow: 6 hours
Start/end point: Loreto

The dirt road into the Sierra de la Giganta is somewhat rough, but passable in a regular car, except during the rainy season (August to November). Ask in town about the road conditions, and don't attempt this drive after hard rains. There are plans to improve the road, since San Javier has become a popular side trip for passengers on cruise ships visiting Loreto. The road is part of the Camino Real (Royal Road), once used by the Spaniards in the 18th century as they established a chain of mission settlements throughout the Californias. San Javier was chosen for some of the New World's first orchards and vineyards because of its exceptionally temperate climate and abundance of fresh water.

Statue of St. Francisco Javier in Misión San Javier

From Loreto (▷ 164), turn south on Highway 1 to the west of town and continue for 2km (1 mile) to the turn-off on the west side of the road, marked San Javier. The road runs southwest, winding up Cerro la Gigántica (1,490m/4,885ft) through low hills. After 10km (6 miles) the road begins to climb steeply and signs to the petroglyphs appear. There is parking near the sign on the left-hand side of the road.

❶ Baja's petroglyphs are one of its great mysteries. No one knows who painted the large figures of humans and animals, although experts have determined that they date from 3000BC to AD1650. The most dramatic petroglyphs, with figures up 4m (12ft) tall, are in remote caves high in the Sierra and are accessible only by hiking or riding a burro (donkey) for several days. The small cluster of paintings on the road to San Javier include faint red, white and black figures of deer and people.

Typical desert terrain near San Javier, which lies in a deep valley in the Sierra de la Giganta

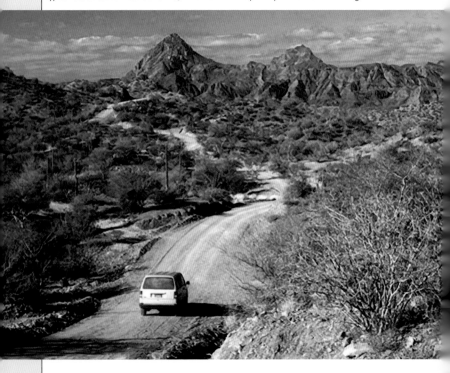

From the petroglyphs, continue 10km (6 miles) on Highway 1 to Rancho las Parras, built in an oasis on both sides of the road.

❷ The private ranch has a small chapel on the east side of the road and tropical fruit orchards on the west, including 5,000 mango trees. Some of the olive, date and fig trees were planted by the Jesuits in the late 1700s. The ranch is not normally open to the public, but if the gates are open and there's someone around, ask to see Juan Angel (also known as Johnny Angel), the manager of the ranch. A garrulous gentleman in his 80s, he loves picking exotic fruits for guests to sample. If he takes you on a tour, offer 50 or so pesos as a gift for his time.

From the ranch the road climbs steeply, twisting along mountainsides with staggering views of canyons, orchards, small ranches and the sea for another 16km (10 miles) to San Javier.

❸ The small settlement of San Javier sits in a deep valley surrounded by towering cliffs. Its 100 or so residents live in whitewashed homes lining the dirt street that ends at the mission church. The stone structure, built from slabs cut from a nearby arroyo (dry stream), was moved from its original location in 1720 to free up the fertile land for orchards. The Jesuits planted grapes, olives, figs and oranges in the valley, which supported a community of more than 500 residents in the mid-1800s.

From the outside the church is rather plain, although the entrance has a subtle Moorish look, with several domes and turrets. Inside, several oil paintings hanging over the main and side altars depict Jesus, Mary, Joseph, the trinity and St. Javier. The church is an important pilgrimage site for people from all over central Baja, and on December 1, 2 and 3 the town is filled with thousands of pilgrims for the Feast of San Javier. Villagers, eager to chat with visitors, sell homemade candies and local produce from stands in front of their homes along the street leading to the church.

Oranges at San Javier (above)
Cacti of all shapes and sizes adorn the landscape (left)
Prehistoric petroglyphs (below)

To return to Loreto, retrace your drive down the mountain, then turn north (left) on Highway 1. Be sure to leave San Javier at least two hours before dusk, as it is not advisable to drive the mountain road in the dark.

TOURIST INFORMATION

Calle Madero at Salvatierra in the City Hall, Loreto
☎ (613) 135 04 11
Mon–Fri 9–3

WHEN TO GO

The best weather is during October and November, and April and May. Summers can be very hot and winter chilly and very windy.

WHERE TO EAT

La Palapa
San Javier
A small restaurant next to the church serves bean and *machaca* (dried shredded beef) *burritos*, homemade cheese and *tortillas*, cold sodas and other simple fare. The cooks are happy to create a basic meal for visitors. Take snacks and water for the drive.
Daily 10–7

Café Olé Calle
Madero 14, Loreto
☎ (613) 135 04 96
Serves *tacos*, *burritos* and sandwiches that can be packaged for a picnic lunch.
Daily 9–7

WHERE TO STAY

Casa de Ana
On the main road at the entrance to San Javier
www.hoteloasis.com
Simple rooms in adobe bungalows with hot showers and electricity for about two hours after dusk. Meals are available. Reserve at the Hotel Oasis, Calle de la Playa (tel (613) 135 01 12), in Loreto.
$35

15. DRIVE

THE SEA OF CORTÉS: LORETO TO MULEGÉ

This route goes from Loreto, site of the first mission in the Californias, to the oasis town of Mulegé. After passing through dry desert terrain with the Sierra de la Giganta looming to the west, the highway reaches the shores of the Sea of Cortés, where there are panoramic views of crystalline bays dotted with small islands.

THE DRIVE

Distance: 270km (167 miles)
Allow: 8 hours
Start/end point: Loreto

Note: Watch for cattle wandering on the roadside and be prepared to drive slowly behind buses and trucks.

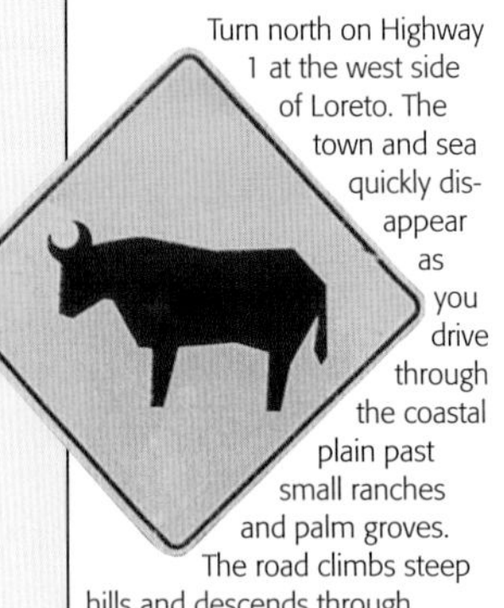

Turn north on Highway 1 at the west side of Loreto. The town and sea quickly disappear as you drive through the coastal plain past small ranches and palm groves. The road climbs steep hills and descends through *vados* (sudden dips in the road). After 23km (14 miles) you approach a military checkpoint where all vehicles must stop for inspection. The officers may ask to look inside the vehicle's trunk (boot) to check for weapons and drugs. After climbing steep hills and negotiating narrow curves for about 45km (28 miles), the Sea of Cortés appears to the east.

❶ The next 40km (25 miles) cover one of Baja's most spectacular drives along Bahía Concepción, a huge bay open to the north and sheltered by Punta Concepción. The entire bay is a national marine preserve that's home to frigates, blue-footed boobies, porpoises, whales and dozens of species of marine mammals, fish and birds. As you drive along the coastline you'll see volcanic islands, white-sand beaches and water in startling shades of blue and green.

Continue for a further 23m (14 miles), then turn east on a dirt road to Playa Buenaventura (there's a sign at the entrance).

❷ Guests swing in hammocks at Hotel San Buenaventura and lunch on ceviche and fried fish at the adjacent restaurant.

If you want to swim or go kayaking in the bay, stay on Highway 1 for another 20km (14 miles) until you reach a small sign on the right-hand side of the road to EcoMundo Baja Tropicales.

❸ This ecologically sensitive camp houses the largest kayaking outfitter on the bay.

The views of the bay continue as you drive north on Highway 1 toward Mulegé, passing Playa Concepción and Playa Santispac, both dotted with recreational vehicles and vacation homes. Continue for another 29km (18 miles) until you reach a large sign for the Hotel Serenidad on the right-hand side of the road. Turn right and follow the dirt road to the Hotel Serenidad on a cliff above the Sea of Cortés.

❹ The view of the sea disappears by the Serenidad and is replaced with lush palm groves and campgrounds.

Drive 10km (6 miles) along this busy stretch of Highway 1. A small bridge passes above the Río Santa Rosalia. Past the river is the turn-off east to the small town of Mulegé. At the intersection of the highway and the road into Mulegé called Calle Moctezuma (you won't see any street signs), turn right. Follow the road as it becomes a one-way street and bears right (southeast). Driving is difficult at this point, as the streets are narrow and unmarked. The main road becomes Calle Madero. There is parking next to Hotel Las Casitas, in Mulegé.

❺ It's best to explore Mulegé (**▷ 166****) on foot. The modest main plaza is a block south of Las Casitas, and there are several small souvenir shops, taco stands and restaurants along the side roads.**

Back in your car, turn southwest on Calle Zaragoza and drive under the highway bridge along the riverbed and up a steep hill to the Misión Santa Rosalia de Mulegé—about 3km (2 miles) from the bridge.

❻ The modest brick mission church of Santa Rosalia is usually locked, but the view from the churchyard over the river is worth a look. Established in 1705, the mission has been restored after a history of hurricane damage and abandonment.

From the church, turn southeast on Calle Moctezuma and then south on Highway 1 to return to Loreto.

TOURIST INFORMATION

Calle Madero at Salvatierra in the City Hall, Loreto
☎ (613) 135 04 11
🕑 Mon–Fri 9–3

WHERE TO EAT AND STAY

EcoMundo Baja Tropicales
Highway 1 Loreto-Mulegé Km 111 at Playa Concepción
☎ (615) 153 04 09/153 03 20
The camp has simple cabañas with cots and hammocks. Communal showers have cold water only. The restaurant serves breakfast and lunch. Kayaks are available for rent.
$12–$20 per person

Hotel Las Casitas
Calle Madero 50, Mulegé
☎ (615) 153 00 19
www.baja-web.com/mulege/casitas.htm

OUT AND ABOUT

Looking out over Santispac Bay (above) and desert landscape (below) in Bahía Concepción

Mulegé Mission (above) Houses along the Río Mulegé (below)

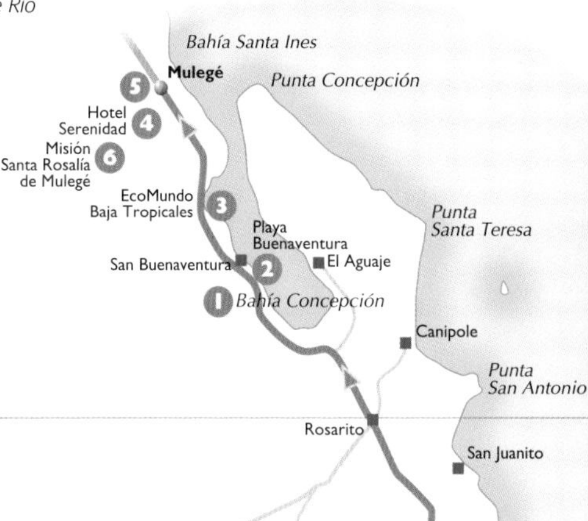

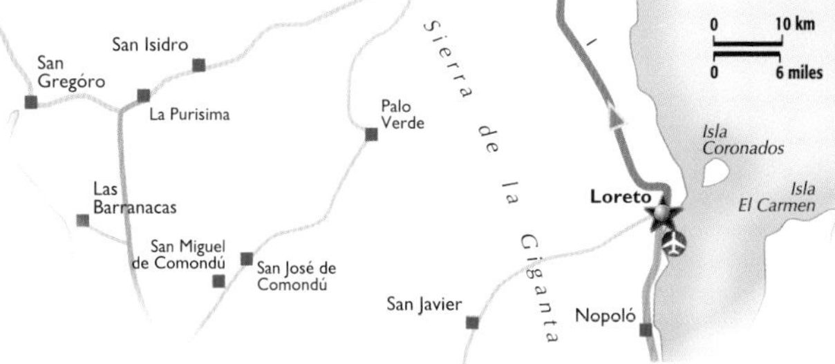

This former home, with eight air-conditioned rooms, is also Mulegé's informal visitor information office. The garden restaurant serves good Mexican food.
$35–$45 double

Hotel San Buenaventura
Highway 1 Loreto-Mulegé Km 91, Playa Buenaventura
(615) 155 56 16
www.hotelsanbuenaventura.com
Simple beachfront *cabañas* cost $25 per night. The restaurant is open for breakfast, lunch and dinner daily. Kayak rental is also available.
$69–$99

Hotel Serenidad
Mulegé, Highway 1
Tel (615) 153 05 30
www.hotelserenidad.com
This is a great place for lunch, with Mexican specials and clean rest rooms. Guests dining here are allowed to use the cool, refreshing swimming pool. Rooms and cottages are both available overnight.
$65–$120

The clear blue waters of Bahía Concepción are ideal for swimming and snorkeling

ORGANIZED TOURS

If you have a special passion for one of Mexico's many facets, be it the country's art and architecture, cuisine, sports or the great outdoors, there are many specialist operators offering in-depth tours. Many of the companies listed here will arange tours for visitors from outside the country where they are based. One very useful website is www.planeta.com

Asociación Mexicana de Turismo de Aventura y Ecoturismo (AMTAVE)
Mariposa 1012-A, Colonia General Anaya, Mexico City
Tel/fax 55 5688 3883
www.amtave.org
A national organization that groups professional operators and promotors of ecotourism and adventure travel in Mexico, actively involving local communities, and with an emphasis on environmental protection. Activities include everything from climbing and caving to rafting, scuba diving, hiking, biking and hot-air ballooning.

Baja Outdoor Activities
P.O. Box 792, Col. Centro, La Paz
Tel (612) 125 56 36
www.kayaktivities.com
Ben and Alejandra Gillam offer a wide selection of excellent tours, including whale watching, sea kayaking around Isla Espíritu Santo, snorkelling, fishing, hiking and trips to the Copper Canyon. Prices start at US$35.

Bicicletas Bravo
Garcia Vigil 409-C, Centro Oaxaca
Tel (951) 516 09 53
www.bikeoaxaca.com
Bicicletas Bravo offers guided bicycle trips in and around the mountains and valleys of the city of Oaxaca. The itineraries are rated from "easy" to "technically challenging" on new aluminum-frame bicycles with front suspension. It's a great way to see the surrounding countryside as well as the villages and craft towns around Oaxaca.

Canyon Travel
900 Ridge Creek, Bulverde, Texas, TX 78163-2872 USA
Tel (830) 885-2000; fax (830) 885-2010
www.canyontravel.com
These seven-day Copper Canyon itineraries go off the beaten track, yet stay in comfortable lodges. They also offer specialist birding tours as well as hiking or biking camping treks.

Dragoman
Camp Green, Debenham, Stowmarket, Suffolk, IP14 6LA, England
Tel +44 (0) 870 499 4475; fax +44 (0)1728 861127
www.dragoman.com
Overland adventure travel company, running adventure tours and activity holidays worldwide. Their trips allow you to experience all aspects of Mexico, including sites, historic monuments, natural beauty and wildlife.

Expediciones Mexico Verde
Mauricio Morales Contel, Murillo Vidal 133 Fraccionamiento Ensueño CP, Xalapa
Tel (228) 812 01 34
www.mexicoverde.com
Rafting specialists, based in the Jalcomulco area of Veracruz and now also in the state of San Luis Potosí, who also offer kayaking, trekking, riding trips and family programs.

Mayan Destinations
Avenida Coba 31, SM 22 Edificio Monaco, Local 1 PB, Cancún
Tel (998) 884 43 08; fax: (998) 887 96 08
www.mayandestinations.com
Tours to popular destinations such as Chichén Itzá, Tulúm, Xcaret and Isla Mujeres.

Promotion of Mexican Culture
Cuña de Allende No 11, interior 04, Col. Centro, San Miguel de Allende
Tel (415) 21630; fax (415) 20121
www.pmexc.com
A variety of tours focusing mainly on archaeology, architecture, art and history. Also walking tours of the town, workshops and language classes, and adventure and nature tours.

Restaurante El Naranjo
Valerio Trujano 203, Col. Centro, Oaxaca
Tel (951) 514 18 78
www.elnaranjo.com.mx
Twice-weekly cooking classes upon request for a maximum of 12 people including the preparation of a four-course meal with *agua fresca* and two salsas. Lunch is also included as is an informative guided visit to the Benito Juárez market and chocolate mill.

Tierra Dentro
Reforma 528-B, 68000 Oaxaca,
Tel (951) 514 92 84
www.TierraDentro.com
One of the leading organizations for adventure tourism, Tierra Dentro specializes in mountaineering and rock climbing; choose from one-day and weekend trips and six-day expeditions to the Mexican volcanoes. Contacts: Livingston Monteverde and Gloria Gracida.

Viajes Pakal
Cuahtémoc 6-A, Centro Histórico, San Cristóbal de las Casas
Tel (967) 678 28 18; 01-800-716 32 81 (freephone)
www.pakal.com.mx
A reliable agency running culturally friendly tours to the Sumidero Canyon, the Lagos de Montebello, Misol Ha, Agua Azul, as well as the towns, villages and archaeological sites of Chiapas.

WINGS Birding Tours Worldwide
1643 N. Alvernon, Suite 109, Tucson, Arizona, AZ85712
Tel (520) 320 9868; (888) 293-6443 (toll-free); fax (520) 320 9373
www.wingsbirds.com
Tours strongly oriented toward birds. The timing and itinerary of the tours is dictated almost entirely by ornithological considerations. They also arrange tours which are designed to combine serious birdwatching with other activities appropriate to the area.

Yucatán Trails
Calle 62 No. 482, Mérida
Tel (999) 928 25 82
Canadian-owned operator offering all-inclusive tours to all the popular destinations such as Uxmal, Celestún, Dzibilchaltún, Progreso and Izamal. Also hacienda tours, snorkeling and swimming in *cenotes* and others.

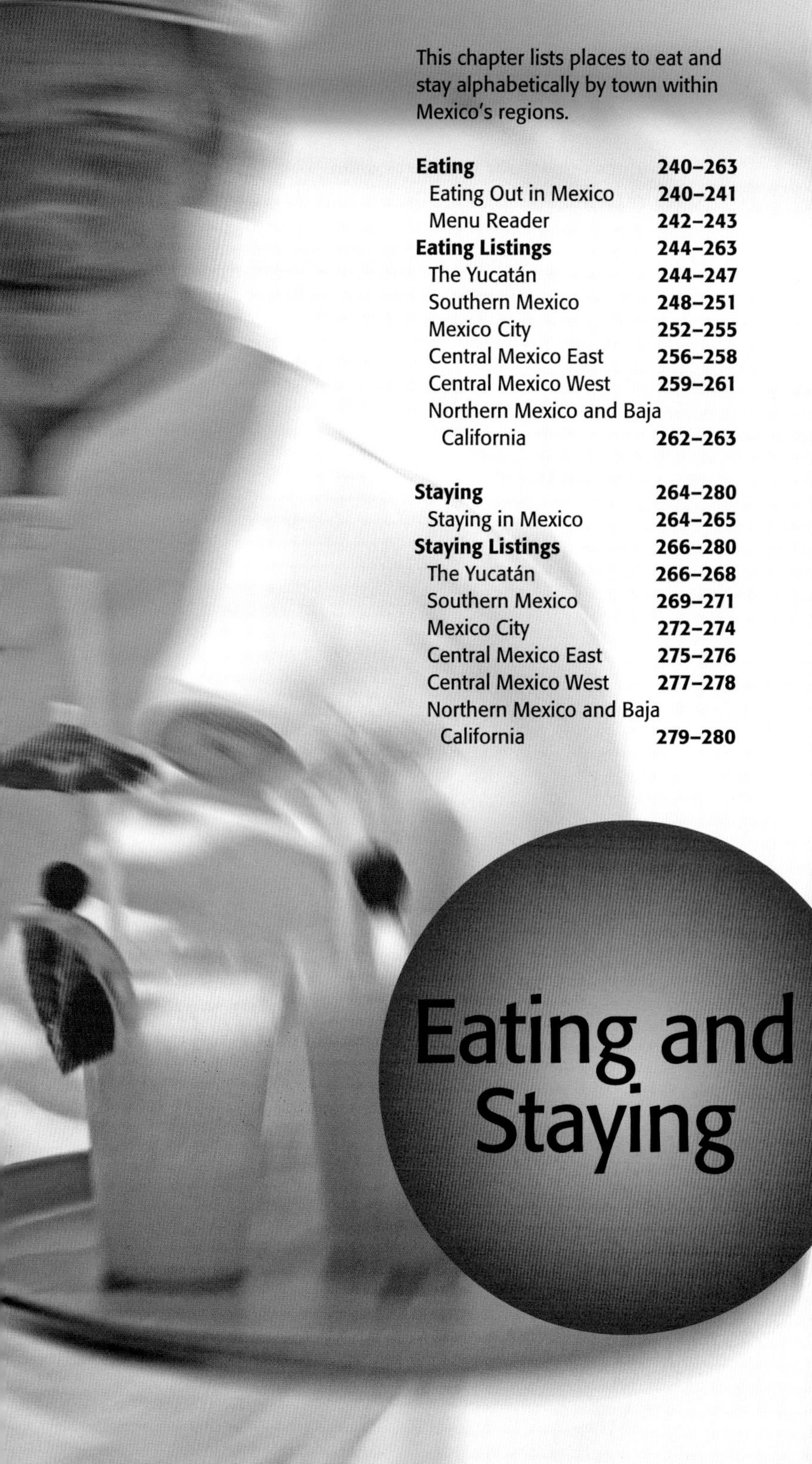

Eating and Staying

This chapter lists places to eat and stay alphabetically by town within Mexico's regions.

Eating **240–263**
- Eating Out in Mexico **240–241**
- Menu Reader **242–243**

Eating Listings **244–263**
- The Yucatán **244–247**
- Southern Mexico **248–251**
- Mexico City **252–255**
- Central Mexico East **256–258**
- Central Mexico West **259–261**
- Northern Mexico and Baja California **262–263**

Staying **264–280**
- Staying in Mexico **264–265**

Staying Listings **266–280**
- The Yucatán **266–268**
- Southern Mexico **269–271**
- Mexico City **272–274**
- Central Mexico East **275–276**
- Central Mexico West **277–278**
- Northern Mexico and Baja California **279–280**

EATING OUT IN MEXICO

Mexican cuisine today is a combination of indigenous and Spanish recipes, seasoned with French influence from the 19th century and topped with the 20th-century additions of Asian dishes and fast food from the US. The result is a very broad mix of styles and tastes to suit all budgets, from street-corner tacos to sophisticated dining—a far cry from the "Tex-Mex" served up elsewhere in the world.

Left to right: dining in Oaxaca; seafood dish; fresh fruit platter; Damiana Restaurant, San José del Cabo

TRADITIONAL MEXICAN FOOD

- *Tortillas* are the staple diet of all Mexicans, whether they are consumed at breakfast, eaten from a food stand by a roadside or enjoyed in a restaurant selling fine cuisine. The classic *tortilla* consists of unleavened corn dough which is pressed into a round, thin pancake then cooked on a hot griddle. They are best when handmade and served fresh, but as demand grows more and more are mass-produced.
- Mexicans eat *tortillas* in many forms as *antojitos,* or *botanas,* savory snacks that may be eaten by themselves or as a starter in restaurants and markets, or from street stands and pushcarts. Loosely translated as "appetizers," the most common of these include *tacos* (*tortillas* stuffed with any filling), *tostados* (*tortillas* topped with shredded meat, cheese, tomatoes and beans), *totopos* or *tostadaditas* (deep-fried and cut *tortillas*, more commonly known as *nachos,* dipped in a hot sauce), *quesadillas* (*tortillas* stuffed with cheese) and *enchiladas* (*tortillas* fried in cheese sauce and smothered in chili sauce).
- In addition to the corn *tortilla,* the chili pepper is another Mexican staple that is never far away from any kitchen. Mexico has more varieties of chili (over 200) than any other country, ranging from the relatively tame *jalapeño* to the red hot *habanero*, which will seriously blow the roof of your mouth off.
- Mexico has a wealth of tropical fruits, from the commonplace banana, mango, pineapple, guava and papaya to the bright pink, plastic-looking dragon fruits (*pitahaya roja*) that taste like sour kiwi fruits, and they all produce fantastic juices.
- The world can thank Mexico for chocolate, as the Mayan Indians first cultivated the cocoa plant in AD600. The Aztec emperor Moctezuma was said to have been the first person to add vanilla pods to chocolate in order to sweeten it. Boiling pots of the stuff are made and mixed with ground cinnamon, almonds and sugar.
- Adventurous palates may wish to taste some of the more unusual culinary offerings, such as *jumiles* (a type of beetle, eaten alive or fried, by themselves or in tacos) from Taxco, *chapulines* (small crickets fried with chili until they turn red and then served with lime) from Oaxaca, or *gusanos de maguey* (maguey worms, fried and seasoned with garlic and served with guacamole) from Tlaxcala. Other strange delicacies include *escamoles* (ant eggs) and for vegetarians there's *huitlacoche* (black corn fungus) which can be served in crêpes, omelettes and *quesadillas*. Note: Recent tests have shown that *chapulines* can have a high lead content and may not be suitable for pregnant women or children.

MEALTIMES AND MENUS

- Breakfast (*desayuno*) is eaten early and often consists of coffee and *pan dulce* (sweet rolls and pastries), or eggs in many and varied forms. Lunch (*almuerzo/comida*) is the main meal of the day, eaten around 2pm, while supper (*cena*) is a light meal, often *antojitos*, eaten around 8pm.
- A meal in the classiest restaurants of Mexico City can cost anything from $15–$40 and more, while more modest establishments will charge from around $7–$12 for an à la carte dinner. The most economical eating by far is the set lunch (*comida corrida*), which will generally cost around $3–$4 and is usually served between 1 and 5 pm. In more expensive restaurants, the set lunch will be called *menu del día* or *menu turístico* and cost from around $5.

EATING

• Always check on local seasonal variations when ordering seafood. For example, lobster is best between April and October.

• Some restaurants give foreigners the menu without the *comida corrida* (set meals), forcing them to order à la carte, which is often double the price. Try to avoid eating in restaurants that don't display a menu.

• McDonald's, Burger King, KFC, Pizza Hut and Domino's are everywhere, should your kids long for a hit of high cholesterol junk food.

• Vegetarians can eat well in Mexico and many national dishes are naturally meat-free. *Chiles rellenos*, *quesadillas* and *tacos* can all come with non-meat fillings. Eggs and cheese are widely available, as are salads, though be wary of restaurants washing vegetables in tap water. Vegetarian restaurants are becoming more widespread in the main resorts and large cities, while in more remote parts you may have to endure a rather bland and monotonous diet of *tortillas* and cheese.

Luaú Chinese restaurant, Mexico City; making tortillas; fruit stall in Benito Juárez market, Oaxaca

TIPPING AND PAYMENT

Tipping in restaurants should be around 10 to 15 percent of the bill. However, even if service is included waiters have been known to deduct a further tip from the change; they will hand it back if challenged.

Unless otherwise stated, the restaurants listed on the following pages accept credit cards.

SMOKING

Smoking is on the increase in Mexico. Strictly speaking, smoking and non-smoking areas in restaurants should be properly separated, but this is not always the case.

MEXICAN TIPPLES

The native alcoholic drinks are tequila, made mostly in Jalisco, and mezcal from Oaxaca, both of which are distilled from agave plants. *Pulque* is a sweet fermented cactus drink and definitely an acquired taste. Also available is the Spanish aniseed spirit, *anís*, which is made locally. Imported whiskies and brandies are expensive, while rum is cheap and good.

Puro de caña (called *chingre* in Chinanteca and *posh* in Chamula) is distilled from sugar cane; stronger than mezcal but with less taste, it is found in Oaxaca and Chiapas.

Tequila is usually drunk in one hit with a lick of salt before (to encourage the thirst) and a suck on a lemon wedge after (to quash the bitter aftertaste). The poorer-quality tequilas are normally used to make cocktails such as margaritas, while the better tequilas, generally graded as *anejo* (aged) or gold, are smooth and should be sipped like a good brandy or malt whisky. The best brands are generally Herradura, Sauza and Cuervo.

Mezcal usually has a *gusano de maguey* (worm) in the bottle, considered by Mexicans to be a particular delicacy. The worm is, in fact, a butterfly larva which crawls into the heart of the agave plant and often ends up in the finished product. Although the larva used is traditionally coral pink, it does tend to fade after time in the bottle.

WATER

Tap water should not be drunk, but there are always plenty of non-alcoholic soft drinks (*refrescos*) and bottled mineral water available. Fresh fruit juices (*jugos*) are many and wonderful. The country's markets are often the best places to sample these juices, or the refreshingly delicious watered-down versions called *aguas frescas,* or *licuados* (milkshakes).

BEER

Mexican beer is excellent, particularly the blond varieties, which include Dos Equis-XX, Montejo, Bohemia, Corona, Sol and Superior. Sometimes these beers are drunk with lime juice and a salt-rimmed glass. Negra Modelo, a dark variety, is one of the country's most distinctive beers.

WINE

Local wine is cheap and improving in quality, especially Domecq, Casa Madero and Santo Tomás. The white wines sold in *ostionerías* (oyster restaurants) are also usually good, especially Cetto Reisling Fumé. Some of the best wines produced in Mexico are those from Monte Xanic, near Ensenada, Baja California, though they are very expensive.

HOT DRINKS

Mexicans often round off a meal with chocolate, coffee (especially *café de olla*—with cinnamon) or *atole*, a sweet maize-based drink with milk.

MEXICAN MENU READER

Each region of Mexico has its own special dishes, based on the best ingredients available locally. Some of the most unusual ones come from central Mexico and the southern states. If you don't speak Spanish (*castellano*) it can be daunting to work out exactly what's on offer. Below is a menu reader to help you familiarize yourself with some of the dishes and foods you are likely to come across. This is not a complete list by any means, but it includes many regional specials.

Left to right: seafood buffet; jalapeño peppers; succulent leaves of the prickly pear cactus

Pescado–Fish
atún tuna
cazón dogfish
dorado dolphin (fish)
huachinango red snapper
jurel yellowtail
mero grouper
pez espada swordfish
robalo bass
tuburón shark
trucha trout

Frutas–Fruits
aguacate avocado
coco coconut
duraznoz peaches
fresa strawberry
granada passion fruit
guayaba guava
higo fig
manzana apple
naranja orange
papaya pawpaw
piña pineapple
plátano banana
sandía watermelon
tamarindo tamarind
zarzamora blackberry

Carne–Meat
albóndigas meatballs
chivo goat
chorizo/salchicha sausage
chuleta chop or cutlet
cordero lamb
costillas ribs
hamburguesa hamburger
hígado liver
jamón ham
lengua tongue
lomo tenderloin
pato duck
pavo turkey
perro caliente hot dog
pollo chicken
puerco pork
res beef
ternera veal
tocino bacon

Mariscos–Seafood
almeja clam
calamares squid
camarones shrimps
cangrejo crab
langosta lobster
ostra oyster
pulpo octopus

Legumbres–Vegetables
aceitunas olives
cebolla onion
chícharos peas
frijoles beans
hongos/champiñones mushrooms
lechuga lettuce
nopales young leaves of the prickly pear cactus
palmito palm heart
rábano radish
zanahoria carrot

Entremés–Side dishes
arroz rice
huevo egg
mantequilla butter
mermelada jam
pan bread
papas fritas french fries
queso cheese

Postres–Desserts/puddings
arroz con leche rice pudding
ate jelly made from quince
flan crème caramel
helado ice cream
membrillo jelly made from any fruit other than quince
torrejas bread soaked in honey and fried
turrón nougat

Bebidas–Drinks
agua mineral con gas/sin gas sparkling mineral water/still mineral water
café coffee
cerveza beer
leche milk
refrescos soft drinks
té tea
vino wine

Cooking methods
a la brasa flame-grilled
a la plancha grilled on a griddle
al horno baked/roasted
asado roast
borracho cooked with wine
frito fried
poché poached
relleno stuffed/filled

SOME REGIONAL SPECIALS

Aquascalientes/Durango
menudo tripe
Chiapas
tamales chiapanecos maize pancake in banana leaves
Chihuahua
machaca con huevo eggs with dried minced beef
Coahuila and **Monterrey**
frijoles charros beans with bacon and chili
Guanajuato
enchiladas mineras large *tortillas* filled with potato, chicken, lettuce and radishes
Oaxaca
mole negro as *mole* (see below) but with sauce based on chili and chocolate
San Luis Potosí
enchiladas potosinas non-spicy coated red *tortillas*
Tlaxcala
sopa tlaxcalteca spicy soup with mushrooms and *tortilla*
Veracruz
huachinango a la veracruziana red snapper in sauce of tomatoes, olives and onion
Yucatán
sopa de lima chicken broth with giblets, fried tortillas, sweet chili and lime

Edible grasshoppers (chapulines)*; fruit-shaped candy; fresh strawberries from Zamora, Michoacán*

OTHER DISHES

caldo de pollo chicken-based broth with vegetables and seasoned with coriander
caldo tlalpeño highly spiced chicken soup, sometimes with rice, and avocado
ceviche raw fish in lime juice with tomatoes, onions, spices and chilis
chalupas fried *tortillas,* shaped like a boat, with sauce and salad
chicharrón pork crackling
chilaquiles rojos as above with red tomato sauce
chilaquiles verdes small fried *tortillas* with green tomato sauce
chiles en nogada stuffed peppers with white almond sauce and red pomegranate seeds, echoing the green, white and red of the Mexican flag
chilorio loin of pork in chili sauce
enchiladas verdes fried *tortillas* filled with chicken with green tomato sauce, sprinkled with onion and cream
enchiladas rojas as above with red *mole*
enfrijoladas fried *tortillas* with a bean-based sauce, with cheese, cream and onion
ensalada de nopales cactus-leaf salad
fajitas anything rolled up in flour *tortilla,* but strictly should contain skirt steak
guacamole mashed avocado and green tomatoes, with onion, coriander and sometimes with chili
huevos ahogados hard-boiled eggs in a tomato-based sauce
huevos a la mexicana scrambled eggs with chili and tomatoes
huevos motuleños fried eggs in a sauce of tomatoes, peas, cheese and fried banana
huevos rancheros fried eggs and diced chili in a tomato sauce on top of a *tortilla*
mixiotes chicken or rabbit wrapped in leaves of the maguey
mole a chili-based sauce, usually used to accompany cooked chicken or turkey
mole poblano (▷256)
picadillo minced beef with tomatoes and other vegetables
pipián chicken or pork in a chili-based sauce with peanuts, almonds or pumpkin seeds
pozole a pot-au-feu with a base of maize and stock
quesadillas doubled-over *tortillas*, heated, slightly crisp, filled with one or more of beef, chicken, cheese, *rajas* (green peppers), spinach, *flor de calabaza* (pumpkin flower), *chorizo* (spicy sausage), *nopal* (cactus leaves) or *huitlacoche* (a fungus that grows on maize)
rope vieja beef pulled into fibrous strips with a tomato-based sauce and peas
salpicón cold cooked beef with salad
sopa Juliana soup made from lentils *(lentejas)* or broad beans *(habas)*
sopa de tortilla tomato-based soup with shredded tortillas
sopa azteca as above but with chili
tacos rolled up tortillas, usually filled with chicken or beef
tamales meat and chili sauce wrapped in corn dough and then in maize or banana leaves and steamed. Sweet *tamales* with pineapple, strawberries and nuts are also delicious, while chili and cheese *tamales* are suitable for vegetarians

THE YUCATÁN

The Yucatán Peninsula has some of the most distinctive Mexican dishes, especially in Mérida, with its French and Lebanese influences. A major characteristic of Yucatecan cuisine is the traditional Maya cuisine that still features on many restaurant menus. One of the main staples is turkey, and *chilmole* is a local dish of turkey served in a very dark, spicy sauce. Another popular meat dish is *cochinita pibil*, pieces of pork marinated in *achiote* (a pungent red paste made from the seed of the annatto tree) and cooked in a stone-lined pit *(pib)*. Fish and seafood also feature heavily and there are many fine seafood restaurants in the coastal towns and resorts serving *pescado tikin-xic*, grouper rubbed with *achiote* and baked in banana leaves, or perhaps a *sopa de mariscos* (seafood soup) using local squid. Other regional dishes include *sopa de lima*, chicken broth with fried *tortillas*, sweet chili and lime, and *chivitas* (little goats), which are actually river snails.

PRICES AND SYMBOLS

The restaurants are listed alphabetically within each town. The prices given for lunch (L) and dinner (D) are for three courses for one person, without drinks. The wine price is for the least expensive bottle.

For a key to the symbols, ▷ 2.

CAMPECHE

LA PARROQUIA

Calle 55 No. 8, Campeche
Tel (981) 816 25 30

There's a good atmosphere at this friendly, family-run restaurant which serves traditional and regional dishes at reasonable prices. It's also very popular with the locals, which is always a good recommendation.

Daily 24 hours
L $3–5, D $4–$7, Wine $3

LA PIGUA

Avenida Migual Alemán 179, Campeche
Tel (981) 811 35 65

Campeche is renowned for its fish and seafood, in particular *camarones* (shrimps) and *pan de cazón* (bread with dogfish), and La Pigua is one of the best places to sample it. This seafood restaurant has played host to many famous visitors, including the late Celia Cruz, Queen of Salsa. The emphasis is on freshness and quality rather than presentation.

Daily noon–5.30
L $12, Wine $14

CANCÚN

LA DOLCE VITA

Boulevard Kukulcán Km 14.5, Hotel Zone, Cancún
Tel (998) 885 01 50
www.cancunitalianrestaurant.com

Opposite the Marriott Hotel and with stunning views of the lagoon, the sophisticated Dolce Vita serves some of the finest Italian cooking in Cancún. Wicker chairs, crisp white tablecloths and a resident saxophonist set the scene. The house special is the *boquinete dolce* (red snapper in puff pastry), and the large selection of fresh pasta dishes includes a very rich green taglioni with lobster and shrimp. The knowledgeable staff are formally attentive. Reservations advisable.

Daily noon–11.30
L $16, D $24, Wine $18

LA HABICHUELA

Calle Margaritas 25, Hotel Zone, Cancún
Tel (998) 884 31 58
www.lahabichuela.com

La Habichuela is one of the oldest and most popular restaurants in Cancún. Maya sculptures, elegant candlelit tables and live jazz music complement the delicious Caribbean cuisine here. The house special is *cocobichuela*—lobster and shrimp in a piquant curry sauce served in a coconut shell ($32). To finish off, try the divine chocolate pyramid of Chichén Itzá. The wine list is excellent and the service gracious and friendly.

Daily noon–midnight
L $27, D $32, Wine $17

PERICOS

Avenida Yaxchilán 61, Cancún
Tel (998) 884 31 52
www.periscoscancun.com

This is an archetypal Cancún eating house—a tacky, *cantina*-style restaurant (local bar serving food) with jovial staff in full bandit costume. Still, it is hugely popular, serving generous portions of food, including jumbo shrimp platters and filet mignon alongside pitchers of frozen margaritas. The atmosphere is ebullient, courtesy of the live *mariachi* music.

Daily noon–midnight
L $16, D $23, Wine $18

CHETUMAL

CAFÉ LOS COCOS

Hotel Los Cocos, Avenida Héroes 134, Chetumal
Tel (983) 832 05 44
www.hotelloscocos.com.mx

Decent restaurants are rather thin on the ground in Chetumal, but Hotel Los Cocos' streetside café, close to the Museo de la Cultura Maya (▷ 70), serves quality regional and international dishes with excellent service and good presentation. There are great healthy breakfasts ($12), with generous portions, and the fish and seafood dishes are surprisingly well priced. On the downside, it is very exposed to the street noise and soaring humidity—and the television can be a little distracting.
Daily 7am–11pm
L $8, D $14, Wine $16

SERGIO'S PIZZA
Avenida Alvaro Obregon 182, Chetumal
Tel (983) 832 08 82
This is the nicest and best-value place in town, two blocks from Avenida Héroes: relaxing, dimly lit and informal, with wooden tables and large windows. The food is well presented, and although the pasta dishes can be bland the pizzas are delicious and the "Sergio salad," with pulses, vegetables, mushrooms and greens tucked inside a *tortilla* shell and topped with grilled chicken breast, is perfect. Good for late-night suppers, with tasty sweet breads and creamy broccoli soup. There'a a good selection of drinks and the service is excellent.
Daily 8am–10.30pm
L $10, D $16, Wine $15

COZUMEL

LA LOBSTERIA
Avenida 5 No. 501, on corner with Calle 7, San Miguel de Cozumel
Tel (987) 800 25 17
This charming, laid-back restaurant occupies an old Mayan house built in 1899 and serves some of the freshest, tastiest lobster, shrimp and fish in Cozumel. The lobster tails are sold by weight and cooked just the way you want them. Also great salads, steak and chicken. No credit cards.
Mon–Sat 4pm–11pm
D $13, Wine $16

LAS PALMERAS
Avenida Rafael Melgar, San Miguel de Cozumel
Tel (987) 872 05 32
Because it is just across from the ferry dock, this restaurant with streetside tables is always jam-packed. It is popular as much for its people-watching opportunities, lively atmosphere and friendly service as for its rather hit-and-miss à la carte international menu, which includes shrimp, lobster and ribs. Guaranteed hits are the satisfyingly generous Mexican and American breakfasts and the industrial-strength margaritas.
Daily 7.30am–11pm
L $16, D $24, Wine $17

LA PRIMA
Avenida Adolfo Rosala Salas 109, San Miguel de Cozumel
Tel (987) 872 42 42
This busy Italian restaurant uses fresh organic ingredients from the owner's garden in its pastas, northern Italian seafood and wood-oven pizzas. The portions are generous and filling, though many dishes are coated rather too liberally with cream or cheese. The presentation and service are good, and there is breezy outdoor seating. Try the fettuccini with prawns and steak prima, followed by a thick slice of key lime pie. There is a non-smoking area.
Daily 4pm–midnight
D $24, Wine $18

ISLA MUJERES

ALUXES COFFEE HOUSE
Avenida Matamoros 1, Isla Mujeres
Tel (998) 845 49 85
Young American Rebecca Lane runs this very popular closet-sized coffee shop with just six tables and a kitchen with barely enough room to swing a cat. There is plenty of reading material, Latin music and a procession of interesting characters to accompany great cappuccinos, bagels smothered with cream cheese, muffins, cookies, granola—be sure to try the truly decadent New York cheesecake. No credit cards.
Daily 6am–10pm
Breakfast/snack $3. No wine

EL BALCÓN DE ARRIBA
Avenida Hidalgo 12, Isla Mujeres
Tel (998) 877 05 13
On the main high street that leads to the Playa Norte, this charming little restaurant runs the gamut of tasty fresh fish and seafood dishes—try the excellent grilled red snapper with *achiote* sauce—and is especially noted for its tempura. The broad menu also includes a couple of vegetarian

options. The portions are large, the staff are friendly, and from its elevated position above Hidalgo it's a good people-watching spot. No credit cards.
Daily 8am–11pm
L $12, D $17, Wine $17

BISTRO FRANCÉS
Avenida Matamoros 29, Avenida Juárez and Avenida Hidalgo, Isla Mujeres
By 8.30am this French bistro—two blocks from the ferry terminal, in the middle of town—is packed cheek by jowl for the best-value and most varied breakfast combinations ($8) you'll find on the island, including crêpes, French toast and *huevos rancheros*. By night a more intimate Gallic ambience holds sway with candlelit dining and French-inspired cuisine, including French onion soup and fresh fish fillet with lime and capers. No credit cards.
Daily 6–noon, 6–midnight (closed one day per week, usually Sat)
D $14, Wine $15

LONCHERÍA LA LOMITA
Avenida Juárez, Isla Mujeres
Known as the house on the hill, this quirky *lonchería* (snack eatery), a five-minute walk from the plaza, serves

bargain home-style cooking in a kitsch canteen. Inflatable sharks float over the TV, and there are white plastic tables and chairs and sticky red plastic tablecloths. Grab one of tables clustered outside on the street for the best free dinnertime entertainment. The house special is *chiles rellenos*—peppers stuffed with cheese, rolled in breadcrumbs, fried, topped with cream and served with rice and beans—delicious. There are also excellent-value garlic prawns, and chicken with *mole*. No credit cards.
Mon–Sat 10am–10.30pm
L $5, D $7, Wine $12 (or bring your own bottle)

MÉRIDA

AMARO

Calle 59 No. 507, between Calle 60 and Calle 62, Mérida
Tel (999) 928 24 51
www.restauranteamaro.com

Amaro is one of the most popular restaurants in Mérida. While the food is rather overpriced, the setting is romantic, with candlelit tables under the stars in the lovely open courtyard and live music from 9pm. The refreshing vegetarian cuisine has plenty of regional twists, including eggplant (aubergine) baked in a white sauce and topped with sautéed vegetables. There are pasta dishes, salads and pizzas, including an avocado thin-crust pizza that has gained quasi-legendary status. Open till late.
Daily 11am–2am
L $10, D $14, Wine $16

DULCERIA Y SORBETERÍA COLÓN

Calle 61 and 62, Mérida
Tel (999) 928 14 97

An essential ritual in Mérida is to take a 20-minute stroll from the *zócalo* along Paseo Montejo and stop and cool off with an ice cream from this legendary parlor, established in 1907. The light and refreshing sorbets and ice creams are made from pure fruit, mixed with water or milk, and there are good explanations of ingredients in English. The breezy, open-air tables overlook the Plaza Grande. No credit cards.
Daily 8am–11pm
$1.70

HACIENDA XCANATUN

Carretera Mérida-Progreso Km 12, Mérida
Tel (999) 941 02 13
www.xcanatun.com

It's worth the taxi fare to get to Hacienda Xcanatun (out of town, on the road to Progreso, ▷ 267) to experience the finest Yucatán cuisine in Mérida. The sumptuous 18th-century hacienda, surrounded by beautiful gardens, is stunning and relaxing. Only the freshest ingredients are used to create delicious regional dishes with Caribbean and French influences, gracefully presented by the charming staff. Try the cream of *poblano chile* with Roquefort, grilled salmon served over creamed leeks or quails marinated in *achiote*.
Daily 1pm–midnight
L $21, D $29, Wine $21

PLAYA DEL CARMEN

CASA TUCAN

Calle 4 between avenidas 10 and 15, Playa del Carmen
Tel (984) 873 02 83
www.casatucan.de

Away from Avenida 5 prices drop considerably and this expertly managed, German-run hotel/restaurant/bar serves wonderful dishes—artfully presented, with a vegetarian slant. Shells encrusted into the tiled floor, snug alcoves, a tree protruding through the roof, and eggyolk-yellow handpainted walls create a tempting breakfast spot. A variety of evening specials include fettuccine with salmon, spinach and goat's cheese salad and fish baked in garlic.
Daily 8am–11pm
L $8, D $14, Wine $10

KAREN'S PIZZA

Avenida 5, between Calle 2 and Calle 4, Playa del Carmen

This large, open-plan restaurant towards the southern end of Playa's main pedestrian strip has a broad menu of fish, meat, pasta—and very good thin-based pizzas. The main draw is the jovial atmosphere, with a marimba band to keep the party spirit up, along with the free margarita tickets (pick one up from the waiter outside, before you come in). While the decor is bland, the food is generally abundant and reliable and the service gracious. It's very popular with Mexican families, always a good recommendation.
Daily 8am–11pm
L $11, D $15, Wine $16

MANDARINA'S CAFÉ

Avenida 5 and Calle 14, Playa del Carmen
Tel (984) 803 12 49

The original Mandarina's opened in Buenos Aires in the late 1990s. Here, the Argentinian owners have added a Caribbean twist with rock pools, bamboo furnishings, fountains, creamy paintwork and plants draped with tiny lights. The menu is all things to all men—pasta served with 20 different sauces, pizza, good salads, crêpes and great lobster-stuffed pies.
Daily 8am–11pm
L $15, D $20, Wine $19

MEDIA LUNA
Avenida 5, between Calle 12 and Calle 14, Playa del Carmen
Tel (984) 873 05 26
Tables here overlook Avenida 5, and background music adds to the hip lounge-bar vibe. The Mediterranean cuisine includes baked squash, Roquefort and caramelized onion salads, chicken with goat's cheese and sun-dried tomatoes, and seafood pasta. The cocktails are great, and the breakfast specials are also worth checking out. No credit cards.
Daily 8am–11.30pm
L $11, D $19, Wine $19

TODO NATURAL
Avenida 5, Playa del Carmen
Tel (984) 873 22 42
Large portions of salads, pasta and rice dishes (as well as the usual Mexican fare), using tasty wholesome ingredients, are served at this health-food restaurant. Candlelight and the leisurely pace of the attentive waiters make for a therapeutic dining experience. Most items on the menu are vegetarian, but there are also inventive fish and chicken dishes. Todo Natural is worth a visit for the goldfish-bowl-sized *jugo* (fruit juice) alone. There is live music at the weekend.
Daily 7am–11pm
L $11, D $17, Wine $18

XLAPAK
Avenida 5, Playa del Carmen
Unassuming from the outside, this small café-juice-bar-restaurant-gallery-internet-café-language-school along the northern stretch of Avenida 5 is a great late-afternoon hang-out. The smoothies are the main draw at just $2, and are a meal in themselves. The Mexican fare, served on earthenware plates, includes stuffed chicken breast coated with tamarind sauce, a tasty rendition of *mole Oaxaqueña* with chicken, and fish stuffed with shrimps. Food is expensive in Playa, and Xlapak's daily *comida corridas* (set lunches) are arguably the best in town. No credit cards.
Daily 8am–11.30pm
L $7, D $18, Wine $16

TULÚM

CABAÑAS COPAL
Carretera Tulum Ruinas Km 5, Tulúm
Tel (984) 806 44 06
www.cabanascopal.com
Candles and classical music set the scene at this beachside *palapa,* an eco-tourism restaurant serving tasty and inventive dishes with a health-conscious, vegetarian slant. Light lunches include *nopal* (cactus leaf) and *chaya* (a large-leafed vegetable) salads, and *tostadas de nopal*. For dinner, there is spaghetti or *fajitas* with shrimp, and one of the house specials, traditional Maya *tikin xik*—broiled fish cooked with spices and sour orange juice, seasoned with herbs and tomato and baked in banana leaves. There's also a good selection of imported wines.
Daily 7.30am–11pm
L $8, D $15, Wine $12

VALLADOLID

HOTEL EL MESÓN DEL MARQUÉS
Calle 30 No. 203, Valladolid
Tel (985) 856 20 73
www.mesondelmarques.com
El Mesón, on the north side of Plaza Principal is one of the best restaurants in town, with romantic, candlelit tables and colonial furnishings. The serene patio with an ornate water fountain and gently strumming folk music makes this one of the most idyllic places to relax after a strenuous day's sightseeing. The broad menu encompasses international and regional fare, including an excellent version of chicken *pibil*. There is even a low-calorie menu featuring a marinaded chicken salad, grilled fish and low-fat ice cream. Not to be missed. No credit cards.
Daily 8am–10.30pm
L $11, D $15, Wine $16

LOS PORTALES
Calle 42 No. 202, Valladolid
Tel (985) 856 32 43
Valladolid may not be renowned for its diversity and quality of restaurants, but with prized seating overlooking the main square, unpretentious, family-run Los Portales, rather than being a tourist trap, serves great-value regional cooking. Just be prepared for the plastic tablecloths, mismatched cutlery, TV blasting in the corner, and traffic horns outside competing with pans crashing in the kitchen. The *pollo motuleño* (chicken with fried banana, tomato, peas, and cheese) is well worth trying.
Daily 8am–11pm
L $8, D $10, Wine $14

RESTAURANTE Y COCTELERÍA LA SIRENITA
Calle 34 No. 188, Fernando Novelo (Rumba Unidad Deportivo), Valladolid
Tel (985) 856 16 55

Despite being slightly off the tourist trail, seven long blocks from the main square, this seafood restaurant is one of the most popular in Valladolid. Dine outside under canopies by the swimming pool or inside with continual *telenovelas* (soap operas) blaring out from the TV. The dishes, which include fish fillet filled with prawns, lobster and king prawns, are excellent value, with the emphasis on freshness and quality rather than presentation and style. No credit cards.
Daily 9–7
L $11, Wine, available by glass only, $2

SOUTHERN MEXICO

No one state can compete with Oaxaca when it comes to the sheer diversity of cuisines on offer. Oaxacan staples such as *tortillas* (known locally as *blandas*) and *frijoles negras* (black beans) are served with the region's many *moles*, which accompany fish, meat and chicken dishes. *Mole negro* is a Oaxacan version of *mole poblano*. One of the main ingredients used in regional cooking is the pasilla oaxaqueña chile, which gives Oaxacan dishes their distinctive hot, smoky taste and deep red hue. Vegetarians need not feel left out. *Flor de Calabaza* are squashed flowers that are used in soups, garnishes and *empanadas* (pasties).

In Chiapas indigenous influences remain strong. *Tamales chiapanecos* are maize pancakes cooked in banana leaves, often spiced with *hoja santa,* an anise-scented herb that has characterized southern Mexican cooking for centuries. Beef is a staple, accompanied by a variety of *moles*. One of the best known is *mole verde,* made from pumpkin seeds (*pipián*), an important ingredient of Chiapan cooking. Fish and seafood are plentiful on the coast, especially bass, grouper, sardines, crab, shrimp and clams. Chiapas also offers some of the country's tastiest desserts, such as the divine *dulce de camote y naranja* (yam and orange sweet) and San Cristobal de las Casas is famed for its sweets and chocolates.

ACAPULCO

PIPO'S

Almirante Breton 3, Acapulco
Tel (744) 484 01 65

One of Acapulco's oldest and best-loved restaurants has been luring the locals for years with its fresh fish, friendly service and reasonable prices. The airy dining room is decorated with the obligatory fishing paraphernalia and the English menu features a good selection of seafood, including clams, crayfish, lobster, shrimp,

crab and octopus. Try the *huachinango Veracruzano* (red snapper baked with tomatoes, peppers, onion and olives). There's another branch at Costera Miguel Alemanand Canadá (tel 748 401 65).

Daily noon–8
L$8, D$18, Wine $9

PRICES AND SYMBOLS

The restaurants are listed alphabetically within each town. The prices given for lunch (L) and dinner (D) are for three courses for one person, without drinks. The wine price is for the least expensive bottle.

For a key to the symbols, ▷ 2.

HUATULCO

LAS CÚPULAS

Quinta Real Hotel, Paseo Benito Juárez 2, Zona Hotelera,Bahía Tangolunda Huatulco
Tel (958) 581 04 28
www.quintareal.com

Stunning panoramic views of Tangolunda Bay make this elegant hotel restaurant one of the best-placed in Huatulco. The furnishings are sumptuous, the service impeccable and the cuisine mouthwatering, with an eclectic menu of regional and international dishes presented with panache: definitely worth splashing out on. For a civilized start to the evening, have a cocktail at the bar next door and soak up the dazzling views. Las Cúpulas is also a popular breakfast venue.

Daily 9am–10pm
L $13, D $17, Wine $18

OAXACA

EL BICHO POBRE II

Calzada de la República 600, Colonia Jalatlaca, Oaxaca
Tel (951) 513 46 36

Both local *Oaxaqueños* and visitors flock to this hugely popular restaurant with its large, airy, open plan—if rather Spartan—dining room. The specialty is the *botano surtido,* a massive platter of regional delicacies including *chalupas, tamales* and *quesadillas*. The *mole negro con pollo* and *sopa azteca* are also highly rated. If you need any guidance the friendly staff and chefs will describe each dish.

Daily 8am–9pm
L $8, D $11, Wine $14

LA BIZNAGA

Calle García Vígia 512, Oaxaca
Tel (951) 516 18 00

Opened at the end of 2003, close to the Iglesia de Santo Domingo, La Biznaga is run by chef and owner Fernando Lopez, whose philosophy is "slow food." The cuisine, fusing traditional Oaxacan ingredients and recipes with intriguing international twists, is served on the patio. Salmon with pesto and cilantro (coriander), garlic prawns with tamarind sauce, beef with goat's cheese, and a sublime chocolate torte with fruit cassis are just some of the gastronomic delights on the changing menu. No credit cards.

Mon–Wed 9am–9.30pm, Thu–Sat 9.30–9, Sun 10am–10.30pm
L $13, D $17, Wine $18

LA BREW COFFEE AND WAFFLEHOUSE

Calle García Vigil 304, Oaxaca
Tel (951) 514 96 73

American Susan McGlynn claims to serve the finest coffee in Oaxaca; try it and get a refund if you disagree! With a comfy sofa, laid-back music, vibrant *artesanía* and warm service, this is a great breakfast or coffee-stop spot. The house special is a fruit-filled waffle

with maple syrup. Other American-style breakfasts include bacon and egg bagels, potato and onion *frittatas,* and fruit topped with yogurt and granola.
Mon–Sat 8–8, Sun 8–2
Breakfast $5, L$7. No wine

CAFÉ ALEX
Avenida Díaz Ordáz 218 and Avenida Trujano, Oaxaca
Tel (951) 514 07 15
Three blocks west of the *zócalo* in the buzzing commercial area, Café Alex serves good breakfasts ranging from a traditional Oaxacan feast of *chilaquiles* with eggs, sour cream and *quesillo,* refried beans and *tortilla* to wholesome fresh-fruit platters topped with granola and yogurt and drenched in honey. The quirkily decorated dining rooms, with rust-red walls combined with 1970s wood paneling, are usually jam-packed with locals and visitors keeping the service brisk and the atmosphere lively. No credit cards.
Mon–Sat 7am–9pm, Sun 7am–noon
$4 (breakfast)

LA CASA DE ALCALÁ
Macedonia Alcalá 303, Oaxaca
Tel (951) 516 81 87
You enter this colonial home on the main pedestrian mall through a wrought-iron arched gateway. Adobe walls decorated with black-and-white photographs of early 19th-century Oaxaca encircle the peaceful patio, with its ornate fountain and cobbled floor. The staff are extremely friendly and efficient, serving traditional Oaxacan dishes and international fare. Try the *pechuga campestre* (chicken filled with pumpkin) and *mole Oaxaqueña*. Breakfast set menus are also very good value. High chairs are available for children.
Daily 8am–11pm
L $9, D $11, Wine $14

CASA OAXACA
Calle García Vigil 407, Oaxaca
Tel (951) 514 41 73
www.casa-oaxaca.com
Chef and manager Alejandro has developed a cult following among Oaxacan artists and it's not hard to understand why. The stylish and serene patio with live music in the evenings is the perfect backdrop to Alejandro's philosophy that food is art. The choice changes weekly but dishes always contain the freshest organic ingredients. Perfectly executed combinations such as sea bass with lime and squash blossoms served with tomato marmalade, or jumbo shrimp with ginger sauce served over *jícama* (raw root vegetable) complement Oaxaqueña specialties such as *chiles en nogada* or black *mole*. The service is impeccable, the wine list monumental and, by international standards, excellent value.
Breakfast 9am–11.30am, dinner 6.30–8.30
D $30, lunch not available. Five-course tasting menu $29, Wine $18

COMO AGUA PARA CHOCOLATE
Calle Hidalgo 612, Oaxaca
Tel (951) 516 29 17
Laura Esquivel's eponymous novel inspired the fresh and expertly run Like Water for Chocolate restaurant just off the *zócalo*. Chicken with *tamarindo* (tamarind) sauce, duck with ginger and orange sauce, and a variety of vegetarian options, including stuffed pumpkin squash and pasta with pesto, line up alongside stylishly presented and well executed Oaxacan specialties. There is a relaxing candlelit bar, but while main course prices are very reasonable, drinks are overpriced.
Daily 9am–11pm
L $11, D $14, Wine $24

LA CRÊPE
Macedonio Alcalá 307, Oaxaca
Tel (951) 516 22 00
With views across Oaxaca from its first-floor balcony, one block from the Iglesia de Santo Domingo, La Crêpe is fresh and modern with an inventive menu of snacks and light meals—perfect for lunch. Owner Vicente began his career with a little pancake cart in Mexico City and has now established a loyal following among locals, expats and visitors. Dishes are always well presented, and include Mediterranean-inspired salads with lashings of olives, pine nuts and heavenly goat cheese, wholesome seeded baguettes, and, of course, sweet and savory crêpes. No credit cards.
Mon–Sat 8am–11pm, Sun 8am–9pm
L $8, D $11, Wine $10

MARÍA BONITA
Macedonio Alcalá 706B, Oaxaca
Tel (951) 516 72 33
Just north of the Iglesia de Santo Domingo, this snug, family-run restaurant with cobbled floors, yellow walls and rustic tables has an extensive menu of delicious Oaxacan cooking served in clay pots or on terracotta earthenware plates. The enthusiastic staff will lovingly list the ingredients and describe the preparation of each recipe. This is a great place to try one of the *moles, quesadilla*-style *tlayudas* with *quesilla* and pumpkin flowers, or chilies stuffed with *chapulines*, and the set menus are great value.
Tue–Sat 9–9, Sun 9–5
L $9, D $13, Wine $14

EL NARANJO
Avenida Trujano 203, Oaxaca
Tel (951) 514 18 78
www.elnaranjo.com.mx
Inspired regional dishes using the finest organic ingredients are served with aplomb in the fragrant courtyard of this 17th-century house, one block from the *zócalo,* south of Avenida Independencia. The seven signature *mole* dishes on the menu provide a great initiation into one of Oaxaca's most memorable tastes and textures. The rolled *tortillas* with *picadillo Oaxaqueño* topped with *mole*, and the *sopa de nuez y chipotle* (pecan and chili soup) are first class.
Mon–Sat noon–11
L $12, D $14, Wine $15

PALENQUE

DON MUCHO
El Panchan Camping
Carretera Zona Arqueológica Km 4.5, Apartado Postal 55, Palenque
Tel (916) 341 48 46
Part of the Palenque experience has to involve stopping for lunch or dinner, or chilling out at least, at the heady jungle retreat of El Panchan. The total antithesis of the func-

tional frenzy of Palenque, the atmosphere is laid back, the vibe offbeat and the music chilled. The Italian-Mexican menu varies from pasta with pesto to *fajitas,* club sandwiches and wood-oven pizzas drizzled with olive oil (after 6pm only). The breakfast deals are the best in town, with a chocolate and banana shake making a suitable initiation. In the evening there are plenty of amateur performances to accompany the gastronomic delights, from fire dancers to circus performersr. No credit cards.

Daily 7am–11pm

L $7, D $11, Wine $12

Take a *colectivo* from the main high street in Palenque, marked "ruinas," and ask the driver to drop you of at El Panchan (2km/1 mile before the ruins). To return after 6.30pm, catch a ride or share a taxi

PIZZERIA PALENQUE

Avenida Juárez 168, Palenque

Tel (916) 345 03 32

It is difficult to miss this small streetside pizzeria in the heart of Palenque town. The proactive waiters usually take it in turns to announce "pizza" to every passerby. Still, for all its lack of subtlety, stark lighting and a fair coating of traffic fumes, the thin-crust pizzas laden with an inventive medley of toppings, served swiftly and with a smile, are the best you'll find in Palenque, with good prices to match. No credit cards.

Daily 1pm–11pm

L $8, D $12, Wine $17

RESTAURANTE LAS TINAJAS

Avenida 20 de Noviembre, esq Absalo Carlos Caraveo Gómez, Palenque

Tel (916) 100 11 47

Backpackers flocked to the original Las Tinajes, famed for its massive portions, in the heart of Palenque. The smaller, original restaurant has now spread its wings to larger premises a couple of doors down, with outdoor seating and a breezy open-plan design. A broad menu includes the house special, *pollo pibil,* huge steaks, *enchiladas, quesadillas,* salads, pasta and club sandwiches. Left-over take-out boxes are the norm. With every dish cooked to order, grumbling tour groups can often wait up to an hour. The breakfast deals are excellent value, although the five-egg omelettes are rather overwhelming.

Daily 8am–11pm (or until the last customer leaves)

L $11, D $14

PUERTO ESCONDIDO

CABO BLANCO

Calle del Moro, Zicatela, Puerto Escondido

Tel (954) 582 03 37

Diners come to this Puerto institution for its excellent grilled fish and seafood, served with inspired sauces. Tasty Asian dishes, including piquant Thai curries, make a refreshing change and inventive vegetarian food usually appears on the menu. After dinner the restaurant turns into a lively beach bar with a true Zicatela vibe, and in the high season there is music on Thursday and Saturdays.

Daily 8am–11pm

L $11, D $14, Wine $17

EL CAFECITO

Calle del Moro, Zicatela Beach, Puerto Escondido

Tel (954) 582 05 16

Under the same ownership as the hugely popular Carmen's patisserie on a path to the beach from the main road, this coffee shop and bistro serves superlative breakfasts—the chocolate bread is particularly good, accompanied by a deliciously robust coffee. The more cosmopolitan restaurant has blissful sea-view dining, and a tropical tone prevails with wicker chairs and relaxed music. Fresh fish draws a loyal clientele who enthuse over the seared tuna steaks and excellent-value shrimp platters. No credit cards.

Wed–Mon 6.30am–10pm

L $7, D $10, Wine $16

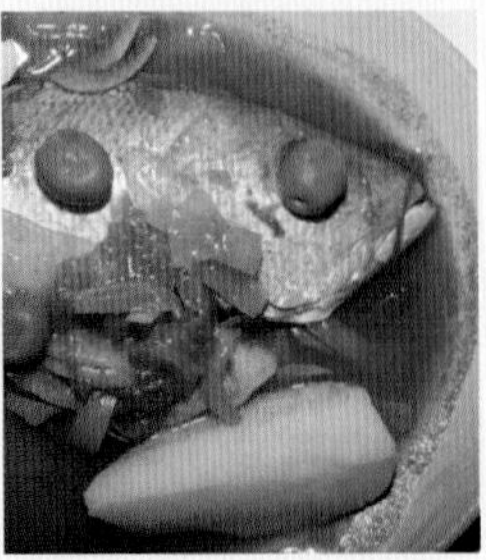

SAN CRISTÓBAL DE LAS CASAS

CASA DEL PAN

Calle Dr. Navarro 10, San Cristóbal de las Casas

www.casadelpan.com

Tel (967) 678 58 95

This fantastic bakery, with a sunny, calm café-restaurant, is one of the best places to start the day in San Cristóbal. Wonderful wholemeal breads and huge fruit platters heaped with granola and honey, hotcakes, omelettes and *huevos rancheros* are all served abundantly and with ceremonial panache by the welcoming staff. There is often live music in the evenings and other cultural activities. The set lunches are good value, and there are sandwiches and refreshing salads for vegetarians. No credit cards.

Daily 8am–11pm

Breakfast $5, L $7, D $10, Wine $14

EL FOGÓN DE JOVEL

Avenida 16 de Septiembre, San Cristóbal de las Casas

Tel (967) 678 11 53

www.atztours.com/fogon

El Fogón is well established on the tour group itinerary for its rather manufactured brand of typical Chiapaneca food. The colonial house, one block from the cathedral, decorated with a bizarre combination of regional handicrafts and international flags, is warmed by open fires and enlivened with marimba. Overpriced main dishes vary in quality, with the house special being a rather greasy pork *pibil*. The appetizers, however, are simple and satisfying with delicious tortillas, guacamole, *salsa verde,* and double-cream cheese. Round off the meal with the local firewater—*posh*.

Daily noon–11pm

L $10, D $15, Wine $18

MADRE TIERRA
Avenida Insurgentes 19, San Cristóbal de las Casas
Tel (967) 678 42 97
This Anglo-Mexican restaurant and bakery, opposite the Iglesia de San Francisco, is worth a visit for its wholemeal breads and chocolate cheesecake alone. By day you can eat in the arcaded courtyard, while inside, candles, intimate alcoves, bookcases and an arty vibe make a snug setting for the cool nights. Lighter snacks, including pizzas, spinach *empanadas* and quiche, are the better choices. as the main dishes, which include curry and spinach cannelloni, can be rather bland and often not very hot. The bakery also sells bagels, cinnamon rolls and chocolate croissants. No credit cards.
Daily 8am–midnight
L $6, D $9, Wine $14

NATURALISSIMO
Calle 20 de Noviembre 4, San Cristóbal de las Casas
Tel (967) 678 99 97
Just one block from the cathedral, deliciously wholesome food is served in a lovely courtyard. Great breakfasts include a help-yourself fruit bar with creamy yogurt, crunchy granola and honey, and other nutty tropical tastes. The main reason to visit however is for the *comida corrida* (set lunch) served from noon–6 daily; three courses including soup, salad bar, *jugo* and a *plato fuerte* (main dish). There is also a bakery where you can buy cakes as well as yogurt. No credit cards.
Daily 7am–11pm
Breakfast $5, L $5, D $9, Wine $12

PALOMA
Avenida Miguel Hidalgo 3, San Cristóbal de las Casas
Tel (967) 678 15 47
Paloma, one of San Cristóbal's more sophisticated restaurants, was reinvented at the end of 2003 and is now geared to a slightly older crowd. An eclectic menu includes delicious salmon with Dijon sauce, chicken in peanut sauce and, for vegetarians, *quesadillas* and ravioli with *acelgas* (a root vegetable) and cheese. There is also a laid-back bar with comfy wicker chairs, a civilized spot to round off an evening listening to jazz (every night from 9.30), maybe with a cappuccino and a slice of chocolate cake.
Daily 9am–11pm
L $8, D $13, Wine $16

PARIS-MEXICO
Calle Francisco 1 Madero 20, San Cristóbal de las Casas
Tel (967) 674 52 88

Parisienne panache meets Mexican piquancy at Paris-Mexico. While the interior is reminiscent of a 1950s brasserie, with arty wooden tables and walls decorated with black-and-white shots, the ambience is pure Mexican. Feisty margaritas, *sopa azteca* and fish à la Villacruzana team up with more Gallic offerings including rough red wine, French onion soup, coq au vin and crêpes with chocolate. Decent pasta and pizza dishes ordered à la carte can be rather pricey. Great breakfast deals with crêpes, eggs, juices and coffee.
Daily 7am–midnight
L $8, D $11, Wine $16

EL PUENTE
Calle Real de Guadalupe 55, San Cristóbal de las Casas
This lively cultural center is three blocks from the *zócalo*. The leafy bar-restaurant with laid-back music, Zapatista posters on the walls and internet access is one of the best spots in San Cristóbal to relax, read and meet other visitors. The broad menu includes leafy spinach salads, pasta dishes, *enchiladas,* soups, sandwiches and juices. There is also a cinema showing Mexican and international films every night; the schedule is posted on the door. No credit cards.
Daily 8am–midnight
L $6, D $9, Wine $14

LA SELVA CAFÉ
Avenida Crescencio Rosas and Cuauhtémoc, San Cristóbal de las Casas
Tel (967) 678 72 43
This sleekly run, continental-style coffee shop is just two blocks south of the *zócalo*. Owned by a coffee growers' collective, there are more than 30 types of delicious organic coffees. The light and airy art gallery gets lively in the evenings with a youthful, bohemian crowd. There are excellent liqueur cappuccinos, thick hot chocolate and sinful cakes, while healthier options include refreshing Mediterranean salads and wholemeal baguettes. No credit cards.
Daily 9am–11pm
Breakfast $5, L $9, D $12

TUXTLA GUTIÉRREZ

LAS PICHANCHAS
Avenida Central Oriente 857, Tuxtla Guttiérez
Tel (961) 612 53 51
www.laspichanchas.com.mx
A lovely *casona* with a pretty courtyard houses the ebullient Pichanchas, established in 1976 and one of the best restaurants in Tuxtla, despite being on the tourist trail. Accompanying the highly rated regional cooking are traditional dance performances and marimba music at 2–5 and 8–11. The restaurant is famous for its *tamales*, and other house specials include *juacané* chicken breast (stuffed with beans and smothered in Hierba Santa sauce).
Daily noon–midnight
L $11, D $15, Wine $17

MEXICO CITY

Mexico City is home to some of the most unusual cuisine in the country, a legacy of its Aztec past. *Chapulines* (fried grasshoppers), best accompanied with avocado, chili and coriander guacamole, can be found on many menus. You might also see *escamoles* (ant eggs) and *gusanos de maguey* (cactus worms), usually fried and often served with *tortillas* for you to make your own *taco* with. Look out too for *huitlacoche,* a highly prized Mexican corn truffle mainly served as a cream sauce on top of soup. And then there's the tender *nopal* cactus, best when cubed and served in a *taco* with *chipotle* chilies. If that all sounds too far-out, there's always *chiles en nogada,* mild chilies cooked with nuts and delicious spices. While Puebla lays claim to the classic Mexican *mole* dish (▷ 256), there are plenty of varieties to be tried in Mexico City too. You'll also find all the classics of Mexican cuisine—*quesadillas, tacos, burritos* and *enchiladas*. And of course, as in any great city, there are plenty of other culinary options, including French, Chinese, Japanese, Argentine and Cuban.

PRICES AND SYMBOLS

The restaurants are listed alphabetically within each town. The prices given for lunch (L) and dinner (D) are for three courses for one person, without drinks. The wine price is for the least expensive bottle.

For a key to the symbols, ▷ 2.

LA BODEGUITA DEL MEDIO

Calle Cozumel 37, Condesa
Tel (55) 55 53 02 46

The Mexico City branch of Ernest Hemingway's favorite Cuban bar, the Bodeguita del Medio, is housed in an attractive early 19th-century house, its walls covered in the signatures of previous diners. This is an atmospheric bar and restaurant—and the ideal place to sip a refreshing *mojito* (a Cuban cocktail made with rum, soda water, sugar and lime) to the sound of Cuban *son*. Try the *tostones* stuffed with seafood, and for real Cuban authenticity ask for the cigars.

Sun and Sat 1.30pm–2am, Mon 1.30–10.30
L $10, D $19, Wine $16
Sevilla

SPECIAL

BAR LA OPERA

Avenida 5 de Mayo
Tel (55) 55 12 89 59

Founded in 1876, this elegant restaurant one block from Bellas Artes oozes lavish belle époque charm and sophistication with its sumptuous red velvet upholstery, large gilt mirrors and mahogany furniture. Bar La Opera's famous clientele include Pancho Villa, who left his mark with a bullet hole you can still see in the ceiling. The eclectic and original dishes include grilled fish in a Veracruzana sauce and *paella* Valenciana.

Mon–Sat 1–midnight, Sun 1–6
L $18, D $30, Wine $8
Bellas Artes

CAFÉ LA BLANCA

Avenida 5 de Mayo 40
Tel (55) 55 10 03 99

You'll come across this no-nonsense eatery halfway along Avenida 5 de Mayo. Open early for excellent-value breakfasts and during the week for two-course set lunches, its menu also lists several Mexican dishes. The large canteen-style, open-plan dining room has a circular soda bar, which, together with the retro orange plastic chairs, gives a classic 1950s feel. Good espresso coffee. No credit cards.

Daily 6.30am–11pm
L $6, D $7, Wine $9
Zócalo, Allende

CAFÉ TACUBA

Calle Tacuba 28
Tel (55) 55 18 49 50/55 21 20 48

One block east of the Museo Nacional de Arte, this immensely popular restaurant occupies a 17th-century mansion. *Quartetos* and *mariachis* play here every evening from 8pm against the backdrop of blue-and-white Spanish tiles. Founded in 1912, the restaurant specializes in Mexican dishes, including excellent *enchiladas, tamales* and fruit desserts. Mexican politician Danilo Fabio Altamirano was assassinated here in 1936. One of the country's most famous rock bands takes its name from the restaurant.

Daily 8am–11pm
L $10, D $18, Wine $15
Allende

CAMBALACHE

Calle Arquímedes 85, Polanco
Tel (55) 52 80 20 80
www.grupocambalache.com

Don't be put off by this Argentine steak house being a chain restaurant: For sizzling steaks in an intimate atmosphere there's none better. Diners tuck into the filling portions under oak beamed ceilings, served by friendly and professional staff. And vegetarians and fish lovers aren't excluded either—there's a decent selection of non-meat dishes, including a succulent salmon fillet layered with crunchy black pepper.

Daily 1pm–1am
L $28, D $40, Wine $20
Polanco

SPECIAL

CANTINA LA GUADALUPANA

Avenida Higuera 14, Coyoacán
Tel (55) 55 54 62 53

A stone's throw from Plaza Hidalgo in the southern neighborhood of Coyoacán, this is one of the best-known *cantinas* (locals bars serving simple food) in Mexico. With its saloon doors, heavy wooden furniture and bulls' heads on the paneled walls, you'd be forgiven for thinking you're in a small town in deepest Mexico with your horse tethered up outside rather than a bustling suburb of Mexico City. Bean soup and squid cooked in its own ink are good options if you're struggling to choose from the extensive menu. Or just come for a drink. Attentive waiters. No credit cards.

Mon–Sat noon–11
L $9, D $14, Wine $9
General Anaya, Viveros

EL CAMPIRANO

Calle Bolivar 20
Tel (55) 55 21 08 15/55 10 09 20

Just off Avenida 5 de Mayo, this smart restaurant-bar is open every day for excellent buffet breakfasts (until 12.30) and buffet lunches (until 6.30). The mouthwatering and temptingly displayed dishes include *mole poblano,* seafood *paella, lomo al higo* (beef in a fig sauce), *chiles rellenos* (stuffed chilies) and an enticing selection of 28 different salads!

Daily 9–6.30
L $10, Wine $7
Allende

CASA DE LOS AZULEJOS

Calle Madero 4
Tel (55) 55 12 13 31

This 16th-century palace (the House of Tiles, ▷ 106), directly across from the Templo de San Francisco, is now home to Sanborn's Restaurant, the flagship establishment of a chain of 36 across the city. As well as the restaurant, in the high-ceilinged central courtyard, overlooked by wooden balconies, there is a drugstore, chocolate shop and bookshop with foreign-language magazines. Serving toned-down but delicious dishes, Sanborn's is an excellent option for those unused to the fire of Mexican cuisine. Many people come just to enjoy the building.

Daily 7.30am–1am
L $8, D $11, Wine $8
Bellas Artes

LA CASA DE LAS SIRENAS

Calle República de Guatemala 32
Tel (55) 57 04 32 25
www.lacasadelassirenas.com.mx

This elegant, sun-drenched terrace restaurant occupies a 1750s colonial house just behind the cathedral. The traditional mahogany wood bar serving 250 types of tequila is linked to the terrace by a series of sloping corridors and staircases filled with period furniture. From the restaurant, where the atmosphere is relaxed and the service impeccable, there is a splendid view over the *zócalo*. The menu covers Mexican specialties, meat and fish dishes and breakfast at weekends.

Mon–Fri 1–11, Sat 8am–11pm, Sun 8–6
L $18, D $20, Wine $14
Zócalo

CENTRO CASTELLANO

Calle República de Uruguay 16–18
Tel (55) 55 18 60 80/55 21 35 16

The best Spanish restaurant in town, Centro Castellano was founded in 1959 by Don Ricardo Vega Velasco and for four decades has excelled in serving the very best Spanish dishes in a warm and welcoming stone-flanked taverna. Cuts of ham and wooden tankards hang from low beams. From among the exquisitely presented dishes, try the superb *gazpacho Andaluz* and the specialties *lechón al estilo Segovia* (suckling pig), *lomo de huachinango a las brasas* (red snapper cooked over charcoal), or the *paellas*.

Mon–Sat 1–11, Sun 1–8
L $10, D $20, Wine $11
San Juan de Letrán

CHEZ WOK

Calle Tennyson 117, Polanco
Tel (55) 52 81 34 10

Renowned chef Kwong Poon Li is at the helm of this gourmet Chinese restaurant just off Avenida Presidente Masaryk. Describing its cuisine as "Imperial China," a good few of Chez Wok's highly original creations also come fused with Mexican ingredients—try the Mexican spring roll with quail. There are good options for vegetarians too. The immaculate dining room is elegant and discreet.

Mon–Sat 1.30–11, Sun 1.30–4.45
L $20, D $28, Wine $11
Polanco

CHUCHO EL ROTO

Calle Madero 8, San Angel
Tel (55) 56 16 20 41

You'll get tasty breakfasts and good-value lunches in this bright, cheerful café, half a block from the Plaza San Jacinto in San Angel. A pretty pattern of lilies decorates the orange and blue walls, and a flower-covered balustrade separates the pine tables from the pavement outside. Highlights on the simple menu include *enchiladas de mole Oaxaqueña* and *enchiladas suizas*. Mexican breakfasts are just $3.

Mon–Fri 8–8, Sat and Sun 9–6.30
L $5
Miguel Ángel de Quevedo

COCINA VERÓNICA

Calle República de Cuba 75
Tel (55) 55 10 42 98

Set yourself up for the day with one of the filling breakfasts from this excellent value eatery and streetside bar two blocks from the Plaza Santo Domingo. Omelettes or scrambled eggs are accompanied by tortillas and a choice of fresh pastries, and washed down with freshly squeezed juices and coffee or tea—all for as little as $3. Burgers and tasty *tortas* make up the lunch menu. No credit cards.

Mon–Sat 9–7, closed Sun
L $4
Allende

FOCOLARE
Calle Hamburgo 87, Zona Rosa
Tel (55) 52 07 85 03/52 07 85 07
This unashamedly touristy restaurant caters to large groups with its evening folk dance show "Noches Mexicanas" (Monday–Saturday 8.45; reservations essential), a spectacle of color and music. The attractive dining room is adorned with local baskets and terracotta tiles, and tables are grouped around a central catwalk stage. Try the original *camarones al tequila* (shrimps with tequila) and the delicious *pato en salsa de Jamaica*. Specializes in Yucatecan cuisine. It costs $5 to take photos of the show.
Mon–Sat 8am–2am, Sun 9am–midnight
L $12, D $17, Wine $14
Insurgentes, Sevilla

LOS GIRASOLES
Calle Tacuba 8–10
Tel (55) 55 10 06 30/55 10 32 81
www.restaurantelosgirasoles.com
Slick waiters in patriotic red, green and white neckties and leather aprons buzz around this lively Mexican restaurant on the Plaza Manuel Tolsa, next to the Museo de Arte Nacional. Oaxacan pottery, flagstones dotted with handsome *azulejo* tiles and roughly hewn walls add to the atmosphere. The extensive menu, also available in English, includes Aztec-inspired dishes such as maguey worms fried in butter and chili, as well as turkey breasts in a tamarind *mole* sauce and the Yucatán-inspired *cochinita pibil*—spicy shredded pork.
Sun–Mon 1–9, Tue–Sat 1–midnight
L $15, D $22, Wine $18
Bellas Artes, Allende

GO FRESH
Hamburgo 141B, Zona Rosa
Tel (55) 52 08 14 03/52 08 17 13
www.gofresh.com.mx
Opened in June 2004, this trendy café two blocks north of metro Insurgentes provides wholesome, healthy food and a welcome break for those feeling jaded with *tacos* and the like. Duck, brie and fig wraps or bagels overflowing with arugula (rocket), Parmesan shavings and lemon zest dressing are the highlights in the selection of light lunch options that also includes homemade breads, juices and organic yogurts. But note: originality doesn't come cheap. No credit cards.
Mon–Fri 9am–11pm, Sat and Sun 10–10
L and D $8
Insurgentes

HACIENDA DE CORTÉS
Fernández Leal 70, Coyoacán
Tel (55) 56 59 37 41
The interior patios and flowering gardens of this colonial-style hacienda tucked behind Plaza la Conchita make this restaurant an exceptionally pleasant place to dine. The large, shaded outdoor patio area lends itself to leisurely breakfasts and the dining room inside is softly lit with brass lamps. Try the delicious fish fillet with butter, almonds and parsley or the plentiful set breakfasts (9–1), which are excellent value at $3.
Mon–Sat 9am–10.30pm, Sun 9–7
L $10, D $13, Wine $10
General Anaya, Viveros

HOSTERÍA DE SANTO DOMINGO
Belisario Domínguez 72
Tel (55) 55 10 14 34/55 26 52 76
Mexico City's oldest restaurant can be found in the former Santo Domingo convent, just half a block from the square of the same name in the historic downtown area. Tables are spread through a labyrinth of rooms on different levels connected by archways and steps under beamed ceilings, in contrast to the cavernously large—and somehow rather soulless—first-floor back area. House specials include chorizo sausage accompanied by a salad of tender *nopal* cactus, chili stuffed with beef, raisins (sultanas), pine nuts and *acitrón* (candied cactus) and *chiles en nogada* (peppers stuffed with minced meat). There is piano music every evening from 8.
Daily 9am–9.30pm
L $12, D $18, Wine $8
Allende, Zócalo

EL HUEQUITO
Calle República de Bolivia 58
Tel (55) 55 10 4199/55 21 02 07
www.elhuequito.com
Three blocks south of Avenida 5 de Mayo, between República de Uruguay and República de El Salvador, this brightly painted and lively American-style diner is casual, cheap and friendly. In addition to the delicious breakfasts, the restaurant serves an extensive choice of tasty, toned down Mexican specials such as *enchiladas al suizo, tacos* and *quesadillas* as well as hamburgers, T-bone steak and ice cream. There is a good children's menu. Live music on Thursdays and Fridays from 8pm.
Mon–Sat 8am–11pm, Sun 8am–9pm
L $7, D $12, Wine $12
San Juan de Letrán

EL JOLGORIO
Avenida Higuera 22 E, Coyoacán
Tel (55) 56 58 83 39
Tucked away down Avenida Higuera, the attractive and fashionable El Jolgorio restaurant specializes in Arabic-Indian-Mexican fusion cuisine. The reasonably priced and inventive dishes are divided on the menu into earth, water, fire and air, and include couscous salads, lightly curried meats and many vegetarian dishes. The restaurant has a superb-value set lunch from Monday to Thursday ($7).
Mon 2–7, Tue 1–7, Wed–Fri 1–11, Sat 2–11, Sun 11–11
L $10, D $15, Wine $10
General Anaya, Viveros

JUGOS CANADÁ
Avenida 5 de Mayo 49, corner with República de Chile
Tel (55) 55 18 37 17
A perfect place for a quick snack and vitamin-C boost, this juice bar is casual and cheap. The walls are covered with tropical fruits, which are plucked, chopped and squeezed in front of you and served in plentiful quantities.

Tortas, hamburgers and hot-dogs are under $3 and the mountainous salad of fresh fruits, yogurt, granola and honey is a must. No credit cards.
Tue–Sat 8am–10pm, Sun 9–9
L and D $5
Zócalo

MESÓN ANTIGUA SANTA CATARINA
Plaza Santa Catarina 6, Coyoacán
Tel (55) 56 58 48 31
Situated on the square of the same name in Coyocán, this pink-and-blue café-restaurant has a rickety wooden staircase that emerges onto a splendid open dining room overlooking the square: a perfect place for enjoying a leisurely afternoon sangria. The good Mexican dishes served on ceramic dishes are very reasonably priced and the breakfasts are delicious.
Daily 8am–11pm
L $8, D $15, Wine $30
General Anaya, Viveros

MEXICO VIEJO
Calle Tacuba 87
Tel (55) 55 10 37 48/ 55 12 97 43
One block north of the *zócalo* on the corner with República de Brasil, this inviting restaurant offers impeccable service in a sunflower-yellow ranch-style dining room. Popular with local business people, it is particularly recommended for its delicious breakfasts of *huevos rancheros* or hotcakes, and for its four-course set lunches on weekdays ($7).
Mon–Sat 8am–9pm, Sun 8–6 (breakfast until 12.30, lunch until 6)
L $11, D $15, Wine $14
Zócalo

LES MOUSTACHES
Río Sena 88 between La Reforma and Río Lerma, Zona Rosa
Tel (55) 55 33 33 90/55 25 12 65
www.lesmoustaches.com.mx
Dine in style in this elegant French restaurant, one of the top eating experiences in town. A gastronomic feast in a Porfiriato-era mansion near the US embassy, Les Moustaches is by reservation only. Choose from such culinary delights as salmon in a saffron sauce with wild rice, and *lenguado Veronique* (sole in a white wine sauce with glazed grapes). The wine list is superb and a sommelier is at hand to offer expert advice should you need it.

Daily 1–11
L $28, D $30, Wine $15
Insurgentes

LOS MURALES
Avenida Liverpool 152, Zona Rosa
Tel (55) 57 26 99 11
www.century.com.mx
Attached to Hotel Century just off Avenida Insurgentes, the strength of this understated business restaurant is its delicious vegetarian lunch buffet. Between numerous trips to the buffet—spread with salads, pastas, Mexican dishes and desserts—the attentive waiters refill your glass with *agua de fruta* and then green tea, all included. There is also an excellent weekend breakfast buffet until 11am.
Daily 7am–10.45pm
L $7, D $18, Wine $13
Insurgentes

SAN ANGEL INN
Calle Diego Rivera 50 at Calle Altavista, San Angel
Tel (55) 56 16 22 22/56 16 05 37
www.sanangelinn.com

For a taste of how the city's elite dine, this exquisitely converted monastery decorated in colonial style with original tiled stone fountains and beautiful interior patios is the place to see and be seen. Throughout its 300-year history, this hacienda, in the delightful colonial district of San Angel, has played host to generals, revolutionaries and ambassadors, and more recently, the likes of Bridget Bardot, Henry Kissinger and Muhammad Ali. Start with a margarita or a martini, then choose from the European cuisine and sumptuous desserts which are served in a delightful, softly lighted dining room, hung with iron chandeliers.
Mon–Sat 1–1, Sun 1–9.30
L $20, D $28, Wine $18
Miguel Angel de Quevedo, then take a taxi

SUSHI ROLL
Avenida 5 de Mayo 15B, corner with Filomeno Mata
Tel (55) 55 12 13 87/55 21 12 17
There are few surprises in this impressively authentic sushi bar, a popular lunch spot with local office workers. The place has a clean look, with white-washed walls and spotlighting. The menu includes everything you might expect, with prices depending on whether the fish is imported or caught locally. This being Mexico, you'll find a bowl of chilies next to the soy sauce.
Mon–Sat 1–8, Sun 1–6
L $9
Bellas Artes

LA TERRAZA, HOTEL MAJESTIC
Avenida Francisco Madero 73
Tel (55) 55 12 86 00
www.majestic.com.mx
For a spectacular vista over the *zócalo*, head to the Hotel Majestic's seventh-floor rooftop restaurant. This is an expensive option but it is a perfect observation point for watching the frenetic action below. Stylish breakfasts until noon; thereafter fairly standard Mexican and international food.
Daily 7am–11pm
L $9, D $9, Wine $9
Zócalo

CENTRAL MEXICO EAST

This region extends from the highlands of Puebla, home to one of Mexico's most eclectic cuisines, to the humid, tropical state of Veracruz, where almost every dish comes with the suffix *Veracruzana*. Puebla is most famous for its *mole poblano*. It's made from a mix of cloves, onion, garlic, sesame seed, chili, cinnamon, almonds, raisins and chocolate, and is served today at weddings, christenings and funerals. There's more to the city than *mole poblano*, however. *Tinga poblano* is beef or chicken meat pulled into fibrous strips in a tomato and chili sauce, while *chile en nogada* (only available July to September, when the ingredients are harvested) is a stuffed pepper with white almond sauce and red pomegranate seeds, echoing the green, white and red of the Mexican flag.

The Spanish influence is felt most strongly in the gulf coast state of Vercacruz, where the regional specialty, *huachinango a la veracruzana* (red snapper in a spicy tomato sauce) relies heavily on imported ingredients such as olives, garlic and capers. Two other popular local dishes are *arroz a la tumbada,* a delicious rice dish baked with a variety of shellfish, and *sopa de mariscos*, a seafood soup claimed to cure hangovers. Veracruz is also a good place to try the ever-popular *ceviche*, which is raw white fish marinated in lime juice and served with onion, tomato, chili and cilantro (coriander), a vital ingredient in much of Mexican cooking.

In the region of the Dos Tuxtlas, look out for *tepache*, a drink made from fermented pineapple, similar in taste to cider. In Xalapa, the heart of the coffee-growing region and home to the ubiquitous *jalapeño* chili pepper, the most satisfying culinary experience is a strong local coffee served with *pan dulce* (sweet bread) in a traditional café.

PRICES AND SYMBOLS

The restaurants are listed alphabetically within each town. The prices given for lunch (L) and dinner (D) are for three courses for one person, without drinks. The wine price is for the least expensive bottle.

For a key to the symbols, ⊳ 2.

CATEMACO

LOS SAUCES

Paseo del Malecón, Catemaco
Tel (294) 943 05 48

Cool breezes from Lake Catemaco waft over the terrace of this fish restaurant, the best choice along the lakeside *malecón*. The specialty is the *mojarro*, small perch from the lake, best sampled with *tachogobi*, a traditional spicy, fresh tomato sauce. Set breakfasts served until midday are also good value and filling. No credit cards.

Daily 8am–10pm
L $8, D $22 Wine $12

COATEPEC

CAFÉ SOLEIL

Calle Lerdo 3, Local 1, Coatepec
Tel (228) 816 35 02

In her brightly painted yellow café, friendly Eugenia makes superb espresso and cappuccino using the aromatic local coffee. Sample it together with her delicious homemade pastries, carrot cake or bagels. Also easily whipped up are melon, passion fruit and pineapple juices, all at excellent prices. No credit cards.

Daily 10.30–2.30, 4.30–9.30
L $5

CASA BONILLAS

Calle Juárez 20 with Calle Cuauhtémoc, Coatepec
Tel (228) 816 00 09

Two blocks from the *zócalo*, this very popular restaurant was established in 1934 and specializes in exquisite seafood dishes. It is justly proud of its prawns in a homemade *salsa verde* made from chili, orange juice and butter. The delightful sun- and flower-filled patio is trimmed with leaf and berry frescoes, and the sound of parrots permeates the air. There is a bar attached with less expensive lunch snacks. No Amex cards.

Daily 10–7; bar closes 11pm Thu–Sat
L $10, D $20, Wine $14

CÓRDOBA

EL BALCÓN

Avenida 1 No. 101, Córdoba
Tel (217) 712 19 89

Situated on the balcony of the historic Portales de Zevallos, where the Treaty of Córdoba (acknowledging Mexican Independence) was signed in 1821, this restaurant affords lovely views of the plaza below, animated by dancers and musicians in the evenings. While away an hour sampling the local Córdoban coffee or the Veracruzana *julep* drink made from dark rum and mint.

Mon–Sat 5.30–10, Sun 2–4.30
L $8, D $20, Wine $16

CUERNAVACA

LA INDIA BONITA

Calle Morrow 15, Cuernavaca
Tel (777) 318 69 67

High walls protect La India Bonita's lush central patio and its murmuring fountains, making it easy to forget you're in the heart of Cuernavaca. Restored in 1992, the house of former US ambassador to Mexico Dwight D. Morrow (father-in-law to aviator Charles Lindbergh) offers comfortable dining at very reasonable prices. Specials include a tender lamb fillet in pulque salsa. From 7pm on Saturdays the restaurant is host to a gregarious Mexican dance show.

Tue–Sat noon–10, Sun noon–6
L $12, D $15, Wine $14

MAGGIO CAFFE
Calle Comonfort 12, Cuernavaca
Tel (777) 310 37 27
The sweet smell of roasting coffee gives away the whereabouts of this small café hidden away on a street off Cerdo de Tejada, to the west of Jardín Juárez. Family-run and extremely hospitable, Maggio Caffe proudly displays its sparkling espresso machines, producing superb cappuccinos, and serves croissants, delicious banana bread and ice-cold fruit smoothies. No credit cards.
Mon–Fri 9–8.30, Sat 10.30–8.30
L $4

LAS MAÑANITAS
Calle Ricardo Linares 107, Cuernavaca
Tel (777) 314 14 66
www.lasmananitas.com.mx

Las Mañanitas, set in a restored hacienda with immaculate grounds, has a well-deserved reputation as one of the finest restaurants in Mexico. Innovative regional cuisine at its best is the order of the day, featuring *sopa de tortilla* and chicken in *mole verde*.
Daily 1pm–5pm, 7pm–11pm
L $30, D $40, Wine $15

PACHUCA

MI ANTIGUA CAFE
Calle Matamoros 115, Pachuca
Tel (771) 107 18 37
On the south side of the *zócalo*, this modern, light café with trendy wrought-iron tables and chairs is the place to come for good espressos and breakfasts of croissants or fruit salad. Also on the menu are light lunches of imaginatively filled baguettes and crêpes, and cheesecakes with pots of Darjeeling tea in the afternoon. No credit cards.
Mon–Sat 8.30am–10.30pm, Sun 9.30–8.30
L and D $7

PUEBLA

CAFE Y LIBRERÍA TEOREMA
Avenida Reforma 540, Puebla
Tel (222) 298 00 28
Delicious coffees are served in a studious atmosphere, the walls lined with books and paintings, and tables scattered with newspapers. Choose from specialty coffees with amaretto, brandy or whisky, lunch snacks, or a coffee-and-cake deal from 5 to 7pm. There's live jazz, trova and rock every evening from 9.30, plus a huge cocktail menu.
Mon–Fri 10am–12.30am, Sat and Sun 10am–2am
L and D $5

FONDA DE SANTA CLARA
Calle 3 Poniente No. 307, Puebla
Tel (222) 242 26 59

This picturesque, taverna-style restaurant one block west of the *zócalo* is something of an institution. It's popular with locals and visitors alike, and has a relaxed family atmosphere in which to sample some of the most original cuisine in Mexico. The *mole poblano* and *chiles en nogada* are house specials.
Daily 8.30am–10pm
L $11, D $15, Wine $14

SAN ANDRÉS TUXTLA

MARISCOS CHAZARO
Avenida Madero 12, San Andrés Tuxtla
Tel (294) 942 13 79
Jorge Chávez Flores, owner of this family-run fish restaurant, prepares exquisite prawn cocktails, which make for a perfect light lunch in the heat of San Andrés. The restaurant is cooled by whirring fans and decorated with the fantastic marine life he has caught. The specialty is the prawns in extra hot *chile chipotle* sauce—only for the brave. No credit cards.
Mon–Sat 8.30–7, Sun 8.30–5
L $9, D $13, Wine $13

TAMPICO

LA TROYA
Inside Hotel Posada del Rey, Calle Madero 218, Tampico
Tel (833) 214 11 55
An excellent view over the animated and rowdy Plaza de la Libertad makes this the most entertaining restaurant in town. It occupies the balcony of a 19th-century art nouveau building, now the Hotel Posada del Rey, one of the oldest in Tampico. On September 11 1829, the Spanish brigadier Don Isidro Barradas surrendered to Mexican authorities here after a final attempt to recuperate the Crown's lost power. A wide choice of Mexican and international cuisine, including a good paella, is on the menu.
Daily 7am–11pm
L $7, D $11, Wine $13

TAXCO

CAFÉ EL ADOBE
Plazuela San Juan 13, Taxco
Tel (762) 622 14 16
Terracotta adobe walls, a mosaic tiled floor, low arches and a very attractive balcony with potted plants lend this restaurant a pleasant colonial, hacienda-style feel. Suitable for all hours of the day, breakfasts are excellent and good value, and the menu includes many variations on the principal Mexican *antojitos* (appetizers), including the original *tacos taxqueños*, as well as seafood, steaks and tempting desserts.
Daily 8am–11pm
L $5, D $15, Wine $12

CAFÉ SASHA
Calle Juan Ruiz de Alarcón 1, Taxco
On the first floor of a colonial building, some of the tables in this intimate and very friendly vegetarian restaurant are squeezed onto tiny balconies overlooking the cobbled street below. Brightly decorated with *artesanía* and candles and lined with comfy sofas, the service is informal but attentive and the food moderately priced and consistently good. Choose from vegetarian pasta dishes, crêpes, Chinese noodles and delicious carrot cake. Breakfast is excellent. No credit cards.
Daily 8am–midnight
L $7, D $11, Wine $12

LA HACIENDA
Hotel Agua Escondida, Plaza de la Borda 4, Taxco
Tel (762) 622 06 63

This restaurant, one of two in the Hotel Agua Escondida, is a popular venue with locals and vistors. Dishes include *cecina hacienda* and *enchiladas hacienda*.
7.30–11.30, 12.30–4.30, 6.30–10.30
L $8, D $9–$10, Wine $7

TEPOZTLÁN

LA TAPATÍA
Avenida Revolución 18, Tepoztlán
Tel (739) 395 10 21
On the south side of the *zócalo*, this informal and very friendly restaurant is decorated with local textiles and tablecloths, and prepares its delicious tropical juices, vegetarian set lunches and Mexican *quesadillas* and *tacos* with natural, organic ingredients. Amex cards not accepted.
Daily 8–8
L $5, D $10, Wine $10

TLACOTALPAN

LAS BRISAS DEL PAPALOAPAN
Calle Ribera, Tlacotalpan
Tel (288) 420 03
www.tlaco.com.mx
As its name suggests, this appealing restaurant on the riverfront benefits from delicious breezes from the Papaloapan—very welcome in this sweltering town. The wooden terrace on stilts over the river has lovely panoramic views, and examples of the day's specialties are displayed on large platters so you can see exactly which sea creature you are ordering. The seafood is prepared in tasty *enchipotlado* chili sauces, and many meat dishes are also available. No credit cards.
Daily 8–8
L $9, D $20, Wine $12

TLAXCALA

LOS PORTALES
Portal Hidalgo 8, Plaza de la Constitución 8, Tlaxcala
Tel (246) 462 23 38
One of the inviting restaurants under the arches that line the eastern side of the *zócalo*, Los Portales is a very pleasant place to watch life go by and sample the local Tlaxcalan cuisine. The delicious *sopa tlaxcala* is made from black beans, *tortilla* chips, avocado and cheese. Also on the extensive menu are Mexican *antojitos* (appetizers), hamburgers and pasta dishes.
Daily 8am–10.30pm
L $8, D $13, Wine $11

VERACRUZ

GRAN CAFÉ DEL PORTAL
Calle Independencia 1187, Veracruz
Tel (229) 932 93 39
A *cafe lechero* (white coffee) and pastry in this famous family-run establishment opposite the cathedral is a must. The Cuban Caldevilla family opened the premises as a candy store in 1824 and Spaniard Don Pepe, whose grandson still owns the café, later created the bustling, social gathering point it is today. Old photos of Veracruz line the walls and waiters are dressed in white coats. The menu includes a choice of meat and fish dishes and Mexican meals.
Daily 8am–11pm
L $6, D $18, Wine $12

NEVERÍA TRIGUEROS
Calle Zaragoza, 147 between Calle Mario Molina and Calle Serdan, Veracruz
Tel (229) 932 39 50
There is nowhere better than this popular, relaxed juice and ice cream bar to sample the traditional Veracruzana *mondonga de fruta*. Consisting of a mountain of chopped tropical fruit topped with a generous dollop of ice cream or yogurt, it is usually a considered a breakfast but also makes a refreshing, if filling, snack during the hot afternoons.
Daily 7am–midnight
L and D $5

TANO EL VERACRUZANO
Calle Mario Molina 20, Veracruz
Tel (229) 31 50 50
Just off the *malecón* and one block from the fish market, this excellent restaurant stands out among the host of small fish restaurants in the area. Every spare inch of wall is covered with photos of the owner, Tano el Dueño, clearly quite a character. Other quirky decorations include the dried eels, turtles and small sharks that hang menacingly from the ceilings. Start with the delicious *Campechano* fresh crab and prawn cocktail with lime and coriander before moving on to the house special, *arroz a la tumbada*, a local paella-style dish. No credit cards.
Daily 9am–10.30pm
L $9, D $13, Wine $10

XALAPA

LA FONDA
Callejón del Diamante with Enriquez, Xalapa
Tel (228) 818 72 82
Tucked away up a side street off Calle Enriquez, this very popular lunch restaurant serves excellent-value three-course set lunches, which include *agua de frutas* (fruit-flavored water) and coffee. The crêpe-paper decorations, frescoes of lilies and bright murals are fitted around the long, open kitchen where cooks in traditional white dresses and head scarves stir great steaming cauldrons of piping hot soups and bake homemade *tortillas* on an open fire. No credit cards.
Mon–Sat 8–5.30
L $3

MANANTIAL DE LAS FLORES
Calle Ursulo Galván 102, Xalapa
Tel (228) 812 45 57
This oasis of peace and quiet and organic delights occupies a colonial house along a cobbled path, its sunny verandah hidden by the explosion of pink bougainvillea. The fruit, yogurt and honey breakfasts are a treat, and the healthy, homemade three-course set lunches come with organic bread and herbal tea. There is also an eco-shop selling organic breads and coffee. No credit cards.
Tue–Sun 9–6
L $4

CENTRAL MEXICO WEST

On the Pacific coast, Manzanillo, in the state of Colima, is a great place to sample some of the country's finest fish and seafood. Restaurants offer local delicacies, including swordfish, red snapper and *ceviche de pescado ahumado* (smoked fish *ceviche*). Carnivores shouldn't feel left out either–good meat dishes are easy to come by, and are especially good in the cattle-rearing areas from Querétaro to Zacatecas. In the western states of Michoacán and Jalisco, *pozole* (a pot-au-feu with a base of maize and stock) and *birria*, a spicy goat stew, feature heavily.

Vegetarians can have a tough time of it in Mexico, but the restaurants and eateries listed below are all vegetarian-friendly. Avocado in Uruapan mustn't be missed, nor should *sopa tarasca*, a soup made with chili and shredded *tortilla* in Pátzcuaro. In Guadalajara you have the home of many of the dishes now considered typically Mexican, including *birria* (mutton or goat and served in a rich tomato sauce) and *pozole*, a pork stew.

The region also specializes in a varied assortment of sweets, treats and candies. Try the Jardín Hidalgo in Guanajuato for *yemitas*, little caramel eggs wrapped in white and blue tissue paper, and the wonderful Mercado de Dulces in Morelia for guava paste rolls and *chongos*, made from milk, honey and cinnamon. Finally, don't miss the extraordinary ice creams in the town of Dolores Hidalgo.

AGUASCALIENTES

CAFÉ PANA

Calle Zaragoza 418, Aguascalientes
Tel (449) 915 25 76

Just outside the Iglesia de Templo de San Antonio and the Museo de Aguascalientes, this is a great spot for both light snacks–try the *molletes* (French bread with a refried bean spread)–and sizeable dinner dishes; the T-bone steak with tomato salsa is recommended. Open to the street and dotted with potted palms, the restaurant has an airy atmosphere, while tables are small and intimate. And the coffee's the best in town.

Mon–Sat 9am–11pm
L $12, D $17, Wine $14

BARRA DE NAVIDAD

SEA MASTER

Avenida Lopez de Legaspi 146, Barra de Navidad
Tel (315) 355 51 19

Sea Master has a front entrance on the main drag and views across the bay to Melaque with waves lapping up on the beach just a few steps from your table. Open-sided, lit by bamboo lampshades and decked out with typical Mexican panache in bright yellows, pinks and blues, style is matched by a quality menu (mainly seafood) that includes a superb red snapper stuffed with shrimp, bacon and pecans. And for ultimate beach hedonism, order a pitcher of daiquiri. The service is great and the drinks are strong. Cash only.

Daily noon–11
L $12, D $16, Wine $14

PRICES AND SYMBOLS

The restaurants are listed alphabetically within each town. The prices given for lunch (L) and dinner (D) are for three courses for one person, without drinks. The wine price is for the least expensive bottle.

For a key to the symbols, ▷ 2.

COLIMA

LOS NARANJOS

Calle Gabino Barreda 34, Colima
Tel (312) 312 00 29

Tasty, fresh and filling breakfasts ($6) are highly recommended in this long-standing restaurant halfway between Parque Nuñez and the Jardín Torres Quintero. Try the *nopales* with eggs à la Mexicana, or the fresh hotcakes dripping with maple syrup. For lunch and dinner there are tender steaks, spicy barbecued chicken drumsticks and good *quesadillas*. Service is polite and efficient and the atmosphere family-friendly.

Daily 8am–11pm
L $10, D $13, Wine $11

GUADALAJARA

EL MEXICANO

Calle Morelos 76, Guadalajara
Tel (33) 658 03 45

A couple of minutes' walk from the Teatro Degollado toward the Hospicio Cabañas is El Mexicano, which specializes in barbecued steaks. The rustic Mexican decoration may be a little over the top, but the atmosphere is consistently lively and fun, with *mariachis* wandering from table to table every evening after 7pm. As well as good meats and *pozole* (soup made with hominy and pork or chicken), the *queso fundido* (a Mexican-style fondue) is recommended, and if you're still hungry, the desserts are satisfyingly large.

Sun–Thu 1–10, Fri 1–11, Sat noon–11
L $16, D $19, Wine $16

RESTAURANT SIN NOMBRE

Avenida Madero 80, Tlaquepaque, Guadalajara
Tel (33) 3635 4520

You'll find this delightful restaurant housed in an 18th-century mansion a couple of blocks north of the Jardín Hidalgo in the southeastern suburb of Tlaquepaque. Candlelit tables are set in a wonderful garden under pergolas shaded with vines and palms. There are good Mexican options—melted cheese with mushrooms and a tasty guacamole—as well as more ambitious international dishes, including tender red snapper in butter and capers.

Mon–Thu 11–10, Fri, Sat 11am–midnight
L $14, D $18, Wine $15

GUANAJUATO

CIAO BELLA

Calle Pocitos 25, Guanajuato
Tel (473) 732 67 64

Just a few steps behind the Museo del Pueblo de Guanajuato, Luis Arturo Tinajero presides over this attractive Italian restaurant with warm hospitality. There is a good wine list and the menu includes both classics and more daring dishes—try the delicious walnut, pear and Parmesan salad, as well as the tasty *fusilli à la boscaiola* (fusilli in mushroom sauce). Tables are set in high-ceilinged rooms painted in oranges and yellows, with wine bottles suspended from the walls. Amex cards not accepted.

Sun–Fri 2–10, Sat 1–10
L $24, D $28, Wine $13

TRUCO 7

Calle del Truco 7, Guanajuato
Tel (473) 732 83 74

Between the university and Jardín de la Unión, Truco 7 is a favorite hangout of local students and visitors alike. Decked out with old radios, engravings and antique candelabras, and spread through a warren of different rooms, this is a great place to linger over a coffee or light meal to the sound of jazz or bossa nova. Homemade hamburgers, *enchiladas*, *tortas* and filling breakfasts are all available. Cash only.

Daily 8.30am–11.30pm
L $5, D $8

MANZANILLO

TOSCANA

Boulevard Miguel de la Madrid 3177, Manzanillo
Tel (314) 333 25 15

French chef Michele Laugeri Giraud's wonderful creations have made Toscana's one of the top landmarks in the Playa Azul zone of Manzanillo—without stratospheric prices. The international menu changes weekly, but includes the likes of *gazpacho*, shrimp ravioli, and sea bass in a mango and ginger marinade. Tables are wafted by sea breezes coming in off the bay, and at weekends there's live music after 9pm. Amex cards not accepted.

Daily 7am–midnight
L $20, D $26, Wine $17

MORELIA

CAFÉ CONSERVATORIO

Calle Santiago Tapia 363, Morelia
Tel (443) 312 86 01

Café Conservatorio opens onto tranquil, tree-lined Jardín de las Rosas, just across from the Palacio Clavijero. With tables and chairs al fresco, this is the perfect place to relax over a good coffee and delicious apple strudel while watching the world go by. The light eats on the menu include huge baguettes and ham- and cheese-filled croissants. There's also the full range of Mexican breakfasts for $5 a head. Cash only.

Mon–Fri 9am–9.30pm, Sat and Sun 1.30–9
L and D $9

LAS MERCEDES

León Guzmán 47
Tel (443) 312 61 13

Three blocks west of the cathedral off Madero, Las Mercedes is a quite enchanting restaurant offering classy dining in a highly original setting. Tables are set in a colonial patio amid a forest of balls of lava called *heodas*, palms, orchids and enormous, locally made vases. Steak fillets, crêpes suzettes and tasty shrimps sizzling in garlic are just some of the menu's highlights. Service is impeccable. Amex cards not accepted.

Mon–Sat 1–1, Sun 1–6
L $25, D $30, Wine $11

PÁTZCUARO

LOS ESCUDOS

Plaza Quiroga, Portal Hidalgo 73, Pátzcuaro
Tel (434) 201 38

Housed under the attractive arcades on the west side of the Plaza Quiroga, Los Escudos is a popular mid-range dining option with a pleasant, family-friendly atmosphere. It is set on two levels under pink-painted beams, and keen staff serve a wide range of breakfasts ($9), including a good

fruit platter. For later in the day, try the tasty *sopa tarasca*, a tasty soup made from toasted *tortillas*, cream and cheese. In the summer there are tables outside. Cash only.

Daily 7am–10pm (breakfast until 1pm)
L $9, D $10, Wine $16

PUERTO VALLARTA

PLANETA VEGETARIANO

Calle Iturbide 270, Puerto Vallarta
Tel (322) 222 30 73
www.planetavegetariano.com

Two blocks along Iturbide from the *malecón*, Planeta Vegetariano offers a superb-value vegetarian buffet in an informal, friendly atmosphere. Humus with pita bread, roasted peppers and zucchini, *tabulé* (a Middle Eastern dip of bulgar wheat, parsley and tomato), soups and fresh salads make up the excellent spread. The price also includes unlimited refills of delicious fresh juices, dessert and a digestive tea. *Chilaquiles*, hotcakes and cereals make up the breakfast menu. Cash only.

Daily 8am–10pm
Buffet L & D $12

THE RIVER CAFÉ

Isla Río Cuale local 4, Puerto Vallarta
Tel (322) 223 07 88
www.rivercafe.com.mx

Tucked under the principal bridge over the Río Cuale three blocks from Puerto Vallarta's old heart, the River Café oozes trendy elegance. Diners can either eat inside at candlelit tables amid cool pastel shades or on the terrace overlooking the river and trees strung with tiny lights. While the crêpes, salads and meat options are

reliably tasty, it's the seafood that really stands out—try the pan-seared yellowfin tuna accompanied by a delicate black truffle risotto.
Daily 9am–11pm
L $26, D $34, Wine $20

QUERÉTARO

LA CUISINE DES ANGES

Calle Reforma 38, Querétaro
Tel (442) 212 05 08
Opened in 2003, this French-run restaurant is a gourmet's heaven in the heart of Querétaro one block south from Plaza de la Constitución. Prepare to be tantalized by an extensive menu that includes *escargots à la Bourgogne*, delicious onion soup and a tender duck *confit*. The restaurant is housed in a wonderful colonial patio painted in vivid blue and yellow amid potted ferns and paintings (displayed on their easels) by local artists.
Tue–Sun 2–10.30
L $11, D $16, Wine $18

SAN MIGUEL DE ALLENDE

CAFE DE LA PARROQUIA

Calle Jesús 11, San Miguel de Allende
Tel (415) 231 61
This very popular restaurant set in a gorgeous patio with a trickling fountain and filtered sunlight makes for a delightful place to start the day. Particularly known for its filling, good-value breakfasts of eggs, fruit and hotcakes, the menu also includes beautifully presented Mexican lunches of *quesadillas* and *enchiladas*.
Mon–Sat 7.30–4, Sun 7.30–2
L $8

TIO LUCAS

Calle Mesones 103, San Miguel de Allende
Tel (415) 152 49 96
Tio Lucas is situated within 50m (55 yards) of the Escuela de Bellas Artes in a pretty colonial house that opens onto an attractive whitewashed patio lit by pink paper lanterns. The pink theme is repeated in the painted tin folk art adorning the walls of the interior dining area. The filet mignon and T-bone steak in a mushroom sauce are particularly good options from a menu that leans towards meat.
Daily noon–11
L $17, D $20, Wine $14

TEQUILA

REAL MARINERO

Paseo Benito Juárez 92, Tequila
Tel (374) 21 674
Should you find yourself in Tequila in need of sustenance to soak up the local tipple, this is the place to head for. On the main square within stumbling distance of the Sauza and José Cuervo distilleries, the Real Marinero restaurant offers good seafood, including a first-class *ceviche*, at very reasonable prices. There are also good set meals available at lunchtime.
Daily 9am–10.30pm (Wed, lunch only)
L $7, D $11

TOLUCA

BIARRITZ

Calle Nigromante 200, Toluca
Tel (722) 214 57 57
This unpretentious café-restaurant within two minutes' walk of the cathedral supplies tasty local delicacies at reasonable prices. Specialties include the *torta Toluqueña*, a roll containing cheese and Toluca's own chorizo sausage, as well as the extravagantly carnivorous *Molcajete*, a stone bowl filled with strips of local chorizo, barbecued ribs, chilies and avocado and accompanied by maize *tortillas*. Filling Mexican breakfasts ($7) make up the morning fare. Amex cards not accepted
Daily 8am–11pm
L $7, D $10, Wine $10

URUAPAN

VENTANAS AL PARAÍSO

Calle Nicolás Bravo 100, Uruapan
Tel (452) 527 59 00
The hotel housing this restaurant may be somewhat sterile, but the views are worth the elevator trip up to the top floor of Uruapan's highest building. The restaurant serves generous portions and the soups are particularly good: *caldo tlalpeño* is a tasty vegetable and chicken soup, and *crema P'urhépecha* is a delicious avocado bisque using exquisite local fruits.
Daily 3–11
D $16, Wine $10

VALLE DE BRAVO

DA CIRO

Calle del Vergel 201, Valle de Bravo
Tel (726) 26 201 22
Five minutes' walk from Valle de Bravo's main square, Da Ciro serves delicious Italian cuisine in a colonial house with heavy beamed ceilings, flagstones and fireplaces. Starters include foie gras with a strawberry and arugula (rocket) salad, while dishes such as spaghetti with porcini and shiitake and a mouthwatering prawn and saffron risotto top the mains. There is an excellent and extensive wine list. Unfortunately, like many of the town's restaurants, Da Ciro is only open on weekends.
Fri 1pm–midnight, Sat 1–1, Sun 1–9
L $21, D $25, Wine $28

ZACATECAS

ACROPOLIS

Avenida Hidalgo, Zacatecas
Tel (492) 922 12 84
Operating since 1943 next to the cathedral at a corner of the González Ortega market, this is Zacatecas' place to see and be seen. American diner-style tables next to the windows are the perfect place to watch the world go by, although they don't leave much legroom. Good Mexican breakfasts are served until 12.30 and there are good *chilaquiles* and *enchiladas*, as well as coffee, cake and ice cream. Amex cards not accepted.
Daily 8am–10pm
L $9, D $12, Wine $13

BURGER QUEEN

Calle Tacuba 101, Zacatecas
Tel (492) 429 58
This unprepossessing eatery just a block south from the Plazuela Goitia has one of Mexico's best-kept secrets: the most mouthwateringly delicious *quesadilla* you're ever likely to taste. The *quesadilla francesa* is made with fresh-flour *tortillas* and contains mushrooms and green peppers as well as cheese. It's divine and unbeatably cheap. If that leaves you unconvinced, the menu also includes good Mexican burgers and *tortas*. Cash only.
Mon–Sat 9am–11pm, Sun 1–10
L $3, D $5

NORTHERN MEXICO AND BAJA CALIFORNIA

In northern Mexico beef dominates the culinary landscape, often accompanied by *frijoles charros* (beans with pork rind and chili) and the typically *norteño* flour *tortillas*. Aside from beef in all its forms, northerners also eat *cabrito* (barbecued goat). In Monterrey and Coahuila *cabrito al pastor*, spit-roast goat, is very popular. Other northern dishes include *huevos rancheros* (fried eggs served with a mild salsa sauce on a bed of tortillas), which have become a national breakfast staple, and *machaca norteña* (eggs scrambled with dried minced beef).

PRICES AND SYMBOLS

The restaurants are listed alphabetically within each town. The prices given for lunch (L) and dinner (D) are for three courses for one person, without drinks. The wine price is for the least expensive bottle.

For a key to the symbols, ▷ 2.

CABO SAN LUCAS

MI CASA

Plaza Mayor, Calle Cabo San Lucas, Cabo San Lucas
Tel (624) 143 19 33

Mi Casa is one of the most highly regarded Mexican restaurants in town. A restored colonial hacienda provides the setting with regional dishes served in a candlelit courtyard. The house special is *chiles en nogado*, a red pepper stuffed with creamy walnut sauce, but the seafood and fish and meat dishes are also recommended —try the *pescado sarandeado* (barbequed red snapper) or the chicken with *mole* sauce. While some dishes can be hard to fault, consistency is reputedly an issue.

Mon–Sat noon–3, 5–10.30
L $15, D $19, Wine $15

LA RÉPUBLICA

Avenida Morelos and 20 de Noviembre, Cabo San Lucas
Tel (624) 143 34 00

La République is one of Cabo's most romantic and expensive restaurants. Regional Mexican dishes with international twists, from three-corn *tortilla* soup to filet mignon in a *guajillo* (burgundy-colored chili pepper) sauce or lamb in *chipotle* sauce, are served on a candlelit patio, with fountains, traditional music and Mexican artworks providing the perfect backdrop for Mexican gastronomy at its finest.

Daily 6pm–11pm
D $23, Wine $19

SANCHO PANZA

Plaza las Glorias, Cabo San Lucas
Tel (624) 143 32 12

Right on the marina, Sancho is one of the most popular and liveliest restaurant-bars in Cabo, serving a delectable feast of pan-Latin tastes ranging from mussels and oysters to lasagna, Cuban fried chicken, cheese fondue and several inventive and bountiful salads. Throughout the spacious dining room a mood of arty elegance prevails with decorations inspired by Dalí, Miró and Picasso, and a collection of Cuban paintings. There is live jazz, salsa and merengue every evening, excellent service and very fair prices—by international standards.

Mon–Sat 11.30am–1am
L $16, D $22, Wine $18

CHIHUAHUA

TONY'S

Avenida Juárez 3901, Chihuahua
Tel (614) 460 29 88

Steeped in the ranching traditions of Chihuahua, this highly regarded restaurant which opened in the 1950s is something of a local institution. The setting, a classical-style adobe building, decorated with photographs of Chihuahua's local legends, is as engaging as the food is satisfying. Huge steaks and succulent *carne asado* (roasted or barbecued meat) are the house specials, served with generous portions of rice, *tortillas* and guacamole. Vegetarians should think twice.

Mon–Sat noon–9.30
L $S17, D $23, Wine $17

ENSENADA

EL CHARRO

Avenida López Mateos 454, Ensenada
Tel (646) 178 38 81

It is hard to miss the aroma of spit-roasted chicken that exudes from El Charro, the locals' favorite. A simple but tasty Mexican repertoire ranges from fresh homemade tortillas with guacamole to fish and meat *tacos* and *burritos*, and even the Oaxacan dish of chicken smothered with deep-flavored *mole*. Serving the masses in a satisfyingly unpolished closet-sized setting since the 1950s, El Charro is worth visiting as much for the gregarious ambience as for excellent cooking. No credit cards.

Daily 11.30am–2am
L $8, D $12, Wine $12

LA EMBOTELLADORA VIEJA

Avenida Miramar 666 and Calle 7, Ensenada
Tel (646) 174 16 60

This smart, Mediterranean-influenced restaurant has a gastronomic panache that makes it arguably the best restaurant in town. Located in the ageing room of the Bodega de Santo Tomás, the Gothic interior with candelabras and exposed brickwork fuses decadence and sophistication with aplomb. The menu has excellent fish, seafood and meat dishes, served with an inspired selection of sauces and a monumental wine list.

Tue, Wed 11.30–10, Thu–Sat 11.30–11, Sun 11.30–5
L $14, D $20, Wine $17

LORETO

CAFÉ OLÉ

Calle Madero 14, Loreto
Tel (613) 135 04 95

Right on the main square in the middle of town, this vibrant and inexpensive café is a great stop-off for breakfasts, light lunches, snacks, decadent cakes and pastries, smoothies, milkshakes and a medley of coffee varieties. The breakfast special is eggs with *nopal* (cactus), but *huevos rancheros*, fish tacos and seafood omelettes all feature on the broad menu and all are more than satisfying. Burgers and chicken dishes cater for the more carnivorous. No credit cards.

Mon–Sat 7am–10pm, Sun 7am–2pm
L and D $11

CHILE WILLIE
Calle López Mateo, Loreto
Tel (613) 135 06 77
On the waterfront at the northern end of the beach, this fine *palapa*-style restaurant has an inventive selection of fish and seafood dishes. The menu is an eclectic fusion of exotic Pan-Latin cuisine and wholesome American classics. Begin with an appetizer of choco clams—named for their color, not taste—followed by a fresh fillet of grilled fish doused in a heady liqueur sauce. Be sure to leave room for one of the delicious American-style diner desserts such as chocolate cake with huge peaks of ice cream swimming in chocolate sauce or a slab of key lime pie.
Daily 11.30–11
L $14, D $20, Wine $15

LOS MOCHIS

EL FARALLÓN
Calle Angel Flores, Los Mochis
Tel (668) 812 14 28
El Farollón is the apogee of dining among the rather slim selection of quality restaurants in Los Mochis. Excellent seafood and fish dishes are cooked to order, or you can chose from one of the chef's special sauces or piquant marinades. The atmosphere is smart but relaxed, the dining room cool, and the attentive and friendly staff are keen to elaborate on the menu's often bewildering descriptions.
Daily 8am–midnight
L $13, D $18, Wine $14

LA PAZ

LA PAZTA
Calle Allende 36, La Paz
Tel (612) 125 11 95
One block from the *malecón*, and next door to the Hotel Mediterrané, this chichi Italian-Swiss restaurant is one of La Paz's hippest eateries. Exposed brick and contemporary art works provide the minimalist backdrop to a maximalist menu with everything from pasta to fondu, wood-oven pizza and Mediterranean meat and fish dishes. The wine list is monumental, the service discreet and the prices very reasonable by international standards. Breakfasts ($14) are also served.
Wed–Mon 7am–10pm
L $12, D $18, Wine $15

QUINTA SOL
Avenida Independenia and Calle Domínguez, La Paz
Tel (612) 122 16 92
This popular café caters to most special dietary regimes with wholesome soya products, gluten-free ingredients and vegetarian and vegan products. Salads, wholemeal sandwiches and vegetarian tacos are all fresh and tasty, and the fresh-fruit smoothies are reason alone for visiting. No credit cards.
Mon–Sat 7am–9.30pm, Sun 8am–2pm
L $9

SAN JOSE DEL CABO

DAMIANA
Plaza, San Jose del Cabo
Tel (624) 142 04 99
Damiana occupies a beautifully restored late 18th-century hacienda in the heart of town, and has several dining options, including a leafy courtyard patio, the perfect setting for an exotic synthesis of tastes and textures. Inside, a bright Mexican theme prevails with burnished orange, terra-cotta tiles and local artworks. The menu includes lobster, jumbo shrimp, filet mignon and a few Mexican vegetarian choices.
Daily 11–10.30
L $15, D $22, Wine $18

MI COCINA
Casa Natalia Hotel, Boulevard Mijares, San Jose del Cabo
Tel (624) 142 51 00
Mi Cocina is widely considered the gastronomic zenith of San Jose del Cabo. The setting is as sublime as the food, with a lush candlelit patio that is romantic, stylish and contemporary. The inspired and consistent menu injects traditional Mexican ingredients and recipes with European and Mediterranean influences. The house special is filet mignon with a rich piquant cream sauce, but the fish and seafood dishes are also delectable with succulent lobster and stir-fried jumbo shrimps. For vegetarians, there is a selection of pasta dishes.
Daily 6.30pm–10pm
D $26, Wine $19

TIJUANA

CIEN AÑOS
Calle José María Velazco 1407, Tijuana
Tel (664) 634 30 39
This classy restaurant is thought by many to be the finest in the city. Mexican *alta cocina* fuses liberally spiced traditional regional recipes, including *mole* and *chile en nogada*, with Maya-inspired twists. The more intrepid diner can munch on an appetizer of mescal worms, or else sample one of the excellent tequilas on offer.
Daily 12.30–midnight
L $15, D $20, Wine $17

LA FONDA DE ROBERTO
La Sierra Motel, Cuauhtémoc Sur Oeste 2800, Tijuana
Tel (664) 686 46 87
Just out of town, La Fonda is as popular with San Diego residents north of the border as it is with the locals. It's a veritable kitsch fest: Fountains laden with plastic fruit, flags and dolls juxtaposed with human skulls provide a kaleidoscopic backdrop. The traditional Mexican dishes are well prepared and presented. Specials include *pechuga de angel* (a breast of chicken with squash flowers), Oaxacan *mole poblano* and *dedos de Montezuma* (cactus stuffed with strips of roast beef coated with a spicy sauce).
Noon–10pm
L $12, D $16, Wine $18

TIJUANA TILLY'S
La Leña, Avenida Revolución, Tijuana
Tel (664) 685 60 24
Tilly's is a monument to historic Tijuana with atmospheric wall-to-wall black-and-white photos and a low-key, unpretentious vibe. Visitors come for the excellent steaks, seafood and Mexican dishes—all served with panache by the friendly staff.
Sun–Thu noon–midnight, Fri–Sat noon–3am
L $12, D $16, Wine $14

STAYING IN MEXICO

While Mexico may not have the range of accommodation options of other popular destinations around the world, there are many international hotel chains in the major resorts and commercially oriented large cities. There are also several small, independent hotels in the lower and middle price brackets, which are good value by US and European standards. Away from the main visitor areas and cities, though, choice becomes more limited.

Left to right: Hotel de Cortés, Mexico City; drinks on the beach; Marquis Hotel, Mexico City;

TAXES

Taxes vary from state to state. Most charge 15 percent, while others impose a 12 percent tax. There is also a hotel (or *hospedaje*) tax, ranging from between 1 percent and 4 percent, depending on the state, although it is generally levied only when a formal bill is issued.

TYPES OF ACCOMMODATION

HOTELS

- Hotels in Mexico can be described as anything from *paradores* to *posadas* (inns), from *casas de huéspedes* (guesthouses) to plain *hoteles*. The name, however, gives little clue to the standards on offer. *Paradores*, for example, bear little relation to their classy Spanish counterparts, while a *casa de huéspedes* can be a rather grand and expensive affair. Prices at the most luxurious resort hotels are the same as you'd pay in Europe and America, but they also offer the same standards of comfort and service, with English spoken almost everywhere. Prices are also usually quoted in US dollars.
- Boutique hotels are spreading across Mexico to meet international demands for more intimate luxury accommodation. Hoteles Boutique de México (www.mexicoboutiquehotels.com) is a network of these small, independent hotels, all of less than 50 rooms and many of which are refurbished 16th- and 17th-century haciendas.
- Though finding a room is rarely a problem, making reservations is a good idea in the peak season (November to April) and during busy times such as the Easter and Christmas holidays. There are often great seasonal variations in hotel prices in the main resorts and discounts can be negotiated in the low season (May to October), though this is more difficult in the most popular regions, such as Yucatán and Baja California.
- All rooms should have an official price displayed in the reception area, though this is not always a reliable guide to quality. Prices are usually based on a room rate, so sharing works out cheaper. Single rooms can cost as much as 80 percent of the price of a double. A room with a double bed (*cama matrimonial*) is normally cheaper than a room with two single beds *(doble)*. Many hotels have large family rooms.
- Check-out time from hotels is generally 11am or noon, but most establishments will be happy to store your luggage till the end of the day.
- Air-conditioning (*aire acondicionado*) adds significantly to the price of a room and often it is better to opt for the alternative of a ceiling fan (*ventilador*), unless, of course, it is unbearably hot and humid where you're staying. Except in the top hotels, air-conditioning units can be so noisy as to render sleep impossible.
- In the highlands, where it can be cold at night, especially in winter, many hotels do not have heating. The cheaper ones often provide only one blanket so you may need a sleeping bag. This applies in popular visitor bases such as San Cristóbal de las Casas, Oaxaca and Pátzcuaro.
- Hotel rooms facing the street may be noisy, so make sure you always ask for the best and quietest available room. The very cheapest hotels are normally found in abundance near bus and railway stations and markets. These often do not have 24-hour water supplies, so ask when the water is available. Also, at this end of the market, reservations can prove meaningless. Ask the hotel if there is anything you can do to secure the room and, if arriving late, make sure they know what time you plan to arrive.

CASAS DE HUÉSPEDES AND POSADAS
Smaller than hotels, and often friendlier, these offer cheap and simple accommodation, though without the services and facilities of a hotel. Some *posadas* are more like small hotels, while others are, effectively, *casas de huéspedes*.

MOTELS
Motels, particularly in northern Mexico, are extremely popular and tend to provide accessible, economical accommodation close to the main roads. Farther south, the term "motel" picks up an altogether seedier interpretation and is used by those with a car who want to get away for an hour or two with their lovers. You can recognize them by curtains over the garage and red and green lights above the door to show if the room is free or not. If you are driving, and wishing to avoid a night on the road, they can often be quite acceptable. They are usually clean, some have hot water, and in the Yucatán, they also have air-conditioning. They also tend to be less expensive than other, "more respectable," establishments.

YOUTH HOSTELS
Youth hostels (*albergues de junventud*) offer a viable alternative to budget hotels. Found mostly in tourist towns such as Oaxaca, San Cristóbal de las Casas, San Miguel de Allende and Mérida, they are usually good value, clean, safe places. While the hostels take non-members, YHA members pay a slightly reduced rate and, after about four nights, it normally works out to be cost effective to become a member. Services vary from place to place, but you often have to pay a key deposit. For information contact Hostelling Mexico I Guatemala 4, Col Centro, Mexico City, tel (55) 52 11 11 13; www.hostellingmexico.com.

CAMPING
Organized campsites in Mexico are few and far between. Those that do exist are called Trailer Parks, and are more suited to RVs or campervans. Most of the Trailer Parks are in the well-traveled parts of the country, especially Baja and the Pacific Coast. Playas Públicas, with a blue-and-white sign of a palm tree, are beaches where camping is allowed. They are usually cheap, often free, and some have shelters and basic amenities, but theft is common. Mosquito netting (*pabellón*) is available by the meter in textile shops and, sewn into a sheet sleeping bag, is adequate protection against insects. You can often camp in or near national parks, although you must speak first with the guards, and usually pay a small fee. In less official campsites, you can rent a hammock and a place to sling it for around the same price as pitching a tent.

Hotel María del Mar, Isla Mujeres; Casa Natalia, San José del Cabo; Camino Real in Loreto and Puebla

CABAÑAS
Cabañas are rustic beach huts, usually with a palm-thatch roof and a bed, or place to sling a hammock, and little else. They cost from around $5 up to $25, though some Caribbean resorts feature luxury versions that can cost up to $100!

APARTMENTS
Self-catering can work out as an economical option, especially for groups of three or more, and there are many apartments for rent in the main resorts and larger towns and cities. Fully furnished and with all modern conveniences, these can cost from as little as $300–$350 per week for a two-bed apartment. Serviced apartments with full maid service are also available, though these are more expensive. A minimum stay of two or more nights is standard practice.

MAJOR HOTEL CHAINS

NAME	DESCRIPTION	CONTACT NUMBER
Best Western	Largest hotel chain in the world with more than 120 mid- to upper-range hotels in towns and cities across Mexico	1-00 528 12 34 (toll-free); www.bestwestern.com
Camino Real	Classy Mexican chain with 18 hotels and more planned	1-800 722 64 66; www.caminoreal.com
Hyatt	Top-end international chain with five hotels and resorts in Mexico	www.hyatt.com
InterContinental	Giant international chain who own Holiday Inn and Crowne Plaza, among others. Mid- to upper-range hotels aimed at businesspeople and tourists in more than 50 towns and cities across the country	1-800 00 999 00 (toll-free) www.ichotelsgroup.com
Radisson Hotels	23 luxury hotels and resorts throughout Mexico	1-888 201 17 18; www.radisson.com

THE YUCATÁN

Accommodation in the Yucatán ranges from exclusive, classy, all-inclusive hotels that span the Riviera Maya to colonial style bed-and-breakfasts and the more rustic, ecologically oriented options within easy reach of Maya ruins. Valladolid provides a charming, economical base to explore the archaelogical sites and is a refreshing antidote to over-commercialized Cancún. Most hotels in Cancún are best arranged as part of a package holiday before you travel.

CAMPECHE

HOTEL BALUARTE

Avenida 16 de Septiembre 128, Campeche
Tel (981) 816 39 11
www.baluarte.com.mx

Hotels in Campeche may not offer the best value, compared with Mérida and other parts of Mexico, but the Baluarte is one of the city's best mid-range options. Just two blocks from the heart of the city, close to the *malecón*, the modern four-story complex has bright, functional rooms with television, and well-stocked bathrooms. There is a small pool area, restaurant and rooftop bar with nighttime views. Parking is available.

$55
102

CHETUMAL

CARIBE PRINCESA

Avenida Obregón 168, Chetumal
Tel (983) 832 09 00

Decent, good-value accommodation in Chetumal is quite hard to come by and this is about the best of the mid-range options. The building is unprepossessing and the old-fashioned lobby unintentional 1970s retro, but the rooms have all been renovated and have a relaxing, fresh feel. Cable television, good air-conditioning units and bathroom counter space add to the comfort factor. The quiet location, just a 10-minute walk from the *malécon* and a 15-minute walk from the Museo de la Cultura Maya, makes it a perfectly adequate base for a couple of nights. Parking is available.

$40
52

HOTEL LOS COCOS

Avenida Héroes 134, Chetumal
Tel (983) 832 05 44
www.hotelloscocos.com.mx

Los Cocos, on the main Avenida Héroes, a five-minute walk from the Museo de la Cultura Maya (⊳ 70), is one of the plusher options in the city, and much better value than the Holiday Inn across the road. Functional rooms are character-free, although equipped with all the basics, but the major draw in hot, humid Chetumal is the swimming pool, surrounded by palms and peaceful gardens. The café/bar (⊳ 244–245), while expensive, serves the best breakfast in town. Parking is available.

$70
85

PRICES AND SYMBOLS

Prices are for a double room for one night. Breakfast is included unless noted otherwise. All the hotels listed accept credit cards unless otherwise stated. Note that rates vary widely throughout the year.

For a key to the symbols ⊳ 2.

CHICANNÁ

CHICANNÁ ECO VILLAGE RESORT

Carretera Escarcega Km 150, Chicanná
Tel (981) 811 91 91

Ideally placed for exploring the rather inaccessible Río Bec archeological sites, this welcoming, rustic eco-lodge surrounded by lush jungle hosts an eclectic mix of travelers. Each cabin is basic but very comfortable with crisp white paintwork, private bath and a table. Also on site is a pool deck with Jacuzzi, a sociable bar area, a satellite television room, a library and hammocks strewn through the extensive gardens. The restaurant, La Biósfera, serves delicious wholesome cooking, including an intriguing banana cream soup. Parking is available.

$90–$110
32 rooms in bungalows

COBÁ

ARCHAEOLOGICAL VILLA (CLUB MED)

Domicilio Conocido, Zona Arqueologica, Cobá
Tel (985) 858 15 26

Overlooking the Cobá lakeshore and just 10 minutes' walk from the ruins, these peaceful villas in landscaped gardens provide a great base to explore (particularly early in the morning before tour groups arrive) the archaeological sites of the Maya Riviera. Family-oriented facilities include a large swimming pool, a library, a television room, a pool table, a boutique and a very good restaurant. Parking is available.

$68
40

ISLA MUJERES

AVALON REEF CLUB

Calle Zahil 7, Islote Yunke, Isla Mujeres
Tel (800) 713 81 70
www.avalonresorts.com

Guest rooms at the Avalon Reef Club overlook the azure waters of Playa Norte. The modern complex is immaculately presented with all the services and facilities you would expect in this price range. The plush rooms have queen-sized beds, fans as well as air-conditioning and cable TV. Suites have living areas, huge terraces with sweeping views and Jacuzzis. The swimming pool, with cooling lounge chairs, looks out onto the ocean. The restaurant serves excellent, very pricey, cuisine. Parking is available.

$169–$220
140

HOTEL PERLA DEL CARIBE

Avenida Francisco Madero 2, Isla Mujeres
Tel (998) 877 04 44
http://perla-del-caribe.myislamuheres.com

This hotel is enviably positioned on the northeastern

STAYING

side of the island, a stone's throw from what is virtually a private sliver of beach. The simple, neutral-toned rooms are airy, flooded with light, very clean and have decent mattresses; most have ocean views. The staff are very friendly and will usually offer discounts for longer stays. No credit cards. Parking is available.

$50

90

MARÍA DEL MAR

Avenida Carlos Larzo 1, Isla Mujeres
Tel (998) 877 01 79
www.cabanasdelmar.com

María del Mar has a variety of accommodation, from top-of-the-range, chilled-out *cabañas* to swanky rooms in the Castle complex, which are fresh and elegant, decorated in neutral magnolia shades and fully equipped with cable television, minibar and sitting area. It is also close to the nicest stretch of beach on the island. Throughout the complex, a relaxed and sociable Caribbean vibe prevails with hammocks, rocking chairs, a swimming pool and a popular bar serving excellent tropical drinks and cocktails.

Castle $121, Tower $99, *cabañas* $112

Castle complex 18, Tower complex 24, *cabañas* 31

NA BALAM

Calle Zazil-Há 118, Playa Norte, Isla Mujeres
Tel (998) 877 02 79
www.nabalam.com

Smack bang on one of the finest stretches of beach on the island, Na Balam combines a relaxed Caribbean vibe with a liberal dousing of eastern spirituality. Tropical thatched bungalows with hammocks slung from each patio, some with private pools, are scattered around labyrinthine pathways dotted with palms. White furnishings and wicker furniture predominate in the reception areas and bar/restaurant, which is one of the best on the island, with dazzling ocean views. There is yoga every morning at 9am and the hotel is often busy with groups on spiritual retreats. Parking is available.

$121 standard

42

MÉRIDA

CASA MEXILIO

Calle 68 No. 495, Mérida
Tel (999) 928 25 05/0-800 538 68 02 (US toll-free)

This elegantly restored colonial guesthouse is the best place by far to stay in the heart of Mérida. There is a romantic *mudéjar*-style courtyard, colonial antiques at every turn, a swimming pool with deck and a garden ablaze with flowers and wild vegetation. Each of the rooms is very comfortable, with Maya, Spanish and eastern themes. The staff are efficient and helpful. Mexilio is always fully booked, so reserve well in advance.

$47–$120

13

CASA SAN JUAN

Calle 62 No. 545A, Mérida
Tel (999) 923 68 23

Pablo, the flamboyant owner, has converted this colonial home into a bed-and-breakfast. It is just three blocks from the *zócalo* and within walking distance of the bus station. The seven spacious rooms with soaring ceilings, each decorated differently, are grouped around a central patio garden where sociable breakfasts are served. A new extension features two light and airy modern rooms with patio windows and kitchenettes, which are great value. Long-stay discounted rates can be arranged. Reserve as far in advance as possible. Advance payment is required and absolutely no refunds are given.

$35

7

HACIENDA XCANATUN

Carretera Mérida-Progreso Km 12, Mérida
Tel (999) 941 02 13
www.xcanatun.com

A palpable sense of history and grandeur pervades each room of this 18th-century hacienda, carefully restored by Jorge Ruz Buenfil, whose father was Alberto Luz-Lullier, the esteemed archaeologist who discovered Pakal's tomb in Palenque. It is equipped with all modern conveniences, in addition to a superlative restaurant (▷ 246), a holistic spa, two swimming pools and a garden retreat. Although some 8km (5 miles) north of Mérida, this is without doubt the most lavish option in the area. Parking is available.

$220–$305

18 suites

PLAYA DEL CARMEN

BLUE PARROT

Calle 12 and 14, Playa del Carmen
Tel (984) 873 00 83/(888) 854 44 98 (US toll-free)
www.blueparrot.com

Sociable and upbeat, the Blue Parrot attracts an eclectic mix of people with its varied accommodation options and fantastic, if pricey, bar on one of the liveliest stretches of the beach. Waterfront *palapas* with hammocks slung outside are basic, while studios and deluxe rooms come with all creature comforts. There are daily yoga classes, massages are available and there is a dive school on site. Note that music and revelry continues until 4am.

$165/$155 (deluxe/double room), beachfront *palapa* ($75)

72

CASA DE GOPOLA

Calle 2 Norte, Playa del Carmen
Tel (984) 873 00 54
www.casadegopola.com

Lush vegetation screens the Casa de Gopola, which provides a peaceful respite from the frenzy of the main strip five minutes' walk away. Large, brightly decorated rooms with large arched windows and vivid Mexican tapestries and throws are equipped with a fridge and fans. On the downside, bathrooms are basic, some rooms could do with upgrading—ask to see several—and the staff could be friendlier. No credit cards. Parking is available.

$52

15

HUL-KÚ

Avenida 20, Playa del Carmen
Tel (984) 873 00 21
www.hotelhulku.com

At the beachside hotels in Playa you'll pay a premium for dingy, basic rooms, but just a couple of streets back from the water there are some excellent-value hotels. This is one. Spotless rooms with cable television and fans are decorated with bamboo furniture and Mexican ceramics. There is a calming, leafy pool area, with hammocks, lounge chairs and plenty of reading material on hand. Good security. No credit cards.

$30

29

VALLADOLID

GENESIS EK-BALAM

Off Highway 295, Valladolid
Tel (985) 852 79 80
www.genesisretreat.com

Close to the archaeological site of Ek-Balam, 25 minutes' drive north of Valladolid, Genesis Ek-Balam is an ecological retreat with a philosophy of low-impact tourism and community integration. Each screened *cabaña* is basic but comfortable and site facilities include "eco showers," a garden bathtub, coffee shop and chemical-free bio-filtered swimming pool. There are lovely gardens in which to observe wildlife, and activities include Maya language classes. You can also rent mountain bikes to explore the nearby ruins and *cenotes*. The restaurant serves wholesome regional dishes, snacks and ice cream.

$20 per person in single or twin *cabañas*

6 *cabañas*, 3 tents

SPECIAL IN TULÚM

CABAÑAS COPAL

Tulúm Beach, Tulúm
Tel (984) 806 44 06
www.cabanascopal.com

This exotic eco-tourism complex and holistic spa makes a harmonious base from which to explore Tulúm. Perched above the spectacular beach, it has a mystical atmosphere with daily yoga classes, an excellent restaurant/bar (▷ 247) and an internet café. This is rustic chic at its finest: each serene *caseta* and *cabaña* has mosquito nets, mosaic tiled bathrooms, and the more expensive cabins have stunning panoramic views. With no electricity or phone, this is a blissful escape. Parking is available.

$65–$85 (*cabaña* for 4), $150 (*caseta*)

45 *palapas*, 15 rooms

HOTEL EL MESÓN DEL MARQUÉS

Calle 30 No. 203, Valladolid
Tel (985) 856 20 73
www.mesondelmarques.com

Character and charm emanate from this 16th-century mansion overlooking Valladolid's main square. The restaurant and lobby are decorated with magnificent chandeliers, Mexican paintings and candles, while a fountain and luxuriant vegetation add an ethereal serenity to the arcaded patio. Rooms, which vary greatly in size and quality—ask to see several—have television and telephone. There is a small manicured pool area with lounge chairs, and a laundry service is available. The staff are professional and the restaurant (▷ 247) is ideal for romantic dining. Parking is available.

$50

90

HOTEL MARÍA DE LA LUZ

Calle 42 No. 193, Valladolid
Tel (985) 856 20 71

Right on the plaza, this unassuming hotel represents very good value. The rooms vary considerably and are often on the dark and musty side, but all have cable television, noisy air-conditioning, fans and decent bathrooms. There is a small pool area and a good restaurant overlooking the action on the square, which serves buffet breakfasts for $4.50. Parking is available.

$30

69

HOTEL SAN CLEMENTE

Calle 42 No. 206, Valladolid
Tel (985) 856 22 08

This inviting hotel next to the cathedral, just off the plaza, is another of Valladolid's excellent-value lodgings options. The peaceful colonial building has plenty of character, with a lovely arcaded patio with a central fountain and benches among palms and flowers humming with birdlife. The swimming pool is equipped with lounge chairs and umbrellas, and each room is spacious and clean with cable television. The staff are friendly and helpful. Parking is available.

$34

63

SOUTHERN MEXICO

Oaxaca, one of the most popular destinations with American and European visitors, has accommodation for all tastes and budgets. At the upper end of the scale are converted monasteries with an ethereal aura, while humble pensions and family-run hotels with traditional courtyards ablaze with flowers cater for the budget-conscious visitor. Along the coast, Puerto Escondido has long been popular with backpackers, and provides an eclectic range of intimate hotels, often with a more alternative vibe. San Cristóbal de las Casas makes a great base to explore explore Chiapas, and here you will find a sprinkling of adobe hotels and converted colonial mansions.

ACAPULCO

LOS FLAMINGOS

Avenida López Mateos, Acapulco
Tel (744) 748 206 90

Los Flamingos was the favored hangout of many Hollywood greats. John Wayne, Johnny "Tarzan" Weissmuller, Cary Grant et al came here and loved it so much they bought it as their own private club. And you can see why. The views from the generous balconies, 150m (500ft) above the pounding surf, are without peer. Rooms are a little bare, with shower-only baths and most without air-conditioning, but the cooling sea breezes are compensation enough. Impeccably tended gardens, polite service and a superb restaurant add to the considerable charm and appeal. Free transport is provided to the beach and downtown.

$85–$130
46 rooms, 2 suites

HUATULCO

HOTEL POSADA ARRECIFE

Colorín 510, La Crucita, Bahias de Huatulco, Huatulco
Tel (958) 587 17 37

This is one of the newer hotels in Huatulco and one of the most economical, 15 minutes' walk from Bahía Santa Cruz and two blocks from the main square. Modern rooms may lack character, but they are fresh and airy, with a TV, a fan or air-conditioning and a safe. There is also a swimming pool, internet access, restaurant and visitor information kiosk on site. Parking is available.

$35
28

PRICES AND SYMBOLS

Prices are for a double room for one night. Breakfast is included unless noted otherwise. All the hotels listed accept credit cards unless otherwise stated. Note that rates vary widely throughout the year.

For a key to the symbols ▷ 2.

MISIÓN DE LOS ARCOS

Gardenia 902 y Tamarindo, Huatulco
Tel (958) 587 01 65
www.misiondelosarcos.com

This homey, characterful hotel in the La Crucita area makes a refreshing change from the rather impersonal, all-inclusive mega-complexes that predominate in Huatulco. Each comfortable room is elegantly finished and has air-conditioning or a fan (less expensive). There is also an excellent coffee shop-cum-ice cream parlor, internet access and a fully equipped gymnasium. Probably the best value for money in Huatulco.

$40
13

OAXACA

CASA OAXACA

Calle García Vigil 407, Oaxaca
Tel (951) 514 41 73
www.casa-oaxaca.com

Just four blocks from the *zócalo*, this distinctive hotel blends clean minimalist furnishings and artful design with elegance. The restored colonial house is popular with the Oaxacan artistic community, and international figures such as Gabriel García Marquez have dined in the restaurant (▷ 249). Guests may find that the emphasis on intimacy and the lack of some facilities that you would expect at this price, including air-conditioning and TV, may not be to their taste. However, there is a sauna.

$160
7

HOSTAL DON MARIO

Cosijopi 219, Oaxaca
Tel (915) 142 0 12
www.hostaldonmario.8m.com

Rufino Tamayo was born in this sunny colonial house in one of the loveliest areas of the city, close to the Arcos de Xochimilco. With a welcoming family feel and patios flushed with jacaranda, and adobe walls draped with creeping vines, this is a great budget choice. Spiral staircases lead to the bedrooms, spread over three floors. While basic, each room is spotless and airy with a fan, and those on the third floor have private bathrooms and access to a patio with views across the city. There is also internet access, information on tours in the area and a small handicraft shop.

$20
9

HOSTAL SANTA ROSA

Trujano 201, Oaxaca
Tel (951) 514 67 14

You'll be at the heart of the action, one block from the *zócalo*, at this pristine *hostal*. Spacious, airy rooms have cable TV, phone and ceiling fans. The large bathrooms, regularly topped up with scented goodies, are surgically scrubbed each day. There is also a tour agency in the lobby and a restaurant offering good-value *comida corrida*. Parking is available.

$45
17

MAELA
Constitución 206, Centro Histórico, Oaxaca
Tel (951) 516 60 22
www.mexonline.com/maela.htm
In a calm, leafy street, close to the Iglesia de Santo Domingo, this mid-range hotel offers great value. A wrought-iron colonial gateway and pretty patio with a central fountain leads to the small lobby decorated with chunky antique furniture. The bright and comfortable rooms with terra-cotta-tiled floors all have cable television, fans and decent-sized bathrooms with hot water. There is a pleasant café where snacks and meals are served. Parking is available.
$45
29 (all non smoking)

LAS MARIPOSAS
Piña Suárez 517, Centro Histórico, Oaxaca
Tel (951) 515 58 54
www.mexonline.com/mariposas.htm
Just four blocks west of Iglesia de Santo Domingo, this inviting adobe house is more of a cultural center than a hotel. Teresa Villareal is a gracious, interesting host and she is very knowledgeable about eco-tourism projects around Oaxaca. Hammocks are strewn from breezy patios ablaze with jacaranda, and sunny alcoves and spiral staircases lead to spotless rooms and studio apartments with small kitchenettes geared towards long-stay guests. Continental or Oaxacan breakfast (included) is served on the patio.
$40 (double room), $45 (studio)
13

STAYING

SAN PABLO HOTEL EX-CONVENTO
Fiallo 102, Oaxaca
Tel (951) 516 25 53/01-800 215 33 90 (toll-free reservations)
www.hotelsanpablo.com
Exposed brickwork, vaulted ceilings, dark cloisters and shadowy porticos evoke a monastic calm at this former 16th-century convent—one of the most luxurious options in the city. The rooms have separate sitting areas with modern appliances, well-stocked minibars and sumptuous bathrooms. Some rooms, while atmospheric, don't have windows, so ask for a room on the upper levels—one of which has a small terrace. A fine American breakfast is served in the arcaded patio. Parking is available.
$190
21

SPECIAL IN OAXACA

CAMINO REAL
Calle 5 de Mayo 300, Centro Histórico, Oaxaca
Tel (951) 516 06 11
www.caminoreal.com
The former convent of Santa Catalina, in the heart of the old town, has been converted into the internationally renowned Camino Real. There are hushed, leafy patios with ornate fountains, while the carved stone arcades are decorated with tapestries and frescoes. Rich fabrics lend a luxurious quality to each tranquil room with views onto the street or the gardens and swimming pool. Impeccable service extends to the excellent El Refectorio restaurant.
$210, $260 Camino Real Club (includes $25 restaurant), $330 junior suite
91 (all non smoking)

PALENQUE

MARGARITA AND ED
El Panchan Camping, Carretera Zona Arqueológica Km 4.5, Apartado Postal 55, Palenque
Tel (916) 341 00 63
Approximately 7km (4 miles) from Palenque, El Panchan—Maya for "heaven on earth"—is host to a fascinating mix of different philosophies, foods and intellectual interests. Don Moisés, founder of Panchan, originally came to Palenque as an archaeologist and was one of the first guides to the ruins. He bought a plot of land and started to raise a family. This is by far the plushest of the accommodation options on the site, comprising comfortable, private, thatched-roof cabins with private bath, sundeck and hot water. A mix of people, evening entertainment, interesting conversation, and more than a whiff of spirituality makes this a perfect place for immersing yourself in the mystique of Palenque. Parking is available.
$16

MAYA TULIPANES
Cañada 6, Palenque
Tel (916) 345 02 01
www.mayatulipanes.com.mx
This modern hotel has one of the best positions in Palenque. The spacious, functional rooms, with cable television and noisy air-conditioning, vary greatly, with many being rather musty and rough around the edges and all generally lacking character. However, the lovely pool area, tropical jungle and pleasant staff make up for these shortcomings. The bar/restaurant also serves very good regional food with candlelit, outdoor seating—and there is internet access. Parking is available.
$80
70

PUERTO ANGEL

CAÑÓN DEVATA
Playa del Panteón, Puerto Angel
Tel (958) 584 31 37
Here, rustic bungalows and guesthouse are surrounded by forest in a landscaped canyon—the result of an ecological project conceived by painter Mateo López. Labyrinthine pathways lead to bright, comfortable bungalows decorated with paintings and sculptures, many the work of Mateo himself. Hammocks, wonderful views, fascinating hosts and an excellent organic restaurant add to the appeal of the *posada*, which is often booked months in advance. Reservations advised. No credit cards.
$35–$50 (bungalows), $25 (guesthouse)
21
Closed May and Jun

PUERTO ESCONDIDO

ALDEA DEL BAZAR
Benito Juárez 7, Fracc. Bacocho, Puerto Escondido
Tel (954) 582 05 08
A veritable sultan's palace, the Aldea del Bazar extends its Moorish theme to the staff, kitted out in Middle Eastern garb. While the rooms are comfortable and spacious, many with twin and double beds and a

sitting room, making it a good choice for families, it's the range of facilities, including an expansive lush garden with palms, a pool, a *temazcal* (pre-Hispanic sauna), and a restaurant serving highly rated cuisine, that makes this hotel so appealing.
$70
47

CASTILLO DE REYES
Avenida Pérez Gasga 210, Puerto Escondido
Tel (954) 582 04 42

While it may lack some creature comforts, this small, unpretentious, friendly hotel is an excellent budget choice. No-frills, clean, airy and quiet rooms have decent bathrooms, piping hot water and firm beds. Some rooms are air-conditioned, but all have fans. The staff are extremely helpful and knowledgeable, and the many long-term and repeat guests testify to the hotel's popularity. No credit cards.
$20
18
Some rooms

SAN CRISTÓBAL DE LAS CASAS

CASA MEXICANA
28 de Agosto 1, San Cristóbal de las Casas
Tel (967) 678 06 98
www.hotelcasamexicana.com
Two blocks from the cathedral, this intimate and romantic hotel bears the imprint of its owner, local artist Kiki Suárez, who also owns the Paloma restaurant (▷ 251). There is a tropical greenhouse overflowing with banana trees, fountains and flowers, a collection of sculptures and paintings, stained-glass windows and a colonial patio. Comfortable, inviting rooms are well equipped with cable television and spacious bathrooms, and services include a boutique, room service, massage and a conference room. On the downside, service can be brusque. Parking is available.
$75
52, 3 suites

MANSIÓN DE LOS ANGELES
Francisco I Madero 17, San Cristóbal de las Casas
Tel (967) 678 11 73
www.mansiondelvalle.com
This elegant, neoclassical building has been converted to a stylish hotel with great facilities, a colonial look and faultless service. All rooms have cable television, telephone and safes. There is a lovely courtyard restaurant, El Patio, which serves extensive buffets and à la carte dishes.
$80
20

NA BOLOM
Vicente Guerrero 33, San Cristóbal de las Casas
Tel (967) 678 14 18
The house where archaeologist Franz Blum and his wife, Gertrude, a Swiss photographer and fervent campaigner for the preservation of the Lacandón Indians, lived is now a cultural complex and guesthouse (▷ 96). Each room has a private bathroom and fireplace and guests enjoy free access to the museum and library. A buffet-style meal is served at 7pm and guests, staff and volunteers from the center sit together at the long dining table where Frida Kahlo, Diego Rivera and François Mitterand—to name a few—were once entertained. For those interested in learning more about the indigenous cultures of Chiapas, this is a must. No credit cards. Parking is available.
$70
15

POSADA EL PARAÍSO
Avenida 5 de Febrero 19, San Cristóbal de las Casas
Tel (967) 678 00 85
www.hotelposadaparaiso.com
Everything in this Mexican-Swiss-owned hotel, from the reception area to the bright

patio bedrooms, is impeccably finished. Decorated throughout in tones of siena and aquamarine, each pristine room has high ceilings with exposed beams, brick bathrooms, comfortable beds, a desk and a telephone. The restaurant serves pricey but faultless food.
$44
14

TUXTLA GUTIÉRREZ

CAMINO REAL
Belisario Dominguez 1195, Tuxtla Gutiérrez
Tel (961) 617 77 77
This modern, five-floor hotel is one of the best in Tuxtla, combining modern conveniences with fabulous service and intoxicating jungle surroundings. The rooms are first class, with cable TV and lavish bathrooms. The *cenote*-style swimming pool, sauna, gym, massage rooms and excellent restaurant make this a great place for tired visitors to relax and be pampered for a few days. Parking is available.
$95
210

VILLAHERMOSA

CENCALI
Juárez y Paseo Tabasco, Villahermosa
Tel (993) 315 19 99
www.cancali.com.mx
Just five minutes' walk from the middle of Villahermosa, this superlative hotel offers excellent value for money. Plush carpeted rooms include balconies, cable TV and bathrooms with tubs. An aura of tranquility and efficiency pervades throughout. The restaurant serves a particularly delicious and abundant breakfast. Parking is available.
$85
120

MEXICO CITY

There are options in Mexico City to suit all tastes and budgets—from hostels to dependable international chains. Excellent accommodation can be found in and around the *zócalo*, as well as around the Alameda. These central locations aren't just the preserve of the top-class hotels—there are some superb budget and mid-range options here, too. The chic district of Polanco offers classy hotels, although this area is not as easy to negotiate on foot as the pedestrian-friendly heart. And then there's the Zona Rosa, popular with business travelers, but equally convenient for restaurants, shopping and nightlife.

PRICES AND SYMBOLS

Prices are for a double room for one night. Breakfast is included unless noted otherwise. All the hotels listed accept credit cards unless otherwise stated. Note that rates vary widely throughout the year.

For a key to the symbols ▷ 2.

CAMINO REAL
Avenida Mariano Escobedo 700, Polanco
Tel (55) 52 63 88 88
www.caminoreal.com/mexico/

Designed by Mexican architect Luis Barragán and opened in 1968, the Camino Real, just minutes from the Museo Nacional de Antropología, is a luxury hotel imbued with daring style. Influenced by pre-Hispanic pyramids and colonial haciendas, the hotel also has a futuristic Starship Enterprise feel to it. Add bubbling fountains and bold colors and you have a wonderfully original hotel. Style aside, there's also a tennis club, spa, massage parlor, swimming pool and gym, as well as a 24-hour café, three restaurants and a trendy bar. All rooms have a view of the attractive gardens, the pool or the interior patios, and are agreeably, if less daringly, furnished.
$175 weekdays; $105 weekends, excluding breakfast ($8)
714
Chapultepec, Polanco

LA CASONA
Avenida Durango 280, corner with Cozumel, Polanco
Tel (55) 52 86 30 01
www.hotellacasona.com.mx
An exquisite pink mansion listed by the National Institute of Fine Arts as a protected building is home to this small and utterly delightful hotel three blocks from metro Sevilla and within 10 minutes' walk of the Bosque de Chapultepec. The lobby is furnished with antique English dressers, while watercolors and Mexican masks adorn the walls. The dining room leads out to a pretty patio with stylish tiled fountain. Rooms are all individually decorated, and are without exception light and pleasant.
$145 including American breakfast
29 (12 non-smoking)
Sevilla

CENTURY
Avenida Liverpool 152, Zona Rosa
Tel (55) 57 26 99 11
www.century.com.mx
A stone's throw from Avenida Insurgentes, the towering Hotel Century caters for a business clientele and offers all the facilities you would expect from its five stars. Views from the outdoor pool on the 22nd story are spectacular. The bedrooms are large, with thick carpets and gleaming bathrooms with large round bathtubs, but otherwise unimaginative. Next door is the excellent Restaurante Los Murales (daily 8am–11pm) offering a mouthwatering breakfasts ($4). Valet parking is available.
$110 including Continental breakfast
140
Outdoor
Insurgentes

GILLOW
Calle Isabel la Católica 17
Tel (55) 55 10 07 91
Next door to the imposing (and sinking) Iglesia de la Profesa, just two blocks from the *zócalo*, this hotel offers an unpretentious atmosphere in a pleasant setting. The airy rooms—all with large beds, writing desks and enormous closets—are built around a tall central well, and those with the best views are on the sixth floor. The restaurant, the Capilla, offers good-value three-course set meals for $8.
$50 excluding breakfast ($4)
103
Allende

HOLIDAY INN
Avenida 5 de Mayo 61
Tel (55) 55 21 21 21
www.holidayinnzocalo.com.mx

Breakfast on the sunny sixth-floor terrace with fantastic views over the *zócalo* is the highlight of this gleaming, swanky hotel. Once the residence of Hernán Cortés, it occupies one of the original colonial buildings on the square. Although a little small, bedrooms have all the expected conveniences and are painted in pastel hues. The super location, slick service and elegant furnishings make this an excellent central choice. Parking is available.
$110 excluding breakfast ($10)
110
Zócalo

STAYING

HOSTAL MONEDA
Calle Moneda 8
Tel (55) 55 22 58 21
www.hostalmoneda.com.mx
The friendly Hostal Moneda is located in the heart of downtown, just one block east of the cathedral, with easy access to Chapultepec Park and Coyoacán. Breakfast is served on the sunny rooftop terrace, which has splendid views of the cathedral. Each room is equipped with lockers and hot water, and internet access is available in the reception area. Other facilities include a laundry and tourist information.
Private rooms and dorms (4, 7 or 10 beds) starting at $10 per person
37
Zócalo

HOTEL DE CORTÉS
Avenida Hidalgo 85
Tel (55) 55 18 21 81/86
www.hoteldecortes.com

This Best Western hotel at the northwestern end of the Alameda is a baroque-style. 17th-century former pilgrims' guesthouse. The rooms overlook the pleasant, brightly painted central courtyard, where breakfast is served, so they can be a little dark. Children under 12 free. Valet parking is available.
$137
29, including 10 suites (12 non-smoking)
Hidalgo

HOTEL SUITES AMBERES
Calle Amberes 64, Zona Rosa
Tel (55) 55 33 13 06
www.suitesamberes.com.mx
Just five minutes' walk from the Insurgentes metro stop is this very pleasant complex of comfortable studio apartments for long stays. The airy apartments come with a fully equipped kitchenette, lounge, terrace, TV television and internet access. Some can sleep up to six people. There is also a rooftop gym and sauna with superb views over the city.
$133 (prices are negotiable for stays longer than 7 days)
28 apartments
Insurgentes

HOTEL TOLEDO
Avenida López 22
Tel (55) 55 21 50 79/55 21 32 49
This budget hotel's superb location—halfway between Bellas Artes and San Juan de Letrán metro stations—is its greatest asset. The convenience of being within a one-minute walk from several budget breakfast and lunch cafés, an ATM and a Sanborn's more than makes up for the fact that the Toledo is past its heyday. Carpets are frayed but rooms are kept clean and all have television. Prices are good for people on their own too. No breakfast room.
$21 excluding breakfast
58
Belles Artes, San Juan de Letrán

ISABEL
Calle Isabel la Católica 63
Tel (55) 55 18 12 13/17
www.hotel-isabel.com.mx
Two blocks from the *zócalo*, the friendly staff and relaxed atmosphere of the Isabel provide welcome respite from the busy pavements outside. The lobby is gloriously original—its orange and blue walls are decorated with ersatz coats of arms with matching axes and swords. The same vivid hues decorate the pleasantly light central patio, around which the large though slightly shabby rooms are grouped. Wrought-iron balconies offer a chance to observe street life below, at least as long as you can stand the fumes.
$45 excluding breakfast ($3.50)
71
Isabel la Católica, Allende

JUÁREZ
Avenida 5 de Mayo 17
Tel (55) 55 12 69 29/55 18 47 18
This small and friendly hotel tucked into a quiet alleyway just off Avenida 5 de Mayo is one of the best budget options in the city, thanks in large part to its excellent location just a minute away from the *zócalo*. Staff are friendly and the rooms, though small, are clean and pleasant and all have television—ask for one with a window. It's popular with budget visitors, so it's definitely worth booking in advance.
$15 excluding breakfast
39
Zócalo

MAJESTIC
Avenida Francisco Madero 73
Tel (55) 55 21 86 00; from US 1-800 528 12 34
www.majestic.com.mx
At the heart of the action on the *zócalo* itself, this elegant hotel occupies a grand and imposing 16th-century building. The attractive lobby, however, is a haven of tranquil Moroccan arches, Spanish tiles and palms. The quiet rooms overlooking the central courtyard are all decorated in a grand 1930s style with enormous beds, soft lighting and bathtubs. The breakfasts served on the seventh-floor La Terraza restaurant (▷ 255) overlooking the *zócalo*, are magnificent. Next door, the El Campanario bar is open until 2am with live music from 7.30pm. Valet parking is available.
$120 excluding breakfast ($4)
85 including 5 suites
Zócalo

MANAGUA
Plaza de San Fernando 11
Tel (55) 55 12 13 12/55 21 49 61
Rooms in this popular budget option are basic but the hotel is 200m (220 yards) from metro Hidalgo, putting you within minutes of the Alameda, not to mention good-value eateries and internet cafés. The quiet square and helpful staff are other pluses. Reservations are recommended.
$17 excluding breakfast ($3)
75
Hidalgo

MARCO POLO
Calle Amberes 27, Zona Rosa
Tel (55) 55 11 18 39
www.marcopolo.com.mx
Small but stylish, the Marco Polo offers everything you need for a comfortable and luxurious stay. Bedrooms are sumptuously furnished—all include a lounge—while bath-

rooms are glitteringly pristine. Also featured in each room are internet access and a bar with complimentary fruit and coffee. Valet parking is available.

$90
60, 4 penthouse suites with Jacuzzi, 12 suites for longer stays

Insurgentes

MARIA CRISTINA
Río Lerma 31, Zona Rosa
Tel (55) 57 03 12 12/55 66 96 88
www.hotelmariacristina.com.mx

A block from La Reforma in the quieter and nicer part of the Zona Rosa, this charming and spacious hotel is decorated in the style of an Andalusian Moorish palace: a blue-and-white tiled lobby with heavy mahogany furniture and wrought-iron chandeliers leads to tranquil interior patios and gardens around trickling fountains. Bedrooms are well appointed, attractive and quiet, and delicious breakfasts are served in the adjoining Río Nansa Restaurant. Parking is available.
$70 excluding breakfast ($5)
148, including 8 suites with Jacuzzi
Insurgentes

MARLOWE
Avenida Independencia 17
Tel (55) 55 21 95 40
México City's airport tourist office refers many visitors to this modern mid-range hotel just one block from Bellas

Artes and the Alameda, and it's easy to see why. This makes a pleasant, simple base offering good value in an excellent location. Rooms are kept scrupulously clean, staff are professional and there is a gym, sauna and restaurant.
$44 excluding breakfast ($5)
105
Bellas Artes

REPÚBLICA
Calle Cuba 57
Tel (55) 55 12 95 17
The República is a good budget option in down-to-earth Calle Cuba, just beyond the more prominently touristy streets to the south yet between the Alameda and *Zócalo*. Rooms with painted wooden balconies surround a central patio, and faded 1950s furniture adds to the charm.
$25 excluding breakfast
53
Allende

EL ROBLE
Calle Uruguay 109
Tel (55) 55 22 78 30/55 22 80 83
www.hotelroble.com.mx
El Roble is the best value mid-range hotel in the vicinity. The polished marbled reception is appealing, as are the rooms, which, although a little dark, are well appointed, clean and carpeted—all with television. Parking is available ($3 per day).
$25 excluding breakfast ($3)
61
Zócalo

EL SALVADOR
Avenida República del Salvador 16
Tel (55) 55 21 12 47/55 21 10 08
www.hotelelsalvador.com
The bustling market street of El Salvador, 10 minutes' walk from Bellas Artes, surrounds this good-value, 3-star option in the city's historic heart. The marble and mirrored lobby is spacious, and bedrooms, although small and conventional, are modern and comfortable. A lively restaurant serves set breakfasts for $3 and an excellent-value four-course *comida corrida* for $6.
$32 excluding breakfast ($3)
110
San Juan de Letrán

SHERATON CENTRO HISTÓRICO
Avenida Juárez 70
Tel (55) 51 30 53 00
www.sheratonmexico.com

The 26-floor Sheraton has fabulous views across the park and east towards Reforma. Opened in 2003, this luxurious hotel, a study in understated elegance, has spacious rooms decorated in cool pastel shades and furnished in stylish dark mahogany. Sliding doors, marble bathrooms and intelligent sensor lighting all add to the Zen-like calm. Modern facilities include satellite television, internet access and a sauna.
$265 excluding breakfast ($8)
427
Hidalgo

VIENA
Calle Marsella 28, corner with Calle Dinamarca, Zona Rosa
Tel (55) 55 66 07 00
This is a friendly, modern, mid-range hotel in the less raucous part of the Zona Rosa on the east side of Avenida Insurgentes. Rooms are decorated in a bright modern colonial style and are all light and clean, with large windows and decent mattresses. There is a jolly mock-alpine restaurant on the ground floor where good-value breakfast is served. Parking is available.
$44 excluding breakfast ($4)
88
Insurgentes, Cuauhtémoc

CENTRAL MEXICO EAST

This region has no shortage of accommodation across the range: luxury 5-star hotels, attractive and family-run middle range *posadas*, and basic hostels. The most unusual places to stay are the "boutique" hotels that occupy converted convents or haciendas. The colonial heartland around Taxco, Cuernavaca and Puebla has some spectacular examples, where rooms individually decorated with antique furniture cluster around gorgeous interior patios. Invariably, they are charming and imaginative and give the visitor a real taste of wealthy colonial Mexico.

Plenty of attractive colonial homes have been converted into comfortable family *posadas*—unpretentious, intimate and extremely good value for European and American visitors.

Two-star hotels and cheap hostels abound in all the major cities, although they tend to be better kept and cleaner in the smaller, provincial towns. Veracruz offers large, modern beach hotels along its *malecón* and in Boca del Río, the new resort 7km (4 miles) away along the coast. Other than here, however, you are unlikely to experience many impersonal, western chain hotels.

Veracruz is completely full around Carnival (the week before Lent), so book ahead. Christmas and New Year, as well as Semana Santa (Holy Week), are busy across the region; again reservations are essential.

CATEMACO

PARQUE ECOLÓGICO NANCIYAGA

Catemaco-Coyame Road Km 7, Catemaco
Tel (294) 943 01 99
www.nanciyaga.com

Situated in the most northerly stretch of tropical rain forest on the planet, 7km (4 miles) from Catemaco on the northern side of Lake Catemaco, this eco-lodge is one of the most original places to stay in southern Veracruz. Comfortable wooden cabins with verandas and hammocks are scattered among the trees. There are canoes for rent, and swimming in the healing spring waters, aromatherapy massages, guided walks in the jungle and a *temazcal* spiritual treatment are all on offer for an extra fee.

$65

10 cabins with fans

COATEPEC

POSADA COATEPEC

Calle Hidalgo 9, Coatepec
Tel (228) 816 05 44

This magnificent hacienda in the middle of Coatepec has a flower-filled interior patio painted with detailed frescoes, 19th-century furniture, vases and a Victorian carriage. Rooms are individually decorated with enormous beds, soft lighting and attractively tiled bathrooms. An ivy-covered walled garden, a swimming pool, a fountain and a sauna add to the appeal.

$88 including Continental breakfast; suites $135

22, 10 with air-conditioning

Some Outdoor

PRICES AND SYMBOLS

Prices are for a double room for one night. Breakfast is included unless noted otherwise. All the hotels listed accept credit cards unless otherwise stated. Note that rates vary widely throughout the year.

For a key to the symbols ▷ 2.

CUERNAVACA

CASA COLONIAL

Calle Netzahualcoyotl 37, Cuernavaca
Tel (777) 312 70 33

This understated, luxurious hotel stands opposite the cathedral, in the heart of Cuernavaca, known as the City of Eternal Spring. It occupies an 18th-century house and garden, and features lofty, beamed ceilings, open fires, heavy dark wood furniture and antique chests. The rooms are all individually decorated and have gleaming, traditionally tiled bathrooms, perfect white linen, terra-cotta-tiled floors and softly lit lanterns.

$80 (at weekends $95); Continental breakfast in hotel restaurant $3.70

16

PACHUCA

HOTEL DE LOS BAÑOS

Calle Matamoros 205, Pachuca
Tel (771) 713 07 00

The corridor leading to the reception of this excellent-value hotel, just one block from the *zócalo*, is lined with gilt mirrors and tiles. More blue-and-white tiles cover the central, enclosed patio of this 19th-century building. Rooms are carpeted and comfortable, with elaborately carved wooden furniture.

$24

56

PUEBLA

CAMINO REAL PUEBLA

Calle 7 Poniente 105, Puebla
Tel (222) 229 09 09
www.caminoreal.com/puebla/

One block from the *zócalo*, this sumptuous hotel occupies the reconverted and beautifully restored El Convento de la Concepción. Founded in 1593, it was a functioning convent until 1861, when it was used as a military barracks. Rooms surround the two interior stone patios, whose deep-yellow walls are covered with their original flowery frescoes, and are exquisitely furnished with huge oak beds, antique wardrobes and colonial-era art. The elegant El Convento restaurant offers exquisite international and Mexican dishes. Parking is available.

$197 ($105 on weekends) excluding breakfast

84 rooms and suites

STAYING

MESÓN SACRISTÍA DE LA COMPAÑÍA
6 Sur 304, Callejón de los Sapos, Puebla
Tel (222) 242 35 54
www.hotelsboutique.com/mesonsacristia
This boutique hotel in a 200-year-old building near the Plazuela de los Sapos has individually and elegantly decorated rooms with four-poster beds, antique dressers, Talavera pottery and exquisite gold-leaf details around the door frames. The public areas are crammed with beautiful objects and paintings, but luckily everything you see in the hotel is for sale, should you fall in love with something. There is also an antique shop on site. Parking is available.
$170
9

TAXCO

AGUA ESCONDIDO
Plaza de la Borda 4, Taxco
Tel (762) 622 11 66

Hotel Agua Escondida put you right at the heart of things, in the *zócalo* district of the town. This great value hotel has the amenities of its larger competitors, such as a swimming pool, restaurant and café/bar, with the added benefits of friendly service and a vibrant, typically Mexican atmosphere. Just sit back on the terrace and enjoy the views of the parish church of Santa Prisca (▷ 130).
$67
50

LOS ARCOS
Juan Ruiz de Alarcón 4, Taxco
Tel (762) 622 18 36
Just one block down the hill from the Plaza Borda, this colonial mansion is set around a delightful courtyard shaded by a handsome jacaranda tree. The lobby is in the former carriageway, opening out onto the stone arches of the courtyard. Rooms are pleasant and bathrooms sparklingly clean. There is a fantastic roof terrace with views of Santa Prisca and the town spreading into the valley below.
$42 excluding breakfast (plenty of cafés serving breakfast in nearby Plaza Borda)
21

TEPOZTLÁN

POSADA DEL TEPOZTECO
Calle Paraíso 3, Tepoztlán
Tel (739) 395 00 10
www.posadadeltepozteco.com.mx
Surely the loveliest place to stay in Morelos state, this beautifully renovated colonial hacienda affords spectacular views over the Tepozteco National Park from its gardens and terraces. The rooms are large, many with a private terrace and Jacuzzi, and the restaurant extends into the flower garden, where there is an ivy-covered fountain and a pleasantly shaded pergola for relaxed al fresco dining.

$140
20 (including 6 suites)

TLACOTALPÁN

POSADA DOÑA LALA
Calle Carranza 11, Tlacotalpán
Tel (288) 884 25 80
Situated on the *zócalo*, with a breezy restaurant terrace at the rear looking over the river promenade, this family-run and very friendly hotel offers simple but attractive rooms with high ceilings, large dark wood beds and crisp white sheets. There is also a pretty garden with a swimming pool and a family restaurant. Parking is available.
$25 excluding breakfast ($2.50)
15
Some rooms
Outdoor

VERACRUZ

GRAN HOTEL DILIGENCIAS
Calle Independencia 1115, Veracruz
Tel (229) 923 02 80
This modern 5-star hotel takes pride of place on the *zócalo*. The grand, marble-covered reception with cool white decor employs extremely efficient, English-speaking staff. Rooms are immaculate if a little soulless. The terrace overlooking the square has an inviting pool and sun-lounge area. Valet parking is available.
$130
60

MOCAMBO
Boulevard Ruiz Cortinez 4000, Mocambo Beach, Veracruz
Tel (229) 922 02 02
www.hotelmocambo.com.mx
This fabulous hotel, 8km (5 miles) south of Veracruz, was built in the 1930s and still retains its air of grandeur, albeit somewhat faded. Its palatial art deco interior is bright and airy. The rooms have air-conditioning, TV and balcony with a view of the gardens or the ocean.

$70–80
123

XALAPA

MESÓN DEL ALFÉREZ
Calle Sebastián Camacho 2–6, corner with Calle Zarargoza, Xalapa
Tel (228) 818 80 113
This is the pleasantest place to stay in the middle of town. Rooms in the converted colonial house are brightly painted, furnished in rustic farmhouse style and open onto the central patio. Rooms looking onto the congested street side can be noisy, so opt for an interior one. Children under 10 stay free.
$32
20, including 2-floor suites

CENTRAL MEXICO WEST

For visitors looking for something different, Central Mexico West offers some true gems—dull concrete towers needn't figure on your itinerary. There is a good choice of hotels, ranging from colonial mansions to idyllic beach eco-resorts.

There's no better way to get a feel for Mexico's colonial past than to stay in its outstanding buildings—from monasteries to mints—where the past comes alive. In the towns of the Bajío, from Zacatecas to Querétaro, and in Jalisco and Michoacán, protected historic monuments with courtyards, fountains and grandiose stairways are now hotels—the Quinta Real in Zacatecas must surely rank as one of the world's most original. To appreciate its transformation, don't miss the photographs of how the bullring looked in the 1950s.

And what's more, you won't necessarily have to pay through the nose for the privilege of staying in such marvelous locations. For visitors from the US and Europe, some of the prices are a bargain given the luxury on offer.

On the coast, you can really get away from it all in exquisite boutique beach hotels where peace and quiet, private beaches and healthy eating are all the norm. You'll need to book in advance though, as these are small, exclusive places with a loyal customer base who, not surprisingly, come back year after year.

BARRA DE NAVIDAD

HOTEL LAS VILLITAS

López de la Gaspez 127, Barra de Navidad
Tel (315) 355 53 54

In the heart of Barra de Navidad, this is a great boutique hotel with its own private entrance to the beach. The comfortable rooms have vaulted ceilings, spacious closets and thick mattresses on enormous beds. The terrace overlooking the beach, with a large Jacuzzi and attractive bamboo loungers, is a perfect place to watch the sunset. Booking essential in summer months.

$60 excluding breakfast (available for $4 per head)
8, including 2 with sea views

GUADALAJARA

HOTEL FRANCÉS

Maestranza 35, Guadalajara
Tel (33) 361 311 90

One block south of the Plaza de Armas, this is Guadalajara's oldest hotel and a protected monument. Rooms are grouped around a two-tiered covered courtyard with a marble fountain, a chandelier and a wonderful old elevator—all with gleaming brass fittings. Rooms are comfortable and elegantly furnished in sober oak with cream walls. Warning for those who go to bed early: on Friday nights from 9pm to 10pm there is *mariachi* music in the lobby. Parking is available.

$50 excluding breakfast ($6)
60, including 10 suites

PRICES AND SYMBOLS

Prices are for a double room for one night. Breakfast is included unless noted otherwise. All the hotels listed accept credit cards unless otherwise stated. Note that rates vary widely throughout the year.

For a key to the symbols ▷ 2.

GUANAJUATO

HOSTAL CANTARRANAS

Cantarranas 50, Guanajuato
Tel (473) 732 52 41

A superb budget option in the heart of Guanajuato, just half a block from the Teatro Juárez and two minutes' walk from the Jardín de la Unión. Rooms are comfortable and clean; some have kitchenettes and others cater to groups as large as six. There is also a roof terrace with superb views up to the Pípila. No credit cards.

$28 in low season, $40 in high season (excluding breakfast)
12

HOSTERIA DEL FRAYLE

Sopeña 3, Guanajuato
Tel (473) 732 11 79

Housed in Guanajuato's original mint, founded in 1673, this is a marvelously convenient hotel just a block from the Jardín de la Unión. Well-appointed rooms are decorated with antiques and colonial religious art; some have balconies and handsome, high windows looking out onto the street below. Staff are professional and friendly. This is a perfect place to be for the Festival Cervantino, although it can be noisy. Amex cards not accepted.

$80 excluding breakfast ($5)
37, including 5 suites

MORELIA

LA CASA DE LAS ROSAS

Guillermo Prieto 125, Morelia
Tel (443) 312 45 45

This tiny hotel is in Morelia's colonial heart, halfway between the Plaza de Armas and the Jardín de las Rosas. Its motto might well be "quality, not quantity"—there are only four rooms, each exquisitely furnished and endowed with huge beds overflowing with bulging down pillows. Staff are attentive to the last detail, and cater to your every whim. Valet parking is available.

$200 excluding breakfast ($7)
4

PÁTZCUARO

MISIÓN SAN MANUEL

Portal Aldama 12, Pátzcuaro
Tel (434) 342 10 50

You'll find this atmospheric hotel in the heart of Pátzcuaro under the arches on the south side of Plaza Quiroga. Beamed balconies, antique gramophones, old typewriters and suits of armor all adorn the

lobby and interior courtyard. The carpeted rooms, meanwhile, come with corner chimney pieces, have good reading lamps and are kept spotlessly clean by the pleasant staff. Cash only. Parking is available.

$80

35

PUERTO VALLARTA

MAJAHUITAS RESORT

Majahuitas, 21km (13 miles) southwest of Puerto Vallarta
Tel (322) 293 45 06

Unforgettable luxury is the order of the day at this divine hotel (accessible only by boat) in a protected cove on the beautiful Bay of Banderas between Quimixto and Yelapa, just 15 minutes south of Puerto Vallarta. Attractive individual and duplex *casitas* (cabin houses) dot the 7ha (18 acres) of private gardens and lush jungle, filled with fruit trees and wildlife. The beach is gloriously pristine and the whole place runs on alternative energy sources. Massages, snorkeling, kayaking, fishing and hiking are all available.

$345 Nov–Apr, $236 Jun–Sep , $300 May–Oct

7 *casitas*

QUERÉTARO

LA CASA DE LA MARQUESA

Madero 41, Querétaro
Tel (442) 212 00 92
www.lacasadelamarquesa.com

A beautiful mansion built in 1756 situated one block west of the Jardín Zenéa, this sumptuous hotel is utterly charming and an aesthete's heaven. Rooms are individually decorated—the Moorish room, for instance, comes with *mudéjar* chests and an Andalucian-style bedstead. Public areas are hung with velvet curtains and scattered with chaise-longues and leather-backed armchairs. Don't forget to take a look inside the private chapel too—you can even ask for it to be set up as a private dining room.

$160

25

MESON DE SANTA ROSA

Pasteur Sur 17, Plaza de la Independencia, Querétaro
Tel (442) 224 26 23

This luxury hotel has been welcoming visitors for centuries: It use to be a caravan stop on the route to the north of the country and still has a drinking trough in the central courtyard. All rooms are tastefully decorated and have cable TV and a minibar; some have views over the central courtyard or the pool courtyard. Facilities include a sauna, Jacuzzi, boutiques, indoor and outdoor pools and a patio restaurant.

$166

21 rooms (15 suites and 6 guestrooms

SAN MIGUEL DE ALLENDE

CASA DE SIERRA NEVADA – QUINTA REAL

Hospicio 35, San Miguel de Allende
Tel (415) 152 70 40
www.quintareal.com

Five magnificently restored colonial houses comprise this beautiful hotel oozing with understated elegance. In each house, rooms are arranged around a tranquil, flower-filled patio; many have a private veranda, and all have massive oak beds, fresh flowers and intricately tiled bathrooms. This hotel is a truly a treat.

$245

33

VALLE DE BRAVO

HOTEL BATUCADA

Bocanegra 207, Valle de Bravo
Tel (726) 262 16 66

Three blocks north of the Plaza Independencia, this is a very appealing hotel ranged around an attractive courtyard with trickling fountain. The nine rooms are individually decorated, but all are furnished with beautiful antique Michoacanense chests and vases, and come with wood-burning fireplaces for cold nights. Bathrooms have antique bathtubs, spotlighting and gorgeously fluffy towels. The corridors are painted in calming sky blue. Parking is available.

$120

9

ZACATECAS

QUINTA REAL

Avenida Ignacio Rayon 434, Zacatecas
Tel (492) 922 91 04
www.quintareal.com

Standing in the shadow of Zacatecas' colonial aqueduct, the great novelty of this luxurious hotel is its incorporation into the beautiful old Plaza de Toros, which functioned as a bullring until 1976. The elegant dining room overlooks the arena, which is spectacularly lit at night and regularly used for wedding photos. Rooms are stunning, with huge beds and sparkling bathrooms. There's a silver shop on site.

$260

49

NORTHERN MEXICO AND BAJA CALIFORNIA

Camping is particularly popular in Northern Mexico and Baja California, where accommodation ranges from inexpensive campgrounds and RV parks to luxurious hotels offering world-class, all-inclusive packages.

CABO SAN LUCAS

DREAMS LOS CABOS

Los Cabos Corridor, Km 18.5 Carretera Transpeninsular
Tel (624) 145 65 00

The main draw here is undoubtably the 18-hole golf course designed Robert Trent Jones, but for non-players there's still plenty to do. This all-inclusive resort has an outdoor pool, tennis courts, a gym and spa. The studios have two double beds, a private bathroom with shower and a terrace with an ocean view. Suites have a separate bedroom with king-sized bed, private bathroom with tub, and a queen-sized sleeper sofa in the living room. The private balconies also have ocean views. All rooms have air-conditioning, satellite TV and a minibar. You can take your meals in one of the five restaurants, then relax in any of the six bars and lounges.

$236–$450
104 suites

FINISTERRA

Domicilio Conocido, Cabo San Lucas
Tel (642) 414 33 33
www.finisterra.com

Perched on promontory near "Land's End," this landmark hotel has fully appointed luxury suites and rooms with air-conditioning, television and views of the bay area. New extensions blend seamlessly with the original 1970s building, part of which was built into the rock face. Facilities include a mammoth swimming pool with a swim-up poolside bar and unsurpassed view, tennis courts and a good restaurant. And, should you get carried away by the romance of it all, there's even a wedding chapel.

$140
287
Outdoor

PRICES AND SYMBOLS

Prices are for a double room for one night. Breakfast is included unless noted otherwise. All the hotels listed accept credit cards unless otherwise stated. Note that rates vary widely throughout the year.

For a key to the symbols ▷ 2.

HACIENDA BEACH RESORT

The north entrance to the harbor, Cabo San Lucas
Tel (624) 143 06 65
www.haciendacabo.com

Dominating the southern end of the bay, this modern, lively resort, nestling in tropical gardens, is designed in traditional hacienda style. The hotel has undergone extensive renovations and offers very comfortable rooms with a fresh contemporary feel, all equipped with air-conditioning, small fridge, television and hairdryer. Activities (besides relaxing by the large pool) include tennis, various watersports, hunting, horseback-riding and parasailing.

$150
102
Outdoor

CHIHUAHUA

HOTEL PALACIO DEL SOL

Avenida Independencia 116, Chihuahua
Tel (614) 416 60 00

Handy for the main plaza, this modern hotel block provides good services and a range of facilities. Each room has a king- or queen-size bed, air-conditioning and television. While the decoration may lack imagination, and be in need of upgrading here and there, the location and amenities—which include two restaurants, a very sociable bar, room service and laundry—and the warm welcome certainly compensate.

$135
200

COPPER CANYON

HOTEL PARAISO DEL OSO

Cerocahui, Copper Canyon
Tel (614) 421 33 72
www.mexicohorse.com

In the middle of the Sierra and less then 2km (1 mile) from Cerocahui, this inviting family-run inn provides a wonderful sense of solitude. The comfortable hacienda-style rooms, with two double beds, are grouped around the central patio and powered by solar energy. A large communal dining room is where meals are served, and there's a sociable living room and a well-stocked library. Welcoming and informative host Dan Rhodes organizes horseback-riding, birdwatching and hiking trips. Reserve well ahead of time.

$155 including 3 meals per day
21

ENSENADA

PUNTA MORRO HOTEL SUITES

3km (2 miles) north of Ensenada on Highway 1, Ensenada
Tel (646) 178 35 07
www.punta-morro.com

A 20-minute stroll from the middle of town, this understated but fine hotel draws a large following of American and international guests with its superlative service, good facilities and comfortable minimalist accommodation. Each pleasantly designed room is fully equipped with air-conditioning, television, hair dryer and a kitchen with a small fridge, and all have wonderful sea views. There is an outdoor heated pool, spa and Jacuzzi, plus a good restaurant and bar. Three-bedroom apartments are available for larger groups.

$95
24
Outdoor

LA PAZ

MEDITERRÁNEO

Allende 36, La Paz
Tel/Fax: (612) 125 11 95
www.hotelmed.com

This intimate hotel overlooking the *malecón* exudes relaxed Mediterranean panache. The whitewashed hotel, set around an idyllic palm-fringed courtyard, fuses Greek and Mexican style with aplomb. Each impeccable room is named after a Greek island and varies in size and design, with original art works. The outstanding La Pazta restaurant serves Greek and Italian dishes fit for the gods. There is also internet access, and bicycles and kayaks are available for rent.

$70
5

LORIMAR

Bravo 110, La Paz
Tel (612) 125 38 22

Just two blocks from the *malecón*, this popular budget option may be lacking in creature comforts but it is very clean, has hot showers and provides an excellent base to meet fellow travelers. Run by a friendly and helpful Mexican-American couple, this is the best value for money in town by a long shot. There is a good-value restaurant and you can organize trips to Tecolote beach. No credit cards.

$27
20

LORETO

CAMINO REAL

Boulevard Misión de Loreto, Loreto
Tel (613) 133 00 10

If watching the sun rise over the Sea of Cortés is your idea of bliss, then this is the hotel for you. The Camino Real is set in its own secluded cove, and all guestrooms have stunning views of the desert, the Giganta Mountains, the Loreto Golf Course or the Sea of Cortés. All rooms have air conditioning and private bathroom, with either a tub or shower, and the suites have a Jacuzzi on the balcony. The hotel complex has two bars, one of which looks out over the Sea of Cortés, and three restaurants: Salvatierra for fine Italian food, buffet-style Guaycura serving Mexican and international food, and the Snack-Shack set in the gardens and surrounded by pools.

$140–$170
156

LA PINTA

Sea of Cortés, 2km (1 mile) north of the *zócalo*, Loreto
Tel (613) 135 00 25

In a beautiful setting right on the seafront, the hacienda-style La Pinta is a pleasantly designed complex of rooms and villas, each with cable television, air-conditioning and safe-deposit boxes. Considered by many to be the best of the original "Presidente" *paradores*, facilities include a large swimming pool, tennis courts, a restaurant and two cocktail bars. This is an ideal base for fishing enthusiasts, and there are boats for rent and organized tours.

$79
48
Outdoor

SAN JOSÉ DEL CABO

POSADA SEÑOR MAÑANA

Alvaro Obregon 1, San José del Cabo
Tel (624) 142 04 62
www.srmanana.com

In a peaceful enclave a short walk from the main square, this neat *posada* is one of the best budget options in San José del Cabo. Meandering walkways connect each of the simple, but clean and bright, rooms to the communal, well-stocked kitchen and leafy courtyard strewn with hammocks shaded by mango trees and lolling palms. It's worth looking at a selection of rooms—those on the lower level have been more recently renovated. There is also a basketball court and pool table.

$35–$58
11

PRESIDENTE INTERCONTINENTAL LOS CABOS

Zona Hotelera, San José del Cabo
Tel (624) 142 02 11
www.loscabos.interconti.com

Right on the beach, against the spectacular backdrop of the Sierra de San Lazaro Mountains, the Intercontinental is the mother of all Mexican all-inclusive resorts. A variety of accommodation packages are available and facilities cater for every whim. If your tendency is to wear your club bracelet with pride, there are six restaurants, seven bars, a cocktail lounge, travel agency, three swimming pools, three tennis courts, car rental and a nearby golf course. Rooms are a good size, well equipped with air-conditioning, television and mini bar, and the large bathrooms are amply stocked with a range of goodies.

$150–$200
402 (108 non smoking)
Outdoor (3)

TIJUANA

GRAND HOTEL TIJUANA

Boulevard Agua Caliente 4500, Tijuana
Tel (664) 681 70 00/1-800 026 60 07 (toll-free in Mexico)

The soaring, monolithic Grand Hotel is grand and lavish. Standard rooms, while rather charmless and lacking any Mexican identity, are plush and well equipped with internet access, hair dryer, mini bar and television and DVD. Extensive facilities include an impressive business complex, golf course, heated swimming pool, Jacuzzi, gym and restaurant. Staff are attentive.

$145–$195
422
Outdoor and indoor

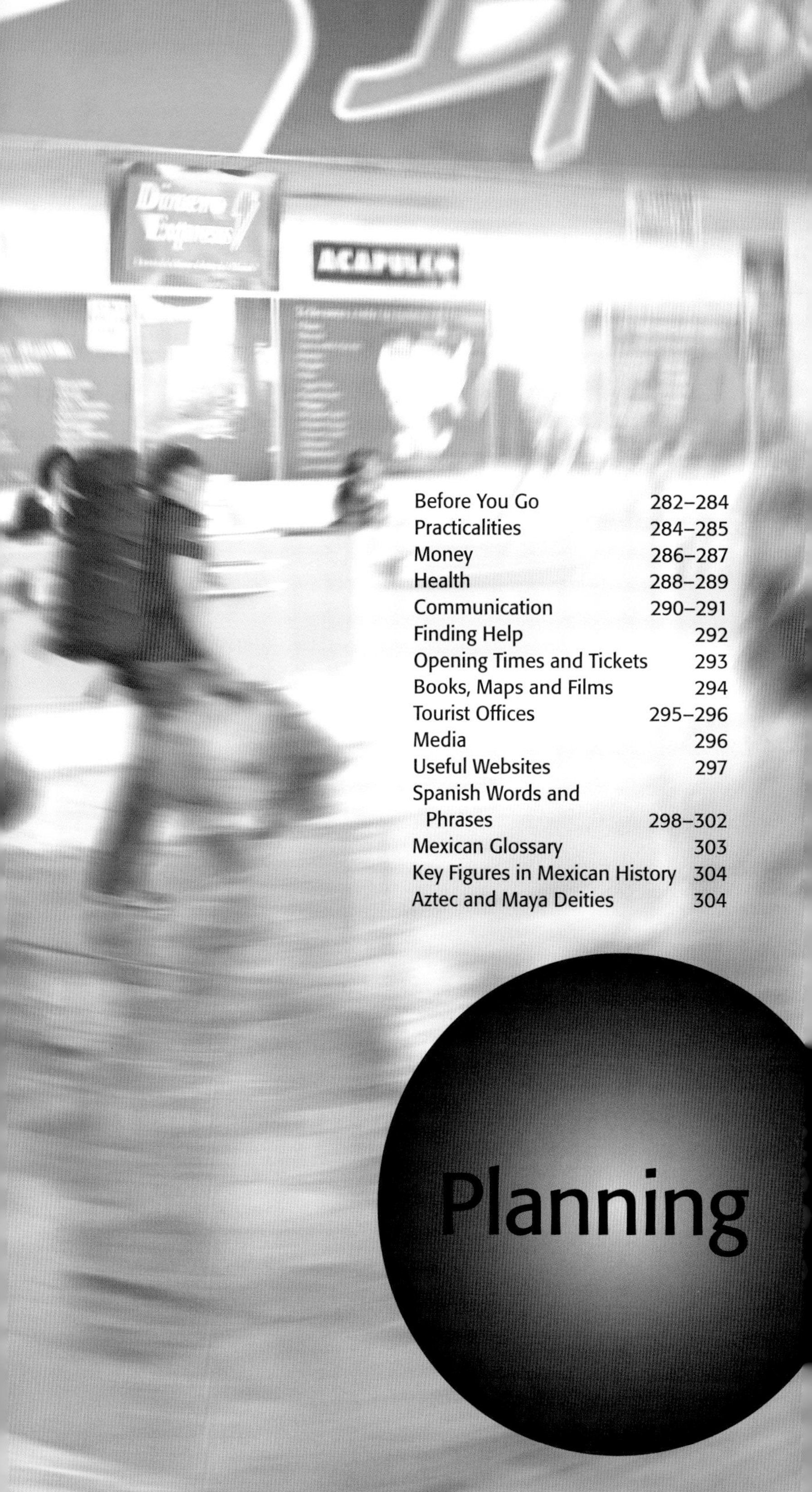

Planning

Before You Go	282–284
Practicalities	284–285
Money	286–287
Health	288–289
Communication	290–291
Finding Help	292
Opening Times and Tickets	293
Books, Maps and Films	294
Tourist Offices	295–296
Media	296
Useful Websites	297
Spanish Words and Phrases	298–302
Mexican Glossary	303
Key Figures in Mexican History	304
Aztec and Maya Deities	304

CLIMATE

In Mexico, climate—as well as scenery, vegetation and even culture—is determined by altitude rather than latitude or longitude. Along the Pacific Coast, for example, things don't change that much from north to south, but head up into the mountains and the differences are immediately apparent. It is difficult, therefore, to make too many generalizations about climate.

The best time to go is the dry season, between October and April, although there are slight regional variations. The rainy season works its way up from the south, beginning in May and running through until August, September and even October. This is also hurricane season in the Caribbean and on rare occasions the Yucatán and Gulf states get hit. Don't be put off by the term "rainy season." Most years, the rains only really affect visitors for an hour or two a day and, especially in the northern states of Baja, Sonora, Chihuahua and Coahuila, it can remain very hot and dry.

The highlands are mostly mild, but with sharp changes of temperature between day and night, sunshine and shade. There are only two areas where rain falls year-round: south of Tampico along the lower slopes of the Sierra Madre Oriental and across the Isthmus of Tehuantepec into Tabasco state; and along the Pacific coast of the state of Chiapas. In southern coastal areas it gets very hot and humid between June and September.

WHEN TO GO

Baja California is popular at different times of year for different reasons. During the winter, US and Canadian "snowbirds" head south to escape the cold and then head back when it warms up in the north. This doesn't put any real pressure upon available hotel rooms, but what does is the spring break influx of students, particularly in Baja California Norte and in the small oasis towns of Baja California Sur.

February to March are the best months for whale-watching in the Guerrero Negro area. Mid-April to mid-June is a good time to visit, too, because it is not too hot and the water is starting to warm up in the Sea of Cortés. October is also good as it is still quiet and the sea is about as warm as it is going to get.

August is vacation time for Mexicans and this can make rooms scarce in the smaller resorts and in popular places close to Mexico City. *Semana Santa* (Easter week) witnesses an exodus from parts of the capital, putting pressure on transportation to, and hotel space within, many attractive regional towns and villages. The *Día de los Muertos* (Day of the Dead) celebrations at the beginning of November and the Christmas holidays can also affect room availability.

For up-to-date weather information for your region in Mexico and for the latest hurricane reports, visit www.accuweather.com.

WHAT TO TAKE

- The key things to remember are travel and health insurance documents, money, credit cards and any medication you will need.
- Also vital are photocopies of essential documents, including passport, visa and travelers' check receipts in case you lose the originals.
- Clothes that are quick and easy to wash and dry are a good idea. Loose-fitting clothes are more comfortable in hot climates

WEATHER STATIONS

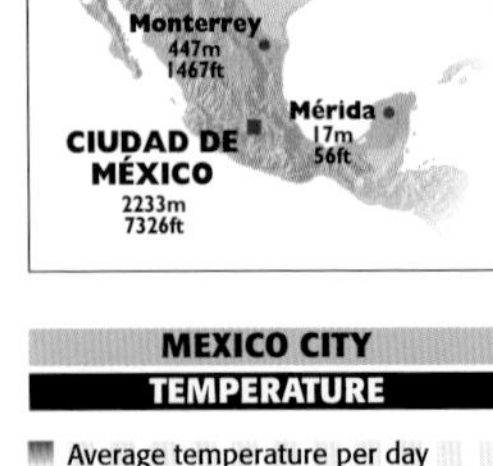

MEXICO CITY TEMPERATURE

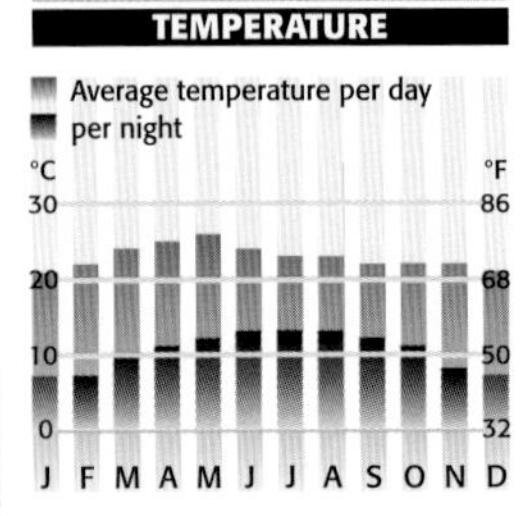

MERIDA TEMPERATURE

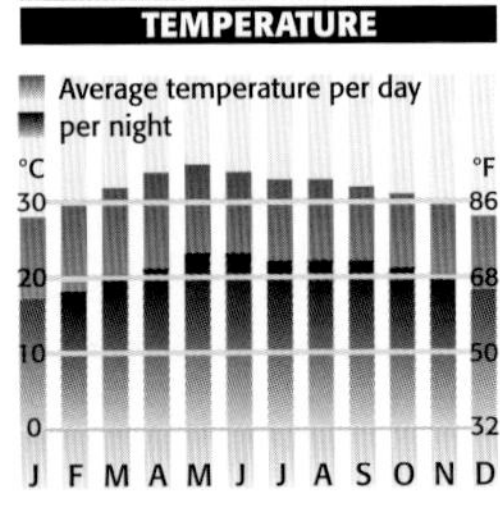

MONTERREY TEMPERATURE

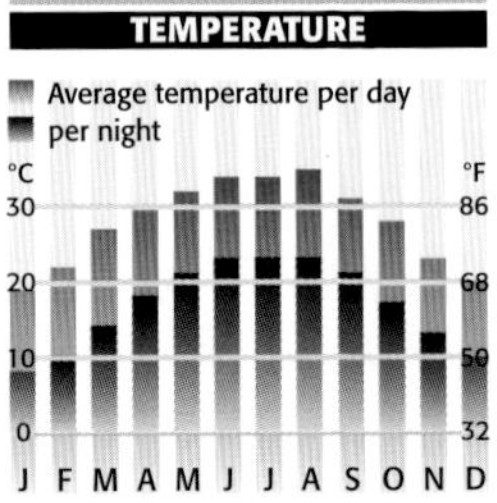

RAINFALL

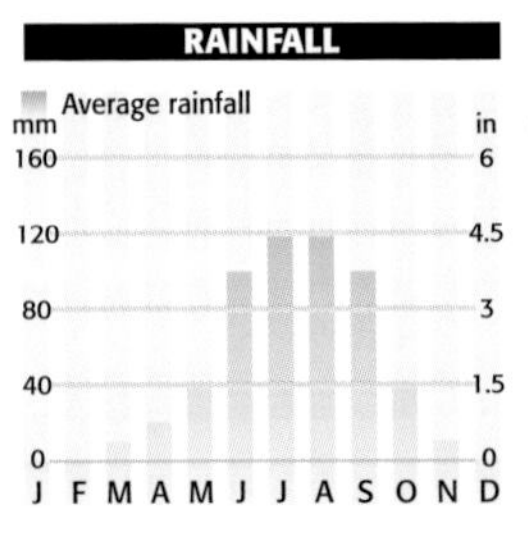

RAINFALL

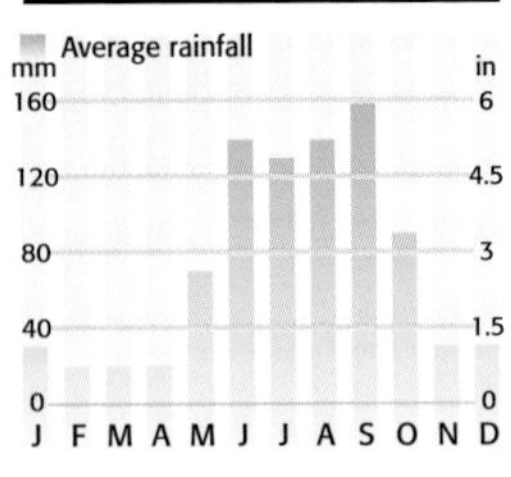

RAINFALL

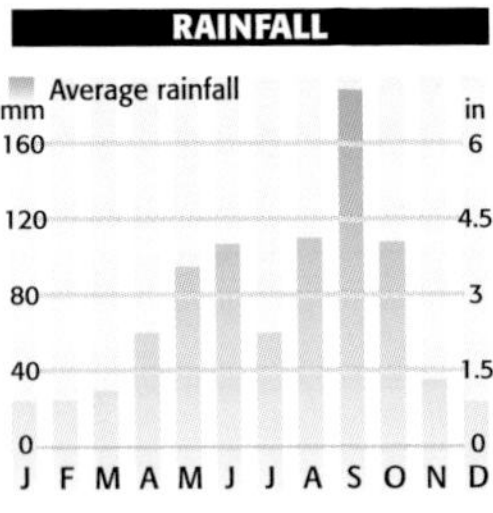

PLANNING

TIMES ZONES

CITY	TIME DIFFERENCE	TIME AT 12 NOON in Mexico
Amsterdam	+7	7pm
Berlin	+7	7pm
Brussels	+7	7pm
Chicago	0	12 noon
Dublin	+6	6pm
Johannesburg*	+7	7pm
London	+6	6pm
Madrid	+7	7pm
Montréal	+1	1pm
New York	+1	1pm
Paris	+7	7pm
Perth, Australia*	+11	11pm
Rome	+7	7pm
San Francisco	-2	10am
Sydney*	+13	1am
Tokyo*	+12	12am

Clocks in Mexico go forward one hour from the first Sunday in April to the last Sunday in October.

* One hour less during Summer Time

CUSTOMS

The list of permitted items is extensive and generally allows for things that could reasonably be considered for personal use. Large quantities of any item may attract suspicion. Those entering by trailer are subject to the same rules based on reasonable personal use. Adults entering Mexico are allowed to bring in up to:

- **20 packs of cigarettes**
- **50 cigars**
- **250g (8.8oz) of tobacco**
- **200g (7oz) of medicines for personal use**
- **3 liters (0.6 gallons) of wine, beer or spirits**
- **A reasonable amount of perfume for personal use**
- **Goods imported into Mexico with a value of more than $1,000 (with the exception of computer equipment, where the limit is $4,000) have to be handled by an officially appointed agent**
- **Gift items not exceeding a total of $300**

Protect yourself against the sun—wear a hat

and can be layered if it gets cooler.

● Sunscreen and a sun hat are essential (see also Health, ▷ 288–289).

● Take all the camera film you will require for the duration of your trip, ideally in a bag that is both water- and dust-proof. Obtaining film in Mexico is getting easier, but you may not be able to get the precise type you want when you want it.

● In the highlands it can be cold at night, especially in winter, and most cheaper hotels do not have heating and provide only one blanket. A light sleeping bag that packs up tightly can be useful.

● Health precautions should be taken; important items include a first-aid kit, sunscreen and painkillers. Also handy are diarrhea treatments, such as Imodium and Pepto-Bismol. An effective mosquito repellent containing Di-ethyltoluamide (DEET) and anti-malarial tablets in key areas are also vital.

TRAVEL INSURANCE

● Insurance is strongly recommended. If you have financial constraints the most important aspect of any insurance policy is medical care and repatriation. Ideally, make sure you are covered for personal items too.

● Read the small print before leaving so you are aware of what is covered and what is not, what is required to submit a claim and what to do in the event of an emergency.

● Don't bring anything you can't afford to replace.

● Check whether your insurer has a 24-hour helpline, and make a note of it.

PASSPORTS AND VISAS

● US citizens need only show an original birth certificate and photo ID to enter Mexico.

● A passport is required for citizens from western European countries, Canada, Australia, New Zealand, Hungary, Iceland, Israel Japan, Singapore, South Korea, Argentina, Bermuda, Chile, Costa Rica, Uruguay and Venezuela.

● Once proof of nationality has been verified, you will receive a Mexican Tourist Card (FM-T) at the point of entry or in advance at a consulate or embassy. The tourist card is issued for up to 180 days and should be returned to immigration officials when departing the country. Citizens of other countries need

MEXICAN EMBASSIES AND CONSULATES ABROAD

COUNTRY	ADDRESS	CONTACT DETAILS
Australia	4 Perth Avenue, Yarralumia, 2600 ACT, Canberra	Tel (02) 6273 3963 www.embassyofmexicoinaustralia.org
Canada	45 O'Connor Street, Suite 1500, K1P 1A4, Ottawa, Ontario	Tel 613 233 8988; www.embamexcan.com
Ireland	43 Ailesbury Road, Ballsbridge 4, Dublin	Tel 260-0699; www.sre.gob.mx/irlanda
New Zealand	111–15 Customhouse Quay, 8th floor, Box 11–510, Wellington	Tel 472 0555; www.mexico.org.nz
South Africa	2nd Floor, Alexandra House, Earlsfort Centre	Tel 01 661 5553
UK	16 St. George Street, Hanover Square, London, W1S 1LX	Tel 020 57499-8586; www.embamex.co.uk
USA	1911 Pennsylvania Avenue, NW, 20006 Washington DC	Tel (202)728-1600; www.sre.gob.mx/eua

to obtain a visa before visiting, so check in advance.

- Tourist cards are not required for cities close to the US border, such as Tijuana and Mexicali.
- Renewal of entry cards or visas must be done at Servicios Migratorios (862 Ejercito Nacional, Mexico City, Mon–Fri 9–1). Only 60 days are given, and you can expect to wait up to 10 days for a replacement tourist card.
- There are immigration offices at international airports, and in cities such as Guadalajara, Oaxaca and Acapulco, which can renew tourist cards. To renew a tourist card by leaving the country, you must stay outside Mexico for at least 72 hours. Take travelers' checks or a credit card as proof of finance.
- Visitors not carrying tourist cards need visas; multiple entry is not allowed and visas must be renewed before re-entry (South Africans and those nationalities not listed here need a visa). Business visitors and technical personnel should apply for the requisite visa and permit.
- At the border crossings with Belize and Guatemala, you may be refused entry into Mexico if you have less than $200 (or $350 for each month of intended stay, up to a maximum of 180 days). Similarly, if you are carrying more than $10,000 in cash or travelers' checks, you must declare it.
- If a person under 18 is touring alone or with one parent, both parents' consent is required, certified by a notary or authorized by a consulate. A divorced parent must be able to show custody of a child. (These requirements are not always checked by immigration and do not apply to all nationalities.) Exact details are available from any Mexican consulate.
- Entry requirements can change at short notice: Always check before you travel.

LONGER STAYS

For a *Visitante Rentista* visa (non-immigrant pensioner) for stays over six months (up to two years) the following are required: passport, proof of income from abroad of $750 per month (or 400 days of the minimum wage), which is reduced by half if you own a house in Mexico, and your tourist card. For information call the Immigration Department of the Mexican consulate (see chart on page 283).

PRACTICALITIES

CONVERSION CHART

FROM	TO	MULTIPLY BY
Inches	Centimeters	2.54
Centimeters	Inches	0.3937
Feet	Meters	0.3048
Meters	Feet	3.2810
Yards	Meters	0.9144
Meters	Yards	1.0940
Miles	Kilometers	1.6090
Kilometers	Miles	0.6214
Acres	Hectares	0.4047
Hectares	Acres	2.4710
Gallons	Liters	4.5460
Liters	Gallons	0.2200
Ounces	Grams	28.35
Grams	Ounces	0.0353
Pounds	Grams	453.6
Grams	Pounds	0.0022
Pounds	Kilograms	0.4536
Kilograms	Pounds	2.205
Tons	Tonnes	1.0160
Tonnes	Tons	0.9842

ELECTRICITY

- Mexico's electricity system is the same as that of the US: 120 volts, 60Hz.
- Any electrical equipment you carry with you that operates at the higher 240 volts rate will need to be dual-voltage, such as hair dryers.
- A lot of electrical equipment (including video cameras, digital cameras, laptops) that operates on 12 volts via a product-specific adaptor will happily cope with dual voltage—check the adaptor and the device instructions to be sure.
- Most plugs in Mexico have two flat prongs. Some have a third, circular prong, and adaptors can be bought for these.

LAUNDRY

- Almost every town and city in Mexico has a number of *lavenderías*. These places normally wash and dry a load (about 3kg/7lb) of laundry for between $2.50 and $4.50.
- Self-service is generally not an option, although more coin-operated machines are beginning to appear.
- Dry-cleaning shops can be found in the larger towns and cities.

MEASUREMENTS

Mexico uses the metric system for all weights and measures.

PUBLIC RESTROOMS

- Almost without exception, used toilet paper should be placed in the receptacle provided, not flushed down the toilet. This applies even in quite expensive hotels. Failing to observe this custom blocks the drain or pan.
- Public restrooms (toilets) are a rare sight, and are often particularly unpleasant. Some now make a small charge for entry, and you'll find these are usually clean and tidy.
- If you cannot find a public restroom, use the facilities at a nearby restaurant or hotel, but make sure that you leave some money for the service provided.
- When you wash your hands, you will see a small, flat box, sometimes with a piece of cloth inside (and usually a couple of coins on it), placed beside one of the sinks. A small tip, depending on the class of establishment, is sufficient.

SMOKING

Smoking is not allowed on most forms of public transportation, including intercity buses, the metro and *colectivos*; there are usually non-smoking areas in the better restaurants.

The attitude toward smoking is more relaxed than in the US and some other countries.

VISITORS WITH DISABILITIES

- As in most Latin American countries, facilities for visitors with disabilities are severely lacking. Most airports, hotels and restaurants in major resorts have wheelchair ramps and adapted toilets (▷ 58).

CLOTHING SIZES

Use the clothing sizes chart below to convert the size you use at home.

UK	Metric	USA		
36	46	36	Men	SUITS
38	48	38		
40	50	40		
42	52	42		
44	54	44		
46	56	46		
48	58	48		
7	41	8	Men	SHOES
7.5	42	8.5		
8.5	43	9.5		
9.5	44	10.5		
10.5	45	11.5		
11	46	12		
14.5	37	14.5	Men	SHIRTS
15	38	15		
15.5	39/40	15.5		
16	41	16		
16.5	42	16.5		
17	43	17		
8	36	6	Women	DRESSES
10	38	8		
12	40	10		
14	42	12		
16	44	14		
18	46	16		
20	46	18		
4.5	37.5	6	Women	SHOES
5	38	6.5		
5.5	38.5	7		
6	39	7.5		
6.5	40	8		
7	41	8.5		

- Sidewalks (pavements) are often in such a poor state of repair that walking is precarious.
- Some travel companies specialize in exciting, tailormade holidays for individuals depending on their level of disability. For those with access to the internet, a Global Access-Disabled Travel Network Site, www.geocities.com/Paris/1502, provides travel information for adventurers with disabilities and has a number of reviews and tips from members of the public.

PLACES OF WORSHIP

Religion plays a vital part in the lives of many Mexicans. For this reason it is important to remain respectful of religious services at all times. Photography is allowed in most churches and cathedrals, but not when there is a service in progress. Avoid wearing shorts or revealing clothing when visiting churches.

Churches in Mexico City

Roman Catholic St. Patrick's, Bondojito 248, Tacubaya (tel (55) 55 15 19 93).
Evangelical Union Reforma 1870, Lomas de Chapultepec (tel (55) 55 20 04 36).
Baptist Capital City Baptist Church, Calle Sur 138 y Bondojito (tel (55) 55 16 18 62).
Lutheran Church of the Good Shepherd, Paseo de Palmas 1910 (tel (55) 55 96 10 34).
Anglican Christ Church, Monte Escandinavos 405, Lomas de Chapultepec (tel (55) 52 02 09 49).
Jewish Beth Israel, Virreyes 1140, Lomas Virreyes, Nidche Israel (Orthodox), Acapulco 70.

LOCAL WAYS

- Casual clothing is adequate for most occasions, although men may need a jacket and tie in some restaurants.
- Topless bathing is increasingly acceptable in parts of Baja California, but take your cues from others.
- Most Latin Americans, if they can afford it, devote great care to their clothes and appearance; it is appreciated if visitors do likewise. How you dress is mostly how people will judge you.
- Remember that politeness—even a little ceremoniousness—is much appreciated. Men should always remove any headgear and say *con permiso* when entering offices. Shaking hands is much more common in Latin America than in Europe or North America.
- Always say *Buenos días* before midday, *Buenas tardes* in the afternoon or *Buenas noches* later in the evening, and wait for a reply before proceeding further.
- In shops and markets, saying *No, gracias* with a smile is always better than an arrogant dismissal.
- Try not to be impatient, and avoid criticizing situations in public; the officials may know more English than you think and gestures and facial expressions are certainly open to interpretation.
- Punctuality is more of a concept than a reality in Latin American countries. The *mañana* culture reigns supreme and any arrangement to meet at, say 7pm, will normally rendezvous about 9pm. However, the one time you are late to catch a bus, boat or plane, it will leave on time; the rule is to arrive on time and be prepared to wait.
- If you have any complaints about faulty goods or services contact Profeco or Procuraduría Federal del Consumidor I, tel 01-800-468-8722; www.profeco.gob.mx, or visit the nearest city branch.
- ID is increasingly required when visiting offices or tourist sites within government buildings. It's handy to have some form of identification (*identificación* or *credencial*; a photocopied passport will usually do). Register your name and leave the ID with the security guard in exchange for a pass.
- There is a charge of $4 to $5 for the use of video cameras at historical sites. If you want to use professional camera equipment, including a tripod, the fee is $150 per day.

Ringing the church bells at Santiago de Jalpan

MONEY

THE PESO

The Mexican peso, usually represented by the dollar sign ($), has the potential of creating great confusion, especially in popular tourist places where prices are higher and often quoted in US$. The one- and two-peso coins and the 10- and 20-peso coins are similar in size; check the number on the coin. US$1 = approximately $11.27 Mexican pesos.

In this book, the dollar sign ($) indicates the US dollar.

BEFORE LEAVING HOME

- The three main ways of carrying money while visiting Mexico are with US dollars cash, US dollars travelers' checks (TCs), or plastic (credit cards). It is recommended that you take all three.
- Check with your credit or debit card company that your card can be used to withdraw cash from Automatic Teller Machines (ATMs) in Mexico. It is also worth checking what fee will be charged for this and what number you should call if your card is stolen.

TIPS

- Dollars are easily changed in all cities and towns at banks and *casas de cambio*, and in the more popular places can sometimes be used if you are running short of pesos.
- Take a mix of large and small denominations—you don't want to get stuck trying to change a US$100 bill in a dusty village in the middle of nowhere.
- In the border states with the US, such as Baja California Norte, the most-used currency is the US dollar.
- Large branches of BITAL bank have been known to change travelers' checks in other currencies if you are stuck.
- Keep your spare money and travelers' checks in your hotel safe until you need them.
- Sell any currency left over at the end of your visit to avoid losing out on the exchange rate.
- If your budget is tight it is essential to avoid situations where you are forced to change money regardless of the rate.
- Watch weekends and public holidays carefully and try not to run out of local currency.
- Take plenty of local currency, in small denominations, when making trips away from the major towns and resorts. It is also very useful for tipping.

TRAVELERS' CHECKS

- Travelers' checks are a safer way of bringing in money as you can claim a refund if they are stolen—but commission can be high when you cash them.
- Checks from any well-known bank can be cashed in most towns if drawn in US dollars; travelers' checks from other currencies (including euros) are harder to cash, and certainly not worth trying to change outside the largest of cities.
- Denominations of US$50 and US$100 are preferable, though you will need a few of US$20. American Express and Visa US$ travelers' checks are the easiest to change.

ATMS

ATMs (*cajero automático*) are now found even in small towns, allowing you to travel without carrying large amounts of cash or traveler' checks. You will need a four-digit PIN number. Amex (American Express), MasterCard and Visa are widely accepted in Mexico. Your card issuer may charge you for withdrawing cash.

BANKS

- Larger branches of main banks in Mexico City are usually open from 8am to 7pm; most are open at least from 9am to 5pm.
- In smaller provincial towns some branches still close at 1.30pm. Larger branches open between 9am and 12.30pm on Saturday mornings.
- Public holidays lead to a complete shutdown in virtually all services, including banks. It is worth keeping an eye on the calendar to avoid changing money on these days.

Money exchanges are easy to find in most towns and cities

CASAS DE CAMBIO

- *Casas de cambio* are generally quicker than banks for exchange transactions, and stay open later; fees are not charged, but their rates may not be as good.
- You may be asked to show your passport, another form of ID or even proof of purchase (but keep it separate from your travelers' checks).

CREDIT CARDS

- MasterCard, Visa and American Express are widely accepted in Mexico, whether you are paying for goods, withdrawing cash from

MEXICAN BILLS (BANKNOTES)

Mexican bills (notes) come in denominations of 20, 50, 100, 200, 500 and 1,000 pesos

ATMs or obtaining cash over the counter from banks.

- Credit cards are useful in hotels, restaurants, shops and when making a deposit to rent equipment.
- Credit card transactions are normally made at an officially recognized rate of exchange and are often subject to sales tax.
- In addition, many charge a fee of about 5 percent on credit card transactions; although it is forbidden by credit card company rules, there is not a lot you can do about this.
- Rates of exchange on ATM withdrawals are the best available for currency exchange, but your bank or credit card company imposes a handling charge.
- If you lose a card, contact the 24-hour helpline of the issuer in your home country immediately (find out the numbers to call before leaving home and keep them in a safe place).
- Most card issuers provide a telephone number where you can call collect from anywhere in the world in case of card loss or theft; be sure to request it before leaving home.

TAXES

- Airport departure tax is around $24 on international flights (dollars or pesos are accepted), but can be higher, depending on the airline you use and your destination; always check when purchasing your ticket if departure tax is included in the price.
- A sales tax of 15 percent is payable on domestic plane tickets bought in Mexico.

WIRING MONEY

If you need to make a transfer ask your bank if they can transfer direct to a Mexican bank without using an intermediary, which usually results in greater delays. Beware of short-changing at all times.

Western Union (www.westernunion.com) has outlets throughout Mexico, but the service is more expensive than a traditional bank wire.

PRICES OF EVERYDAY ITEMS (MEXICO CITY)

ITEM	PESOS
Loaf of bread	13.50
Bottled mineral water (per liter)	5.50
Coffee and pastry at specialty coffee house eg. Starbucks	70
Petrol (per liter)	6.71
Diesel (per liter)	6.50
Buses (local)	1–15
Buses (national)	50–1,000
Camera film (36 exposures)	43
20 cigarettes (on average)	17
33cl bottle of beer	8

TIPPING

Restaurants	10–15 percent
Bell boys	equivalent of US$0.20
Lavatories	equivalent of US$0.20–0.25 depending on class of establishment
Fuel stations	3–5 percent of cost of fuel
Taxis	none, unless some kind of exceptional service provided

It is not usually necessary to tip a taxi driver

HEALTH

BEFORE YOU GO

- Ideally, see your doctor or travel clinic at least six weeks before departure for general advice on travel risks, malaria and vaccinations; know your own blood group, and if you suffer a long-term condition such as diabetes or epilepsy make sure someone knows, or that you have a Medic Alert bracelet/ necklace with this information.
- Get a dental checkup, especially if you are going to be away for more than a month.
- Take out adequate travel insurance (▷ 283).
- Check with your doctor whether you are up to date with BCG (against TB; recommended if staying for more than a month), tetanus and polio.
- Make sure you have received vaccinations (and that they are still valid) for: hepatitis A, typhoid and yellow fever. Mexico has no yellow fever and wants to keep it that way. If you arrive from Africa or South America the authorities may want to see your yellow fever certificate. You may also want to consider vaccination against rabies.
- Be aware of the risk of malaria in Mexico. Rural areas are at risk, including resorts in the rural areas of the following states: Campeche, Chiapas, Guerrero, Michoacán, Nayarit, Oaxaca, Quintana Roo, Sinaloa and Tabasco. Before travel, go to your doctor to check whether any anti-malarial medication should be used.

WHAT TO TAKE

It is a good idea to carry a first-aid kit with you, especially if you have children in tow. This could include the following:

Antiseptic cream
Insect repellent
Antihistamine cream for insect bites or stings
Band aids/plasters
Water sterilization tablets or water purifier
Bandages
Calamine lotion
Cotton wool
Imodium (Lomotil) for emergency diarrhea treatment
Rehydration sachets
Painkillers such as paracetamol or aspirin
Wet wipes

GETTING TREATMENT

- The Social Security hospitals are restricted to members, but will take visitors in emergencies; they are more up-to-date than the *Centros de Salud* and *Hospitales Civiles* found in most towns, which are very cheap and open to everyone.
- Most medium- and larger-sized towns and cities have at least one hospital or clinic. In an emergency, an ambulance will take you to a nearby hospital for treatment. Your doctor may refer you to a local clinic or hospital, for example to get broken bones/sprains attended to.

FINDING A DOCTOR

- Your hotels will be able to recommend local English-speaking doctors.
- Most of the higher-quality hotels that cater to foreign

HEALTHY FLYING

- Visitors to Mexico from as far as Europe, Australia or New Zealand may be concerned about the effect of long-haul flights on their health. The most widely publicized concern is Deep Vein Thrombosis, or DVT. Misleadingly called "economy class syndrome," DVT is the forming of a blood clot in the body's deep veins, particularly in the legs. The clot can move around the bloodstream and could be fatal.
- Those most at risk include the elderly, pregnant women and those using the contraceptive pill, smokers and the overweight. If you are at increased risk of DVT see your doctor before departing. Flying increases the likelihood of DVT because passengers are often seated in a cramped position for long periods of time and may become dehydrated.

To minimize risk:

Drink water (not alcohol)
Don't stay immobile for hours at a time
Stretch and exercise your legs periodically
Do wear elastic flight socks, which support veins and reduce the chances of a clot forming

EXERCISES

1 ANKLE ROTATIONS

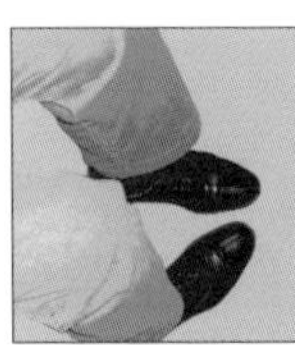

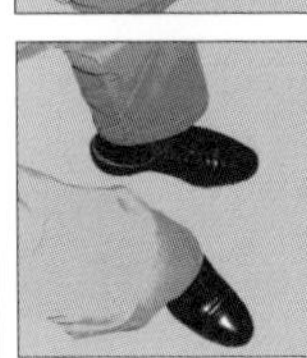

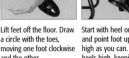

Lift feet off the floor. Draw a circle with the toes, moving one foot clockwise and the other counterclockwise

2 CALF STRETCHES

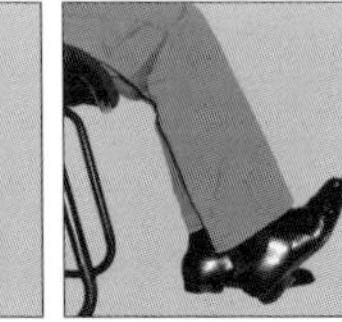

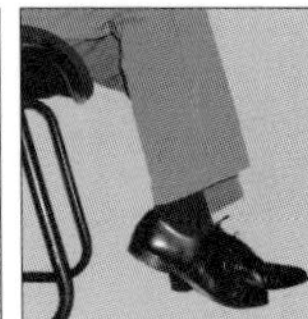

Start with heel on the floor and point foot upward as high as you can. Then lift heels high, keeping balls of feet on the floor

3 KNEE LIFTS

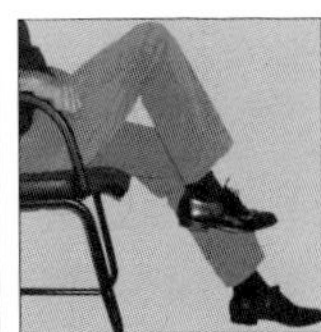

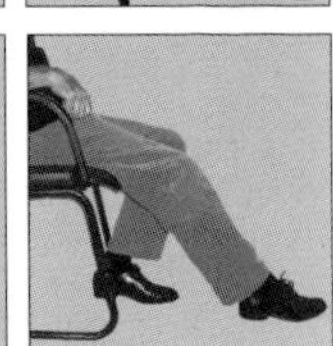

Lift leg with knee bent while contracting your thigh muscle. Then straighten leg, pressing foot flat to the floor

Other health hazards for flyers are airborne diseases and bugs spread by the plane's air-conditioning system. These are largely unavoidable, but if you have a serious medical condition seek advice from a doctor before flying.

USEFUL TELEPHONE NUMBERS	
Emergencies (police, ambulance, fire): *emergencias*	**060/080**
To report a crime	**061**
Federal Highway Police: *Policia Federal de Caminos*	**(55) 5684 2142**
Anti-Rabies Center: *Centro Antirabbico*	**(55) 5607-4093/4658**
AIDS Information: *SIDA*	**(55) 5644 7603**
AIDS Support: *Telsida y Conasida*	**(55) 5666 7432**
Tourist Safety: *Infotur Seguridad Turistica*	**(55) 5250-0123** **(01) 800 903 9200**
Emergencies (English spoken)	**(55) 52 50 04 93**

visitors have a doctor on call at all times. Ask at reception.

- Most embassies have a list of recommended doctors.

FINDING A HOSPITAL

- Parts of rural Mexico are very poor and health services are often basic; communicable diseases are an ever-present threat. However, in the capital and large cities there is a thriving private sector and standards are high.
- In the event of an emergency requiring treatment, your embassy or consulate, or the larger hotels, should be able to recommend a local clinic or hospital.
- If you have the opportunity, ask your medical insurer whether they are satisfied that the establishment you have been referred to is of a suitable standard.
- A list of English-speaking private, public and specialist hospitals can be found on the website for the US embassy in Mexico, www.usembassy-mexico.gov/medical.

DENTAL TREATMENT

- There are many dentists all over Mexico. In the more touristy areas, it is possible to find dental surgeries offering the same services and technology that you might expect from your own country.
- Dental practices are easily found through the local directory and also simply by walking around a town or a city and enquiring at any places that look appropriate.
- Many dentists speak English and the cost is likely to be much cheaper than elsewhere in the world. However, be careful of those who are not adequately qualified.
- Despite the relatively low cost of dental work, it is still worth checking that your insurance plan covers you for it. Have a dental checkup before you go.

OPTICIANS

- Pack a spare pair of glasses or spare contact lenses and your prescription in case you break or lose them.
- Opticians can be found in the local directory under *Opticas*, or ask at the nearest pharmacy.

PHARMACIES

- Many of Mexico's pharmacies are open 24 hours a day. Some close at around 10pm, others stay open all night. In smaller towns, pharmacies take turns staying open on the "all night" shift—ask locally for details. They are recognizable by the green cross and *Farmacia* sign.
- Although you can buy almost any medicine you ask for over the counter in Mexico, you should only buy medicines that you know are safe to self-prescribe.
- If you think you need something stronger see a doctor and get a prescription; don't just take the pharmacist's advice.
- Most medicine is quite inexpensive in Mexico, but keep receipts for claims on medical insurance where appropriate.
- In Mexico City and some of the other major cities in Mexico, the larger supermarkets usually have a good pharmacy attached.

TAP WATER

- Use bottled or mineral water for drinking, except in hotels that normally provide *agua de garrión* (purified drinking water). Take care with ice; make sure it is made from *agua purificada*. Remember that coffee water is not necessarily boiled.
- Bottled water is available everywhere and is safe, but always make sure the cap is sealed as it is not unknown for bottles to be filled from the tap and passed off as bottled water.
- If bottled water is not available, it is essential that you purify drinking water with a preparation containing chlorine (for example Puritabs), widely available in pharmacies.
- There are a number of water filters now on the market available in personal and expedition size. They work either on mechanical or chemical principles, or may do both. Make sure you take the spare parts or spare chemicals with you.

HAZARDS

- Both dengue fever and cholera are on the rise in Mexico, so seek the relevant advice before visiting and be mindful about getting bitten or drinking non-purified water once in the country.
- Although most insect bites are more of a nuisance that an actual hazard, proper insect repellent,

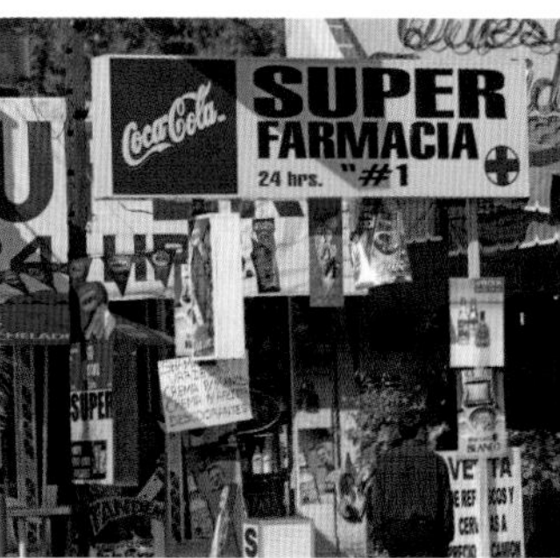

as well as covering your skin with clothing will make your stay much more comfortable.

- There is a risk of malaria in the low-lying tropical zones—consult your own doctor on whether any anti-malarial medication will be necessary for your trip.
- Altitude sickness is a very real problem when visiting Mexico. The ideal prevention for this is to get acclimatized—do not try to reach the highest levels on your first few days of your visit. Mexico City lies at an altitude of 2,240m (7,347ft), so you will have this as well as pollution to contend with.
- The burning power of the tropical sun, especially at high altitude, is phenomenal. Always wear a wide-brimmed hat and use high-factor sunscreen.
- The high glare of the sun can also cause conjunctivitis, so a good-quality pair of sunglasses is essential—both at high altitude and at the beach.

COMMUNICATION

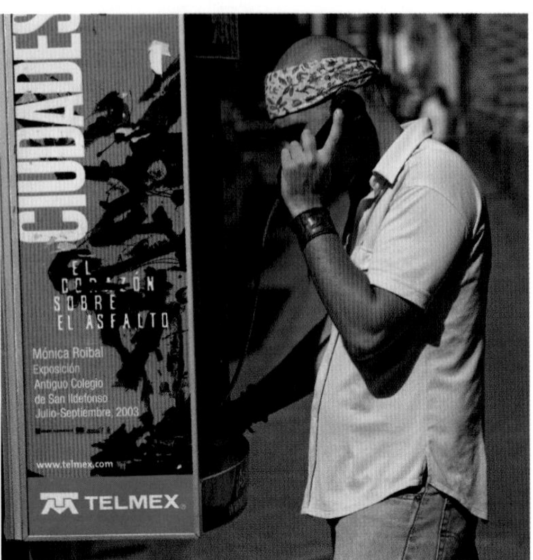

TELEPHONES

- Calls made to Mexican numbers are either local, regional or international.
- Most destinations have a 7-digit number (except Mexico DF, Guadalajara and Monterrey, which have 8-digit numbers).
- Most regions have a 3-digit code (except Mexico DF, Guadalajara and Monterrey, which have 2-digit codes).
- See chart listing the phone codes of the major regions in Mexico.
- The format of a number, depending on the type of call, should be as follows:

Local: use 7- or 8-digit numbers
Between regions: long-distance access (01), plus regional code (2- or 3-digit code), plus 7- or 8-digit number
International: international access, plus country code (52), plus regional code, plus 7- or 8-digit number.

- To call Mexico from the UK dial 00 52, followed by the regional code (2 or 3 digits, depending on the area) and then the 7- or 8-digit number.
- To call the UK from Mexico, dial 00 44, then drop the first zero from the relevant area code.
- To call Mexico from the US dial 011 52, followed by the regional code (2 or 3 digits) and then the relevant 7- or 8-digit number.
- To call the US from Mexico, dial 00 1, followed by the number.

CALL CHARGES

- There is a fixed charge for a local call, regardless of how long the call lasts. National and international calls vary in price according to time of day and distance.
- International calls are very expensive by US, European and Australian standards.

PAYPHONES

- Most public phones take phone cards only (Ladatel), costing 30 or 50 pesos from shops and news kiosks everywhere. AT&T's US Direct service is available; for information in Mexico dial 412-553-7458, ext. 359. From LADA phones (see below), dial 01, similar for AT&T credit cards. To use calling cards to Canada tel 95-800-010-1990.
- Commercially run *casetas*, or booths (for example Computel), where you pay after phoning, are up to twice as expensive as private phones, and charges vary

AREA CODES FOR MAJOR CITIES	
Acapulco	744
Aguascalientes	449
Campeche	981
Cancún	998
Chihuahua	614
Cozumel	987
Cuernavaca	777
Durango	686
Guadalajara	33
Guanajuato	473
La Paz	612
Mérida	999
Mexico City	55
Monterrey	81
Morelia	443
Oaxaca	951
Puebla	222
Querétaro	442
San Cristóbal de las Casas	967
San José del Cabo	624
San Miguel de Allende	415
Taxco	762
Tijuana	664
Veracruz	229
Xalapa (Jalapa)	228
Zacatecas	492

INTERNATIONAL DIALING CODES	
Australia	00 61
Belize	00 501
Canada	00 1
Costa Rica	00 506
Germany	00 49
Guatemala	00 502
Honduras	00 504
Ireland	00 353
Italy	00 39
New Zealand	00 64
Spain	00 34
UK	00 44
US	00 1

GUIDE TO TELEPHONE PRICES

TYPE OF CALL	(PER MINUTE)/LOWEST PRICE	HIGHEST PRICE
National calls	1.32 pesos	2.60 pesos
International (USA/Canada)	6.32 pesos	12.64 pesos
Other international calls	9.92 pesos	14.84 pesos
Mobile phones	2.50 pesos	

NB. Call charges vary and change, therefore it is important to check before making a call.

POSTAGE GUIDE PRICES	UNDER 20g	20–50g	500g–1kg
North America, Central America and the Caribbean	8.50 pesos	14 pesos	87 pesos
South America and Europe	10.50 pesos	16.50 pesos	120.50 pesos
Asia, Africa and Oceania	11.50 pesos	19.50 pesos	153.50 pesos

NB. Postal rates are subject to change.

from place to place. Computel have offices countrywide with long opening hours. It is better to call collect (reverse charge) from private phones, but better still to use the LADA system.

- Collect calls on LADA can be made from any blue public phone; ask for *"llamar por cobrar"*; silver phones are for local and direct long-distance calls, some take coins. Others take foreign credit cards (Visa, MasterCard, not Amex; not all phones that say they take cards accept them, others that say they don't, do).
- Pre-paid phone cards (such as Ladatel, above) are available, but expensive for international calls.
- Of other pre-paid cards, the best value are those issued by Ekofon, available at various airport and other outlets.
- Ekofon provides a pre-chargeable account service, which may be opened from anywhere (including outside Mexico) by internet; go to www.amistadbm.org.mx and then to the Ekofon link.
- Accounts may be opened with as little as $5 and are rechargeable.
- Calls, which can be made from any telephone in the country, cost 3 pesos per minute to the US, 5 pesos per minute to Europe, 2.75 pesos per minute to Asia.
- The same account can be used for calls made from the US and Canada, at even cheaper rates.

MOBILE PHONES

- If you want to be able to talk on the move, you can rent a mobile phone while you are in Mexico, or if you have a triband GSM (Global System for Mobile) phone, you can take yours with you, but beware as the charges are high.
- Your telephone provider back home must enable international roaming on your account before you go, and have a reciprocal arrangement with Telmex in Mexico.
- If you are going to be in Mexico for a while, the best bet is to buy a Mexican mobile phone.
- Mexico's dominant telephone company, Telmex, has been rolling out its GSM network in Mexico. This means that users of GSM phones (Europe, Australia, et al) will soon be able to take their phones to Mexico and use them as if they were at home.

POST OFFICES

- You'll find a post office (*Oficina de Correos*) in almost every town and in every city in Mexico.
- In the major cities, opening hours are long, Monday to Friday 9 to 7, Saturday 9 to 1.
- In the more remote areas, post offices may only open in the morning.

SENDING A LETTER

- International services have improved and the bright red mailboxes found in many parts of the country are reliable for sending letters.
- Stamps can be bought from post offices or stamp machines, located outside post offices, at bus stations, airports and some commercial establishments (but not many).
- Airmail letters have to be weighed at the post office and stamps to the postage value bought.
- Rates are raised periodically in line with the devaluation of the peso against the dollar, but occasionally vary between towns.
- Parcel counters often close earlier than other sections of the post office in Mexico.
- Not all of these services are obtainable outside Mexico City; delivery times in or from the interior may well be longer than those from Mexico City.
- Poste Restante (*lista de correos* in Mexico) functions quite reliably; mail is returned to the sender after 10 days if not collected (for an extension write to the Jefe de la Administración of the post office holding your mail; any other post office will help with this). Address *Favor de retener hasta llegada* on envelope.

INTERNET ACCESS

- Internet access in Mexico is extensive and often easier and more reliable than the phone. Every major town now has at least one internet café, with more springing up daily.
- If money is tight and you have time, look around; prices vary from place to place, but are normally $1–$2 an hour.
- Visit www.cybercafes.com for a selection of some of those in Mexico.

Outside the post office in Mexico City

PLANNING

FINDING HELP

EMERGENCY PHONE NUMBERS

General emergency number (police, ambulance, fire)

060/080

Tourist police are very helpful

PERSONAL SECURITY

Mexico is generally a safe country to visit, although precautions over personal safety should be taken, especially in Mexico City and other large cities, especially when taking a taxi in the street.

- Make sure you have adequate insurance to cover any health emergencies, thefts or legal costs that could arise.
- Never carry valuables visibly or in easily picked pockets.
- Leave passports, tickets and important documents in a hotel safety deposit, not in your room.
- Never leave possessions visible inside the car and at night park in hotel parking areas.
- Avoid using the bus at night, particularly in Guerrero, Oaxaca, Veracruz and Chiapas; if at all possible make journeys in daylight.

In most towns the police station is on the main square

- Couples and women on their own should avoid lonely beaches.
- Be prepared for short-changing and overcharging.

LOSS OF PASSPORT

- If possible, scan the relevant pages of your passport and email them to yourself at an email account you can access anywhere (like www.hotmail.com).
- Always keep a separate note of your passport number and a photocopy of the page that carries your details, in case of loss or theft.
- If you do lose your passport or it is stolen, report it to the police and then contact your nearest embassy or consulate.

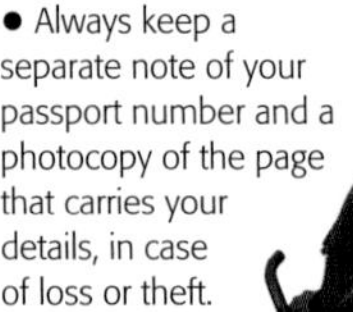

Policing the streets is easier on a bicycle

POLICE

The police service has an equivalent to the *Angeles Verdes* (Green Angels, ▷ 55), who help victims of crime to file a report. US citizens should present this report to the nearest embassy or consulate. Otherwise, try to avoid the police if possible; they are rarely helpful and tend to make complicated situations even worse. Should you come into contact with them, try to stay as calm and polite as possible. Never offer a bribe unless you are fully conversant with the customs of Mexico.

EMBASSIES AND CONSULATES IN MEXICO CITY

COUNTRY	ADDRESS	CONTACT DETAILS
Australia	Ruben Dario 55, Colonia Polanco, 11580 Mexico DF	tel (55) 11 01 22 00 www.mexico.embassy.gov.au
Canada	Calle Schiller 529, Colonia Polanco (Rincón del Bosque) 11580 Mexico DF	tel (55) 57 24 79 00 www.canada.org.mx
Germany	Lord Byron 737, Colonia Polanco, 11560 Mexico DF	tel (55) 52 83 22 00 www.embajada-alemana.org.mx
New Zealand	Jaime Balmes No. 8, 4th Floor, Colonia Los Morales, Polanco, 11510 Mexico DF	tel (55) 52 83 94 60
Spain	(Consulate General) Galileo 114, Colonia Polanco, 11560 Mexico DF	tel (55) 53 80 43 83
UK	Río Lerma 71, Colonia Cuauhtémoc, 06500 Mexico DF	tel (55) 52 42 85 00 www.embajadabritanica.com.mx
US	Paseo de la Reforma 305, Colonia Cuauhtémoc, 06500 Mexico DF	tel (55) 50 80 20 00 www.usembassy-mexico.gov

OPENING TIMES AND TICKETS

It's very difficult to generalize about opening times for museums, tourist offices and shops in Mexico. Even when times are posted, they are not necessarily adhered to. The hours of business in Mexico City are extremely variable and in other parts of the country vary considerably according to climate and local custom. The siesta, though slowly disappearing in large cities, is still commonplace, particularly in hotter areas such as the Gulf coast and Yucatán, and many places will close for a few hours in early afternoon, usually from around 1 till 3 or even 4.

NATIONAL HOLIDAYS

If any of these holidays falls on a Thursday or a Tuesday, they are usually an excuse for a *puente*, a bridge or long weekend (which can have implications for travel, hotel accommodation and services). Sunday is a statutory holiday. Saturday is also observed as a holiday, except by the shops. There is no early-closing day.

January 1	New Year
February 5	Constitution Day
March 21	Birthday of Benito Juárez
March/April	Maundy Thursday, Good Friday and Easter Saturday
May 1	Labor Day
May 5	Battle of Puebla
September 1	*El Informe* (Presidential Message)
September 16	Independence Day
October 12	*Día de la Raza* (Discovery of America)
November 20	*Día de la Revolución* (Revolution Day)
December 25	Christmas Day

BANKS

- Both larger branches of main banks in Mexico City and those in the rest of the country are generally open Monday to Friday 9 to 5. Head offices and some larger branches are open 9 to 12.30 on Saturday mornings. In smaller provincial towns some branches still close at 1.30.
- Public holidays lead to a complete shutdown in virtually all services, including banks. It is worth keeping an eye on the calendar to avoid having to change money on such days.

Always take care when visiting Mexico's eco parks

SHOPS

- Shops in big towns and cities are normally open daily from 9 till between 8 and 10pm. Smaller towns will have more limited opening hours, and in hotter, non-tourist regions, will close between 1pm and 3 or 4pm for siesta. In smaller towns shops may close on Sundays, except tourist spots in high season.
- Christmas and Easter public holidays are observed; on other public holidays you'll find most things open in cities, bigger towns and resorts.

MUSEUMS, GALLERIES AND ARCHEOLOGICAL SITES

- Museums and galleries tend to open from around 9 to 1 and from 3 to 6, but hours vary across the country and are seasonal; check locally. Many close on Monday, but again this can vary.
- Many museums and archaeological sites offer free entry on Sundays.
- Archaeological sites are normally open all day, from 8 or 9 till 5.

RESTAURANTS, BARS AND CAFÉS

- Opening times vary wildly, depending on location and season. In Mexico City and large towns and tourist areas, places tend to open longer, often from 8 or 9 in the morning till 11 or 12 at night, though some are open only from lunch (1pm).
- Cafés serving breakfast may open from around 6.30 or 7am.
- Bars will open from lunchtime onwards, but again times vary around the country. Many are open till around 2 or 3 in the morning, or even later in tourist hotspots in high season.

POST OFFICES

In the major cities, opening hours are Monday to Friday 9 to 6 and Saturday 9 to 1. Smaller branches open shorter hours, often 9 to 3, and Saturdays from 9 to 1. In the more remote areas, post offices may only open in the morning on weekdays.

PHARMACIES

Many of Mexico's pharmacies are open 24 hours a day. Some close at around 10pm, others stay open all night. In smaller towns, pharmacies take turns staying open on the "all night" shift—ask at your hotel for details.

CONCESSIONS

- Although an international student identity card (ISIC) offers student discounts, only national Mexican student cards permit free entry to archaeological sites, museums, etc.
- SETEJ (Mexican Students' Union) issues student cards and offers ISIS insurance. To obtain a national student card you need two photos, passport, confirmation of student status and $13.
- For elderly visitors (age 60 plus, retirees or those on a long vacation) who can provide proof of address, a special card is available from the Instituto Nacional de la Senectud (INSEN), which gives free admission to museums, use of the metro, and 50 percent off bus and theater tickets.
- Children can often travel for reduced rates on buses, and free entry is usually given to them on sightseeing tours to museums etc. Also check out cheaper flights for children.

BOOKS, MAPS AND FILMS

BOOKS

There is a wide selection of travel literature on offer, including Carl Franz's *The People's Guide to Mexico* (John Muir Publications, Santa Fe, NM, 1998), which is practical and entertaining.

Isabella Tree's *Sliced Iguana* (2001) is a wonderful piece of writing in which she describes her travels to various parts of Mexico, showing it as an exciting, diverse and delightful country.

Works from a national perspective are equally abundant as Mexico has produced some widely respected writers, among them Carlos Fuentes. Of his many works, both *Terra Nostra* (1975) and *The Old Gringo* (1985) are well worth a read.

Laura Esquivel's *Like Water for Chocolate* (1993) was the novel about desire, love and rebellion that led to big-screen success.

There are dozens of works about Mexico from a foreign perspective. Among the most well known and most popular are Malcolm Lowry's *Under the Volcano* (1947), Graham Greene's *The Power and The Glory* (1940), and D. H. Lawrence's *The Plumed Serpent* (1926). Although these works are not contemporary, they provide a vivid and insightful view into Mexican life and culture that holds true today.

For an insight into different aspects of Mexican culture and the people's own perceived place in the world around them, try Octavio Paz's *The Labyrinth of Solitude and Other Writings* (1985).

Coe, MD, *The Maya* (Pelican Books, or large-format edition, Thames and Hudson) is essential reading for the Maya archaeological area.

There are many good works on Mexican history, among which William Prescott's *History of the Conquest of Mexico* (1849) remains a popular choice.

A more up-to-date perspective can be found in Hugh Thomas' *Conquest: Cortes, Montezuma, and the Fall of the Old Mexico* (1995).

The informative annual *Travelers Guide to Mexico* (editor and publisher Chris Luhnow) can be found in more than 35,000 hotels rooms across Mexico.

MAPS AND LEAFLETS

Do not expect to find leaflets or books available at all the archaeological sites. Bloomgarden, Richard Panorama Guides and Easy Guides are all reliable, widely available and have plans and good illustrations.

Also available are Miniguides to archaeological and historical sites, published in various languages by INAH, $0.75 each.

The AAA (US) produces a Mexican map predominantly for the independent visitor. There is also a road atlas for the US, Canada and Mexico combined. To order a copy, look up www.theAA.com.

The Instituto Geográfico Militar sells topographical maps, scale 1:100,000 or 1:50,000. The physical features shown on these are usually accurate; the trails and place names less so. National Parks offices also sell maps.

Specialist Map Shops

UK

National Map Centre, 22–24 Caxton Street, London SW1H 0QU, tel 020 7222 2466, www.mapsnmc.co.uk

Stanfords, 12–14 Long Acre, Covent Garden, London WC2E 9LP, tel 020 7836 1321, www.stanfords.co.uk

US

The Complete Traveler, 199 Madison Avenue, New York, NY 10022, tel 212/685-9007

Map Link inc, 30 S La Patera Lane, Unit 5, Santa Barbara, CA 93117, tel 805/692-6777, www.maplink.com

FILMS

On the international big screen Mexico has probably suffered more than most from stereotypical images painting the whole nation as a bunch of lazy, good-for-nothing scoundrels, crooks and corrupt officials, but things began to change with the international success of the 1992 movie, *Como Agua Para Chocolate (Like Water for Chocolate)*.

Mexico's new film image was further enhanced by the 2002 hit *Frida*, which celebrated the life of the painter Frida Kahlo and her relationship with Diego Rivera, but it was the Oscar-nominated and Bafta-winning *Amores Perros* (*Love's a Bitch*, 2001), and *Y Tu Mamá También* (*And Your Mother Too*, 2001) that really put Mexican cinema on the map, as well as launching the glittering careers of Latin heartthrob Gael García Bernal and director Alejandro González Iñárritu (▷ 18).

The Mexican landscape has always featured on the international film scene and the Western genre relied heavily on the scenic locations around Durango, producing classics from the 1950s through the works of Sam Peckinpah up to the all-star *Mask of Zorro* (1998) starring Antonio Banderas.

Many other US productions have used Mexico's tropical locations for films, such as *Night of the Iguana*, *Romancing the Stone* and *Medicine Man*, and the 1997 blockbuster *Titanic*, which was shot at Rosarito, Baja California, close to Tijuana.

TOURIST OFFICES

TOURIST INFORMATION OFFICES IN MEXICO

Aguascalientes
Avenida Universidad No. 1001, Edifico Torre Plaza Bosques 8 Piso, CP 20127 Aguascalientes, AGS (tel (449) 912 35 11)

Baja California Norte
Boulevard Díaz Ordáz s/n, Edificio Plaza Patria Nivel 3, CP 22400 Tijuana, BAJ (tel (664) 634 63 30)

Baja California Sur
Carretera Al Norte Km. 5.5 Fracc. Fidepaz, CP 23090 La Paz, BCS (tel (612) 124 01 00)

Campeche
Avenida Ruiz Cortines s/n, Plaza Moch-Couoh, Centro, CP 24000 Campeche, CAM (tel (981) 811 92 00)

Chiapas
Boulevard Belisario Dominguez No. 950, Planta Baja, CP 29060 Tuxtla Gutiérrez, CHI (tel (961) 613 93 96)

Coahuila
Boulevard Luis Echeverría No. 1560, Edificio Torre Saltillo Piso 11, CP 25286 Saltillo, COA (tel (884) 415 17 14)

Colima
Portal Hidalgo No. 96 Centro, CP 2800 Colima, COL (tel (312) 312 28 57)

Distrito Federal (Mexico City)
Amberes No. 54, 2 Piso, CP 06600 Mexico DF (tel (55) 55 53 87 59)

Durango
Hidalgo No. 408 Sur, CP 34000 Durango, DUR (tel (618) 811 31 60)

Guanajuato
Plaza de la Paz No. 14, CP 36000 Guanajuato, GNJ (tel (473) 732 15 74)

Guerrero
Avenida Costera Miguel Alemán 4455, Centro Cultural y de Convenciones de Acapulco, CP 39850 Acapulco, GUE (tel (44) 484 24 23)

Hidalgo
Carretera Mexico-Pachuca km 93.5, Colonia Venta Prieta, CP 42080 Pachuca, HID (tel (771) 717 81 17)

Jalisco
Morelos No. 102, Plaza Tapatia, CP 44100 Guadalajara, JAL (tel (333) 668 16 02)

Mexico (state)
Urawa No. 100, Edificio Centro de Servicios Admvos. Puerta No. 110, CP 50150 Toluca, MX (tel (722) 212 59 98)

Michoacán
El Nigromate No. 79, Palacio Clavijero, Centro, CP 58000 Morelia, MIC (tel (443) 312 52 44)

Morelos
Avenida Morelos Sur No. 187, Las Palmas, CP 62050 Cuernavaca, MOR (tel (777) 314 38 72)

Nayarit
Calzada del Ejército y Avenida México s/n, Ex-Convento de la Cruz de Zacate, CP 63168 Tepic, NAY (tel (311) 214 80 71)

Nuevo Leon
Zaragoza No. 1300 Sur, Edificio Kalos Nivel A-1 Desp. 137, CP 64000 Monterrey, NL (tel (81) 8344 4343)

Oaxaca
Independencia No. 607 esq. García Vigil, CP 68000 Oaxaca, OAX (tel (951) 516 07 17)

Puebla
5 Oriente No. 3, Centro Histórico, CP 72000 Puebla, PUE (tel (222) 246 20 44)

Querétaro
Avenida Luis Pasteur No. 4, Norte, Centro Histórico, CP 76000 Querétaro (tel (442) 212 14 12)

Quintana Roo
Avenida Cobá, CP 77500 Cancún, QUI (tel (998) 884 65 31)

San Luis Potosí
Alvaro Obregón No. 520, CP 78000 San Luis Potosí, SLP (tel (444) 812 99 39)

Sinaloa
Avenida Camarón Sabalo esq. Tiburon, Edificio Banrural 4 Piso, CP 82100 Mazatlán, SIN (tel (667) 916 51 60)

Sonora
Centro de Gobierno, Edif Estatal Norte 3er Nivel, CP 83280 Hermosillo, SON (tel (662) 217 00 76)

Tabasco
Avenida Los Ríos s/n, Calle 13 Tabasco 2000, CP 86035 Villahermosa, TAB (tel (993) 316 51 34)

Tamaulipas
16 Rosales No. 272, CP 87000 Ciudad Victoria, TAM (tel (834) 312 10 57)

Tlaxcala
Avenida Juárez esq, Lardizábal, CP 90000 Tlaxcala, TLA (tel (246) 462 00 27)

Veracruz
Bouevard Cristóbal Colón No. 5, CP 91190 Xalapa, VER (tel (228) 812 85 00)

Yucatán
Calle 59 No. 514 entre 62 y 64, Centro, CP 97000 Mérida, YUC (tel (999) 924 93 89/930 37 66)

Zacatecas
Avenida Hidalgo No. 403 Segundo Piso, CP 98000 Zacatecas, ZAC (tel (492) 924 05 52)

MEXICAN TOURIST OFFICES ABROAD

Canada
1610-999 West Hastings Street, Suite 1110, Vancouver, British Columbia V6C 2W2 (tel +1-604-669-2845)

France
4 rue Notre Dame des Victories, Paris 75002 (tel +33-1-42 86 96 12)

Germany
Taunusanlage 21, Franfurt-am-Main D60325 (tel +49-69-71 03 38 95)

Italy
Via Barberini No. 3, 7° piso, Rome 00187 (tel +39-06-487-46 98)

Spain
Calle de Velázquez No 126, Madrid 28006 (tel +34-1-561-3520)

UK
Wakefield House, 41 Trinity Square, London EC3N 4DJ (tel +44-20-7488-9392)

US
10100 Santa Monica Boulevard, Suite 450, Los Angeles, CA 90067; 1880 Century Park East, Suite 511, Los Angeles CA 90067 (tel +1 310 282 9112); 375 Park Avenue, Floor 19, Suite 1905, NY 10152 (tel +1 212 308 2110); 5875 Sunset Drive, Suite 305, South Miami, FL 33143 (tel +1 786 621 2909); 4507 San Jacinto, Suite 308, Houston TX 77004 (tel +1 713 772 2581)

GETTING INFO

For most visitors, the first port of call for information and maps is the Secretaría de Turismo (SECTUR), the Mexican Government Ministry of Tourism, which has offices throughout the country and abroad. As well as providing free information and various brochures and maps, these tourist offices—also known as *turismos*—will book your hotel. It's a good idea, however, to stock up on as many freebies as you can before leaving, as many offices in Mexico either run out or don't stock them. As well as SECTUR offices, there are offices run by state and municipal authorities.

- Standards of service vary greatly from place to place. Many people are extremely friendly and helpful, while others appear not to know much about the town in which they live.
- In Mexico City there are sporadically manned tourist booths dotted around which have handy maps and can provide information.
- Information is also available in the capital at Tourist Information Centers operated by the Mexico City Government at several places throughout the city. The website www.mexicocity.gob.mx gives comprehensive information on a wide range of topics, from business to pleasure, and even film locations.
- You can refer complaints to the Tourist Information Centers or to the Tourist Police, in blue uniforms, who are usually very friendly.
- The SECTUR main office in Mexico City can be called from anywhere in the country at local rates (tel 1-800/903-9200).

MEDIA

TELEVISION

- The national television network is largely controlled by Televisa, which owns and runs four of the six national channels, while the other two are owned and run by TV Azteca.
- Mexican television basically consists of adverts, soap operas *(telenovelas)*, sports (predominantly soccer/football), movies and comedy. As a general rule, the networks refrain from showing any material containing nudity, violence or offensive language.
- Once TV and Canal 22 are two channels that offer a much more cultural selection of viewing.
- It is only through satellite and cable television that visitors are likely to find channels that they recognize.
- The main providers, Multivisíon and Cablevision, offer the now widely known Cartoon Network, MTV, ESPN and CNN. However, these are likely to be found only in mid- to upper-range hotels.

RADIO

- Mexico has approximately 1,000 short-wave and long-wave stations and so a short-wave (world band) radio offers a practical means to brush up on the language, sample popular culture and absorb some of the richly varied regional music.
- There are also radio stations available if you want to catch up on events at home or around the world. International broadcasters offer this service, often both in English and Spanish. Among the most popular is the BBC World Service: 648 kHz LW; check www.bbc.co.uk/worldservice/index.shtml for schedules and the relevant short-wave frequencies depending on your location.
- The Voice of America website, www.voa.gov, gives all schedules and frequencies for Mexico and the rest of Latin America.

NEWSPAPERS

- The influential national dailies are: *Excelsior*, *Novedades*, *El Día*, *Uno Más Uno*, *El Universal*, *El Heraldo*, *La Jornada* (www.jornada.unam.mx, more to the left), *La Prensa* (a popular tabloid, with the largest circulation) and *El Nacional*, which is effectively the mouthpiece of the government.
- There are influential weekly magazines such as *Proceso*, *Siempre*, *Epoca* and *Quehacer Político*. *Los Agachados* is a weekly political satirical magazine. *The News*, an English-language daily, is currently not available.
- The New York edition of the *Financial Times* and other British and European papers are available at Mexico City Airport and from the Casa del Libro, Calle Florencia 37 (Zona Rosa), Hamburgo 141 (Zona Rosa) and Calle Homero (Polanco), all in Mexico City. The *Miami Herald* is stocked by most newspaper stands.

Newspaper vendors, Mexico City

USEFUL WEBSITES

MAJOR SIGHTS QUICK WEBSITE/PAGE FINDER		
SIGHT/TOWN	**WEBSITE**	**PAGE**
Acapulco	www.sectur.guerrero.gob.mx	82
Aguascalientes	www.aguascalientes.gob.mx	138
Barranca del Cobre	www.coppercanyon-mexico.com	158–159
Campeche	www.campeche.gob.mx	62
Cancún	www.cancunmx.com	63
Chichén Itzá		64–67
Cozumel	www.islacozumel.com.mx	68–69
Cuernavaca	www.cuernavaca.gob.mx	124
Guadalajara	www.guadalajara.gob.mx	141
Guanajuato	www.guanajuato.gob.mx	142–144
Mérida		73
Monte Albán	www.oaxaca.gob.mx	86–87
Monterrey		165
Morelia		147
Museo Nacional de Antropológia	www.mexicocity.com.mx/musantro.html	108–111
Oaxaca	www.oaxaca.gob.mx	88–91
Palenque	www.palenquemx.com	92–95
Puebla		126–127
San Cristóbal de las Casas	www.turismochiapas.gob.mx	96
San Miguel de Allende	www.sanmigueldeallende.gob.mx	149
El Tajín		129
Taxco	www.guerrero.gob.mx	130
Tijuana		168
Tulúm		75
Uxmal		78–79
Veracruz	www.veracruz-puerto.gob.mx/turismo	135
Xalapa (Jalapa)	www.xalapa.net/sitios/xalapa.htm	136
Zacatecas	www.turismozacatecas.gob.mx	154–155

www.visitmexico.com
Website of Mexico Tourist Board, a comprehensive multilingual site with information on the entire country.

www.sectur.gob.mx
Website of Tourism Secretariat with less glossy links but equally comprehensive information.

www.mexicanwave.com and www.mexperience.com
Well-constructed site updated daily, with current affairs, feature articles and advice on travel in Mexico. Look out for the forum where comments from fellow visitors are exchanged.

www.mexconnect.com
A massive and comprehensive site devoted to Mexico. Although you will have to sign up as a member, the level of information, news and articles on offer is vast and well worth a look.

Gorp.com/gorp/location/latamer/mexico.htm
An option for adventurers, with lots of detailed information, including good suggestions and tips on more adventurous travel.

www.wtgonline.com/data/mex/mex.asp
The online presence of The World Travel Guide Mexico, with an overview of Mexico for visitors, and a useful Essentials section with facts on visas, public holidays, money and health.

www.lanic.utexas.edu/la/mexico/
Mexico Reference Desk, a huge site containing a variety of information about Mexico ranging from anthropology to sport and trade. Rather academic in tone, it is nevertheless an excellent source for background information.

www.mexonline.com
Another good source for information of all types on Mexico. It offers everything from places to stay, eat and visit as well as more general information on Mexico's history, culture and everyday life.

www.cybercaptive.com
A site that holds a database of the location of many cyber cafés in Mexico.

www.eluniversal.com.mx
This online version of the popular *El Universal* newspaper has stories primarily in Spanish, but also offers translations into English on the major stories and articles. A useful tool to keep abreast of current events in Mexico.

www.jornada.unam.mx
The *La Jornada* newspaper is the most popular national daily in Mexico. This online site is only in Spanish, but is very useful for any who can read the language.

www.mexicocity.com.mx
An excellent site that caters specifically for Mexico City. With a large amount of information on restaurants, transportation, embassies and much more, it's a comprehensive resource if you are spending time in the capital.

www.planeta.com
Website run by Ron Mader. Forum for various environmental issues, but also features Mexican stories and travel articles.

SPANISH WORDS AND PHRASES

A little Spanish will make a difference to your visit. Once you have learned a few basic rules, it's an easy language to speak: It is phonetic and, unlike English, particular combinations of letters are always pronounced the same way. When a word ends in a vowel, an n or an s, the stress is usually on the penultimate syllable; otherwise, its on the last syllable. If a word has an accent, this is where the stress falls.

a	as in	pat	**ai, ay**	as **i** in	side
e	as in	set	**au**	as **ou** in	out
i	as **e** in	be	**ei, ey**	as **ey** in	they
o	as in	hot	**oi, oy**	as **oy** in	boy
u	as in	flute			

Consonants as in English except:

c before **i** and **e** as **th**, *although some pronounce it as* **s**
ch as **ch** in church
d at the end of a word becomes **th**
g before **i** or **e** becomes **ch** as in loch
h is silent
j as **ch** in loch
ll as **lli** in million
ñ as **ny** in canyon
qu is hard like a k
r usually rolled
v is a **b**
z is a **th**, *but sometimes pronounced as s*

COLORS

black
negro

orange
naranja

blue
azul

pink
rosa

brown
café

purple
purpúreo

cerise
cereza

red
rojo

gold
oro

silver
plata

green
verde

turquoise
turquesa

grey
gris

white
blanco

mauve
malva

yellow
amarillo

CONVERSATION

What is the time?
¿Qué hora es?

I don't speak Spanish
No hablo español

Do you speak English?
¿Habla inglés?

I don't understand
No entiendo

Please repeat that
Por favor repita eso

Please speak more slowly
Por favor hable más despacio

What does this mean?
¿Qué significa esto?

Can you write that for me?
¿Me lo puede escribir?

My name is...
Me llamo...

What's your name?
¿Como se llama?

Hello, pleased to meet you
Hola, encantado/a

I'm from...
Soy de...

I live in...
Vivo en...

Where do you live?
¿Dónde vive usted?

Good morning/afternoon
Buenos días/buenas tardes

Good evening/night
Buenas noches

Goodbye
Adiós

This is my wife/husband/son/daughter/friend
Esta es mi mujer/marido/hijo/hija/amigo

See you later
Hasta luego

That's all right
Está bien

I don't know
No lo sé

You're welcome
De nada

How are you?
¿Cómo está?

USEFUL WORDS

yes **sí**	thank you **gracias**	here **aquí**	how **cómo**	I'm sorry **Lo siento**	small **pequeño**
no **no**	there **allí**	when **cuándo**	why **por qué**	excuse me **perdone**	good **bueno**
please **por favor**	where **dónde**	who **quién**	free **gratis**	large **grande**	bad **malo**

TIMES/DAYS/MONTHS/HOLIDAYS

morning
la mañana

afternoon
la tarde

evening
la tarde/ noche

day
el día

night
la noche

today
hoy

yesterday
ayer

tomorrow
mañana

now
ahora

later
más tarde

spring
primavera

summer
verano

autumn
otoño

winter
invierno

Monday
lunes

Tuesday
martes

Wednesday
miércoles

Thursday
jueves

Friday
viernes

Saturday
sábado

Sunday
domingo

month
el mes

year
el año

January
enero

February
febrero

March
marzo

April
abril

May
mayo

June
junio

July
julio

August
agosto

September
septiembre

October
octubre

November
noviembre

December
diciembre

Easter
Pascua

Christmas
Navidad

New Year
El Año Nuevo

All Saints' Day
Todos los Santos

vacation (holiday)
las vacaciones

pilgrimage
una romería

MONEY

Is there a bank/bureau de change nearby?
Hay un banco/una oficina de cambio cerca?

Can I cash this here?
¿Puedo cobrar esto aquí?

I'd like to change dollars/sterling into pesos
Quisiera cambiar dólares libras para pesos

Can I use my credit card to withdraw cash?
¿Puedo usar la tarjeta de crédito para sacar dinero?

What is the exchange rate?
¿Cómo está el cambio?

GETTING AROUND

Where is the information desk?
¿Dónde está el mostrador de información?

Where is the timetable?
¿Dónde está el horario?

Does this train/bus go to...?
¿Va este tren/autobús a...?

Does this train/bus stop at...?
¿Para este tren/autobús en...?

Do I have to get off here?
¿Me tengo que bajar aquí?

Do you have a subway/bus map?
¿Tiene un mapa del metro/de los autobuses?

Can I have a single/return ticket to...
¿Me da un boleto sencillo/de ida y vuelta para...?

Can I have a standard/first-class ticket to...
Quisiera un boleto de segunda/primera clase para...

I'd like to rent a car
Quiero alquilar un coche

Where are we?
¿Dónde estamos?

I'm lost
Estoy perdido

Is this the way to...?
¿Es esto el camino para ir a...?

I am in a hurry
Tengo prisa

Where can I find a taxi?
¿Dónde puedo encontrar un taxi?

Please take me to...
Me lleva a..., por favor

Please slow down
Vaya más despacio por favor

Can you turn on the meter
Podría poner el metro

How much is the journey?
¿Cuánto cuesta el viaje?

Could you wait for me?
¿Me podría esperar aquí?

POST AND TELEPHONES

Where is the nearest post office?
¿Dónde está la oficina de correos más cercana?

What is the postage to...
¿Cuánto vale mandarlo a...?

I'd like to send this by air mail
Quiero mandar esto por correo aéreo

Hello this is...
Bueno, habla...?

I'd like to speak to...
¿Podría hablar con...?

Who is speaking?
¿Con quién hablo?

What is the number for...
¿Cuál es el número de...?

Please put me through to...
Comuníqueme con..., por favor

Where can I buy a phone card?
¿Dónde puedo comprar una tarjeta de teléfono?

Extension..., please
La extensión..., por favor

SHOPPING

Could you help me please?
¿Me podría atender por favor?

How much is this?
¿Cuánto vale esto?

I'm looking for...
Estoy buscando...

When does the shop open/close?
¿A qué hora abre/cierra la tienda?

I'm just looking
Sólo estoy viendo

Do you have anything less expensive/smaller/larger
¿Tiene algo más barato/pequeño/grande?

Do you have this in...?
¿Tienen esto en...?

This is the right size
Esta talla está bien

I'll take this
Me llevo esto

Do you have a bag for this?
¿Tiene una bolsa para esto?

Can you gift wrap this?
¿Me lo envuelve para regalo?

Do you accept credit cards?
¿Aceptan tarjetas de crédito?

I'd like ... grams
Me pone ... gramos, por favor

I'd like a kilo of ...
Me da un kilo de...

I'd like ... slices of that
Me pone ... pedazos de eso

This isn't what I want
Esto no es lo que quiero

Can I help myself?
¿Puedo servirme?

bakery
la panadería

bookshop
la librería

pharmacy
la farmacia

supermarket
el supermercado

market
el mercado

sale
las rebajas

NUMBERS

1 **uno**	6 **seis**	11 **once**	16 **dieciséis**	21 **veintiuno**	70 **setente**
2 **dos**	7 **siete**	12 **doce**	17 **diecisiete**	30 **treinta**	80 **ochenta**
3 **tres**	8 **ocho**	13 **trece**	18 **dieciocho**	40 **cuarenta**	90 **noventa**
4 **cuatro**	9 **nueve**	14 **catorce**	19 **diecinueve**	50 **cincuenta**	100 **cien**
5 **cinco**	10 **diez**	15 **quince**	20 **veinte**	60 **sesenta**	1,000 **mil**

HOTELS

Do you have a room?
¿Tiene una habitación?

I have a reservation for ... nights
Tengo una reservación para ... noches

How much per night?
¿Cuánto es por noche?

Double room
Habitación doble con cama de matrimonio

Single room
Habitación sencilla

Twin room
Habitación doble con dos camas

With bath/shower
Con baño/ducha

Swimming pool
La alberca

Air conditioning
Aire acondicionado

Non smoking
Se prohibe fumar

Is breakfast included?
¿Está el desayuno incluido?

When is breakfast served?
¿A qué hora se sirve el desayuno?

May I see the room?
¿Puedo ver la habitación?

Is there an elevator?
¿Hay elevador?

I'll take this room
Me quedo con la esta habitación

The room is dirty
La habitación está sucia

The room is too hot/cold
Hace demasiado calor/frío en la habitación

Can I pay my bill?
La cuenta por favor

Could you order a taxi for me?
¿Me pide un taxi por favor?

See also the menu reader on pages 242–243.

I'd like to reserve a table for .... people at...
Quisiera reservar una mesa para ... personas para las...

A table for ..., please
Una mesa para ..., por favor

We have/haven't booked
Tenemos una/no tenemos reservación

What time does the restaurant open?
¿A qué hora se abre el restaurante?

We'd like to wait for a table
Queremos esperar a que haya una mesa

Could we sit here?
¿Nos podemos sentar aquí?

Is this table free?
¿Queda libre esta mesa?

Are there tables outside?
¿Hay mesas afuera?

Is there a car park?
¿Hay aparcamiento?

Where are the lavatories?
¿Dónde están los baños?

Can I have an ashtray?
¿Me da un cenicero?

I prefer non-smoking
Prefiero no fumadores

Could you warm this up for me?
¿Me podria calentar esto?

Could we see the menu/ wine list?
¿Podemos ver la carta/ carta de vinos?

We would like something to drink
Quisiéramos algo a beber

What do you recommend?
¿Qué nos recomienda?

Can you recommend a local wine?
¿Puede usted recomendar un vino de la región?

Is there a dish of the day?
¿Hay un plato del día?

I am a vegetarian
Soy vegetariano

I am diabetic
Soy diabético(a)

I can't eat wheat/sugar/salt/ pork/beef/dairy/nuts
No puedo tomar trigo/azúcar/sal/cerdo/carne (de res)/ productos lácteos/nueces

Could I have a bottle of still/sparkling water?
¿Me podría traer una botella de agua mineral sin/con gas?

Could we have some more bread?
¿Nos podría traer más pan?

Could we have some salt and pepper?
¿Nos podría traer sal y pimienta?

How much is this dish?
¿Cuánto es este plato?

This is not what I ordered
Esto no es lo que había pedido

I ordered...
Habia pedido...

I'd like...
Quisiera...

May I change my order
¿Puedo cambiar la orden?

I'd prefer a salad
Prefiero una ensalada

How is it cooked?
¿Cómo está hecho?

is it very spicy?
¿Esta muy picante?

The food is cold
La comida está fría

... is too rare/overcooked
... está demasiado crudo/ demasiado hecho

We would like a coffee
Quisieramos tomar café

May I have the bill, please?
¿Me trae la cuenta, por favor?

Is service included?
¿Está incluido el servicio?

What is this charge?
¿Qué es esta cantidad?

The bill is not right
La cuenta no está bien

We didn't have this
No tomamos esto

Do you accept this credit card (travelers' checks)?
¿Acepta usted esta tarjeta de crédito (cheques de viajero)?

I'd like to speak to the manager
Quisiera hablar con el jefe

The food was excellent
La comida fue excelente

We enjoyed it, thank you
Nos ha gustado, muchas gracias

breakfast
el desayuno

lunch
la comida

dinner
la cena

starters
los antojitos/botanas

main course
el plato principal

dessert
el postre

dish of the day
el plato del día

bread
el pan

sugar
el azúcar

wine list
la carta de vinos

knife/fork/spoon
el cuchillo/tenedor/ la cuchara

waiter/waitress
El mesero/la mesara

TOURIST INFORMATION

Where is the tourist information office?
¿Dónde está la oficina de turismo?

Do you have a city map?
¿Tiene un mapa de la ciudad?

Can you give me some information about…?
¿Me podría dar información sobre…?

What sights/hotels/restaurants can you recommend?
¿Qué lugares de interés/hoteles/restaurantes nos recomienda?

Can you point them out on the map?
¿Me los podría señalar en el mapa?

What time does it open/close?
¿A qué hora se abre/cierra?

Are there guided tours?
¿Hay visitas con guía?

Is there an English-speaking guide?
¿Hay algún guía que hable inglés?

Can we make reservations here?
¿Podemos hacer las reservaciones aquí?

What is the admission price?
¿Cuánto es la entrada?

Is photography allowed?
¿Se permite tomar fotos?

Is there a discount for senior citizens/students?
¿Hay descuento para los mayores/los estudiantes?

Do you have a brochure in English?
¿Tiene un folleto en inglés?

What time does the show start?
¿A qué hora empieza la función?

How much is a ticket?
¿Cuánto vale una entrada?

IN THE TOWN

church
la iglesia

castle
el castillo

museum
el museo

park
el parque

cathedral
la catedral

bridge
el puente

gallery
la galería de arte

river
el río

no entry
prohibido el paso

entrance
entrada

exit
salida

lavatories
los baños

men/women
caballeros/señoras

open
abierto

closed
cerrado

ILLNESS AND EMERGENCIES

I don't feel well
No me siento bien

Could you call a doctor?
¿Podría llamar a un médico?

I feel nauseous
Tengo ganas de vomitar

I have a headache
Tengo dolor de cabeza

I am allergic to…
Soy alérgico a…

I am on medication
Estoy tomando medicamentos

I am diabetic
Soy diabético

I have asthma
Soy asmático

hospital
el hospital

How long will I have to stay in bed/hospital?
¿Cuánto tiempo tendré que quedarme en la cama/el hospital?

How many tablets a day should I take?
¿Cuántas pastillas debéna de tomar diario?

Can I have a painkiller?
¿Me da un analgésico?

I need to see a doctor/dentist
Necesito ver un médico/dentista

I have bad toothache
Tengo un dolor de muelas horrible

Help!
Socorro

Stop thief!
Al ladrón

Call the fire brigade/police/ambulance
Llame a los bomberos/la policía/una ambulancia

I have lost my passport/wallet/purse/handbag
He perdido me pasaporte/la cartera/el monedero/la bolsa

Is there a lost property office?
¿Hay una oficina de objetos perdidos?

I have had an accident
Tuve un accidente

I have been robbed
Me han robado

Where is the police station?
¿Dónde está la comisaría?

MEXICAN GLOSSARY

Ahuehuete: giant cypress, Mexico's national tree
Alameda: large plaza or city park
Animalitos: little clay animals, produced in Chiapas
Arbol de la vida: tree of life
Ayuntamiento: town hall or government
Aztec: dominant empire in Central Mexico from the 14th century till Spanish Conquest
Avenida: avenue
Azulejo: decorative glazed tile
Bahía: bay
Baluarte: bastion, bulwark
Barranca: canyon
Barrio: suburb or area within a town or city
Cabo: cape, headland
Calle: street
Calzada: avenue
Campesino: peasant farmer
Cantina: bar, usually only frequented by men
Capilla: chapel
Casa: house
Cascada: waterfall
Cenote: freshwater sinkhole, often used by divers
Cerro: hill
Chac Mool: carved figure used for holding sacrifical offerings
Chaltun: underground water cistern for storing rainwater
Charrería: rodeo
Chinampas: floating gardens whose plants eventually root themselves to the lake bed
Churrigueresque: highly elaborate and decorative form of baroque architecture seen in many Mexican churches, named after 17th-century Spanish architect
Colectivo: small bus
Convento: convent or monastery
Criollo: Mexican-born Spaniard
Don/Doña: Sir/Madam
Ejido: communal farmland
EZLN: Ejército Zapatista de Liberación Nacional (Zapatista Army of Liberation), Chiapas guerilla group
Feria: fair/market
Fuente: fountain
Fuerte: fort
Finca: ranch or plantation
Fonart: government agency responsible for promoting crafts
Fonda: basic restaurant or boarding house
Gachupin: person of pure Spanish blood
Gringo: general term for a foreigner, especially North American, but not an insult
Gruta: grotto
Guayabera: style of man's shirt originally from Cuba
Hacendado: estate owner
Hacienda: large country house or estate
Henequen: hemp fibre used to make rope
Huipil: Maya women's embroidered blouse
Indigena: person of indigenous birth
IVA: 15 percent value-added tax
Lancha: small fishing boat
Luz y sonido: light and sound
Malecón: seafront promenade
Maquiladora: assembly plant using US imported material for re-export
Mariachis: famed wandering musicians notable for their sentimental ballads
Maya: still extant pre-Hispanic tribe who inhabited Southeast Mexico, Guatemala, Belize, Honduras and El Salvador
Mercado: market, usually where local farmers and artisans sell their produce and wares
Mestizo: person of mixed Spanish and Indian blood
Mezcal: alcoholic spirit made from any of the maguey (agave) family of plants. The worm found in some bottles is actually the larva of a moth that lives in the agave plant
Mirador: look-out point
Mixtec: ancient tribe from Oaxaca
Modernidad: modernity
Mudéjar: Spanish architectural style based on Moorish forms
Muelle: pier or jetty
NAFTA: North American Free Trade Agreement which includes Mexico, the US and Canada
Nahuatl: Aztec language
Norteño: northern, used to describe a style of food or music
Obsidian: a type of volcanic glass used to make mirrors, jewelry and weapons such as knives, arrow tips and spear heads
Palacio: mansion
Palacio de Gobierno: state/federal authority headquarters
Palacio Municipal: Municipal local government headquarters
Palapa: palm-thatched hut
Palenque: cockpit (for cockfighting)
PAN: Partido de Acción Nacional (National Action Party), conservative party (currently in power)
Paseo: broad avenue or ritual evening stroll
Pemex: national oil company, Mexico's only provider of gas and oil products
Porfiriato: era of dictator Porfirio Díaz, also used for grandiose architecture of the time
Posada: inn
PRD: Partido Revolucionario Democrático (Party of the Democratic Revolution), left-wing opposition party
PRI: Partido Revolucionario Insitucional (Party of the Institutional Revolution), ruling party for 71 years until 2000 elections
Pulque: alcoholic drink made from fermented maguey
Quetzal: a rare Central American bird, prized by the Maya for its feathers
Retablo: decorative painted wooden altarpiece
Romería: procession
Sacbé (plural sacbeob): literally a "white road"; a stone causeway linking Maya buildings and settlements
Sierra: mountain range
Stela: large freestanding carved stone monument erected to commemorate a Mayan event
Talavera poblano: considered the crème de la crème of decorative azulejos (tiles)
Tenochtitlán: Aztec capital, site of present-day Mexico City
Teotihuacán: ancient city north of Mexico City
Tequila: alcoholic spirit made from the blue maguey plant only (see also Mezcal)
Toltec: tribe which ruled Central Mexico before the Aztecs
Tula: Toltec capital
Tzompantli: Aztec skull rack displaying skulls of sacrificial victims
Virreinal: period of Spanish viceroys
Wetback: illegal Mexican migrant in the US
Zapotec: tribe which ruled in Oaxaca until around eighth century AD
Zócalo: main or central plaza in any town or city

KEY FIGURES IN MEXICAN HISTORY

Ignacio Allende: (1779–1811) Mexican soldier and Independence hero
Luís Barragán: (1902–1988) one of Mexico's most influential 20th-century architects
Miguel Cabrera: (1695–1768) Oaxacan artist
Plutarco Elías Calles: (1877–1945) president of Mexico (1924–28)
Cuauhtémoc Cárdenas: (born 1934) mayor of Mexico City and leader of the PRD
Lázaro Cárdenas: (1895–1970) president of Mexico (1934–40)
Venustiano Carranza: (1859–1920) president of Mexico (1917–20)
Bartolome de las Casas: (1474–1566) Spanish priest, known as a protector of Indians and a defender of their rights
Hernán Cortés: (1485–1547) Spanish conquistador and conqueror of Mexico
Cuauhtémoc: (1495–1525) the last Aztec emperor (1520–21)
Porfirio Díaz: (1830–1915) president of Mexico (1876–80 and 1884–1911)
Vicente Fox: (born 1942) president of Mexico (2000–)
Carlos Fuentes: (born 1928) Mexican novelist, playwright and diplomat
Juan de Grijalva: (1489–1527) Spanish conquistador, one of the earliest to explore the shores of Mexico
Vicente Guerrero: (1782–1831) president of Mexico (1829)
Miguel Hidalgo: (1753–1811) enlightened Catholic priest and leader of the Independence movement, famous for his "grito" (call to arms)
Victoriano Huerta: (1854–1916) president of Mexico (1913–14)
Agustín de Iturbide: (1783–1824) Mexican soldier and emperor (1821–23)
Benito Juárez: (1806–72) Zapotec lawyer who became president of Mexico (1861–63 and 1867–72)
Frida Kahlo: (1907–54) influential Mexican artist, married to Diego Rivera
Diego de Landa: (1524–79) Bishop of Yucatán, infamous for destroying all Maya documents, then writing an account of the Mayan civilization—*Relaciones de las Cosas de Yucatán*—around 1566
Ricardo Legorreta: (born 1931) one of Mexico's most renowned architects
Francisco Indalecio Madero: (1873–1913) president of Mexico (1911–13)
La Malinche: (c1505–c1528) daughter of a nobleman, and later consort and interpreter for Hernán Cortés. She played a significant role in the downfall of the Aztec empire
Maximilian of Habsburg: (1832–67) Emperor of Mexico (1864–67)
Moctezuma II: (Montezuma; 1466–1520) the penultimate Aztec emperor (1502–20)
José María Morelos: (1765–1815) Mexican patriot who took over leadership of the Independence movement after the death of Hidalgo in 1811
Álvaro Obregón: (1880–1928): president of Mexico (1920–24)
Juan O'Gorman: (1905–82) Mexican architect; studied painting under Diego Rivera
José Clemente Orozco: (1883–1949) one of the greatest mural painters of the 20th century
Octavio Paz: (1914–98) leading Mexican poet, particularly known for *The Labyrinth of Solitude* (1950)
José Guadalupe Posada: (1851–1913) considered Mexico's greatest lithographer, whose engravings and etchings satirized tyrannical politicians
Vasco de Quiroga: (1479–1565) Spanish priest who did much to help the Tarascans in Michoacán
Diego Rivera: (1886–1957) Mexican painter, famous for his murals depicting the life and history of the Mexican people
Antonio López de Santa Anna: (1797–1876) soldier and president of Mexico (periodically1833–55)
David Alfaro Siqueiros: (1896–1974) one of Mexico's most original and eminent painters, renowned for his murals
Rufino Tamayo: (1899–1991) one of the great Mexican artists of the 20th century
Miguel Alemán Valdés: (1905–83) president of Mexico (1946–52)
Francisco "Pancho" Villa: (1877–1923) legendary Mexican bandit, real name Doroteo Arango
Emiliano Zapata: (1879–1919) peasant hero of Mexico and rebel leader during the Mexican Revolution

AZTEC AND MAYA DEITIES

Ah Mucen Cab: Maya god of bees
Ah Puch: Maya god of death
Centeotl: Aztec god of corn
Chac: Maya god of rain
Chalchiuhtlicue: Aztec goddess of running water; sister of Tláloc
Chaob: Maya god of the wind
Chicomecoatl: Aztec goddess of corn and fertility
Coatlicue: Aztec earth goddess—she of the serpent skirt
Coyolxauqhui: Aztec god of the moon
Ehécatl: Aztec god of the wind
Ekahau: Maya god of travelers and merchants
Huitzilopochtli: Aztec god of war and the sun, supreme god
Itzamná: Maya god of creation
Ix Chel: Maya goddess of the moon
Ixtab: Maya goddess of suicide
Kukulkán: Maya name for Queztalcóatl
Mictlantecuhtli: Aztec god of death
Nacon: Maya god of war
Queztalcóatl: the plumed serpent, the most powerful and important of all Mexican gods
Tlacolotl: Maya god of evil
Tlaloc: Toltec/Aztec god of rain
Tonatiuh: Aztec sun god
Xochipilli: Aztec god of flowers
Yum Cimil: Maya god of death
Yum Kaax or Yumil Kaxob: Maya god of maize

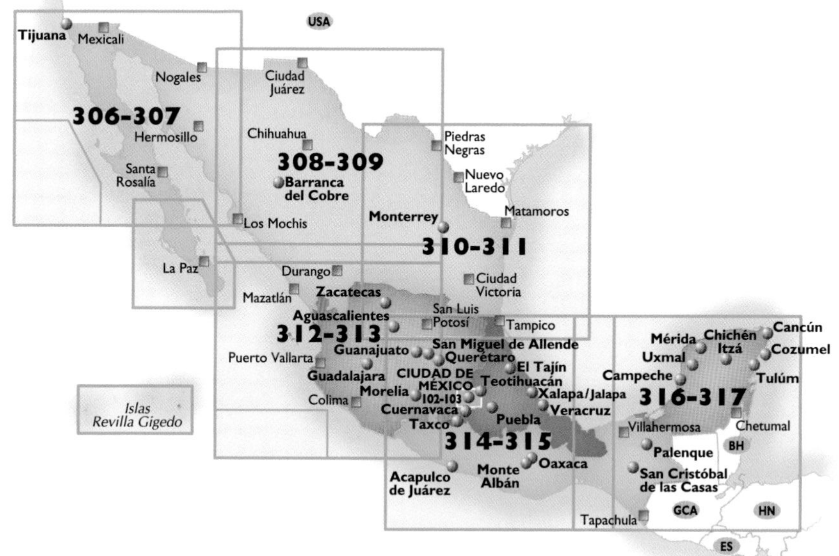

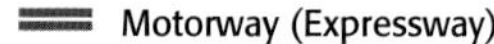
Motorway (Expressway)

National road

Regional road

Main road

Other road

Built-up area

City / Town

National park / Reserve

Featured place of interest

Other place of interest

Airport

621 Height in metres

Ferry route

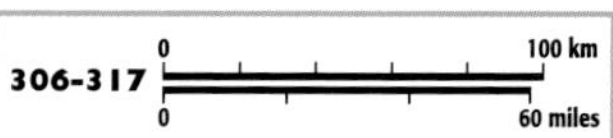

Maps

San Diego
Tijuana
Tecate
Mexicali
San Luis Río Colorado
Ensenada
BAJA
CALIFORNIA
NORTE
San Quintín
San Felipe
El Rosario
Guerrero Negro
Isla Cedros
Loreto
Ciudad Constitución
SUR
La Paz
Topolobampo
Mazatlán
Cabo San Lucas
San José del Cabo
Puerto Vallarta
Sierra de Juárez
Sierra de San Pedro Mártir
Sierra de la Giganta
Sierra de la Laguna
Parque Nacíonal Sierra de San Pedro Mártir
3078 Picacho del Diablo
Bahía Sebastián Vizcaíno
Laguna Ojo de Liebre
Isla Magdalena
Isla Santa Margarita
Isla Espíritu Santo
Isla Cerralvo
Isla San José
Isla Santa Catalina
Isla El Carmen

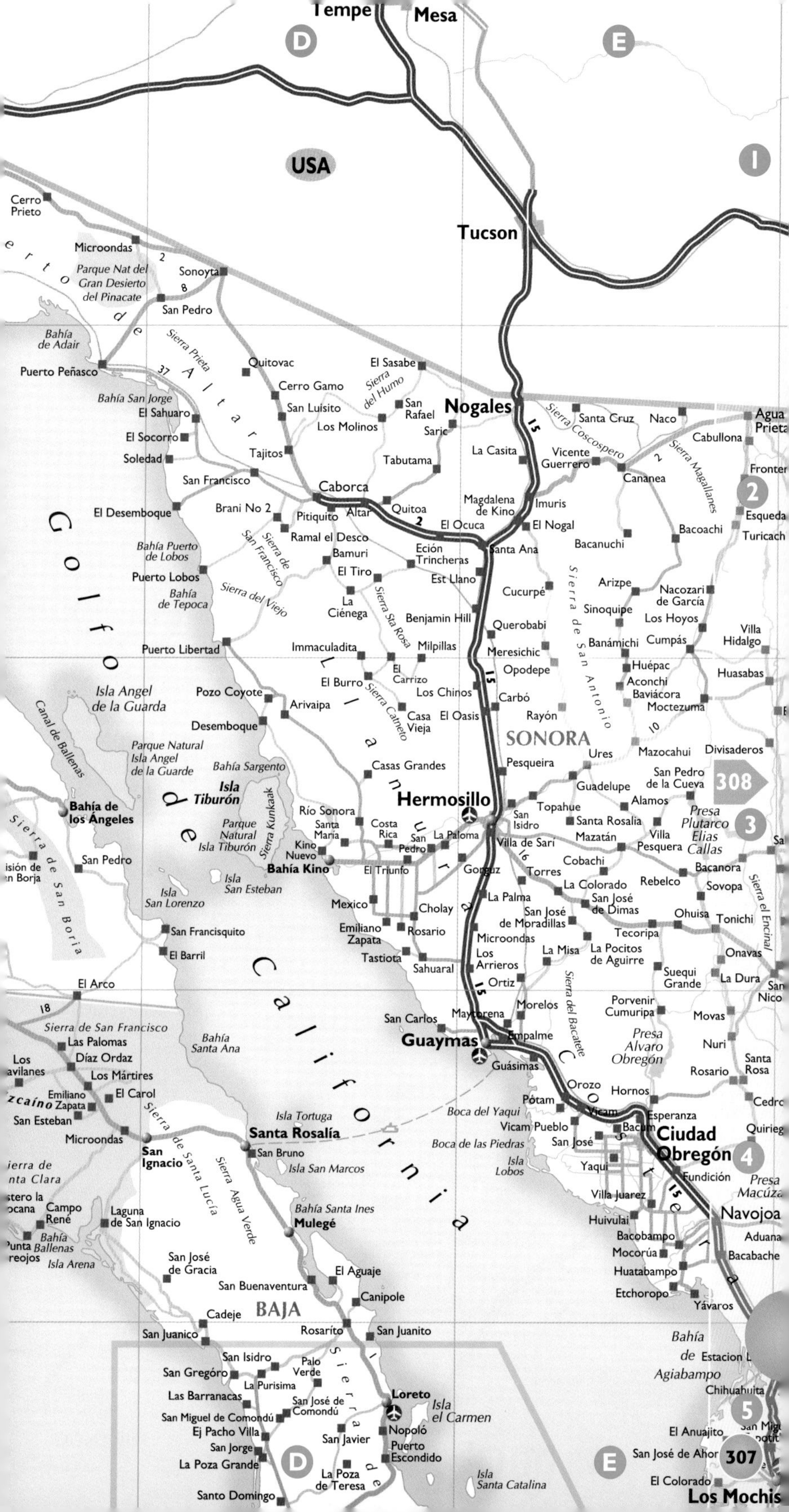

Tempe
Mesa
D
E
USA
I
Tucson
Cerro Prieto
Microondas
Parque Nat del Gran Desierto del Pinacate
Sonoyta
San Pedro
Bahía de Adair
Puerto Peñasco
Sierra Prieta
Desierto de Altar
Quitovac
El Sasabe
Cerro Gamo
Sierra del Humo
San Luisito
San Rafael
Nogales
Los Molinos
Saric
Bahía San Jorge
El Sahuaro
El Socorro
Soledad
Tajitos
Tabutama
La Casita
Santa Cruz
Naco
Agua Prieta
Sierra Coscospero
Vicente Guerrero
Cananea
Sierra Magallanes
Cabullona
Fronter
San Francisco
Caborca
Magdalena de Kino
Imuris
El Desemboque
Brani No 2
Pitiquito
Altar
Quitoa
El Ocuca
El Nogal
Esqueda
Ramal el Desco
Santa Ana
Bacanuchi
Bacoachi
Turicach
Bahía Puerto de Lobos
Sierra de San Francisco
Bamuri
Ención Trincheras
Puerto Lobos
El Tiro
Est Llano
Bahía de Tepoca
Sierra del Viejo
La Ciénega
Sierra Sta Rosa
Cucurpé
Arizpe
Nacozari de García
Sinoquipe
Benjamin Hill
Querobabi
Los Hoyos
Puerto Libertad
Immaculadita
Milpillas
Meresichic
Banámichi
Cumpás
Villa Hidalgo
Golfo de California
Isla Angel de la Guarda
Pozo Coyote
El Burro
El Carrizo
Los Chinos
Opodepe
Huépac
Aconchi
Huasabas
Sierra Catneto
Carbó
Baviácora
Moctezuma
Arivaipa
Casa Vieja
El Oasis
Rayón
Sierra de San Antonio
Canal de Ballenas
Desemboque
Llanura
SONORA
Parque Natural Isla Angel de la Guarde
Ures
Mazocahui
Divisaderos
Bahía Sargento
Casas Grandes
Pesqueira
San Pedro de la Cueva
308
Isla Tiburón
Sierra Kunkaak
Guadelupe
Alamos
Bahía de los Ángeles
Hermosillo
Presa Plutarco Elías Callas
Río Sonora
Topahue
3
Parque Natural Isla Tiburón
Santa María
Costa Rica
San Isidro
Santa Rosalía
San Pedro
La Paloma
Mazatán
Villa Pesquera
Kino Nuevo
Villa de Sarí
Bahía Kino
Cobachi
Bacanora
El Triunfo
Gorguz
Torres
Sierra de San Borja
Isla San Esteban
La Colorado
Rebelco
Sovopa
Isla San Lorenzo
La Palma
San José de Dimas
Sierra el Encinal
Mexico
San José de Moradillas
Cholay
Ohuisa
Tonichi
Emiliano Zapata
Rosario
Tecoripa
San Francisquito
Microondas
El Barril
Tastiota
La Pocitos de Aguirre
La Misa
Sahuaral
Los Arrieros
Suequi Grande
Onavas
La Dura
El Arco
Ortiz
Sierra del Bacatete
Porvenir Cumuripa
Morelos
San Carlos
Maytorena
Movas
Sierra de San Francisco
Las Palomas
Bahía Santa Ana
Guaymas
Empalme
Presa Alvaro Obregón
Nuri
Díaz Ordaz
Los Avilanes
Los Mártires
Guásimas
Santa Rosa
Rosario
El Carol
Emiliano Zapata
Vizcaíno
Orozo
Hornos
San Esteban
Isla Tortuga
Boca del Yaqui
Pótam
Vicam
Esperanza
Cedro
Microondas
Sierra de Santa Lucía
Santa Rosalía
Vicam Pueblo
Bacum
Ciudad Obregón
Quirieg
San Ignacio
San Bruno
Boca de las Piedras
San José
4
Isla San Marcos
Sierra Agua Verde
Isla Lobos
Yaqui
Fundición
Presa Macúza
Sierra de Santa Clara
Campo René
Laguna de San Ignacio
Bahía Santa Ines
Villa Juarez
Mulegé
Navojoa
Huivulai
Bahía Ballenas
Punta Abreojos
Isla Arena
Bacobampo
Aduana
Mocorúa
Bacabache
San José de Gracia
El Aguaje
Huatabampo
San Buenaventura
Etchoropo
Yávaros
Canipole
BAJA
Cadeje
Rosarito
San Juanito
San Juanico
Bahía de Agiabampo
Estacion
San Isidro
Palo Verde
San Gregório
La Purisima
Chihuahuita
Las Barranacas
San José de Comondú
Loreto
Isla el Carmen
5
San Miguel de Comondú
Ej Pacho Villa
Sierra de la Giganta
Nopoló
El Anuajito
San Javier
Puerto Escondido
San Jorge
La Poza Grande
San José de Ahor
307
La Poza de Teresa
Isla Santa Catalina
El Colorado
Santo Domingo
Los Mochis

E
F
G
El Paso
Ciudad Juárez
Rodrego M Quevedo
Zaragoza
Jesús Carranza
San Isidro
Mezquite
Samalayuca
Naco
Agua Prieta
Cabullona
San Bernardino
Nogales
Guzmán
Barreal
Guadalupe de Bravo
El Porvenir
Candelaria
Progreso
Sierra Magallanes
Fronteras
Ascensión
El Barreal
El Mirador
Janos
Sabinal
Esqueda
San Miguelito
Bacoachi
Turicachi
Sierra San Diego
Tres Alamos
El Roble
Banderas
Cajoncitos
Lucero
El Cuarenta
Ojos Calientes
Hidalgo
San Pedro Corralitos
El Oro
Nuevo Casas Grandes
Casas Grandes
Juárez
El Carrizal
Villa Ahumada y Anexas
Alamos de Peña
Villa Ahumada
La Máquina
Sierra del Huesco
Bavispe
Bacerac
Nacozari de García
Los Hoyos
Cumpás
Villa Hidalgo
Huachinera
San Diego
Pacheco
Francisco I Madero
Galeana
Progreso
Benito Juárez
Moctezuma
El Veinticuatro
Mata Ortiz
Aribabi
Huasabas
Moctezuma
Bacadehuachi
Nacori Chico
Buenaventura
R Flores Magón
El Sueco
Ojo de Carrizo
Gallego
San Lorenzo
La Mesa del Huracán
307
Divisaderos
Chuhuichupa
Zaragoza
La Esperanza
San Pedro de la Cueva
Tecoriname
El Alamillo
Las Varas
Gómez Farías
Cruces
El Carrizalillo
Arados
Loma
Presa Plutarco Elías Callas
San José de Bavícora
La Pinta
Santa Clara
Madera
Namiquipa
Benito Juárez
El Pastor
El Peñol
Hormigas
Bacanora
Sahuaripa
Oscar Soto Máynes
El Molino
Yepómera
Arivachi
Natora
Sierra el Encinal
Temosachic
El Morrión
Placer de Guadalupe
Sovopa
Matachic
El Saúz
Cumbres de Majalca
Aldama
Trancas
Ohuisa
Tonichi
Bachiniva
Sianapuchic
P N Cumbres de Majalca
Tejolocachic
Santo Tomás
Alvaro Obregón
Guizamopa
San Antonio El Grande
Chihuahua
Aquiles Serdán
San Diego de Alcalá
Suequi Grande
Onavas
Santa Rosa
Maycoba
Tosanachic
Ciudad Guerrero
La Junta
Anáhuac
Riva Palacio
La Dura
Yepachic
Cuauhtémoc
Bachimba
San Nicolás
Yécora
Temochic
Pedernales
Lázaro Cárdenas
Julimes
Movas
Ocampo
Basaseachic
San Miguel
Gran Morelos
General Trías
Meoqui
Cascada de Basaseáchic
Parque Natural Cascada de Basaseachic
Cajurichic
Pichachic
San Bernabé
La Paz
CHIHUAHUA
El Salitre
Delicias
Presa Alvaro Obregón
Nuri
Tutuaca
Rosario
Santa Rosa
San Juanito
Carichi
El Rebalse
Saucillo
Batopilas
Bocoyna
Satevó
Est Conchos
Cedros
Uruachic
Creel
Sisoguichic
San Francisco de Borja
Santa María de Cuevas
Santa Gertrudis
Naica
Parque Natural Barranca del Cobre
Cusarare
Río Conchos
El Porvenir
Ciudad Camargo
Ciudad Obregón
Quiriego
San Bernardo
Monterde
El Divisadero
Valerio
La Laguna
Presa de la Boquilla
Presa Macúzari
Chinipas
Barranca del Cobre
Basihuare
Nonoava
Boquilla de Abajo
Valle de Zaragoza
La Boquilla del Conchos
Fundición
Témoris
Norogachic
San Felipe de Jesús
Búfalo
Tanques
Navojoa
Milpillas
Samachique
Humariza
Valle del Rosario
La Higuera
La Bufa
Recheáchic
San Javier
El Dorado
Aduana
Santa Matilde
Huejotitán
Alamos
Batopilas
Yoquivo
Gral Carlos Pacheco
Hidalgo del Parral
Pueblito de Allende
Bacabache
El Tule
Tasajeras
Guachochic
San Pablo Balleza
San Francisco del Oro
Valle de Allende
Baca
Choix
El Ojito
Santa Bárbara
Villa Matamoros
Yávaros
Bahía de Agiabampo
Aserradero San Rafael
La Estancia
Río Fuerte
El Fuerte
San Simon
Baborigame
Estacion Don
El Vergel
Villa de Orestes
Las Nieves
Chinobampo
Yecorato
Villa Ocampo
Chihuahuita
San José de Gracia
San Juan Nepomuceno
La Catedral
Cerro Prieto
Torreón de Cañas
Guadalupe y Calvo
El Anuajito
San Miguel Zapotitlan
San Blas
Ocoroni
San José de Ahome
Charay
Aserradero Yerbitas
Guanacevi
San Bernardo
Ahome
Mochicahui
Sinaloa de Leyva
Soyatita
El Colorado
Naranjo
Bajíos de Agua Blanca
El Salitre
Santa María del Oro
Los Mochis
Tetamechi
Bacubirito
Zape
Topolobampo
Est Leon Fonseca
Santiago de los Caballeros
Ciénega de Escobar
Guasave
Guamuchil
Copalquín
La Brecha
Isla de San Ignacio
Las Glorias
Mocorito
General Galeana
Angostura
Tepantita
Cebollin
Tepehuanes
Buenavista
Presa Adolfo López Mateos
San José de la Boca
Baturi
Topía
Presidios
Pichilingüe
Potrero de Los Sánchez
Las Herreras
Mesa de Guadalupe
La Templadera del Derrumbe
Isla Altamura
Pericos
El Varejonal
Santiago Papasquiaro
Culiacancito
Tamazula
Culiacán
San Nicholás de Ariba
Aguaruto
DURANGO
Altata
Comedero
SINALOA
312
Los Remedios
La Alameda
Los Puentes
Tabala
Quila
Santa Crúz
Huajuapan
Sierra Madre Occidental
2
3
4
5
10
15
16
24
45
308

H
J
K
USA
2
3
4
5
6
COAHUILA
Piedras Negras
Nueva Rosita
Monclova
Saltillo
Torreón
Gómez Palacio
Ciudad Acuña
Ojinaga
Jiménez
Río Grande
Río Bravo
Río Álamos
Río Sabinas
Río Nazas
Presa la Amistad
La Amistad
P N la Amistad
P N Carmen
Parque Nacional Los Novilllos
Parque Int del Río Bravo
Serranías del Burro
Sierra del Carmen
Sierra El Pino
Sierra Hermosa de Santa Rosa
Sierra de la Purísima
Sierra de la Palma
Sierra de Parras
Sierra Grande
Sierra Madre Oriental
Llanos de los Cristianos
Llanos de los Caballos Mesteños
Meseta del Norte
Bolsón de Mapimí
Desierto Laguna de Mayrán
Lomas de Arena
San Antonio el Bravo
Barranco de Guadalupe
Los Conchas
El Paradero
Cuchillo Parado
Coyame
San Pedro
El Pueblito
Maclovio Herrera
Boquilla del Mezquite
Potrero del Llano
Manuel Benavides
Polvorillas
Charco de la Peña
La Morita
Charco de la Aguja
La Perla
San Francisco
Santa Anita
Minas de Hércules
Alicante
La Selva
Piedritas
Alamos de Márquez
La Rosita
San Miguel
El Milagro
Boquillas del Carmen
La Linda
Las Norias
Morelos
Los Picos
El Salado
Santa Rosa
Chupadero de Caballo
Santa Eulalia
La Muralla
San Carlos
El León
El Remolino
Terreros
El Tule
Zaragoza
Morelos
Río Bravo
Nava
Allende
Villa Unión
Guadalupe
Mezquitosa
Agujita
Sabinas
Palau
San Juan de Sabinas
Melchor Múzquiz
Las Esperanzas
Minas de Barroterran
El Sauz
La Luz
Progreso
Don Martín
Ramírez
Juárez
La Cuesta
La Babia
La Rosita
Acebuches
El Guaje
El Revés
Santa Elena
La Mora
El Caballo
Cenzontle
San Isidro
Ocampo
Los Laureles
San Blas
Villa Escobedo
Abasolo
Primero de Mayo
Los Rodríguez
San Buenaventura
Nadadores
Lampazos de Naranjo
Candela
Beatriz Microondas
Maravillas
Sierra Mojada
El Oro
La Vibora
El Magueyal
Laguna del Rey
Matrimonio
Zacatosa
Guimbalete
El Oso
San Juan
Lamadrid
Sacramento
Cuatrociénegas de Carranza
Villa Frontera
Socorro
Carrillo
Mohovano
Villa López
Microondas
Rellano
Escalón
Coronado
Guadalupe Bahues
Ceballos
Yermo
San Fermín
Villa Hidalgo
El Venado
La Soledad
Castaños
Tanque Nuevo
El Papalote
Las Palomas
Gloria
Bajan
Bustamante
Villaldama
Espinazo
Dolores
Tlahualillo de Zaragoza
San Francisco de Horizonte
El Cantabro
San Pedro de las Colonias
Tacubaya
Francisco I Madero
Matamoros
Entronque La Cuchilla
Emiliano Zapata
Paila
Pastora
La Rosa
Paredon
Fraustro
Santa Cruz
Hipólito
El Tule
Ramos Arizpe
Grutas de García
Santa Catarina
Garza García
Arteaga
P N Cumbres de Monterrey
General Cepeda
Chapula
San Antonio de los Alazanes
Agua Nueva
San Rafael
La Zarca
La Recholera
San Rafael
Bermejillo
Mapimí
El Casco
El Palmito
San Pedro del Gallo
Ciudad Lerdo
León Guzman
Villa Juárez
San Luis del Cordero
La Perla
Abasolo
Rodeo
Nazas
Paso Nacional
Pedriceña
Viesca
Jimulco
Parras de la Fuente
Bajío de Ahuichila
Santa Victoria
San Jerónimo
Gómez Farías
Avalos
Mazapil
Cedros
Concepción
Ejido Hidalgo
San Juan de Guadalupe
Benito Juárez
Est Simón
General Simón Bolivar
La Mancha
Cuencamé
Peñon Blanco
Yerbanis
Donato Guerra
Guadalupe Victoria
Luis Moya
Santa Clara
310
313
45
49
30
40
57
53
54
2
29
16
23
D

La Linda
Parque Nacional Los Novillos
P N la Amistad
La Amistad
Chisos Mts
3
J
K
Boquillas del Carmen
Las Norias
Chupadero de Caballo
P N Carmen
Ciudad Acuña
Santa Eulalia
La Muralla
Jiménez
Morelos
Sra del Carmen
Los Picos
El León
San Carlos
El Moral
El Milagro
Parque Int del Río Bravo
Piedritas
Burro
El Remolino
Piedras Negras
Alamos de Márquez
San Miguel
La Cuesta
Terreros
Santa Rosa
Zaragoza
La Rosita
La Babia
El Tule
Sierra El Pino
Sierra Hermosa de Santa Rosa
La Rosita
Río Álamos
Morelos
Río Bravo
Nava
Guerrero
Acebuches
Allende
Guadalupe
Villa Unión
Río Bravo del Norte
Río Grande
El Guaje
El Revés
San Juan de Sabinas
Nueva Rosita
Mezquitosa
Santa Elena
Melchor Múzquiz
Palau
Agujita
Sabinas
La Mora
Las Esperanzas
Villa Hidalgo
El Caballo
4
COAHUILA
Minas de Barroterran
El Sauz
Río Sabinas
Juárez
Colombia
La Luz
Don Martin
Nuevo Laredo
San Isidro
Progreso
Los Laureles
San Blas
Ocampo
Ramírez
El Oro
San Lorenzo
Villa Escobedo
309
Anáhuac
Camarón
La Vibora
El Magueyal
Abasolo
Primero de Mayo
Los Rodriguez
Nuevo Anáhuac
Laguna del Rey
Matrimonio
El Oso
San Juan
Lamadrid
San Buenaventura
Lampazos de Naranjo
Casa Blanca
Zacatosa
Cuatrociénegas de Carranza
Sacramento
Nadadores
La Gloria
Río Salado
Socorro
Villa Frontera
Monclova
Candela
El Venado
Estación Candela
Presa Falcón
Mohovano
La Soledad
Castaños
Guerrero
Tanque Nuevo
Vallecillos
Nueva Ciudad Guerrero
Sierra de la Purísima
Gloria
Bajan
Bustamante
Sabinas Hidalgo
El Alamo
Parás
El Papalote
Las Palomas
Villaldama
Mier
Cd Miguel Alemán
Agualeguas
Espinazo
Tlahualillo de Zaragoza
Dolores
Los Nogales
NUEVO
General Treviño
Camargo
Los Comales
Mamulique
Cerralvo
San Francisco de Horizonte
Desierto Laguna de Mayrán
Sierra de la Palma
Mina
San Nicolas de la Garzas
Higueras
Los Aldamas
Doctor Coss
5
El Cantabro
Paredon
Grutas de García
Marín
Los Herreras
San Pedro de las Colonias
Fraustro
Santa Cruz
Santa Catarina
Dr Gonzáles
General Bravo
Francisco I Madero
Tacubaya
Paila
Hipólito
MONTERREY
Juárez
China
Entronque La Cuchilla
Pastora
El Tule
Garza García
Guadalupe
San Juan
Matamoros
Torreón
Emiliano Zapata
La Rosa
Ramos Arizpe
P N Cumbres de Monterrey
Cadereyta
Palmitos
La Barranca
Villa Juárez
Parras de la Fuente
Saltillo
Arteaga
Santiago
San Antonio
El Fraile
General Terán
Viesca
General Cepeda
Sierra de Parras
San Antonio de los Alazanes
Nuncio
Chapula
Jimulco
Bajio de Ahuichila
Agua Nueva
San Rafael
Mesa de las Tablas
Allende
Montemorelos
Vaquer
Santa Victoria
LEÓN
San Rafael
Rayones
San Jerónimo
Hediondilla
Gómez Farías
Linares
Hualahuises
La Mancha
Est Simón
Avalos
Potosí
Galeana
Cedros
Mazapil
San Roberto
Iturbide
General Simón Bolivar
Benito Juárez
San Juan de Guadalupe
Ejido Hidalgo
Santa Clara
Concepción del Oro
Villa Mainero
San Carlos
Est Camacho
El Salvador
San José de Raices
Camarones
Villagran
Juan Aldama
Santa Cruz del Oregano
Est Opal
La Ascensión
6
Norias
Grunidora
Est el Salado
El Caneol
Hidalgo
General Francisco Murguía
Atotonilco de los Martinez
San Felipe Nuevo Mercurio
San Tiburico
Huertecillas
El Tecolote
La Escondida
El Barreta
Pacheco
San Francisco del Oro
Est Vanegas
Aramberri
Est Cruz
Guemez
Ciudad de Río Grande
Valle del Salado
General Ignacio Zaragoza
Ciudad Victoria
ZACATECAS
Cedral
Cruz de Elorza
Real de Catorce
San Andrés
Doctor Arroyo
Est Cañitas de Felipe Pescador
El Jarro
Matehuala
Miquihuana
313
Villa de Guadalupe
Mier y Noriega
Jaumave
Lavin
Monte Mariana
El Mezquite
El Rucio
Santo Domingo
Bustamante
Llera de Canales
La Chicharrona
Villa de Cos
San Juan del Salado
Cerritos de Bernal
San Ignacio
Palmillas
Fresnillo
Est Ojuelos
González Ortega
El Barril
El Reventon
Gómez Farías
de Cabrales
Charcas
La Ventana
Tula
Ermita de Correa
Victor Rosales
Hernandez
Herradura
Miguel Hidalgo
Xicoténcatl
7
Morelos
Zacatecas
Villa de Ramoz
Venado
El Huizache
SAN LUIS
Ocampo
Limón
Tacualeche
Pozas de Santa Ana
Lucio Vázquez
Ciudad Mante
Jerez de Salinas
Guadalupe
Troncoso
Salinas de Hildago
Moctezuma
Espíritu Santo
Arista
Guadalcázar
El Salto
Nuevo Morelos
Mal Paso
Ojo Caliente
Villa González Ortega
Villa Hidalgo
Palomas
Ciudad del Maíz
Chicomostoc
Cerritos
Villanueva
Cosío
Luis Moya
Ahualulco
Villa Juárez
Santo Domingo
El Estribo
Santa María de los Angeles
Rincos de Romos
Loreto
San Luis Potosí
Armadillo
San Nicolás Tolentino
Est Las Tablas
POTOSÍ
Tepezala
Pinos
Tayahua
AGUASCALIENTES
Villa García
Soledad Diéz Gutiérrez
Villa de Pozos
Est stora
San Francisco
Alaquines
Jesús María
San Martin
La Pila
Zaragoza
314
Cardenas
Ciudad Valles
310
Tabasco
Aguascalientes
Dolores
Atotonilco
Huanusco
Calvillo
Chinampas
Ojuelos de Jalisco
Villa de Reyes
Santa María del Río
Río Verde
Rayón
Benuelas
San Bartolo
P N Gogorrón

San Antonio
USA
Corpus Christi
Valadeces
Los Altos
Reynosa
Río Bravo
Brownsville
Playa Lauro Villar
Matamoros
Gomeño
Santo Domingo
Dieciocho de Marco
Valle Hermoso
Cándido Aguilar
Santa Apolonia
El Horcón
F G Villarreal
Santa Teresa
Mezquital
Méndez
Burgos
El Corral
Guadalupe Victoria
San Fernando
Las Adjuntas
Cruilas
an Nicolás
La Coma
La Carbonera
El Encinal
El Temascal
Morales
Santander Jiménez
Abasolo
Nuevo Padilla
Guadalupe
El Chamal
Soto la Marina
La Pesca
Sierra de Tamaulipas
San José de las Rusias
AMAULIPAS
Los Lavaderos
Agua Nueva
Calles
La Cruz
González
Aldama
Maxcaltzin
Manuel
Est Chocoy
Laguna de San Sandrés
Los Aztecas
Lomas del Real
Cuauhtémoc
Ciudad Madero
Antonio Rayón
Altamira
Ebano
Tampico
Canoas
Tampico Alto
Tamuin
Pánuco
Alto de la Zapupera
El Higo
La Laja

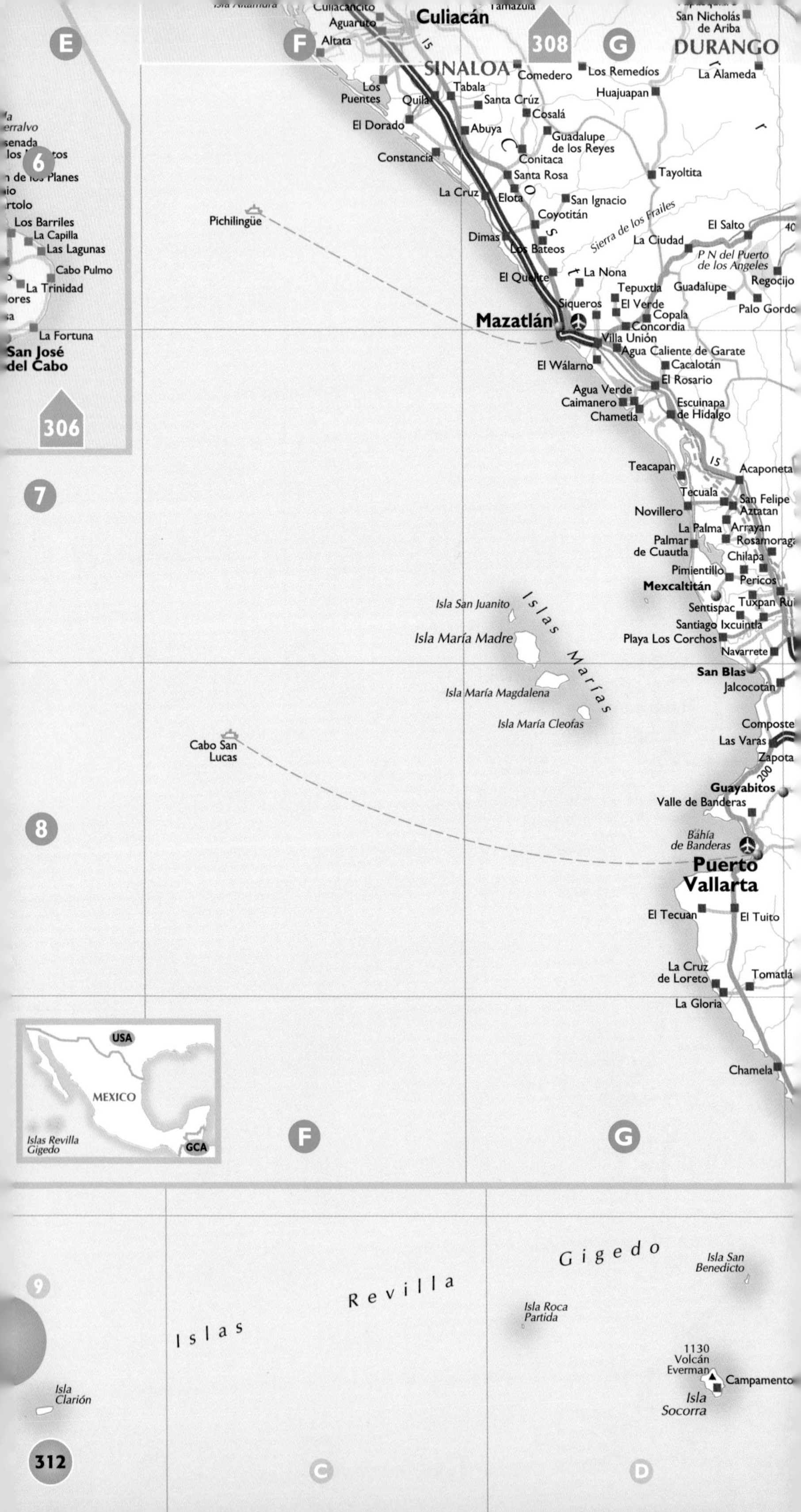
Culiacancito
Aguaruto
Culiacán
Altata
308
DURANGO
SINALOA
San Nicholás de Ariba
Comedero
Los Remedíos
La Alameda
Los Puentes
Quila
Tabala
Santa Crúz
Huajuapan
Cosalá
El Dorado
Abuya
Guadalupe de los Reyes
Constancia
Conitaca
Tayoltita
Santa Rosa
La Cruz
Elota
San Ignacio
Coyotitán
Sierra de los Frailes
El Salto
Dimas
Los Bateos
La Ciudad
P N del Puerto de los Angeles
El Quelite
La Nona
Tepuxtla
Guadalupe
Regocijo
Siqueros
El Verde
Palo Gordo
Mazatlán
Copala
Concordia
Villa Unión
Agua Caliente de Garate
El Wálarno
Cacalotán
El Rosario
Agua Verde
Caimanero
Chametla
Escuinapa de Hidalgo
Pichilingüe
Los Barriles
La Capilla
Las Lagunas
Cabo Pulmo
La Trinidad
La Fortuna
San José del Cabo
306
Teacapan
Acaponeta
Tecuala
San Felipe Aztatan
Novillero
La Palma
Arrayan
Palmar de Cuautla
Rosamorada
Chilapa
Pimientillo
Pericos
Mexcaltitán
Tuxpan
Sentispac
Santiago Ixcuintla
Playa Los Corchos
Navarrete
San Blas
Jalcocotán
Isla San Juanito
Islas Marías
Isla María Madre
Isla María Magdalena
Isla María Cleofas
Cabo San Lucas
Las Varas
Guayabitos
Valle de Banderas
Bahía de Banderas
Puerto Vallarta
El Tecuan
El Tuito
La Cruz de Loreto
Tomatlá
La Gloria
Chamela
USA
MEXICO
Islas Revilla Gigedo
GCA
Islas Revilla Gigedo
Isla San Benedicto
Isla Roca Partida
1130 Volcán Everman
Campamento
Isla Socorra
Isla Clarión
E
F
G
6
7
8
9
C
D

309
310
314
313
H
J
K
6
7
8
9
10
Durango
Peñon Blanco
Cuencamé
La Mancha
Est Simón
San Jerónimo
San Rafael
Gómez Farías
Hediondilla
Avalos
Potosí
Guatimape
San Juan del Río
Yerbanis
General Simón Bolivar
San Juan de Guadalupe
Ejido Hidalgo
Cedros
Mazapil
Canatlán
Donato Guerra
Guadalupe Victoria
Luis Moya
Santa Clara
Benito Juárez
Est Camacho
Concepción del Oro
El Salvador
Venustiano Carranza
Francisco I Madero
General Calixto Contreras
Juan Aldama
Santa Cruz del Oregano
Est Opal
Moncill
Abraham Gonzales
Cuauhtémoc
Miguel Auza
Norias
Gruñidora
Est El Salado
Otinapa
Hidalgo
Ramón Corona
General Francisco Murguía
Atotonilco de los Martinez
San Felipe Nuevo Mercurio
San Tiburico
Huertecillas
El Tecolote
Tuitán
La Ochoa
Pacheco
San Francisco del Oro
Est Vanegas
El Arenal
Villa Unión
Flores Gracía
Ciudad de Río Grande
Valle del Salado
Cedral
Ciénega
Nombre de Dios
Vicente Guerraro
ZACATECAS
San Andrés
Real de Catorce
San José de la Parilla
Est Cañitas de Felipe Pescador
Matehuala
Bayas
Suchil
Sombrerete
Sierra Madre Occidental
Sierra de Durango
Mezquital
Chalchihuites
El Rucio
Santo Domingo
Villa de Guadalupe
Temascal
Monte Mariana
El Mezquite
Tajicaringa
Jiménez de Teul
La Chicharrona
Villa de Cos
San Juan del Salado
Cerritos de Bernal
Buenavista
Fresnillo
González Ortega
El Barril
El Reventon
Santa María de Ocatán
San Fco de Cabrales
Est Ojuelos
Charcas
SAN LUIS
Hernandez
Herradura
El Huizache
Ermita de los Correa
Victor Rosales
Venado
San Mateo
Morelos
Villa de Ramoz
Potrero de Gallegos
Valparaiso
Zacatecas
Tacualeche
Sierra de Zacatecas
Guadalupe
Jerez de García Salinas
Troncoso
Salinas de Hildago
Moctezuma
Arista
Espíritu Santo
Santa Teresa
Huejuquilla el Alto
Mal Paso
Ojo Caliente
Villa González Ortega
Villa Hidalgo
Tepetongo
Chicomostoc
Mezquitic
Luis Moya
Ahualulco
Mesa del Nayar
Huejúcar
Villanueva
Cosío
Loreto
San Luis Potosí
Armadillo
Villa Juárez
Monte Escobedo
Rincos de Romos
Nayar
Santa María de los Angeles
Tepezala
Pinos
Soledad Díez Gutiérrez
Villa de Pozos
Colotlan
AGUASCALIENTES
Villa García
Tayahua
San Martin
La Pila
Zaragoza
Villa Guerrero
Momax
Jesús María
Aguascalientes
Dolores
Atotonilco
Río Atengo
Tabasco
Chinampas
Villa de Reyes
Santa María del Río
NAYARIT
Tlaltenango
Huanusco
Calvillo
Ojuelos de Jalisco
P N Gogorrón
Atolinga
Benuelas
San Bartolo de Berrios
Tepechitlán
Va Hildago
Matanzas
El Jarailillo
Tepic
Jalpa
Encarnación de Díaz
El Puesta
Ocampo
San Diego de la Unión
Tierra Nueva
Teul Ganzález Ortega
Santa María del Oro
Juchipila
Cuarenta
San Felipe
San Pedro Lagunillas
Teocaltiche
Lagos de Moreno
Nochistlan
San Juan de los Lagos
Dolores Hidalgo
Santo Domingo
Moyahua
García de la Catena
Jalostotitlan
Tlacuitlapa
León
Mineral de Pozos
Chapalilla
Ixtlán del Río
Yahualica
Valle de Guadalupe
San Miguel el Alto
Duarte
Guanajuato
Ahuacatlán
San Cristóbal de la Barranca
Magdalena
San Julián
San Fransisco del Rincón
Silao
San Miguel de Allende
San Sebastian
San Marcos
Tequila
Santa María del Valle
Amatlán de Cañas
Amatitán
Ixtlahuacan del Río
Tepatitlán
Ciudad Manuel Doblado
GUANAJUATO
Guachinango
El Arenal
Tesistán
Arandas
Irapuato
Neutla
Comonfort
Atajo
Etzatlan
Zapopan
GUADALAJARA
Ahualulco de Mercata
Tala
Zapotlanejo
Mascota
Ahuisculco
Santa Anita
Tlaquepaque
Atotonilco el Alto
Cueramaro
Salamanca
Ameca
Ayo el Chico
Atenquillo
Mixtlán
Villa Corona
Santa Rosa
Ocotlán
Degollado
Laguna Larga
Pénjamo
Villagrán
Celaya
Tlajomulco
Yurécuaro
Cortázar
Los Volcanes
Cocula
Atequiza
Abasolo
Valle de Santiago
Tarimoro
Zacoalco de Torres
Ajijic
Chapala
La Barca
La Piedad
Cuautla
Tenamaxtlán
Jocotepec
Lago de Chapala
Villa Hermosa
Numaran
Angamacutiro de la Unión
Yuriria
Salvatierra
JALISCO
Cojumatlán
Zinaparo
Uriangato
Ayutla
Techaluta
Tuxcueca
Patzimaro
Purándiro
Santiago Maravatío
Jerecuaro
Juchitlán
Amacueca
Manzanilla
Sahuayo
Panindicuaro
Acámbaro
Unión de Tula
Tapalpa
Concepcion de Buenos Aires
Jiquilpan
Zamora
Tarandacuao
Huantacareo
Autlán de Navarro
Tonaya
Mazzamitla
Jacona
Purepero
Zacapu
Zinapécuaro
El Grullo
Venustiano Carranza
Cotija de la Paz
Tangancícuaro
Carapán
Comanjá
Queréndaro
Tlalpujahua
Purificación
Ciudad Guzman
Paracho de Verduzco
Cheran
Quiroga
Morelia
Cd Hidalgo
La Huerra
Manatlán
P N Volcán de Colima
Zapotitic
Tamazula de Gordiano
Tocumbo
Volcán Paricutín
Nahuatzen
Tzintzuntzán
Mil Cumbres
Tuxpan
Cuautitlan
San Antonio
Tonila
Tuxpan
Ziracuaretiro
Pátzcuaro
Reserva Ecologica El Campanario
Minatitlán
Comala
Tecalitián
Uruapan del Progreso
Barra de Navidad
Chandiablo
Cuauhtemoc
Jilotlán de los Dolores
Buenavista Tomatlán
Tancitaro
Cutzota
Taretán
Opopeo
Heroica Zitácuaro
Colima
Ario de Rosales
Tecámbaro de Collados
Cihuatlán
Pihuamo
Benito Juárez
COLIMA
Tepalcatepec
MICHOACÁN
Santiago
Colomos
Santa Rita
Los Tepames
Apatzingán de la Constitución
Nueva Italia de Ruiz
Puruarán
Manzanillo
Ixtlahuacan
Inguarán
Curácuaro de Morelos
Armeria
Tecomán
Uspero
Gambara
La Huacana
Coalcomán de Matamoros
Zicuirán
Tiquicheo
Coahuayana
Aguilillla
Huetamo de Nuñez
Aquila
Sierra de Coalcomán
Tumoiscatio del Ruíz
Nuevo Churumuco
Cuenca del Balsas
San Lucas
Cañas
Cutzamala de Pinzón
Ziraándaro
Arteaga
Coahuayutla
Cd Altamirano
Pomaro
Infiernillo
Coyuca de Catalán
Tlapehuala
Tupitina
Ajuchitlán del Progreso
Nexpa
Las Peñas
Playa Azul
Lázaro Cárdenas
La Union
Bahía de Petucalco
Ixtapa
Zihuatanejo
San Jeronimito
Petatlán
Santa Rosa
Tecpan
57
54
23
49
45
80
80D
37
84
70
51
15
15D
110
200
134

J
K
L
310
7
8
9
10
11
313
314
San Luis Potosí
Aguascalientes
Ciudad Valles
Tamuin
POTOSÍ
Villa Juárez
Santo Domingo
Est Las Tablas
El Estribo
Antonio Rayón
Altamira
Armadillo
Soledad
Villa de Pozos
Zaragoza
Atotonilco
Santa María del Río
Río Verde
Cardenas
Rayón
Alaquines
San Francisco
La Jarille
Canoas
Pánuco
Gargaleote
San Vicente Tancuayalab
El Higo
Tancuime
Antonio Santos
Tanquián de Escobedo
Ozuluama
Tempoal de Sánchez
Pinos
Villa García
San Martin
La Pila
Dolores
Villa de Reyes
P N Gogorrón
San Bartolo de Berrios
Ojuelos de Jalisco
Chinampas
Matanzas
El Jarailillo
El Puesta
Ocampo
Cuarenta
San Diego de la Unión
San Felipe
Tierra Nueva
Pedro Montoya
Río Santa María
Lagunillas
Arroyo Seco
Xilitla
Tampacan
San Martín Chalchicuautla
Tantoyuca
Lagos de Moreno
Dolores Hidalgo
San Luiz de la Paz
Xichu
Jalpan
Ahuacatlan
Landa de Matamoros
Platón Sanchez
Tamazunchale
Chontla
León
Tlacuitlapa
San Miguel el Alto
Duarte
Guanajuato
Mineral de Pozos
Dr Mora
San José Iturbide
Chapulhuacan
Huejula de Reyes
Huautla
San Julián
San Fransisco del Rincón
Silao
San Miguel de Allende
Tolimán
San Joaquin
Jacala
P N Los Marmoles
Atlapexco
Chicontepec de Tejeda
Canali
Molango
La Guadalupe
Cd Manuel Doblado
GUANAJUATO
Irapuato
Neutla
Comonfort
Colón
QUERÉTARO
Encarnación
Iztacoyotla
Santuario
Zacualtipán
Tlachichilco
Salamanca
Querétaro
Cadereyta
Cardonal
Metztitlán
Huayacocotla
Ayo
El Chico
Laguna Larga
Cueramaro
Pénjamo
Villagrán
Celaya
Tequisquiapan
Capula
Metzquititlán
Degollado
Yurécuaro
Cortázar
San Juan del Río
La Cruz
Jonacapa
Ixmiquilpan
Xicotepec de Juárez
La Piedad
Abasolo
Valle de Santiago
Tarimoro
El Terrero
Entronque Palmillas
Huichapan
HIDALGO
Metepec
Min del Chico
Numaran
Zináparo
Angamacutiro de la Unión
Yuriria
Salvatierra
Amealco
Polotitlán
Arroyo Zarco
Mixquiahuala
Actopan
Tulancingo
Patzimaro
Purándiro
Uriangato
Santiago Maravatío
Jerecuaro
Coroneo
Aculco
Tula de Allende
Pachuca de Soto
Zamora
Panindicuaro
Acámbaro
Tarandacuao
Contepec
Pathe
Apaxco
Cuautepec
Zacatlán
Purepero
Huantacareo
Maravatío
Tepeji del Río
Tequixquiac
Metepec
Tangancícuaro
Carapán
Zacapu
Zinapécuaro
El Oro
Atlacomulco
Zumpango
Tizayuca
Chignahuapan
Tepeapulco
Paracho
Cheran
Comanjá
Queréndaro
Tlalpujahua
Carmona
Tepotzotlán
Cuautitlán
Otumpa
Apan
de Verduzco
Quiroga
Morelia
Cd Hidalgo
Angangueo
CIUDAD DE MÉXICO
Ecatepec
Teotihuacán
Tlaxco
Nahuatzen
Tzintzuntzán
Mil Cumbres
Tuxpan
Chiconcuac
Juarez
Ziracuaretiro
Pátzcuaro
Reserva Ecologica el Campanario
MEXICO
Nezahualcoyotl
DF
Cutzota
Taretán
Opopeo
Heroica Zitácuaro
Dos Casos
Toluca
San Angel
Coyoacán
Cacaxtla
Tlaxcala
Ario de Rosales
Tecámbaro de Collados
Benito Juárez
Metepec
Capulhuac
Xochimilco
Iztaccíhuatl
5286
Chiautempan
MICHOACAN
Valle de Bravo
Temascaltepec
P N Nev de Toluca
Tepoztlán
5452
Popocatépetl
PUEBLA
Puruarán
Nva Italia de Ruiz
Inguarán
NP Nanchititla
Tenancingo
Malinalco
Cuernavaca
Cholula
Amozoc
Uspero
Gambara
La Huacana
Curácuaro de Morelos
Texcaltitlan
Coatepec
Ocuilán
Yautepec
Atlixco
Zicuirán
Tiquicheo
Tejupilco de Hidalgo
Sultepec
Xochicalco
Cuautla de Morelos
Atoyatempan
Nuevo Churumuco
Huetamo de Nuñez
Amatepec
Zacualpan
Ixtapan de la Sal
MORELOS
Tepeojuma
Cacahuamilpa
Zacatepec
Janteteico
PUEBLA
Tepexi de Rodríguez
Cañas
San Lucas
Cutzamala de Pinzón
Tlatlaya
Taxco
Jojutla de Juárez
Tepalcingo
Atencingo
Izúcar de Matamoros
Ziraándaro
Iguala
Tilzapotla
Axochiapan
Infiernillo
Coahuayutla
Cd Altamirano
Coyuca de Catalán
Arcelia
Teloloapan
Huitzuco
Tlancualpicán
Tehuitzingo
Chiautla
Tepecoacuilco
Jolalpan
Tlapehuala
Ajuchitlán del Progreso
San Miguel Totolopán
Apaxtla de Castrejón
Balsas
Atenango del Río
Yeloixtlahuacan
Tecomatlán
Copalillo
Ixcamilpa
Mariscal de Juárez
La Union
Tetela del Río
Mezcala
Xochihuehuetlán
Lázaro Cárdenas
Bahía de Petucalco
Tlacotepec
Huitziltepec
Huamuxtitlán
Santiago Tamazola
Ixtapa
Zihuatanejo
GUERRERO
Chichinuaco
Tixtla de Guerrero
Zitlala
Alpoyeca
San Jeronimito
Petatlán
Chilpancingo de los Bravos
Chilapa
Zapotitlán Tables
Tlapa del Comonfort
Mochitlán
Petaquillas
Nieves Ixpantepec
Santa Rosa
Colotlipa
Xalpatláhuac
San Sebastián Tecomaxtlahuaca
Tecpan de Galeana
El Praiso
Cuatepin
El Ocotito
Tlacoapa
San Luis San Pedro
Nuxco
Atoyac de Álvarez
Tierra Colorada
Metlatonoc
Coicoyán de las Flores
San Jerónimo
Xaltianguis
Ayutla de los Libres
Rancho Viejo
Laguna Mitla
Coyuca de Benitez
Las Mesas
Tecoanapa
La Sabana
Hidalgo
Santa María Zacatepec
Acapulco de Juárez
Tres Palos
San Marcos
San Luis Acatlán
Igualapa
Cruz Grande
Azoyú
Ometepec
Chapultepec
La Viga
Cacahuatepec
Copala
Marquelia
Juchitán
San Sebastián Ixcapa
Cuajinicuilapa
Pinotepa Nacional

Madero
Tampico
Tampico Alto
Alto de la Zapupera
M
311
N
7
La Laja
Naranjos
Tamiahua
Cerro Azul
Potrero del Llano
Alamo
Tuxpan de RC
Santiago de la Peña
Tihuatlán
Barra de Cazones
Poza Rica de Hidalgo
Villa de Cazones
Tenixtepec
8
Tecolutla
El Tajín
Papantla de Olarte
Gutiérrez Zamora
Espinal
180
San Rafael
Nautla
Barra de Palmas
Tenampulco
Ayotoxco
Tlapacoyan
Martinez de la T
Vega de Alatorre
Cuetzalán
Misantla
Teziutlán
Jalacingo
Yecuatla
Juchique de F
Palma Sola
Altotonga
Plan de las Hayas
Tlacolulan
Las Vigas
Xalapa/ Jalapa
Perote
Actopan
Banderilla
140
El Limón
Cempoala
Coatepec
Ursulo Galván
Oriental
José Cardel
Antigua
Guadalupe Victoria
Teocelo
Bahía de Campeche
Totutla
Paso de Ovejas
Veracruz
Zacatepec
Huatusco de Ch
VERACRUZ
Boca del Río
5760
Pico de Orizaba
Paso del Toro
Antón Lizardo
9
Cd Serdán
Barranca de Metlac
Soledad de Doblado
La Piedra
Orizaba
Córdoba
150D
Mecayucan
Alvarado
Cotaxtla
Yanga
Coitlahuac
La Tinaja
Lerdo de Tejada
La Nueva Victoria
316
Nogales
Cd Mendoza
Omealca
Tlacotalpan
Montepío
Acultzingo
Joachín
145
Angel R Cabada
Chapulco
Cozolapa
Acatlán
Acula
N P Laguna de Catemaco
Tupilco
Tehuacán
D
Cosamaloapan
Santiago Tuxtla
Catemaco
Sánchez Magallanes
Ajalpan
Tierra Blanca
150
Carlos A Carrillo
San Andrés Tuxtla
Barra de Tonalá
Zinacatepec
Presa Miguel Alemán
Los Naranjos
Chacaltianguis
Santa Ana
TABASCO
Coxcatlán
Huautla de Jiménez
Temezcal
Tres Valles
Tuxtilla
Palmarillo
Coatzacoalcos
Allende
Agua Dulce
Aleman
Zapotitlán de Salinas
Alemán
Villa Azueta
J Diaz Covarrubias
Nanchital
La Venta
Santiago Chazumba
Teotitlán del Camino
San Juan Bautista Tuxtepec
Loma Bonita
Isla
Chinameca
Minatitlán
180
El Limon
San Pedro y San Pablo
Santa Ma Tecomavaca
San Juan Chiquihuitlán
Santa María Jacatepec
J Rodriguez Clara
Acayucan
Cosoleacaque
Jáltipan de Morelos
Filisola
Las Choapas
Huajuapan de León
San Miguel Chicahua
San J Bautista Cuicatlán
San José Chiltepec
Playa Vicente
Villa Juanita
Sayula de Alemán
Texistepec
Francisco Rueda
Huima
175
185
Hidalgotitlán
Quiotepec
Valle Nacional
El Juile
Tenochtitlán
Chontalpa
Soyaltepec
Xochiapa
Medias Aguas
El Chichón
Teposcolula
Comaltepec
Nuevo Ixcatlán
Vasconcelos
Yanhuitlán
P N Benito Juárez
Istmo de Tehuantepec
Ixtapa
Asunción Nochixtlán
San Miguel Aloapan
San Miguel Talea d C
Jalahuy
Jesús Carranza
Yodocono
Jayacatlán
Ixtlán de Juárez
Choapan
Pueblo Viejo
10
San Juan Achiuta
Telixtlahuaca
Guelatao
Sierra de Villa Alta
147
Presa Nezahuacóyotl
Tilantongo
Huitzo
Yalalag
Totontepec
Palomares
Tlaxiaco
Nazareno Etla
Yalina
Oaxaca
Xagacia
Monte Albán
El Tule
Ayutla
San Juan Guichicovi
OAXACA
Zaachila
Yagul
Santa María Chimalapa
San Antonio Huitepec
Tiacolula
Mitla
Matías Romero
Lázaro Cárdenas
Cintalapa de Figueroa
Santiago Yosondua
Zimatlán
Matatlán
Juquila Mixes
Santo Domingo Petapa
San Miguel Chimalapa
Huixtepec
Lachiguiri
Santa María Guiennagati
San Mateo Yucutindo
Tlapacoyan
Ocotlán
Chichicapan
190
Santa Ana Tavela
185
Santo Domingo Niltepec
Las Cruces
Jiquipilas
Ayoquezco
Totolapan
Amoltepec
Santa Ma Sola
Ejutla
Santa María Zoquitlán
El Camarón
Nejapa de Madero
Cd Ixtepec
La Ventosa
190
Santo Domingo Zanatepec
Nuevo México
San Miguel Sola de Vega
San José Lachiguiri
SC Yautepec
Magd Tequisistlán
Ixtaltepec
U Hidalgo
Santa Isabel
Santiago Jamiltepec
131
Yogaña
175
Miahuatlán
Asunción Tlacolulita
Santo Domingo Tehuantepec
190
Juchitan de Zaragoza
San Pedro Tapanatepec
Sierra de Miahuatlán
Juquila
San Juan Lachao
Tamazulapan
Arriaga
San Sebastián Coatlán
San Pedro Suchixtepec
Santa Ma Ecatepec
San Mateo del Mar
Puerto Palomas
Tonalá
Tututepec
Nopala
San Gabriel Mixtepec
Salina Cruz
Paredón
Río Grande
San Pedro el Alto
San Pedro Huamelula
200
200
Santa María Colotepec
Candelaria Loxicha
Santa Ma Huatulco
Xadani
Santiago Astata
Golfo de Tehuantepec
Puerto Arista
Cacalotepec
Puerto Escondido
200
San Pedro Pochutla
Santa Cruz Huatulco
11
Barra Santa Elena
Puerto Angel
M
N
315

P
Q
7
8
9
10
11
Reserva de la Biósfera Celestún
Celestún
Chunchucmil
La Costa
Tankuché
Hampolol
Campeche
China
Seybaplaya
Tixmucuy
Haltunchén
Sihochác
Champotón
Santa Cruz
Chencán
Pixtun
Sabancuy
Xcabacab
Puerto Real
Chekubul
Chicbul
Dieciocho de Marzo
Escárcega
Bahía de Campeche
Ciudad del Carmen
Nuevo Campechito
Frontera
Atasta
Zacatal
Laguna de Términos
Mamantel
División del Norte
Matamoros
Aguada Seca
Buenavista
Candelaria
Salsipuedes
Monclova
Nueva Coahuila
315
Tupilco
Puerto Ceiba
Chiltepec
Alvaro Obregón
El Vapor
Sánchez Magallanes
Paraiso
Hidalgo
Tecoluttilla
Comalcalco
Palizada
Santa Ana
El Espino
TABASCO
Jonuta
San Joaquín
Barra de Tonalá
Allende
Agua Dulce
Aleman
Nacajuca
Villahermosa
La Venta
Cárdenas
Cunduacán
José Colomo
Minatitlán
Nanchital
El Limon
Bonito Juárez
Ciudad Pemex
Chablé
El Triunfo
Jáltipan de Morelos
Filisola
Las Choapas
La Reforma
Pueblo Nuevo
Tepetitlán
Catazajá
Balancán
San Pedro
Aguila
Hidalgotitlán
Francisco Rueda
Huimanguillo
Astapa
Jalapa
Macuspana
La Libertad
Tulipan
La Revancha
Tenochtitlán
Mezcalapa
Tacotalpa
Tenosique de Pino Suárez
Vasconcelos
El Chichón
Chontalpa
Juárez
Salto de Agua
Palenque
Gregório Méndez
Istmo
Pichucalco
Teapa
La Palma
Ixtacomitán
Mísol-Há
Río Chancalá
Raudales de Malpaso
Amatán
Agua Azul
Pueblo Veijo
Ostuacán
Huitiupan
Tzinteel
de
Tapilula
Simojovel de Allende
Yajalón
Río Usumacinta
Presa Nezahuacóyotl
Tecpatán
Rayón
Chilón
Tehuantepec
Apic Pac
Copainala
Pueblo Nuevo
El Bosque
Temo
Montañas del Norte de Chiapas
Santa María Chimalapa
Jitotol
Cancuc
Ocosingo
Yaxchilán
Cañon del Sumidero
Bochil
Soyaló
Tenejapa
Lacanjá
San Miguel Chimalapa
Tuxtla Gutiérrez
Zinacantán
Santo Tomás
Altamirano
Bonampak
Cintalapa de Figueroa
Chiapa do Corzo
San Cristóbal de las Casas
El Vergelito
Santo Domingo
Las Cruces
Jiquipilas
Suchiapa
Acala
Teopisca
Amatenango del Valle
Niltepec
Santo Domingo Zanatepec
Nuevo México
Benito Juárez
CHIAPAS
La Ventosa
U Hidalgo
Santa Isabel
Domingo Chanona
Zaragoza
Venustiano Carranza
Las Rosas
Las Margaritas
San Pedro Tapanatepec
El Brillante
San Francisco Pujiltic
Tzimol
Comitán de Domínguez
N P Lagunas de Montebello
San Mateo del Mar
Puerto Palomas
Arriaga
Villa Flores
Revolución Mexicana
Presa de la Angostura
La Trinitaria
Tziscao
Lagunas de Montebello
Tonalá
Sierra Madre de Chiapas
La Concordia
Buenavista
Santa Inés
Paredón
Jaltenango de la Paz
San Antonio
Puerto Arista
Tres Picos
San Gregorio
El Jocate
Golfo de Tehuantepec
Chicomuselo
Custepec
Frontera Comalapa
Pijijiapan
Reserva de la Biósfera el Triunfo
Siltepec
El Carmen
Mapastepec
Motozintla de Mendoza
Acacoyagua
Escuintla
Acapetagua
Va Comaltitlán
Unión Juárez
Huixtla
Cacahoatan
Tapachula
El Carmen
Mazatán
Frontera Hidalgo
Puerto Madero
180
186
261
221
195
187
203
199
190
200
225
316

R
S
T
7
Isla Holbox
Porvenir
San Felipe
Río Lagartos
El Cuyo
Parque Natural San Felipe
Parque Natural Río Lagartos
Dzilam de Bravo
Chiquilá
Isla Mujeres
Telchac Puerto
Yalsihon
295
Puerto Chicxulub
Dzilam González
Panabá
Kikil
Yucatán
Kantunil Kin
Cancún
Puerto Juárez
Progreso
176
Sucilá
Buenaventura
Leona Vicario
180
Chelem
Dzidzantún
Cansahcab
Buctzotz
Tizimín
Tixcancal
El Rey
Dzibilchaltún
Dzemul
Baca
Tixbacab
Calotmul
Popolnah
Sisal
Fucu
Conkal
Motul
Temax
Espita
Ek-Balam
El Cedral
307
Tixkokob
Tekantó
Cenotillo
Vicente Guerrero
Puerto Morelos
Mérida
Cacalchén
Izamal
Tunkás
180D
El Ideal
Hoctún
Sudzal
Temozón
X-Can
Uman
Seye
Kantunil
Dzitás
Tinúm
Tres Reyes
Playa del Carmen
Chocolá
Tekik
Hocaba
Holca
Piste
Uayma
Valladolid
Xcaret
180
Tecoh
Libre Unión
Tekom
Chemax
Paamul
Isla del Cozumel
Yaxcopil
Cuzamá
Huhi
Chichén Itzá
Cozumel
Xcanú
Opichén
18
Sotuta
Grutas de Balankanché
Cobá
YUCATÁN
Akumal
Cedral
Maxcanú
Mama
PN de Quintana Roo
Muna
Maní
Teabo
Chikindzonot
Xel-Há
Punta Celarain
8
Calkiní
Ticul
Oxkutzcab
Tahdzibichén
Tepich
Tulúm
Uxmal
Santa Elena
Akil
Tekax de AO
Ichmul
Peto
Tihosuco
Chunyaxché
Boca Paila
Dzibalché
295
Chumpón
Hecelchakán
261
Xul
Thul
Sabán
Reserva
Tzucacab
Santa Rosa
Dzoyola
Señor
307
Bolonchén de Rejón
Becanchen
Dzuiché
José María Morelos
Vigía Chico
Emiliano Zapata
Hunto Chac
Candelaria
de la Biósfera
Península
Nohalal
Xiatil
184
Hopelchén
Felipe Curillo Puerto
Edzná
Xcupil
El Naranjal
Polyuc
Konchén
Iturbide
Chunhuhub
Chankán Veracrut
Sian Ka'an
de Yucatán
San Isidro Poniente
Pres Juárez
293
Laguna Kaná
Dzibalchén
Kopchén
Puerto Madero
QUINTANA ROO
Xmaben
Valle Hermoso
Palmas
Los Lirios
Nohbec
Limones
Placer
Emiliano Zapata
Lázaro Cárdenas
Cafetal
CAMPECHE
Rio Escondido
Reforma
307
Puerto Bravo
Ursulo Galván
9
Meseta de Zohlaguna
San Román
Bacalar
Laguna Bacalar
Majahual
Calderitas
Becán
Ucum
Conhuas
Nicolás Bravo
186
Chetumal
Chicanná
Xpujil
Kohunlich
Xcalak
Pucté
Bonfil
Tomás Garrido
Agua Blanca
La Esperanza
Calakmul
Villahermosa
BH
BELMOPAN
10
Golfo de Honduras
GCA
11
HN
GUATEMALA
R
S
T

A

Acala 316 P10
Acapulco de Juárez 314 K10
Acatlán 315 M9
Acatlán de Osorio 314 L9
Acatzingo 315 L9
Actopan 314 L8
Aduana 308 F4
Agua Azul 316 Q10
Agua Caliente de Garate 312 G7
Agua Dulce 315 P9
Agua Flores 306 B1
Agua Prieta 308 E2
Aguascalientes 313 J7
Agua Verde 312 G7
Aguila 316 Q10
Ajalpan 315 M9
Ajijic 313 H8
Akumal 317 S8
Alamo 315 M8
Alamos 308 F4
Aleman 316 P9
Alicante 309 H4
Altamira 311 L7
Altamirano 316 Q10
Alvarado 315 N9
Alvaro Obregón 308 G3
Alvaro Obregón 316 P9
Amatenango del Valle 316 Q10
Amatitán 313 H8
Amozoc 314 L9
Anáhuac 308 G3
Anáhuac 310 K4
Angangueo 314 K9
Angostura 308 F5
Antigua 315 M9
Antiguo Morelos 310 L6
Apaxco 314 L8
Aquila 313 H9
Arados 308 G3
Arandas 313 J8
Arizpe 307 E2
Armería 313 H9
Arriaga 316 P11
Arroyo Seco 314 K8
Arroyo Zarco 314 K8
Arteaga 310 K5
Arteaga 313 J9
Ascensión 308 F2
Astapa 316 P10
Asunción 315 M11
Atenango del Río 314 L10
Atenquillo 313 H8
Atlacomulco 314 K9
Atlixco 314 L9
Atolinga 313 H7
Atotonilco 314 K7
Atotonilco el Alto 313 J8
Atoyac de Alvarez 314 K10
Autlán de Navarro 313 H9
Ayutla 313 H8
Ayutla 315 M10
Aztatan 312 G7

B

Baborigame 308 F5
Bacalar 317 S9
Bacoachi 307 E2
Bacobampo 307 E4
Bacubirito 308 F5
Bacum 307 E4
Bahía Asunción 306 C4
Bahía de los Ángeles 307 C3
Bahía Kino 307 D3
Bahía Magdalena 306 D6
Bahia Santa Maria 306 C2
Bahía Tortugas 306 B4
Bajío de Ahuichila 309 J5
Bajios de Agua Blanca 308 G5
Balancán 316 Q10
Balsas 314 K10
Banámichi 307 E2
Banderas 308 G2
Barra de Cazones 315 M8
Barra de Navidad 313 H9
Barra de Palmas 315 M8
Barranca del Cobre 308 F4
Barra Santa Elena 315 M11
Barreal 308 G2
Basaseachic 308 F4
Basihuare 308 F4
Bataques 306 C1
Batopilas 308 F4
Baturi 308 F5
Bavispe 308 F2
Beatriz Microondas 309 H4
Becán 317 R9
Benito Juárez 316 P10
Benuelas 313 J7
Bermejillo 309 H5
Boca del Río 315 M9
Boca Paila 317 S8
Bochil 316 P10
Bocoyna 308 F4
Bonampak 316 Q10
Boquilla del Mezquite 309 H3
Boquillas del Carmen 309 J3
Buenaventura 317 S8
Burgos 311 L6

C

Cabo Pulmo 306 E6
Caborca 307 D2
Cabo San Lucas 306 E7
Cacahoatan 316 Q11
Cacahuamilpa 314 L9
Cacahuatepec 314 L10
Cacalotepec 315 M11
Cacaxtla 314 L9
Cadeje 307 D4
Calakmul 317 R9
Calderitas 317 S9
Calkiní 317 R8
Calotmul 317 S8
Calvillo 313 J7
Camalú 306 B2
Camarón 310 K4
Camarones 310 K6
Campeche 316 Q8
Cananea 307 E2
Cañas 313 J9
Canatlán 313 H6
Cancún 317 S7
Candelaria 317 R8
Candelaria Loxicha 315 M11
Canipole 307 D4
Canoas 311 L7
Cañon del Sumidero 316 P10
Cantamar 306 B1
Carapán 313 J9
Cárdenas 316 P10
Carichi 308 G4
Carmona 314 K9
Carrillo 309 H4
Casas Grandes 308 F2
Casa Vieja 307 D3
Cascada de Basaseáchic 308 F4
Castaños 310 K5
Cataviña 306 C2
Catazajá 316 Q10
Catemaco 315 N9
Ceballos 309 H5
Cedral 317 S8
Celaya 314 K8
Celestún 316 Q8
Cempoala 315 M9
Cenotillo 317 R8
Cenzontle 309 H4
Cerralvo 310 K5
Cerritos 310 K7
Cerritos de Bernal 310 J7
Cerro Azul 315 M8
Cerro Gamo 307 D2
Chamela 312 G9
Chametla 312 G7
Champotón 316 Q9
Chandiablo 313 H9
Chankán Veracrut 317 S9
Chapala 313 J8
Chapalilla 313 H8
Chapulco 315 M9
Chapulhuacan 314 L8
Chapultepec 314 L10
Charco de la Peña 309 H3
Chekubul 316 Q9
Cheran 313 J9
Chetumal 317 S9
Chiapa do Corzo 316 P10
Chicanná 317 R9
Chicbul 316 Q9
Chichén Itzá 317 R8
Chichicapan 315 M10
Chicomostoc 313 J7
Chihuahua 308 G3
Chihuahuita 308 E5
Chilapa 312 G7
Chilón 316 Q10
Chilpancingo de los Bravos 314 L10
Chinameca 315 N10
Chinampas 313 J7
Chinipas 308 F4
Chinobampo 308 F5
Chiquilá 317 S7
Cholula 314 L9
Chontalpa 316 P10
Chumpón 317 S8
Chunhuhub 317 R9
Chunyaxché 317 S8
Chupadero de Caballo 310 J3
Ciénega 313 H6
Ciénega de Escobar 308 G5
Cihuatlán 313 H9
Cintalapa de Figueroa 316 P10
Ciudad Acuña 310 K3
Ciudad Altamirano 314 K9
Ciudad Camargo 308 H4
Ciudad Constitución 306 D5
Ciudad del Carmen 316 Q9
Ciudad del Maíz 310 K7
Ciudad de México 314 K9
Ciudad de Río Grande 313 J6
Ciudad Guerrero 308 F3
Ciudad Guzman 313 H9
Ciudad Hidalgo 314 K9
Ciudad Ixtepec 315 N10
Ciudad Juárez 308 G2
Ciudad Lerdo 309 H5
Ciudad Obregón 307 E4
Ciudad Pemex 316 P10
Ciudad Serdán 315 M9
Ciudad Valles 314 L7
Ciudad Victoria 310 L6
Coahuayutla 313 J9
Coatepec 315 M9
Coatzacoalcs 315 N9
Cobá 317 S8
Cocula 313 H8
Cojumatlán 313 J8
Colima 313 H9
Colombia 310 K4
Colomos 313 H9
Colotlan 313 H7
Comala 313 H9
Comalcalco 316 P9
Comanjá 313 J9
Comitán de Domínguez 316 Q11
Comonfort 314 K8
Compostela 313 H8
Concepción del Oro 310 J6
Concordia 312 G6
Conitaca 312 G6
Conkal 317 R8
Constancia 312 F6
Copala 312 G6
Córdoba 315 M9
Coroneo 314 K8
Cortázar 314 K8
Cotaxtla 315 M9
Coxcatlán 315 M9
Coyoacán 314 L9
Coyotitán 312 G6
Coyuca de Benitez 314 K10
Coyuca de Catalán 314 K9
Cozumel 317 S8
Creel 308 F4
Cruces 308 F3
Cruz Grande 314 L10
Cuajinicuilapa 314 L11
Cuarenta 313 J8
Cuauhtémoc 308 G3
Cuautepec 314 L8
Cuautillán 314 L9
Cuautitlan 313 H9
Cuautla 313 H8
Cuautla de Mor 314 L9
Cucurpé 307 E2
Cuernavaca 314 L9
Culiacán 308 F6
Culiacancito 308 F6
Cumbres de Majalca 308 G3
Cusarare 308 F4
Custepec 316 P11
Cutzota 313 J9

D

Degollado 313 J8
Delicias 308 G4
Desierto Vizcaíno 306 C4
Díaz Ordaz 307 C4
Dieciocho de Marco 311 L5
Dimas 312 G6
Dolores 310 J5
Dolores Hidalgo 314 K8
Donato Guerra 313 H6
Don Martin 310 K4
Dos Casos 314 K9
Durango 313 H6
Dzibalché 317 R8
Dzibalchén 317 R9
Dzibilchaltún 317 R8
Dzilam de Bravo 317 R7
Dzitás 317 R8
Dzoyola 317 S8

E

Edzná 317 R9
Ejido Bonfil 306 B2
Ejido Eréndira 306 B2
Ejido Hidalgo 313 J6
Ejido Morelas y Pavon 306 C3
Ejido Uruapan 306 B1
Ejutla 315 M10
Ek-Balam 317 S8
El Aguaje 307 D4
El Alamillo 308 F3
El Alamo 310 K5
El Anuajito 308 E5

El Arco 307 C4
El Arenal 313 H6
El Atajo 313 H8
El Barretal 310 L6
El Burro 307 D3
El Caballo 309 J4
El Cajete 306 E6
El Camarón 315 M10
El Cantabro 309 J5
El Cardón 306 C3
El Carol 307 C4
El Carrizal 308 G2
El Carrizo 307 D3
El Cedral 317 S8
El Centenario 306 E6
El Chamal 311 L6
El Chichón 316P10
El Chinero 306 C1
El Cipres 306 B2
El Coloradito 306 C2
El Colorado 308 E5
El Corral 311 L6
El Coyote 306 B1
El Crucero 306 C3
El Cuarenta 308 G2
El Cuyo 317 S7
El Descanso 306 B1
El Desemboque 307 D2
El Divisadero 308 F4
El Dorado 312 F6
El Encinal 311 L6
El Faro 306 B1
El Fuerte 308 F5
El Golfo de Santa Clara 306 C1
El Guaje 309 J4
El Horcón 311 M5
El Huizache 310 K7
El Ident 317 S8
El Jarailillo 313 J8
El Jarro 310 K6
El Juile 315 N10
El León 310 J3
El Magueyal 309 J4
El Marrón 306 C3
El Mayor 306 B1
El Mezquite 313 J6
El Milagro 309 J3
El Mirador 308 G2
El Moral 310 K3
El Naranjal 317 R8
El Nogal 307 E2
El Oasis 307 E3
El Ocuca 307 D2
El Ojito 308 G4
El Olvido 310 L6
El Oso 309 J4
Elota 312 G6
El Palmito 309 H5
El Papalote 309 J5
El Pescadero 306 E6
El Porvenir 308 G2
El Porvenir 308 G4
El Puesta 313 J8
El Quelite 312 G6
El Refugio 306 D5
El Remolino 310 K3
El Reventon 310 K7
El Rey 317 S8
El Rosano 306 B2
El Rucio 313 J6
El Sahuaro 307 D2
El Salado 309 J3
El Salto 312 G6
El Salvador 310 K6
El Sasabe 307 D2
El Saúz 308 G3
El Sauz 310 K4
El Sauzar 306 B1
El Socorro 307 D2
El Tajín 315 M8
El Tecolote 310 K6
El Tecuan 312 G8
El Temascal 311 L6
El Tiro 307 D2
El Triunfo 306 E6
El Triunfo 316 Q10
El Tuito 312 G8
El Tule 315 M10
El Varejonal 308 F5
El Veinticuatro 308 G2
El Verde 312 G6
El Vergel 308 G5
El Vergelito 316 Q10
El Wálarno 312 G7
Empalme 307 E4
Encarnación 314 L8
Encarnacion de Díaz 313 J8
Ensenada 306 B1
Entronque La Cuchilla 309 J5
Entronque Palmillas 314 K8
Escalón 309 H5
Escárcega 316 Q9
Escuintla 316 P11
Esperanza 307 E4
Espinazo 310 K5
Espíritu Santo 310 J7
Est el Salado 310 K6
Estero la Bocana 307 C4
Est las Tablas 310 K7
Est Leon Fonseca 308 F5
Est Llano 307 E2
Est Opal 313 J6
Est Simón 309 J6
Etzatlan 313 H8

F

Felipe Curillo Puerto 317 S8
Francisco I Madero 308 F2
Francisco I Madero 309 J5
Fresnillo 313 J7
Frontera 316 P9
Frontera Comalapa 316 Q11
Frontera Hidalgo 316 Q11
Fronteras 308 E2
Fundición 307 E4

G

Galeana 308 F2
Galeana 310 K6
Gallego 308 G3
Gambara 313 J9
García de la Catena 313 H8
Garza García 310 K5
General Bravo 310 L5
General Carlos Pacheco 308 G4
General Cepeda 310 J5
General Simón Bolivar 313 J6
General Treviño 310 L5
General Trías 308 G4
Gloria 310 K5
Gomeño 311 M5
Gómez Farías 308 F3
Gómez Palacio 309 H5
González 311 L7
Gorguz 307 E3
Gran Morelos 308 G4
Gregório Méndez 316 Q10
Gruñidora 310 J6
Grutas de Balankanché 317 S8
Grutas de García 310 K5
Guadalajara 313 H8
Guadalcázar 310 K7
Guadalupe 313 J7
Guadalupe de Bravo 308 G2
Guadalupe de los Reyes 312 G6
Guadalupe Victoria 313 H6
Guadalupe Victoria 311 L6
Guadalupe Victoria 315 M9
Guadelupe 307 E3
Guamuchil 308 F5
Guanacevi 308 G5
Guanajuato 314 K8
Guasave 308 F5
Guásimas 307 E4
Guatimape 313 H6
Guayabitos 312 G8
Guaymas 307 E4
Guelatao 315 M10
Guemez 310 L6
Guerrero 310 K5
Guerrero Negro 306 C4
Gutiérrez Zamora 315 M8
Guzmán 308 F2

H

Haltunchén 316 Q9
Hampolol 316 Q8
Hecelchakán 317 R8
Hermosillo 307 E3
Hernandez 313 J7
Heroica Zitácuaro 314 K9
Herradura 310 J7
Hidalgo del Parral 308 G4
Higueras 310 K5
Hipólito 310 K5
Hocaba 317 R8
Hoctún 317 R8
Hopelchén 317 R8
Hormigas 308 G3
Hornos 307 E4
Huachinera 308 F2
Huajuapan 312 G6
Huajuapan de León 315 M10
Hualahuises 310 K6
Huantacareo 314 K9
Huatabampo 307 E4
Huautla 314 L8
Huejotitán 308 G4
Huejúcar 313 J7
Huejuquilla el Alto 313 H7
Huépac 307 E3
Huertecillas 310 K6
Huichapan 314 K8
Huimanguillo 316 P10
Huitzo 315 M10
Huixtepec 315 M10
Huixtla 316 Q11
Humariza 308 G4

I

Ichmul 317 R8
Iguala 314 L9
Immaculadita 307 D2
Imuris 307 E2
Indé 308 H5
Infiernillo 313 J9
Irapuato 313 J8
Isla Holbox 317 S7
Isla Mujeres 317 S7
Isla Tiburón 307 D3
Iturbide 317 R9
Ixmiquilpan 314 L8
Ixtacomitán 316 P10
Ixtaltepec 315 N10
Ixtapa 313 J10
Ixtapan de la Sal 314 K9
Ixtlahuacan 313 H9
Ixtlahuacan del Río 313 J8
Ixtlán de Juárez 315 M10
Ixtlán del Río 313 H8
Izamal 317 R8
Izúcar de Matamoros 314 L9

J

Jacala 314 L8
Jacona 313 J8
Jalacingo 315 M9
Jalahuy 315 N10
Jalapa (Xalapa) 315 M9
Jalapa 316 P10
Jalcocotán 312 G8
Jalostotitlan 313 J8
Jalpa 313 J8
Jalpan 314 L8
Jaltenango de la Paz 316 P11
Jáltipan de Morelos 315 N10
Janos 308 F2
Janteteico 314 L9
Jaumave 310 L6
J Diaz Covarrubias 315 N10
Jerecuaro 314 K8
Jerez de García Salinas 313 J7
Jesayo 306 B1
Jesús Carranza 308 G2
Jesús Carranza 315 N10
Jilotlán de los Dolores 313 J9
Jiménez 309 H4
Jimulco 309 J5
Jiquilpan 313 J8
Joachín 315 M9
Jocotepec 313 H8
Jolalpan 314 L9
Jonacapa 314 L8
Jonuta 316 P10
José Cardel 315 M9
José Mariá Morelos 317 R8
J Rodriguez Clara 315 N10
Juan Aldama 313 H6
Juarez 314 L9
Juárez 316 P10
Juchipila 313 J8
Juchitán 314 L10
Juchitan de Zaragoza 315 N11
Juchitlán 313 H8
Julimes 308 G4
Juquila Mixes 315 N10
Juxtlahuaca 314 L10

K

Kikil 317 S7
Kino Nuevo 307 D3
Kohunlich 317 R9
Konchén 317 R9
Kopchén 317 S9

L

La Alameda 312 G6
La Amistad 310 K3
La Ascensión 310 K6
La Babia 309 J3
La Barca 313 J8
La Barranca 310 L5
La Bolsa 306 C1
La Boquilla del Conchos 308 G4
La Brecha 308 F5
La Bufa 308 F4
La Bufadora 306 B1
Lacanjá 316 Q10
La Carbonera 311 L6
La Casita 307 E2
La Catedral 308 G5
La Chicharrona 313 J7
La Ciénega 307 D2
La Ciudad 312 G6
La Colorado 307E3
La Coma 311 L6
La Concordia 316 P11
La Cruz 312 G6
La Cruz 314 K8
La Cruz de Loreto 312 G8
La Cuesta 309 J3
La Dura 308 E3
La Escondida 310 K6
La Esperanza 317 R9
La Estancia 308 G5
La Florida 306 D5

La Fortuna 306 E6
La Gloria 310 K4
La Gloria 312 G8
Lagos de Moreno 313 J8
La Grullita 306 C1
La Guadalupe 314 L8
Laguna Bacalar 317 S9
Laguna de Chapala 306 C3
Laguna Ojo de Liebre 306 C4
Laguna de San Ignacio 307 C4
Laguna Kaná 317 S9
Laguna Larga 313 J8
Lagunas de Montebello 316 Q11
Lagunillas 314 K8
La Higuera 308 F4
La Huerra 313 H9
La Junta 308 F3
La Laguna 308 H4
La Libertad 316 Q10
La Linda 309 J3
La Mancha 309 J6
La Máquina 308 G2
La Misa 307 E3
La Misión 306 B1
La Mora 309 J4
La Morita 309 H3
Lampazos de Naranjo 310 K4
La Muralla 310 K3
Landa de Matamoros 314 L8
La Nona 312 G6
La Nueva Victoria 315 N9
La Palma 312 G7
La Palma 316 Q10
La Paloma 307 D3
La Paz 306 E6
La Perla 309 H5
La Pesca 311 L6
La Piedad 313 J8
La Piedra 315 M9
La Pila 314 K7
La Pinta 308 F3
La Pocitos de Aguirre 307 E3
La Poza de Teresa 306 D5
La Poza de Teresa 307 D5
La Poza Grande 307 D5
La Purisima 306 D5
La Purisima 307 D5
La Recholera 309 H5
La Reforma 316 P10
La Rosa 310 J5
La Rosita 309 J3
La Rosita 310 J4
La Rumorosa 306 B1
Las Adjuntas 311 L6
Las Barranacas 306 D5
Las Brujas 310 L6
Las Cruces 306 E6
Las Cruces 316 P10
Las Cuevas 306 E6
La Selva 309 H3
Las Encantades 306 C2
Las Glorias 308 F5
Las Herreras 308 G5
Las Isabeles 306 B1
Las Lagunas 306 E6
Las Nieves 308 G5
Las Norias 309 J3
La Soledad 310 J5
Las Palomas 307 C4
Las Palomas 309 J5
Las Peñas 313 J10
Las Rosas 316 Q10
Las Vigas 315 M9
La Tinaja 315 M9
La Trinidad 306 E6
La Trinitaria 316 Q11
La Union 313 J10
La Venta 316 P10
La Ventana 306 C1
La Ventana 310 K7
La Ventosa 315 N10
La Viga 314 L10
La Zarca 309 H5
Lázaro Cárdenas 313 J10
Lázaro Cárdenas 317 S9
León 313 J8
Leona 317 S8
León Guzman 309 H5
Lerdo de Tejada 315 N9
Limón 310 L6
Limones 317 S9
Linares 310 L6
Llera de Canaies 310 L6
Loma 308 G3
Loma Bonita 315 N10
Loreto 307 D5
Los Arrieros 307 E3
Los Aztecas 311 L7
Los Barriles 306 E6
Los Chinos 307 E3
Los Gavilanes 307 C4
Los Herreras 310 L5
Los Hoyos 307 E2
Los Laureles 309 J4
Los Lavaderos 311 L6
Los Lirios 317 R9
Los Mártires 307 C4
Los Mochis 308 F5
Los Molinos 307 D2
Los Naranjos 315 M9
Los Nogales 310 K5
Los Picos 309 J3
Los Remedíos 312 G6
Los Rodriguez 310 K4
Lucio Vázquez 310 K7

M

Maclovio Herrera 309 H3
Madera 308 F3
Magdalena 313 H8
Magdalena de Kino 307 E2
Magdalena Tequisistlán 315 N11
Majahual 317 S9
Malinalco 314 L9
Mal Paso 313 J7
Mama 317 R8
Manatlán 313 H9
Maneadero 306 B1
Maní 317 R8
Manuel 311 L7
Manzanilla 313 J8
Manzanillo 313 H9
Mapastepec 316 P11
Mapimí 309 H5
Maravatío 314 K9
Maravillas 309 H4
Marquelia 314 L10
Martinez de la T 315 M8
Mascota 313 H8
Matachic 308 F3
Matamoros 311 L5
Matanzas 313 J7
Mata Ortiz 308 F3
Matatlán 315 M10
Matehuala 310 K6
Matías Romero 315 N10
Matrimonio 309 J4
Maxcaltzin 311 L7
Maxcanú 317 R8
Maytorena 307 E4
Mazapil 310 J6
Mazatán 307 E3
Mazatán 316 Q11
Mazatlán 312 G6
Mazocahui 307 E3
Mazzamitla 313 J9
Medias Aguas 315 N10
Méndez 311 L5
Meoqui 308 G4
Meresichic 307 E2
Mérida 317 R8
Mesa de Guadalupe 308 G5
Metepec 314 K9
Metepec 314 L9
Metztitlán 314 L8
Mexcaltitán 312 G7
Mexicali 306 B1
Mexico 307 D3
Mezcala 314 K10
Mezcalapa 316 P10
Mezquite 308 G2
Mezquitic 313 H7
Mezquitosa 310 K4
Mier 310 L5
Mier y Noriega 310 K6
Miguel Hidalgo 310 K7
Mil Cumbres 314 K9
Milpillas 307 D2
Milpillas 308 F4
Mina 310 K5
Minas de Barroterran 310 K4
Minas de Hércules 309 H4
Minatitlán 313 H9
Minatitlán 315 N10
Miquihuana 310 K6
Miraflores 306 E6
Misión de San Borja 307 C3
Misión de San Fernando 306 B2
Misión de San Telmo 306 B2
Mísol-Há 316 Q10
Mitla 315 M10
Mixquiahuala 314 L8
Mixtlán 313 H8
Mochicahui 308 F5
Mocorito 308 F5
Mocorúa 307 E4
Moctezuma 310 K7
Molango 314 L8
Momax 313 H7
Moncill 313 H6
Monclova 310 K4
Monclova 316 Q9
Monte Albán 315 M10
Monte Mariana 313 J6
Montemorelos 310 K5
Montepío 315 N9
Monterde 308 F4
Monterrey 310 K5
Morales 311 L6
Morelia 314 K9
Morelos 307 E4
Morelos 308 G5
Morelos 309 J3
Morelos 310 K4
Morelos 313 J7
Motul 317 R8
Moyahua 313 J8
Mulegé 307 D4
Muna 317 R8

N

Naco 307 E2
Nacori Chico 308 F3
Nacozari de García 307 E2
Namiquipa 308 F3
Nanchital 315 N10
Naranjo 308 F5
Naranjos 315 M8
Nautla 315 M8
Nava 310 K4
Navojoa 308 E4
Nazas 309 H5
Neji 306 B1
Nexpa 313 J10
Nezahualcoy 314 L9
Nicolás Bravo 317 R9
Nogales 307 E2
Nombre de Dios 313 H6
Nonoava 308 G4
Nopoló 306 D5
Norias 313 J6
Norogachic 308 G4
Nueva Ciudad Guerrero 310 L5
Nueva Coahuila 316 Q10
Nueva Rosita 310 K4
Nuevo Campechito 316 P9
Nuevo Casas Grandes 308 F2
Nuevo Churumuco 313 J9
Nuevo Ixcatlán 315 N10
Nuevo Laredo 310 K4
Nuevo México 316 P10
Nuevo Morelos 310 L6
Nuevo Padilla 311 L6
Numaran 313 J8
Nuxco 314 K10

O

Oaxaca 315 M10
Ocampo 308 F4
Ocampo 313 J8
Ocosingo 316 Q10
Ocotlán 313 J8
Ocotlán 315 M10
Ohuisa 307 E3
Ojinaga 309 H3
Ojo Caliente 313 J7
Ojo de Carrizo 308 H3
Ojos Negros 306 B1
Opichén 317 R8
Opodepe 307 E3
Opopeo 313 J9
Oriental 315 M9
Orizaba 315 M9
Orozo 307 E4
Ortiz 307 E3
Otinapa 313 H6
Oxkutzcab 317 R8
Ozuluama 314 L8

P

Paamul 317 S8
Pacheco 313 J6
Pachuca de Soto 314 L8
Paila 309 J5
Palau 310 K4
Palenque 316 Q10
Palmar de Cuautla 312 G7
Palmarillo 315 N10
Palmas 317 S9
Palma Sola 315 M9
Palmillas 310 L6
Palmitos 310 K5
Palo Gordo 312 G6
Palomares 315 N10
Palomas 310 K7
Palo Verde 306 D5
Pánuco 311 L7
Papantla de Olarte 315 M8
Paracho de Verduzco 313 J9
Paracuaro 313 J9
Paraiso 316 P9
Parás 310 K5
Paredon 310 K5
Parque Nacional Sierra de San Pedro Mártir 306 B2
Parras de la Fuente 309 J5
Paso de Ovejas 315 M9
Pastora 310 J5
Pathe 314 K8
Pátzcuaro 313 J9
Patzimaro 313 J8
Pedernales 308 G3
Pedro Montoya 314 K7
Pénjamo 313 J8
Pericos 312 G7
Perote 315 M9

Pesqueira 307 E3
Petatlán 314 K10
Peto 317 R8
Pichachic 308 F4
Pichilingüe 306 E6
Pichucalco 316 P10
Piedras Negras 310 K3
Pihuamo 313 H9
Pimientillo 312 G7
Pinos 310 J7
Pinotepa Nacional 314 L11
Piste 317 R8
Pixoyal 316 Q9
Placer de Guadalupe 308 G3
Platón Sanchez 314 L8
Playa Azul 313 J10
Playa del Carmen 317 S8
Playa Lauro Villar 311 M5
Playa los Corchos 312 G7
Playa Vicente 315 N10
Polotitlán 314 K8
Polyuc 317 S8
Pomaro 313 H9
Pomuch 317 R8
Porvenir 317 S7
Porvenir Cumuripa 307 E4
Pótam 307 E4
Potosi 310 K6
Potrero de Gallegos 313 H7
Potrero del Llano 309 H3
Potrero del Llano 315 M8
Potrero de Los Sánchez 308 F5
Poza Rica de Hidalgo 315 M8
Pozas de Santa Ana 310 K7
Pozo Coyote 307 D3
Pres Juárez 317 S9
Presidios 308 G5
Progreso 308 G2
Progreso 308 G2
Progreso 310 K4
Progreso 317 R8
Pucté 317 S9
Puebla 314 L9
Pueblito de Allende 308 G4
Pueblo Veijo 316 P10
Puerto 316 Q9
Puerto Angel 315 M11
Puerto Adolfo López Mateos 306 D5
Puerto Bravo 317 S9
Puerto Cancún 306 D6
Puerto Catarina 306 B3
Puerto Chicxulub 317 R8
Puerto Cortés 306 D6
Puerto Escondido 315 M11
Puerto Juárez 317 S7
Puerto Libertad 307 D2
Puerto Lobos 307 D2
Puerto Madero 316 Q11
Puerto Madero 317 S9
Puerto Magdalena 306 D6
Puerto Morelos 317 S8
Puerto Nuevo 306 C4
Puerto Nuevo 306 B1
Puerto Palomas 316 P11
Puerto Peñasco 307 C2
Puerto Vallarta 312 G8
Punta Cabras 306 B1
Punta Coyote 306 E6
Punta Eugenia 306 B4
Punta Final 306 C2
Punta Prieta 306 C3
Punta Prieta 306 C4
Punta Radar 306 C2
Purándiro 313 J8
Purepero 313 J9
Purificación 313 H9
Puruarán 313 J9
Pustunich 316 R9

Q

Querendaro 314 K9
Querétaro 314 K8
Querobabi 307 E2
Quila 312 F6
Quiriego 308 E4
Quiroga 313 J9
Quitoa 307 D2

R

Ramírez 310 K4
Ramón Corona 313 H6
Rayones 310 K6
Real 316 Q9
Real de Catorce 310K6
Rechéachic 308 G4
Reforma 317 S9
Rellano 309 H4
Reserva de la Biósfera el Triunfo 316 P11
Reserva de la Biósfera Sian Ka'an 317 S8
Reserva Ecologica el Campanario 314 K9
Reynosa 311 L5
R Flores Magón 308 G3
Rincos de Romos 313 J7
Río Bravo 310 K4
Río Bravo 311 L5
Río Chancalá 316 Q10
Rio Escondido 317 R9
Río Grande 315 M11
Río Lagartos 317 S7
Río Sonora 307 D3
Riva Palacio 308 G3
Rodeo 309 H5
Rodrego M Quevedo 308 F2
Rosamoraga 312 G7
Rosario 308 E4
Rosarito 306 B2
Rosarito 306 C3
Rosarito 306 B1
Rosarito 307 D5
Ruiz 312 G7
Ruiz Cortines 316 R9

S

Sabán 317 S8
Sabancuy 316 Q9
Sabinas 310 K4
Sabinas Hidalgo 310 K5
Sacramento 310 J4
Sahuaral 307 D3
Sahuaripa 308 E3
Sahuayo 313 J8
Salamanca 314 K8
Salina Cruz 315 N11
Salinas de Hildago 310 J7
Salsipuedes 316 Q9
Saltillo 310 K5
Salto de Agua 316 Q10
Salvatierra 314 K8
Samachique 308 F4
Samalayuca 308 G2
San Agustin 306 C2
San Alicia 306 B1
San Andrés 310 J6
San Andrés Tuxtla 315 N9
San Ángel 306 C3
San Angel 314 L9
San Antonio 306 E6
San Antonio 313 H9
San Antonio 316 Q11
San Antonio del Mar 306B2
San Bartolo 306 E6
San Bernardino 308 F2
San Bernardo 308 F4
San Bernardo 308 G5
San Blas 312 G8
San Buenaventura 307 D4
San Carlos 307 D4
San Cristóbal de las Casas 316 P10
San Diego 308 F2
San Esteban 307C4
San Fco de Cabrales 313 J7
San Felipe 306 C2
San Fermín 309 H5
San Fernando 311L6
San Francisco 307 D2
San Francisco 310 K7
San Francisco de Borja 308 G4
San Fransisco del Rincón 313 J8
San Gabriel Mixtepec 315 M11
San Hipólito 306 C4
San Ignacio 307 D4
San Isidro 306 D5
San Isidro 307 E3
San Isidro 308 G2
San Isidro Poniente 317 R9
San Javier 306 D5
San Javier 308 G4
San Jeronimito 314 K10
San Jerónimo 309 J6
San Jerónimo 314 K10
San José 307 E4
San José Chiltepec 315 M10
San José de Ahome 308E5
San José de Dimas 307 E3
San José de Gracia 307 D4
San José de Gracia 308 F5
San José de la Boca 308 G5
San José de las Rusias 311 L6
San José del Cabo 306 E7
San José del Progreso 315 M11
San José de Moradillas 307 E3
San José de Raices 310 K6
San José Iturbide 314 K8
San José Lachiguiri 315 M11
San Juan Bautista Tuxtepec 315 M10
San Juan de Guadalupe 313 J6
San Juan de la Costa 306 E6
San Juan de la Zorra 306 B1
San Juan de los Planes 306 E6
San Juan del Río 314 K8
San Juan del Salado 310 J7
San Juanico 307 D5
San Julián 313 J8
San Lorenzo 310 J4
San Lucas 314 K9
San Luis 306 C3
San Luis Potosí 310 K7
San Luis Río Colorado 306 C1
San Luis San Pedro 314 K10
San Luiz de la Paz 314 K8
San Marcos 313 H8
San Marcos 314 L10
San Mateo 313 H7
San Mateo del Mar 315 N11
San Miguel de Allende 314 K8
San Miguel el Alto 313 J8
San Miguelito 308 F2
San Miguel Zapotitlan 308 E5
San Pablo Balleza 308 G4
San Pedro 306 E6
San Pedro 307 C3
San Pedro 307 D3
San Pedro 309 H3
San Pedro 316 Q10
San Pedro Corralitos 308 F2
San Pedro de la Cueva 307 E3
San Pedro del Gallo 309 H5
San Pedro Huamelula 315 N11
San Pedro Pochutla 315 M11
San Pedro Suchixtepec 315 M11
San Pedro Tapanatepec 315 P11
San Quintín 306 B2
San Rafael 307 D2
San Rafael 309 H5
San Rafael 310 K6
San Rafael 315 M8
San Roberto 310 K6
San Román 317 R9
San Roque 306 C4
San Salvador 314 L9
San Sebastian 313 H8
San Sebastián Ixcapa 314 L11
San Simon 308 F5
Santa Ana 307 E2
Santa Anita 309 H4
Santa Anita 313 H8
Santa Bárbara 308 G4
Santa Catarina 306 B1
Santa Catarina 306 B2
Santa Catarina 310 K5
Santa Clara 313 H6
Santa Cruz 307 E2
Santa Cruz 310 K5
Santa Cruz 316 Q9
Santa Cruz del Oregano 313 J6
Santa Cruz Huatulco 315 M11
Santa Elena 309 J4
Santa Elena 317 R8
Santa Eulalia 310 K3
Santa Inés 316 Q11
Santa Isabel 316 P11
Santa María 307 D3
Santa María de Cuevas 308 G4
Santa María del Oro 308 G5
Santa María del Oro 313 H8
Santa María del Río 314 K7
Santa María del Valle 313 J8
Santa María Huatulco 315 M11
Santa María Jacatepec 315 M10
Santa María Zacatepec 314 L10
Santa Matilde 308 F4
Santander Jiménez 311 L6
Santa Rita 306 D6
Santa Rita 313 H9
Santa Rosa 306 E6
Santa Rosa 308 E4
Santa Rosa 308 F3
Santa Rosa 310 J3
Santa Rosa 312 G6
Santa Rosa 313 J8
Santa Rosa 314 K10
Santa Rosa 317 R8
Santa Rosalía 307 D4
Santa Teresa 311 L5
Santa Victoria 310 J5
Santiago 306 E6
Santiago 313 H9
Santiago de la Peña 315 M8
Santiago Ixcuintla 312 G7
Santiago Jamiltepec 315 M11
Santiago Papasquiaro 308 G5
Santiago Tuxtla 315 N9
San Tiburico 310 J6
San Tiburico 313 J6
Santo Domingo 306 D5
Santo Domingo 307 D5
Santo Domingo 310 J6
Santo Domingo 310 K7
Santo Domingo 311 L5
Santo Domingo 313 H8
Santo Domingo 315 N10
Santo Domingo Tehuantepec 315 N11
Santo Tomás 306 B1
Santo Tomás 308 F3
San Vicente 306 B1
Satevó 308 G4
Saucillo 308 G4
SC Yautepec 315 M10
Sentispac 312 G7
Seye 317 R8

Sierra Mojada 309 H4
Silao 313 J8
Sinoquipe 307 E2
Siqueros 312 G6
Sisal 317 R8
Sisoguichic 308 F4
Socorro 309 J4
Soledad 307 D2
Sombrerete 313 H6
Sonora 306 C1
Sonoyta 307 D1
Soto la Marina 311 L6
Sotuta 317 R8
Sovopa 307 E3
Soyaló 316 P10
Soyatita 308 F5
Suchil 313 H6

T

Tabasco 313 J7
Tacubaya 309 J5
Tahdzibichén 317 R8
Tajicaringa 313 H6
Talpa de Allende 313 H8
Tamazula 308 G6
Tamazula de Gordiano 313 J9
Tamazunchale 314 L8
Tampacan 314 L8
Tampico 311 L7
Tampico Alto 311 L7
Tamuin 314 L7
Tancitaro 313 J9
Tangancicuaro 313 J9
Tanque Nuevo 309 J5
Tanques 308 F4
Tapachula 316 Q11
Tapalpa 313 H8
Tapilula 316 P10
Tarandacuao 314 K8
Taretán 313 J9
Tasajeras 308 F4
Tastiota 307 D3
Taxco 314 K9
Tayahua 313 J7
Teabo 317 R8
Teacapan 312 G7
Teapa 316 P10
Tecalitián 313 H9
Tecamachalo 315 M9
Tecate 306 B1
Tecoh 317 R8
Tecolutla 315 M8
Tecomán 313 H9
Tecpan de Galeana 314 K10
Tecuala 312 G7
Tehuacán 315 M9
Tehuitzingo 314 L9
Tejolocachic 308 F3
Tejupilco de Hidalgo 314 K9
Tekantó 317 R8
Tekax de AO 317 R8
Tekik 317 R8
Telchac Puerto 317 R7
Temascal 313 H6
Temascaltepec 314 K9
Temax 317 R8
Temezcal 315 M9
Temochic 308 F4
Temosachic 308 F3
Temozón 317 S8
Tenabó 316 R8
Tenamaxtlán 313 H8
Tenancingo 314 K9
Tenejapa 316 P10
Tenixtepec 315 M8
Tenochtitlán 315 N10
Tenosique de Pino Suárez 316 Q10
Teotihuacán 314 L9
Teotitlán del Camino 315 M10
Tepalcatepec 313 J9
Tepantita 308 F5
Tepatitlán 313 J8
Tepechitlán 313 H7
Tepehuanes 308 G5
Tepeji del Río 314 L9
Tepeojuma 314 L9
Tepetitlán 316 Q10
Tepetongo 313 J7
Tepetzintla 315 L8
Tepic 313 H8
Tepich 317 S8
Tepotzotlán 314 L9
Tepoztlán 314 L9
Tepuxtla 312 G6
Tequila 313 H8
Tequisquiapan 314 K8
Tequixquiac 314 L9
Tetamechi 308 F5
Teul Ganzález Ortega 313 H8
Texistepec 315 N10
Teziutlán 315 M9
Tiacolulan 315 M9
Ticul 317 R8
Tierra Blanca 315 M9
Tihosuco 317 S8
Tihuatlán 315 M8
Tijuana 306 B1
Tilzapotla 314 L9
Tinum 316 R8
Tinúm 317 S8
Tixbacab 317 S8
Tixcancal 317 S8
Tixkokob 317 R8
Tixmucuy 316 R9
Tizimín 317 S8
Tlachichilco 314 L8
Tlacolula 315 M10
Tlacotalpan 315 N9
Tlajomulco 313 H8
Tlalpujahua 314 K9
Tlaltenango 313 H7
Tlapacoyan 315 M10
Tlapacoyan 315 M8
Tlaquepaque 313 H8
Tlatlaya 314 K9
Tlaxcala 314 L9
Tlaxco 314 L9
Tlaxiaco 315 M10
Tocumbo 313 J9
Todos Santos 306 E6
Toluca 314 K9
Tomatán 306 C3
Tomatlán 312 G8
Tonalá 316 P11
Tonaya 313 H9
Tonila 313 H9
Topolobampo 308 E5
Torreón 309 H5
Torreón de Cañas 308 G5
Torres 307 E3
Tosanachic 308 F3
Totolapan 315 M10
Totontepec 315 N10
Totutla 315 M9
Tres Picos 316 P11
Tres Reyes 317 S8
Tula 310 K7
Tula de Allende 314 L8
Tulancingo 314 L8
Tulipan 316 Q10
Tulúm 317 S8
Tupilco 316 P9
Tuxcueca 313 J8
Tuxpan 313 H9
Tuxpan 314 K9
Tuxpan de RC 315 M8
Tuxtla Gutiérrez 316 P10
Tzintzuntzán 313 J9
Tzucacab 317 R8

U

Uaymá 317 S8
Ucum 317 S9
U Hidalgo 315 N10
Uman 317 R8
Unión de Tula 313 H8
Unión Juárez 316 Q11
Ures 307 E3
Uriangato 313 J8
Ursulo Galván 315 M9
Ursulo Galván 317 S9
Uruachic 308 F4
Uruapan del Progreso 313 J9
Uxmal 317 R8

V

Va Comaltitlán 316 P11
Va Hildago 313 J7
Valerio 308 G4
Valladolid 317 S8
Valle de Allende 308 G4
Valle de Banderas 312 G8
Valle de Bravo 314 K9
Valle de Guadalupe 313 J8
Valle del Rosario 308 G4
Valle de Santiago 314 K8
Valle de Zaragoza 308 G4
Valle Hermoso 311 L5
Valle Hermoso 317 S9
Valle Las Palmas 306 B1
Valle Nacional 315 M10
Valparaiso 313 H7
Vaquería 310 L5
Vasconcelos 315 N10
Vega de Alatorre 315 M8
Venado 310 K7
Venustiano Carranza 306 B2
Venustiano Carranza 313 H6
Venustiono Carranza 313 H9
Venustiano Carranza 316 P10
Veracruz 306 C1
Veracruz 315 M9
Vicam 307 E4
Vicam Pueblo 307 E4
Vicario 317 S8
Vicente Guerrero 307 E2
Vicente Guerraro 313 H6
Vicente Guerrero 317 S8
Viejo 306 B1
Viesca 309 J5
Vigia Chico 317 S8
Villa Ahumada 308 G2
Villa Ahumada y Anexas 308 G2
Villa Coronado 308 H5
Villa de Cazones 315 M8
Villa de Guadalupe 310 K6
Villa de Orestes 308 G5
Villa de Pozos 310 K7
Villa de Ramoz 310 J7
Villa de Reyes 314 K7
Villa de Sarí 307 E3
Villa Flores 316 P11
Villa Frontera 310 J4
Villa García 313 J7
Villago Hidalgo 306B2
Villa González Ortega 310 J7
Villagrán 314 K8
Villagran 310 L6
Villa Guerrero 313 H7
Villahermosa 316 P10
Villa Hidalgo 308 E2
Villa Hidalgo 309 H5
Villa Hidalgo 310 K4
Villa Hidalgo 310 K7
Villa Insurgentes 306 D5
Villa Jesús Maria 306 C3
Villa Juanita 315 N10
Villa Juarez 307 E4
Villa Juárez 309 H5
Villa Juárez 310 K7
Villaldama 310 K5
Villa López 309 H4
Villa Mainero 310 L6
Villa Matamoros 308 G5
Villanueva 313 J7
Villa Ocampo 308 G5
Villa Pesquera 307 E3
Villa Unión 310 K4
Villa Unión 312 G7
Villa Unión 313 H6

X

Xagacia 315 M10
Xalapa (Jalapa) 315 M9
Xcabacab 316 Q9
Xcalak 317 S9
X-Can 317 S8
Xcaret 317 S8
Xcupil 317 R8
Xel-Há 317 S8
Xiatil 317 S8
Xicotepecde Juárez 314 L8
Xilitla 314 L8
Xochicalco 314 L9
Xochihuehuetlán 314 L10
Xochimilco 314 L9
Xonacatlan 315 M9
Xpujil 317 R9
Xul 317 R8

Y

Yagul 315 M10
Yahualica 313 J8
Yajalón 316 Q10
Yalina 315 M10
Yalsihon 317 S7
Yanga 315 M9
Yanhuitlán 315 M10
Yaqui 307 E4
Yautepec d Z 314 L9
Yávaros 307 E4
Yaxchilán 316 Q10
Yaxcopil 317 R8
Yécora 308 F3
Yecorato 308 F5
Yeloixtlahuacan 314 L10
Yerbanis 313 H6
Yermo 309 H5
Yucatán 317 S7
Yurécuaro 313 J8
Yuriria 314 K8

Z

Zaachila 315 M10
Zacatal 316 Q9
Zacatecas 313 J7
Zacatlán 31 4L9
Zacatosa 309 J4
Zamora 313 J8
Zapopan 313 H8
Zapotan 312 H8
Zapotitic 313 H9
Zaragoza 308 F3
Zaragoza 308 G2
Zaragoza 310 K3
Zaragoza 310 K7
Zaragoza 315 M9
Zaragoza 316 P11
Zicuirán 313 J9
Zihuatanejo 313 J10
Zinacantán 316 P10
Zinacatepec 315 M9
Zináparo 313 J8
Zinapécuaro 314 K9
Zitlala 314 L10

Page numbers in **bold** indicate the main reference.

A

Acancéh 212
Acapulco **82**, 186
  airport 41–42
  beaches 82
  Fuerte de San Diego 82
  hotels 269
  La Quebrada 82
  restaurants 248
accidents and breakdowns 55–56
accommodation 264–265
  apartments 265
  cabañas 265
  camping 265
  casas de huéspedes 264, 265
  children 178
  motels 265
  posadas 264, 265
  self-catering 265
  taxes 264
  words and phrasesl 300
  youth hostels 265
  see also hotels
Actopan 122
Acuario Mazatlán 165
agave 151
agriculture 5, 20, 21
Agua Azul 83
Aguascalientes **138**, 203
  Museo de Aguascalientes 138
  Museo José Guadalupe Posada 138
  Palacio de Gobierno 138
  restaurants 259
  Teatro Morelos 138
Ahuacatlán 226
air travel 40–42, 58
  airports 40–42
  domestic 45, 50–51
  health hazards for flyers 288
Aktun Chen 210
Akumal **61**, 210
Alameda 100, 104, 220
Alamos 157
  Museo Costumbrista de Sonora 157
alejibres 188, 189
Alhóndiga de Granaditas, Guanajuato 143–144
Allende, Ignacio 149, 304
altitude sickness 289
Amatenango del Valle 214
Angahuan 153
apartments 265
archaeological site opening hours 293
archaeological sites
  Bonampak 83
  Casas Grandes (Paquimé) 160
  Cempoala 123
  Chicanná 70
  Chicomostoc 139
  Cholula **123**, 224, 225
  Dainzú 218
  Ek-Balam 71
  El Tajín 9, 23, 26, **129**
  Kohunlich 72
  Sayil 212
  Teotihuacán 9, 26, 27, **132–134**
  Tzintzuntzán 230
  Xlapak 212
  Xochicalco 131
  see also Aztec, Maya, Olmec, Toltec and Zapotec sites
architecture
  baroque 10, 33, 73, 90, 96, 126, 154, 216, 225, 226
  Churrigueresque 33, 107, 130, 131, 143, 144, 150, 151
  colonial 8, 62, 75, 96, 117, 167
  contemporary 14, 15
  neoclassical 73, 143
artesanía 170
arts 14–15
Atlantes figures 153
ATMs 286
Aztec deities 304
Aztec sites
  Malinalco 145
  Plaza de las Tres Culturas, Mexico City 116
  Templo Mayor 118–119
  see also Tenochtitlán
Aztecs 30–31

B

Bacalar 72
Bahía de los Angeles 157
Bahía Concepción 236
Bahía Kino 157
  Museo de los Seris 157
Bahía Magdalena 157
Bahía de Navidad 138
Bahía San Carlos 162
Baja California 7
  see also Northern Mexico and Baja California
Bajío 228–229
Balankanché Caves 71
ball courts 66, 67, 86, 98, 129, 131, 153
ball game 29, 66
Ballet Folklórico 172, 192
Baluarte de Santiago, Veracruz 135
Banco Chinchorro 72, 80
Banderas Bay 147
banks 286, 293
Barra de Navidad **138**, 259
  hotel 277
Barragán, Luis 14, 15, 165, 304
Barranca del Cobre 9, **158–159, 232–233**
Barranca de Metlac 122
bars and nightclubs 173, 293
baseball 174
Basílica de Guadalupe, Mexico City 104
Basílica de la Soledad, Oaxaca 90, 216
Batopilas 159
Becal 180
Becán 61
beer 241
Belize 44
Benito Juárez 218
Bernal 176, 226
Bernal, Gael García 18
best of Mexico 8–10
Biblioteca Francisco Burgoa, Oaxaca 90, 216, 217
Biblioteca Palafoxiana, Puebla 126
bird-watching 61, 71, 74, 184, 238
Boca del Río 135
Bodega de Santo Tomás 162
Bonampak 83
border crossings 43–44, 284
Bosque de Chapultepec, Mexico City 105
bullfighting 84, 107, 168, 174, 194–195, 205
Burton, Richard 148
buses 45, 46, 52–53, 58
  cities 57
  long-distance 45, 52, 53
  Mexico City 46
  safety 45, 53

C

cabañas 265
Cabo San Lucas **159**, 204, 206
  hotels 279
  restaurants 262
Cacahuamilpa 122
Cacaxtla 122
Café Tacuba 19
cafés 293
Calakmul 61
Calakmul Biosphere Reserve 61
calendars 27, 30
Camino Real (Royal Road) 234
Campeche **62**, 180
  Baluarte de la Soledad 62
  Casa de Teniente del Rey 62
  Catedral de la Concepción 62
  Circuito baluartes (bastions) 62
  Fuerte de San Miguel 62
  hotels 266
  Jardín Botánico Xmuch'Haltun 62
  luz y sonido 62
  Museo de la Cultura Maya 62
  Museo Regional de Campeche 62
  restaurants 244
camping 265
Cañadas de Cotlamani 174
Cancún 8, **63**, 180–181, 185, 210
  hotels 266
  restaurants 244
Cañon del Diablo 166
Cañon del Sumidero 10, **83**, 186
canyoning 174
Capilla del Rosario, Puebla 33, 126, 224
Carnival 9, 179, 185, 199, 206
Carrillo, Chávez 139
Carrillo-Gil, Álvaro 112
Casa del Adivino, Uxmal 78
Casa de Amado Nervo, Tepic 150
Casa de los Azulejos, Mexico City 106
Casa de Don Ignacio de Allende, San Miguel de Allende 149
Casa de La Malinche, Mexico City 223
Casa de León Trotsky, Mexico City 223
Casa de las Monjas, Uxmal 78
Casa de Mundaca, Isla Mujeres 72, 209
Casa Natal de Morelos, Morelia 147
Casa del Risco, Mexico City 117, 222, 223

Casa de las Tortugas, Uxmal 79
Casas Grandes (Paquimé) 160
casas de huéspedes 264, 265
Cascada de Basaseáchic 160
Cascado de Texolo 123
Catedral Metropolitana, Mexico City 20, **106–107**
Catedral San Ildefonso, Mérida 73
Catemaco **123**, 256, 275
cave diving 75
cave paintings (petroglyphs) 234–235
caves
  Aktun Chen 210
  Grutas de Balankanché 71
  Grutas de Cacahuamilpa 122
  Grutas de Loltún 212
  Grutas de García 162
  San Ignacio 167
caving 174
Celaya 138–139
  Convento de San Francisco 139
  Templo del Carmen 139
  Torre Hidráulica 139
Celestún 61
Celestún Biosphere Reserve 61, 177
Cempoala 123
Cenote Azul 72
cenote diving 174–175, 185
Cenote Sagrado, Chichén Itzá 66
Cenote X-Kekén 185
Cenote Xlacah 70–71
Cenote Zací 75, 185
Central Mexico East 7, 9, **121–136**
  drive 224–225
  festivals and events 199
  hotels 275–276
  map 121
  restaurants 256–258
  sights 122–136
  what to do 196–199
Central Mexico West 7, 9, **137–155**
  drives 226–231
  festivals and events 203
  hotels 277–278
  map 137
  restaurants 259–261
  sights 138–155
  what to do 200–203
Centro de Desarrollo de la Medicina Maya, San Cristóbal de las Casas 96
Centro Ecológico de Sonora 163
Centro de Investigaciones de las Culturas Olmecas (CICOM), Villahermosa 98
Centro Mexicano de la Tortuga 85, 188
ceramics 171, 188, 197
Cerro de La Bufa 154
Chahué 84
Chan Bahlum 92, 94, 95
Chapala 139
charrería 10, 176
charros 9
Chetumal 70
  hotels 266
  Museo de la Cultura Maya 70
  restaurants 244–245
Chiapa del Corzo 83, 186
Chicanná **70**, 266
Chichén Itzá 10, **64–67**, 185
  Casa de las Monjas 66
  Cenote Sagrado 66
  Chichén Viejo 66
  El Caracol 66
  El Castillo 10, 64
  Juego de Pelota 66, 67
  site plan 67
  Templo de los Guerreros 66
Chicomostoc 139
Chihuahua **160**, 204
  Catedral Metropolitana 160
  hotels 279
  Museo Histórico de la Revolución Mexicana 160
  Museo Regional 160
  Quinta Luz 160
  restaurants 262
Chihuahua al Pacifico 9, 49, 159, 164
children 178, 293
China Poblana 24
chocolate 29, 240
cholera 289
Cholula **123**, 224, 225
Chumayel 212
cigar factories 128
cinema 18, 172, 294
Cinema Museum, Durango 161
Citlatépetl 175
Ciudad Cuauhtémoc 44
Cíudad Hidalgo 44
Cíudad Juárez 43
Ciudad Universitaria, Hermosillo 163
Ciudad Universitaria, Mexico City 107
Clausell, Joaquín 112
cliff diving 82
climate 4, 282
climbing 175
clothing sizes 285
cloud forest 85, 175
Coatepec **123**, 196
  hotels 275
  restaurants 256
Cobá **70**, 211, 266
cocoa 29
Cocula 23
coffee growing 123
Cofre de Perote 4
colectivos, combis and *peseros* 57
Colegio de San Ildefonso, Mexico City 107
Colegio de San Nicolás de Hidalgo, Morelia 147
Colima **139**, 200
  Jardín de Libertad 139
  Museo de las Culturas de Occidente María Ahumada 139
  Museo Regional de Historia 139
  Palacio de Gobierno 139
  restaurants 259
Comalcalco 84
concessions 293
Condesa, Mexico City 8
Convent and Puuc routes 212–213
Convento Franciscano de San Miguel de Huejotzingo 224, 225
Convento de San Antonio de Padua 72
conversion chart 284
Copper Canyon 9, **158–159**, **232–233**, 279
copper mining 167
Córdoba **125**, 256
Coronel, Pedro and Rafael 154
Cortés, Hernán 16, 31, 32, 101, 106, 112, 123, 124, 304
La Costa Alegre 138
Cousteau, Jacques 69
Coyoacán 8, **106**, 222–223
Cozumel 8, **68–69**, 181
  archaeological sites 68
  beaches 68
  El Cedral 69
  Museo de la Isla Cozumel 68
  Parque Chankanaab 69
  Parque Punta Sur 69
  Punta Celarain 68, 69
  restaurants 245
crafts 22, 170, 218
credit cards 170, 241, 286, 287
Creel 9, 159, 205
crime and personal safety 45, 53, 100, 292
Cristero War 37
cruise ships 44
Cuauhtémoc (Aztec emperor) 130, 304
Cuauhtémoc 160–161
  Mennonite Museum 161
Cuernavaca **124**, 196–197
  Catedral de la Asunción 124
  hotels 275
  Jardín Borda 124
  Museo de Historia Cuauhnáhuac 124
  Museo Robert Brady 124
  Palacio de Cortés 124
  restaurants 256–257
Cuesta del Palmarito 167
cultural tours 238
Cumbres de Monterrey National Park 174
Cunningham, Osvaldo Barra 138
currency 286
currency exchange 286–287
customs regulations 283
cycling 57, 188, 206, 38

D

Dainzú 218
Day of the Dead 9, 22, 24, 179
demography 5
dengue fever 289
dental treatment 289
department stores 170
Desierto Vizcaíno 161
Día de los Muertos 9, 22, 24, 179
Díaz, Porfirio 34, 36, 304
Diego, Juan 33, 104
disabilities, visitors with 58, 284–285
  specialist tour operators 58, 285–285
  travel 58
diving 8, 61, 63, 68, 69, 80, 175, 181, 182, 183, 184, 185, 205
doctors 288–289
Dolores Hidalgo 9, 34, **139–140**, 228
  Iglesia de Nuestra Señora de los Dolores 139
  Museo Casa Hidalgo 139
dress code 285
drinking water 241, 289
driving 45, 54–56
  accidents and breakdowns 55–56
  border crossings 43–44
  car crime 45, 292
  car ferries 49
  cities 48
  distances 54
  documents 54
  fuel 56
  regulations 55
  road signs 56
  speed limits 54
  toll roads 45, 54–55
drug trade 13, 56
Durango 10, **161**
  Cinema Museum 161
duty-free allowances 283
Dzibilchaltún 70–71

E

earthquakes 13, 17, 139
Easter 22, 179
eating out 240–243
  mealtimes and menus 240–241, 293

menu reader 242–243
Mexican cuisine 240, 243
tipping 241
vegetarian food 241
words and phrases 301
see also restaurants
Eco-Park Kantún Chí 181
eco-tourism 186, 188, 238
EcoMundo Baja Tropicales 236
economy 5, 13
Edificio de los Danzantes, Monte Albán 86
Edzná 71
Ek-Balam 71
El Anfiteatro 219
El Arco 159
El Campanario Ecological Reserve 9, **148**
El Castillo de Kukulkán, Chichén Itzá 10, 64
El Castillo, Tulúm 75
El Cedral 69
El Divisadero 9, 232
El Fuerte 162
El Garrafón 72, 182, 209
El Palomar, Uxmal 79
El Tajín 9, 23, 26, **129**
ball courts 129
Pirámide de los Nichos 129
Tajín Chico 129
voladores 23, 129
El Triunfo Biosphere Reserve **85**, 175, 177
El Tule 218, 219
El Vizcaíno Biosphere Reserve 161
electricity 284
embassies and consulates
abroad 283
Mexico City 292
emergencies 292
emergency telephone numbers 289, 292
words and phrases 302
Ensenada **162**, 205, 206
Bodega de Santo Tomás 162
hotels 279
Museo de Historia de Ensenada 162
Museo Histórico Regional 162
restaurants 262
entertainment 172
Mexico City 192–193
Erongarícuaro 230
Estacahuite 85
Explora Science Museum, León 145, 201

F

family holidays 178
feminist movement 38
Feria Nacional de San Marcos 138, 203
ferries 49, 58
festivals and events 9, 22–24, 179
Central Mexico East 199
Central Mexico West 203
Mexico City 195
Northern Mexico and Baja California 206
Southern Mexico 189
Yucatán 185
Finca Prusia 85
first-aid kit 288
fishing 63, 69, 145, 157, 162, 164, 167, 176–177, 204, 205, 206
flamingos 61, 74
folk art 24
food and drink
alcohol 241
beer 241
chapulines 89, 240
chiles en nogada 126
chocolate 240
cooking classes 238
drinking water 241, 289
hot drinks 241
pulque 151, 173, 241
tequila 10, 241
tortillas 13, 240
wine 241
see also eating out; restaurants
Fox, Vicente 13, 38, 144, 304
Freedom Bell 35
fuel 56
Fuentes, Carlos 15, 21, 294 304
Fuerte de San Diego, Acapulco 82
Fuerte de San Miguel, Campeche 62

G

gardens
Centro de Desarrollo de la Medicina Maya, San Cristóbal de las Casas 96
Jardín Borda, Cuernavaca 124
Jardín Botánico Cosmovitral, Toluca 151
Jardín Botánico Dr. Alfredo Barrera Marin 210
Jardín Botánico, Mexico City 107
Jardín Botánico Xmuch'Haltun, Campeche 62
Jardín Centenario, Mexico City 106
Jardín Etnobotánico, Oaxaca 90, 216, 217
gay and lesbian scene 173
geography 4
go-karting 202
Goitia, Francisco 155
golf 175, 195, 201
Grutas de Balankanché 71
Grutas de Cacahuamilpa 122
Grutas de Loltún 212
Grutas de García 162
Guadalajara **141**, 200–201, 203
airport 42
Basilica of Zapopán 141
hotels 277
Huichol Museum 141
Instituto Cultural Cabañas 141
Museo Regional de Guadalajara 141
Palacio de Gobierno 141
restaurants 259
Tlaquepaque 141
Zoológico Guadalajara 201
Guadalupe **140**, 201
Convento de Guadalupe 140
Museo de Arte Religioso 140
Guanajuato 9, **142–144**, 201, 203, 228
Alhóndiga de Granaditas 143–144
Basílica de Nuestra Señora de Guanajuato 143
Callejón del Beso 143
Casa del Conde de la Valenciana 144, 201
El Pípila Monument 144
hotels 277
Iglesia de la Compañía 143
Iglesia de La Valenciana 144, 228
Iglesia de San Diego 143
Jardín de la Unión 143
Museo Diego Rivera 144
Museo Iconográfico del Quijote 144
Museo de las Momias 144, 228
Museo del Pueblo 144
restaurants 260
Teatro Juárez 143
Guatemala 44
Guayabitos 140
Guaymas 162
Guelaguetza 22, 189
Guerrero Negro 162–163
Gutiérrez, José Maria 35

H

Hacienda Casa de Santa Anna, Xalapa 136
Hadad, Astrid 19
Half Moon Bay 61
hammocks 171
hang-gliding 150
health 288–289
dental treatment 289
doctors 288–289
drinking water 241, 289
first-aid kit 288
hazards 288, 289
health hazards for flyers 288
hospitals 289
malaria 288, 289
medical treatment 288–289
opticians 289
pharmacies 289, 293
sun safety 178, 289
vaccinations 288
words and phrases 302
Hermosillo 163
Centro Ecológico de Sonora 163
Ciudad Universitaria 163
Museo Regional de Sonora 163
Hidalgo del Parral 163
Casa Griensen 163
La Prieta 163
Templo San Juan de Dios 163
Hidalgo y Costilla, Father Miguel 34, 139, 144, 148, 160, 304
Hierve el Agua 218–219
Higuerillas 226
hiking and walking 175
see also walks and drives
history 26–38
Aztecs 30–31
civil society politics 38
colonialism 32, 33
Cristero War 37
independence 34–35
key figures 304
Maya 27, 28–29, 33
Mexican Revolution 36–37
Mexican-American War 35
Mexico City 101
Olmecs 26, 27
Pastry War 35
prehistory 26–27
Spanish conquest 31, 32–33, 101
horse racing 195
horseback riding 188
hospitals 289
hotels 264
Central Mexico East 275–276
Central Mexico West 277–278
chains 265
Mexico City 272–274
Northern Mexico and Baja California 279–280
Southern Mexico 269–271
words and phrases 300
Yucatán 266–268
Huatulco **84**, 186–187
hotels 269
restaurants 248
Huejotzingo 224
Convento Franciscano 224, 225
Huichols 23
huipiles 12, 184, 212
Huitzilopochtli 31, 304
human sacrifice 29, 30, 31, 66, 78
Humboldt, Baron von 130

I

identity documents 285
Iglesia de Nuestra Señora de los Dolores, Dolores Hidalgo 139
Iglesia de San Bernardino de Siena, Mexico City 120
Iglesia de Santo Domingo, Oaxaca 10, 88, 89, 90, 216
Independence Monument, Mexico City 115
indígenas (indigenous people) 4, 5, 12
insect repellent 289
Instituto Cultural Cabañas, Guadalajara 141
insurance 283
Insurgentes, Mexico City 107
Internet access 291
Isla de los Alacranes 139
Isla Angel de la Guarda 157
Isla Holbox 71
Isla Magdalena 157
Isla de los Monos 123
Isla Mujeres **72**, 181–183, 209
  hotels 266–267
  restaurants 245–246
Isla de Pajaros 71
Isla Santa Margarita 157
Isla Tiburón 163
Isthmus of Tehuantepec 4, 12
Ixcateopan de Cuauhtémoc 130, 199
Ixtapa-Zihuatanejo 84
Ixtapan de la Sal 140
Ixtlán del Río 140
  Los Toriles 140
Izamal 72
  Convento de San Antonio de Padua 72
  Pirámide Kinich Kakmó 72
Iztaccíhuatl 4, 17, **125**, 175

J

jaguar 27
jai alai 168, 175–176
Jalisco 9
Jalpan 226
Jaltenango 85
Janitzio 147
Jardín Borda, Cuernavaca 124
Jardín Botánico Cosmovitral, Toluca 151
Jardín Botánico Dr. Alfredo Barrera Marin 210
Jardín Botánico, Mexico City 107
Jardín Botánico Xmuch'Haltun, Campeche 62
Jardín Centenario, Mexico City 106
Jardín Etnobotánico, Oaxaca 90, 216, 217
jewelry 171
Juárez, Benito 34, 91, 135, 150, 304
Juchitán 12

K

Kabah 212
Kahlo, Frida 14, 24, 106, 117, 304
kitesurfing 184
Kohunlich 72

L

La Costa Alegre 138
La Crucecita 84
La Malinche 32, 223, 304
La Paz **164**, 205, 206
  hotels 280
  Museo Antropológico de Baja California Sur 164
  restaurants 263
La Quebrada, Acapulco 82
La Venta 97
Labná 212
lacquerwork 153, 171, 203
Lago Cobá 70
Lago Macanxoc 70
Lago de Pátzcuaro 230–231
Laguna Bacalar 72
Laguna Bosque Azul 84
Laguna Ojo de Liebre 9, **164**
Laguna San Ignacio 167
Lagunas de Montebello 84
Landa, Father Diego de 33, 72, 212, 304
landscape 4, 16
language 5
  indigenous languages 5, 12
  menu reader 242–243
  Mexican glossary 303
  Spanish words and phrases 298–302
Las Coloradas 74
Las Pinturas 70
laundry and dry-cleaning 284
Lawrence, D. H. 218
leatherwork 171
Legorreta, Ricardo 14, 15, 304
León **145**, 201
  Explora Science Museum 145, 201
  Templo Expiatorio 145
Liberty Bell, Mexico City 115
literature 14, 15, 21
local etiquette 285
logging 17
Loltún 212
Loma Bonita 85
long stays 284
Loreto **164**, 205, 234, 236
  hotels 280
  restaurants 262–263
Los Mochis **164**, 263
Los Toriles 140

M

Macanxoc 70
Madero, Francisco 36, 304
Magdalena Contreras 176
malaria 288, 289
Malinalco 145
  Templo y Ex-Convento del Divino Salvador 145
La Malinche 32, 223, 304
Mama 212
Maní 212
Manzanillo **145**, 201
  restaurants 260
Mapastepec 85
Mapimi Biosphere Reserve 17, 177
maps
  airports 41
  atlas 305–317
  Central Mexico East 121
  Central Mexico West 137
  Mexico City (location) 99
  Mexico City (public transport) 47
  Mexico City (streetplan) 102–103
  Northern Mexico and Baja California 156
  regions 7
  road network 55
  sources 294
  Southern Mexico 81
  walks and drives 208
  Yucatán 60
mariachis 9, 23, 115, 172
markets 170
  Mexico City 112, 192
  Oaxaca 90–91
  Toluca 151
Marquez, Gabriel García 15
masks 150, 171, 230
Mata Ortiz 160
Matlalcueyetl 4
Maximilian, Emperor 35, 105, 124, 125, 148, 304
Maya 27, 28–29, 33
Maya deities 304
Maya sites
  Becán 61
  Calakmul 61
  Chiapa del Corzo 83, 186
  Chicanná 70
  Chichén Itzá 8, 10, 64–67, 185
  Cobá 70
  Comalcalco 84
  Dzibilchaltún 70–71
  Edzná 71
  Izamal 72
  Kabah 212
  Labná 212
  Mayapán 212
  Palenque 8, 92–95
  San Gervasio 68
  Toniná 214
  Tulúm 8, 75, 184–185
  Uxmal 8, 78–79
  Xpujil 80
  Yaxchilán 98
Mayapán 79, 212
Mazatlán **164–165**, 205, 206
  Acuario Mazatlán 165
  Museo Arqueológico de Mazatlán 165
Mazunte 85
measurements and sizes 284, 285
medical treatment 288–289
Melaque 138
Mennonite community, Cuauhtémoc 160–161
Mennonite Museum, Cuauhtémoc 161
Mercado de Abastos, Oaxaca 10, 90–91
Mérida **73**, 183, 185
  Catedral San Ildefonso 73
  hotels 267
  Museo de Antropología e Historia 73
  Museo de la Canción Yucateca 73
  Museo Macay 73
  Palacio de Gobierno 73
  Pinacoteca Juan Gamboa Guzmán 73
  restaurants 246
  Teatro Peón Contreras 183
mestizos 4, 12
Metepec 24
Mexcaltitán 145
Mexicali 43
Mexican-American War 35
Mexican Revolution 36–37
Mexico City (Ciudad México) 7, 8, 13, 20, 21, **99–120**
  airports 40–41
  Alameda 100, **104**, 220
  Auditorio Nacional 105
  Basílica de Guadalupe 104
  Bazar Sábado 117
  Bosque de Chapultepec 105
  bullring 107, 174, 194–195
  Capilla de San Antonio Panzacola 222
  Casa de los Azulejos **106**, 221
  Casa de La Malinche 223
  Casa de León Trotsky 106, 223
  Casa del Risco 117, 222, 223
  Catedral Metropolitana 20, **106–107**
  Centro Cultural San Angel 117
  Centro Historico 220–221
  Ciudad Universitaria 107
  Colegio de San Ildefonso 107
  Condesa 8
  Convento de Santo Domingo 220

Coyoacán 8, **106**, 222–223
El Sagrario 107
entertainment 192–193
Estadio Olímpico 107
festivals and events 195
Foro Cultural de Coyoacán 106, 193
history 101
hotels 272–274
Iglesia de Corpus Christi 104
Iglesia de Loreto 220
Iglesia de San Bernardino de Siena 120
Iglesia de San Jacinto 117
Iglesia de San Juan Bautista 106
Independence Monument 115
Insurgentes 107
Jardín Botánico 107
Jardín Centenario 106, 222
map (location) 99
map (streetplan) 102–103
markets 192
Mercado de la Merced 112
Monumento a General Alvaro Obregón 222
Monumento a los Niños Héroes 105
murals 104, 105, 107, 115, 116
Museo Anahuacalli 112
Museo de Arte Carrillo-Gil 112
Museo de Arte Moderno 105
Museo de la Ciudad de México 112
Museo Colonial del Carmen 117, 222, 223
Museo Estudio Diego Rivera 117, 222
Museo Franz Mayer 112–113
Museo Frida Kahlo 106, 223
Museo José Luis Cuevas 220, 221
Museo de la Medicina Mexicana 115, 220, 221
Museo Mural Diego Rivera 8, 104
Museo Nacional de Antropología 8, **108–111**
Museo Nacional de Arte **113**, 220
Museo Nacional de Culturas Populares 106
Museo Nacional de Historia 105
Museo del Papalote 113
Museo Rufino Tamayo 105
Museo de San Carlos 113
Museo Universitario de Ciencias y Arte (MUCA) 107
nightlife 193–194
orientation 100–101
Palacio de Bellas Artes 8, 104, 220
Palacio de Iturbide 113
Palacio Nacional 115
Parque Zoológico Chapultepec 195
Paseo de la Reforma 115
Plaza de las Esculturas 104
Plaza Garibaldi 8, **115**
Plaza México 107, 174, 194–195
Plaza Santo Domingo 115
Plaza de las Tres Culturas 116
Polanco 8, 15, **116**
Polyforum Cultural Siqueiros 107
public transport 46–48
restaurants 252–255
San Angel 8, **117**, 222–223
San Sebastián Martir 222
Secretaría de Educación Pública **116**, 220
shopping 190–192
sights 100–120
sports and activities 194–195
streetplan index 102–103
Teatro de los Insurgentes 107
Templo Mayor 118–119
Templo de San Francisco 116
Torre Latinoamericana 104, 220
walks 220–223
Xochimilco 120
Zócalo 100, **120**
Zona Rosa 120
Mina El Edén, Zacatecas 155, 203
Minas Nuevas 157
Misión de Concá 226
Misión de Landa de Matamoros 227
Misión de Nuestra Señora de Loreto 164
Misión de Santa Gertrudis 161
Misión de Santa Rosalía de Mulegé 166, 236
Misión de Tancoyol 227
Misión de Tilaco 227
Misol-Há 83
Mitla 84-85, 218
Museo Frissell de Arte Zapoteca 218
Mixtecs 26, 98
mobile phones 291
Moctezuma II 30, 31, 101, 112, 304
monarch butterflies 9, 16, 148
money 286–287
ATMs 286
banks 286, 293
credit cards 170, 241, 286–287
currency 286
currency exchange 286–287
everyday items and prices 287
taxes 264, 287
tips 286
travelers' checks 286
wiring money 287
words and phrases 299
Monte Albán 8, 86–87
ball court 86
Edificio de los Danzantes 86
Gran Plaza 86
Montejo, Francisco 67
Monterrey 165
airport 42
Faro del Comercio 165
Museo de Arte Contemporaneo de Monterrey (MARCO) 165
Museo de Historia Mexicana 165
Monumento a General Alvaro Obregón, Mexico City 222
Morado, José Chávez 136, 144
Morelia 15, 146–147, 201–202
Casa Natal de Morelos 147
Colegio de San Nicolás de Hidalgo 147
hotels 277
Museo Casa de Morelos 147
Museo del Estado 147
Palacio Clavijero 147
Palacio de Gobierno 15, 147
restaurants 260
Morelos y Pavón, José María 147, 304
motels 265
mountain biking 188, 202
mountaineering 238
Mulegé 166, 236
Misión de Santa Rosalía de Mulegé 166, 236
Museo Mulegé 166
Mundaca, Fermín 209
murals 14, 15, 30, 34, 35, 37, 73, 104, 105, 107, 115, 116, 131, 138, 139, 141, 144, 147, 154
museum and gallery opening house 293
museums and galleries
Alhóndiga de Granaditas, Guanajuato 143–144
Casa de Amado Nervo, Tepic 150
Casa de Don Ignacio de Allende, San Miguel de Allende 149
Casa de León Trotsky, Mexico City 223
Cinema Museum, Durango 161
Explora Science Museum, León 145, 201
Huatápera, Uruapan 153
Huichol Museum, Guadalajara 141
La Casa del Jade, San Cristóbal de las Casas 188
Mennonite Museum, Cuauhtémoc 161
Museo de Aguascalientes 138
Museo Amparo, Puebla 127
Museo Anahuacalli, Mexico City 112
Museo de Antropología, Xalapa 8, 136
Museo de Antropología e Historia, Mérida 73
Museo Antropológico de Baja California Sur, La Paz 164
Museo Arqueológico de Mazatlán 165
Museo de Arte Carrillo-Gil, Mexico City 112
Museo de Arte Contemporaneo de Monterrey (MARCO) 165
Museo de Arte Contemporáneo de Oaxaca 91, 216, 217
Museo de Arte Moderno, Mexico City 105
Museo de Arte Religioso, Guadalupe 140
Museo de Arte Virreinal, Taxco 130
Museo de Artes Populares, Pátzcuaro 147
Museo de Artes y Tradiciones Populares, Tlaxcala 131
Museo de la Canción Yucateca, Mérida 73
Museo Casa Hidalgo, Dolores Hidalgo 139
Museo Casa de Morelos, Morelia 147
Museo Casa de la Señora Juana C. Romero, Tehuantepec 97
Museo de Cera de Tijuana 168
Museo de la Ciudad de México, Mexico City 112
Museo del Cobre, Santa Clara del Cobre 230

Museo Colonial del Carmen, Mexico City 117, 222, 223
Museo Costumbrista de Sonora, Alamos 157
Museo de la Cultura Maya, Campeche 62
Museo de la Cultura Maya, Chetumal 70
Museo de Cultura Popular, Villahermosa 98
Museo de las Culturas de Oaxaca 90, 217
Museo de las Culturas del Norte, Casas Grandes 160
Museo de las Culturas Occidente de María Ahumada, Colima 139
Museo Diego Rivera, Guanajuato 144
Museo de El Fuerte 162
Museo del Estado, Morelia 147
Museo Estudio Diego Rivera, Mexico City 117
Museo de la Fotografía, Pachuca 125
Museo Francisco Goitia, Zacatecas 155
Museo Frida Kahlo, Mexico City 106, 223
Museo Frissell de Arte Zapoteca, Mitla 85, 218
Museo Guillermo Spratling, Taxco 130
Museo de Historia Cuauhnáhuac, Cuernavaca 124
Museo de Historia de Ensenada 162
Museo de Historia Mexicana, Monterrey 165
Museo de Historia Natural, Puebla 197
Museo de Historia de Tabasco, Villahermosa 98
Museo Histórico Regional, Ensenada 162
Museo Histórico de la Revolución Mexicana, Chihuahua 160
Museo Iconográfico del Quijote, Guanajuato 144
Museo de las Identidades Mexicanas, Tijuana 168
Museo de la Isla Cozumel 68
Museo José Guadalupe Posada, Aguascalientes 138
Museo José Luis Cuevas, Mexico City 220, 221
Museo de Los Altos, San Cristóbal de las Casas 96
Museo Macay, Mérida 73
Museo de la Máscara, San Luis Potosí 150
Museo de la Medicina Mexicana, Mexico City 115, 220, 221
Museo de la Minería, Pachuca 125
Museo de las Momias, Guanajuato 144, 228
Museo Mulegé 166
Museo Mural Diego Rivera, Mexico City 8, 104
Museo Nacional de Antropología, Mexico City 8, 108–111
Museo Nacional de Arte, Mexico City 113
Museo Nacional de Culturas Populares, Mexico City 106
Museo Nacional de Historia, Mexico City 105
Museo Nacional de La Venta 97
Museo Nacional de Tequila 151
Museo Nacional del Vírreinato, Tepotzotlán 151
Museo de Naturaleza y Cultura, Bahía de los Angeles 157
Museo del Papalote, Mexico City 113
Museo Pedro Coronel, Zacatecas 154
Museo de la Pintura Mural Teotihuacana 134
Museo del Pueblo, Guanajuato 144
Museo Rafael Coronel, Zacatecas 154
Museo Regional de Antropología Carlos Pellicer, Villahermosa 98
Museo Regional de Campeche 62
Museo Regional de Chiapas, Tuxtla Gutiérrez 97
Museo Regional de Guadalajara 141
Museo Regional de Historia, Colima 139
Museo Regional Potosino, San Luis Potosí 150
Museo Regional de Sonora, Hermosillo 163
Museo Religiosa de la Soledad, Oaxaca 90
Museo de la Revolución Mexicana, Puebla 127
Museo Robert Brady, Cuernavaca 124
Museo Rufino Tamayo, Mexico City 105
Museo Rufino Tamayo, Oaxaca 90, 216
Museo Salvador Ferrando, Tlacotalpan 131
Museo de San Carlos, Mexico City 113
Museo de Santa Mónica, Puebla 127
Museo de los Seris, Bahía Kino 157
Museo de Sitio Casa de Juárez, Oaxaca 91
Museo Toma de Zacatecas 154
Museo Tuxtleco, Santiago Tuxtla 128
Museo Universitario de Ciencias y Arte, Mexico City 107
Palacio de Bellas Artes, Mexico City 8, 104
Pinacoteca Juan Gamboa Guzmán, Mérida 73
Templo Mayor 118–119
music
  classical music, dance and opera 172
  festivals 157, 185, 206
  Latin rock 19, 172
  live music 172
  mariachis 9, 23, 115, 172
  popular 18
  traditional 22, 23

N

Nanciyaga Ecological Reserve 10, 123
national holidays 293
national parks
  Cañon del Sumidero 10,83
  Cumbres de Monterrey 174
  El Garrafón 72, 182, 209
  Lagunas de Montebello 84
  Parque Chankanaab 69
  Parque Nacional El Tepozteco 128
  Parque Nacional de La Venta 97
  Parque Nacional Sierra de San Pedro Mártir 166
  Sierra de los Organos 161
Navidad 179
Nervo, Amado 150
Nevado de Toluca 4
newspapers and magazines 296
nightlife 8, 173
  Mexico City 193–194
Noche de Rábanos 23
Nogales 43
Nohoch Mul 70
Nohoch Nah Chich 175
Nopoló 164
North American Free Trade Agreement (NAFTA) 12, 13, 20
Northern Mexico and Baja California 7, 9, 156–168
  festivals and events 206
  hotels 279–280
  map 156
  restaurants 262–263
  sights 157–168
  walks and drives 232–237
  what to do 204–206
nudist beaches 85

O

Oaxaca City 8, 10, 88–91, 187–188, 189, 216–217
  Arcos de Xochimilco 216
  Basílica de la Soledad 90, 216
  Biblioteca Francisco Burgoa 90, 217
  Camino Real 216, 270
  Centro Cultural Santo Domingo 90, 216
  Cerro de Fortín 90
  hotels 269–270
  Iglesia de San Juan de Dios 216
  Iglesia de Santo Domingo 10, 88, 89, 90, 216, 217
  Jardín Etnobotánico 90, 217
  Macedonia Alcalá 216
  markets 10, 89, 90–91, 216
  Museo de Arte Contemporáneo 91, 216
  Museo de las Culturas de Oaxaca 90, 217
  Museo Religiosa de la Soledad 90
  Museo Rufino Tamayo 90, 216
  Museo de Sitio Casa de Juárez 91
  Palácio del Gobierno 89
  restaurants 248–249
  San Agustín 217
  walk 216–217
  what to do 187–188
  zócalo 89–90, 216
Ocosingo 214
O'Gorman, Juan 105, 107, 117, 147, 304
Olmec heads 27, 97, 128
Olmec sites
  Cacaxtla 122
  San Lorenzo 26
  La Venta 97
Olmecs 26, 27, 29, 128
opening hours 170, 173, 293
opticians 289
organized tours 238
Orizaba 4, 125, 175
Orozco, José Clemente 14, 37, 105, 106, 107, 112, 125, 141, 304
Otay Mesa 43
Oxkutzcab 212

P

Pacheco, Fernando Castro 73
Pachuca 125

hotels 275
Museo de la Fotografía 125
Museo de la Minería 125
Reloj Monumental 125
restaurants 257
packing tips 282–283
Pakal 92, 94, 95
Palacio de Bellas Artes, Mexico City 8, 104
Palacio del Gobernador, Uxmal 79
Palacio de Iturbide, Mexico City 113
Palacio Nacional, Mexico City 115
Palacio de Quetzalpapálotl, Teotihuacán 134
Palenque 8, **92–95**
El Palacio 92
Grupo de la Cruz 94–95
hotels 270
museum 95
restaurants 249–250
site plan 95
Templo de las Inscripciones 92, 94
Templo del Sol 94
Palenque town 95
panama hats 180
Papantla 9, 23
Voladores de Papantla 9, 22, 23, 129
Parque Chankanaab 69
Parque Chupícuaro 230
Parque Ecoturístico Cañon del Sumidero 186
Parque Nacional El Tepozteco 128
Parque Nacional de La Venta 97
Parque Nacional Sierra de San Pedro Mártir 166
Parque Natural de la Ballena Gris 164
Parque Punta Sur 69
Parque Yumká 98, 189
Parque Zoológico Chapultepec 195
parrots 17
passports and visas 283–284
lost passport 292
Pastry War 35
Pátzcuaro 9, **147**, 202, 230
Basílica de Nuestra Señora de la Salud 147
hotels 277–278
Museo de Artes Populares 147
restaurants 260
Paz, Octavio 14, 304
Pelican Rock 159
Pellicer, Carlos 97
Peñón de Bernal 176, 226
petroglyphs (cave paintings) 234–235
peyote 22, 23
pharmacies 289, 293
photography 283, 285
Pichilingüe Peninsula 164
Pico de Orizaba 4, 125, 175
Pinacoteca Juan Gamboa Guzmán, Mérida 73
Pinal de Amoles 226
Pirámide Kinich Kakmó, Izamal 72
Pirámide de la Luna, Teotihuacán 134
Pirámide de los Mascarones, Kohunlich 72
Pirámide de los Nichos, El Tajín 129
Pirámide de Quetzalcóatl, Xochicalco 131
Pirámide de la Serpiente, Cacaxtla 122
Pirámide del Sol, Teotihuacán 133–134
Pirámide de Tepanapa, Cholula 123
places of worship 285
Playa Buenaventura 236
Playa del Carmen **74**, 183–184, 210
hotels 267–268
restaurants 246–247
Playa del Norte 209
Playa Paraíso 209
Playa Zicatela 85
Polanco 8, 15, **116**
police 292
politics and government 5, 38
pollution 20, 21, 100
Polyforum Cultural Siqueiros, Mexico City 107
ponchos 171
Popocatépetl 4, 17, **125**, 175
popular culture 18–19
population 4, 12
Posada, José Guadalupe 24, 37, 138, 304
posadas 264, 265
post offices 291, 293
postal services 291
words and phrases, useful 299
Presa Ignacio Allende 229
public transportation *see travel*
Puebla 9, 21, **126–127**, 197, 224–225
Biblioteca Palafoxiana 126
Capilla del Rosario 33, 126, 127, 224
Catedral de la Inmaculada Concepción 126, 224
Ex-Convento de Santa Rosa 127
hotels 275–276
Museo Amparo 127
Museo de Historia Natural 197
Museo de la Revolución Mexicana 127
Museo de Santa Mónica 127
Patio de los Azulejos 126
restaurants 257
San Cristóbal 126
San Francisco 127
San José 126–127
zócalo 126
Puerto Adolfo López Mateos 157
Puerto Angel **85**, 270
Puerto del Cielo 226
Puerto Escondido 85
hotels 270–271
restaurants 250
Puerto Magdalena 157
Puerto Morelos **74**, 184, 210
Puerto Vallarta **147–148**, 202
airport 41
hotels 278
restaurants 260–261
pulque 151, 173, 241
Punta Allen 74
Punta Celarain 69
Punta Chueca 157
Punta Entrada 157
Punta Eugenia 161
Punta Maroma 210
Punta Sur Ecological Reserve 181\

Q

Querétaro 9, **148**, 202, 226
Convento de la Santa Crux 148
hotels 278
Museo Regional 148
restaurants 261
Quetzalcóatl 31, 101, 304
Quiroga 148, 230
Quiroga, Vasco de 33, 148 304

R

rabies 178
radio 296
rainfall 4, 282
Rancho las Parras 235
rappelling 199
Real de Catorce 166
Casa de la Moneda 166
Iglesia de San Francisco 166
Iglesia de Virgen del Guadalupe 166
regions 7
religion 5
reserves
Isla Angel de la Guarda 157
Isla Tiburón 163
Mapimi Biosphere Reserve 17, 177
Punta Sur Ecological Reserve 181
Reserva de la Biósfera Calakmul 61
Reserva de la Biósfera Celestún 61, 177
Reserva de la Biósfera El Triunfo 85, 175, 177
Reserva de la Biósfera El Vizcaíno 161
Reserva de la Biosfera Sian Ka'an 8, 74
Reserva Ecológica Nanciyaga 10, 123
Reserva Ecologica El Campanario 9, 148
restaurants
Central Mexico East 256–258
Central Mexico West 259–261
Mexico City 252–255
Northern Mexico and Baja California 262–263
Southern Mexico 248–251
words and phrases, useful 301
Yucatán 244–247
see also eating out
restrooms 284
Riley, John 35
Rio Antigua/Pescados 177
Río Lagartos **74**, 184
Rivera, Diego 8, 14, 15, 24, 30, 37, 104, 105, 112, 115, 116, 117, 144, 304
Riviera Maya 210–211
road signs 56
rock climbing 176, 238
rodeos 10, 176, 195, 201
Rodríguez, Antonio Pintor 154
Rosarito 205–206
rural population 20, 21
Ruz Lhuillier, Alberto 92

S

sacbeob 70, 71
sacred white roads 70, 71
San Agustinillo 85
San Andrés Tuxtla 128
cigar factories 128
restaurants 257
San Angel 8, **117**, 222–223
San Antonio Arrazola 188
San Bartolo Coyotepec 188
San Blas **150**, 202
San Cristóbal de las Casas 8, **96**, 188–189, 214, 215
Centro de Desarrollo de la Medicina Maya 96
hotels 271
Iglesia y Ex-Convento de Santo Domingo 96
La Casa del Jade 188
Museo de Los Altos 96
Na Bolom 96, 215
restaurants 250–251
San Felipe 166
San Felipe fort 72

San Francisco Acatepec 224–225
San Francisco de la Sierra 167
San Gervasio 68
San Ignacio 167
San Isidro Roaguía 218
San Javier 234, 235
San Jerónimo Tlacochahuaya 218
San José del Cabo **167**, 206
hotels 280
restaurants 263
San Juan Chamula 214
San Juan de Ulúa, Veracruz 135
San Lorenzo 26
San Luis Potosí 23, **150**
Capilla de Aranzazú 150
Museo de la Máscara 150
Museo Regional Potosino 150
Templo del Carmen 150
San Martín Tilcajete 189
San Miguel de Allende 9, **149**, 202–203, 229
Casa de Don Ignacio de Allende 149
El Chorro 149
Escuela de Bellas Artes 149
hotels 278
Instituto Allende 149
restaurants 261
San Patricio Melauqe 138
San Pedro Ayutla 218
San Quintín 167
San Tomás Jalieza 189
Santa Ana del Valle 218
Santa Anna, Antonio López de 35, 136, 304
Santa Clara del Cobre 230
Santa Cruz Huatulco 84
Santa Rosa 228
Santa Rosalia 167
Santana, Carlos 18, 19
Santiago Tuxtla **128**, 199
Museo Tuxtleco 128
Santuario Maya a la Diosa Ixchel 209
Sayil 212
Scammon's Lagoon 9, **164**
Sea of Cortés 177, 236
sea kayaking 176
self-catering 265
Semanta Santa 22
seniors 293
Serdán, Aquiles 127
Seri 157, 163
Serra, Fray Junípero 226
shamanism 23, 27
shopping 170–171
crafts 170
department stores 170
gifts and souvenirs 170–171
markets 170
Mexico City 190–192
opening hours 170, 293
payment 170
words and phrases, useful 300
Sian Ka'an Biosphere Reserve 8, **74**
Sierra de la Giganta 234–235
Sierra Gorda 226–227
Sierra Madre Occidental 16, 17
Sierra Madre Oriental 16
Sierra de los Organos 161
Sierra de San Pedro Martír National Park 166
Sierra Tarahumara 159
silver mining 125, 130, 144, 155, 157, 166
Siqueiros, David Alfaro 14, 37, 105, 107, 112, 304
skydiving 184
smoking etiquette 178, 241, 284
soccer 176, 195
Sombrerete 161
Southern Mexico 7, 8, **81–98**
festivals and events 189
hotels 269–271
map 81
restaurants 248–251
sights 82–98
walks and drives 214–219
what to do 186–189
spas 140, 178, 196, 202
sports and activities 174–177
baseball 174
bird-watching 61, 71, 74, 184, 238
bullfighting 84, 107, 168, 174, 194–195, 205
canyoning 174
cave diving 75
caving 174
cenote diving 174–175
climbing 175
diving 8, 61, 63, 68, 69, 80, 175, 181, 182, 183, 184, 185, 205
fishing 63, 69, 145, 157, 162, 164, 167, 176–177, 204, 205, 206
go-karting 202
golf 175, 195, 201
hang-gliding 150
hiking and walking 175
horse racing 195
horseback riding 188
jai alai 175–176
kitesurfing 184
mountain biking 188, 202
mountaineering 238
rappelling 199
rock climbing 176, 238
rodeos 10, 176, 195, 201
sea kayaking 176
skydiving 184
soccer 176, 195
surfing 85, 150, 167, 177, 202
whale and dolphin watching 9, 140, 157, 162, 164, 167
whitewater rafting 177
wrestling 18, 19, 177
stamps 291
Steinbeck, John 157, 159
student travelers 293
Sumidero Canyon 10, **83**, 186
sun safety 178, 289
Super Barrio 13
surfing 85, 150, 167, 177, 202

T

Talavera tiles 9, 126, 127
Talismán 44
Tamayo, Rufino 90, 105, 304
Tampico **128**, 257
Tangolunda 84
Tapalpa 150
Tarahumara 232
Tarascans 33
Taxco **130**, 198
hotels 276
Iglesia de Santa Prisca 130
Museo de Arte Virreinal 130
Museo Guillermo Spratling 130
restaurants 257–258
Teleférico 130
taxes 264, 287
taxis 48, 57
Taylor, Elizabeth 148
Tecoh 212
Tehuantepec 8, 12, **97**
Casa de la Cultura 97
Museo Casa de la Señora Juana C. Romero 97
Tekit 212
Telchaquillo 212
telenovelas 18, 19
telephones 290–291
words and phrases 299
television 296
Templo del Dios Descendente, Tulúm 75
Templo de los Guerreros, Chichén Itzá 66
Templo de las Inscripciones, Palenque 92, 94
Templo Mayor 118–119
Templo de San Francisco, Mexico City 116
Tenejapa 214
Tenochtitlán 30, 31, 101, 118, 119
Teocicca Valley 214
Teotihuacán 9, 26, 27, **132–134**
La Ciudadela 133
Museo de la Pintura Mural Teotihuacana 134
Palacio de los Jaguares 134
Palacio de Quetzalpapálotl 134
Pirámide de la Luna 134
Pirámide del Sol 133–134
Teotitlán del Valle 189, 218
Tepic 150
Casa de Amado Nervo 150
Museo Regional 150
Tepotzotlán 151
Museo Nacional del Vírreinato 151
Tepoztlán **128**, 198
hotels 276
María de la Natividad 128
restaurants 258
Tequila 9, **151**
Museo Nacional de Tequila 151
La Rojena 151
restaurants 261
Tequila Sauza 151
tequila (drink) 10, 241
Tequila Express 49
Tequisquiapan 151
Tetas de Cabra 162
textiles 171, 189, 218
theater 172
theme and water parks 80, 196–197, 199
thermal baths
Ixtapan de la Sal 140
Tequisquiapan 151
Ticul 184, 212
Tijuana 43, **168**, 206
bullrings 168
Centro Cultural Tijuana 168
hotels 280
Jai Alai Palace 168
Museo de Cera de Tijuana 168
Museo de las Identidades Mexicanas 168
restaurants 263
time zones 283
tipping 241
Tírado, Dr. Alfonso Ortiz 157
Tlacolula 218
Tlacotalpan 131
hotels 276
Museo Salvador Ferrando 131
restaurants 258
Tlaquepaque 141
Tlaxcala 131
Basílica de Ocotlán 131
Museo de Artes y Tradiciones Populares 131
restaurants 258
Xicoténcatl 131
Tocuaro 230
toilets 284
toll roads 45, 54–55
Toltec sites
Los Toriles 140
Tula de Allende 153
Toltecs 30, 79

Toluca 151
Jardín Botánico Cosmovitral 151
restaurants 261
Tonalá 141
Tonantzintla 224
Toniná 214
topless bathing 285
Torre Latinoamericana, Mexico City 104, 220
tortillas 13, 240
tourism 5
tourist offices 295
words and phrases 302
tours, organized 238
traditions 22–24
trains 9, 45, 49, 58, 159, 164
travel
air travel 40–42, 45, 50–51, 58
border crossings 43–44
buses 45, 46, 52–53, 57, 58
city transportation 46–48, 57
colectivos, combis and *peseros* 57
concessions 178
cruise ships 44
cycling 57
disabilities, visitors with 58
ferries 49, 58
information 45
taxis 48, 57
trains 9, 45, 49, 58, 159, 164
words and phrases 299
see also driving
travel insurance 283
travel literature 294
travelers' checks 286
Tree of Life 24
Tres de Mayo 85
Tres Ríos 10, 181, 210
Tresguerras, Francisco Eduardo 139
Triunfo Biosphere Reserve 85
Trotsky, León 223
Tula de Allende 153
Tulúm 8, 10, **75**, 76–77, 184–185, 210–211
El Castillo 75
restaurants 247
Templo del Dios Descendente 75
turtles 17, 61, 188, 210
Tuxtepec 97
Tuxtla Gutiérrez 97
hotels 271
Museo Regional de Chiapas 97
restaurants 251
Zoológico Miguel Alvarez del Toro 97
Tzintzuntzán 230

U

Urique Canyon 159, 232
Uruapan **153**, 203
Casa del la Cultura 153
Huatápera 153
Parque Nacional 153
restaurants 261
US–Mexican border 21, 43–44
Uxmal 8, **78–79**, 212
Casa del Adivino 78
Casa de las Monjas 78
Casa de las Tortugas 79
El Palomar 79
Palacio del Gobernador 79

V

vaccinations 288
Valenciana 144, 228
Valladolid **75**, 185
hotels 268
restaurants 247
Valle de Bravo **153**, 261, 278
Valley of the Giants 161
vegetarian food 241
La Venta 97
Ventanilla 189
Veracruz 9, **135**, 198–199
aquarium 199
Baluarte de Santiago 135
hotels 276
Museo de la Ciudad 135
restaurants 258
San Juan de Ulúa 135
Veta Grande 155
Villa, Pancho 36, 37, 138, 154, 160, 163, 221, 304
Villahermosa **98**, 189
Centro de Investigaciones de las Culturas Olmecas (CICOM) 98
hotels 271
Museo de Cultura Popular 98
Museo de Historia de Tabasco 98
Museo Regional de Antropología Carlos Pellicer 98
Virgin of Guadalupe 33, 104, 179
Vizcaíno Peninsula 161
Voladores de Papantla 9, 22, 23, 129
Volcán Paricutín 10, **153**
volcanoes 4, 16, 17, 125, 153
Volkswagen Beetle 21
Volpi, Jorge 15

W

walks and drives
Bajío silver towns 228–229
Convent and Puuc routes 212–213
Copper Canyon 232–233
craft villages 218–219
indigenous villages 214–215
Isla Mujeres 209
Lago de Pátzcuaro 230–231
Loreto to Mulegé 236–237
map 208
Mexico City 220–223
Oaxaca City 216–217
organized tours 238
Puebla churches 224–225
Riviera Maya 210–211
Sierra de la Giganta 234–235
Sierra Gorda missions 226–227
waterfalls
Agua Azul 83
Cascada de Basaseáchic 160
Cascado de Texolo 123
Hierve el Agua 218–219
websites 297
whale and dolphin watching 9, 140, 157, 162, 164, 167
what to do
Central Mexico East 196–199
Central Mexico West 200–203
Mexico City 190–195
Northern Mexico and Baja California 204–206
Southern Mexico 186–189
Yucatán 180–185
whitewater rafting 177
wildlife 8, 9, 16, 17, 177
see also reserves
wines 162, 241
witchcraft 123
wrestling 18, 19, 177

X

Xalapa (Jalapa) 9, **136**, 199
Hacienda Casa de Santa Anna 136
hotels 276
Museo de Antropología 9, 136
restaurants 258
Xcacel 210
Xcalak 80
Xcaret **80**, 210
Xel-Há 80
Xicoténcatl 131
Xlapak 212
Xochicalco 131
ball courts 131
Pirámide de Quetzalcóatl 131
Xochimilco 120
Xochitécatl 122
Xochitiotzin, Desiderio Hernández 131
Xpujil 80

Y

Ya Kul lagoon 61, 210
Yagul **98**, 218, 219
Yaxchilán 98
youth hostels 265
Yucatán 7, 8, **60–80**
festivals and events 185
hotels 266–268
map 60
restaurants 244–247
sights 61–80
walks and drives 209–213
what to do 180–185

Z

Zacatecas **154–155**, 203
Casa de la Mala Noche 154
Catedral Basílica Menor 154
Cerro de La Bufa 154
hotels 278
Mina El Edén 155
Museo Francisco Goitia 155
Museo Pedro Coronel 154
Museo Rafael Coronel 154
Museo Toma de Zacatecas 154
restaurants 261
teleférico 154
Zalce, Alfredo 15
Zapata, Emiliano 37, 138, 304
Zapatista National Liberation Army (EZLN) 12
Zapotec sites
Mitla 84–85
Monte Albán 8, 86–87
Yagul 98, 218, 219
Zapotecs 12, 26
Zihuatanejo 84
Zinacantán 214
Zipolite 85
Zona del Silencio 17
Zoológico Guadalajara 201
Zoológico Miguel Alvarez del Toro, Tuxtla Gutiérrez 97

ACKNOWLEDGMENTS

Abbreviations for the credits are as follows:
AA = AA World Travel Library, t (top), b (bottom), c (centre), l (left), r (right), bg (background)

UNDERSTANDING MEXICO

4 Mexico Tourism Board; **5l, 5c, 5r** Mexico Tourism Board; **6** Mexico Tourism Board; **8tl, 8tr, 8bl** Mexico Tourism Board; **8rct** Alamy; **8rcb** AA/C Sawyer; **8br** AA/R Strange; **9tl** AA/C Sawyer; **9tr** AA/S L Day; **9lct, 9cr** AA/R Strange; **9lcb** Mexico Tourism Board; **9bl** Photodisc; **9br** Alamy; **10tr** Mexico Tourism Board; **10rct, 10l** Alamy; **10c, 10rcb, 10br** AA/R Strange.

LIVING MEXICO

11 Mexico Tourism Board; **12tl, 12tr, 12cl** AA/C Sawyer; **12c, 12b** AA/R Strange; **12cr** Mexico Tourism Board; **13tl, 13tr, 13cl, 13cr, 13ct, 13c, 13b** AA/C Sawyer; **12/3bg** AA/R Strange; **14tl, 14tr, 14cr** AA/R Strange; **14cl, 14bl** AA/C Sawyer; **14c** Bettmann/Corbis; **14/5** AA/P Wilson; **15tc, 15r, 15cl, 15cr** AA/C Sawyer; **15tl, 15tr** AA/R Strange; **14/5bg** AA/R Strange; **16tl, 16tr** Mexico Tourism Board; **16c** AA/S L Day; **16cl, 16ccl, 16t, 16cr, 16b** AA/R Strange; **17tl, 17cl, 17cr, 17tc** Mexico Tourism Board; **17tr** AA/N Sumner; **17ccr** AA/R Strange; **17c** AA/C Sawyer; **16/7bg** AA/R Strange; **18tl, 18tr** AA/C Sawyer; **18cl** Danny Lehman/Corbis; **18c** AA/P Wilson; **18ctr, 18cr** AA/R Strange; **18br** Henry Diltz/Corbis; **19tl, 19tr, 19cr, 19cbl** AA/C Sawyer; **19cl** Rex Features; **19c** Lynsey Addario/Corbis; **18/9bg, 19cbr** AA/R Strange; **20tl** Greg Smith/Corbis; **20tr, 20cl, 20r** Mexico Tourism Board; **20c, 20b** AA/R Strange; **21tcr, 21tl** AA/P Wilson, **21tr** Mexico Tourism Board; **21lc, 21lct, 20/1bg** AA/C Sawyer; **21r** AA/R Strange; **22/3bg, 22tc, 22cl, 22cr, 22br** AA/R Strange; **22tl, 22bl** AA/C Sawyer; **22** Mexico Tourism Board; **23tl** Danny Lehman/Corbis; **23tc** AA/C Sawyer; **23cr, 23c** AA/R Strange; **23tr, 23cl** Mexico Tourism Board; **24tl, 24cl** AA/R Strange; **24tr** Mexico Tourism Board; **24t** Reuters/Corbis; **24cr** AA/C Sawyer, **24bl** Alamy; **24bg** AA/P Wilson.

THE STORY OF MEXICO

25 Mexico Tourism Board; **26tl, 26cl, 26bc** AA/R Strange; **26tr** AA/P Kenward; **26bl** AA/P Wilson; **26/7bg, 26/7b** AA/F Dunlop; **27tl, 27tr, 27bl, 27bc** AA/R Strange; **27br** AA/C Sawyer; **28tl, 28tr, 28bl, 28/9b, 28/9bg** AA/R Strange; **28tc** AA/T Souter; **29tl** AA/R Strange; **29tr, 29cl, 29bl, 29br** AA/C Sawyer; **30tl** AA/P Wilson; **30tr, 30/1b, 30/1bg** AA/R Strange; **30bl** AA/C Sawyer; **31tl, 31cl, 31br, 31bl** AA/R Strange; **31tc** AA/C Sawyer; **31tr** Archivo Iconografico/Corbis; **32t, 32bl, 32/3bg** AA/R Strange; **32br** Bettmann/Corbis; **33t, 33bl** AA/R Strange; **33bc, 33br** AA/C Sawyer; **34tr, 34c, 34/5b, 34/5bg** AA/R Strange; **34bl** AA/P Wilson; **35tl** Bettmann/Corbis; **35tc** Stadtische Kunsthalle, Mannheim, Germany/Bridgeman Art Library; **35bl, 35br** AA/R Strange; **36t, 36/7b** South American Pictures; **36cl, 36bl, 36/7bg** AA/R Strange; **37tl, 37bl** AA/R Strange; **37tc** Museo Nacional de Historia, Mexico City, Mexico, Giraudon/Bridgeman Art Library (We have been unable to trace the copyright holder of 'Portrait of General Emiliano Zapata' by Mexican School and would be grateful to receive any information as to their identity); **37br** AA/L Dunmire; **38tl, 38tr** Reuters/Corbis; **38cl** Les Stone/Corbis; **38cr, 38c, 38bl, 38br, 38bg** AA/C Sawyer.

ON THE MOVE

39 AA/C Sawyer; **40/1** Digital Vision; **41l, 41r** AA/C Sawyer; **42t** Digital Vision; **42b** AA/C Sawyer; **43t** AA/C Sawyer; **44/5t** AA/C Sawyer; **44c** AA/R Strange; **45c** AA/C Sawyer; **46/7t, 46c, 46cr** AA/C Sawyer; **46b** Mexico Tourism Board; **48t, 48l** AA/C Sawyer; **48r** AA/R Strange; **49t** AA/C Sawyer; **49r** Ferrocarril Mexicano; **50/1t** Digital Vision; **50** Aeromexico; **52/3t, 53** AA/C Sawyer; **54/5t** AA/C Sawyer; **55r** AA/F Dunlop; **56t, 56c** AA/C Sawyer; **57t, 57l** AA/C Sawyer; **57b** AA/R Strange; **58t** AA/C Sawyer.

THE SIGHTS

59 AA/R Strange; **61tl, 61c, 61tr** AA/P Wilson; **61l** AA/T Souter; **62t, 62b** AA/C Sawyer; **63t** Mexico Tourism Board; **63r** AA/C Sawyer; **64t, 64l, 64c, 64r** AA/R Strange; **65** AA/R Strange; **66/7, 66tl, 66cl** AA/R Strange; **67r** AA/R Strange; **68t** AA/C Jones; **68l** AA/R Strange; **69main** AA/R Strange; **68/9c** AA/R Strange; **70tl, 70c, 70tr** AA/R Strange; **71l, 71r** AA/C Sawyer; **72l, 72c** Mexico Tourism Board; **72r** AA/C Sawyer; **72b** AA/N Sumner; **73t** AA/C Sawyer; **73r** AA/R Strange; **74tl, 74c, 74r** AA/C Sawyer; **74b** AA/N Sumner; **75l** AA/P Wilson; **75r** AA/C Sawyer; **76/7** AA/R Strange; **78t, 78c** AA/ R Strange; **79tl, 79tr, 79cr, 79br** AA/R Strange; **80l** Mexico Tourism Board; **80c, 80r** AA/R Strange; **80cl** AA/C Sawyer; **82 main** Mexico Tourism Board; **82tr** AA/R Strange; **82bl** AA/C Sawyer; **83tl** AA/R Strange; **83tr** Mexico Tourism Board; **84l, 84c, 84r** AA/R Strange; **85tl, 85tr** AA/R Strange; **85b** Mexico Tourism Board; **86t, 86l** AA/R Strange; **87t, 87c** AA/R Strange; **88** AA/P Wilson; **89t, 89cl, 89c, 89cr** AA/R Strange; **90tl** AA/R Strange; **90cl** Mexico Tourism Board; **91** AA/R Strange; **92t** AA/R Strange; **92cl, 92c, 92cr** AA/C Sawyer; **93** AA/R Strange; **94/5** AA/C Sawyer; **96** AA/R Strange; **97tl, 97tr** Mexico Tourism Board; **97tc** AA/C Sawyer; **97b** AA/R Strange; **98tl, 98b** AA/R Strange; **98tr** S Wilkins; **100t, 100l** AA/C Sawyer; **101rt** AA/R Strange; **101ctr, 101cr** AA/C Sawyer; **101cbr, 101br** AA/R Strange; **101l** Mexico Tourism Board; **104tl** Mexico Tourism Board; **104tr, 104br** AA/R Strange; **105t, 105r** AA/C Sawyer; **106tl, 106b** AA/R Strange; **106tr** AA/C Sawyer; **107tl, 107tr, 107c** AA/R Strange; **107br** AA/C Sawyer; **108t** AA/R Strange; **108cl** Mexico Tourism Board; **108c, 108cr** AA/R Strange; **109** Mexico Tourism Board; **110t, 110c, 110b** AA/R Strange; **111** AA/R Strange; **112tl, 112tr** AA/C Sawyer; **112tc, 112c** AA/R Strange; **113tl, 113tc, 113tr, 113b** AA/C Sawyer; **114** AA/C Sawyer; **115tl** AA/C Sawyer; **115tc** AA/R Strange; **115tr** Mexico Tourism Board; **115b** AA/P Wilson; **116tl, 116tc, 116b** AA/C Sawyer; **116tr** AA/R Strange; **117t, 117cr, 117br** AA/C Sawyer; **118t** AA/R Strange; **118cl, 118/9c** AA/C Sawyer; **119c, 119r** AA/C Sawyer; **120tl** AA/R Strange; **120tr** Mexico Tourism Board; **120b** AA/C Sawyer; **122tl** AA/P Wilson; **122tr, 122b** AA/R Strange; **123tl, 123tc, 123tr** AA/R Strange; **124l** AA/C Sawyer; **124r** AA/R Strange; **125tl, 125b** AA/C Sawyer; **125tc, 125tr** AA/R Strange; **126t, 126cl, 126/7c** AA/C Sawyer; **127l** AA/R Strange; **127r** AA/C Sawyer; **128tl, 128tc, 128tr** AA/C Sawyer; **129t, 129cr** AA/R Strange; **129b** Mexico Tourism Board; **130t, 130l** AA/R Strange; **131tl, 131tc** AA/C Sawyer; **131tr, 131b** AA/R Strange; **132** AA/R Strange; **133t, 133c, 133cr** AA/R Strange; **133cl** AA/C Sawyer; **134tl** AA/C Sawyer; **134b** AA/R Strange; **135t** AA/C Sawyer; **135cr** AA/R Strange; **136t** AA/C Sawyer; **136l** AA/P Wilson; **138tl, 138cl, 138tr** AA/P Wilson; **138br** AA/C Sawyer; **139tl, 139tr** AA/R Strange; **140tl, 140tr, 140b** AA/R Strange; **140tc** AA/C Sawyer; **141tl, 141tr, 141cr** AA/R Strange; **142/3** AA/P Wilson; **142c** AA/C Sawyer; **143r** AA/R Strange; **144tl, 144cl** AA/R Strange; **145tl, 145b** AA/C Sawyer; **145tr** AA/R Strange; **146** AA/R Strange; **147l** Mexico Tourism Board; **147r** AA/R Strange; **148tl** AA/R

Strange; **148tr, 148b** AA/C Sawyer; **149t, 149b** Mexico Tourism Board; **150tl, 150c** AA/R Strange; **150tr** AA/C Sawyer; **151tl, 151tc, 151tr** AA/C Sawyer; **151b** AA/R Strange; **152** AA/C Sawyer; **153tl, 153tr, 153b** AA/R Strange; **153tc** Mexico Tourism Board; **154t, 154/5c** AA/R Strange; **154l** AA/C Sawyer; **155l, 155r** AA/R Strange; **157tl** Mexico Tourism Board; **157tr** AA/P Wilson; **157b** AA/P Baker; **158 main** Macduff Everton/Corbis; **158 inset** Ferrocarril Mexicano; **159tl** AA/F Dunlop; **159tr** AA/L Dunmire; **160tl, 160tr** AA/P Wilson; **160tc** Mexico Tourism Board; **161tl** AA/L Dunmire; **161tc** AA/R Strange; **161tr, 161b** AA/P Wilson; **162tl** AA/L Dunmire; **162tc, 162tr** AA/P Wilson; **163tl** Mexico Tourism Board; **163tc** AA/P Wilson; **163tr, 163b** AA/R Strange; **164tl, 164tr** AA/L Dunmire; **165tl, 165tr, 165b** Mexico Tourism Board; **166tl** Mexico Tourism Board; **166tc** AA/R Strange; **166tr** AA/F Dunlop; **167tl** Mexico Tourism Board; **167tc** AA/P Wilson; **167tr** AA/L Dunmire; **167b** Mexico Tourism Board; **168t** Alamy; **168l** AA/L Dunmire.

WHAT TO DO

169 AA/C Sawyer; **170t** AA/C Sawyer; **170cl, 170cr** Mexico Tourism Board; **171t** AA/C Sawyer; **171cl** Mexico Tourism Board; **171cr** AA/R Strange; **172t** Mexico Tourism Board; **172cl** AA/C Sawyer; **172cr** AA/R Strange; **173t, 173cl, 173cr** AA/C Sawyer; **174t, 174cr** Mexico Tourism Board; **174c** AA/R Strange; **175t, 175cl** Mexico Tourism Board; **175cr** AA/C Sawyer; **176t, 176cl** Mexico Tourism Board; **176cr** AA/L Dunmire; **177t, 177cr** Mexico Tourism Board; **178t** AA/C Sawyer; **179t, 179cl, 179c, 179cr** Mexico Tourism Board; **180t, 180c** AA/C Sawyer; **181t, 181c** AA/C Sawyer; **182t, 182c** AA/C Sawyer; **183t** AA/C Sawyer; **183c** A/R Strange; **184t** AA/C Sawyer; **184c** Mexico Tourism Board; **185t** AA/C Sawyer; **186t** Mexico Tourism Board; **186c** AA/P Wilson; **187t, 187c** Mexico Tourism Board; **188t** Mexico Tourism Board; **188c** AA/C Sawyer; **189t** Mexico Tourism Board; **189c** AA/R Strange; **190t, 190c** AA/C Sawyer; **191t, 191cr** AA/C Sawyer; **192t, 192c** AA/C Sawyer; **193t, 193c** AA/C Sawyer; **194t** AA/C Sawyer; **194c** Mexico Tourism Board; **195t** A/C Sawyer; **196t** AA/C Sawyer; **196c** Mexico Tourism Board; **197t, 197c** AA/C Sawyer; **198t, 198c** AA/C Sawyer; **199t** AA/C Sawyer; **200t** AA/R Strange; **200c** AA/C Sawyer; **201t** AA/R Strange; **201c** Mexico Tourism Board; **202t, 202c** AA/R Strange; **203t** AA/R Strange; **204t** Brand X Pictures; **204cl** Mexico Tourism Board; **205t** Brand X Pictures; **205c** AA/F Dunlop; **206t** Brand X Pictures.

OUT AND ABOUT

207 AA/C Sawyer; **208bl, 208br** Mexico Tourism Board; **211tl, 211tr 211cl, 211b** AA/C Sawyer; **211cl** AA/R Strange; **213tl, 213tc, 213br** AA/P Wilson; **213tr, 213bl, 213bc** AA/C Sawyer; **214** AA/C Sawyer; **215tl, 215cl, 215bl, 215br** AA/C Sawyer; **215tr** AA/R Strange; **217tl** AA/C Sawyer; **217tr, 217cl, 217br** AA/R Strange; **219tl** AA/R Strange; **219tr** Mexico Tourism Board; **218/9** AA/R Strange; **219bc** Mexico Tourism Board; **219br** AA/P Wilson; **220** AA/C Sawyer; **221tl, 221c** AA/C Sawyer; **221tr, 221b** AA/R Strange; **222** AA/C Sawyer; **223l, 223r** AA/C Sawyer; **224** AA/C Sawyer; **225t, 225cr** AA/C Sawyer; **225cl, 225bl** AA/R Strange; **225br** Mexico Tourism Board; **226** Galen Rowell/Corbis; **227l, 227r** AA/C Sawyer; **228t** Mexico Tourism Board; **228b** AA/R Strange; **229t** AA/R Strange; **229cl, 229cr, 229b** Mexico Tourism Board; **230** AA/C Sawyer; **231tl, 231tr, 231cr, 231bl, 231br** AA/C Sawyer; **232** Mexico Tourism Board; **233t** Setboun/Corbis; **233cl** AA/F Dunlop; **233br** Bob Krist/Corbis; **234t** Macduff Everton/Corbis; **234** Corbis; **235tr** AA/P Baker; **235cl** AA/L Dunmire; **235cr** David Muench/Corbis; **236bl, 236/7** AA/L Dunmire; **237tl** Mexico Tourism Board; **237tr, 237cr, 237br** AA/L Dunmire.

EATING AND STAYING

239 AA/C Sawyer; **240l, 240cl** Mexico Tourism Board; **240cr** AA/P Wilson; **240r** AA/L Dunmire; **241l** AA/C Sawyer; **241c, 241r** AA/R Strange; **242l** Mexico Tourism Board; **242c, 242r** AA/R Strange; **243l** AA/R Strange; **243c, 243r** Mexico Tourism Board; **244cl, 244b, 244cr** AA/C Sawyer; **245l** AA/R Strange; **245r** AA/C Sawyer; **246l, 246c** AA/C Sawyer; **246r** Photodisc; **247tc** AA/M Chaplow; **247r** AA/C Sawyer; **248cl** Mexico Tourism Board; **248bl** AA/C Sawyer; **250c** AA/C Sawyer; **250r** AA/P Wilson; **251c** AA/C Sawyer; **251r** AA/P Kenward; **252l, 252r** AA/C Sawyer; **253c** AA/C Sawyer; **254** AA/P Wilson; **255c, 255r** AA/R Strange; **256** AA/C Sawyer; **257l** AA/R Strange; **257c** AA/C Sawyer; **258** AA/C Sawyer; **259** AA/C Sawyer; **260l, 260r** AA/C Sawyer; **263** Mexico Tourism Board; **264l, 264cl** AA/C Sawyer; **264cr** Mexico Tourism Board; **264/5** AA/C Sawyer; **265cl, 265cr** AA/L Dunmire; **265r** AA/C Sawyer; **267l, 267tr, 267br** AA/C Sawyer; **269** AA/C Sawyer; **271l, 271c** AA/C Sawyer; **272l, 272r** AA/C Sawyer; **273** AA/C Sawyer; **274tl** Marco Polo; **274r** Starwood Hotels & Resorts Worldwide; **274cl** AA/R Strange; **274tc** AA/C Sawyer; **275** AA/C Sawyer; **276l, 276c, 276r** AA/C Sawyer; **277** AA/R Strange; **278tl, 278tc, 278tr** AA/C Sawyer; **279** AA/C Sawyer; **280t** AA/L Dunmire; **280r** Presidente InterContinental Los Cabos Resort.

PLANNING

281 AA/C Sawyer; **283** AA/C Sawyer; **285** AA/C Sawyer; **286t** AA/C Sawyer; **286r** AA/L Dunmire; **287b** AA/C Sawyer; **289** AA/C Sawyer; **290** AA/C Sawyer; **291** AA/C Sawyer; **292tl, 292tr, 292c** AA/C Sawyer; **293t** Currency information courtesy of MRI Bankers Guide to Foreign Currency; **293b** AA/C Sawyer; **294** AA/C Sawyer; **296t, 296b** AA/C Sawyer; **297** Digital Vision.

Project editor
Karen Kemp

Design work
David Austin

Picture research
Bea Ray, Carol Walker

Cover design
Tigist Getachew

Internal repro work
Michael Moody, Susan Crowhurst, Ian Little

Production
Lyn Kirby, Helen Sweeney

Mapping
Maps produced by the Cartography Department of AA Publishing

Main contributors
Carolyn Bointon, Vanessa Hadley, Peter Hutchison, Caroline Lascom, Maribeth Mellin, Alan Murphy, Rafe Stone, Nicholas Watson

Copy editor
Rebecca Snelling

See It Mexico ISBN 1-4000-1588-X

Published in the United States by Fodor's Travel Publications and simultaneously in Canada by Random House of Canada Limited, Toronto. Published in the United Kingdom by AA Publishing.

Color separation by Keenes
Printed and bound by Leo, China

Important note: Time inevitably brings changes, so always confirm prices, travel facts, and other perishable information when it matters. Although Fodor's cannot accept responsibility for errors, you can use this guide in the confidence that we have taken every care to ensure its accuracy.